Nineveh

Asshur

MEDIA

BABYLONIA

Babylon

Sidon

Tyre

Acco

Megiddo

SAMARIA

Mesad
Hashavyahu

Jericho

Jerusalem

JUDAH

Lachish

MOAB

Beer-sheba

Arad

PHILISTINES

Glimpses of Lehi's Jerusalem

J GLIMPSES OF LEHI'S
JERUSALEM

EDITED BY JOHN W. WELCH
DAVID ROLPH SEELY • JO ANN H. SEELY

FOUNDATION FOR ANCIENT RESEARCH AND MORMON STUDIES (FARMS)
BRIGHAM YOUNG UNIVERSITY
PROVO, UTAH

Cover design by Diane Schultz

Foundation for Ancient Research and Mormon Studies (FARMS)
Institute for the Study and Preservation of Ancient Religious Texts
Brigham Young University
PO Box 7113
University Station
Provo, Utah 84602

Library of Congress Cataloging-in-Publication Data

Glimpses of Lehi's Jerusalem / edited by John W. Welch, David Rolph Seely,
Jo Ann H. Seely.
    p. cm.
Includes bibliographical references and index.
ISBN 0-934893-74-8
1. Book of Mormon—Criticism, interpretation, etc. 2. Jerusalem in the Book of
Mormon. 3. Lehi (Book of Mormon figure) 4. Nephi (Book of Mormon figure)
I. Welch, John W. (John Woodland). II. Seely, David Rolph. III. Seely, Jo Ann H.,
1958–
BX8627.G59 2004
289.3'22—dc22
                                           2003023797

Contents

About the Authors

William James Adams Jr. (Ph.D., University of Utah Middle East Center) is now retired.

Terry B. Ball (Ph.D., Brigham Young University) is Associate Dean of Religious Education at Brigham Young University.

Margaret Barker (M.A., Cambridge, England) is an independent scholar and author. She is a former president of the Society for Old Testament Study.

S. Kent Brown (Ph.D., Brown University) is Professor of Ancient Scripture and Director of Ancient Studies at Brigham Young University.

Ariel E. Bybee (B.A., Brigham Young University) is a Ph.D. candidate in Early Christianity and Patristics at Duke University in Durham, North Carolina.

Jeffrey R. Chadwick (Ph.D., University of Utah Middle East Center) is Associate Professor of Church History at Brigham Young University.

Kevin Christensen (B.A., San Jose State University) is a contract technical writer living in Lawrence, Kansas.

John Gee (Ph.D., Yale University) is the William "Bill" Gay Assistant Research Professor of Egyptology at the Institute for the Study and Preservation of Ancient Religious Texts at Brigham Young University.

Wilford M. Hess (Ph.D., Oregon State University) is Professor of Botany at Brigham Young University.

Robert D. Hunt (M.A., Brigham Young University) works in an appraisal office in Park City, Utah.

Dana M. Pike (Ph.D., University of Pennsylvania) is Associate Professor of Ancient Scripture at Brigham Young University.

Bruce Satterfield (Ph.D., University of Idaho) is on the faculty in the Department of Religious Education at Brigham Young University—Idaho.

Aaron P. Schade (M.A., University of Toronto) is a Ph.D. candidate in Northwest Semitic epigraphy at the University of Toronto.

David Rolph Seely (Ph.D., University of Michigan) is Professor of Ancient Scripture at Brigham Young University.

Jo Ann H. Seely (M.A., Brigham Young University) is an instructor of Ancient Scripture at Brigham Young University.

Jeffrey P. Thompson (J.D., Brigham Young University) is working in the Farmers Insurance San Francisco legal office.

John S. Thompson (M.A., University of California at Berkeley) is a Ph.D. student of Egyptology at the University of Pennsylvania. He also is a coordinator for the Church Educational System in the Philadelphia, Pennsylvania, area.

John W. Welch (J.D., Duke University) is the Robert K. Thomas Professor of Law at Brigham Young University. He is also editor in chief of *BYU Studies* and director of publications for the Joseph Fielding Smith Institute for Latter-day Saint History.

Fred E. Woods (Ph.D., University of Utah) is Associate Professor of Church History and Doctrine at Brigham Young University.

INTRODUCTION

Imagine the world of Jerusalem around 600 B.C. This was the world of Lehi, Sariah, Laban, and Zoram. It was also the world of Josiah, Jeremiah, Nahum, and Urijah. What was that world like? How did people live in that day and age? How can an understanding of that world help as we read the prophecies of Ezekiel or the records of Nephi?

This book tries to answer such questions and to glimpse parts of that world. Much of that era was lost forever, of course, when the warnings of many prophets came to pass as Jerusalem was destroyed by the Babylonians shortly after Lehi left Jerusalem. The Temple of Solomon and the walls of the city were torn down. Buildings were burned. Treasuries were looted. People were killed or deported. Many records were destroyed, and certain religious beliefs were changed or extinguished. Most of what we know about these events comes from accounts written by a few of the survivors and influenced by their biases. Archaeological and textual evidence allows us to snatch only a glimpse of this and a peek at that. Carefully linked together, however, these snapshots blend into a helpful and interesting vista.

Chapters in histories discuss these years, and articles focus on one particular person or point. Rarely, however, has an entire book been devoted to this quarter century. Perhaps because this episode has an unhappy ending, historians and general readers feel its pain and turn away. Readers of the Book of Mormon, however, will see light at the end of this dark historical tunnel and a silver lining around these dark clouds of destruction.

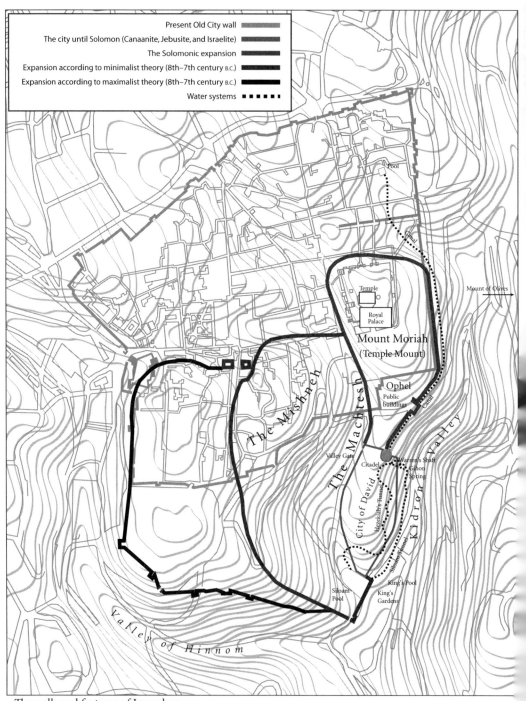

Pool

Canal

Temple

Royal Palace

Mount Moriah
(Temple Mount)

Mount of Olives →

The Mishneh

The Machtesh

Ophel

Public buildings

Canal

Kidron Valley

Valley Gate

Citadel

Warren's Shaft
Gihon Spring

City of David

Hezekiah's Tunnel

Siloam Tunnel

Siloam Pool

King's Pool
King's Gardens

Valley of Hinnom

The walls and features of Jerusalem.

To understand this world, historians strive to identify significant changes that occurred at that time. Many cultural features remained relatively constant in the ancient world from one century to the next, but during certain decades, dramatic developments occurred. Lehi's Jerusalem was one such time of turbulence and transformation. Locally, the kingdom of Judah rose to new heights under the reforms of King Josiah, only to crash to new lows a few years later with his death at Megiddo in 609. Internationally, the world was in wild flux as the Assyrian empire collapsed and the Babylonian kingdom came to power. Lehi can be understood in this setting, as he cried out against imprudent changes and improvident actions.

These developments around 600 B.C. were extremely interesting and influential. Events of this axial period shaped the contours of civilizations for centuries to come. This world was also the incubator in which the seeds of Nephite civilization germinated. Lehi and his family left from this world, carrying with them certain amounts of religious, linguistic, social, political, and cultural baggage. Knowing as much as possible about that world yields important glimpses into the backgrounds of the Book of Mormon.

In this book we have invited a variety of scholars with training in many disciplines to discuss what is known about Jerusalem around 600 B.C. Their topics range from ordinary domestic life to extraordinary religious institutions. We hope that readers will find these glimpses into Lehi's world fresh and lively. All these studies are published here for the first time, with the exception of chapters 13 and 15.

Following a "culturegram," a register of people in Lehi's world, and a photo essay that introduce a hypothetical traveler into the world of Jerusalem in that day, three studies focus on the daily life of people at this time. Jeffrey Chadwick helps

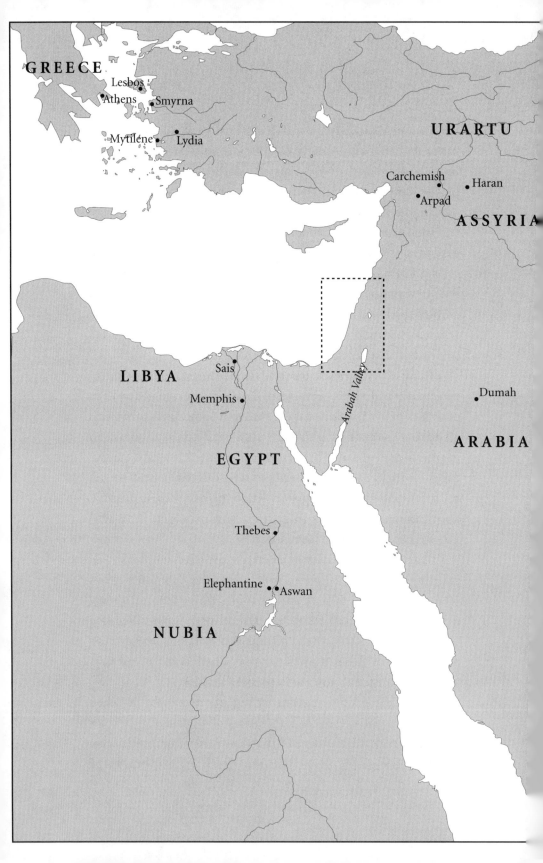

readers to understand the configuration of a typical preexilic Israelite house, which helps us to imagine what the house of Lehi and Sariah would have been like. Consistent with the fact that Lehi had gold and silver and other precious things, his was probably an upper- or solid middle-class home.

Essential to the survival of people in the ancient world were the diverse and valuable contributions of women, as the chapter by Ariel Bybee informatively discusses. Women were key members in the fabric of Lehi's society. Men in Lehi's world were predominantly involved in farming. Thus, the study by Terry Ball and Wilford Hess helps explain the agricultural concerns of men in Judah, which provides a context in which to better understand scriptural images that draw on horticultural symbols, such as the olive tree in 1 Nephi 10.

Language, literacy, and record keeping were important parts of Lehi's life. Dana Pike employs archaeological and paleographic tools to comprehensively survey the written artifacts from preexilic times. William Adams uses linguistic tools to examine four features of the Hebrew language that changed over time. Both of these authors relate their findings to the Book of Mormon.

Internationally, Lehi's Jerusalem had connections with Egypt. John Thompson shows that these relationships were at a high point during Lehi's day. John Gee skillfully sketches what Egyptian society was like at that time. Aaron Shade recounts the history of the kingdom of Judah during the century before Lehi. These chapters are especially interesting to readers of the Book of Mormon because Lehi knew Egyptian and was influenced by the scribal traditions of that world.

Main institutions in the world of Jerusalem 600 B.C. were the temple, the monarchy, wisdom teachers, legal administrators, and prophetic spokesmen. John Welch analyzes the trial of Jeremiah and what Lehi would have learned from Jeremiah's narrow escape. David and Jo Ann Seely compare the prophetic missions of Lehi and Jeremiah. David Seely discusses the importance of covenant and the Temple of Solomon, which is the temple that Lehi and his contemporaries knew, and Welch explains the calling of Lehi as a prophet in terms of contemporaneous expectations. Kevin Christensen distills the many relevant insights of British scholar Margaret Barker, and her 2003 BYU Forum address on the reforms of Josiah offers new perspectives on the changes and losses that occurred in Israel during Lehi's lifetime.

The "seething pot" of Babylonia finally boiled over and spilled into Judah. John Gee gives fascinating information about the political powers that destroyed Jerusalem in 587/586 B.C. The divine justification for that catastrophe is discussed by Bruce Satterfield, and domestic and theological reasons allowing it are explained by David Seely and Fred Woods.

Knowing of the impending fate that hung over the city of Jerusalem, Lehi led his family out into the Arabian desert. The pattern of fleeing into the wilderness to escape wickedness was a pattern in Lehi's world, made attractive by the Rechabites, as is discussed by Welch and Jeffrey Thompson. Kent Brown concludes by providing details about Arabian connections with Jerusalem in Lehi's day, helping modern readers to travel a few days' journey alongside the footprints of Lehi.

With Lehi's vision that Jerusalem would be destroyed came the assurance that the mercies of the Lord would be over those who would repent and turn their hearts again to the ways of righteousness. Sensing the precariousness of wickedness, as well as trusting in the Lord's continuous generosity, are strong Book of Mormon themes pertinent at the beginning of the twenty-first century.

Of course, some details in these reconstructions remain uncertain and, as a result, readers should not expect to find complete agreement among these authors. For example, assessments of Josiah's reforms vary, and the state of the law at this time is debatable. In addition, dates of certain events cannot always be stated with precision. Indeed, the date 600 B.C. only approximates the year of Lehi's departure. Even the Nephite record keepers were not sure exactly when Lehi left: in Mosiah 6:4 the best that could be said of the key date that links the small plates to King Mosiah was that his reign commenced "in the whole *about* four hundred and seventy-six years from the time that Lehi left Jerusalem." Also, Hebrew words have been transliterated using the SBL popular style with variations to suit author preference.

We highly recommend further reading about this historic era. The reading list at the end of this book highlights our favorites. Other useful books are mentioned throughout this volume in footnotes.

Many people have helped significantly in bringing this book together. The skillful copyediting of Shirley Ricks and the competent typesetting of Jacob Rawlins are especially appreciated. Angela Clyde Barrionuevo, Alison Coutts, Julie Dozier, Ellen Henneman, Paula Hicken, Linda Sheffield, David Solorzano, Sandra Thorne, and Elizabeth Watkins assisted in various ways. Andrew Livingston and Michael Lyon assisted with the illustrations, which were chosen centrally for the entire book with help from a couple of the authors. We thank research assistants, students who have explored many of these topics with us, and family members who have traveled these roads with us.

As we journey, we hope you will keep your eyes peeled and that you will enjoy the trip.

Chapter 1

Culturegram: Jerusalem 600 b.c.

John W. Welch and Robert D. Hunt

Dear Reader and Ancient Traveler,

Welcome to these glimpses of Lehi's Jerusalem, the world from which Lehi and Sariah, the patriarch and matriarch of the main Book of Mormon peoples, left a little after 600 b.c. We hope that you will have an interesting and enjoyable trip back into that world twenty-six hundred years ago as you immerse yourself in the available, fascinating information about that time and place.

As you prepare for this journey, we suggest that you begin by reading the following culturegram, a brief report about the people, geography, politics, emergent history, prevailing customs, and daily life of that country or region. Modern culturegrams, which give answers to frequently asked questions, prepared originally under the direction of the David M. Kennedy Center for International Studies at Brigham Young University, are recognized as popular and useful guides for international travelers. We thought that you might like to know what you might expect to see if you were to travel with us back into Lehi's world.

The following culturegram of the ancient city of Jerusalem goes beyond the basic data that one would expect to find in an encyclopedia article or travel brochure about the Holy City today. This profile takes you out into the streets of Jerusalem on an introductory guided tour of its many surprising features and exotic sights and sounds. Until a person has actually been to a place, however, it is very difficult to visualize its personality or appreciate the ambience of routine life there. We recommend that you, in preparation for this journey, read especially Philip J. King and Lawrence E. Stager's *Life in Biblical Israel,* Roland de Vaux's *Ancient Israel,* and Oded Borowski's *Daily Life in Biblical Times.*[1]

How do we get there?

Traveling from western Europe to Jerusalem around 600 B.C., we obviously will not be arriving at the Tel Aviv airport. No such city, let alone airport, existed there at this time. And you will not need to worry about having a passport. No border guards patrol Lehi's world; in fact, there were no international borders at all.

We will probably see if we can catch a ride on a small Phoenician ship leaving Spain, but these vessels sail only sporadically. There is no travel agency to book us passage in advance. The sea voyage will be long, uncomfortable, and risky. We may need to lay over at several small ports in North Africa, Sicily, southern Italy, Greece, Asia Minor, Rhodes, and Cyprus. Finally, we hope to arrive safely at either the exotic port of Sidon or the heavily fortified harbor of Tyre.

From our port of arrival, we will need to travel about a hundred miles down one of the caravan roads, picking up either the Way of the Sea or an internal, local road, and eventually climbing up to the highlands in northern Judah, where Jerusalem is located, about twenty-five hundred feet above sea level. On this expedition, you will be traveling much differently from what you are used to.² Obviously, we have no cars or buses nor modern-day transportation vehicles. Beyond that, you may be surprised by what we do have. Most of us will be riding on a donkey or walking on foot. Riding donkeys is very uncomfortable, so you may prefer to walk. If you are extremely wealthy, we may be able to get a horse for you, but we cannot guarantee this since horses are fairly rare. It may be possible to get a few camels, but we will need to buy them; they are not available for rent.

With luck, we may get an ox-drawn wagon or two. But please travel light. These wagons have poor wooden axles and irregular wheels with no bearings and thus cannot carry many suitcases. Some of the wagons are covered. You will also notice that the harnesses are marginal—mostly just a rope around the animal's neck. Good harnesses will not be developed until the Middle Ages. Also, because horseback riding is rare, you will find nothing resembling a saddle with stirrups. We will have to learn how to ride these donkeys the same way the ancients did—sit toward the rear of the donkey's back, grip with your knees, and hold on for dear life. We will have to use our sleeping blankets as saddle pads.

We will look for a caravan and see if we can convince its leaders to let us travel with them. Traveling in a group is a necessity because ancient roads are very dangerous. Even the international roadways can be narrow winding paths mired with mud or dusty and rutted from use. If we are to see paved streets at all, it would be in the city, and, even then, they would be just dirt roads overlaid with stones. We will need help getting through, especially in the event of accidents or break-downs. Being with a caravan will also protect us from the wild beasts and bandits that are a common threat to all ancient travelers. Under no circumstances can you stray from the path or wander away from the caravan—it is just too dangerous. Our water will be rationed, partly because our daily headway will be slow (about seventeen to twenty-three miles per day) and also because we must carry what we need. Such things as modern convenience stores, gas stations, restaurants, motels, or even drinking fountains are unheard of.

The other important thing for you to know is that much of our travel will be done at night, which helps to alleviate some of the danger from fatigue, heat, or robbers. You may assume that our caravan will be accompanied by armed guards and will be sponsored by a king or high-level aristocrat. Private caravans are very rare because of the cost. As you look around, you will notice that oxen, and not horses, pull the carts that we do have. Using horses as draft animals is not common in the ancient world, except for pulling chariots.

Exhausted after several weeks on the road, we will jubilantly celebrate our safe arrival. Of course, it is still unclear where we will stay. But let us turn our attention to the reason for our journey—namely, trying to understand what has been happening in this turbulent city in recent decades and what is likely to happen here in the near future. As we walk through the city, we will spend the next little while coming to terms with its many interesting features.

What is the land itself like?

We will notice as we travel that the geography of this area varies significantly. Some of us may have imagined this land to be mostly desert, but it is a land of contrasts, covered with fertile valleys, sloping hills, mountains, and, yes, deserts. The area known today as the Negev is a desert, but in the mountains in the north, especially on Mount Hermon, some snow falls. In between these two extremes are the west coastal plain, with its humid summers and somewhat mild winters, and the lowest point on earth not covered by water, the land around the Dead Sea in the Jordan Rift Valley, which is thirteen hundred feet below sea level.

These Israelites focus on Jerusalem and commonly refer to their capital city when speaking about their country, calling it the "Land of Jerusalem." Of course, the very words *country* and *capital city* are misnomers in this ancient world. Ancient societies did not view themselves as countries with capital cities, a concept we might find hard to grasp.

Scattered throughout this land are villages whose inhabitants rarely travel outside the village and its environs. However, the law of Moses dictates that they are to travel to Jerusalem for certain feasts and festivals (see Deuteronomy 31:10–11). This directive also contributes to ancient Israel's focus on Jerusalem.

What will we see when we first get there?[3]

One of the first things you will notice is the relatively small size of Jerusalem, at least by modern standards. By ancient standards it is a good-sized city, but still only about twenty-five thousand people live here, enough to fill only half of a typical football stadium. You will need to be on good behavior since visitors are uncommon here, and you will stand out.

Even the fabled walls of Jerusalem are not yet that impressive, standing only about fifteen feet high. Those of you familiar with Jerusalem's walls and gates at the time of Jesus or in medieval times will be surprised by the walls of Lehi's Jerusalem. They are much smaller than in Jesus' day, most significantly around the Temple Mount, which has not yet been built up and expanded into a very large platform. Looking down on the city from one of the surrounding hills to the east, you can see the Temple of Solomon, the focal point of the upper city. The temple is smaller than you might have expected, at least in comparison with the Temple of Herod as it appears in most drawings or paintings of Jerusalem. The Temple of Solomon has some gold on it, but not much. Part of the king's palace complex comprises buildings that descend south down the hill away from the temple. The temple and palace stand in the middle of a court-yard called the great court. The houses inside the walled city are built on the hillsides in a sort of terraced manner. Even the big-gest of these homes is not large, although most homes are two stories high. The second story is more like a loft covered by the main roof. Notice also the colors, which are mostly natural. The houses are light tan because they are, by and large, built from local stone with some mud and wood. Inside, wood beams and joists support the roofs. Paint is rarely used.

You will want to take a close look at the gates of the city as we enter through them. Most cities in the ancient world have gates. In this world, gates grant security, protection, and

All illustrations in this chapter © Michael P. Lyon

regulation of traffic and serve as venues for conducting trials and important official business. Many cities hold city council meetings and judicial hearings here.[4] When we get to the gates, be prepared to see crowds of people and a fair amount of congestion. These areas are not as crowded as downtown freeways at rush hour, but gates in the ancient world are busy centers of activity. Most shopping is done here in a market, in a bazaarlike manner. Nothing is actually "sold." You first become "friends," greeting one another in an informal way, saying *shalom* and possibly shaking hands and patting each other on the shoulder. Of course, you must keep in mind that men and women have little or no contact in public. Then you sit together for a while if you do not know each other already; after this you *give* what you have (gold, silver, precious things), and the merchant *gives* you what you have bargained for. As the sons of Lehi learned in their negotiations with Laban, you should be careful what you ask for and how you ask (see 1 Nephi 3:11, 22–24). Do not expect to see any retail prices listed since bartering characterizes their manner of trade. Be sure to keep your money in a secure place.

Away from the bustle of the marketplace, you will soon be struck by how quiet things have become—no radios or loudspeakers, no cars or trucks, no honking horns or blaring sirens, guns, explosions, bells, or any of the usual noises of a modern city are present. In fact, the silence here can be rather uncanny. The sound of a ram's horn blown by a priest will signal times for prayer, and even without amplification you can hear its distinctive squeal all over town.

What languages do people speak here?[5]

About the only language we will need to know to get around Jerusalem is Hebrew. Of course, knowing Modern Hebrew will help only a little. The Hebrew spoken at this time in ancient

Jerusalem is archaic when compared to the Hebrew spoken at the time of Christ. The square Hebrew letters with which you may be familiar have not yet come into use, so the shapes of the letters of the Hebrew alphabet at this early period may come as a surprise to you. But do not worry too much since there are few road signs and no menus or newspapers to read anyway.

Depending on how international you are, it may help to know a little Egyptian, Aramaic, or Greek, probably in that order. Greek is not yet the lingua franca of the eastern Mediterranean, as it will become in about three hundred years, after the conquest of Alexander the Great, and as it will be during the days of Jesus. Aramaic, also in contrast to its role in the days of Jesus, is not spoken widely in this area and does not become prominent in Judah until after the return of the Jews from their exile in Aramaic-speaking Babylon.

What sort of calendar do they use?[6]

Like most things in ancient Israel, the calendar is largely governed by religion. Each week has seven days, ending with a Sabbath. Days are determined from sundown to sundown, so watch out: on this trip when we say "Thursday night," we mean the night *before* Thursday day. The night is divided into three "watches"—first, midnight, and last (or morning) watch. The daylight hours are counted approximately, but since no one has clocks or wristwatches, don't worry too much about being on time; schedules are less of a concern here—things just happen when they happen. The year is lunar and the months are called *yerah* (which means "moon") or *hodesh* (which means "new moon"). These months determine religious festivals, which we will talk about a little later. Months alternate between twenty-nine and thirty days.

What about money and coins?[7]

Currency exchange will also present a few problems for you, especially since coins have not yet entered Israel's history. The commercially revolutionary invention of coinage in the kingdom of Lydia is just over the historical horizon. Payments in Jerusalem during our visit will be made by weight—chiefly in silver, but also in copper or gold. In earlier centuries, a person's wealth was counted in terms of sheep and cattle. In Lehi's era, however, gold and silver have become indicators of wealth (1 Nephi 2:4) and are common media of exchange (1 Nephi 3:24). Different values are placed on those metals by weight. The most basic measure, and the one with which we will become the most familiar as we travel here, is the *sheqel*. This word in Hebrew simply means "to weigh." Fifty *sheqalim* make a *mina,* which is a substantial amount of money. Below the *sheqel* are the *pim,* the *beqaʿ,* and the *gerah* (in that order). There are also

larger sums, called "talents" in New Testament times, but we will not be dealing with such large sums. So, despite your desire to have exact values given to these weights like at home, we will learn to cope with these more ambiguous values here. In most cases, silver or gold is melted into ingots of different sizes or shapes or is fashioned into discs, bars, brooches, or rings. If you have any gold or silver, you may want to bring it along.

What is a cubit?

While we are traveling here, we will become familiar with the cubit. Much of the ancient world of this time period used this measurement. One Hebrew cubit is approximately twenty-one inches, or fifty centimeters. This is a hard measurement for us to gauge, but just think of it as two feet minus a couple of inches. Do not be too concerned about exact distance measurements; similar to currency exchange, ancient people tend to estimate and do not use precise measurements.

What can we eat? Do we get any meat?[8]

We will eat the customary three meals a day. Breakfast is usually fruit or bread; lunch consists of bread, olives, and figs; and the typical main meal—eaten after sunset with the whole family—consists of a stew sopped with bread. Cooking is typically done in the open courtyard, and most people eat with their hands and rarely use utensils, reclining as they eat.

Little if any meat will be included in our menus for two reasons. First, meat is expensive in 600 B.C. and hard to come by. There is no corner market or butcher shop selling the latest cut of beef or a good lamb chop. Second, when meat is eaten, it is usually done in a sacrificial, religious setting, where it is roasted; otherwise, it is boiled. If we are lucky, we may get to sample some fish, but Jerusalem is far from Galilee and the Mediterranean Sea, and this commodity can be hard to come by. Do not be disappointed, however, since plenty of variety is found in the different fruits and vegetables, beans, and olives. Animals are kept for food, including cheese and milk. Actually, the most common milk is goat's milk. Sheep's milk is also used, but cow's milk only rarely. We must quickly drink any milk that we have and not try to store it. Pasteurization is obviously over two thousand years away, and few means exist to keep food cold. This means that almost everything we drink will be lukewarm. We will mostly be drinking juice or wine. Stay away from the water, which is not very clean and could make you sick.

What kinds of crops are raised, and how are they stored and marketed?[9]

This society is agrarian—most people farm at least minimally for their sustenance, raising wheat, barley, beans, and vegetables. The most important tool is the plow. The storage of food can be problematic since only some of the foods harvested can be stored for lengthy periods of time. If people need to keep things cold, they must pay for ice that is shipped from Mount Hermon, north of here. Obviously, only the very rich can afford to do this, so most food products are eaten immediately or they spoil. One of the staples of an ancient Israelite's diet—the olive—however, has proved to be superior in this regard. Olives can be pickled and stored for up to two years. Other foods like grapes, figs, and dates are easily dried and pressed into cakes. Storing their food is serious business for these Israelites. Their storage must provide sufficient food not only for the entire year but also for periods of famine, which can hit these people hard and with little notice.

Ancient Israelites store most of their produce in pottery jars, which are placed in special, designated buildings. Often, they store their grain in pits. Before this grain reaches the pit, however, it must be harvested (reaped or picked), transported to the threshing floor, dried, threshed (to separate the grain from the stalks), winnowed and sieved (to separate the grain from the chaff), and then measured. Harvesting was hard, backbreaking work.

Water is always a chief concern for these people. Preserving water for use in the city is of paramount importance. Water is collected from rain and runoff during the rainy seasons in cisterns located underground. Farmers terrace the land to make better use of the rainwater, and this same technique is used in Israel today. Even though ancient Israelites, in living the law of Moses, are cleaner than most other ancient people, this water is not very clean. These cisterns are just holes in the ground and are sometimes lined with clay plaster or some other sealant. Three underground water systems in Jerusalem originate from the Gihon Spring.

Produce is sold in market areas from small stands. People in their own area usually set up a market in the town or village square and run the market privately with the assistance of their families. The farmer conducts his business on a very small scale, selling directly to the consumer without any middleman.

What kinds of clothing are worn?[10]

As we progress through the streets, you will want to notice the clothing these people are wearing. The robes, headdresses, cloaks, and sandals may be what you were expecting, but if you get a chance, feel some of the robes and other clothing for sale. Not very soft, is it? The clothing is mostly made of dark shades of wool—grays, browns, and blacks. Some flax, goat's hair, and leather is used. Sometimes dyes are added for color; white clothing is extremely hard to find and very expensive. Linen is used, but only by the elite and sometimes by the priests. The clothing for women and men is roughly similar, although women wear a shawl or veil. Undergarments are usually made from linen and resemble a kilt or loincloth. Everyone wears sandals except the very poor, and no one wears shoes inside the homes. Men sometimes wear head coverings resembling turbans, and members of the upper class wear a loose-fitting robe over their clothes.

You will recognize a priest by his white robes. Only priests and the very rich can afford such clothing. Imagine what it means for these priests if their robes get stained, as is often the case when they perform their sacrificial duties. With no laundromat or laundry detergent available, stains remain on clothes. This is an additional reason why white cloth is not used much and gives added insight to scriptures that talk about having our robes white or washed white in Christ's blood (see Alma 5:21). Getting clothes this white is particularly difficult, if not impossible, especially if they are stained. The high-end clothes are not too uncomfortable, though. Skilled weavers are able to make cloth from wool that is not too scratchy.

What will the weather be like?[11]

The weather will be moderate while we are here during the springtime. As mentioned above, much of the time the weather is dry. But when it does rain in the winter months, it can come down in torrents. Only rarely does snow fall in Jerusalem. The amount and timing of the rain are vital to the Israelites living in and around Jerusalem. If the rain comes too soon or too late, it can spell disaster for agricultural pursuits.

What will our accommodations be like?[12]

The current political situation has led many inhabitants of Jerusalem to be suspicious of outsiders. Remember that this city has only twenty-five thousand people, a small city by modern standards. Strangers can be quickly and easily noticed. The characteristic Near Eastern hospitality prevails among friends and family, but the people may be reserved and guarded with outsiders. The law of Moses commands the Israelites to welcome and care for traveling strangers (see Leviticus 19:33–34), but only the father of a

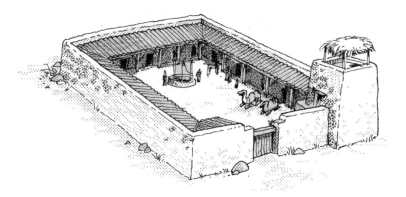

household has the right to invite such a wanderer into his home as a guest. Once the guests enter, the host washes their feet.

Hotels—at least like the ones we are used to—do not exist in this world. We sometimes mistakenly think that Mary and Joseph stayed in a motel-like inn at Bethlehem, but where they stayed was certainly no inn by modern standards. Travelers are few and far between in the ancient world and would not support a system of hotels. Instead, people use rooms on the upper level of homes as guestrooms, or groups would "camp" together in what are known as caravanserai (see above), which are most equivalent to large, dense campsites with many different families and groups. Caravanserai are rarely found inside a city. We will be staying at such campsites as we travel to and from Jerusalem.

Where do we sleep and what do we sleep on?[13]

Only the very rich sleep in what we would consider a decent bed. Most people here sleep on a mat or just curl up with their cloak and sleep in their clothes with no pillows or down comforters. Pajamas are not used, except by the rich, who may have special clothes to sleep in. Most people sleep on their roofs during the hotter months and, if they have some sort of protection up there, will sleep there in the winter as well. Some travelers will even sleep in the streets if accommodations are unavailable. The way homes are designed in this part of the world, most houses have an upper story or room that in many cases is designated the living area of the house, while the ground level is used for storage and animal space. In other homes, the ground area serves as the living area during the day and then at night is transformed into sleeping quarters as each family member lays out his or her bedding.

Additionally, a regular sleep schedule is not as common as today. People may get up in the night to do different things. If the moon is particularly bright, some may even try to do a little work at night. These nocturnal habits mean that many take naps during the day, especially when the weather is the hottest. After dark, oil lamps provide light, but remember that sleeping quarters are shared—if the light is on for one, it is on for all.

What about washing and bathing?[14]

Some of the areas we are visiting have conditions that seem more primitive than one would expect for the advanced city that Jerusalem is for its time. However, most Israelites are pretty clean compared to the ancient world in which they live. The law of Moses mandates ritual cleansing anytime a person is defiled, which can happen in numerous ways. Basic hygiene is also stipulated by the law of Moses; thus those who faithfully observe it, even if just a portion of it, are reasonably clean. But we also want to point out that the ritual hand washing we are familiar with from the New Testament comes later and is found in the Talmud but not the Old Testament. Foot washing is also common, as is smearing oil on the body after bathing. Perfume is also worn, by both men and women.

Special places outside the cities—usually near certain gates (like the Dung Gate)—are designated as lavatories, but, unfortunately, they are not furnished with toilet paper. Ritual purity and cleanliness are closely related and are all set out by the law of Moses. In a society full of epidemic diseases, famine, and wars and natural calamities such as hailstorms, locusts, and lice, uncleanliness abounds. We can see the divine wisdom in the requirements for cleanliness found in the law of Moses.

Is there a doctor in the house?[15]

Of course, uncleanliness leads to sickness. Even common ailments like the flu and colds can be disastrous for these people. Also, they can get very little relief for common discomforts like headaches or sore throats. Often, the priests are involved with cases of injury and sickness. The law of Moses stipulates that priests diagnose and take care of the dreaded disease of leprosy. Basic remedies include isolation, quarantine, and cleansing the sick area. Any healing of sickness or disease is viewed as religious. Naturally, many people try their own home remedies, but in many cases they do little to alleviate the problem. Be sure to bring your medicines with you since we will not find any pharmacies, hospitals, emergency rooms, or medical equipment. Even in Greece, anything like a medical science is still several centuries in the future.

What is the social class structure here?[16]

As in any society, a class structure is present here in ancient Jerusalem. However, social classes in ancient Israel do not exist in the modern sense in which groups are conscious of their particular interests and are opposed to one another. Some of the different groups in Jerusalem include the *zᵉqanim,* or "elders" of each village or city, and, similarly, the *sarim,* or "chiefs" of families. When we remember that Israel is a patriarchal society with chiefs of the families who are also the chiefs of the villages and cities, this connection becomes obvious. These *sarim* can also be officials of the king (military or civil). Similar to these are *nᵉdibim,* "the excellent," and the *horim,* which groups are the "ruling class," or "men of good birth." Differing from this class is the *ᶜam haʾrets,* who represent the general body of citizens. This term should not be confused with its usage after the exile, when it began to have a derogatory nuance. *Gerim* are aliens, or strangers from other nations. Although they have many of the same rights, they are not treated as highly as other Israelites. A clear indication of this is that *gerim* are usually poor because all the land belongs to Israel.

What does a household consist of?[17]

The main social unit here is the household, which is more than just a family. The head of the household is the father, or *ʾab* in Hebrew. A household consists of multiple homes built close together and usually comprises the *bet ʾab,* his sons and unmarried daughters and any aging parent, uncle, or unmarried aunt. In most cases the homes surround an outdoor courtyard where much of the cooking and social activities take place.

Can women appear in public? What will the women in town be doing?[18]

Contrary to some assumptions, women are not considered property and have more rights in ancient Israel than is usually assumed. The mother of a household has legitimate and significant authority and influence in the decision making. Both men and women have designated jobs that they perform. Women work around the house making clothes, cleaning, cooking, washing, and raising the children. While the men are in the fields working, the women take charge of the household and make sure things run smoothly. We will see some women in the city performing various chores such as drawing water. Some will be veiled, but some women wear a veil only on special public occasions. Women also take part in the worship ceremonies of their community.

Will we see many children?[19]

You will notice many children as we travel through this area. Israelites consider it a coveted honor to have many children, and childlessness is considered a curse. A midwife assists and, in many cases, is in charge of the birth and early years of a child. Of course, ancient Israelites value sons over daughters. Sons perpetuate the family line and fortune and preserve the ancestral inheritance, while daughters leave the family when they marry. The eldest son is favored and given a double inheritance because it is his responsibility to take care of the family when the father dies. According to the law of Moses, all male children are to be circumcised on the eighth day after birth. Depending on the affluence of the family, the father, a physician, or a specialist performs this rite, but it is not performed in the temple or by a priest.

Little children spend most of their time playing in the streets around their homes. They do have clay models and dolls to play with, but not many. Notice that many of the younger children are naked, which is typical in this ancient society. (As mentioned before, the hygiene in this ancient setting is not as meticulous as you might want or expect.) As the children get older, their responsibilities around the house increase.

While children are young, their mother provides most of their education at home. When a son is old enough, his father assumes the responsibility to teach him the law of Moses and a trade (see Deuteronomy 6:7; Alma 36–42). Trades are most often passed down through the generations. Rites of passage for young men are common and mirror the present-day bar mitzvah for young Jewish boys. We must remember, however, that in this ancient society, instruction of the law of Moses does not include the Talmud like it does today. In fact, there will be no Talmud until after the third or fourth century A.D. Many Israelites, not just the wealthy, learn how to write. However, most teaching is done orally as national traditions and religious stories and practices are passed down. In general, girls remain at home and receive their education from their mothers in areas of housekeeping and learning their duty as wives.

What is the employment situation like?[20]

The workforce is divided into a few main categories:

Craftsmen. A variety of different occupations in this society—many located right here in Jerusalem—include millers, bakers, weavers, barbers, potters, fullers, locksmiths, and jewelers. As we travel through this city, try to spot the names given to different streets and quarters. Each quarter of the city specializes in a certain craft; for example, we might see a bakers' street (see Jeremiah 37:21), a fuller's field (see Isaiah 7:3), or a goldsmiths' quarter (see Nehemiah 3:31–32). The surrounding

villages each specialize in a particular industry. Heavier trades involve woodworkers, iron founders, and linen workers. These crafts are divided into groups or guilds and are ruled by a father. They are called *mishpahoth,* implying the members are united in kinship or grouped like families.

Daily wage earners.[21] In addition, free men hire themselves for a definite job for a certain time at an agreed wage. Unfortunately, poverty has increased, and more and more Israelites have been forced to this labor. In the early days it was mostly agricultural workers who did this—herdsmen, harvesters, and grape pickers. These workers hire themselves out for a day or by the year. Often these laborers are taken advantage of, with unjust wages paid by those who hire them despite the law stipulating that workmen are to be paid every evening. Much of the land is owned by the king, who then leases the land to workers.

Merchants.[22] Other Israelites make their living as merchants. These men essentially work for the king since this type of big business belongs to royalty. Solomon built a fleet in the Red Sea and financed desert caravans.

Slaves.[23] Slavery is a reality in the ancient world. Even some Israelites have slaves, although Hebrew slaves are treated differently from foreign slaves. Moreover, slavery in the ancient world is different from our modern, postcolonial ideas. Israelites consider slaves as members of the family; if the household has any slaves, it is usually a small number—only one or two. Certain statutes in the law of Moses protect slaves, at least when society follows the law. According to the law, Israelite slaves are set free after six years of servitude. Sometimes a slave will decline to be freed. His master then pierces his ear, not as a brand but as a symbol of his attachment to the family. The law also protects slaves or servants from harsh treatment or physical abuse. Slaves are also allowed to take part in Israelite religious rites, circumcision, Sabbath observance, sacrificial meals, and religious feasts like Passover.

What has been happening politically here in recent years?[24]

The decade from 610 to 600 B.C. has been rife with political and social upheavals. For the last few hundred years, Assyria has ruled the Mesopotamian and Levantine world with an iron fist. However, in 612 B.C., the Babylonians and the Medes destroyed Nineveh, the Assyrian capital, thus ending Assyrian domination. Egypt and Babylon vied for control over the western portion of Assyria, which included Judah. In 609, Judah was rocked when Necho II, pharaoh of Egypt, led a large force to Carchemish on the Euphrates River to aid the Assyrian ruler Asshur-uballit in a desperate effort to retake Haran from the Babylonians. Near Megiddo, about sixty miles from Jerusalem, Josiah the king of Judah tried to stop Necho. Josiah's motive most certainly included trying to prevent an Egypto-Assyrian victory, which would have put him at the mercy of Egypt's ambitions. Disaster struck for the Judahites. Josiah was killed in battle, and his son Jehoahaz replaced him as king. Pharaoh Necho's assault on Haran failed, though, and he returned home. Along the way he deposed Jehoahaz and deported him to Egypt. Judah was now a vassal to Egypt. Necho appointed Jehoahaz's brother Eliakim (whose name was changed to Jehoiakim) as king and laid upon him and Judah a heavy tribute.

From 609 to 605, Judah remained under Egyptian control but only while Babylon campaigned in the East, in Armenia. During this time the king, Jehoiakim, remained a vassal of the pharaoh, and the internal situation of Judah was bleak. In addition to Egyptian oppression, Jehoiakim was a ruthless tyrant who disregarded his subjects' needs and by so doing incurred the wrath of Jeremiah the prophet. The recent reforms of King Josiah were neglected and then opposed as paganism, and immorality ran rampant.

In 605, however, the Babylonians defeated the Egyptians at Carchemish and sent them back to Egypt. Even though Nebuchadnezzar, the Babylonian general, was delayed from marching into Judah, he resumed his campaigns in September 604. In 603, Jehoiakim pledged allegiance to Nebuchadnezzar and became his vassal. Another battle between Egypt and Babylon forced Nebuchadnezzar to return to Babylon and re-group his forces. Foolishly, Jehoiakim decided to rebel against Babylon. In December 598, Jehoiakim died, and his eighteen-year-old son, Jehoiakin, became king. Also in this month, Nebuchadnezzar returned to lay siege on Jerusalem. Within three months the city surrendered. The Babylonians took Jehoiakin and his family to Babylon, and the king's uncle Zedekiah was set up in his place.[25]

Obviously, this has been a time of momentous turmoil. Civil wars, international conflict, rising and falling fortunes, and shifting cultural pressures and loyalties have raised anxieties and uncertainties throughout the region. As whole civilizations have faced the prospect of extinction, a great urge to recapture and preserve the records of the past is also evident among these people. In Assyria, scribes have been busily engaged in copying and preserving royal libraries. In Jerusalem, the most precious records have been inscribed on metal plates for safekeeping in the temple treasury, as well as on small silver scrolls that can be worn as amulets for personal protection.

What will be the mood in the city?

You will notice as you spend more time here that the events of the last ten years have left a deep pall on Jerusalem. However, this is not the only feeling here. Some of these people really believe that God will still save them from total destruction despite their wickedness. The moral fiber of Judah has increasingly unraveled since Josiah was killed; the nationalistic pride has also increased. Despite their defeats, these people believe that the temple will never fall. As evidenced in the cases of Jeremiah, Urijah ben Shemaiah, and Lehi, those who speak out against these ideals are threatened and reviled.

Is Jerusalem a cosmopolitan city?

Despite all the calamities that this city has seen in the last ten years, for the most part it is business as usual. Many different people travel to and from Jerusalem at any given time; Egyptian, Syrian, Arab, and other merchants make their way here on a regular basis. Right now, Babylonian officials and their entourage live here, but just a few years ago it was the Egyptians who controlled the city.

How did the loss of the northern kingdom affect life here in the south?[26]

The loss of the northern kingdom a century ago is still remembered with grief by the people of Jerusalem. To be sure, since Israel broke away from Judah, they have alternated between being allies and enemies, but there was always a feeling that they were one people. They were "Israel," and they were brethren. The idea of the federation of the twelve tribes has remained. The people were united by their traditions and their religion. After the Assyrians destroyed the northern kingdom, there were many refugees in Judah. The difficulty was trying to find where to put them and how to support them. Because of this, some Jerusalemites regard these "northerners" as riffraff. Although the northerners have, for the most part, been settled, some are unhappy with this settlement.

What kinds of public services are offered by the king and his government?[27]

At this time in Jerusalem, all the important enterprises are in the king's control. The king's revenues and the kingdom's are the same because he is responsible for the administration and upkeep of the army, national defense, and public works. Any profits he maintains come from his royal estate and from his commercial and industrial enterprises. Depending on the king, taxes—including those paid by the caravan merchants—and tribute of vassal states contribute to his treasury.

What is the tax rate?[28]

The law stipulates that the people of Judah pay a tax in the form of a tithe on their fields, vineyards, and herds. In addition, each king can institute additional taxes to pay for specific expenses. Starting with Solomon, various kings employed forced labor for their personal building programs or other projects. At this point in Judah's history, most of the taxes they pay goes to Babylon, not Jerusalem.

How do people feel about their king?[29]

Judah during this century is a monarchy, and the dynastic principle is accepted. Accession to the throne is viewed as a divine choice—a man is king because God wants him to be king. Each enthronement means a renewal of the Davidic covenant and adoption of the new sovereign by God. Separation between church and state is foreign to these people. Anointing the king is a religious rite that makes the king inviolable and holy. He is looked upon as a protector and savior to his people but, despite this adoration and despite the Israelite idea that the king is not merely a man like other men, he is still not viewed as a god.

Will we get to see the king's palace? Is it dominant in the life of the city?[30]

The king's palace is situated on the Temple Mount, just south of the temple. In effect, the king's palace is just one part of a large temple/palace complex. Just a few years ago, Jehoiakim used forced labor to completely renovate his old palace. The resulting beautiful building came at great cost in human toil. As you can see, the Temple Mount, including all the buildings, plays a dominant role in the city life of Jerusalem. It is situated above most of the city and occupies a large percentage of the total square acreage. But keep in mind that this Temple Mount is small in comparison to the one Herod will build, the one that Jesus will know during his earthly ministry.

What government officers should we expect to encounter?

In any monarchy the royal court is saturated with officials, and Jerusalem is no different. The royal family is surrounded by a court of officials and household servants who are all called the king's servants, although specific offices bear different names. The expression *ᶜebed hammelek* (king's servant) when used in the singular may sometimes denote a special office. *Soferim* (royal scribes) are also present along with a *yoᶜets* (counselor). The royal scribe acts as a kind of regal private secretary and secretary of state. All correspondence as well as the temple collections fall under his jurisdiction. The *ʾasher ᶜal habbayit* (man of the house) is the master of the palace; he supervises the whole palace. All the affairs of the kingdom pass through his hands. The *sarisim,* a number of high-ranking officials, or ministers, aid the king in the administration of the kingdom and serve as his confidential advisors. Eunuchs supervise the harem and royal family. Singers, musicians, cupbearers, bakers, and carvers are present in abundance to see to the king's every need. The king has a squire and a royal guard who act as his bodyguards along with "runners" who run before the king's chariot.

Also, there are commanders of the army, heralds, and commanders of the guards. The *mazkir,* or herald, is the man who calls, names, reminds, and reports. He is in charge of the palace ceremonies and introduces people to audiences. He reports to the king on the concerns of the people of the country and also passes on to the people the commands of their sovereign.

What about a military presence? Does Jerusalem have a standing army?[31]

Obviously the Israelites now have no army in Jerusalem as they languish under the weight of a Babylonian tribute. When Israel is sovereign, however, the king employs bodyguards, and a small standing army made up of foreign mercenaries is supplemented with a few Israelites. Additionally, each man aged twenty and above is responsible to answer the call to arms when it occurs—sometimes with a trumpet sounding or with messengers being sent around to the tribes. In spite of this mass call-up, the number of fighting men is usually small, nothing to compete with the large armies of Assyria, Egypt, or Babylon.

Men ready to fight assemble in short cloaks called *halutsim,* which literally means unclothed, or stripped. Each man provides his own simple arms—the usual weapons are swords and slings. The units of the army are based on those of society. The unit is the *mishpahah* (clan), which in theory provides a contingent of one thousand men, though in fact the number is usually far smaller. When the people take up arms, they are referred to as "the thousands of Israel" because these units are commanded by a leader of a thousand, *sar ʾelef.*[32] These units are composed of smaller groups of one hundred and fifty men.

We may be reminded of the powerful Laban, whom Laman and Lemuel describe as a man powerful enough to command fifty (1 Nephi 4:1). One of the king's duties is to lead his army into battle. Solomon instituted chariots among the Israelite army, but when the kingdom split, the majority of the chariots went to the northern kingdom.

The Babylonian occupation does not stop Judah from rebelling against Babylon at least three times during this period. We can only imagine what the loss of so many young men does to this ancient society.

Will we see soldiers in the streets? What will they wear and what weapons will they have?[33]

During the time that Israel was autonomous, few, if any, soldiers roamed the streets. Maybe you picture Roman soldiers patrolling the walls of the city, but at this time, Rome is only a very distant spot on the future's horizon. Before Judah was a Babylonian vassal, the only armed men here were the bodyguards of the king. If you do spot any soldiers in the streets now, you can be sure they are Babylonian and not Judahite. Notice the weapons they are carrying. The main offensive weapon in the ancient world is the *hereb,* or sword, but spears, slings, clubs, maces, axes, bows, and shields are also common. Most soldiers wear helmets and breastplates, which are often made of leather.

How does the old temple compare to Herod's temple?[34]

We want to emphasize that this is not that same city that we may be familiar with from the time of Jesus. This city is smaller, and the temple complex is very different. During his lifetime, Herod will expand the Temple Mount area and completely rebuild the actual temple. Solomon's temple and temple complex are much less grandiose. Solomon's temple is basically rectangular in shape, containing the *hekhal,* the holy place or main room, where most of the religious rites take place, and the *debir,* or holy of holies, where the ark of the covenant is located. No one is allowed in the holy of holies except the high priest on the Day of Atonement. The holy of holies is raised up from the holy place. We can see the two large, hollow, bronze pillars that stand outside the main door of the temple and give it such a magnificent look.

Outside the temple is the altar of bronze and the sea of bronze supported by twelve bronze bulls. Inside the temple, in the holy place, are the altar of incense, the table of shewbread, and ten candlesticks. The ark of the covenant and two large cherubim are in the holy of holies. This distinguishes this temple from Herod's temple. After the destruction of Jerusalem by the Babylonians, the ark is lost and the temple destroyed. This Temple Mount will become a heap of rubble. Many Israelites, however, will make pilgrimages to this area to mourn the loss of their beloved temple and to remember better days.

The temple is surrounded on two sides and the back with three-story auxiliary buildings that the priests use on a daily basis; they are not actually part of the temple itself. The temple is 165 feet long and 84 1/2 feet wide, including these outside chambers and storerooms that surround it. Just like modern-day temples, this temple was constructed with the utmost care and quality of materials. The builders used stone and brick overlaid with cedar panels that were beautifully carved and overlaid with gold and other precious metals. Many times during Jerusalem's history, kings and conquerors have stripped the temple of its precious metals, in many cases to pay tribute to conquering empires, such as the Babylonians. Solomon built this temple as large and as magnificent as ancient conventions allowed.

What happens on a normal day at the temple?[35]

As we approach the temple, you will notice all the activity that is going on there. Since we are here during the morning, we will be able to see the morning sacrifice. The priests sacrifice every morning and every evening, while simultaneously burning incense. In addition, the high priest offers a separate morning and evening sacrifice. The temple itself is just the main building, whereas the buildings attached to the sides of the temple are used for auxiliary purposes. Some of them are apartments for the priests, and some are kitchens and storage rooms. The temple must perform a variety of purposes, and such rooms are a necessity.

Each day a number of men may bring their animal sacrifices to the temple to be offered by the priests. The different animals offered are oxen, sheep, and goats, but, for the poor, birds, turtledoves, or pigeons suffice (see Leviticus 1:14). First, the man lays his hands on the victim and blesses it. Then he cuts the throat of the victim some distance from the altar. The actual slaughtering is not the responsibility of the priests and Levites unless the offering is public. Only the actual pouring of the blood on the altar and sacrificial burning are the priests' responsibility. In addition, the priests get at least some of the meat of the offering to eat. The priests skin and cut up the sacrifice and then place the four quarters of the animal on the altar, where it is burned. You can see the priests at work. Some are eating, some are cleaning, and others are sacrificing. The temple is a busy place nearly every day.

What happens in town on the Sabbath day?[36]

Many ancient cultures during this time set aside a type of "sabbath." For ancient Israelites, however, Sabbath observance takes deeper meaning. Some of you may be familiar with the typical activities observant Jews perform on the Sabbath today, including Friday evening dinner, synagogue attendance, and prayers. Most of these customs would appear foreign to an ancient Israelite, for whom the Sabbath is much simpler. The basic rudiments of Sabbath observance seen in modern Jerusalem were also present in seventh-century B.C. Jerusalem. It is a day of rest, a joyful feast day, when men visit sanctuaries and normal, heavy work is interrupted, as are commercial transactions. The strict, detailed rules that some of us are familiar with from the New Testament will develop after the Jews return from exile in Babylon. But still be careful. One man mentioned in the book of Numbers was put to death for gathering sticks on the Sabbath day (Numbers 15:32–36), so although the specific rules are not spelled out in great detail at this time, people take the observance of the Sabbath very seriously.

Will we see any festivals? How are they celebrated?[37]

The various feasts and festivals of ancient Israel prescribed by the law of Moses are very important. These holy days are also observed as "sabbath" days, in accordance with the law of Moses. These celebrations are usually taken seriously by the majority of Israel and form a viable part of the ancient Israelites' existence as they renew their loyalty to their God, purify themselves as a group from all unholiness, and strengthen their commitment to revealed principles of personal and community righteousness. These feasts and festivals have not yet developed into the array of detailed minutiae that they are under modern Jewish practice. They are still relatively simple, relying on the Lord's description of them as outlined in the Torah. The New Moon feast celebrates the first day of the lunar month and is similar to the Sabbath as a day of rest and feasting. Additionally, the law of Moses requires ancient Israel to celebrate three main holy convocations each year. We are familiar with the first one from the story of Israel's exodus from Egypt. In Hebrew it is called Pesach, but we call it Passover. This holy day began the Feast of Unleavened Bread. During Passover, no leaven may be found in a house. The feast commences with the offering of the paschal lamb.

Anyone familiar with the Acts of the Apostles in the New Testament will remember the second holy day, Shavuot or Pentecost, which occurs fifty days after Passover. This festival is agricultural in nature since it marks the beginning of the harvest. As part of the celebration an omer, or a measure of barley, is brought to the temple. On this day, the Jews at Jerusalem also celebrate the giving of the law on Mount Sinai.

The third festival encompasses three holy days. This festival is celebrated in the fall and is made up of Rosh ha-Shanah, or New Year; Yom Kippur, Day of Judgment, or Day of Atonement; and Sukkot, or Feast of Tabernacles. Today, Jews celebrate these days as separate, distinct holidays but here in the ancient world Israelites looked upon them as one large and single season of celebration. During Yom Kippur the priests perform impressive temple rituals. Outside Jerusalem, most Israelites feel the spirit of the holiday as they abstain from food and pleasure and participate in the set prayers recited outside the temple. After Yom Kippur, ancient Israelites begin to build their *sukkot,* or their booths. This part of the festival is to give thanks for the harvest and to commemorate God's protection. The king gives a public reading of the law of Moses during this time.

Most of us are familiar with the holiday Hanukkah. This celebration will not develop for another few hundred years. It will come about after the Maccabean war in the second century B.C. Another popular holiday among Jews today, Purim (which celebrates Esther's rescue of the Jews from destruction in Persia), will come about after the exile. The Israelites in Lehi's day are completely unfamiliar with such holidays.

How do people know all these rules and regulations?[38]

The public reading of the law of Moses is very important in the lives of these ancient Israelites. The law of Moses stipulates that it is to be read every seventh year during the Festival of Booths (Sukkot). Israelites who are willing and able make a pilgrimage to Jerusalem during this festival. During this time, the king or high priest reads the whole law, or at least large portions of it, while a grand assembly of Israelites listens. The way the law is preserved for us today shows that much of it was written specifically to be heard.

Which books of the Bible are available at this time? Does oral custom prevail, or is the written law predominant?

Only a few of the books in the Bible have been written by this time, so the body of scripture available in Jerusalem is relatively small. The Pentateuch, the five books of Moses, exists in some form, but some editing and revising is still going on. Certain histories and genealogies of the people and kings of Israel exist, as do the words of early prophets such as Amos, Hosea, Isaiah, and a few others. But many parts of the Old Testament are yet to be written and assembled.

Regarding the law, the Ten Commandments in Exodus 20 are clearly in effect. Their two tablets are kept in the ark of the covenant in the holy of holies in the temple. A version of the Code of the Covenant, found in Exodus 21–23, along with portions of the Holiness Code in Leviticus 17–26, legal sections found at various places in the book of Numbers (Numbers 5–6, 30–36), and other such normative texts, are also in place.

Just a few years ago, a book of the law, thought to be our book of Deuteronomy, was discovered while Josiah's men were renovating the temple. This book had been neglected for many years. Its discovery has had a significant impact on legal and religious attitudes in Jerusalem, especially by centralizing worship of Jehovah at the temple in Jerusalem, rooting out apostasy and false prophets, limiting the power of kings, providing charity to the poor, and promising blessings and threatening curses. This law is read out loud to the people at the temple every seventh year.

Largely because of the scarceness of written records, especially out in the villages, custom and the spirit of the law usually prevail over the technical letter of the law. Judges are told to judge righteously and to apply the law faithfully, with fear (or respect) for the Lord, and with a perfect heart. If we get to watch an actual lawsuit, it will probably strike you as quite chaotic and imprecise. Various charges may be thrown around at any time, different parties speak up without clear jurisdictional authority, a judge may be called as a witness, and the lines between divine law and secular powers are very porous.

Still, the legal system works fairly well. Most people in town know each other very well, and thus honor and shame are powerful enforcement mechanisms in the society. The system is efficient: there are no paid judges, no policemen, no prisons, and trials usually last less than a day. The real threat of capital punishment (usually by stoning) keeps most people well within the bounds of the law.

Are we having fun yet? What is the amusement and entertainment scene like?[39]

Even though life in this society can be hard and unforgiving, these people still do not forget to have fun and take advantage of some spare time. As in most societies throughout time, music is an important aspect for ancient Israel. Some of the purposes of music include soothing a child, making work (such as treading grapes or digging irrigation channels) more enjoyable, and celebrating major events in a person's life. In a land where so many of the people are involved in pastoral and agricultural activities, planting, harvesting, and sheep shearing are occasions for group gatherings and celebrations. In addition to such celebrations, key events of people's lives (such as weddings, births, royal coronations, and military rallies) are marked with music. Many of these festivities are accompanied by dancing as well.

Typically, the marriage ritual at a wedding includes a feast, preceded by a staged meeting between the bride's and groom's parties to the accompaniment of music. Births have their own form of ceremony and ritualized singing. Coronations of kings are announced with trumpets and singing. During such a grand event, priests and aristocrats march through the streets of Jerusalem up to the temple, accompanied by singers and other musicians. Of course, the rich can hire people to provide music. This has become one of the trappings of power. The military uses

music to marshal its forces and to guide and signal its troops. And, of course, any victories are marked with spontaneous celebration and joy.

Music is also played for religious purposes. Mourning or lamentation and funerals are marked with music, including wailing flutes. Pilgrimages to Jerusalem or other sacred shrines usually include music and singing with special pilgrim songs. Temple choirs and other musicians are employed, and although these musicians were more prominent in the Second Temple period, they exist during this time as well. The musical instruments include harps, lyres, and lutes.

What is the dating scene like?

There is no dating—marriages are arranged and negotiated by the fathers of the bride and groom (compare the marriages of Lehi's sons to Ishmael's daughters in 1 Nephi 16:7). Most marriages are arranged when the children are very young.

What happens at a local wedding?[40]

Marriage in this eastern world is viewed a little differently than in our own. Typically, marriage is considered an economic arrangement made between two families of the same or closely related tribes. This is not to say that love and romance do not exist in such a relationship, but these people are more focused on survival, perpetuation of their family, and family honor than on pleasure and sensuality. This mentality leads to a more practical approach to relationships, especially between husband and wife. As part of the marriage arrangements, the groom gives the bride's father an agreed-upon amount of money, called the *mohar* (bride-price).

This acts as a type of compensation for the loss of the daughter from the household and in many cases is used as a part of her dowry or old-age security.

The beginning of the marriage is actually the betrothal. The bride's father and the groom or his father sign a contract and form a covenant and bond. This period can last for many months or even a couple of years. During this time the bride and bridegroom have no contact. Their first private encounter after the betrothal is when they enter the wedding chamber. But this does not happen until after the wedding festivities. The bride and her entourage make their way from her house to the groom's household where, after much feasting and music, the husband escorts his bride away to the wedding chamber.

What goes on in a typical funeral?[41]

In such a primitive existence as ancient Israel, death and funerals are common. As we make our way down a street in town, you may well see a funeral procession up ahead. You will hear the cries from the family members and friends who carry the bier upon which the body is laid. Notice that the men and women are in separate mourning groups. You can see that the Israelites do not embalm their dead. The warm climate here and the ancient Israelites' belief that dead bodies are ritually impure mean that the dead are taken outside the city and buried as soon as possible after death. The funeral procession will most likely make its way to a family tomb, a cave, or a rock-cut tomb. If you look closely, you will see some of the family members have torn a part of their clothing to indicate their mourning. They will also veil their faces, remove any type of headdress, cut their beards and hair, put on sackcloth, and sit in ashes. You may find it interesting that some of the people may actually be professional mourners hired by the family. You can hear the wailing and crying from them and also from the family. This method of mourning is typical and is a way for them to honor their dead.

Let's Go

The journey to Jerusalem will be arduous, but fascinating. Come prepared to soak up all the sights, sounds, and smells. We will meet a lot of interesting people and collect memories that will last a lifetime. We hope that the other materials in this book will prepare you further for the things we will encounter in the world of Lehi, around 600 B.C. We look forward to having you join us for this trip and wish all a bon voyage!

Sincerely, your tour guides,

John W. Welch
Robert D. Hunt

Notes

1. Philip J. King and Lawrence E. Stager, *Life in Biblical Israel* (Louisville, Ky.: Knox, 2001); Roland de Vaux, *Ancient Israel*, 2 vols. (New York: McGraw-Hill, 1965); and Oded Borowski, *Daily Life in Biblical Times* (Atlanta: Society of Biblical Literature, 2003).

2. King and Stager, *Biblical Israel*, 114–18, 176–89; King and

Stager's book provides an excellent source for further study of daily life in ancient Israel; see also Barry J. Beitzel, "Travel and Communication," in *Anchor Bible Dictionary,* ed. David Noel Freedman (New York: Doubleday, 1992), 6:644–46.

3. De Vaux, *Ancient Israel,* 1:229–31; Lewis B. Paton, "Jerusalem in Bible Times," *Biblical World* 30 (1907): 7–17; Victor H. Matthews, *Manners and Customs in the Bible* (Peabody, Mass.: Hendrickson, 1991), 102–15; King and Stager, *Biblical Israel,* 21–28, 201, 332.

4. King and Stager, *Biblical Israel,* 191, 234; Victor H. Matthews and Don C. Benjamin, *Social World of Ancient Israel 1250–587 BCE* (Peabody, Mass.: Hendrickson, 1993), 123; Matthews, *Manners,* 106–9.

5. Stephen A. Kaufman et al., "Languages (Aramaic)," in *Anchor Bible Dictionary,* 4:173–205.

6. De Vaux, *Ancient Israel,* 1:178–94; King and Stager, *Biblical Israel,* 8.

7. De Vaux, *Ancient Israel,* 1:204–7; Daniel C. Snell, "Trade and Commerce," in *Anchor Bible Dictionary,* 6:625–29.

8. Edwin Firmage, "Zoology," in *Anchor Bible Dictionary,* 6:1120–27; King and Stager, *Biblical Israel,* 19, 33, 63, 67, 85–122; Matthews, *Manners,* 19–20.

9. De Vaux, *Ancient Israel,* 1:78; David C. Hopkins, *The Highlands of Canaan: Agricultural Life in the Early Iron Age* (Sheffield: Almond, 1985), 143, 169, 173, 225, 243, 268; King and Stager, *Biblical Israel,* 86–106, 122–29; Matthews and Benjamin, *Social World,* 37–51; Matthews, *Manners,* 42, 49–50.

10. Firmage, "Zoology," in *Anchor Bible Dictionary,* 6:1126–28; King and Stager, *Biblical Israel,* 146–63, 259–80; Matthews and Benjamin, *Social World,* 41; Matthews, *Manners,* 117–22.

11. King and Stager, *Biblical Israel,* 85–92.

12. James Wells, "Bible Hospitality," *Expository Times* 10 (1898–99): 62–64; King and Stager, *Biblical Israel,* 61–63; Matthews and Benjamin, *Social World,* 82–95.

13. Samuel S. Kottek, "Hygiene and Health Care in the Bible," in *Health and Disease in the Holy Land,* ed. Manfred Waserman and Samuel S. Kottek (Lewiston, N.Y.: Mellen, 1996), 37–65; Thomas H.

McAlpine, *Sleep, Divine and Human, in the Old Testament* (Sheffield: Sheffield Academic, 1987), 80–85; King and Stager, *Biblical Israel,* 35; Matthews and Benjamin, *Social World,* 41.

14. Kottek, "Hygiene and Health Care," 37–65; Abraham P. Bloch, *The Biblical and Historical Background of Jewish Customs and Ceremonies* (New York: Ktav, 1980), 61; King and Stager, *Biblical Israel,* 69–71.

15. Kottek, "Hygiene and Health Care," 37–65; Bernard Palmer, ed., *Medicine and the Bible* (Exeter: Paternoster, 1986), 15–18; King and Stager, *Biblical Israel,* 71–75; Matthews, *Manners,* 125–26.

16. De Vaux, *Ancient Israel,* 1:23, 69–75; Bruce V. Malchow, *Social Justice in the Hebrew Bible* (Collegeville, Minn.: Liturgical, 1996), 11–12; King and Stager, *Biblical Israel,* 5; Matthews, *Manners,* 115–17.

17. King and Stager, *Biblical Israel,* 4, 21, 36–38, 49.

18. Ibid., 49–53; Matthews, *Manners,* 19–26.

19. De Vaux, *Ancient Israel,* 1:41–49; King and Stager, *Biblical Israel,* 41–47, 50, 300–317; Matthews and Benjamin, *Social World,* 142–54; Matthews, *Manners,* 73–74.

20. De Vaux, *Ancient Israel,* 1:77; King and Stager, *Biblical Israel,* 37; Matthews and Benjamin, *Social World,* 37–66.

21. Léon Epsztein, *Social Justice in the Ancient Near East and the People of the Bible,* trans. John Bowden (London: SCM, 1983), 118; Malchow, *Social Justice,* 23.

22. De Vaux, *Ancient Israel,* 1:78; King and Stager, *Biblical Israel,* 189–95.

23. De Vaux, *Ancient Israel,* 1:23, 82–90; Malchow, *Social Justice,* 41; Matthews and Benjamin, *Social World,* 199–210; Matthews, *Manners,* 136–38.

24. John Bright, *A History of Israel* (Philadelphia: Westminster, 1981), 325–28.

25. John W. Welch, "They Came from Jerusalem: Some Old World Perspectives on the Book of Mormon," *Ensign,* September 1976, 27–29.

26. De Vaux, *Ancient Israel,* 1:96–99.

27. Ibid., 1:139–42.

28. Ibid., 1:142.

29. Ibid., 1:104–12; Matthews, *Manners,* 86–102.

30. Malchow, *Social Justice,* 39; King and Stager, *Biblical Israel,* 202–10; see especially picture of Jerusalem during the time of Solomon on page 205.

31. De Vaux, *Ancient Israel,* 1:220–27; King and Stager, *Biblical Israel,* 239–45; Matthews and Benjamin, *Social World,* 162–63; Matthews, *Manners,* 144–50.

32. De Vaux, *Ancient Israel,* 1:130; Matthews and Benjamin, *Social World,* 96–109; several scholars have suggested that the Hebrew term *ʾelef* does not necessarily designate literally "thousand" but sometimes refers to a subdivision of a tribe. If this theory is correct, it may be one explanation for some of the astounding and in some cases unrealistically high numbers found in the biblical accounts; see for example King and Stager, *Biblical Israel,* 240–41.

33. De Vaux, *Ancient Israel,* 1:220–27; King and Stager, *Biblical Israel,* 163, 223–58.

34. Carol Meyers, "Temple, Jerusalem," in *Anchor Bible Dictionary,* 6:355–58; Paton, "Jerusalem in Bible Times," 7–17; King and Stager, *Biblical Israel,* 332–37; Matthews, *Manners,* 141–44.

35. De Vaux, *Ancient Israel,* 2:416–23, 468; King and Stager, *Biblical Israel,* 46, 319–63; Matthews and Benjamin, *Social World,* 187–98.

36. De Vaux, *Ancient Israel,* 2:480; Bloch, *Jewish Customs,* 111–18; King and Stager, *Biblical Israel,* 353–63.

37. John W. Welch and Stephen D. Ricks, eds., *King Benjamin's Speech: "That Ye May Learn Wisdom"* (Provo, Utah: FARMS, 1998), 148–59, 190–91; Bloch, *Jewish Customs,* 141–46, 163–69, 181–83, 245, 295; De Vaux, *Ancient Israel,* 2:484–506; King and Stager, *Biblical Israel,* 353–63; Matthews, *Manners,* 138–41.

38. James W. Watts, *Reading Law: The Rhetorical Shaping of the Pentateuch* (Sheffield: Sheffield Academic, 1999), 16–29.

39. Ivor H. Jones, "Music and Musical Instruments," in *Anchor Bible Dictionary,* 4:931–33; King and Stager, *Biblical Israel,* 285–300; Matthews, *Manners,* 123–25.

40. King and Stager, *Biblical Life,* 54–57; Matthews and Benjamin, *Social World,* 13–17; Matthews, *Manners,* 72–73.

41. De Vaux, *Ancient Israel,* 1:56–58; King and Stager, *Biblical Israel,* 363–81; Matthews, *Manners,* 127–30.

Chapter 2

Dramatis Personae:
The World of Lehi (ca. 700–562 b.c.)

David Rolph Seely and Robert D. Hunt

The following kings, pharaohs, and prophets are listed in chronological order.[1] Lehi could well have known or known of these people.

Kings of the Neo-Assyrian Empire

Sennacherib (704–681 b.c.). Son of Sargon II. Sennacherib was a powerful king who subdued revolts in Babylon and in the west, including Judah. In 701 he invaded and decimated Judah during the reign of Hezekiah; the destruction of Lachish is depicted in his palace reliefs. He besieged Jerusalem, but, miraculously, his army was destroyed (2 Kings 18:13–19:36). He claimed to have deported many Judahites to Assyria. Eventually he was murdered by two of his sons (2 Kings 19:37).

Esarhaddon (680–669 b.c.). Son and successor of Sennacherib. He put down a rebellion and consolidated his father's kingdom by continuing to collect heavy tribute from the west (including Judah) and from Egypt. The Israelite king Manasseh may have been transported to Babylon during his reign (2 Chronicles 33:11). He conquered Egypt and looted Memphis.

Assurbanipal (668–627 B.C.). Son and successor of Esarhaddon and last of the great Neo-Assyrian kings. He inherited a relatively peaceful empire except for Egypt, which he invaded to put down a rebellion. He captured and utterly destroyed the great city of Thebes. His brother Shamash-shuma-ukin sat on the throne of Babylon and eventually led the Babylonians in a bloody revolt that was resolved with the victory of Assurbanipal. No record remains of the last twelve years of his forty-one-year-long reign. Assurbanipal is the only Assyrian king that claimed to be literate. His library at Nineveh was discovered in A.D. 1852, and its wealth of historical, economic, religious, and literary texts was instrumental in the decipherment of the Akkadian language and in the reconstruction of Assyrian history, culture, and thought.

After the reign of Assurbanipal, the Assyrian empire quickly disintegrated under the rule of several kings. A resurgent Babylon, led by Nabopolassar, declared independence and led the revolt that finally toppled Assyria. The Medes destroyed Assur in 614, and in 612 Nineveh fell. A small Assyrian contingent held out in Haran until 609, and the final remnants of the Assyrian army, along with their Egyptian allies, were defeated by Nebuchadnezzar's Babylonian forces at Carchemish in 605.

Kings of the Babylonian/Chaldean Empire

Nabopolassar (626–605 B.C.). The first king of the Chaldean dynasty. A Babylonian general in the Assyrian army, he rebelled against Assyria and led his armies, allied with the Medes, in a series of battles against Assyria that led to the independence of Babylon and the eventual downfall of the Assyrian empire in 609 B.C.

Nebuchadnezzar (605–562 B.C.). Son and successor of Nabopolassar, he was the greatest of the Babylonian kings, ruling for forty-three years. He consolidated and expanded his father's empire following the final destruction of the Assyrian empire at the battle of Carchemish, where he defeated the Assyrians and the Egyptians. He campaigned in Syria and Palestine in 597 and sent a large contingent of Judahites to exile in Babylon (2 Kings 24). In 586, after laying siege and capturing Jerusalem, he destroyed the temple and deported another group of Judahites into captivity in Babylon (2 Kings 25; Jeremiah 52). During his reign, Babylon, renowned for its extravagance, became the economic and administrative center and showpiece of the ancient world—and hence a symbol of worldliness in the scriptures.

Evil-merodach (562–560 B.C.). Son and successor of Nebuchadnezzar. At the death of his father, he released the king of Judah, Jehoiachin, from prison and gave him an allowance (2 Kings 25:27–30; Jeremiah 52:31–34). Eventually the Babylonian empire would be conquered by the Persians under King Cyrus in 539 B.C.

Pharaohs of Egypt

Dynasty 25: The Nubian/Kushite Dynasty (747–656 B.C.)

Pianki (747–716 B.C.). Reestablished the Nubian dynasty over the Libyan dynasty.

Shabaka (716–701 B.C.). Brother of Pianki. Monuments copied from the past and erected during his reign include the famous Memphite Theology (or Shabako Stone), containing one of the oldest known texts of temple dedications.

Shabataka (701–689 B.C.). Son of Pianki and nephew to Shabaka. He sided with the Palestinian/Phoenician revolt against Assyria. In 701 Sennacherib came west to put down the uprising and destroyed many cites in Judah, including Lachish.

Taharqa (689–664 B.C.). Son of Pianki and nephew to Shabaka. During his reign, the Assyrian king Esarhaddon invaded Egypt and destroyed Memphis. Taharqa took it back, but shortly thereafter Assurbanipal defeated him and drove him to the Sudan.

Tanutamani (664–656 B.C.). Taharqa's cousin, heir, and for a time coregent. He envisioned a resurgence of the Nubian dynasty and recaptured Aswan, Thebes, and Memphis from the Assyrians before Assurbanipal reacted and captured Memphis and destroyed and sacked Thebes. Tanutamani fled to the south and died in 656 after the Assyrian-appointed Psammetichus had begun the Saite dynasty.

Dynasty 26: Saite Renaissance (664–525 B.C.)

Psammetichus (also Psamtik) I (664–610 B.C.). Confirmed by Assurbanipal and ruled with Assyrian approval. Psammetichus consolidated his rule throughout Egypt.

Necho II (610–595 B.C.). After the fall of Nineveh, Necho led an army through Palestine and Syria to aid the remnant of the Assyrian armies against the Babylonians, headed by Nabopolassar. Josiah, king of Judah, decided to attempt to stop the Egyptian forces and was killed (2 Kings 23:28–30; 2 Chronicles 35:20–24). Presumably the Egyptians preferred the survival of the weakened Assyrian empire to the Babylonian empire and perhaps thought that they would achieve supremacy of the west with an Assyrian victory. After Josiah was killed, Necho and Egypt ruled Palestine from 609 to 605. In 605, at the battle of Carchemish, Nebuchadnezzar and the Babylonians defeated the Assyrians and the Egyptians (under the command of Necho) and eventually conquered

Syria and Palestine. Necho retreated to Egypt and successfully repelled Nebuchadnezzar at the border of Egypt.

Psammetichus II (595–589 B.C.). In connection with a brief incursion into southern Palestine against the Babylonians, Psamtik II encouraged a Judean revolt against the Babylonian rule, culminating in the eventual destruction of Jerusalem in 586 B.C. and the exile of many of the people.

Apries (589–570 B.C.). He encouraged Palestinian revolt against Babylon. His reign ended in civil war.

Amasis (570–526 B.C.). He was a general on the winning side of the civil war. Amasis established extensive trade with the Greeks.

Psammetichus III (526–525 B.C.). He lost his rule to the invasion of the Persians under the command of Cambyses in the battle of Pelusium in 525.

Kings of Judah

Hezekiah (715–687 B.C.). Son of Ahaz and Abi, daughter of Zechariah. Hezekiah was judged by the author of the books of Kings to be one of the most righteous kings of Judah and reigned as king during most of the ministry of Isaiah. His reign is recounted in 2 Kings 18–20, Isaiah 36–39, and 2 Chronicles 29–32. He was a religious king and was remembered for his construction projects fortifying Jerusalem against the Assyrian siege in 701 B.C. He initiated religious reform in an attempt to reverse the importation of Assyrian religious practices and the idolatry of his father, Ahaz. Hezekiah purified the temple at Jerusalem, began to remove the Israelite and Canaanite high places, and renewed the celebration of Passover. Eventually Hezekiah revolted against Assyria, leading to Sennacherib's invasion of Judah and the siege of Jerusalem in 701 B.C. The Assyrian army was miraculously destroyed and Jerusalem delivered. At the trial of Jeremiah, the fact that King Hezekiah allowed Micah to prophesy of the destruction of Jerusalem without executing him is given as legal precedent for not sentencing Jeremiah to death for similar prophecies (Jeremiah 26:18–19).

Manasseh (687–642 B.C.). Son of Hezekiah and Hephzibah. Manasseh was judged by the author of Kings to be the most wicked king of Judah. His reign was characterized by idolatry, pagan worship, child sacrifice, and witchcraft, as recounted in 2 Kings 21:1–17; 23:26–27; 24:3–4; and 2 Chronicles 33:1–20. According to Chronicles, he was exiled to Babylon where he repented and then returned to Judah and initiated religious reform (2 Chronicles 33). The abominations of his reign are remembered by Jeremiah as the reason for the eventual destruction of Jerusalem (Jeremiah 15:4; cf. 2 Kings 21:12–16). Lehi was probably born in the last years of the reign of Manasseh.

Amon (642–640 B.C.). Son of Manasseh and Meshullemeth, daughter of Haruz of Jotbah. Amon reigned for only two years, as recounted in 2 Kings 21:19–25 and 2 Chronicles 33:21–25. The author of Kings judged him to be a wicked king who continued in the idolatrous practices of his father. He was assassinated as a result of a conspiracy by his officials, who in turn were executed by the people. His young son Josiah was put on the throne in his place.

Josiah (640–609 B.C.). Son of Amon and Jedidah, daughter of Adaiah of Boscath. Josiah was eight when he was put on the throne. His reign is recorded in 2 Kings 21:26–23:30 and 2 Chronicles 34–35. According to the author of Kings, he was a righteous king following in the ways of his ancestor David (2 Kings 22:2). His long reign of thirty-one years coincided with the fall of the Assyrian empire, a time full of internal and external turmoil in Judah. The most noteworthy event of his reign was his so-called reform of Judah in which the temple in Jerusalem became the only accepted site of worship and sacrifice (as recorded in Deuteronomy 12) and the idolatrous worship of other deities throughout the land was forbidden.[2] The evidence suggests that his reforms were instituted in conjunction with a nationalistic revival declaring independence from Assyria and an attempt to reestablish the Davidic empire. In conjunction with this reform (either before or after its commencement), a book of the law was discovered in the temple, which many scholars believe was some form of the book of Deuteronomy. The prophetess Huldah was consulted as to the authenticity of this book. For some reason Josiah chose to lead his armies to Megiddo, where he attempted to block the advance of Pharaoh Necho II, who was going to deliver a remnant of Assyrians from the Babylonians in 609. Perhaps he preferred the Babylonians over the Assyrians, or else he was attempting to solidify his independence against both by defeating the Egyptians. He was killed in battle. Upon his death, the Egyptians essentially gained control over Judah. Jeremiah remembered Josiah as a righteous king who cared for the poor (Jeremiah 22:15–16). After his death he was succeeded by two of his sons: Jehoahaz and Jehoiakim.

Jehoahaz (609 B.C.). Son of Josiah and Hamutal, daughter of Jeremiah (not the prophet) of Libnah. Also known as Shallum, Jehoahaz was only twenty-three years old when he was proclaimed king. His reign, characterized by wickedness, is recorded in 2 Kings 23:31–34 and 2 Chronicles 36:1–4. The Egyptians removed Jehoahaz from the throne in favor of his older brother, who was deemed to be more pro-Egyptian. Jehoahaz was taken to Egypt in chains, where he died. Jeremiah composed a lament on the occasion of his deportation in which he predicted that Jehoahaz would never return to his native land (Jeremiah 22:10–12).

Jehoiakim (609–598 B.C.). Son of Josiah and Zebidah, daughter of Pedaiah of Rumah in Galilee. Jehoiakim's given name was Eliakim. His reign is recorded in 2 Kings 23:36–24:7 and

2 Chronicles 36:5–8. At the age of twenty-five, he was placed on the throne by Pharaoh Necho to replace his brother Jehoahaz. Jehoiakim was a faithful vassal to Egypt until 605, at which time Syria and Palestine came under Babylonian rule following Nebuchadnezzar's victory over the Assyrians and the Egyptians at Carchemish. Jehoiakim served Babylon for three years (2 Kings 24:1) and then led a revolt—probably encouraged by a series of Babylonian military setbacks in Egypt. Nebuchadnezzar responded by besieging and capturing Jerusalem in 597. Jehoiakim was taken to Babylon (2 Chronicles 36:6) where, according to Jewish tradition, he was executed. He was replaced by his eight-year-old son Jehoiachin. Jehoiakim was judged as a wicked king by the writer of the book of Kings. Jeremiah was an outspoken critic of conditions in Jerusalem and Judah during Jehoiakim's reign. It would seem that the positive results of Josiah's reforms did not continue. Jeremiah depicts Jehoiakim as a corrupt king and condemned him for his "covetousness, and for to shed innocent blood, and for oppression, and for violence" (Jeremiah 22:17), while Josiah was just and righteous (Jeremiah 22:15). Additionally, Jeremiah opposed Jehoiakim's pro-Egyptian stance and advocated obedience to the Lord's plea to submit to Babylon. Jeremiah experienced constant conflict with King Jehoiakim, which came to a climax in Jeremiah 36: Jehoiakim, after hearing the word of the Lord read to him from Jeremiah's scroll, had the scroll burned.

Jehoiachin (598 B.C.). Son of Jehoiakim and Nehushta, daughter of Elnathan of Jerusalem. Also called Coniah. Jehoiachin's short reign is recounted in 2 Kings 24:6–16 and 2 Chronicles 36:9–10. He came to the throne after his father's death during the Babylonian siege of Jerusalem and reigned only three months before he was taken to Babylon by Nebuchadnezzar and replaced on the throne by his uncle Zedekiah. He was considered a wicked king by the author of Kings in that he continued in the ways of his father. Upon the death of Nebuchadnezzar in 562 B.C., Jehoiachin, the crown prince of Judah, was released from prison in Babylon (2 Kings 25:27–30). Jeremiah likened his short reign to a signet ring pulled from a hand and given to Babylon as well as to a broken pot hurled into exile (Jeremiah 22:24–30).

Zedekiah (597–586 B.C.). Son of Josiah and Hamutal, daughter of Jeremiah of Libnah, half brother of Jehoiakim, and therefore Jehoiachin's uncle. His original name was Mattaniah. After Nebuchadnezzar captured Jerusalem, he put Mattaniah on the throne and changed his name to Zedekiah. He was twenty-one. His reign is recounted in 2 Kings 24:17–25:7 and 2 Chronicles 36:11–21. The situation in the opening chapters of the Book of Mormon in which the prophet Lehi describes the Lord sending prophets to his people during the reign of Zedekiah is reflected in 2 Chronicles 36:15–16: "And the Lord God of their fathers sent to them by his messengers, rising up betimes, and sending; because he had compassion on his people, and on his dwelling place; But they mocked the messengers of God, and despised his words, and misused his prophets, until the wrath of the Lord arose against his people, till there was no remedy." Jeremiah was one of these prophets. Zedekiah was weak and vacillating, on the one hand consulting Jeremiah for the will of the Lord and on the other having him thrown into prison for revealing the Lord's will. Eventually, contrary to the word of the Lord that was delivered to him on numerous occasions, Zedekiah chose to trust in the Egyptians and revolted against the Babylonians. This resulted in the catastrophic siege and destruction of Jerusalem and its temple in 586 and in the exile of many more Judahites to Babylon. Zedekiah was taken to Riblah (in modern Syria), where he was forced to watch the execution of all of his sons except Mulek. He then had his eyes put out and was taken into exile in Babylon, where he died.

	ROME	GREECE/ ASIA MINOR	EGYPT	JUDAH	ISRAEL
750	Traditional founding of Rome by Romulus (753)	P=Poet Ph=Philosopher L=Lawgiver		Ahaz (735–715)	Pekah (735–732) Hoshea (732–724) INVAS 732 B
725					
			DYNASTY 25 Shabaka (716–701)	*Isaiah*	Fall of Samaria 722 B.C.
				Hezekiah (715–687)	
700					INVASION (Jerusalem Prese 701 B.C.
			Shabataka (701–689) Taharqa (689–664)	Manasseh (687–642)	
675				SACK OF MEMPHIS 671 B.C.	
			Tanutamani (664–656)	SACK OF THEBES 663 B.C.	
			DYNASTY 26 Saite Renaissance (716–701) Psammetichus I (664–609)		
650		Archilochus of Paros (P, 650) Solon of Athens (L, 630–560) Thales of Miletus (Ph, 624–545)		Amon (642–640) Josiah (640–609) *Zephaniah Jeremiah Nahum*	
625		Draco of Athens (L, 621) Alcaeus of Mytilene (P, 620–580) Sappho of Lesbos (P, 610–550)	Necho II (609–594)	*Habakkuk Huldah* Jehoahaz (609) Jehoiakim (609–598) *Lehi, Urijah Daniel*	
600		Anaximander of Miletus (Ph, 610–546) Peisistratus of Athens (L, 600–527) Pythagoras of Samos (Ph, 582–500)	Psammetichus II (594–588) Apries (588–568)	Jehoiachin (598) Zedekiah (597–586) Lehi leaves *Ezekiel* Jerusalem Destroyed 586 B.C.	JERUSALEM CAPTURED 597 B.C.
575		Cleisthenes of Athens (L, 570–508)			
550					
525	Prepared by David Rolph Seely		EGYPT CONQUERED 525 B.C.		

	MESOPOTAMIA			FAR EAST	
	ASSYRIA	BABYLON	PERSIA	INDIA	CHINA
750	Tiglath-pileser III (745–727)				
725	Shalmaneser V (726–722)				
	Sargon II (721–705)				
700	Sennacherib (704–681)				
	Esarhaddon (680–669)	Assur-nadin-shumi (699–694) Nergal-ushezib (693) Mushezib-Marduk (692–691)			
675	Assurbanipal (668–627)	Shamash-shuma-ukin (667–648)			
650		Kandalanu (647–627) **Neo-Babylonian Empire**			
625		Nabopolassar (626–605)	Zoroaster (628–551)		
	Fall of Assur (614) Fall of Nineveh (612) Fall of Haran (609) Assur-uballit II (611–605) **Fall of Assyria 605 B.C.**	Nebuchadnezzar (605–562)		Upanishads composed (ca. 600)	
				Gautama Buddha (ca. 563–483)	Lao Tsu (ca. 6th century)
			Persian Empire Cyrus (558–530)		Confucius (ca. 551–479)
		Fall of Babylon 539 B.C.		Vardhamana Mahavira Jina (ca. 540–468)	
			Cambyses (529–522)		

Prophets

And in that same year there came many prophets, prophesying unto the people that they must repent, or the great city of Jerusalem be destroyed. (1 Nephi 1:4)

Isaiah (740–701 B.C.). Son of Amoz. Isaiah's prophecies for which we have a date range from 740 to 701 B.C., during the reigns of Kings Uzziah, Ahaz, Hezekiah, and possibly Manasseh. They deal with the destruction of the north and the south, the scattering and gathering of Israel, the coming of the Messiah, the restoration of the covenant in the latter days and the second coming, the millennium, and the end of time. According to Jewish tradition, Isaiah was killed by Manasseh (687–640). Isaiah's prophecies were preserved on the brass plates, and Nephi quoted them to his brothers in order to "more fully persuade them to believe in the Lord their Redeemer" (1 Nephi 19:23; cf. 5:13). Passages from Isaiah (including 2–14 and portions of 29, 48–49, and 52–54, as quoted by Nephi, Jacob, and the Savior) figure prominently in the Book of Mormon.

Zephaniah (ca. 640–609 B.C.). "The son of Cushi, the son of Gedaliah, the son of Amariah, the son of Hizkiah" (Zephaniah 1:1). A prophet during the reign of Josiah (640–609). Because of his references to idolatrous worship in Jerusalem, which was abandoned through Josiah's reforms, some argue that he had an influence for good on King Josiah.

Jeremiah (626–580 B.C.). Son of Hilkiah the priest. Throughout his forty-year ministry, Jeremiah was called to deliver the word of the Lord during the reigns of the Judahite kings Josiah, Jehoahaz, Jehoiakim, Jehoiachin, and Zedekiah. The Old Testament book contains the history of his times and many of his writings, and his prophecies are also contained on the brass plates (1 Nephi 5:13). Biographical details about the prophet's life are found throughout the book of Jeremiah, but particularly in chapters 34–45. Though King Jehoiakim and King Zedekiah sought his counsel, they opposed the Lord's advice to submit to Babylon; they thus rejected Jeremiah as a prophet and his attempts to call them to repentance. Jeremiah's unsuccessful attempts to get Judah to repent resulted in his prophecy of the imminent destruction of Jerusalem and the temple and the scattering of his people. Jeremiah declined an invitation from the Babylonians to go to Babylon and remained with his people in Judah to witness the fulfillment of his prophecies. When the Babylonian-appointed governor Gedaliah was killed by Ishmael and his conspirators, a group of Judahites, fearing retribution by the Babylonians, fled to Egypt and forced Jeremiah and his scribe Baruch to accompany them (Jeremiah 41–43). Jeremiah probably died in Egypt.

Huldah (ca. 621 B.C.). A prophetess and wife of Shallum "the keeper of the wardrobe." Huldah lived in Jerusalem in the quarter called the Mishneh (Heb. "second"; KJV "college").[3] When the book of the law was discovered in the temple during Josiah's reforms, Josiah sent the priest Hilkiah and four others to Huldah to ascertain the authenticity of the book as well as to receive a prophecy from the prophetess. She affirmed that the book came from the Lord and pronounced a prophecy of judgment against Judah detailing the destruction that would come after the death of Josiah (2 Kings 22:14–20; 2 Chronicles 34:22–28).

Nahum (ca. 630–612 B.C.). Nahum was a prophet from the village of Elkosh in southern Judah. He prophesied the destruction of the Assyrian city of Nineveh, which took place in 612 B.C.; thus his prophecies must be dated to some time before then.

Habakkuk (ca. 622–605 B.C.). While the book of Habakkuk in the Old Testament is undated, mention is made of "the Chaldeans" (Habakkuk 1:6); thus most scholars believe that he prophesied in Jerusalem during the tumultuous period of the fall of the Assyrian empire and the rise of the Babylonians.

Daniel (ca. 606–536 B.C.). A prophet in exile in Babylon noted for his righteousness and wisdom. Daniel 1:1 records that he went into exile in 606 B.C., though some scholars believe this exile occurred in 597 B.C.[4] The stories of his life are an example to covenant people of how to live in exile: observe dietary laws, pray, and avoid idolatry. In addition, Daniel prophesied the future history of the world, including the changing empires and eventually the restoration, the second coming, and the end of the world.

Ezekiel (ca. 594–574 B.C.). Son of Buzi. A prophet of Judah called to minister to the people in exile in Babylon. He was a priest and prophesied in vision the idolatry in Jerusalem, the destruction in 586 B.C., and the scattering of Israel (Ezekiel 8–11). He also prophesied about the future coming of a Messiah, the gathering of Israel, and the restoration of the temple.

Urijah (ca. 609 B.C.). Son of Shemaiah from Kiriath Jearim. A prophet in Jerusalem at the time of Jeremiah. After escaping from Jerusalem to Egypt, Urijah was captured by the king, brought back to Jerusalem, and killed for his prophecy against Judah and Jerusalem (Jeremiah 26:20–23). Although Jeremiah delivered the same message as Urijah, Jeremiah was preserved through the influence of his friends at the royal court. The story of Urijah illustrates the real danger to Lehi's life as recorded in the Book of Mormon (1 Nephi 1:19–20).

Other People Whom Lehi May Have Known

These people are arranged in alphabetical order. An indication is made at the beginning of the entries of those who figure prominently in Jeremiah's story. A plus sign (+) means they were supportive of Jeremiah, and a minus sign (–) means they were opposed to him.

Abdon son of Micah. One of the group of messengers to whom Josiah gave the book of the law to take to Huldah (2 Chronicles 34:20; cf. list in 2 Kings 22:12).

Achbor son of Micaiah. One of the officials sent by Josiah to consult the prophetess Huldah on the occasion of the finding of the book of the law (2 Kings 22:12; cf. list in 2 Chronicles 34:20).

– **Ahab son of Kolaiah.** A false prophet in Babylon. Jeremiah wrote a letter to the exiles there condemning Ahab and Zedekiah (another false prophet) for immoral behavior and false prophecy (Jeremiah 29:21).

+ **Ahikam son of Shaphan.** One of the group of messengers to whom Josiah gave the book of the law to take to Huldah (2 Kings 22:12; 2 Chronicles 34:20). Ahikam gave Jeremiah protection following his famous temple sermon and trial of 609 (Jeremiah 26:24).

Asahiah (Asaiah). A servant to the king. One of the group of messengers to whom Josiah gave the book of the law to take to Huldah (2 Kings 22:12; 2 Chronicles 34:20).

Asaph. A member of a guild of singers put in charge of the singing at Josiah's Passover (2 Chronicles 35:15).

+ **Baruch son of Neriah son of Maaseiah.** Baruch was a faithful friend and scribe to Jeremiah. He is a prominent character in Jeremiah 32, 36, 43, and 45. He wrote Jeremiah's prophecies (Jeremiah 36:4, 32), and he was a witness to Jeremiah's purchase of the family land in Anathoth (Jeremiah 32:11–15). Following the destruction of Jerusalem, he remained with Jeremiah and was eventually taken with him to Egypt (Jeremiah 43:6).

+ **Delaiah son of Shemaiah.** A member of Jehoiakim's royal cabinet and one of the three who unsuccessfully attempted to get King Jehoiakim not to burn Jeremiah's scroll (Jeremiah 36:12, 25).

+ **Ebed-melech.** His name means "servant of the king." Ebed-melech was an Ethiopian servant of Zedekiah who rescued Jeremiah from a cistern used as a dungeon (Jeremiah 38:7–13). As a reward for his service, Jeremiah promised him that his life would be spared at the destruction of Jerusalem (Jeremiah 39:15–18).

+ **Elasah son of Shaphan.** A messenger sent by Zedekiah to Babylon carrying with him a letter written by Jeremiah to the exiles (Jeremiah 29:3).

Elishama. A secretary, or scribe, during the reign of Jehoiakim (Jeremiah 36:12, 20–21).

Elnathan son of Achbor. A royal official during the reign of Jehoiakim. He was sent by the king to capture and bring back the fugitive prophet Urijah, who had fled to Egypt (Jeremiah 26:22). He was among the Judahite officials who unsuccessfully attempted to dissuade King Jehoiakim from burning the scroll dictated by Jeremiah (Jeremiah 36:12, 25). This Elnathan may be the one whose daughter married Jehoiakim (2 Kings 24:8).

+ **Gedaliah son of Ahikam.** A royal official. Gedaliah was appointed governor of Judah by the Babylonians after the destruction of Jerusalem (2 Kings 25:22–26; Jeremiah 40:6–41:18). He was aided in his rule by Jeremiah but was assassinated after only two or three months by a group of Judahite nationalists. After his death his supporters fled to Egypt, forcing Jeremiah and Baruch to go with them.

– **Gedaliah son of Pashur.** One of the four officials of King Zedekiah who demanded that Jeremiah be put to death for the treasonable content of his prophecies urging surrender to the Babylonians. Zedekiah granted their demand and gave Jeremiah over to them to be cast into a dry cistern to die (Jeremiah 38:1–6). Jeremiah was saved by Ebed-melech (Jeremiah 38:7–13).

+ **Gemariah son of Hilkiah.** Zedekiah sent Gemariah with Elasah as messengers to Nebuchadnezzar. They carried a letter from Jeremiah to the exiles (Jeremiah 29:1–3).

+ **Gemariah son of Shaphan the scribe.** Son of the royal secretary and brother of Ahikam. Gemariah had a chamber in the temple complex where Baruch read Jeremiah's prophecies. He was among the officials who urged Jeremiah and Baruch to hide and urged King Jehoiakim not to burn the scroll (Jeremiah 36:10–26).

Hanameel son of Shallum. The cousin of Jeremiah whose field at Anathoth the prophet purchased as a symbol of the future return of Israel to their land (Jeremiah 32:7–15).

– Hananiah son of Azur. A false prophet from Gibeon who prophesied the imminent liberation of the Judahites from Babylonian rule and the return of the temple vessels from Babylon within two years (Jeremiah 28). This was in contrast to Jeremiah's warning that Judah should accept the rule of the Babylonians. Jeremiah accused him of false prophecies and correctly foretold Hananiah's death within a year (Jeremiah 28:17).

Heman. A member of a guild of singers put in charge of the singing at Josiah's Passover (2 Chronicles 35:15).

Hilkiah. A Levitical priest from Anathoth and the father of Jeremiah (Jeremiah 1:1). Possibly he was a descendant of Bather, the last high priest of the house of Eli, who was exiled to Anathoth at the time of Solomon (1 Kings 2:26–27).

Hilkiah son of Shallum. A Levitical high priest who was active during the reign of King Josiah. It was Hilkiah who found the book of the law in the temple. He played a role in Josiah's reforms (2 Kings 22–23; 2 Chronicles 34–35) and provided the sacrifices for Josiah's Passover celebration (2 Chronicles 35:8). Hilkiah was one of the group of messengers to whom Josiah gave the book of the law to take to Huldah (2 Kings 22:12; 2 Chronicles 34:20). He gave a Passover offering to the priests and Levites (2 Chronicles 35:8).

– Irijah son of Shelemiah. A sentry at the Benjamin Gate in Jerusalem who arrested Jeremiah and had him thrown in prison when he was accused of deserting to the Babylonians (Jeremiah 37:13–14).

– **Ishmael son of Nethaniah.** A member of the royal family who went to Gedaliah at Mizpah after the destruction of Jerusalem (Jeremiah 40:8–41:18; 2 Kings 25:23–25). He betrayed Judah by organizing a conspiracy to assassinate the governor, Gedaliah, along with other supporters. He captured the residents of Mizpah, including Jeremiah, but was driven off by others loyal to Gedaliah. He escaped to live among the Ammonites.

Jaazaniah son of Jeremiah (not the prophet). Presumably the head of the Rechabite community (Jeremiah 35). During the reign of King Jehoiakim, the prophet Jeremiah tested Jaazaniah and the Rechabites before the people of Judah by asking them to drink wine, which they would not do because it was against their beliefs. Jeremiah used the Rechabites as an example of obedience and faithfulness in contrast to the Judahites, who did not always live according to their beliefs.

Jaazaniah (Jezaniah) son of a Maachathite. A commander of the troops under the governor Gedaliah at Mizpah (2 Kings 25:23; cf. Jeremiah 40:8).

Jahath son of Merari. A Levite who oversaw the work on the temple during the reign of Josiah (2 Chronicles 34:12).

Jeduthun. The king's seer and a member of a guild of singers put in charge of the singing at Josiah's Passover (2 Chronicles 35:15).

Jehiel. A ruler at the temple at the time of Josiah who gave a Passover offering to the priests and Levites (2 Chronicles 35:8).

Jehucal son of Shelemiah. Royal official sent by King Zedekiah to Jeremiah to get the prophet to pray to the Lord for Judah (Jeremiah 37:3).

Jehudi son of Nethaniah. A royal official sent to summon Baruch to bring Jeremiah's prophecies before King Jehoiakim (Jeremiah 36:14). Later he brought the scroll, read portions of it to the king, and cut off and burned portions of it (Jeremiah 36:12–23).

Jerahmeel son of Hammelech ("son of the king"). A royal official assigned police duties under King Jehoiakim sent to seize Jeremiah and Baruch after the scroll containing Jeremiah's prophecies was burned (Jeremiah 36:26). It is not certain if "son of the king" is an honorary title or a designation of actual relationship to the royal family. He may have been the son of King Jehoiakim or of another one of the kings of Judah. See Malchiah son of Hammelech (below).

– **Jezaniah son of Hashanah.** A military commander (Jeremiah 42:1). Probably the same person as Azariah who opposed Jeremiah's advice not to flee to Egypt (Jeremiah 43:2).

Joah son of Joahaz the recorder. One of the messengers sent by Josiah to repair the temple (2 Chronicles 34:8).

– **Johanan and Jonathan sons of Kareah.** Judahite commanders who joined Gedaliah in Mizpah (Jeremiah 40:8) and later, against of the advice of Jeremiah, led a group of people to Egypt, taking Jeremiah and Baruch with them (Jeremiah 42:1–43:7).

Jonathan. A royal official who held the position of scribe. His house was used as a temporary prison for Jeremiah (Jeremiah 37:15, 20; 38:26).

– **Jucal/Jehucal son of Shelemiah.** One of the four officials of King Zedekiah who demanded Jeremiah be put to death for the treasonable content of his prophecies advocating surrender to the Babylonians (Jeremiah 38:1–6). Zedekiah granted their demand and gave Jeremiah over to them to be cast into a dry cistern to die. He was saved by Ebed-melech (Jeremiah 38:7–13).

Maaseiah. A governor of Jerusalem during the reign of Josiah who was assigned to repair the temple (2 Chronicles 34:8).

+ **Maaseiah son of Shallum.** A doorkeeper of the temple at the time of Jeremiah (Jeremiah 35:4).

Malchiah son of Hammelech. A member of the royal family and owner of the cistern in which Jeremiah was imprisoned (Jeremiah 38:6). The word *hammelek* in Hebrew means "the king"; thus Malchiah son of Hammelech can be translated as "Malchiah the son of the king" (NRSV "the king's son"). The name Malchiah means "Jehovah is king." Latter-day Saint scholars have argued that the shortened form of this name may be Mulek and that Malchiah the son of Hammelech may be a reference to Mulek son of King Zedekiah (Helaman 6:10; 8:21).[5]

Meshullam. One of the overseers of the work on the temple during the reign of Josiah (2 Chronicles 34:12).

Michaiah son of Gemariah. He reported the reading of Jeremiah's scroll to the court officials of King Jehoiakim in 605 B.C. (Jeremiah 36:11–13).

Nathan-melech. A chamberlain (eunuch) at the time of Josiah. Josiah had the horses dedicated to the sun removed from their quarters near Nathan-melech's room (2 Kings 23:11).

Obadiah son of Merari. A Levite who oversaw the work on the temple during the reign of Josiah (2 Chronicles 34:12).

Offerers of gifts at Passover. A passage in 2 Chronicles 35:9 lists several individuals who offered gifts to the Levites at the Passover of Josiah, including Cononiah, Shemaiah, Nethaneel, Hashabiah, Jeiel, and Jozabad.

– **Pashur son of Immer.** A priest and official in the temple (Jeremiah 20:1–6). After hearing Jeremiah's prophecy of destruction, Pashur had Jeremiah beaten, put in stocks, and imprisoned overnight. The next day Jeremiah prophesied that Pashur and his family and friends would be taken to Babylon, where they would spend the rest of their lives.

– **Pashur son of Malchiah.** One of the four officials of King Zedekiah who demanded that Jeremiah be put to death for the treasonable content of his prophecies to surrender to the

Babylonians (Jeremiah 38:1–6). Zedekiah granted their demand and gave Jeremiah over to them to be cast into a dry cistern to die. He was saved by Ebed-melech (Jeremiah 38:7–13).

Seraiah son of Azariah. High priest of Jerusalem, and one of the Judahite royal officials put to death in Riblah by Nebuchadnezzar after the destruction of Jerusalem in 586 B.C. (Jeremiah 52:24–27; 2 Kings 25:18–21).

Seraiah son of Azriel. A royal officer under King Jehoiakim sent to seize Jeremiah and Baruch after the scroll containing Jeremiah's prophecies was burned (Jeremiah 36:26).

+ **Seraiah son of Neriah and brother of Baruch.** A high official in the court of King Zedekiah and a friend and protector of Jeremiah and supporter of his ministry (see Jeremiah 50–51). Seraiah accompanied Zedekiah in his visit to Babylon in the fourth year of his reign. On this occasion Jeremiah instructed him to take a scroll containing the prophecies of destruction against Babylon, read them to the people there, and then throw the scroll into the Euphrates with a stone tied to it, also uttering the words of a curse (Jeremiah 51:59–64).

Seraiah son of Tanhumeth. A Judahite military commander who gathered to Gedaliah at Mizpah (Jeremiah 40:8).

Shallum father of Hanameel. Jeremiah's uncle, whose son Hanameel sold Jeremiah a field in the family hometown of Anathoth during the siege of Jerusalem as a sign of the eventual return of Judah to her land (Jeremiah 32:6–12).

+ **Shaphan son of Aziliah and father of Ahikam, Elasah, and Gemariah.** A prominent scribe to King Josiah who was sent to distribute the wages to the workers on the temple in 622 B.C. when the book of the law was discovered. Shaphan read the book to Josiah and was sent with several others to take it to Huldah to verify its authenticity (2 Kings 22:3–20; 2 Chronicles 34:8–22). His sons Ahikam (Jeremiah 26:24), Elasah (Jeremiah 29:3), and

Gemariah (Jeremiah 36:10–26)—also scribes during the ministry of Jeremiah (2 Kings 22:3, 12; Jeremiah 29:3; 36:10)—helped the prophet. His grandson Gedaliah son of Ahikam was the governor set over Judah by Nebuchadnezzar after the destruction of Jerusalem (2 Kings 25:22–26; Jeremiah 40:6–41:18).

Shelemiah son of Abdeel. A royal official under King Jehoiakim sent to seize Jeremiah and Baruch after the scroll containing Jeremiah's prophecies was burned (Jeremiah 36:26).

– Shemaiah a Nehelamite. A false prophet living among the exiles in Babylon (Jeremiah 29:24–32). Shemaiah prophesied the imminent return of the people to Judah and urged the priests in Jerusalem to rebuke and imprison Jeremiah for prophesying that the exile would last a long time. Jeremiah prophesied that Shemaiah would not have descendants among the people of Judah and would not live long enough to return from exile.

– Shephatiah son of Mattan. One of the four officials of King Zedekiah who demanded that Jeremiah be put to death for the treasonable content of his prophecies advocating surrender to the Babylonians (Jeremiah 38:1–6). Zedekiah granted their demand and gave Jeremiah over to them to be cast into a dry cistern to die. He was saved by Ebed-melech (Jeremiah 38:7–13).

Sons of Ephai the Netophathite. Some of the Judahite commanders who gathered to Gedaliah at Mizpah after the destruction of Jerusalem (Jeremiah 40:8).

Sons of Hanan son of Igdaliah, a man of God. The sons of Hanan had a room near the chamber of the princes where Jeremiah brought the Rechabites (Jeremiah 35:4). Their father is called a "man of God," which may mean he was a prophet.

Uzza. A man who owned a garden in Jerusalem during the reign of Amon. King Amon was buried in a sepulcher in his garden (2 Kings 21:26).

Zechariah. One of the overseers of the work on the temple during the reign of Josiah (2 Chronicles 34:12).

Zechariah. A ruler at the temple at the time of Josiah who gave a Passover offering to the priests and Levites (2 Chronicles 35:8).

Zedekiah. An otherwise unknown son of King Jehoiakim (1 Chronicles 3:16).

Zedekiah son of Hananiah. A royal official in the court of King Jehoiakim who was among those who listened to Michaiah's report of Baruch's reading of Jeremiah's prophecies (Jeremiah 36:12).

– **Zedekiah son of Maaseiah.** A false prophet contemporary with Jeremiah. Jeremiah accused him of false prophecy—of not being sent by the Lord—and immoral behavior and predicted his death (Jeremiah 29:21–23).

+ **Zephaniah son of Maaseiah.** He was the "second priest" in rank to the high priest Seraiah (Jeremiah 52:24). Twice Zephaniah served as an emissary from King Zedekiah to Jeremiah asking him to inquire of the Lord as to what Zedekiah should do (Jeremiah 21:1; 37:3). The false prophet Shemaiah who was exiled to Babylon wrote Zephaniah a letter rebuking him for not having Jeremiah imprisoned (Jeremiah 29:24–28); Zephaniah read the letter to Jeremiah (Jeremiah 24:29).

Notes

1. The names of the individuals are taken from 2 Kings 21–25; 2 Chronicles 33–36; and the book of Jeremiah. For a more limited list of these names, see "The *Dramatis Personae* in the Book of Jeremiah," in Jack R. Lundbom, *Jeremiah: A New Translation with Introduction and Commentary* (New York: Doubleday, 1999), 882–84. The Mesopotamian rulers and chronologies are found in A. Leo Oppenheim, *Ancient Mesopotamia: Portrait of a Dead Civilization,*

rev. ed. (Chicago: University of Chicago Press, 1977), 335–40. The Egyptian rulers are found in William W. Hallo and William Kelly Simpson, *The Ancient Near East: A History* (New York: Harcourt, Brace, Jovanovich, 1971), 299–302.

2. See Margaret Barker, "What Did King Josiah Reform?" in this volume, pages 523–42.

3. See Jeffrey R. Chadwick, "Lehi's House at Jerusalem and the Land of His Inheritance," in this volume, pages 81–130.

4. This point is covered by Robert F. Smith, "Book of Mormon Event Structure: The Ancient Near East," *Journal of Book of Mormon Studies* 5/2 (1996): 117–18; see John J. Collins, *Daniel: A Commentary on the Book of Daniel* (Minneapolis: Fortress, 1993), 130–33.

5. H. Curtis Wright, "Mulek," in *Encyclopedia of Mormonism,* 2:970.

*A*nd in that same year there came many prophets, prophesying unto the people that they must repent, or the great city Jerusalem must be destroyed. (1 Nephi 1:4)

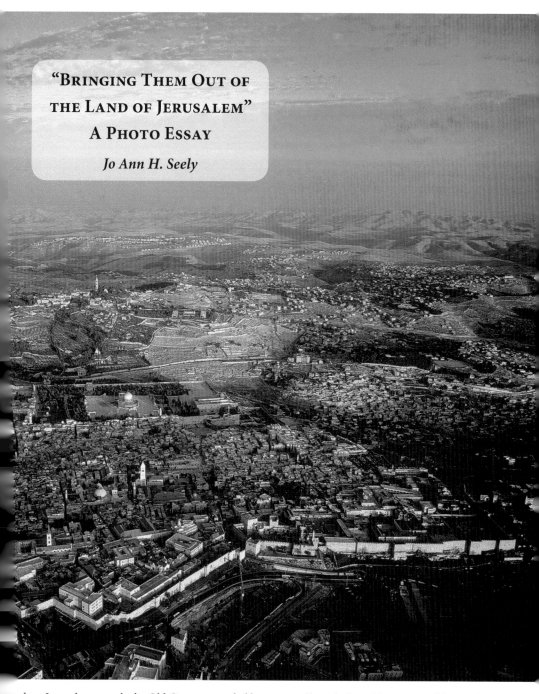

"Bringing Them Out of the Land of Jerusalem" A Photo Essay

Jo Ann H. Seely

odern Jerusalem reveals the Old City surrounded by stone walls with the golden Dome of the Rock in the ter of the Temple Mount. Jerusalem at the time of Lehi was the small area that sloped down the hill to right of the Temple Mount. In this photo looking east, the Mount of Olives can be seen directly above Temple Mount with the Judean Hills in the background. © Albatross Photography

*W*herefore it came to pass that my father, Lehi, as he went forth prayed unto the Lord, yea, even with all his heart, in behalf of his people. (1 Nephi 1:5)

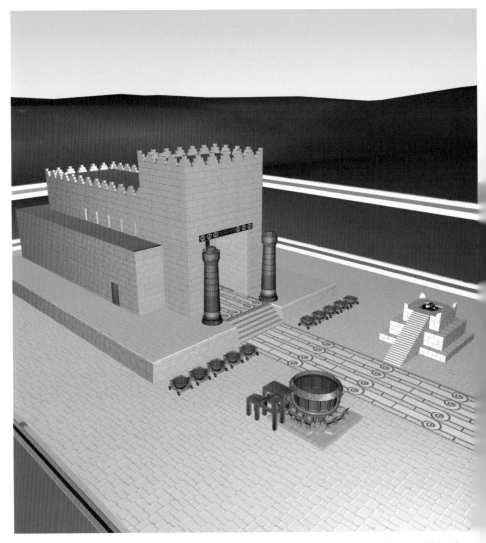

The Temple of Solomon, as seen in this artist's rendition, was nearly four hundred years old by the time of Lehi and was a monumental building for its time. The temple was the focal point of worship and prayer for all of Israel. Lehi would have been present here on several occasions. Many people at the time of Lehi did not believe Jerusalem would be destroyed, as Lehi's sons Laman and Lemuel verbalized (1 Nephi 2:13). Most Jerusalemites viewed the temple as a visible symbol of their security (Jeremiah 7). In front of the temple stood two pillars, the brazen sea, and the altar of burnt offering

nd I, Nephi, did build a temple; and I did construct it after the manner of the temple of Solomon save it were not built of so many precious things. (2 Nephi 5:16)

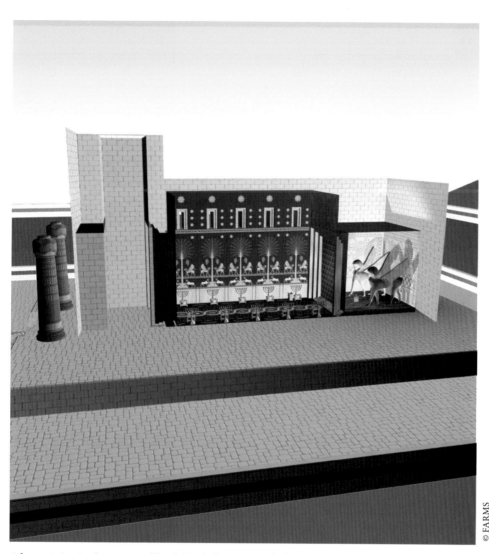

After arriving in the promised land, Nephi built a temple following the pattern of the temple in Jerusalem. This cutaway view shows the three distinct rooms of the temple: the porch just behind the pillars; the holy place in the center, including the menorahs, shewbread tables, and incense altar; and, just beyond the veil, the holy of holies, where the cherubim stood on each side of the ark of the covenant.

*A*nd it came to pass that he [Lehi] returned to his own house at Jerusalem. (1 Nephi 1:7)

This model shows Jerusalem of the First Temple period from the south. The city, surrounded by walls, sloped down the hill from the Temple Mount with valleys on both the east and the west. By the time of Lehi the city had expanded beyond the walls to the west, with new settlement areas known as the Mishneh and Makhtesh. It is likely that Lehi lived in the expanded area of the city with many other families from the northern tribes that had moved south during the Assyrian occupation. Jerusalem of Lehi's time had a population of approximately 25,000 inhabitants in an area of about 125 acres. (From Magen Broshi, "Estimating the Population of Ancient Jerusalem," *Biblical Archaeology Review* 4/2 [June 1978]: 12.)

𝒴ea, and many things did my father read concerning Jerusalem—that it should be destroyed, and the inhabitants thereof; many should perish by the sword, and many should be carried away captive into Babylon. (1 Nephi 1:13)

Images on this page: Staatliche Museen zu Berlin, Vorderasiatisches Museum, Berlin (Jürgen Liepe)\bpk 2003

Reassembled Ishtar Gate from ancient Babylon (in the Pergamon Museum, Berlin). Located on the eastern bank of the Euphrates River, Babylon maintained a civilization in Mesopotamia for nearly 2,000 years and was at its peak during the reign of Nebuchadnezzar (604–562 B.C.). It was a vast city of approximately 2,125 acres and had numerous palaces and 43 cultic sites. The Ishtar Gate was part of the Processional Way through which images of the gods were carried during the New Year festival. It was made of baked glazed bricks and was over 12 meters high. (See Joan G. Westenholz, ed., *Royal Cities of the Biblical World* [Jerusalem: Bible Lands Museum, 1995], 208.)

Cuneiform tablet recording the food allowance of Jehoiachin, king of Judah, living in exile in Babylon (see 2 Kings 25:27).

Behold he [Lehi] went forth among the people, and began to prophesy . . . And it came to pass that the Jews did mock him; . . . they were angry with him; yea, even as with the prophets of old, . . . and they also sought his life. (1 Nephi 1:18–20)

One of the few representations of the population of ancient Palestine. Note the multicolored knee-length garments of the women and the beards worn by the men. (Procession of Asiatics from Palestine, painted on the Tomb of Khnumhotep III, Beni-Hasan, Egypt, ca. 1900 B.C.)

Seals from the First Temple period (8th–6th centuries B.C.). Seals were used in the ancient world to protect property and to authenticate transactions or documents. The king's seal represented his authority. Representing personal identity, the seals were also used by scribes, merchants, and property owners. They bear the names of both men and women.

(Right top) Barren hills of the Ju wilderness to the east of Jerus

(Right bottom) The wilderne the Red Sea (seen in the uppe There are several possible route: Jerusalem to the Red Sea that Le his family may have traveled; e them involved diverse terrain a nificant distance. The Red Sea is ap mately 200 miles from Jeru

*T*he Lord commanded my father . . . that he should take his family and depart into the wilderness. . . . And he left his house, and the land of his inheritance, . . . and took nothing with him, save it were his family, and provisions, and tents, and departed into the wilderness. (1 Nephi 2:2, 4)

© FARMS

*A*nd he traveled in the wilderness in the borders which are nearer the Red Sea; and he did travel in the wilderness with his family, which consisted of my mother, Sariah, and my elder brothers, who were Laman, Lemuel, and Sam. (1 Nephi 2:5)

© Albatross Photography

He pitched his tent in a valley by the side of a river of water.
(1 Nephi 2:6)

Modern Bedouin tents may be similar to those used thousands of years ago.

© Werner Braun

Altar located in th
Judean city of Ara
and made of unhe
stones as prescrib
by the law of Mos
(Exodus 20:25), u
from approximat
the tenth to the
beginning of the
enth centuries B.

And it came to pass that he built an altar of stones, and made an
offering unto the Lord, and gave thanks unto the Lord our God.
(1 Nephi 2:7)

*T*he Lord hath commanded me that thou [Nephi] and thy brethren
shall return to Jerusalem. . . . Go unto the house of Laban, and seek
the records, and bring them down hither into the wilderness. (1 Nephi 3:2, 4)

Part of a home excavated in Jerusalem dating to the Iron Age II period. Known as the house of
Ahiel, it was destroyed in the Babylonian siege of 587/586 B.C. The drawing below is an artist's
reconstruction of the house. This type of home would most likely have belonged to someone of
prominence or wealth in the community. The artist's reconstruction shows a pillared, Israelite
four-room home with three additional rooms added on the north end, including an indoor toilet.

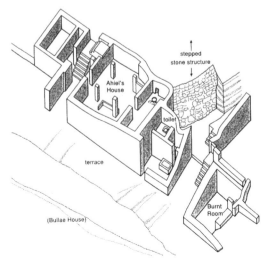

Pottery recovered from Jerusalem from
the final phase of the Iron Age II period
(720–586 B.C.), contemporary with Lehi.

*A*nd *behold, it came to pass that Laban was angry, . . . and he would not that he [Laman] should have the records. . . . Wherefore, let us be faithful in keeping the commandments of the Lord; therefore let us go down to the land of our father's inheritance, for behold he left gold and silver, and all manner of riches. (1 Nephi 3:13, 16)*

The land of Lehi's inheritance may have been located in the tribal inheritance of Manasseh, which was located north of both Jerusalem and the hills of Ephraim and was on both the east and west sides of the Jordan River. This view looks east past the Jordan River to the area of Gilead, which was part of the tribal area of Manasseh.

(Right top) Silver pieces and trea
were often hidden in jars like these ╪
at Eshtemoa, a site south of Jerus
These five jars located in situ cont
over sixty pounds of silver an╪
to approximately 8C

(Right bottom) Silver pieces from tʰ
found at Eshtemoa after cleʰ

$\mathcal{A}$nd it came to pass that we went in unto Laban, and desired him that he would give unto us the records which were engraven upon the plates of brass, for which we would give unto him our gold, and our silver, and all our precious things. (1 Nephi 3:24)

© Ze'ev Yeivin

© Israel Antiquities Authority

__A__nd now I, Nephi, proceed to give an account upon these plates. . . . Yea, even six hundred years from the time that my father left Jerusalem, a prophet would the Lord God raise up among the Jews—even a Messiah, or, in other words, a Savior of the world. (1 Nephi 10:1, 4)

Ancient book written on six gold plates (measuring 5 cm in length and 4.5 cm in width) bound by gold rings found in southwestern Bulgaria. The book is written in Etruscan characters and dates to approximately 600 B.C. The content suggests that it belonged to a member of the Orpheus cult. Lehi's family obtained the brass plates from Laban in Jerusalem, and Nephi made two other sets of plates: one to chronicle the history (large plates of Nephi) and a second set to preserve a spiritual record (small plates of Nephi).

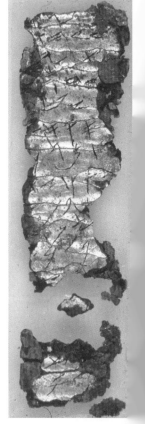

This silver amulet is inscribed with a version of the priestly benediction from Numbers 6:24–26: "The Lord bless thee, and keep thee: The Lord make his face shine upon thee, and be gracious unto thee: The Lord lift up his countenance upon thee, and give thee peace." It is written in archaic Hebrew and dates from the early sixth century B.C.

*A*nd we did sojourn for the space of many years, yea, even eight years in the wilderness. And we did come to the land which we called Bountiful, because of its much fruit and also wild honey; and all these things were prepared of the Lord. . . . And we beheld the sea. (1 Nephi 17:4–5)

Wilderness area near Nihm about 25 miles northeast of Sana'a, capital of the Republic of Yemen, an area Lehi and Sariah may have traversed during their journey. Nihm is likely the location of Nahom, where Ishmael was buried (1 Nephi 16:34).

© FARMS

Looking west across Wadi Sayq to the inlet bay of Khor Kharfot in southern Oman, which has been proposed as a possible site for the area of Bountiful. (See *Journal of Book of Mormon Studies* 7/1 [1998]: 4–21.)

© Warren Aston

*T*he Lord spake unto me, saying: Thou shalt construct a ship, after the manner which I shall show thee, that I may carry thy people across these waters. . . . The Lord told me whither I should go to find ore, that I might make tools. And it came to pass that I, Nephi, did make a bellows wherewith to blow the fire. . . . After I had finished the ship, according to the word of the Lord, my brethren beheld that it was good. . . . After we had sailed for the space of many days we did arrive at the promised land. (1 Nephi 17:8, 10–11; 18:4, 23)

Ancient bellows used in metallurgy excavated at Tell edh-Dhibai, Iraq, ca. 1750 B.C. A skin was attached to the top of the bellows, which was pumped to force air out of the opening into the furnace to produce the heat required to smelt ore. © Chris Davey

Crucible found near copper mines in Sinai, ca. 1500 B.C., used for smelting and casting bronze. © The Petrie Museum

ehi . . . rehearsed unto them, how great things the Lord had done for them in bringing them out of the land of Jerusalem. . . . For, behold, said he, I have seen a vision, in which I know that Jerusalem is destroyed; and had we remained in Jerusalem we should also have perished. (2 Nephi 1:1, 4)

© The British Museum

Cuneiform tablet of the Babylonian Chronicle for the years 605 to 594 B.C. during the reign of Nebuchadnezzar. The events recorded include the siege and capture of Jerusalem (597 B.C.), the appointment of King Zedekiah, and the removal of Judahite exiles to Babylon.

© Israel Exploration Society

Arrowheads found in situ in a layer of ash at the base of an Israelite tower used to defend Jerusalem from the Babylonian siege of 587/586 B.C. Three of them are flat, leaf-shaped, iron arrowheads typical of those used in Israel during this period. The fourth is a triple-bladed bronze arrowhead of the "Scythian" type used from the seventh century B.C., often by foreign mercenaries.

© Yigael Shiloh

The black ash left from the Babylonian siege of Jerusalem in 587/586 B.C. is visible in the remains of the structure known as "the Burnt Room" due to the thick layer of charred debris found on its floor.

We have obtained a land of promise, a land which is choice above all oth[er] lands; a land which the Lord God hath covenanted with me should be [a] land for the inheritance of my seed. (2 Nephi 1:5)

West coast of Guatemala, a possible location for the arrival of Lehi and his family in the promised land. © John W.

Lake Atitlan, west of Guatemala City. Photograph by Daniel Bates, courtesy David A. Palmer and S.E.H.A.

Wherefore, I, Lehi, have obtained a promise, that inasmuch as those who[m] the Lord God shall bring out of the land of Jerusalem shall keep his com[m]mandments, they shall prosper upon the face of this land; . . . and they shall dwe[ll] safely forever. (2 Nephi 1:9)

Chapter 4

Lehi's House at Jerusalem and the Land of His Inheritance

Jeffrey R. Chadwick

Where did Lehi and his family live before their departure into the wilderness? Nephi reported that Lehi had "dwelt at Jerusalem in all his days" (1 Nephi 1:4) and that he had "his own house at Jerusalem" (1 Nephi 1:7). We also read of a "land of his inheritance" (1 Nephi 2:4), which, along with his house and his riches, Lehi left behind when he took his family into the wilderness. But what was the connection between the two: Jerusalem and Lehi's land of inheritance? Indeed, was there any connection at all? I will examine evidence in 1 Nephi concerning these questions and will supplement those passages with a significant amount of background information from the Old Testament, ancient Near Eastern historical records, and the findings of modern Israeli archaeology.

After assessing all the data, I will suggest that Lehi's house was located in the city quarter of ancient Jerusalem called the Mishneh (the same location today is part of the Jewish Quarter of Jerusalem's Old City). I will further suggest that Lehi's land of inheritance was a piece of real estate about fifty kilometers (thirty miles) north of Jerusalem, in the former tribal area of

Manasseh, which Lehi owned by virtue of having inherited a deed to the property and which he probably visited on occasion in order to manage the affairs of the land. However, I will suggest that he maintained no residence at the land of inheritance. Reading through the evidence from which my data is culled may seem, for some readers, somewhat long and circuitous. Those readers may trust, however, that by the end of this study they will be much more informed about the world of Lehi preceding 1 Nephi and that the above conclusions will be logically supported and understandable.

Before examining the evidence, it will be necessary to dismiss a misconception that has been in circulation among Latter-day Saint students for many years. In his 1952 book *Lehi in the Desert,* Hugh Nibley suggested the following about the residence of Lehi: "Though he 'dwelt at Jerusalem,' Lehi did not live in the city, for it was after they had failed to get the plates in Jerusalem that his sons decided to 'go down to the land of our father's inheritance' (1 Nephi 3:16), and there gather enough wealth to buy the plates from Laban."[1]

The oft-repeated notion that Lehi's house was not inside the city of Jerusalem but somewhere well outside the city on his land of inheritance is simply incorrect. Also incorrect is the idea that Lehi's land of inheritance was a plot of real estate close enough to the city of Jerusalem to be within the boundaries of the greater land of Jerusalem. Lehi's house is sometimes said to have been "at Jerusalem" but not *in* the city Jerusalem, but this whole notion is not tenable since it does not correspond to the information in the Book of Mormon text. To his credit, Nibley himself later realized this error and offered a correction in his 1958 work, *An Approach to the Book of Mormon:*

> He [Lehi] had "his own house at Jerusalem" (1 Nephi 1:7);
> yet he was accustomed to "go forth" from the city from time

to time (1 Nephi 1:5–7), and his paternal estate, the land of his inheritance, where the bulk of his fortune reposed, was some distance from the town (1 Nephi 3:16, 22; 2:4).[2]

Here Nibley correctly alluded to the facts that Lehi's house at Jerusalem was inside the city itself and that his land of inheritance was a distinctly different location from both his house and Jerusalem. In this conclusion Nibley was certainly correct, although he offered no specifics concerning the questions of the location of the land of inheritance or its direction from Jerusalem, nor did he attempt to locate Lehi's house in any specific location within Jerusalem's walls. We may now address both of those issues by turning to the text of 1 Nephi itself.

The Land of Jerusalem versus the Land of Inheritance

It seems clear that Nephi meant for readers of his record to understand that his father Lehi lived in the city of Jerusalem itself, not somewhere outside the city walls. In the same verse in which he reported that his father had "dwelt at Jerusalem in all his days," Nephi called Jerusalem "the great city" (1 Nephi 1:4)—in other words, by saying "Jerusalem" Nephi was making reference to the city itself, not merely the land of Jerusalem region in which the city was located. When Lehi "went forth" to pray (1 Nephi 1:5), he was probably exiting the city walls, just as Nephi himself did later when he said, "I went forth unto my brethren, who were without the walls" (1 Nephi 4:27). It is entirely possible that Lehi went eastward from the walls of Jerusalem. Immediately east of Jerusalem is the Mount of Olives, a perfect place for Lehi's private prayer—he would even have been able to gaze over the Temple Mount and Solomon's temple from that location. Perhaps the Mount of Olives was where Nephi and his brothers went to "hide themselves without the walls" (1 Nephi 4:5), although that would more likely have taken place directly adjacent to the city wall. In any event, Lehi's house clearly seems to have been located within the walls of Jerusalem.

Lehi's land of inheritance is first alluded to in 1 Nephi 2:4. Later, speaking to his brothers, Nephi called it "the land of our father's inheritance" (1 Nephi 3:16). But the real estate seems to have been destined to be passed on to Lehi's sons, for Nephi also called it "the land of our inheritance" (1 Nephi 3:22). The land of inheritance is not to be confused with the land of Jerusalem first mentioned in 1 Nephi 3:9. From the text of 1 Nephi as a whole, two things are obvious about the land of Jerusalem region: (1) The city of Jerusalem is obviously within the boundaries of the land of Jerusalem, and (2) the land of Jerusalem is a totally different region from Lehi's land of inheritance.

These observations are demonstrated by a three-step examination of Nephi's text:

1.   Nephi and his brothers returned from the valley of Lemuel *up* to the land of Jerusalem (1 Nephi 3:9).

2.   They then went *down* to the land of inheritance to collect Lehi's gold and silver (1 Nephi 3:16, 22).

3.   Finally, Nephi and his brothers returned back *up* again to Jerusalem (1 Nephi 3:23).

It is important to remember that in the idiom of Nephi one always went *up* to come to the Jerusalem region, and one always went *down* when exiting the Jerusalem region. This is also the Hebrew idiom employed in the Bible, where persons in both the Old and New Testaments typically are said to go *down* to leave Jerusalem (see, for example, 2 Samuel 5:17; Luke 10:30; and Acts 8:15) and go *up* to come to Jerusalem (see, for example, 2 Chronicles 2:16 and Matthew 20:18). Nephi adhered to this Hebrew idiom throughout his account—whenever his party is reported to have gone to Jerusalem, they went *up* (see 1 Nephi 3:9; 4:4; 5:6; 7:3–4), and whenever the reference is to leaving the Jerusalem region, they went *down* (see 1 Nephi 2:5; 3:4, 16, 22; 4:35; 5:1; 7:2, 5). It should be clear, then, that when Nephi and his brothers go *down* to the land of inheritance, they are in fact leaving the region of Jerusalem. The land of Jerusalem is clearly *not* the same as the land of inheritance. Since the location of Jerusalem has not changed, the question now becomes: Where was the land of inheritance?

For reasons that will become obvious in this discussion, Lehi's land of inheritance was most likely not located within the borders of the southern kingdom of Judah. The most likely location for Lehi's ancestral real estate in the ancient land of Israel was the region of Manasseh. Lehi is reported to have been a descendant of Manasseh, the son of Joseph who was sold into Egypt (see 1 Nephi 5:14 and Alma 10:3). The ancient tribe of Manasseh possessed large tracts of land on both sides of the Jordan River (see photo essay, p. 74). As described in the Bible (Joshua 13:29–31 and 17:7–10), the territory of Manasseh east of the Jordan was equivalent to the area of Bashan (the modern Golan) and the northern part of Gilead (north of modern Amman). West of the Jordan, Manasseh held territory in what came to be known as the Samaria region, from the Jezreel Valley on the north to Tappuah on the south—Tappuah being about thirty-five kilometers (twenty-one miles) north of Jerusalem (see fig. 1). Historical considerations suggest that the area west of Jordan and north of Tappuah—specifically between ancient Tirzah on the east and modern Jenin on the west—was more likely than any other segment of Manasseh to have been the location of Lehi's ancestral land tract. We will now explore those considerations and how it was that people of Manasseh came to live in Jerusalem, making it possible for

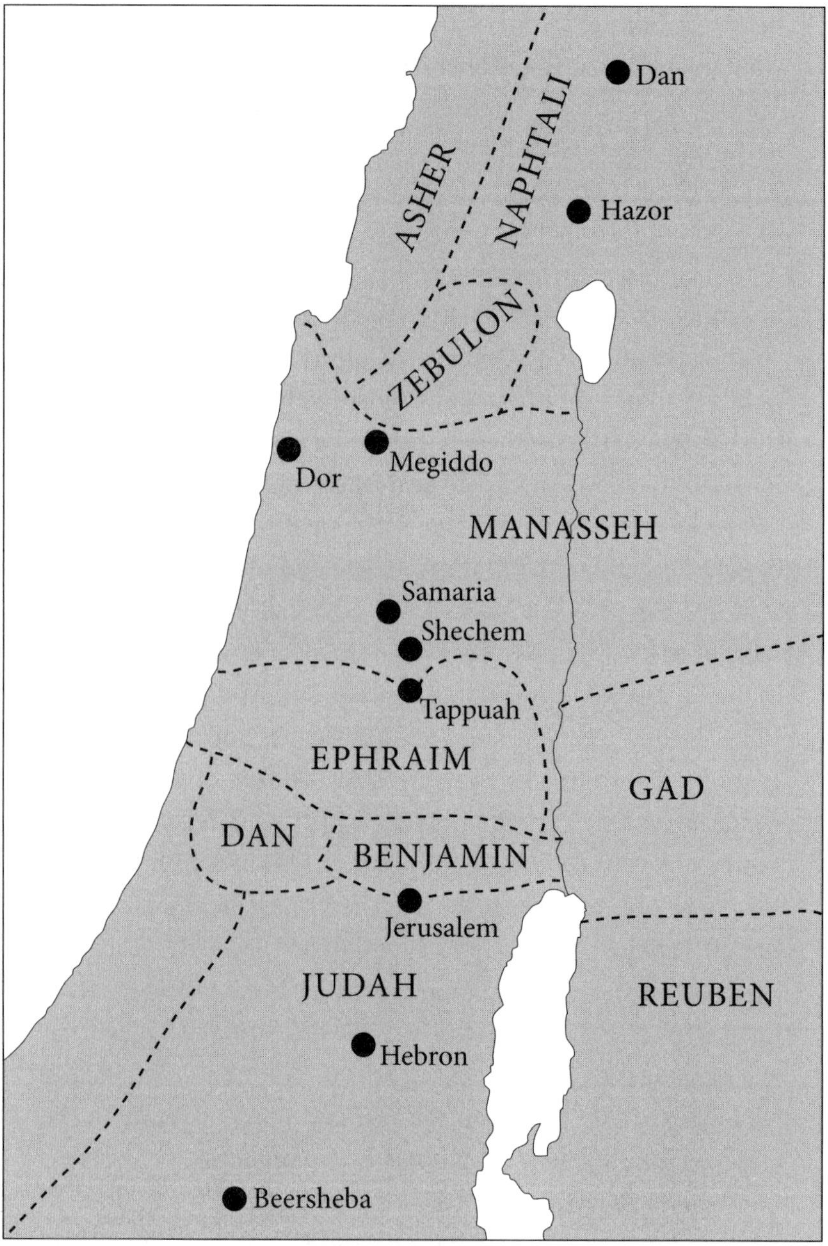

Figure 1. Traditional territories of the tribes of Israel.

Lehi to have been born there and to have dwelled there all his days until the time of his exodus in 1 Nephi 2.

Lehi's Ancestors—From Manasseh to Jerusalem

At least two significant migrations of Israelites from the Manasseh tribal areas to Jerusalem are now known. The first is reported in the Bible, and the second (for our investigation the more significant) has been discerned through the efforts of Israeli archaeologists working in Jerusalem. The first account, found in 2 Chronicles, reports that a number of Israelites from northern tribes left the northern kingdom of Israel and defected to the southern kingdom of Judah during the fifteenth year of Asa, king of Judah (about 900 B.C.). In speaking of Asa, the record reports that "he gathered all Judah and Benjamin, and the strangers with them out of Ephraim and Manasseh, and out of Simeon: for they fell to him out of Israel in abundance" (2 Chronicles 15:9).

While it is possible that these early defectors from Manasseh were the ancestors of Lehi, it is highly improbable. Political factors work against it. For example, Judah and Israel, led by King Asa and King Baasha respectively, were enemies at the time. In leaving Baasha's northern kingdom to join Asa's Judah, the defectors essentially forfeited all rights and privileges they might have claimed in the north, including title to their lands. It is most unlikely that Lehi would have had any claim to land in Manasseh if he were descended from those who left the region to ally with Asa in the south. Moreover, since Lehi's family was living around 600 B.C., nearly three hundred years after Asa, it is unlikely that any record or even memory of land ownership would have remained with them if they had been descended from the early defectors.

It is far more probable that Lehi was the grandson or great-grandson of people who left western Manasseh as refugees around 724 B.C. and fled south to settle in Jerusalem. The Bible reports that many people of the northern Israelite tribes were deported from the land of Israel in connection with Assyrian conquests between 732 and 722 B.C. These deportations occurred in several different actions. The earliest action, carried out by the Assyrian emperor Tiglath-pileser III and known as the First Northern Deportation, involved the transfer of Israelites from the northern part of the land of Israel and also from across the Jordan in Gilead (where half of Manasseh's territory was found; see fig. 2). This First Northern Deportation occurred about 732 B.C., and 2 Kings 15 reports it thus:

> In the days of Pekah king of Israel came Tiglath-pileser king of Assyria, and took Ijon, and Abel-beth-maachah, and Janoah, and Kedesh, and Hazor, and Gilead, and Galilee, all the land of Naphtali, and carried them captive to Assyria. (2 Kings 15:29)

A subsequent series of deportations, known collectively as the Second Northern Deportation, was carried out by the Assyrian emperors Shalmaneser V and Sargon II between 724 and 722 B.C., resulting in the transfer of Israelites from the hill country of Samaria—the area of Ephraim and the western area of Manasseh (see fig. 2). Second Kings 17 reports it this way:

> Then the king of Assyria came up throughout all the land, and went up to Samaria, and besieged it three years. In the ninth year of Hoshea the king of Assyria took Samaria, and carried Israel away into Assyria, and placed them in Halah and in Habor by the river of Gozan, and in the cities of the Medes. (2 Kings 17:5–6)

The two northern deportations involved many thousands of Israelites of all the northern tribes. A line from the Display Inscriptions of Sargon II contains a specific number of deportees that were taken from the city of Samaria: "I besieged and conquered Samaria [and] led away as booty 27,290 inhabitants

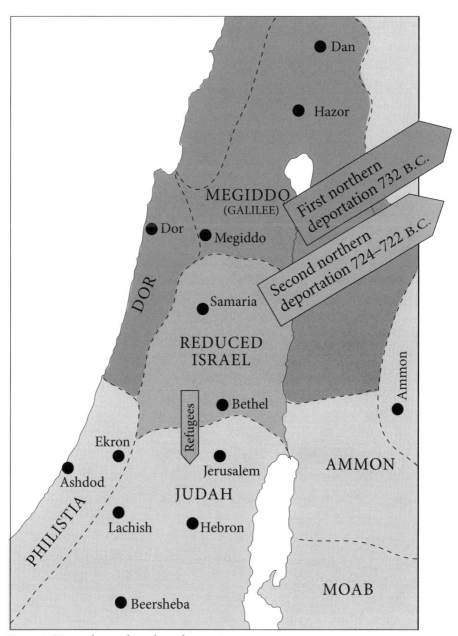

Figure 2. First and second northern deportations.

of it."[3] The so-called Annals of Sargon II make it clear that the Samaria spoken of was not the whole countryside—which naming convention the Assyrians subsequently adopted—but the Israelite capital city itself, which had endured the three-year siege, only to fall in 722 B.C.:

> At the begi[nning of my royal rule, I . . . the town of the Sama]rians [I besieged, conquered] (2 lines destroyed) [for the god . . . who le]t me achieve (this) my triumph. . . . I led away as prisoners 27,290 inhabitants of it. . . . [The town I] re[built] better than (it was) before and [settled] therein people from countries which [I] myself [had con]quered. I placed an officer of mine as governor over them and imposed upon them tribute as (is customary) for Assyrian citizens.[4]

Those 27,290 deportees taken when the city of Samaria fell, and many thousands more from all parts of the northern kingdom of Israel, were resettled far away among gentile peoples and gradually merged with those foreign cultures, eventually forgetting their Israelite lineage and heritage. (Inscriptions with all the specific numbers have not been discovered, but the total number of Israelite deportees probably exceeded one hundred thousand and could possibly have been as high as two hundred thousand.) Collectively, they became the lost tribes of Israel, not because they did not know *where* they were, but because they ultimately forgot *who* they were.

But not *all* the northern Israelites were deported and lost. Though not directly reported in the Bible, a significant number of Israelites appear to have fled the doomed northern kingdom and migrated as refugees to Judah in the south, settling in Jerusalem and other cities of the southern kingdom. This probably began around 724 B.C., incident to the initial attack of Shalmaneser V against Israel in that year (the commencement of the Second Northern Deportation), although refugee movement southward

probably continued for several years thereafter. This refugee
movement has been demonstrated by archaeologists who excavated at Judean sites during the 1970s. They discerned unusually
large population increases at Jerusalem and other locations from
levels dating to the last quarter of the eighth century B.C.—the
exact period of the Assyrian attacks on the northern kingdom. In
terms of this phenomenon in Jerusalem, Israeli archaeologist and
Hebrew University of Jerusalem Professor Nahman Avigad, who
directed excavations in Jerusalem's Jewish Quarter, reported:

> Archaeological finds in the Jewish Quarter clearly show
> that this area was settled in the period of the First Temple,
> from the 8th century B.C. on. . . . Our evidence indicates
> that Israelite houses were spread over the entire plateau of
> the Western Hill. To date, with the exception of a few iso-
> lated sherds, no pottery from before the 8th century B.C. has
> been found here. . . . It can be assumed that the expansion
> of Jerusalem in biblical times, to an area several times that
> of the original city, was brought about largely by the influx
> of refugees from the northern Kingdom of Israel, after the
> Assyrian conquest of Samaria.[5]

The northern kingdom refugees flooding south into Judah
between 724 and 722 B.C. were probably followed by others
who were not initially deported from Israel by the Assyrians
but who felt compelled to move southward in the years between 722 and 715 B.C. because of the destruction of their land
and government and because of the Assyrian importation of
large numbers of gentile foreigners (see 2 Kings 17:24). Those
foreigners became known as Samaritans and continued to live
for centuries in the region the Assyrians called Samaria. The
Israelites who migrated south represented not only Manasseh
and Ephraim but other northern Israelite tribes as well. Passages in 2 Chronicles indicate that these displaced northern

Israelites ("you, that are escaped out of the hand of the kings of Assyria"; 2 Chronicles 30:6) were invited by their new king, Hezekiah of Judah, to come to Jerusalem for the Passover festival he was reintroducing into Judah. King Hezekiah became sole monarch of Judah in 715 B.C., and his Passover invitations were probably extended soon thereafter. The passages in 2 Chronicles seem to refer to northern refugees who were already in Judah but may also have included Israelites who had remained in Samaria and the Galilee and then moved to Judah specifically at Hezekiah's behest:

> Hezekiah sent to all Israel and Judah, and wrote letters also to Ephraim and Manasseh, that they should come to the house of the Lord at Jerusalem, to keep the passover. (2 Chronicles 30:1)

> Ye children of Israel, turn again unto the Lord God of Abraham, Isaac, and Israel, and he will return to the remnant of you, that are escaped out of the hand of the kings of Assyria. (2 Chronicles 30:6)

> Divers [Heb. ʾanashim, literally "men"] of Asher and Manasseh and of Zebulun humbled themselves, and came to Jerusalem. (2 Chronicles 30:11)

> A multitude of the people, even many of Ephraim, and Manasseh, Issachar, and Zebulun (did) eat the passover. (2 Chronicles 30:18)

> And all the congregation that came out of Israel, and the strangers [Heb. gerim can also be rendered "refugees"] that came out of the land of Israel, and that dwelt in Judah, rejoiced. (2 Chronicles 30:25)[6]

These passages indicate that northern Israelites of several tribal lines, including Manasseh and Ephraim, had made their way to Judah to escape the Assyrians and were living at Jerusalem and at other locations in the southern kingdom by the time of King Hezekiah's Passover (ca. 715 B.C.).

The Mishneh of Jerusalem

As indicated earlier in the quotation from Avigad, those recently arrived refugees who decided to settle at Jerusalem began to build new homes on the western hill of the ancient city, an area that is known today as the Jewish Quarter of the Old City. By Lehi's day, this area had become known by the Hebrew name Mishneh, a term that means "addition." (In the King James Version of 2 Kings 22:14 and 2 Chronicles 34:22, the term is confusingly translated as "college," but in Zephaniah 1:10 it is more literally translated as "second.") The Mishneh was a second, or additional, part of ancient Jerusalem, which began essentially as a refugee camp for the arrivals from the north after 724 B.C. but was eventually considered part of the city of Jerusalem proper (see fig. 3). Other parts of the city, populated centuries earlier than the Mishneh, were the city of David (2 Samuel 5:9), the Temple Mount (2 Chronicles 3:1), and the Makhtesh (Zephaniah 1:11). We even know, within a window of roughly four years, just when this Mishneh was physically annexed to Jerusalem—sometime between 705 and 701 B.C. And we can deduce with some certainty that it was to that original Mishneh refugee camp on Jerusalem's western hill that Lehi's Manassite grandparents must have relocated sometime between 724 and 701 B.C. We know all this because of Sennacherib.

Some twenty years after the fall of the Israelite capital at Samaria, the Assyrians attacked the kingdom of Judah, destroying the entire southern kingdom (except for Jerusalem) and deporting hundreds of thousands of people. This dreadful event took place in the aftermath of King Hezekiah's decision to

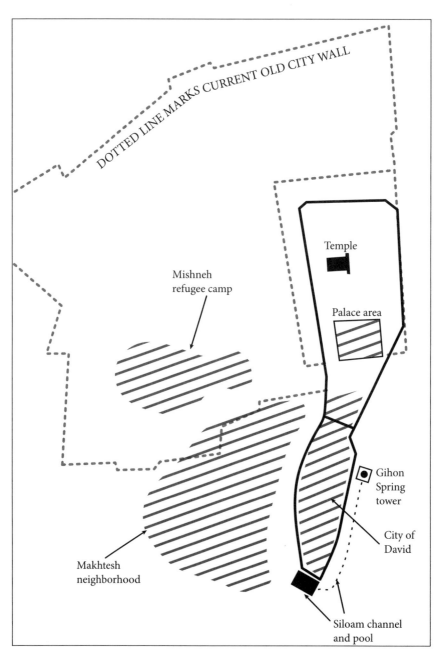

Figure 3. Jerusalem after 724 B.C.

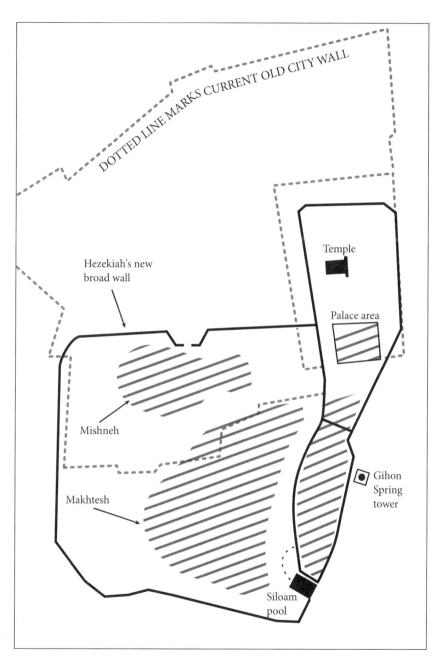

Figure 4. Jerusalem after 705 B.C.

withdraw Judah from the alliance with Assyria that his father, King Ahaz, had entered into around 733 B.C. Against the wishes of the Lord and the advice of the prophet Isaiah (see 2 Kings 16 and Isaiah 7–8), King Ahaz had concluded a treaty with the Assyrians that made Judah a client kingdom to their empire. Ahaz's actions resulted, among other things, in Assyrian idolatry being introduced into the temple at Jerusalem and in Judah agreeing to pay a hefty tribute to the Assyrian empire. But it had also made Judah safe from Assyrian attack, which made the southern kingdom a haven for northern kingdom refugees at the time Assyria was destroying Israel. King Hezekiah, however, was unhappy with the negative aspects of the arrangement his father had forged, and when the Assyrian emperor Sargon II died in 705 B.C., Hezekiah unilaterally canceled the alliance and withheld annual tribute.

Knowing that the new Assyrian king, Sennacherib, would not let this defection go unchallenged, Hezekiah undertook several efforts between 705 and 701 B.C. to strengthen Judah against the retaliatory attack he knew would come. He instituted weapons production, food storage, and water projects all over the southern kingdom (see 2 Chronicles 32:1–8). In Jerusalem, Hezekiah had his famous tunnel constructed to bring water to a pool (reservoir) inside the city (see 2 Kings 20:20; 2 Chronicles 32:30). This allowed Jerusalemites to access their water supply without leaving the safety of their city wall in time of siege.

As for that wall, Hezekiah not only repaired the existing rampart around the City of David but had a huge additional wall built to surround the outer suburbs of Jerusalem, including both the Makhtesh and the Mishneh refugee camp on the western hill (see fig. 4). In 2 Chronicles 32, this wall was referred to as "another wall without," meaning *an additional wall outside the original wall:* "Also he strengthened himself, and built up all the wall that was broken, and raised it up to the towers, and another wall without" (2 Chronicles 32:5). What 2 Chronicles called "another wall" was later called the "broad wall" in Nehemiah 3:8. The name was fitting, for the wall was constructed of solid stone and measured seven meters thick (23 feet) at the base. Remnants of this massive rampart, which stood approximately eight meters high (nearly 27 feet), were also discovered during Avigad's excavation of the Jewish Quarter (see fig. 5). Commenting on the sixty-five-meter section of the broad wall he unearthed in 1970, Avigad concluded: "Apparently, the new wall was the 'another wall' built by Hezekiah, as noted in 2 Chronicles 32:5."[7]

Hezekiah's new wall around the western hills of Jerusalem afforded the northern Israelite refugee residents of the Mishneh camp (which probably included the great-grandparents and

Figure 5. Remains of Hezekiah's "broad wall," discovered by archaeologists in the Jewish Quarter of Jerusalem's Old City during the 1970s, are seen in the bottom portion of this photograph.

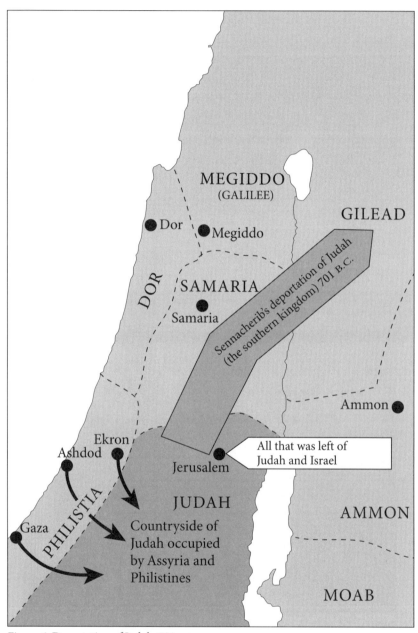

Figure 6. Deportation of Judah, 701 B.C.

grandparents of Lehi) safety from the attack of Sennacherib's Assyrian forces in 701 B.C. But the people of Jerusalem were the *only* ones who were spared the devastating effects of the Assyrian invasion (see fig. 6).

The Assyrian Attack on Judah

The biblical account in 2 Kings reports that every city of Judah other than Jerusalem was taken by the Assyrians in Sennacherib's attack on the country in 701 B.C.: "Now in the fourteenth year of king Hezekiah did Sennacherib king of Assyria come up against all the fenced [i.e., walled] cities of Judah, and took them" (2 Kings 18:13; see also Isaiah 36:1).

The story of horror, suffering, torture, and death implicit in this abbreviated statement is not always obvious to readers moving quickly through the Bible. But more details of the attack were recorded by Sennacherib himself. The account is preserved in cuneiform on a hexagonal pottery relic known as Sennacherib's Prism (see fig. 7). It details Hezekiah's rebellion against the emperor and notes both the number of Judean cities destroyed and the huge total of Judean deportees carried away into captivity:

> As to Hezekiah the Jew, he did not submit to my yoke, I laid siege to 46 of his strong cities, walled forts, and to the countless small villages in their vicinity, and conquered (them)

© The British Museum

Figure 7. The Prism of Sennacherib; a cuneiform account of the Assyrian King Sennacherib's attack upon and deportation of Judah is found upon this hexagonal pottery artifact.

by means of well stamped (earth-)ramps and battering rams. . . . I drove out (of them) 200,150 people, young and old, male and female, horses, mules, donkeys, camels, big and small cattle beyond counting, and considered (them) booty. Himself I made a prisoner in Jerusalem, his royal residence, like a bird in a cage. I surrounded him with earthwork in order to molest those who were leaving his city's gate. His towns which I had plundered, I took away from his country and gave them (over) to Mitinti, king of Ashdod, Padi, king of Ekron, and Sillibel, king of Gaza. Thus I reduced his country, but I still increased the tribute.[8]

The total of Judean deportees was staggering! And although large, the number 200,150 is probably a fairly exact count, within a few persons, of the number of Israelites taken from Judah after the 701 B.C. debacle. The Assyrians employed their policies of deportation in order to secure newly conquered territories, like Israel and Judah, into their empire. Deportation served to break the nationalism and identity of conquered populations, thereby minimizing the chances of those populations successfully rebelling against the empire. The Assyrians were also accomplished accountants. Their conquests were designed not only to establish their military hegemony, but also to create a great *Pax Assyriana,* a stable and peaceful empire that would grow into the economic powerhouse of the ancient Near East in the seventh century B.C. They captured lands and also created new economic and agricultural master plans for those lands and markets for the products of the territories they added to their expanding borders. An example of this activity was the vast expansion of Ekron, a Philistine city thirty-five kilometers (twenty miles) west of Jerusalem, which grew from ten to fifty acres and developed a large olive oil industry (which relied on the Assyrian/Philistine use of Judean fields for olive gardens) all within a short period in the seventh century B.C.[9] The Assyrian macroeconomy required careful accounting, not just of money and territory, but also of people. The Assyrians knew exactly how many people were killed in their battles (careful counts of casualties were kept) and how many were taken as live prisoners.[10] They knew just how many people they would be deporting, where the deportees were coming from, and where they were being resettled. Preparation for the movement of the newly conquered and planning for their arrival in other provinces throughout the empire required having accurate counts. These are the same numbers to which the composers of Sennacherib's Prism would have had access. Thus, figures like 200,150 for the count of deportees from the whole country of Judah in 701 B.C., as well 27,290 from the single city of Samaria alone in 722 B.C., may be confidently taken as fairly accurate counts—they are probably accurate to within ten people, since one figure ends with 50 and the other with 90.

Notably, Sennacherib does not claim to have conquered or destroyed Jerusalem. Although he boasted that he had trapped Hezekiah within the city "like a caged bird," he does not claim to have got inside the cage to get the bird. Both Assyrian sources[11] and the Bible suggest that Jerusalem survived the attack, that Hezekiah continued to reign, and that the city's Judean inhabitants were *not* deported. The biblical record preserves details of Jerusalem's survival in parallel accounts found in 2 Kings 18–19 and Isaiah 36–37, as well as in 2 Chronicles 32. In calling for Jerusalem's surrender, Sennacherib's *rav shakeh,* or chief cup bearer (the KJV transliteration "Rab-shakeh" is not the man's name, but his title; see 2 Kings 18:17, 19, 26–28, 37; 19:4, 8),[12] promised that the city's inhabitants would be spared, but nonetheless would be deported:

> Thus saith the king, Let not Hezekiah deceive you: for he shall not be able to deliver you out of his hand: Neither let

> Hezekiah make you trust in the Lord, saying, The Lord will
> surely deliver us, and this city shall not be delivered into the
> hand of the king of Assyria. Hearken not to Hezekiah: for
> thus saith the king of Assyria, Make an agreement with me
> by a present, and come out to me, and then eat ye every man
> of his own vine, and every one of his fig tree, and drink ye
> every one the waters of his cistern: Until I come and take you
> away to a land like your own land. (2 Kings 18:29–32)

The account in 2 Kings 19 (and repeated in Isaiah 37) proceeds to explain how Hezekiah prayed to the Lord for the preservation of Jerusalem and how the Lord answered back through
the prophet Isaiah. The conclusion of the Lord's answer was the
guarantee that Jerusalem would not fall to the Assyrians, and
that the city's inhabitants ("the remnant that is escaped of the
house of Judah") would survive, not to be deported, but eventually to reconstitute the kingdom of Judah ("again take root
downward, and bear fruit upward"):

> And the remnant that is escaped of the house of Judah
> shall yet again take root downward, and bear fruit upward.
> For out of Jerusalem shall go forth a remnant, and they that
> escape out of mount Zion: the zeal of the Lord of hosts shall
> do this. Therefore thus saith the Lord concerning the king
> of Assyria, He shall not come into this city, nor shoot an
> arrow there, nor come before it with shield, nor cast a bank
> against it. By the way that he came, by the same shall he
> return, and shall not come into this city, saith the Lord. For
> I will defend this city, to save it, for mine own sake, and for
> my servant David's sake. (2 Kings 19:30–34)

The concluding account does not specify the exact nature
of misfortune sent by the Lord upon the Assyrian forces, but
it relates that 185,000 (a more plausible translation is "185
troops")[13] were killed in the divine intervention that caused
Sennacherib to abandon the campaign against Jerusalem:

And it came to pass that night, that the angel of the Lord went out, and smote in the camp of the Assyrians an hundred fourscore and five thousand: and when they arose early in the morning, behold, they were all dead corpses. So Sennacherib king of Assyrian departed, and went and returned, and dwelt at Nineveh. (2 Kings 19:35–36)

So Jerusalem was spared, even though every other city of Judah had been destroyed, and over two hundred thousand of their survivors were deported to eastern regions of the Assyrian empire (see fig. 6). It is estimated that no more than about twenty thousand persons lived inside the city of Jerusalem in 701 B.C., a figure about one-tenth of the population of Judah that the Assyrians deported.[14] It is important to remember that, after 701 B.C., those twenty thousand or so residents of Jerusalem were essentially all that was left of Judah. Indeed, those twenty thousand represented the only remnant of the entire house of Israel that was not taken away by the Assyrians. This is the reality reflected in the first chapter of Isaiah, composed incident to the 701 B.C. siege:

Your country is desolate, your cities are burned with fire: your land, strangers devour it in your presence, and it is desolate, as overthrown by strangers. And the daughter of Zion is left as a cottage in a vineyard, as a lodge in a garden of cucumbers, as a besieged city. Except the Lord of hosts had left unto us a very small remnant, we should have been as Sodom, and we should have been like unto Gomorrah. (Isaiah 1:7–9)

The "daughter of Zion" refers to Jerusalem, and the images of a "cottage in a vineyard" and "a lodge in a garden," while verbally pleasant in English translation, are less elegant in the Hebrew original and refer to harvest shacks left behind in the midst of harvested lands. All of Israel and Judah had been "harvested" so to speak—only Jerusalem had been spared

Figure 8. Scene from the engraved stone panels discovered at Sennacherib's palace at Nineveh, depicting Israelite Judeans being deported from Judah by Sennacherib's Assyrian forces. The figure with a spear is an Assyrian; the other three are Israelite Judeans.

destruction and deportation. It has often been maintained that the northern kingdom of Israel was destroyed and deported by the Assyrians but that the southern kingdom of Judah remained essentially unaffected. In the case of Judah, however, nothing could be further from the truth. Some ninety percent of the kingdom of Judah—consisting not only of people whose tribal heritage was Judah, but of many refugees and other citizens of Judah whose tribal heritage was of Ephraim or Manasseh, Dan or Asher, Zebulon or Naphtali—was also taken away and became part of "lost Israel" (see fig. 8). In this regard, it is perhaps more accurate to speak not of the ten lost tribes, but of the *twelve lost tribes* (or at least the *11.9 lost tribes*) since the majority of *all* twelve tribes, including Judah, was carried away captive by the Assyrians. This was a fact clearly understood in Nephi's day, even though it is not so well known in our own. In fact, Nephi himself spoke of this around 600 B.C., just a century after the 701 B.C. attack:

> And behold, there are many who are already lost from the knowledge of those who are at Jerusalem. Yea, the more part of all the tribes have been led away; and they are scattered to and fro upon the isles of the sea; and whither they are none of us knoweth, save that we know that they have been led away. (1 Nephi 22:4)

The Land of Inheritance—Somewhere in Western Manasseh

The point of reporting this involved history of the Assyrian deportations of both Israel and Judah is to demonstrate where Lehi's great-grandparents must have settled after leaving Manasseh and where his grandparents must have lived—they had to have settled and lived in Jerusalem. Had they settled and lived anywhere else in Judah, they would have either been killed or deported in the Assyrian attack of 701 B.C. This is important not only in locating Lehi's house (which seems most likely to have been in Jerusalem's Mishneh, as will be explained below) but particularly in locating the land of his inheritance. Models that suggest that the land of inheritance was somewhere in Judah very near Jerusalem, in other words in the greater land of Jerusalem, are likely incorrect. If Lehi's ancestors had obtained land and settled anywhere outside the actual limits of Hezekiah's Jerusalem walls, those people would have disappeared (along with the memory of their having owned any land) in the 701 B.C. debacle. And models that suggest that the land of inheritance was somewhere in southwest Judah (the so-called Beit Lei area and the tomb mistakenly called the Lehi Cave) are not supported by the evidence.[15] Had Lehi's ancestors obtained land and settled in that region, or anywhere else outside Jerusalem, they would likely have fallen victim to the Assyrians—having been killed or deported—and Lehi would not have eventually been born at Jerusalem. Two things about Lehi's heritage emerge very clearly from the study of Assyrian actions in Israel and Judah: (1) Lehi's eighth century B.C. progenitors *have* to have settled in Jerusalem and cannot be expected to have obtained land elsewhere in Judah; therefore, (2) Lehi's land of inheritance must have been a tract in the north—a tract in western Manasseh—for which his ancestors, perhaps his great-grandparents, had retained a written deed when they fled around 724 B.C.

Why *western* Manasseh? The answer to this question requires us to explore yet another page of historical geography. For over half a century following the 701 B.C. attack, the Assyrian empire controlled all territory in Judah. Even though Sennacherib had lifted his siege of Jerusalem and gone back to Nineveh, he left occupying troops behind. He granted the Philistines, Judah's neighbor-enemies to the west on the coastal plain, permission to occupy and farm the hilly, fertile lands of Judah left behind after the deportation of their Israelite inhabitants. As previously noted, Sennacherib's Prism reported those lands being assigned to "Mitinti, king of Ashdod, Padi, king of Ekron, and Sillibel, king of Gaza."[16] This was a significant and, in retrospect, very fortunate departure from the normal Assyrian practice of importing subjugated peoples from other areas of their empire to be resettled in newly conquered regions, such as had taken place in the Galilee and in Samaria. Even though the immediate result was that Judean land, like the Galilee and Samaria, was possessed by foreigners (as Isaiah 1:7 puts it: "your land, strangers devour it in your presence"), the Philistines were not strangers from afar—they had come from right next door and could be forced back out of Judah to their own coastal home when Judah eventually revived as a nation released from Assyrian domination.

By 652 B.C. Judah's territory had been under Assyrian dominion and Philistine occupation for some fifty years. During those five decades what existed of the actual kingdom of Judah was found essentially within and directly around Jerusalem's limits. For thirty-five of those fifty years, beginning in 687 B.C., the city-kingdom was ruled by King Manasseh, a wicked man given over to collaboration with his Assyrian overlords (2 Kings 21:1 reports that Manasseh was king for fifty-five years, but this includes ten years of a probable coregency from 697 B.C. with his father Hezekiah—his sole regency was probably from 687 to 642 B.C.). Also, by 652 B.C. the Assyrian empire had stretched itself to the limits of its capacity to control its far-flung territories both in the east and in the west. In that year, the Babylonians rebelled against the Assyrian empire in the east, causing the movement of Assyrian military assets from the west to the east in order to meet the challenge. This spelled the beginning of the end for Assyria along the Mediterranean coast, including its control of Judah, which meant that it was probably only after 652, late in Manasseh's reign, that Judah was again able to control areas outside the immediate vicinity of Jerusalem. Second Chronicles notes that Manasseh "put captains of war in all the fenced cities of Judah" (2 Chronicles 33:14). Even though the Babylonian revolt was put down by 648 B.C., by the time of Manasseh's death in 642 B.C. the Assyrian control of both Judah and Philistia had loosened considerably, and Judah was able to act with an increased measure of autonomy. Manasseh's son Amon was assassinated after only two years on the Judean throne (642–640 B.C.), and his son Josiah was installed as king of Judah in 640 B.C. at only eight years of age (2 Kings 22:1). Josiah had been born in 648 B.C., and it may be surmised that Lehi and Ishmael, as well as the prophet Jeremiah, were probably born about this time (the 640s)—all of them born into a Judah ready to rise again. Judean freedom to act continued to grow during Josiah's younger years on the throne. When Josiah was twenty-one (627 B.C.), the emperor Assurbanipal died, and the Assyrians completely withdrew from the western part of their former empire in order to concentrate on defending the east. Judah became fully independent under the adult King Josiah, and many Judeans were able to move from the crowded precincts of Jerusalem back to the sites of cities in the Judean countryside, forcing Philistine farmers off Judean lands and resettling and re-building towns from Beersheba and Arad in the south to Lachish and Azekah in the west to Gibeon and Mizpah in Judah's north.

Josiah's Judah was not only able to reclaim its own territory, but it also moved into lands of the former northern kingdom of Israel (see fig. 9). Josiah sent forces north to take control of the tribal lands of Manasseh, Ephraim, Simeon, and Naphtali in the regions of Samaria and the Galilee (2 Chronicles 34:6–7), lands that the Assyrians had abandoned but where the gentile popu-lations they had fostered continued to live and work. By 622 B.C., when Josiah reinstituted the Passover festival (see 2 Kings 23:21–23—by this time Lehi had reached adulthood, and Nephi was just about to be born), Josiah's government controlled both the ancient kingdom of Judah and the territory of the former kingdom of Israel, from Dan in the north to Beersheba in the south. However, his dominion ended at the Jordan River. Ancient Israelite territory east of Jordan was not brought under Judah's umbrella—lands east of Jordan were controlled by Ammon, Judah's traditional rival. In terms of the ancient lands associated with Manasseh, this meant that Josiah's Judah only controlled the western part of Manasseh. But it also meant that any Judean whose great-grandparents had owned property in western Manasseh (or any other former northern kingdom territory west of Jordan) could lay claim to that land if they happened to

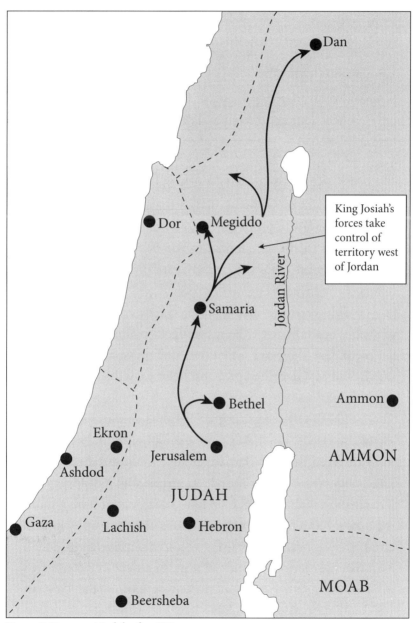

Figure 9. Resurgent Judah after 627 B.C.

be in possession of century-old deeds to such real estate. Lehi seems to have been in just this situation.

Conclusions about the Land of Inheritance

Now, at last, I may present, or least recapitulate, some tentative conclusions about Lehi and the land of his inheritance—tentative because they are based on a series of plausible assumptions:

1.   Since his tribal heritage was Manasseh, Lehi's land of inheritance was probably located in the ancient tribal land of Manasseh and was probably a plot abandoned by his great-grandparents, who were forced to flee as refugees from Israel to Judah around 724 B.C. to avoid death or deportation at the hands of the invading armies of Assyria.

2.   Lehi's refugee ancestors (likely his great-grandparents) probably brought with them the deed to the property they left behind in Manasseh when they fled south to Jerusalem in Judah, and that deed had probably been passed down to Lehi's parents and finally to Lehi.

3.   Lehi's refugee great-grandparents cannot have settled anywhere else in Judah but Jerusalem, or else they would not have survived the Assyrian attack of 701 B.C.—had they been killed or deported in that episode, as virtually all Judeans outside Jerusalem were, Lehi would not have been born at Jerusalem in the mid-seventh century B.C. In no case was the land of inheritance likely to have been within the traditional borders of Judah itself (not near Jerusalem and not near the so-called Beit-Lei area in southwest Judah) because of the ramifications of the Assyrian attack and deportation of Judah.

4.   Neither Lehi's grandparents nor his parents would have been able to travel north from Jerusalem to lay claim to their

family land since it was part of the Assyrian province of Samaria and was occupied and farmed by gentiles called Samaritans.

5. However, by the time Lehi was an adult, the Assyrians had completely withdrawn not only from Judah, but also from Samaria and the Galilee, and Judah's subsequent extension of control over Samaria meant that Lehi could lay claim to the property whose deed he would have inherited from his great-grandfather through his grandfather and father.

6. Because Lehi's sons could apparently travel to and operate on this land of inheritance freely and without fear (see 1 Nephi 3:22), that property was most likely in western Manasseh rather than in the Manassite areas east of Jordan since it was only the area west of Jordan where Judah had reasserted control (eastern areas were controlled by Ammon—see fig. 10).

7. That Lehi could now claim and control his ancestral property in western Manasseh does not mean he maintained a house or household on the property—all indications are that his domestic residence was always at Jerusalem (see 1 Nephi 1:4).

8. Lehi's land of inheritance was quite probably farmed by gentile Samaritans whose fathers had paid rent to the Assyrian administration during its tenure of control over the province of Samaria and who themselves were probably under the necessity of paying rent to Lehi after Judah asserted control in Samaria (such rental receipts would have added to Lehi's personal wealth).

Even though Lehi did not live on the land of inheritance, he had "left gold and silver and all manner of riches" on the property—these were probably buried in caches known only to the family. A common practice during the Iron Age II period, when Lehi lived, was to place loose silver in ceramic jugs and then bury those containers for safekeeping (see photo essay, p. 75). Lehi probably hid (buried) the bulk of his wealth at a secret location on his land of inheritance in Manasseh because

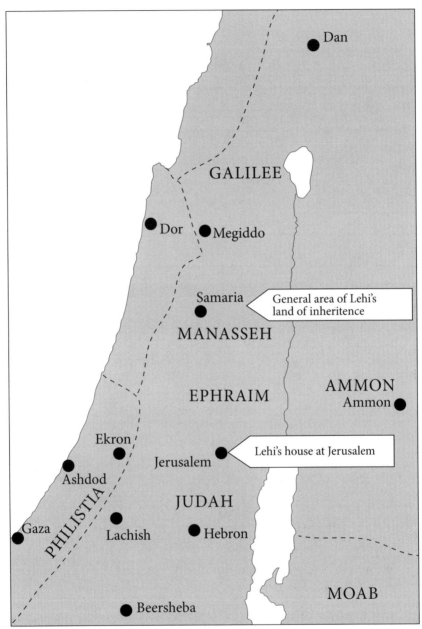

Figure 10. Judah at the height of Josiah's reign, 610 B.C.

he knew those riches would not be safe in Jerusalem—he knew the Babylonians would eventually destroy and loot the city or, as Nephi put it:

> Let us go down to the land of our father's inheritance, for behold he left gold and silver, and all manner of riches. And all this he hath done because of the commandments of the Lord. For he knew that Jerusalem must be destroyed. (1 Nephi 3:16–17)

Life and Work for Lehi in Jerusalem

If, as proposed above, Lehi's recent ancestors had come to Jerusalem as refugees from the north, they would have found themselves landless in Judah. This was not an ideal situation in a society where farming was the way much of the population made its living. Upon establishing themselves in the refugee camp that eventually became known as the Mishneh of Jerusalem, Lehi's great-grandparents and grandparents would have to have figured out a way to support themselves without any land to farm—something that they could do living inside the city wall that Hezekiah had built between 705 and 701 B.C. As first pointed out by John Tvedtnes, indications in the writings of Nephi suggest that both he and his father Lehi were professional metalsmiths.[17] Such a vocation would have been ideal for Lehi's ancestors to learn since it would not require the ownership or rental of property outside the city. Like most professionals of that age, Nephi would have apprenticed with and learned the metalworking trade from his father. Lehi had likely learned it from his father, who in turn learned it from his father, the man who came to Judah as a refugee, who had learned it in order to survive as a landless resident of Jerusalem's Mishneh.

Expertise in smithing precious metals such as silver and gold, particularly in smithing iron and hardening it into steel, is not something a person picked up as a hobby or sideline skill. Smithing, and in particular iron and steel smithing, was the high-tech profession of Lehi's day—the period that archaeologists call Iron Age II. Evidence of Lehi's and Nephi's expertise in all sorts of metals—in other words, evidence that smithing was their profession—is found in several passages of Nephi's writings. A convenient list of ten such passages may be considered:

1. 1 Nephi 2:1. Lehi left behind gold and silver, two precious metals likely to have been used in expert jewelry smithing. While the population at large often utilized silver as money, in the form of cut pieces and small jewelry (no coins were in use in Judah during Iron Age II), to possess gold was very rare—gold was not used as a medium of common monetary exchange. For Lehi to possess both gold and silver suggests that he worked with gold, which in turn suggests gold smithing (gold and silver are also mentioned in 1 Nephi 3:16, 22, and 24).

2. 1 Nephi 4:9. Nephi's evaluation of the sword of Laban includes his assessment that the hilt was of pure gold. This suggests that, at his young age, he was experienced in gold working (nonexperts are rarely able to judge the purity or content of gold-colored metal). He also mentioned the blade of the sword as being of "the most precious steel" and said that "the workmanship thereof was exceedingly fine," assessments that suggest he was experienced in iron and steel work (see fig. 11).

3. 1 Nephi 5:19. Lehi predicts that the "plates of brass should never perish; neither should they be dimmed any more by time"—a surprisingly accurate statement that could probably be made only by a person experienced with the properties of copper-based alloys like bronze and brass (bronze is a combination of copper and tin, and brass a combination of copper and zinc). Whereas iron, the hardest metal of Lehi's day (it

could even be hardened into steel by Lehi's time), will oxidize and rust away over time if neglected, copper alloys such as bronze and brass will not. Even the most damp conditions will not cause plates of copper to "perish." And while it is possible over time for bronze or brass items to be "dimmed . . . by time" with a greenish or greyish patina, even minimal maintenance on a regular basis would prevent this.

4. 1 Nephi 8:19. Lehi "beheld a rod of iron" (see 1 Nephi 8:24 and 30). It is noteworthy that no other artificial object in his dream is described with such specificity. He does not, for example, mention the material from which the large building was constructed. That he actually noted what specific metal the rod was made of, rather than just calling it a rod or handrail, suggests that Lehi was especially sensitive to or interested in metals, as a smith would naturally be.

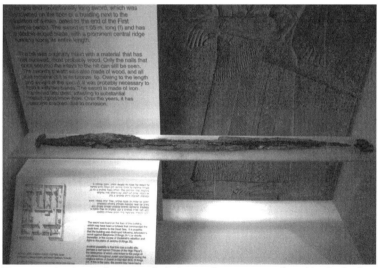

Figure 11. Ancient Judean sword, dating to about 600 B.C., found in the Jordan Valley near Jericho (on display at Israel Museum, Jerusalem). As noted in the caption, "The sword is made of iron hardened into steel, attesting to substantial metallurgical know-how." This weapon may be similar to the sword of Laban and other swords Nephi taught his people to make.

5. 1 Nephi 16:10. Nephi describes what eventually became known as the Liahona (see Alma 37:38). He notes that it was made of "fine brass" and was of "curious workmanship." These are the types of assessments that one who has experience with quality brass work, such as a smith, would make.

6. 1 Nephi 17:9–16. Nephi knew how to smelt metallic ore from rock and forge tools with the metal made from the ore. This is obvious evidence that he was skilled in all aspects of the metallurgical knowledge of the period. Note that Nephi *does not* know how to work with wood or how to design a seagoing vessel—these skills are taught him by God (see 1 Nephi 18:1–2)—but he *does* know, without divine tutorial, how to work in metal and forge tools, indicating it was a previously mastered skill.

7. 1 Nephi 18:25. On arrival in ancient America, Lehi's party found "all manner of ore, both of gold, and of silver, and of copper." The inclusion of these items in their assessment of resources available to them indicates not only their value but implies the ability to use them in metalworking.

8. 1 Nephi 19:1. Nephi made "plates of ore" and lists the various records that he had "engraven" upon them—in other words, Nephi was experienced not only in ore smelting and metalworking but also in engraving long texts on the metal he worked.

9. 2 Nephi 5:15. Nephi taught his people to erect buildings and work wood, using only general terms for those activities, but then he reports specifically each type of metal he taught them to work in—iron, copper, brass, steel, gold, silver, and other precious ores. Not only does this clearly indicate that Nephi himself is a metalsmith but serves as something of a resumé of his varied smithing experience and abilities.

10. 2 Nephi 5:29–31. Nephi again mentions the two sets of metal plates that he had personally made in order to write the

two separate records he was keeping. The thinness and uniformity of size of these plate collections would require considerable skill in metallurgy and smithing.

This ample evidence that Nephi and his father Lehi were experienced in mining metallic ores and smithing a variety of precious and utilitarian metals sheds light on a number of interesting questions often asked about 1 Nephi. For example, why did Lehi and Nephi both seem to have been competent in Egyptian language and writing as well as their native Hebrew? The fact that Egypt was a primary center for gold trade could suggest that Lehi had regularly traveled there to conduct gold business or procure gold supplies. Why did Lehi and Nephi seem to have readily known the way from Jerusalem to the Red Sea (Gulf of Eilat) and back without the aid of the Liahona, which they later needed in Arabia? The fact that copper ore was mined in several locations near the Gulf of Eilat and in northern Sinai (see fig. 12) could suggest that Lehi and Nephi had traveled to the region several times over the years to obtain copper supplies and knew the route well prior to their permanent departure from Jerusalem in 1 Nephi 2. Certainly, however, their expertise in metalworking suggests this had been their primary vocation in Jerusalem. Their standard of living would have been comfortable by itself since metalworking was a respected middle-class occupation. When the rental monies Lehi was presumably able to collect from Samaritans living on and farming his land of inheritance are factored in (income which Lehi's father and grandfather would not have enjoyed, but which became available by the time Lehi was an adult), the combined wealth probably placed Lehi's family in an economic situation approaching Jerusalem's upper class. Thus it is no surprise to read that, in addition to gold and silver, Lehi had possessed "precious things" (1 Nephi 2:4; 3:22) and "all manner of riches" (1 Nephi 3:16).

Living in the Mishneh and Working in the Makhtesh

The typical house found throughout Israel and Judah during the period when Lehi lived is called by archaeologists the "pillared" or "four-room" house.[18] The basic plan, which first appeared in the twelfth century B.C. and which, with improvements and variations, endured for over six centuries, featured three rectangular, parallel rooms on a long axis tied into a single rectangular room on a broad or perpendicular axis (see fig. 13 for plan and drawing). The outer three rooms were roofed and formed a squared U around the middle long room, which was an open-air courtyard. The walls on either parallel side of the open-air courtyard sometimes featured pillars instead of closed walls, hence the

Figure 12. Ancient copper mines at Timna in southern Israel near the Red Sea. Timna was a copper-mining area during both the Bronze and Iron ages and may have been where Lehi and his sons traveled to obtain copper for their metalworking.

term *pillared house.* The outer three rooms often featured interior walls that divided them into yet smaller chambers. Frequently, the forward chambers in the two outer long rooms were used for storage or as domestic animal stalls. The basic domestic living areas were generally in the chambers of the broad room but could also occupy half or all of one or both long rooms, depending on the size and situational needs of the family. The breadth of wall foundations and the presence of stone stairs discovered by archaeologists in some four-room houses suggest that they often supported a second floor, which doubled the number of living chambers possible in the four-room plan. The average dimensions of a four-room house were about 10 x 12 meters (33 x 40 feet). The total ground level floor space of Israelite and Judean four-room houses varied, but could be as much as 110 square meters (about 1,200 square feet).[19] The interior space of these houses was complemented by additional floor space (as much as 800 square feet) on the flat roof, which by law featured a waist-high, upright safety ledge, or battlement (see Deuteronomy 22:8). Domestic activities such as household work, socializing, and even sleeping could take place on the roof in the dry weather that lasted much of the year. The main entrance to the household was at the end of the enclosed (but open-air) courtyard, which also served as an area for gathering and working as well as for dry-weather cooking. Expansion of the house was possible not only by adding an upper floor, but by adding additional long rooms as annexes to the basic plan, or even by building a second four-room structure attached to the first (perhaps even sharing one of the long walls). This allowed for extended family expansion in limited available space, such as areas within walled cities like Jerusalem's Mishneh.

Lehi's house at Jerusalem was probably a large version of the typical pillared or four-room style with as much as 2,000 square feet of living space on two floors, representative of a family with

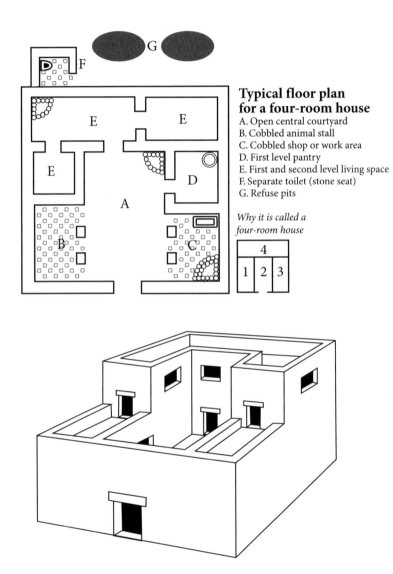

Typical floor plan for a four-room house

A. Open central courtyard
B. Cobbled animal stall
C. Cobbled shop or work area
D. First level pantry
E. First and second level living space
F. Separate toilet (stone seat)
G. Refuse pits

Why it is called a four-room house

Figure 13. Typical four-room house from the period of Lehi.

considerable means in his day. Although the Mishneh area had begun as a refugee settlement in the eighth century B.C. and Lehi's grandparents would likely have plied their presumed metalsmithing trade in the courtyard of their own four-room house, the nature of the Mishneh changed in the eighty years between the completion of Hezekiah's wall in 701 B.C. and Josiah's Passover festival of 622 B.C. (by which time Lehi was likely a young father). By then the Mishneh had evolved into a rather upscale neighborhood, as evidenced by the fact that Huldah the prophetess and her husband, Shallum, the "keeper of the wardrobe" (i.e., the royal clothier), lived there (see 2 Kings 22:14, but beware that Mishneh is curiously translated as "college"). This fact led Avigad to conclude that "the Mishneh was probably a well-to-do residential quarter."[20] Lehi's relative wealth would have placed him at home in such a quarter. But upscale neighborhoods, even in ancient settings, tended to eschew industrial or heavy commercial operations in their midst. The relatively small plot of city property in the Mishneh that Lehi probably inherited from his father, or that he acquired nearby, was of adequate size for a comfortable four-room house but was no longer a place where smithing could be carried on as it had been in his grandfather's day. The question then becomes: If Lehi and his sons were indeed metalsmiths, where in Jerusalem did they conduct their metalworking and marketing operations? The answer may be that they did so in the other Jerusalem quarter previously mentioned—the Makhtesh.

The Hebrew word *makhtesh* means mortar, crater, or hollow. The ancient Jerusalem quarter called the Makhtesh was located in the southern part of Jerusalem's central valley (sometimes called the Tyropoean Valley) on the slope of the hill directly west of the much older City of David (see fig. 14). Topographically, it is easy to understand why the ancient inhabitants of Jerusalem would call this area the Makhtesh, since the narrow central valley is bounded by steep hills rising up on both the west and the east—to the east

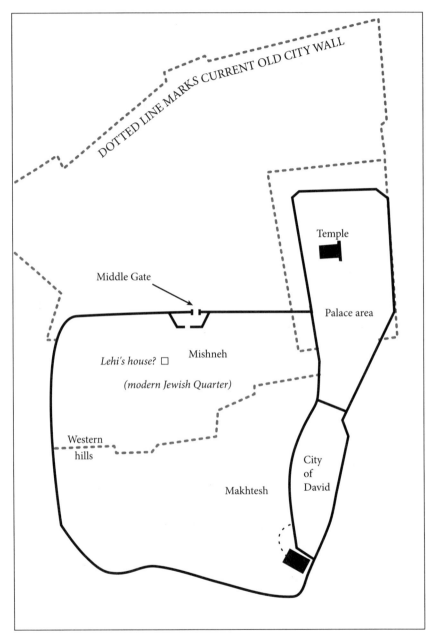

Figure 14. Jerusalem at Lehi's departure.

by the hill upon which sat the City of David and to the west by the larger hill known today as Mount Zion. Building activity in the Makhtesh may have begun as early as the tenth century B.C., when population growth in Jerusalem, the capital of Solomon's empire, would have begun to exceed the land available inside the walled City of David. The new quarter probably experienced only modest growth during the ninth and eighth centuries B.C., and it should be emphasized that those who lived and worked in the Makhtesh were local Judean Jerusalemites. When the northern kingdom refugees began arriving at Jerusalem in the last quarter of the eighth century, they were unlikely to have settled in the Makhtesh alongside the longtime Judean residents (most local populations are initially reticent to allow potentially transient refugees to integrate into their already established communities); thus the original Mishneh camp was located well to the north of the Makhtesh neighborhood (see again fig. 3). The Makhtesh had the advantage that it was nearer to the Siloam Pool, Jerusalem's water supply, than was the Mishneh. In the first few decades after the Assyrian attacks, the Makhtesh probably remained primarily native Judean, if only for proprietary reasons, and the Mishneh became the haven for Ephraimites, Manassites, and other northern Israelites. This situation gradually altered in the century after Hezekiah built his wall around both exterior neighborhoods in 701 B.C., physically annexing them to the City of David and the Temple Mount (see again fig. 4). By the time of King Josiah (640–609 B.C.), the Makhtesh area seems to have become the downtown of Jerusalem—it was *down* from both the City of David and the Mishneh, and for purely residential purposes it was topographically inferior to both, sitting in the Tyropoean hollow where traffic to the Siloam Pool was heavy. While the Mishneh was growing into a higher-class Jerusalem neighborhood, the Makhtesh downtown seems gradually to have evolved into a quarter of commerce and industry, as mirrored in a prophecy of Zephaniah uttered during Josiah's reign:

And it shall come to pass in that day, saith the Lord, that there shall be the noise of a cry from the fish gate, and an howling from the second [Heb. *mishneh*] and a great crashing from the hills. Howl, ye inhabitants of Maktesh, for all the merchant people are cut down; all they that bear silver are cut off. (Zephaniah 1:10–11)

Avigad contrasts the Mishneh with the Makhtesh in Zephaniah's day:

> That the *Mishneh* was probably a well-to-do residential quarter is evidenced by the fact that Huldah the Prophetess and her husband, a high court official, lived there. In contrast, the *Maktesh* was probably a commercial and industrial section located apparently in the lower Central Valley.[21]

It is entirely possible that while Lehi's upscale home was located in the Mishneh, his metalsmithing shop, where he also likely marketed his work, was in the Makhtesh quarter of Jerusalem among the merchant people and "they that bear silver" mentioned in Zephaniah 1:11. This is admittedly conjecture, but it is at least plausible.

The Middle Gate into Lehi's Jerusalem

One more feature of Lehi's Jerusalem is worthy of mention before concluding. When Hezekiah built his wall around the Mishneh and the Makhtesh, his builders created a baylike deviation in the middle of the otherwise straight east-to-west course of the northern wall line (see fig. 15). The likely reason for this feature was the topography of that exact spot. Jutting off of the so-called Transversal Valley, a small north-south ravine existed just at the point in question, and the baylike deviation skirted this ravine on its south side. A significant portion of its foundation was unearthed during Avigad's excavation of the Jewish Quarter in the Old City during the 1970s[22] and has been preserved for visitors to examine (see fig. 5). Avigad suggested that the topography of the spot and the deviation in the wall line there made it likely this was also the location of a gate in the northern wall. The small ravine served as the alley to the gate entrance. The actual opening of that gate was even detected in Avigad's excavation.[23] During the seventh century B.C., however, almost surely during the reign of Josiah, a second phase of construction took place that resulted in another gateway that cut directly across the ravine just north of the first gate, straightening out the line of the northern wall (see fig. 15). Avigad found it difficult to propose a cause for this change, but it may have been that the ravine alley leading to the earlier gate offered a potential attacker too much opportunity to undermine the earlier gate and wall at that spot. In any event, the second gate was in use at the end of the seventh century B.C., when Lehi was living in the city. Doubtless, Lehi and his family passed through the gate on numerous occasions. Avigad even believed that this particular gate is mentioned in the Bible:

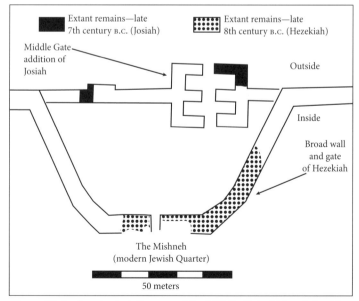

Figure 15. Archaeological diagram of the Middle Gate. (After Avigad.)

In trying to identify our reconstructed gate 2 with one of the gates known from the Scriptures, we seem to have no better candidate than the "Middle Gate" (*sha'ar ha-tawekh*) mentioned only in Jer. 39:3. As can be observed on the plan . . . our gate is situated right in the middle of the northern defence wall of the city. The biblical narrator mentions the Middle Gate as the meeting place of the Babylonian generals after the forcing of the north wall of Jerusalem during the siege in 586 B.C.[24]

The restored remains of the eastern corner of this Middle Gate are open for visitors to Jerusalem to view (see fig. 16). Avigad's team also discovered evidence of a battle on the excavated surface in front of the gate (i.e., on its north side): charred wood, ashes, soot, and a group of five arrowheads, four of iron and one of bronze. The veteran archaeologist felt this find was most significant: "It seems that what we found is the first tan-

© Garo Nalbandian

Figure 16. Tower of the Middle Gate discovered by archaeologists during the 1970s while excavating in the Jewish Quarter of Jerusalem's Old City. This gate would have been in the north wall of Jerusalem during Lehi's day and would have led directly into the Mishneh.

gible evidence of the fateful battle for the walls of Jerusalem, which terminated in the destruction of the entire city and the burning of Solomon's Temple."[25] Lehi had prophesied of this very destruction at the hands of the Babylonians (see 1 Nephi 1:13). Coincidentally, his own house had likely been located not far inside that Middle Gate, in the Mishneh of Jerusalem.

Conclusions about Lehi's House at Jerusalem

Finally, I give some tentative conclusions about Lehi, his family, and his house at Jerusalem—tentative, again, because of the series of assumptions on which they are based:

1. Since his tribal heritage was Manasseh, but he had "dwelt at Jerusalem in all his days" (1 Nephi 1:4), Lehi was probably a descendant of Manassite refugees who had fled south to Judah with others of the northern kingdom when the Assyrians attacked, destroyed, and deported Israel in 724–722 B.C.

2. Because they settled at Jerusalem, Lehi's great-grandparents were part of the refugee camp that was surrounded by a new, seven-meter-wide city wall that King Hezekiah had built to protect the neighborhoods on the western hills and to annex them physically to the older parts of Jerusalem. The refugee camp area became known as the Mishneh, a "second" or "additional" part of the city.

3. Protected by Jerusalem's wall, Lehi's great-grandparents and their fellow Jerusalemites were not deported by the Assyrians in Sennacherib's 701 B.C. attack on Judah. While the rest of Judah was thoroughly destroyed and over 200,150 other Judeans were taken away into captivity, Lehi's ancestors were spared to live on, resulting in Lehi's eventual birth in Jerusalem.

4. Lehi's great-grandparents and grandparents were under the necessity of finding a way to make a living in Jerusalem, being landless sojourners to the area. They seem to have taken up the practice of metalsmithing, a high-tech vocation that did not require farm land outside the city. This vocation seems to have

been passed down through the generations to Lehi and Nephi themselves, who were apparently expert in working both precious and industrial metals.

5. Lehi was probably born around 645 B.C., a contemporary of both the prophet Jeremiah and King Josiah (born 648 B.C.). He would have been a young man when Assyrian occupation forces finally departed Judah after 630 B.C. and an adult by the time of Josiah's Passover in 622 B.C.—a witness to the renewed independence and resurgence of Judah under King Josiah.

6. Lehi would probably have inherited the house and plot of land owned by his grandparents and parents in the Mishneh or would have acquired a lot nearby in the same neighborhood. In either case, by the time he was an adult, the Mishneh had transformed itself from an eighth-century B.C. refugee camp to an upscale quarter of the city where wealthy types like Shallum the royal clothier and Lehi himself lived, as well as possibly Laban (a Josephite captain of fifty) and Ishmael the Ephraimite.

7. With the evolution of the Mishneh into a wealthier neighborhood and the likelihood that industrial work would not have continued to be carried out in such surroundings, it is possible that Lehi's metalsmithing and marketing operation was located well to the south of his residence, in the Makhtesh quarter of Jerusalem, where commercial and industrial enterprise were apparently operating during Josiah's reign (Zephaniah 1:10–11).

8. Since the Middle Gate of Jerusalem was in use in Lehi's day, just before 600 B.C., it could very well have been the gate he used to exit the city as "he went forth," perhaps circling the Temple Mount on its north side and crossing the Kidron Valley to ascend the Mount of Olives, where he "prayed unto the Lord . . . in behalf of his people" (1 Nephi 1:5). If so, it was likely through the same Middle Gate that "he returned to his own house at Jerusalem; and cast himself upon his bed, being overcome with the Spirit and the things which he had seen" (1 Nephi 1:7).

9. The Middle Gate may well have been the portal through which Nephi entered Jerusalem on the night he "crept into the city and went forth towards the house of Laban," who, being also of northern descent, may have lived in the Mishneh as well. In that event, it was probably just outside that northern city wall that Nephi had directed his brothers to "hide themselves without the walls" (1 Nephi 4:5).

Thus, when modern visitors to Jerusalem's Old City walk through the restored Jewish Quarter, photograph the seven-meter-wide remains of Hezekiah's wall, descend into a nearby basement to inspect the tower of the Middle Gate, and rest for lunch in the pleasant open-air plaza near the Rambam Synagogue, they are in the very area of the ancient Mishneh of Jerusalem where Lehi's house was most probably found.

NOTES

1. Hugh Nibley, *Lehi in the Desert, The World of the Jaredites, There Were Jaredites* (1952, 1st ed.; Salt Lake City: Deseret Book and FARMS, 1988), 7.

2. Hugh Nibley, *An Approach to the Book of Mormon,* 3rd ed. (1958, 1st ed.; Salt Lake City: Deseret Book and FARMS, 1988), 46–47.

3. James B. Pritchard, ed., *The Ancient Near East* (Princeton, N.J.: Princeton University Press, 1958), 1:195.

4. Ibid.

5. Nahman Avigad, *Discovering Jerusalem* (Nashville, Tenn.: Nelson, 1983), 54–55.

6. William L. Holladay, *A Concise Hebrew and Aramaic Lexicon of the Old Testament (Based upon the Lexical Work of Ludwig Koehler and Walter Baumgartner)* (Leiden: Brill, 1988), 64.

7. Avigad, *Discovering Jerusalem,* 60.

8. Pritchard, *Ancient Near East,* 1:200.

9. Seymour Gitin, "Ekron of the Philistines—Part II: Olive-Oil Suppliers to the World," *Biblical Archaeology Review* 16/2 (1990): 34–42.

10. Will Durant, *Our Oriental Heritage* (New York: Simon and Schuster, 1963), 1:271.

11. Both Sennacherib and Esarhaddon mention Manasseh's Judah; see Pritchard, *Ancient Near East,* 1:201.

12. Siegfried H. Horn and P. Kyle McCarter, "The Divided Monarchy," in *Ancient Israel: A Short History from Abraham to the Roman Destruction of the Temple,* ed. Hershel Shanks, rev. and expanded ed. (Washington, D.C.: Biblical Archaeology Society, 1999), 180.

13. The Hebrew word *ʾelef* is correctly rendered as "thousand" in the King James Version, but in this passage and some others, it may have been vocalized as *ʾaluf* (same consonantal spelling), indicating a single individual, like a tribal chief (as in Genesis 36) or a professional soldier. See Holladay, *Concise Hebrew and Aramaic Lexicon,* 17; and David Alexander and Pat Alexander, eds., *Eerdmans Handbook to the Bible* (Grand Rapids, Mich.: Eerdmans, 1973), 191–92.

14. The estimate is conservative but based on the two-thirds ratio of ancient to modern architectural capacity of the land area of the current Old City of Jerusalem.

15. LaMar C. Berrett, "The So-Called Lehi Cave," *Journal of Book of Mormon Studies* 8/1 (1999): 64–66.

16. Pritchard, *Ancient Near East,* 1:200.

17. John Tvedtnes, "Was Lehi a Caravaneer?" in *The Most Correct Book: Insights from a Book of Mormon Scholar* (Salt Lake City: Cornerstone, 1999), 94–97. The suggestion was made by Tvedtnes as early as 1984 in "Was Lehi a Caravaneer?" (FARMS Preliminary Report, 1984), 13.

18. B. S. J. Isserlin, *The Israelites* (London: Thames and Hudson, 1998), 124.

19. Amihai Mazar, *Archaeology of the Land of the Bible* (New York: Doubleday, 1990), 486.

20. Avigad, *Discovering Jerusalem,* 54.

21. Ibid., 54.

22. Ibid., 57.

23. Ibid., 59.

24. Ibid.

25. Ibid., 54.

Chapter 5

A Woman's World in Lehi's Jerusalem

Ariel E. Bybee

The scriptures leave little doubt that the public world of ancient Israel was a man's domain. The texts of the Old Testament are largely concerned with preserving the stories and deeds of great prophets, the dealings of God with men, and the civic and priestly laws by which men were to govern themselves and interact with each other. Of course, stories appear of particularly exceptional women, such as Esther, who saved her people from destruction; Ruth, who showed unusual devotion to her family; and Miriam, a prophetess and the sister of Moses. The Old Testament is more interested in preserving patrilineal genealogies and priesthood lines than it is with the daily functioning of families and households, where women's roles were most significant. Women in scripture were not systematically ignored any more than the majority of men were; they simply wielded their influence in a more intimate, less visible sphere.[1]

In a similar fashion and often to an even greater degree, the authors of the Book of Mormon mostly recorded the broader dealings of God with men and of men with each other. For

The name Hannah appears on this Israelite seal, providing evidence that women owned seals that were used for official transactions and to safeguard property.

example, 1 and 2 Nephi recount in great detail the struggle of Nephi's brothers Laman and Lemuel against the patriarchal and religious authority of God; their father, Lehi; and their righteous brothers as they journey in the wilderness outside of Israel. Only faint images appear in the account of the women who accompanied them: their wife or mother, Sariah, as well as the nameless wives and sisters of the sons of Lehi. Nevertheless, these women played significant roles in the story of this Israelite family. Unfortunately, little is known from the text about their specific contributions, personalities, and lifestyles—who they really were.

Only by piecing together bits of archaeological evidence that remain and by looking comparatively at earlier and later sources, especially from the world of the Old Testament, can we attempt to reconstruct a likely picture of how these women might have lived in the late seventh century B.C. Examining and understanding the complexities of marriage, family relation-ships, and motherhood, as well as household, educational, and religious responsibilities within their society, will give greater insight into who Sariah and her daughters and daughters-in-law were and the critical parts they played in Lehi's family.

Marriage

As described and documented in several surveys of life in biblical times, the most significant event in the life of a woman in ancient Israel was marriage.[2] From birth, a woman was pre-pared by her parents to become a wife and mother. All of her training and education within the household was focused on the time when she would leave her parents' home and enter her husband's. Generally, a woman was considered to be of mar-riageable age at twelve to fourteen years. But marriage was not a matter of individual choice, especially for the woman herself. The choosing of a spouse, whether for a son or for a daughter, was a selective process that involved the entire household.[3] A marriage was often contracted for the purpose of extending political or economic relations with new families.[4] However, although a woman was brought into the house of her husband's family upon marriage,[5] she remained somewhat of an outsider for the remainder of her life. It was, therefore, also desirable for her to marry into a household that was close in terms of consanguinity.[6] For this reason, cross-cousin marriages were a time-honored Israelite tradition.[7]

The family patriarch had the final say in the selection pro-cess, and he, or the closest living male relative, negotiated with the suitor. The potential groom, who usually initiated these negotiations, might have become acquainted with the bride as a kinswoman or as a neighbor in the village and, with the prior consent of his own father, now sought to make her his wife.

Once an agreement had been reached between the groom and the bride's father, either a document would be drafted or witnesses would be called in and informed of the details. The contract of betrothal was considered legally binding upon both parties and often included such specifications as the amount of the *mohar,* or bride-price, which the groom would pay the bride's family; a bridal dowry (*zebed* or *silluhim*), which would be returned to the bride in the case of divorcement; and stipulations, such as whether the groom could take another wife.[8] The betrothal generally lasted a year or more before the actual marriage was finalized by a wedding meal and the delivery of the bride to the groom's residence.[9]

Under ancient law, a man could take more than one wife. Several instances of plural marriage are mentioned early in the Old Testament (for example, Jacob in Genesis 29:15–30; 30:1–9; and Esau in Genesis 26:34; 28:9; 36:1–5). But by the time of the monarchy, monogamy seems to have been the most common practice outside the royal household. Most men were not economically able to support more than one or two spouses, and the Torah contains several discouraging accounts of the domestic strife that occurred within, or as a result of, multiple marriages. As mentioned, the contract of betrothal could—and often did—restrict the husband from taking another wife.[10] Therefore, it was unlikely that most men in Lehi's day would marry more than once unless death or divorce occurred.[11] Lehi himself restricted his sons to having a single wife and no concubines (Jacob 3:5).

Nephi's account in the Book of Mormon refers only vaguely to the marriage of his brothers and himself to Ishmael's daughters: "And it came to pass that I, Nephi, took one of the daughters of Ishmael to wife; and also, my brethren took of the daughters of Ishmael to wife; and also Zoram took the eldest daughter of Ishmael to wife" (1 Nephi 16:7).[12] It is not unimaginable that Nephi, his brothers, and Zoram were married in a simplified version of the traditional fashion that would have included an oral agreement with Ishmael, a wedding meal, and the deliverance of the bride to the bridegroom's tent. However, it is likely that Sariah had become Lehi's wife in a more elaborate and formalized manner, as Lehi was a man of significant wealth, had connections with political power and prestige, and dwelt in or near the city. Her marriage contract, perhaps both written out and witnessed by significant family members and friends, was probably concluded with the immediate payment of the bride price by the bridegroom and with the giving of rich gifts to both the bride herself and her family. Sariah's father might also have bestowed an elaborate dowry upon her, such as a piece of land, if he were prosperous. The nuptials would have been celebrated with many guests, feasting, and an elaborate procession, such as that which became more common in New Testament times.[13]

The daughters of Ishmael were patriarchally descended from Ephraim,[14] while Lehi's family was of the tribe of Manasseh (see 1 Nephi 5:14; Alma 10:3). However, it is not known whether some sort of blood relationship existed between the two families through Sariah or the wife of Ishmael. The Israelite tradition of cross-cousin marriage makes this kinship both possible and likely. But whether the two families shared a blood relationship or not, consanguinity was technically achieved in both physical and spiritual senses because they both claimed Israel (Jacob) as a common ancestor and held his God as their own. It is also possible that Lehi and Sariah were closely related.[15]

Family Relationships and Motherhood

For an Israelite woman, marriage meant the transfer of her guardianship from her father (or the male relative who was the head of the house) to her husband.[16] In ancient Israel, as a son was subject to the authority of his father for the duration of the father's life, so a woman also came to be just as much under the guardianship of her father-in-law as of her husband, if not more. Often a newly espoused couple resided in the house of the groom's father, either in the same building or in another part of a larger complex. Sometimes a married couple would live in a new residence away from the father's property, but he continued to have absolute authority over them until his death.[17]

Cultural and archaeological evidences show that during the First Temple period, the average *bet ʾab*—the "house of the father," or ancestral household—consisted fundamentally of two parents and between two and four children. In addition to her father- and mother-in-law, a new bride could often expect to find within her husband's larger household his grandparents; his brothers and their wives and children; his unmarried, divorced, or widowed sisters; one or more adopted children; household servants and slaves; or other dependents, such as resident aliens.[18] Her greatest challenge as a new wife was to find her place within this household hierarchy.

The most effective and long-lasting way for a woman to establish status and a sense of belonging within her husband's family was to bear children. In an era when both infant and maternal mortality rates were extremely high, child bearers had "an importance . . . nearly inconceivable to those of us living in an age facing overpopulation."[19] Children were not only critical to the continuation of the family bloodline but were also economically important for a society based on subsistence agriculture. Motherhood was expected of every wife and was rewarded with great honor, insomuch that children, especially sons, were associated with great prestige. Conversely, barrenness was considered the greatest curse upon a woman, and ancient biblical laws generally provided for the divorce or expulsion of a wife who bore no children.[20]

Sariah seems to have been fortunate in her marriage to Lehi. Lehi's house was located on his inherited lands, but by the time that he and his family left Jerusalem, it is clear that they were living separately from any other relatives (see 1 Nephi 2:4–5). Perhaps all his relations had already passed away. But it seems more likely that this piece of land was his by inheritance. In any case, since Lehi and Sariah lived there at least from the time of Lehi's father's death and perhaps earlier, Sariah would have been spared the politics of her father-in-law's household for at least some of her marriage. The pressure and prestige of childbearing, though still a big factor in her life, would not have been as severe as it must have been in a larger household. The fact that Lehi's land was in or near the city also eased the pressure that would have existed for her to bear children to become agricultural laborers. It was perhaps due in part to these favorable circumstances that the family that Sariah and Lehi brought into the desert—namely, a nuclear family dwelling separately, consisting of two parents, four sons, and at least two daughters—though small in comparison to those of earlier generations, seems to have exceeded the average family size for the time period.[21]

It is difficult to assess the effect that the interfamilial marriages had upon the status of Ishmael, his wife, and his children. However, it does seem that Ishmael's family as a whole was brought into a type of wilderness *bet ʾab* and became subordinate to the will and inspiration of Lehi as patriarchal head, even though rebellions against this authority periodically occurred. Without knowing the prior relationship between Lehi and Ishmael, it is reasonable to assume that Ishmael accepted Lehi's leadership due to his prophetic call rather than any familial precedence. Because Ishmael himself is never said to have rebelled against this order of things, presumably he felt comfortable with his own place in the hierarchy. This extended family-tribe consisted, then, of a patriarchal head, his wife, their sons and their wives and children, their daughters (who were presumably unmarried, or they would have been mentioned in terms of their husbands rather than themselves), and several other dependents. The latter included the two sons of Ishmael and their wives and families (1 Nephi 7:6); Zoram, who had served as an important administrator in the house of Laban and who became like an adopted son in the house of Lehi; and Ishmael and his wife, who, due to their age, probably held status comparable to that of grandparents in the house of Lehi. This type of tribal organization clearly resembled earlier models in ancient Israel and would not have seemed more than slightly unusual to those within it.

Posterity was clearly of great importance to Lehi's family. His sons returned to Jerusalem to get Ishmael and his daughters so that they could "take daughters to wife, that they might raise up seed unto the Lord in the land of promise" (1 Nephi 7:1). The birth of children to the family both ensured the perpetuation of the bloodline and provided additional laborers to till, plant, hunt, and build upon their arrival in the New World, thus making it economically advantageous as well. Because this type of frontier subsistence relied so heavily upon the reproductive abilities of its women for success, motherhood would have afforded women within Lehi's family as much status as it did in Israel at that time period, if not more (see Genesis 30:22–24; 1 Samuel 1:10–20). Sariah apparently bore at least six sons and two daughters under the pressures of agrarian and nomadic living, perhaps even while accompanying her husband to Egypt or other lands. In her world, children were important to the survival of the household and the economy (see 1 Nephi 18:7).

Considering the high infant and maternal mortality rates within the cities during ancient times, Nephi's account of childbirth in the wilderness becomes even more significant:

> And we did travel and wade through much affliction in the wilderness; and our women did bear children in the wilderness. And so great were the blessings of the Lord upon us, that while we did live upon raw meat in the wilderness, our women did give plenty of suck for their children, and were strong, yea, even like unto the men; and they began to bear their journeyings without murmuring. (1 Nephi 17:1–2)

The increased risk for these women, who were living under the harshest nomadic conditions and even subsisting on raw meat, added greatly to the prestige and respect they received within the household—even so much that Nephi, with sincere admiration, thought that their physical abilities almost equaled those of men (1 Nephi 17:2). And Lehi, in blessing his two youngest sons before his death, referred to their births in the wilderness in terms calculated to remind them of their mother's hardship and risk on their behalf (2 Nephi 3:1, 3; see also 2:1–2).

Household, Educational, and Religious Responsibilities

The household was the center of a woman's life in Israel and the place in which she held the most power.[22] Even though a child was born into "the house of the father," the mother was the first and most abiding influence upon the child's life from the day of birth, instilling the most basic sociocultural values, modes of behavior, and religious beliefs. In Proverbs, the mother is seen as both a nurturer and educator whose teachings are complementary to those of the father (see Proverbs 1:8; 6:20). Since there is no evidence concerning formal schooling in Israel before the Hellenistic period,[23] it is most likely that children were taught to read and write at home.[24] In a family setting,

Excavation of an Israelite house in Beersheba from the late Iron Age. Israelite homes usually consisted of four rooms built around a courtyard. In this photo, the remains of the columns in the courtyard are visible as well as the stairs leading to the upper story of the home. (See pages 118–21 of this volume for a discussion of Israelite homes at the time of Lehi.)

both girls and boys would have been taught the rudimentary skills of literacy, probably by both parents.[25]

Children would also have learned to perform primary chores at the side of their mother. Early on, both girls and boys would have been taught to contribute to the functioning of the family household, perhaps by performing such small labors as caring for the younger children, gathering fuel, or helping to prepare food.[26]

As the children matured, work diverged according to gender. At a certain point, a boy was taken out of the household and into his father's workplace, whether it was in the field or in a trade. A girl, however, remained at home under the tutelage of her mother, where she was taught to perform the domestic labors associated with running a household. Not only were women responsible for the care and the discipline of the children, but also for the feeding and clothing of the entire household. Food preparation alone was exceedingly time-consuming. Six days a week, women sorted, cleaned, parched, and ground grain, kneaded and baked bread, drew water, collected fuel for cooking, butchered and cleaned small animals, milked, churned butter, made cheese and yogurt, tended vegetable gardens and fruit trees, and preserved meat and fruits for storage. The women prepared raw wool and flax fibers, which were then spun, woven, sewn, and tailored into clothing for their families. They often produced many of the common household tools, such as cooking and cleaning implements, lamps, and candles. The burden of daily cleaning and washing also fell on the shoulders of the women in the household (see Proverbs 31:10–31).[27]

Women not only taught their children literacy and labor skills but were also a critical part of their religious education.[28] Children learned the proper observance of important features

© Zev Radovan

Reconstruction of a home interior from the fourth century A.D., located in northern Israel. Most homes were furnished simply with facilities for food preparation, provisions for sleeping, and a place to keep animals in the winter.

© Zev Radovan

Replica of a typical cooking stove from Roman Jerusalem.

of ancient Israelite religion by watching their mother's daily ritual of washing herself, offering sacrifice with her husband, and praying.[29] A good deal of this religious teaching would also have taken place on the Sabbath, when both women and men laid aside their daily chores to worship. The Sabbath was a day of rejoicing and rest, particularly for the labor-weary woman. Both she and her husband spent the day reading from the Torah, singing hymns of praise, and teaching their children the beliefs and rituals of their religion.[30] Children living in Jerusalem around 600 B.C. probably would have observed their mother attending local assemblies or gatherings to worship alongside their father. Women actively participated in religious festivals and national celebrations (Deuteronomy 31:12)—singing and dancing—and brought sacrifices of thanksgiving to the temple, teaching their children through their example.

The women within Lehi's household would have been occupied from daybreak to sundown performing such daily tasks as these and perhaps more, depending on where they lived and what the circumstances of the family were. It is likely that Sariah's specific responsibilities changed once she came into the desert; in the city, she had been a rich man's wife, probably with several servants and some leisure time. In the desert, she would have carried more responsibilities, and her tasks might have varied. It is likely that the women also contributed to many uncommon tasks that Nephi and his brothers undertook in the desert. Perhaps the women and children gathered fuel for the fire or brought water to aid Nephi as he made tools to build the ship. Women would have been instrumental in the gathering of seeds, fruit, meat, and other provisions for the journey to the promised land, and they would have helped to till, plant, and harvest crops or tend flocks, especially during their first years in the promised land.

Nephi makes it clear from the first verse of his account that he was grateful to both of his parents for his upbringing. "I, Nephi, having been born of goodly parents, therefore I was taught somewhat in all the learning of my father" (1 Nephi 1:1). Apparently his education was given to him by these "goodly parents," righteous and devoted people who had taken the time to teach him reading, writing, the language of the scriptures, and the learning of his father. But the implication of Nephi's statement is even deeper than that. He also refers to an inherited spiritual knowledge and a familiarity with religion and the God whom his parents worshipped. In his account of her sons' return from Jerusalem with the brass plates, Nephi recalls the powerful words of Sariah, who had been extremely troubled and anxious for their safety during their absence:

> Now I know of a surety that the Lord hath commanded my husband to flee into the wilderness; yea, and I also know of a surety that the Lord hath protected my sons, and delivered them out of the hands of Laban, and given them power

whereby they could accomplish the thing which the Lord hath commanded them. (1 Nephi 5:8)

Against all odds, her sons had succeeded, which built Sariah's testimony into a sure knowledge that God's hand was directing Lehi and the family's course. Sariah and Lehi then offered sacrifice and burnt offerings in thanks for the safety of their sons. Her fervent statement of belief obviously made an impression on Nephi, who painstakingly inscribed the account in considerable detail. This manifestation of Sariah's faith was probably only one example of many that served as religious teaching devices to her children and influenced their own belief systems.

Conclusion

We have examined the Israelite woman in her most important roles within the ancient world: wife, mother, housekeeper, and educator. Each of these roles was critical to the success of the family, in terms of both perpetuation and economic viability. Thus the tremendous importance of women in the ancient world can be better understood.

In particular, the nature and significance of the lives of the women in Lehi's family are clarified, and new dimensions are added to the characters of Sariah, her daughters, and her daughters-in-law. What is so often forgotten about the realities of the social context of the Israelite family is that it was an interdependent unit, despite the decidedly male orientation of the written record. These women who toiled beside their husbands, fathers, brothers, and sons through the wilderness, over the ocean, and in the promised land were not mere, passive shadows in the context of men's lives. On the contrary, Sariah and her faithful daughters and daughters-in-law became women of quiet but powerful conviction, hand-chosen by the Lord to help found a new and fruitful branch of Israel. It is interesting that Nephi's detailed accounts of murmurings and rebellions rarely include the women. This is negative evidence, certainly, but coupled with it are Sariah's testimony (1 Nephi 5:8), at least two of her daughters' decision to follow Nephi (2 Nephi 5:6), Ishmael's wife's and daughter's defense of Nephi in a moment of violent crisis (1 Nephi 7:19), and Nephi's admiration of the women's strength in the wilderness (1 Nephi 17:2). They were active and contributing members of a family unit that was as dependent on them for survival as it was on its male members.

NOTES

1. See Camille S. Williams, "Women in the Book of Mormon: Inclusion, Exclusion, and Interpretation," *Journal of Book of Mormon Studies* 11 (2002): 66–79.

2. Roland de Vaux, *Ancient Israel* (New York: McGraw-Hill, 1965), 1:24–34; Philip J. King and Lawrence E. Stager, *Life in Biblical Israel* (Louisville: Westminster John Knox, 2001), 54–57; Victor H. Matthews and Don C. Benjamin, *Social World of Ancient Israel 1250–587 BCE* (Peabody, Mass.: Hendrickson, 1993), 13–17; Leo G. Perdue et al., *Families in Ancient Israel* (Louisville: Westminster John Knox, 1997). For a brief survey and bibliography of recent scholarship on marriage in the Old Testament, see Gordon P. Hugenberger, *Marriage as a Covenant: Biblical Law and Ethics as Developed from Malachi* (Grand Rapids, Mich.: Baker Books, 1994), 1.

3. See John H. Otwell, *And Sarah Laughed: The Status of Woman in the Old Testament* (Philadelphia: Westminster, 1977), 32–37.

4. Matthews and Benjamin, *Social World of Ancient Israel,* 13, 31.

5. De Vaux, *Ancient Israel,* 1:28.

6. Joseph Blenkinsopp, "The Family in First Temple Israel," in *Families in Ancient Israel* (Louisville, Ky.: Westminster John Knox, 1997), 59.

7. The Old Testament is especially rich in examples of this. For a fuller discussion of cross-cousin marriage, see Robert A. Oden Jr., *The Bible without Theology: The Theological Tradition and Alternatives to It* (San Francisco: Harper & Row, 1987), 106–30.

8. James R. Baker, *Women's Rights in Old Testament Times* (Salt Lake City: Signature Books, 1992), 39. Also see Ze'ev W. Falk, *Hebrew Law in Biblical Times: An Introduction,* 2nd ed. (Provo, Utah: Brigham Young University Press and Eisenbrauns, 2001), 135–50, for a more detailed discussion of marriage contracts.

9. Falk, *Hebrew Law in Biblical Times,* 145. The weddings of Isaac to Rebekah (Genesis 24) and of Jacob to Rachel and Leah (Genesis 29) are early demonstrations of these types of contracts, as well as of cross-cousin marriages.

10. Baker, *Women's Rights,* 39.

11. Monica Alama Laparra, "Mujer, familia y matrimonio en el antiguo Israel bíblico," in *Actas del primer seminario de estudios sobre la mujer en la antigüedad (Valencia, 24–25 abril, 1997),* ed. Carmen Alfaro Giner and Alejandro Noguera Borel (Valencia, Spain: Universitat de Valencia, 1998), 27–28. Laparra discusses the difficult relationships of Sarah with Hagar and Rachel with Leah and then points out that in the books of Samuel and Judges, which cover the monarchy period, there is only one recorded instance of plural marriage outside the royal house, that of Samuel's father and his two wives.

12. Of interest is how Nephi's repeated usage of the wording "took . . . to wife" parallels Old Testament phrasing: Jacob is commanded not to "take a wife" of the daughters of Canaan (Genesis 24:3); Abraham commands his servant to "take a wife" for Isaac (Genesis 24:4, 7); the sons of God "took them wives" of the fair daughters of men (Genesis 6:2).

13. A good example of this is the marriage in the parable of the ten virgins (see Matthew 25:1–13).

14. Erastus Snow, *Journal of Discourses,* 23:184, reported: "The Prophet Joseph informed us that . . . Ishmael was of the lineage of Ephraim, and that his sons married into Lehi's family, and Lehi's sons married Ishmael's daughters."

15. See generally Hugh W. Nibley, *An Approach to the Book of Mormon,* 3rd ed. (Salt Lake City: Deseret Book and FARMS, 1988), 73.

16. Falk, *Hebrew Law in Biblical Times,* 123–24.

17. Laparra, "Mujer, familia y matrimonio," 8.

18. Blenkinsopp, "Family in First Temple Israel," 52.

19. Otwell, *And Sarah Laughed,* 49–50. He cites the facts that Rehoboam's seventy-eight consorts bore only eighty-eight children (2 Chronicles 11:21) and Abijah's fourteen wives bore only thirty-eight (2 Chronicles 13:21) as evidence for the high mortality rate of both women and children.

20. Phyllis A. Bird, "Women, Old Testament," in *The Anchor Bible Dictionary,* ed. David Noel Freedman (New York: Doubleday, 1992), 6:953–54. Bird fully discusses biblical references to this subject.

21. Nephi mentions his sisters after their arrival in the promised land (2 Nephi 5:6), but it is not known how many of them there were or when and where they were born. John L. Sorenson, "The Composition of Lehi's Family," in *By Study and Also by Faith: Essays in Honor of Hugh W. Nibley,* ed. John M. Lundquist and Stephen D. Ricks (Salt Lake City: Deseret Book and FARMS, 1990), 2:174–96, is of the opinion that the daughters were born in Jerusalem before their departure and speculates—based on the statement of Elder Erastus Snow quoted in note 14 above—that at some point they married Ishmael's sons. If so, they apparently left their husbands and followed Nephi when the Nephites and Lamanites separated.

22. See Carol Meyers, "The Family in Early Israel," in *Families in Ancient Israel,* 24–47, for a fuller discussion and reconstruction of ethnographical information on this subject.

23. James L. Crenshaw, *Education in Ancient Israel* (New York: Doubleday, 1998), 86.

24. Matthews and Benjamin, *Social World of Ancient Israel,* 27–28.

25. Carol Meyers, *Discovering Eve: Ancient Israelite Women in Context* (New York: Oxford University Press, 1988), 149–54.

26. Meyers, "Family in Early Israel," 27.

27. Bird, "Women, Old Testament," 954; Meyers, *Discovering Eve,* 142–48. For an illuminating exposition of the proverbial portrayal

of the ideal woman in the Persian period, shortly after Sariah's time, see Christine Roy Yoder, "The Woman of Substance: A Socioeconomic Reading of Proverbs 31:10–31," *Journal of Biblical Literature* 122/3 (2003): 427–47.

28. Matthews and Benjamin, *Social World in Ancient Israel*, 28–29.

29. See Abraham P. Bloch, *The Biblical and Historical Background of Jewish Customs and Ceremonies* (New York: Ktav, 1980), 61–65, for a more detailed description of daily religious observances.

30. Ibid., 107–40. Deuteronomy 6:7 requires parents to teach their children the words of the law. That requirement would have applied to mothers as well as to fathers, as the law was read to the entire population.

Chapter 6

Agriculture in Lehi's World: Some Textual, Historical, Archaeological, and Botanical Insights

Terry B. Ball and Wilford M. Hess

Introduction

The title page of the Book of Mormon declares that the purpose of the text is "to show unto the remnant of the House of Israel what great things the Lord hath done for their fathers; and that they may know the covenants of the Lord, that they are not cast off forever—And also to the convincing of the Jew and Gentile that Jesus is the Christ." As the authors of the book recorded the teachings, doctrines, and history that would accomplish this purpose, they also offered incidental insights into the everyday lives of Lehi and his descendants. Combining those textual insights with current historical, archaeological, and scientific information can help the reader better reconstruct, understand, and appreciate the world in which Lehi and his family lived. This approach can be especially helpful in understanding Book of Mormon agriculture.[1]

Textual Overview

From the Book of Mormon text, we learn that agriculture played an important role in the lives of the Lehites.[2] At the command of the Lord, Lehites and Jaredites alike brought crop and fruit seeds from the Old World (1 Nephi 8:1; 18:6; Ether 1:40–41; 2:1–3), which "did grow exceedingly" in the promised land (1 Nephi 18:23–24). Successful agriculture was often a hallmark of a righteous people (e.g., 2 Nephi 5:10–11; Enos 1:21), while the wicked frequently subsisted solely on wild beasts or on produce that they could rob, extort, or plunder from the righteous (e.g., Enos 1:20; Mosiah 7:22; 9:14; 21:21; 3 Nephi 4:2–6, 18–20). In times of war, agriculture often suffered—raising, protecting, and distributing crops became a matter of great concern and hardship (e.g., Mosiah 10:2–4, 19–21; 21:17–18; Alma 3:1–2; 4:2; 58:3–8; 60:3, 9; 3 Nephi 3:22; 4:2–6, 18–20). Often the Lord used crop failure and the resulting famine to chasten and humble his rebellious people (e.g., Mosiah 12:4–7; Helaman 11:4–17; Ether 9:28–35). Thus agriculture played a major role not only in the day-to-day subsistence of the people, but also in their relationship with God.

Plants of Lehi's World

A number of food plants are mentioned by name in the Book of Mormon, either as cultivars the people were actually utilizing, or in allegories and imagery used to teach gospel principles and truths.[3] The list includes wheat, barley, grapes, olives, corn or maize, neas, and sheum.[4] Two plant species with industrial uses may also be implied: flax, which could be the source of the linen mentioned in the record, and perhaps mulberry, which is required to make the fabric we know as silk. Other plant names and a wide variety of botanical terms can be found sprinkled throughout the text. Tables 1 and 2 summarize these names and terms. Many of these species of plants and their botanical terms have Old World origins or cognates about which history, botany, and archaeology have revealed important insights.

All Manner of Grains

Grain was perhaps the most important food crop cultivated by the Book of Mormon people. The grain harvest became a measure of prosperity and favor with the Lord (e.g., Mosiah 21:16; Alma 1:29; Helaman 6:12; 11:13, 17; Ether 10:12). Grain crops were often a target or casualty of robbers and invading or occupying enemies (e.g., Mosiah 7:22; 11:3; 21:21; Alma 3:2; 4:2). Indeed, the availability of grain influenced the outcome of wars, and warring peoples labored to preserve this important commodity (e.g., Mosiah 21:18; 23:1; 24:18; 3 Nephi 3:22; 4:6; 6:2). When the grain crop failed, famine followed (e.g., Helaman 11:13; cf. Mosiah 12:6). The Lehites raised "all manner of grain" (Enos 1:21; cf. 1 Nephi 8:1; Mosiah 10:4; Alma 62:29; 3 Nephi 6:2; Ether 9:17), including wheat, barley, corn, and perhaps neas and sheum (Mosiah 9:9).

While corn is a New World crop that was probably unknown to Lehi and his contemporaries, Lehi and his family apparently brought wheat and barley with them on their journey from the Old World to the New World. The seeds certainly could have remained viable and survived the journey, which took several years. Viability is dictated by seed moisture content and storage temperature. J. Derek Bewley and Michael Black state that for each 1 percent decrease in seed moisture content, the storage life of a seed is doubled and that for each 10°F (5.6°C) decrease in seed storage temperature, the storage life of a seed is doubled.[5] These authors also point out that at moisture contents of 18–20 percent seeds will respire and that with poor ventilation heat will kill the seeds. Below 8–9 percent moisture content there is little or no insect activity in seeds, and below 4–5 percent moisture content seeds are immune from attack by insects and storage fungi, but the seeds may deteriorate faster than seeds maintained at a slightly higher moisture content. They point out that seeds in a natural history museum in Paris retained their viability for 55 to 158 years, as discussed by M. Paul Becquerel.[6] Wheat and barley grains have sufficient longevity, even under less-than-ideal storage conditions, to survive for more than a decade. Moreover, it is possible that these grains were grown and harvested by Lehi and his family at one or more locations en route to the promised land, thus increasing their chance of viability, although this is not recorded in the Book of Mormon. According to a tradition among the native Jiballi of Dhofar (that region of Oman where Lehi and his family in all likelihood built their ship),[7] wheat was grown there anciently, and one can see the rope marks in the cliffs above the Wadi Sayq where baskets of wheat were raised and lowered to coastal plains.[8]

By the time Columbus arrived in the New World, both wheat and barley apparently had disappeared and had to be reintroduced. Their disappearance is easily explained. The cultivated species of wheat and barley the Lehites would have had available to them were already highly domesticated by the seventh century B.C. Domesticated plants generally cannot survive without human intervention. As David Rindos clarifies, "the most highly developed cultivated plants are incapable of survival in the wild."[9] The very morphological changes that make a plant a good domesticate also inhibit its ability to compete in the wild and thus tie the survival of the plant to the activities of humans. For example, cultivated barley and the best cultivated wheats have nonbrittle ears that allow the spikes or seed heads to stay intact after ripening rather than shattering and dispersing their seeds. Of course this trait is an advantage to the farmer since it allows him to gather and thresh the grain without losing it in the field. However, nonbrittle mutations can survive only under domestication, for without the ability to spontaneously and widely disperse seeds, the plants cannot adequately compete and reproduce in the wild.[10] Thus, although these grains may have been imported by Lehi, if in subsequent years they were not planted, tended, harvested, and stored, they doubtless would not have survived, particularly in a humid climate. The Book of Mormon text suggests that such may have been the case. From about A.D. 322 to 400 the people were at constant war, perhaps to the point that farming was not possible. "It was one complete revolution throughout all the face of the land," Mormon records (Mormon 2:8). By about A.D. 401 Moroni was the only Nephite to survive the great wars and presumably did not grow crops while wandering and hiding (Mormon 8:3–5). The wicked Lamanites, who traditionally did not practice agriculture, continued to fight and were "exceedingly fierce among themselves" (Moroni 1:2). Moroni's observation suggests that the culture continued to be unstable even after the Nephites became extinct. Highly domesticated plants like wheat and barley would probably not have survived the neglect that may have accompanied so many years of war and political upheaval.[11]

Some would suggest that the fact that wheat and barley were not being cultivated in the New World when Columbus arrived indicates that these crops were never in the New World before his arrival and therefore call into question the veracity of the Book of Mormon. However, archaeologists have actually recovered pre-Columbian barley in North America near downtown Phoenix, Arizona, where a Hohokam culture was present from about 300 B.C. to A.D. 1450;[12] at sites in Oklahoma and Illinois dating to about two thousand years ago;[13] and in areas populated during the Late Woodland cultural periods (A.D. 600–1050), as reported by Vorsila Bohrer.[14] While physical evidence of pre-Columbian wheat has not been discovered by archaeologists, one should not conclude that wheat was not cultivated anciently in the New World. Generally, archaeologists understand that failure to find something mentioned in a text does not discredit the text. They recognize that the likelihood of an organic artifact being preserved is very small and that if an organic artifact is indeed preserved, the chance that it will be discovered and correctly identified is even more remote.[15] Accordingly, within their discipline, archaeologists typically accept the axiom that the absence of evidence is not evidence of absence. Thus the Book of Mormon text itself—added to what we know about wheat cultivation in the world from which the Lehites came—may be the best sources for insights to help us understand the earliest cultivation of wheat and barley in the Americas.

Wheat

Wheat is mentioned twice in the Book of Mormon, once as one of the crops raised by Zeniff's colony in the land Lehi-Nephi (Mosiah 9:9) and again in a simile used by the resurrected Lord to warn his disciples of Satan's evil designs to "sift them as wheat" (3 Nephi 18:18).[16] Bread, perhaps made from wheat, is mentioned over twenty times in the text, and the word *chaff* (the remaining by-product of threshing grains such as wheat) is present in six verses (see table 2).

The wheat Zeniff's people sowed (Mosiah 9:9) probably descended from seed stock originally imported from the Old World by Lehi and his family. Wheat is prehistoric in the Old World. Egyptian monuments indicate that it was already established before the Hebrew scriptures came into existence, and when the Egyptians and Greeks speak of its origin they refer to mythology.[17] The evidence indicates that wheat was first domesticated in the Old World, although the exact location of the event is a matter of debate. The earliest known grains of domesticated wheat have been found with barley and pulses in the Fertile Crescent, in Anatolia and the Balkans, and date to as early as 7500–6500 B.C.[18] Simcha Lev-Yadun, Avi Gopher, and Shahal Abbo note that it is generally agreed that plant domestication first took place in the Jordan Valley and areas of the southern Levant (present-day Israel and Jordan).[19] They suggest, however, that since the remains of wild forms of einkorn wheat, emmer wheat, barley, chickpea, lentil, bitter vetch, flax, and perhaps pea, have been found in a small cove area in the Fertile Crescent near the upper reaches of the Tigris and Euphrates Rivers, the northern Levant (present-day southeast Turkey and north Syria) is also a candidate for the location of domestication of these species. They conclude that agriculture in the region was first based upon three cereals (einkorn wheat, emmer wheat, and barley), four pulses (lentil, pea, chickpea, and bitter vetch), and a fiber crop (flax).

In contrast, Israeli researcher Eviator Nevo observes that the wild progenitors of wheat and barley are especially rich in adaptive genetic diversity in the Fertile Crescent, most particularly in Israel, suggesting that Israel is the center of origin and diversity of these plants.[20]

Molecular genetics provides another avenue to investigate the question of the location and process of wheat domestication. This research tool can be used to assign approximate dates to domestication events and identify wild progenitors of a domesticate. Using this kind of genetic analysis, researchers have identified a wild group of *Triticum monoccocum boeticum* (wild einkorn wheat) from southeast Turkey as the probable progenitor of cultivated einkorn varieties, thus suggesting that the domestication of einkorn wheat began in that region.[21] Other investigators in molecular genetics have concluded that einkorn, the most primitive of wheats, was domesticated only once, but that emmer, a slightly more advanced species, might have been domesticated more than once.[22] Li Huang et al. studied Israeli populations of wild emmer wheat (*Triticum turgidum* var. *dicoccoides*).[23] They sampled twelve domesticated landraces (ancient varieties) and both primitive and modern cultivars of *T. turgidum*. They reported high levels of diversity and a large number of alleles (units of genetic material) that were not detected in wild emmer populations. Their observations led them to conclude that emmer wheat underwent a long-term domestication process in which wild, semidomesticated, and domesticated plant types grew sympatrically (side by side), resulting in continuing introgression (introduction of new genetic material through interbreeding) from the wild populations and possibly gene flow from transspecific sources (species other than wheat).

While we do not know for certain the exact location and means by which wheat was first domesticated, these findings argue strongly that the domestication process was in or near the Fertile Crescent. By the time Lehi and his family left the region, wheat and the bread made from it fed the world as he would have known it. It was the main field crop in both Judah and Egypt. In Judah fields of wheat were raised primarily without irrigation, depending instead on rainfall, which was sometimes scarce. Consequently, famine in years of poor rainfall was common. In contrast, Egypt was a land with abundant water for irrigation[24] and was the land to which Israelites looked in time of famine (e.g., Genesis 41–45).[25]

Wheat was important in other areas of the ancient Near and Far East as well. The Chinese name for wheat was *mai,* the Sanskrit names were *sumama* and *gôdhûma,* the Hebrew name was *hittah,* Egyptians called it *br,* and the Basque name was *ogaia* or *okhayi.* The Chinese grew wheat, which was considered a gift from heaven, by at least 2700 B.C.[26] Wheat was also commonly mentioned in the Hellenistic records[27] and in ancient documents in Mycenean Greek.[28] Thus, considering the importance and ubiquity of wheat in the diet of the Old World peoples, one can safely assume that as Lehi and his family gathered seeds to bring with them on their voyage to the New World (1 Nephi 8:1), they certainly would have included this most valuable of all grains.

Moshe Feldman points out that since its domestication, an incredible amount of variation has developed in wheat, some seventeen thousand different varieties having been produced.[29] Varieties now exist that will grow in nearly every region and climate of the world. The species of wheat that Lehi and his family may have brought with them on their journey to the promised land is not certain. Jane Renfrew recognized two wild and fourteen cultivated species of wheat.[30] These wheats have been divided into three groups on the basis of chromosome number, and they can be further divided into species whose seed heads (spikelets) remain intact after threshing (i.e., hulled grain) and those whose grains thresh free from their glumes (chaff) and are called naked grains. The wheats form a polyploid series (multiples of chromosome sets) with fourteen, twenty-eight, and forty-two chromosomes.[31] These are referred to as diploid, tetraploid, and hexaploid wheats respectively. Hybrids can be attained from crosses between tetraploid and hexaploid wheats. Three different genomes (sets of genetic material), each composed of seven chromosomes, are found in the wheat genus

(*Triticum*), and are labeled as A, B, and D. The diploid wheats have only the A genome. The tetraploid wheats have both A and B genomes. The hexaploid wheats have all three genomes A, B, and D. The diploid form appears to be the most primitive and the tetraploids apparently originated from hybrids between the diploid wheat and another diploid species with the B genome. After hybridization a doubling in the chromosome number resulted in the tetraploid wheats, which subsequently hybridized with yet another diploid species to donate the D genome and form the hexaploid wheats.[32] "The sources of the B and D genomes appear to be in the closely related genus *Aegilops*. The B genome is believed to have been donated by an ancestor of the present-day *Aegilops speltoides* whose genomes SS appear to be closely similar to the BB genomes of tetraploid wheat."[33] Possibly *Aegilops squarrosa* is a donor of the D genome.[34]

Daniel Zohary and Maria Hopf outlined the wheat types exceptionally well.[35] They pointed out that wheat falls into four cytogenetic groups. The groups include one diploid, two tetraploid, and one hexaploid. Forms within each group are interfertile. However, hybrids between groups are highly sterile. They outlined four principal species recognized today in the genus *Triticum*.

- Diploid *T. monococcum* L., or einkorn wheat (AA), is made up of both wild and cultivated forms. Cultivated einkorn, which contained hulled grains, was an important grain crop in the past, but it is not often cultivated in modern times.
- Tetraploid *T. turgidum* L. (AABB) includes wild emmer wheat, cultivated emmer wheat, durum wheat, and several other cultivated tetraploid forms. This wheat was important from the beginning of agriculture and gave rise to many of the present-day, free-threshing, tetraploid durum-type wheats that are favorites for pasta.

- Tetraploid *T. timopheevi* Zhuk (AAGG) includes both wild and cultivated hulled forms. This wheat is only grown in a small area in Georgia.

- Hexaploid *T. aestivum* L., or bread wheat (AABBDD), probably originated under cultivation by the addition of the DD chromosome complement from *Aegilops squarrosa* L. to the tetraploid AABB *turgidum* wheats. This group includes the most important wheats of today.[36]

At the time Lehi and his family left the Old World, they may have had several species of wheat from which to choose and may in fact have brought more than one species with them. Einkorn wheat (*T. monococcum*) was still cultivated, though not widely, and bread wheat (*T. aestivum*) may have been present as well. Most likely, however, they would have brought one of the tetraploid wheats such as durum wheat (*Triticum turgidum* var. *durum*) or emmer wheat (*Triticum turgidum* var. *dicoccon*). These two species were the most abundantly cultivated varieties in Israel and adjacent countries, with durum being the favorite. Emmer wheat is significantly inferior to durum wheat, since it cannot be as easily and freely threshed as durum. Durum wheat is still, as it was in the time of the Bible, the dominant field crop commonly grown for bread in warm, temperate countries.[37]

Growing wheat anciently was a labor-intensive undertaking. First the land had to be tilled (or plowed) and then leveled, after which seeds were sown in rows. When the seed heads ripened, the farmer used a sickle to cut the stalks, which were then tied into sheaves and taken to the threshing floor (a flat area of hard, compacted earth) for threshing. This was usually accomplished in Lehi's day by dragging a heavy threshing sled over the wheat, which would grind, cut, and crush the seed heads, thereby separating the naked kernels from the chaff (cf. Isaiah 28:24–28).

© Zev Radovan

Winnowing was done by hand, allowing the chaff (or husks) to be separated from the grain.

Winnowing followed. On a breezy day the farmer would use his winnowing fork to pick up the chaff and grain mixture from the threshing floor and throw it into the air. The wind would blow the light chaff away, while the heavier grain would fall back to the earth in a pile. The clean grain would then be collected and stored in barns or garners. The stubble left in the field would be plowed back under or often burned in preparation for planting in the next growing season. That Book of Mormon peoples were familiar with these grain-growing practices is suggested by the use of terms throughout the text such as plowing, tilling, sowing, reaping, chaff, stubble, and sickles (see table 2).

Barley

It is probable that barley is included in the "grain of every kind" (1 Nephi 8:1) brought by Lehi and his family from the Old World to the promised land in the New World.[38] It is specifically mentioned by name as one of the cereals raised by Zeniff's colony (Mosiah 7:22; 9:9) and apparently was a standard upon which the Nephite monetary system was based: "A senum of silver was equal to a senine of gold, and either for a measure of barley, and also for a measure of every kind of grain" (Alma 11:7; cf. 11:15). Interestingly, barley also appears to have been a standard for biblical monetary systems as well: "Two barley grains made a finger's breadth, 16 made a hand's breadth, 24 a span, and 48 were the biblical cubit—about 41 cm"[39] (cf. Leviticus 27:16; 2 Kings 7:1, 16, 18).

Barley was a founder crop (basic, staple crop) of Old World Neolithic food production and is still one of the main cereals cultivated in the Mediterranean agricultural belt. In the archaeological record, barley is commonly found with wheat.[40] It appears to have been "the most abundant grain of the ancient Near East and the cheapest. It was the standard fare of the poor, the ration of the solider, serf and slave, and the staff of life for the Greek peasantry."[41] Michael Zohary reports that barley is mentioned more than thirty times in the Bible and no fewer than thirteen times in company with wheat. However, barley was considered inferior to wheat for human consumption and was less valued (e.g., Revelation 6:6). Consequently, it became the poor people's bread. The advantage barley has over wheat is that it will grow in relatively poor, salty, and arid soils in which wheat may not grow. Moreover, since barley ripens a month or more before wheat, it provided the first new flour each year, and in fact was apparently taken for the omer offerings at the Passover feast. For these reasons, even though wheat is more palatable, barley was perhaps a more important crop in ancient Israel.[42]

Jack Harlan observes that barley was apparently domesticated from wild races found today in southwestern Asia and was one of the earliest crops domesticated in the Near East. Wild forms with fragile ears (seed heads) have been found in Syria and date to perhaps as early as 8000 B.C. Similar remains have been found in the southern Jordan highlands, dating to about 6800 B.C., and at Jarmo and the Zargos hills in Iraq around the same time. The first cultivated barley appears in Iran, Syria, Palestine, and Turkey at times ranging between 6000 and 7000 B.C. and is commonly found with remains of other important crops such as emmer wheat, einkorn grain, flax, peas, and lentils. Irrigated barley was present by 6000 B.C. and possibly earlier at Jericho.[43] Zohary likewise concludes that the cultivation of barley appears to have begun about 8000 B.C. in southwestern Asia, where the wild progenitor of the primitive two-rowed barley (*Hordeum spontanum*) is widespread.[44] Later, the more advanced six-rowed types of cultivated barley were derived under domestication.[45]

The species of barley Lehi and his family would have known are limited. Eighteen species of barley are recognized today, but only two, *Hordeum distichum* (two-rowed barley), and *H. hexastichum* (six-rowed barley) have been cultivated.[46]

> Barley ears have a unique structure. They contain triplets of spikelets arranged alternately on the rachis [axis of the barley ears containing spikelets]. According to the morphology of the spikelets, barley under domestication can be divided into two principal types:
>
> 1. Two-rowed forms, traditionally called *Hordeum distichum* L., in which only the median spikelet in each triplet is fertile and usually armed with a prominent awn [or beard—bristles that protrude upward from the spikelets]. The two lateral spikelets are reduced, they are born on longer stalks and are grainless and awnless. Each ear thus contains only two rows of fertile spikelets.
>
> 2. Six-rowed forms, traditionally referred to as *H. hexastichum* L., in which the three spikelets in each triplet bear seeds and usually all are armed. Ears in these varieties therefore have six rows of fertile spikelets.[47]

Lehi and his family would probably have brought one or perhaps both of these barley species with them on their journey to the New World.

Corn/Maize

Although *corn* is a general term used to refer to grain or kernels of grain in the King James Version of the Bible (e.g., Genesis 41:5; Exodus 22:6; Isaiah 28:28),[48] when corn is referred to in the Book of Mormon (Mosiah 7:22; 9:9, 14), we assume that Joseph Smith was referring to maize (*Zea mays* L.), or corn as it is known in America today.[49] That the Prophet Joseph was not using the term in the generic biblical sense is perhaps evidenced in Mosiah 9:9: "And we began to till the ground, yea, even with all manner of seeds, with seeds of corn, and of wheat, and of barley, and with neas, and with sheum, and with seeds of all manner of fruits; and we did begin to multiply and prosper in the land." As previously mentioned, the appearance in this passage of the Nephite terms *neas* and *sheum* suggests that Joseph Smith was not familiar with the plants to which they referred and so left the terms in their original language.[50] In contrast, he would have been amply familiar with wheat, barley, and maize, or "corn," as he would have called it, and accordingly translated the Nephite terms for these grains into English.

Maize is a New World plant first domesticated in the Americas, possibly in more than one area. It is generally believed that maize originated in Mexico and was domesticated from wild maize (*teosinte*) in south central or southwestern Mexico[51] in semiarid regions at elevations above 4,500 feet.[52] DNA sequence data between two morphologically similar *teosinte* taxa indicate that the wild species of maize diverged about seven hundred thousand years ago from a common ancestor.

The domestication process was relatively recent and may have been based on a relatively small number of founding individuals that retained a substantial proportion of the genetic variation of their progenitors and diverged rapidly in morphology.[53] Maize similar to current types has been important in highland Mexico for millennia. Perhaps the earliest appearance of domesticated maize in the area can be found at Tehuacán (Mexico) at levels that may date to as early as 5000 B.C.,[54] though recent studies with maize starch suggest dates between 5000 and 3000 B.C.[55] Phytolith analysis[56] suggests that by 2450 B.C. maize cultivation had reached Ecuador.[57] By the time early explorers came to America maize was being cultivated from Canada to Chile.[58]

Although maize cultivation was ancient and widespread in the New World, evidence to date indicates that it was not known in the Fertile Crescent at the time Lehi left.[59] It is not possible to know from the Book of Mormon text when the Lehites first learned of and began maize cultivation in the New World, but it is clear that approximately 450 years after their arrival, corn had become a valued part of their sustenance in the land of Lehi-Nephi (Mosiah 7:22; 9:9, 14). They would probably have learned of maize long before then from other peoples already living in the land when they arrived.[60]

Neas and Sheum

Neas and sheum are included in the list of crops grown by Zeniff's colony in the land of Lehi-Nephi around 200 B.C. (Mosiah 9:9).[61] As discussed above, these words are apparently Nephite terms used to refer to plants with which Joseph Smith was unfamiliar and which he therefore did not translate into English equivalents. John Tvedtnes suggests that because the terms appear in a list of cereal grains including corn, wheat, barley, and other seeds, perhaps sheum and neas are grain food crops as well (Mosiah 9:9).[62] He notes that in the ancient Akkadian language a term cognate to *sheum* was used to refer to cereal grains, often either wheat or barley. Hildegard Lewy identifies the term *sheum* with the ancient Assyrian term used to refer to barley,[63] and John Brinkman et al. view the term *še'u* as referring to barley, grains, and sometimes pine nuts.[64]

Tvedtnes further suggests that neas may be compared with a Late Babylonian term for an unidentified plant and that the ending or last two letters may be related to a Sumerian word referring to either wheat or cereal grains. Moreover, he postulates that "the initial element may be from Sumerian *ni,* which is known in the word *ni-gig,* denoting something of grain."[65]

While neas and sheum were most certainly crop plants, it is also tenable that they were not grains. The list of crops in which the terms appear reads: "And we began to till the ground, yea, even with all manner of seeds, with seeds of corn, and of wheat, and of barley, and with neas, and with sheum, and with seeds of all manner of fruits" (Mosiah 9:9). The wording suggests that while corn, wheat, barley, and fruits were clearly propagated from seeds, perhaps neas and sheum were not. While cereals are always propagated from seeds, some plants are propagated from tubers and others from slips or cuttings. Anciently, there were many nongrain food crops being utilized by the indigenous people in the Americas that would have been unknown to Joseph Smith. For example, at Guitarrero Cave in Peru, researchers found the remains of the oldest cultivated plants in the New World dating to approximately ten thousand years ago. These plants were used for bedding, food, and apparel. They found tubers and rhizomes including *oca* and *ulluco* and a number of fruits and tubers including *lacuma, pacae,* and *Solanum hispidum* (potato). The fruits and tubers could have been gathered wild since they are native to the area. However, they also found common bean (*Phaseolus vulgaris*), lima bean (*P. lunatus*), and chili pepper (*Capsicum* sp.), which must have been cultivated because they are not native to the region. Since Native Americans were cultivating these plants, they may have cultivated the local plant types as well.[66] We know that Native Americans domesticated and cultivated a wide variety of plants that produce starch-rich roots and tubers. Harlan lists sweet potato, manioc, arrowroot, and jícama as root crops that originated in Mesoamerica.[67] Dolores Piperno and others have identified manioc, yams, and arrowroot starch grains on milling stones from Panama that date between 5000 and 3000 B.C.[68] Perhaps neas and sheum were Nephite terms for some of these food plants used from antiquity in the New World.

All Manner of Fruits

In addition to cereal crops, the text clearly indicates that "all manner of fruits" were raised by the Nephites. The diet of New World peoples during Nephite times included a wide variety of fruits. Two Old World fruits, olives and grapes, are also mentioned in the text in metaphorical contexts by Old World prophets or by Christ.

Grapes

In a passage of Isaiah quoted by Nephi, the prophet likened the good works he hoped the covenant people would bring forth to grapes and bemoaned the fact that they brought forth "wild grapes" instead (2 Nephi 15:2, 4). Later, the resurrected Savior also used grapes in a metaphor for the works of men (3 Nephi 14:16). These references constitute the only direct mention of grapes in the Book of Mormon text, and although they give no direct evidence that grapes were actually cultivated by the Lehites, their metaphorical usage suggests that the descendants of Lehi were familiar with the fruit.

While grapes cannot be directly confirmed as a crop among the Lehites, they certainly had wine. Wine is mentioned in thirty-two verses in the Book of Mormon. Typically, wine is produced from the juice of grapes, although sometimes the word refers to beverages made from other fruits. While there are alcohol-free wines today, it is unlikely that "wine" would have referred to nonalcoholic juices either during biblical (Luke 1:15; 5:38–39)[69] or Book of Mormon times. Several references to wine in the Book of Mormon indicate that its use could cause one to be inebriated. For example, on one occasion the captive people of Limhi paid a tribute of wine to their Lamanite guards, who became so "drunken and asleep" that Limhi and all his people were able to escape from the land (Mosiah 22:7, 10). Later, Moroni used a similar ploy to incapacitate Lamanite guards (Alma 55:4–24; cf. Alma 55:31).

Lehi and his family would certainly have known of grapes in the Old World. As Zohary explained: "From the dawn of man's history the vine and its fruit were widely cultivated in the Old Testament world: 'Noah was the first tiller of the soil. He planted a vineyard' (Genesis 8:20). . . . The identification of the Hebrew *gefen* with 'vine' is as unquestionable as *kerem* with 'vineyard' and *anavim* with 'grapes.' Innumerable words in the Bible are associated with planting, pruning, vintage and wine production, and various terms designate the parts of the plant and its fruit varieties."[70] The vine grows wild in temperate regions of western Asia, southern Europe, Algeria, and Morocco. It also appears in Armenia, to the south of the Caucasus and the Caspian Sea. Anciently it was mentioned in Bactriana, Kabul, Kashmir, and in Badakkhan to the north of the Hindu Kush. Seeds of the grape have been found in lake dwellings near Parma and Switzerland. It was assumed that both Semitic and Aryan nations knew the use of wine and may have introduced it into all of the countries into which they migrated, which would include India, Egypt, and Europe. Winemaking in Egypt goes back five or six thousand years. And of course the Phoenicians, Greeks, and Romans used it extensively. The Chinese did not cultivate the vine in their provinces before about 122 B.C., but the existence of several wild vines has been documented in northern China.[71]

H. P. Olmo reports that an estimated ten thousand cultivars of the Old World grape are thought to derive from a single species, *Vitis vinifera* L.[72] The wild species is thought to have originated in Middle Asia and is still found from northern Afghanistan to the southern borders of the Black and Caspian Seas. The cultivated grape is closely related to wild vine forms distributed throughout Europe and western Asia. Botanists thought these wild grapes were an independent species, *V. sylvesteres,* but since the wild forms are so closely related to the domestic forms, most botanists now regard the wild *sylvesteres* as a race of the cultivated crop.[73] Olmo further suggests that domestication began when migratory nomads marked forest trees that supported fruitful vines—such as poplar, pear, willow, plum, or fig—in order to be able to return to them. Vineyards developed later when they could be protected from domesticated sheep and goats by high, mud walls. In the Near East, cultivation of the grape is thought to have occurred as early as the fourth millennium B.C. Domesticated varieties from Asia Minor and Greece were dispersed westward by Phoenician sea routes. The spread of the Christian faith during the Roman period also helped to disseminate domesticated varieties. The spread of grapes followed the main river valleys—the Danube, Rhone, Rhine, Tiber, and Douro. Olmo also suggests that grapes were introduced to the New World when it was discovered. Spanish and Portuguese voyages helped the spread of grapes.[74]

Wild New World grapes were apparently harvested by Native Americans, but there is no evidence that they ever tried to cultivate them. Early Europeans in the New World used some wild and weedy species such as the fox grape (*V. labrusca*), which grows well in forest margin habitats along the edges of woods and fence rows. After early settlers converted forests to farms, this forest margin habitat was increased significantly and provided conditions appropriate for hybridization of various species of grape. Some of the better known American grapes were selected from such hybrid populations. Early attempts were made to introduce the European grape (*V. vinifera*) germ plasm by crossing it with American species. Most of the early attempts were not successful.[75] However, in modern times, a number of wild species native to America have been successfully used for breeding new varieties of grape or as hardy stock for grafting.[76]

The Lehites probably did not bring Old World grapes with them to the New World. Anciently, domesticated grapes were cloned from cuttings, as is the practice today. Some grape clones date back hundreds of years, perhaps more than a thousand years in some instances.[77] Grape seeds are considered too genetically variable to reliably reproduce domesticated plants, often growing into plants that produce "wild," nondesirable fruit.[78] If the Nephites wanted to grow grapes at their new location, they would have taken cuttings, but cuttings would in all probability not have survived the journey. Accordingly, it is our opinion that any grapes that may have been cultivated by the Lehites came from native stock or that the wine to which the text refers was produced from some other fruit.

Olives

Olives are mentioned frequently in the books of 1 Nephi and Jacob (see table 1), but, as with grapes, they are used in the context of metaphors rather than referred to as an agricultural crop cultivated by the Lehites, leaving us with no direct confirmation that they actually grew olives in the New World. However, coming from the Old World, the Lehites certainly would have been familiar with olive culture. From antiquity, the olive was important in the diet of the inhabitants of the Mediterranean basin, and its oil was used for holy anointing of kings and priests, anointing the sick, and lighting, as well as for a solvent for spices, incense, and aromatics used as perfumes and in cosmetics.[79] Indeed, the olive was perhaps the most important plant, having both culinary and religious significance in ancient Israel.[80] Wilford Hess et al. offer an extensive discussion of olive culture, particularly as related to Jacob 5, making it evident that olives have been an important crop throughout the Mediterranean since about 3000 B.C.[81] Daniel Zohary and Pinhas Spiegel-Roy report that olive stones and wood charcoal were found in Chalcolithic Horizons (3200 B.C.) in Tel Masos near Beersheva in early Bronze Age deposits, which date approximately from 2900 to 2700 B.C.[82] Likewise, J. Boardman observes that olives were cultivated in Palestine by at least the early part of the third millennium B.C. and possibly as early as the fourth millennium.[83]

It is commonly held that olive cultivation began in the region that includes northern Palestine and southern Syria. There are three Chalcolithic sites in the Jordan valley that have plant microremains indicating early olive tree cultivation and an economy based largely on the olive tree.[84] Some writers conclude that the olive was not first cultivated in Palestine. For example, Colin Renfrew suggests that the olive was domesticated

© Zev Radovan

Stone olive press used for extracting oil from olives.

in the Aegean region rather than in the Levant.[85] However, W. B. Turrill notes that mythological legends in Greece suggest that the cultivated olive came into Greece from an external source.[86] Archaeological evidence confirms the importance of olives in Greece from early Minoan times, about 1300 B.C. Regardless of the exact location of domestication, certainly olives were important very early on throughout the Mediterranean region and would have played a significant role in Lehi's Old World life.

Because of the olive's importance in the Old World, it would not be unreasonable to postulate that the Lehites attempted to bring the fruit with them to the New World, but it is our opinion that they would not have succeeded. During Old and New Testament times,[87] and even today,[88] the propagation of olive trees has involved taking cuttings from desirable trees rather than attempting to propagate trees by seeds. Seeds are too genetically variable to reliably produce quality plants that provide good fruit and oil. Domesticated plants with desirable characteristics have been propagated by cuttings since before recorded history.[89] Accordingly, we can assume that Lehi and his family were amply familiar with the olive culture practices of the day and, had his family attempted to bring olives with them, they would have brought cuttings rather than seeds. Unfortunately, as with grape cuttings, it is improbable that olive cuttings would have survived the journey to the New World. Moreover, even if the cuttings remained viable, they likely would not have survived in the new climate. Olives are adapted to the Mediterranean climate with warm, wet winters and hot, dry summers. The plants require winter chilling but will not tolerate an average temperature below 34°F (1.3°C) for the coldest winter month. They will grow at elevations up to about 550 meters above sea level and even up to 600 meters for some varieties. The plants thrive on calcareous schistose sandy or even rocky soils with good drainage.[90] The only places olives thrive in the Americas are areas with Mediterranean climates, including regions of California, Chile, and Argentina.[91] It is interesting to note that the olive is not mentioned in the Book of Mormon after Jacob 6, perhaps a further indication that olive culture was not actually practiced by the Lehites.

All Manner of Cloth

Both the Lehites and Jaredites developed a textile industry, with the production of "precious clothing" sometimes being viewed as a sign of industry and favor with God (e.g., Alma 1:29; Ether 9:17; 10:24), but more often as a mark of pride and worldliness (e.g., 1 Nephi 13:7, 8; Alma 4:6). While all the types of cloth produced by the Lehites are not clearly identified in the text, two of the most prized fabrics, linen and silk, are specified. If the linen and silk of Lehi's world are the same fabrics we recognize today, then linen would have been produced from plants and silk from silkworms raised on plants that may have been cultivated by the Lehites.

Linen

"Fine-twined linen" or "fine linen" is mentioned throughout the Book of Mormon text (see table 2).[92] The Lehites would have been well-acquainted with linen, the fabric made from the fibers of the flax plant, in the Old World. Flax was probably the oldest cultivated plant used for weaving clothing and, until recently, was extensively grown from the Atlantic coast of Europe in the west, to Russia and India in the east, and to Ethiopia in the south.[93] Flax fibers are stronger than cotton or wool and anciently were the principal vegetable fiber used for weaving textiles in Europe and western Asia. In modern times, flax has gradually been replaced by cotton as the fiber plant of choice.[94]

Researchers have concluded that cultivated flax (*Linum usitatissimum* L.) was derived anciently from a single species composed of several slightly different forms.[95] Archaeological evidence indicates that flax belongs to a group of plants that were present during the start of agriculture in the Near East, where it is thought to have first been domesticated. No definitive evidence indicates the precise start of domestication of flax in the Near East, but the gradual increase in seed size and use of linen indicate that flax cultivation in the region was apparently practiced before 6000 B.C.[96] In the traditional capital of Crete, flax was well known.[97]

Linen's popularity spread throughout the ancient Near East because the flax plant is easily disseminated by seeds. Flax was possibly associated with the earliest records of civilization in deposits of the Swiss Lake Dwellers. Cultivated flax appeared by at least 1000 B.C. in Egypt and the Middle East. The Egyptians wore linen and used linen to wrap their mummies, and linseed oil was used for embalming. The early Greeks and Romans cultivated flax for both fiber and seed, and the plant, or its products, is also mentioned by Virgil, Ovid, Cicero, and Pliny.[98]

Flax is commonly mentioned in the Bible. According to M. Zohary, during biblical times it was exclusively a fiber plant, and its cultivation dates back to 5000 B.C. in the Middle East, including the land of Israel, where he assumes domesticated flax originated.[99] The fibers for spinning, the linen produced, and the flax plant itself are all expressed by the Hebrew word *pishtah*. Flax was a principal oil and fiber source in the Old World and probably the earliest cultivated plant used for weaving clothes.[100] The famous Shroud of Turin, thought to have an image of the Savior, is linen.[101]

Flax found its way to the New World as well. Liberty Bailey observes that cultivated flax was "widely distributed, probably originally from Asia; escaped in waste places in N. Amer."[102] Thus, when translating the Book of Mormon, the Prophet Joseph certainly would have been familiar with linen, and we can assume that he translated the term accurately. We can also assume that the Lehites would have included flax among the "seed of every kind" which they brought with them to the New World. The Jaredites had linen as well, and in all probability they brought flax seeds with them on their trek to the promised land. Since the plant grows well in the wild, flax was possibly already established by the time the Lehites arrived.

Silk

A textile that Joseph Smith identified as silk or silks was produced by both the Lehites and Jaredites in times of prosperity (see table 2).[103] While Joseph Smith was most likely familiar with silk, it was not a fabric produced at that time in the Americas nor was it the most common cloth encountered in his backwoods upbringing. Accordingly, it is our opinion that while the fabric he identified as silk from the Book of Mormon text may have indeed been the silk we know today, it is also tenable that the fabric was something silklike. True silk is a fabric produced from fibers made by silkworms feeding on mulberry leaves. The mulberry tree (*Morus* L.) is not mentioned in the Book of Mormon text, but in parts of the Old World, the trees have been cultivated since antiquity for edible fruit and leaves for silkworm forage. There are only twelve species of mulberry, but because of morphological variability within some species, approximately ten times that many have been described.[104] The two most common species are white mulberry (*Morus alba* L.) and black mulberry (*M. nigera* L.). White mulberry is preferred for silk production. Silk has long been produced in China and Japan where the number of different varieties of white mulberry grown suggests that cultivation dates from ancient times. The white mulberry probably reached western Asia and southern Europe after monks brought the silkworm to Constantinople under Justinian in the sixth century A.D. If the white mulberry did not originally exist in Persia and the regions of the Caspian Sea, it must have penetrated there a very long time ago as well. The names *tutti* and *tuta*—which are Persian, Arabic, Turkish, and Tartar—have a similarity to the Sanskrit name *tula*. The white mulberry has been commonly used in Europe for raising silkworms. A variety of this plant is also commonly cultivated in India, and some varieties grow wild in northern India. However, no biblical Hebrew name is known for the plant.[105]

Black mulberry is more valued for its fruit than for its leaves and is distinguished from the white by several characteristics besides the color of the fruit. It also has a greater number of varieties than white mulberry.[106] P. M. Smith notes that the black mulberry is native to Iran and Asia Minor but has been cultivated in the Mediterranean area for many centuries.[107] He observes that not only is it referred to in the Bible, but also by Greek and Roman writers. Zohary notes that although silk is mentioned several times in the Bible, neither biblical nor post-biblical literature refers to its production.[108] He suggests that the rendition of *tut* in Maccabees as "mulberry tree" is tenable, though the words *sycamine* in Luke 17:6 and *mesukan* in Isaiah 40:20 may or may not be mulberry. He points out that *mesukan* is clearly related to the Sumerian *messikanu* or *sakannu*, which are thought to refer to mulberry. Zohary also notes that "The black mulberry, possibly a derivative of the white, grows wild in northern Persia, on the shores of the Caspian Sea and in ancient Colchis, whence it was introduced long ago into the lands of the Bible. Such early introduction from Persia and its neighbors was true of the apple, the pomegranate, the fig and the pistachio."[109] John Sorenson and Carl Johannessen suggest that some species of mulberry were in the New World before Columbus and that the bark from the trees may have been used for making paper and cloth.[110]

Although mulberries were obviously present in Israel during Lehi's time, there is no evidence of silk production in the area. In light of the fact that the Lehites were probably not familiar with silk production and because mulberry is not directly referred to in the Book of Mormon, we cannot confidently conclude whether the silk of the Lehites was true silk produced from silkworms or was from a plant fiber.

Other Textiles of Lehi's World

In the Old World, both plant and animal fibers were used for textiles, though Mosaic law prohibited the mixing of plant and animal fibers like linen and wool (e.g., Leviticus 19:19).

Since the Lehites "did cause that the women should spin, and toil, and work, and work all manner of fine linen, yea, and cloth of every kind" (Mosiah 10:5), we may assume that they used animal fibers as well.

Cotton was probably an important source of plant fiber. There are both Old World and New World cotton varieties. The diploid species of *Gossypium herbacium* and *G. arboreum* were cultivated in the Old World at least five thousand years ago. *G. arboreum* became the dominant species throughout Asia and Africa.[111] Early evidence of cotton in the New World has been found at Tehuacán dating to the same time period as maize, 5000 to 3000 B.C. In Peru, naturally colored types of cotton are still grown today.[112] Interestingly, world cotton production in modern times is based primarily on the species *G. hirsitum,* which is actually a cross between an Old World species (*G. herbacium*) and a Peruvian species (*G. raimondii*). Researchers postulate that the first cross of these two species may have initially taken place as far back as the start of the Pleistocene. It apparently took place long enough ago for at least four known species to have evolved from it and for one of those evolved species to have reached the Hawaiian Islands.[113] Considering the importance of cotton in the Old World, it is possible that the Jaredites or Lehites brought cotton with them to the New World and that they encountered, recognized, and used New World varieties when they arrived.

Conclusion

Agriculture played an important role in Lehi's world. Raising, harvesting, and securing crops were major concerns of the Lehites. They cultivated "all manner" of grains, fruits, and textile crops. Many of the crops identified by name were important in the Old World—which Lehi left behind on his journey to the promised land in the Americas—and were likely brought with his family on their pilgrimage. Once here, some of those crops, such as wheat and barley, were successfully propagated and cultivated, at least for a time, and continued to provide sustenance for the Lehites. As one would expect, the Lehites also adopted New World crops into their diets, most specifically corn (maize), and perhaps neas and sheum. For the Lehites, successful agricultural endeavors became a mark not only of prosperity, but of favor with God as well. Future research applying genomics to trace plant ancestry[114] may yet help us identify any remnants of crop plants that the Lehites brought from the Old World and further elucidate Old and New World affinities for the plants we have discussed.

TABLE 1

Summary of Plants Mentioned in the Book of Mormon

Plant	Reference
Barley	Mosiah 7:22; 9:9; Alma 11:7, 15
*Briers	2 Nephi 15:6; 17:23–25; 19:18; 20:17
*Cedars	2 Nephi 12:13; 19:10; 24:8
Corn	Mosiah 7:22; 9:9, 14
*Figs	3 Nephi 14:16
*Fir	2 Nephi 24:8
*Grapes	2 Nephi 15:2, 4; 3 Nephi 14:16
*Lilies	3 Nephi 13:28
Neas	Mosiah 9:9
*Olive	1 Nephi 10:12, 14; 15:7, 12, 16; Jacob 5:3–46; 6:1
Sheum	Mosiah 9:9
*Sycamores	2 Nephi 19:10
Thistles	Mosiah 12:12; 3 Nephi 14:16
Wheat	Mosiah 9:9; 3 Nephi 18:18

Entries marked with an asterisk are plants and terms that are used metaphorically by Old World prophets or by Christ. See note 3.

TABLE 2

Summary of Agricultural or Botanical Terms
Found in the Book of Mormon

Term	Reference
*Barns	3 Nephi 13:26
Blossoms	2 Nephi 15:24; Mosiah 12:12
Bread	2 Nephi 8:14; 13:1, 7; 14:1; Alma 5:34; 8:21, 22; 3 Nephi 14:9; 18:1–6; 20:3–8; 26:13; Moroni 4:3
Chaff	2 Nephi 15:24; 26:18; Mosiah 7:30; Alma 37:15; Mormon 5:16, 18
Crops	Alma 34:24
*Digging	2 Nephi 15:6; 17:25; Jacob 5:5–76
*Dunging	Jacob 5:47, 64, 76
Famine	1 Nephi 5:14; 2 Nephi 1:18; 6:15; 8:19; 10:6; 24:30; Mosiah 1:17; 9:3; 12:4; Alma 9:22; 10:22, 23; 45:11; 53:7; 62:35, 39; Helaman 10:6; 11:4–15; 12:3; 13:9; Ether 9:28, 35; 10:1; 11:7
Forests	1 Nephi 18:25; 2 Nephi 19:18; 20:18, 19, 34; 27:28; Enos 1:3; Mosiah 8:21; 18:30; 20:8; 3 Nephi 20:16; 21:12; Ether 10:19
Fruit[115]	1 Nephi 8:1, 10–35; 11:7; 15:36; 17:5, 6; 18:6; 2 Nephi 2:15, 18, 19; 14:2; 15:1; 20:18; 27:28; Jacob 5:8–77; 6:7; Enos 1:21; Mosiah 3:26; 9:9; 10:4; Alma 5:34, 52, 62; 12:21–23; 32:37–43; 33:1; 42:3; Helaman 6:26; 11:13, 17; 3 Nephi 14:16–20; 24:11; Ether 9:17, 35
Garners	Alma 26:5
Grafting	1 Nephi 10:14; 15:13, 16; Jacob 5:8–68; Alma 16:17

Grain	1 Nephi 8:1; Enos 1:21; Mosiah 7:22; 10:4; 11:3; 12:6; 21:16, 18, 21; 23:1; 24:18; Alma 1:29; 3:2; 4:2; 11:7; 62:29; Helaman 6:12; 11:6, 13, 17; 3 Nephi 3:22; 4:6; 6:2; Ether 9:17; 10:12
Grass	2 Nephi 8:12; 13:30
Groves	3 Nephi 21:18
Harrow	2 Nephi 9:47; Alma 14:6; 15:3; 26:6; 29:4; 36:12, 17, 19; 39:7; Mormon 5:8
Hoe	Ether 10:25
Linen	1 Nephi 13:7, 8; 2 Nephi 13:23; Mosiah 10:5; Alma 1:29; 4:6; Helaman 6:13; Ether 9:17; 10:24
Plowing	2 Nephi 12:4; Ether 10:25
*Pruning	2 Nephi 12:4; 15:6; Jacob 5:4–76; 6:2
Reaping	2 Nephi 5:11; 26:10; Mosiah 7:30, 31; Alma 3:26; 9:28; 26:5; 32:43; 3 Nephi 13:26; Ether 10:25
Ripening[116]	Jacob 5:37, 58; Mosiah 12:12; Alma 26:5
Roots	2 Nephi 15:24; 21:1, 10; 24:29, 30; Jacob 5:8–73; 6:4; Mosiah 14:2; Alma 5:52; 32:37–42; 46:40; 3 Nephi 25:1
Seeds[117]	1 Nephi 8:1; 16:11; 18:6, 24; 2 Nephi 5:11; 15:10; 16:13; Mosiah 9:9; Alma 32:28–39; 33:1; Ether 1:41, 43; 2:3
Sheaves	Alma 26:5; 3 Nephi 20:18
Sickles	Alma 26:5
Silk	1 Nephi 13:7, 8; Alma 1:29; 4:6; Ether 9:17; 10:24
Sowing	2 Nephi 5:11; Mosiah 7:30, 31; 3 Nephi 7:8; 13:26; Ether 10:25
Stalks	Mosiah 12:11
Straw	2 Nephi 21:7; 30:13

Stubble	1 Nephi 22:15, 23; 2 Nephi 15:24; 26:4, 6; 3 Nephi 25:1
Thickets	2 Nephi 19:18; 20:34; Mosiah 18:5
Threshing	Ether 10:25
Threshing Floor	3 Nephi 20:18
Tilling	1 Nephi 18:24; 2 Nephi 2:19; Enos 1:21; Jarom 1:8; Mosiah 6:7; 9:9, 14; 10:4, 21; 23:5, 25, 31; Alma 42:2; 62:29; Ether 6:13, 18; 10:25
Timber	Helaman 3:5–10
Trees	1 Nephi 8:10–30; 10:12–14; 11:4–25; 15:7–36; 2 Nephi 2:15; 16:13; 17:2; 20:19; 24:8; Jacob 4:6; 5:3–74; 6:1; Mosiah 18:5; Alma 5:34, 52, 62; 12:21, 23, 26; 26:36; 32:37–43; 33:23; 42:2–6; Helaman 3:9; 3 Nephi 4:28; 14:17–19; Ether 2:17
Vines	1 Nephi 15:15; 2 Nephi 15:2; 17:23; Alma 16:17; 3 Nephi 24:11
Vineyards	2 Nephi 13:14; 15:1–10; Jacob 5:3–77; 6:2–3; Mosiah 11:15; Alma 13:23; 28:14
Wood	1 Nephi 16:23; 2 Nephi 5:15; 17:2; 20:15; Jarom 1:8; Mosiah 11:8–10; Helaman 3:11; 3 Nephi 8:21

Notes

1. Agriculture is typically thought to include animal husbandry, but this report will focus only on farming and botany.

2. We will use the term *Lehites* to refer to the descendants of Lehi, both Nephite and Lamanite.

3. Old World prophets quoted in the Book of Mormon—such as Isaiah, Zenos, and even Christ—often used botanical imagery in their teachings and prophecies. In some instances, there is little

current evidence to indicate that the agricultural practices were actually followed or that the plants they mention were in fact found in the New World, but their very mention suggests that the audience was somehow familiar with the terms.

4. The appearance of the two foreign words *neas* and *sheum* in the text warrants a note about the translation process. In addition to its internal complexity and doctrinal consistency, one of the remarkable aspects of the Book of Mormon is that it was translated in only eighty-five days, often under extreme difficulties. See Larry C. Porter, "The Book of Mormon: Historical Setting for Its Translation and Publication," in *Joseph Smith: The Prophet, the Man,* ed. Susan Easton Black and Charles D. Tate Jr. (Provo, Utah: BYU Religious Studies Center, 1993), 49–64. In discussing the astonishing process by which the Book of Mormon was translated, B. H. Roberts, "Translation of the Book of Mormon," *Improvement Era,* April 1906, 427, raised a question concerning the role of the Urim and Thummim in the process. He states: "We have no statement at first hand from Martin Harris at all, only the statement of another, Edward Stevenson, as to what he heard Martin Harris say was the manner of translation. This was as follows: 'By aid of the seer stone, sentences would appear, and were read by the prophet, and written by Martin, and when finished he would say, "Written," and if correctly written that sentence would disappear, and another appear in its place; but if not written correctly, it remained until corrected so that the translation was just as it was engraven on the plates precisely in the language then used' [Edward Stevenson, 'One of the Three Witnesses,' *Millennial Star* 44 (6 February 1882): 86–87]." Elder Roberts observes that if this account were accurate then it would lead one to assume that the "Urim and Thummim did the translating, not Joseph the Seer." Such a conclusion would imply that the translation would be a "word for word bringing over from the Nephite language into the English language, a literal interpretation of the record. Therefore the language of translation would not be Joseph's, "but the divine instrument's." This would further imply that New England localisms, modern phrases from the English translation of

Hebrew scripture, and words from other sources would be present in the original Nephite record. Elder Roberts concludes that there are difficulties involved in such a theory of translation. It would be impossible to have a word-for-word translation from one language to another, for doing so would produce unintelligible jargon. Since the language of the English translation of the Book of Mormon is in the English idiom, and since errors in grammar can be found in the translation, it seems obvious that the translator is responsible for the language and grammar of the text, and any errors in the record are the faults of man, not of God. Elder Roberts further observes that this assumption should not cast any doubt upon Joseph's role as a seer. Any human imperfections certainly do not detract from the message of the book. Roberts, "Translation of the Book of Mormon," 428. As Joseph worked with the text, he translated Lehite terms and phrases into the terms and idioms of his day. Apparently not having an English equivalent for *neas* and *sheum,* he left them in their original language.

5. J. Derek Bewley and Michael Black, *Seeds: Physiology of Development and Germination,* 2nd ed. (New York: Plenum, 1994), 93.

6. M. Paul Becquerel, "Biologie Végétale: La longévité des graines macrobiotiques," *Comptes Rendus Hebdomadaires des Séances de l'Academie des Sciences* 199 (1934): 1662. Certainly, barley and wheat seeds are not viable after storage for thousands of years in ancient tombs, as is commonly reported. Bewley and Black, *Seeds,* 89.

7. See Terry B. Ball, S. Kent Brown, Arnold H. Green, David J. Johnson, and W. Revell Phillips, "Planning Research on Oman: The End of Lehi's Trail," *Journal of Book of Mormon Studies* 7/1 (1998): 12–21.

8. This information was provided by Mr. Ali Saaid Akaak, a Jiballi from Dhofar, in a personal conversation with Terry Ball.

9. David Rindos, *The Origins of Agriculture: An Evolutionary Perspective* (Orlando, Fla.: Academic, 1984), 140.

10. Daniel Zohary and Maria Hopf, *Domestication of Plants in the Old World: The Origin and Spread of Cultivated Plants in West Asia, Europe, and the Nile Valley,* 2nd ed. (Oxford: Clarendon, 1993), 25, 28.

11. John L. Sorenson and Carl L. Johannessen, "Biological Evidence for Pre-Columbian Transoceanic Voyages" (unpublished, expanded manuscript of a paper presented at the conference "Contact and Exchange in the Ancient World," Philadelphia, Pa., 5 May 2001) note that millet apparently likewise disappeared from regions where it had first been introduced and cultivated in the New World.

12. Daniel B. Adams, "Last Ditch Archaeology," *Science* 83 (December 1983): 32, 37.

13. Nancy B. Asch and David L. Asch, "Archeobotany," in *Deer Track: A Late Woodland Village in the Mississippi Valley,* ed. Charles R. McGimsey and Michael D. Conner (Kampsville, Ill.: Center for American Archaeology, 1985), 79–82.

14. Vorsila L. Bohrer, "Domesticated and Wild Crops in the CAEP Study Area," in *Prehistoric Cultural Development in Central Arizona: Archaeology of the Upper New River Region,* ed. Patricia M. Spoerl and George J. Gumerman, Center for Archaeological Investigations, Occasional Paper 5 (Carbondale, Ill.: Southern Illinois University, 1984), 249, 252.

15. While organic artifacts of wheat have not been and may not ever be found in the New World, analysis of inorganic opaline plant microfossils, called phytoliths, may yet reveal evidence of pre-Columbian wheat cultivation. Researchers are currently developing phytolith classification paradigms for Old World cereals in an effort to produce research tools to explore the possibility. Terry B. Ball, John S. Gardner, and Nicole Anderson, "Identifying Inflorescence Phytoliths from Selected Species of Wheat (*Triticum monococcum, T. dicoccon, T. dicoccoides,* and *T. aestivum*) and Barley (*Hordeum vulgare* and *H. spontaneum*)," *American Journal of Botany* 86/11 (1999): 1615–23.

16. See John L. Sorenson, *An Ancient American Setting for the Book of Mormon* (Salt Lake City: Deseret Book and FARMS, 1996), 184–85.

17. Alphonse de Candolle, *Origin of Cultivated Plants* (1886; reprint, New York: Hafner, 1967), 354–55.

18. Moshe Feldman, "Wheats," in *Evolution of Crop Plants,* ed. Norman W. Simmonds (London: Longman, 1976), 124.

19. Simcha Lev-Yadun, Avi Gopher, and Shahal Abbo, "The Cradle of Agriculture," *Science* 288 (2 June 2000): 1602.

20. Eviatar Nevo, "Genetic Diversity in Wild Cereals: Regional and Local Studies and Their Bearing on Conservation ex Situ and in Situ," *Genetic Resources and Crop Evolution* 45/4 (1998): 355.

21. Manfred Heun et al., "Site of Einkorn Wheat Domestication Identified by DNA Fingerprinting," *Science* 278 (14 November 1997): 1312.

22. T. A. Brown, "How Ancient DNA May Help in Understanding the Origin and Spread of Agriculture," in *Philosophical Transactions of the Royal Society of London, Series B, Biological Sciences* 354 (29 January 1999): 89.

23. Li Huang et al., "Restriction Fragment Length Polymorphism in Wild and Cultivated Tetraploid Wheat," *Israel Journal of Plant Sciences* 47/4 (1999): 213–24.

24. Michael Zohary, *Plants of the Bible: A Complete Handbook to All the Plants* (Cambridge: Cambridge University Press, 1982), 74.

25. In this biblical text the term *corn* is used to refer to cereal grains and likely means wheat. When the King James Version was translated, corn was the common name in England for wheat or grain. Wheat or grain is still commonly referred to as corn today in the UK and in India, which was influenced by colonizers from the UK. However, the Book of Mormon references to corn appear to refer to maize, which Americans call corn.

26. De Candolle, *Origin of Cultivated Plants,* 355.

27. Michael I. Rostovtzeff, *The Social and Economic History of the Hellenistic World* (Oxford: Clarendon, 1959), 240, 335, 359, 1164, 1168, 1187, 1450.

28. Michael Ventris and John Chadwick, *Documents in Mycenaean Greek* (London: Cambridge University Press, 1973), 213–15.

29. Feldman, "Wheats," 120.

30. Jane M. Renfrew, *Paleoethnobotany: The Prehistoric Food Plants of the Near East and Europe* (New York: Columbia University Press, 1973), 40.

31. Tetsu Sakamura, "Kurze Mitteilung über die Chromosomen-

zahlen und die Verwandtschaftsverhältnisse der *Triticum*-Arten," *Botanical Magazine (Tokyo)* 32 (1918): 151–52.

32. Renfrew, *Paleoethnobotany,* 41.

33. Ibid.

34. Ibid.

35. Zohary and Hopf, *Domestication of Plants,* 24.

36. There are many other classification paradigms for wheat, but for the sake of simplicity and consistency we will use this cytogenetic classification in this paper.

37. Zohary, *Plants of the Bible,* 74; Zohary and Hopf, *Domestication of Plants,* 39.

38. See "Barley in Ancient America," in *Reexploring the Book of Mormon,* ed. John W. Welch (Salt Lake City: Deseret Book and FARMS, 1992), 130–32; and Sorenson, *Ancient American Setting,* 184–86.

39. Richard M. Klein, *The Green World: An Introduction to Plants and People,* 2nd ed. (New York: Harper and Row, 1987), 298.

40. Zohary and Hopf, *Domestication of Plants,* 54.

41. Jack R. Harlan, "Barley," in *Evolution of Crop Plants,* 95.

42. Zohary, *Plants of the Bible,* 76.

43. Harlan, "Barley," 93–94.

44. Zohary, *Plants of the Bible,* 76.

45. Daniel Zohary, "The Progenitors of Wheat and Barley in Relation to Domestication and Agriculture Dispersal in the Old World," in *The Domestication and Exploitation of Plants and Animals,* ed. Peter J. Ucko and G. W. Dimbleby (Chicago: Aldine, 1969), 55.

46. There are hundreds of modern varieties of these two cultivated barleys and thousands of landraces. Zohary and Hopf, *Domestication of Plants,* 55. They are currently cultivated from the polar regions to the tropics. Zohary, *Plants of the Bible,* 76.

47. Zohary and Hopf, *Domestication of Plants,* 55.

48. See note 25 above.

49. See John L. Sorenson, *Images of Ancient America: Visualizing Book of Mormon Life* (Provo, Utah: Research Press, 1998), 35, 37; and Sorenson, *Ancient American Setting,* 28, 98–99, 139–40, 184.

50. See note 4 above.

51. Major M. Goodman, "The History and Evolution of Maize," *Critical Reviews in Plant Sciences* 7 (1988): 197. Richard S. MacNeish, "The Archaeological Record on the Problem of the Domestication of Maize," *Maydica* 30 (1985): 171–78; Richard S. MacNeish, *The Origins of Agriculture and Settled Life* (Norman: University of Oklahoma Press, 1992), 76–78.

52. H. Garrison Wilkes, "Maize and Its Wild Relatives," *Science* 177 (22 September 1972): 1072.

53. Holly Hilton and Brandon S. Gaut, "Speciation and Domestication in Maize and Its Wild Relatives: Evidence from the *Globulin-1* Gene," *Genetics* 150/2 (1998): 863.

54. Major M. Goodman, "Maize," in *Evolution of Crop Plants,* 130.

55. Dolores P. Piperno et al., "Starch Grains Reveal Early Root Crop Horticulture in Panamanian Tropical Forest," *Nature* 407 (19 October 2000): 895. MacNeish, *Origins of Agriculture,* 117; and Emily M. De Tapia, "The Origins of Agriculture in Mesoamerica and Central America," in *The Origins of Agriculture: An International Perspective,* ed. C. Wesley Cowan and Patty Jo Watson (Washington, D.C.: Smithsonian Institution Press, 1992), 143–71, concur with the early dates, while Austin Long et al., "First Direct AMS Dates on Early Maize from Tehuacán, Mexico," *Radiocarbon* 31/3 (1989): 1039, and especially Karen Hardy, "Preceramic Lithics in Central Mexico: An Examination of the Tehuacán and Oaxaca Chronological Sequences" (Ph.D. diss., University College, London, England, 1993), want a more recent date. Hardy's study pointing to more recent dates for Tehuacán culture has been questioned by Kent V. Flannery, "In Defense of the Tehuacán Project," *Current Anthropology* 38/4 (1997): 660–62; and Richard S. MacNeish, "In Defense of the Tehuacán Project," *Current Anthropology* 38/4 (1997): 663–72, but she later defended her position. Karen Hardy, "On the Tehuacán Project: Reply to Flannery and MacNeish," *Current Anthropology* 40/1 (1999): 63–69.

56. See note 15 above.

57. Deborah M. Pearsall, "Phytolith Analysis of Archeological

Soils: Evidence for Maize Cultivation in Formative Ecuador," *Science* 199 (13 January 1978): 177–78.

58. Hudson T. Hartmann et al., *Plant Science: Growth, Development, and Utilization of Cultivated Plants,* 2nd ed. (Englewood Cliffs, N.J.: Prentice Hall, 1988), 490.

59. Sorenson and Johannessen, "Biological Evidence," review the literature arguing the possibility of pre-Columbian *Zea mays* (corn) appearance in Eurasia and Africa, but no one suggests its appearance in the Levant before 600 B.C. See also Carl L. Johannessen and Anne Z. Parker, "Maize Ears Sculptured in 12th and 13th Century A.D. India as Indicators of Pre-Columbian Diffusion," *Economic Botany* 43/2 (1989): 164–80; Walton C. Galinat, "Evolution of Corn," *Advances in Agronomy* 47 (1992): 203–31; Jonathan D. Sauer, *Historical Geography of Crop Plants: A Select Roster* (Boca Raton, Fla.: CRC, 1993).

60. The text suggests that the Book of Mormon people, for the most part, lived and fought in a relatively small area, perhaps two hundred square miles. The archaeological record indicates that there were other peoples preceding and contemporary with the Lehites throughout the Americas. Sorenson, *Ancient American Setting,* 9–23, 146.

61. See ibid., 185.

62. See John A. Tvedtnes, *The Most Correct Book: Insights from a Book of Mormon Scholar* (Salt Lake City: Cornerstone, 1999), 346, who attributes some of his etymological suggestions to Robert F. Smith.

63. Hildegard Lewy, "On Some Old Assyrian Cereal Names," *Journal of the American Oriental Society* 76/4 (1956): 202.

64. John A. Brinkman et al., eds., *The Assyrian Dictionary of the Oriental Institute of the University of Chicago* (Chicago: Oriental Institute, 1992), 17:2:345–55.

65. Tvedtnes, *Most Correct Book,* 346.

66. Michael E. Moseley, *The Incas and Their Ancestors: The Archaeology of Peru* (London: Thames and Hudson, 1992), 96–97.

67. Jack R. Harlan, *Crops and Man,* 2nd ed. (Madison, Wis.: American Society of Agronomy and Crop Science Society of America, 1992), 77.

68. Piperno et al., "Starch Grains," 895.

69. Klein, *Green World,* 300–301.

70. Zohary, *Plants of the Bible,* 54.

71. De Candolle, *Origin of Cultivated Plants,* 191–94.

72. H. P. Olmo, "Grapes," in *Evolution of Crop Plants,* 295.

73. Cf. Zohary and Hopf, *Domestication of Plants,* 144.

74. Olmo, "Grapes," 295.

75. Harlan, *Crops and Man,* 132.

76. Zohary and Hopf, *Domestication of Plants,* 148.

77. Researchers using DNA testing in studies of Neolithic pottery have determined the genetic past of grapes. Patrick E. McGovern, "Searching for the Beginnings of Winemaking," *Expedition* 41/1 (1999): 4–5. One such study determined that one of the world's most successful clones, the Cabernet Sauvignon grape, is a hybrid. "Secrets of the Cabernet," *Economist* 343 (3 May 1997): 72.

78. Grape seeds were likely disseminated by birds long ago, even before fruit was cultivated. De Candolle, *Origin of Cultivated Plants,* 191–92.

79. Zohary and Hopf, *Domestication of Plants,* 137.

80. David Eitam and Michael Heltzer, eds., *Olive Oil in Antiquity: Israel and Neighboring Countries from the Neolithic to the Early Arab Period* (Padova: Sargon, 1996); Rafael Frankel, *Wine and Oil Production in Antiquity in Israel and Other Mediterranean Countries* (Sheffield: Sheffield Academic Press, 1999), 38.

81. Wilford M. Hess, Daniel J. Fairbanks, John W. Welch, and Jonathan K. Driggs, "Botanical Aspects of Olive Culture Relevant to Jacob 5," in *The Allegory of the Olive Tree: The Olive, the Bible, and Jacob 5,* ed. Stephen D. Ricks and John W. Welch (Salt Lake City: Deseret Book and FARMS, 1994), 484–562.

82. Daniel Zohary and Pinhas Spiegel-Roy, "Beginnings of Fruit Growing in the Old World," *Science* 187 (31 January 1975): 319–20.

83. J. Boardman, "The Olive in the Mediterranean: Its Culture and Use," in *Philosophical Transactions of the Royal Society of London Series B* 275 (1976): 194.

84. Reinder Neef, "Introduction, Development and Environmen-

tal Implications of Olive Culture: The Evidence from Jordan," in *Man's Role in the Shaping of the Eastern Mediterranean Landscape,* ed. S. Bottema, G. Entjes-Nieborg, and W. Van Zeist (Rotterdam: Balkema, 1990), 295.

85. Colin Renfrew, *The Emergence of Civilisation: The Cyclades and the Aegean in the Third Millennium* B.C. (London: Methuen, 1972), 304; Ventris and Chadwick, *Documents in Mycenaean Greek,* 50, 217.

86. W. B. Turrill, "Wild and Cultivated Olives," *Kew Bulletin* 3 (1951): 437–42.

87. Hess et al., "Botanical Aspects of Olive Culture," 484–562; Wilford M. Hess, "Botanical Comparisons in the Allegory of the Olive Tree," in *The Book of Mormon: Jacob through Words of Mormon, To Learn with Joy* (Salt Lake City: Bookcraft, 1990), 87–102.

88. N. Jacobini, M. Battaglini, and P. Preziosi, "Propagation of the Olive Tree," in *Modern Olive-Growing,* ed. J. Humanes Guillén and J. M. Philippe (Rome: United Nations Development Programme [UNDP] Food and Agriculture Organization of the United Nations [FAO], 1977), 27.

89. Hess et al., "Botanical Aspects of Olive Culture," 495–96, 498–99, 541.

90. Renfrew, *Paleoethnobotany,* 133–34.

91. Hess et al., "Botanical Aspects of Olive Culture," 553–54; see Sorenson, *Ancient American Setting,* 232.

92. "Possible 'Silk' and 'Linen' in the Book of Mormon," in *Reexploring the Book of Mormon,* 162–64.

93. A. Durrant, "Flax and Linseed," in *Evolution of Crop Plants,* 191–92; Zohary and Hopf, *Domestication of Plants,* 119.

94. Zohary and Hopf, *Domestication of Plants,* 119.

95. De Candolle, *Origin of Cultivated Plants,* 120.

96. Zohary and Hopf, *Domestication of Plants,* 126.

97. Ventris and Chadwick, *Documents in Mycenaean Greek,* 295.

98. Durrant, "Flax and Linseed," 191.

99. Zohary, *Plants of the Bible,* 78.

100. Zohary and Hopf, *Domestication of Plants,* 119.

101. Thaddeus J. Trenn, "The Shroud of Turin: A Parable for Modern Times?" *Journal of Interdisciplinary Studies* 9/1–2 (1997): 121.

102. Liberty H. Bailey, *Manual of Cultivated Plants: Most Commonly Grown in the Continental United States and Canada* (New York: Macmillan, 1949), 604.

103. "Possible 'Silk' and 'Linen' in the Book of Mormon," 162–64; and Sorenson, *Ancient American Setting*, 232.

104. Bailey, *Manual of Cultivated Plants*, 336.

105. De Candolle, *Origin of Cultivated Plants*, 149–51.

106. Ibid., 152.

107. P. M. Smith, "Minor Crops," in *Evolution of Crop Plants*, 316.

108. Zohary, *Plants of the Bible*, 71.

109. Ibid.

110. Sorenson and Johannessen, "Biological Evidence."

111. L. L. Phillips, "Cotton," in *Evolution of Crop Plants*, 197–98.

112. James M. Vreeland, "Coloured Cotton," *International Development Research Centre Reports* 10/2 (1987): 4–5.

113. Phillips, "Cotton," 198–99. Sorenson and Johannessen, "Biological Evidence," provide a nice review of pre-Columbian transoceanic crossing of cotton theories.

114. Jeffrey Bennetzen, "Opening the Door to Comparative Plant Biology," *Science* 296 (5 April 2002): 60–63; Steven H. Strauss, "Genomics, Genetic Engineering, and Domestication of Crops," *Science* 300 (4 April 2003): 61–62.

115. References using fruit in regard to one's posterity (e.g., "fruit of his loins") or the product of something (e.g., "fruit of one's labors") have not been included in this list.

116. References to "ripening in iniquity" have not been included in this list.

117. References to seed meaning one's posterity have not been included in this list.

Chapter 7

Israelite Inscriptions from the Time of Jeremiah and Lehi

Dana M. Pike

The greater the number of sources the better when investigating the history and culture of people in antiquity. Narrative and prophetic texts in the Bible and 1 Nephi have great value in helping us understand the milieu in which Jeremiah and Lehi received and fulfilled their prophetic missions, but these records are not our only documentary sources. A number of Israelite inscriptions dating to the period of 640–586 B.C., the general time of Jeremiah and Lehi, provide additional glimpses into this pivotal and primarily tragic period in Israelite history.

The number of inscriptions discovered from ancient Israel and its immediate neighbors—Ammon, Moab, Edom, Philistia, and Phoenicia—pales in comparison to the bountiful harvest of texts from ancient Assyria, Babylonia, and Egypt. However, known Israelite inscriptions do shed important light on the text and the historical and cultural context of the Hebrew Bible (the Christian Old Testament), including the time period of Jeremiah and Lehi.

The Babylonians conquered Jerusalem and Judah in 597 B.C. and returned and destroyed Solomon's temple in 586 B.C., killing and exiling thousands of Judahites in the process. Israelite history in the land of Canaan prior to 586 B.C. is conveniently referred to by scholars as both the preexilic (i.e., before the Babylonian exile) and the First Temple period (Solomon's temple stood from ca. 960 to 586 B.C.).

Appendix 1 (below) provides a convenient overview of the major preexilic Israelite inscriptions, along with a few of the more noteworthy inscriptions from Israel's immediate neighbors. Only the best preserved inscriptions from the latter portion of the preexilic period, 640–586 B.C., are highlighted in this chapter. They are all from the kingdom of Judah (the northern kingdom of Israel was conquered and incorporated into the Assyrian empire in 722 B.C.). Small or ill-preserved inscriptions from this time period are listed in appendix 1 but are not discussed below. Postexilic Israelite inscriptions are neither listed nor discussed.

The Value of Inscriptions

Archaeological excavation produces two broad types of evidence: nontextual artifacts—ranging in size from beads and seeds to monumental architecture—and inscriptions or texts. Both types must be coordinated with each other in any serious effort to understand the life and times of ancient Israelites or any other people. While inscriptions may seem more readily accessible and understandable than many artifacts are, they, like artifacts, require careful interpretation in order to be employed productively. Authentic Israelite inscriptions (distinguished from forgeries, for which there is, sadly, a flourishing market) are available to us as they existed over twenty-five hundred years ago. They are valuable primary documents not susceptible to tampering or editing, having no transmission history (in contrast to the Bible). As such, ancient inscriptions are of great importance to any study of Israel's past.

However, all archaeological evidence must be coordinated with biblical data to effectively understand ancient Israel. On the one hand, because of its vast size and the great span of time it covers, the Bible preserves historical, cultural, and religious data that would otherwise be unknown if we had only the relatively small corpus of ancient Israelite inscriptions. On the other hand, the Bible has inherent limitations for students of ancient Israelite history and culture because of its focus on religious themes. For example, little if anything is recorded in the Bible about King Ahab's political or military activity during his twenty-year reign or about the plight of the agrarian class of Judahites who remained in the land after many from the upper and middle classes were deported to Babylonia in the 590s and 580s B.C. Thus biblical data must be carefully employed and coordinated with what is learned from inscriptions and artifacts.

Inscriptions help to broaden and deepen our understanding of the various dimensions of Israelite history and society. For example, some preserve Hebrew language features and vocabulary not found in the Bible. They also present evidence of scribal and administrative practices not otherwise attested. Some inscriptions highlight socioeconomic matters, such as an appeal to local authorities for justice, the allocating of provisions to royal officials or to mercenaries, and the authorizing and sealing of official documents. Historical inscriptions, like those from ninth-century Dan and eighth-century Jerusalem, provide information that augments the biblical account. Votive inscriptions help demonstrate Israelite religious inclinations. Tomb inscriptions invoke curses on robbers, who almost inevitably disturbed the remains of the deceased in their quest for treasure or trinkets. Some inscriptions provide a view of the personality of ancient Israelites, allowing us to hear their "voice" in a fascinating way. For example, an Israelite military officer named Hoshaiah indignantly wrote to his superior: "My lord said, 'You do not know how to read a letter!' As

YHWH lives, no one has ever attempted (i.e., had) to read a letter to *me!* For I can read any letter which is sent to me, and moreover, I can recite it back in order" (Lachish ostracon 3; see text and discussion below). Israelite inscriptions thus provide avenues to explore the language, history, and culture of ancient Israel that are not available using the Bible alone.

The Media of Inscriptions

Preexilic Israelite inscriptions survive mainly on stone or pottery and as impressions in lumps of clay. Only rarely are they preserved on papyrus or metal. Stone, with the exception of the softer limestone in the Judean hills, provided a durable medium for inscriptions. For example, the face of unquarried stone was generally smoothed prior to engraving for tomb and other types of inscriptions (e.g., the Silwan and the Hezekiah/Siloam Tunnel inscriptions).[1] Quarried stone was fashioned into stelae that could be engraved (e.g., the Tel Dan inscription; compare the Jaredite monumental inscription that Mosiah₁ translated, as recounted in Omni 1:19–22). Unfortunately, only a few relatively short or fragmentary preexilic Israelite inscriptions in stone have been discovered in Israel, and none of them dates to 640–586 B.C., the time period discussed herein.[2]

Stamp seals represent another type of stone inscription. They are small conical or scaraboid-shaped objects, the flat surface of which is about the size of a person's thumbnail. Seals were generally made from semiprecious stone, although ivory and bone were occasionally employed. The brief, identifying inscription on each seal, carved in mirror image, usually consists of a person's name and patronym or official title. Sometimes a picture is included as well. A few Israelite seals have only a picture and title but no name. Stamp seals were usually pressed into a lump of clay to leave an impression of what was carved into the seal (see photo essay, page 70). Papyrus documents were "sealed" in this manner after they had been folded and wrapped around with a string. Such clay lumps containing seal impressions are called *bullae* (plural; the singular, *bulla,* is the Latin word meaning "bubble"). Many bullae preserve impressions of string and papyrus fibers on the back. Over seven hundred preexilic Israelite seals and seal impressions have been discovered.[3] However, most of them were not found during controlled archaeological excavations. Looters of ancient sites have discovered some, but there is legitimate concern that some are forgeries.[4]

Given the ubiquitous nature of pottery in antiquity, potsherds (broken pieces of fired pottery) provided a ready, inexpensive source of "scrap paper." Ostraca (inscriptions on potsherds) were usually produced by writing with a pen and ink, although the texts of a small number of ostraca were incised with a stylus on a fired potsherd. (Additionally, stamp seals and styli were sometimes used to mark the handles or shoulders of pots to indicate ownership or the place of production before such pots were fired.) Ostraca typically functioned as memos and short letters. They were generally utilized for temporary notations and communications. Texts of any import that were written on ostraca were eventually transferred to other media, especially papyrus. Significant collections of ostraca from the Judahite cities of Arad and Lachish (discussed below) date to the time of Jeremiah and Lehi.

Hazards to preservation—such as moisture, fire, war, and time—have combined to diminish the number of inscriptions that have been found on stone and pottery and to almost totally eliminate four other media on which ancient Israelite texts were no doubt produced: papyrus, metal, plaster, and leather. Evidence from the Bible (e.g., Jeremiah 36) and from the contemporary practices of nearby Egypt suggests that many ancient Israelite texts were written on papyrus. The large number of bullae that have survived the papyrus documents they originally sealed further attests to the numerous Israelite papyri that have perished. Such documents were written with ink on single sheets of papyrus as well as on scrolls formed by gluing multiple sheets together. Only a fragment of one pre-exilic Israelite papyrus text has been discovered to date (Wadi Murabbaʿat papyrus 17, from about 700 B.C.).

While metal was occasionally used as a medium for texts in the ancient Near East, very little evidence of this practice has survived from ancient Israel. The small inscriptions on two rolls of silver foil discovered at Ketef Hinnom in western Jerusalem (discussed below) that date to the time of Jeremiah and Lehi are rare indeed. No bronze plates (or "brass," as it is rendered in the Book of Mormon), such as those Nephi acquired from Laban (1 Nephi 4), have been discovered in Israel by archaeologists.[5]

Another medium of inscriptions for which there is little archaeological evidence from ancient Israel is ink on plaster. Moses instructed the Israelites that after crossing the Jordan River and subduing the land of Canaan under Joshua's direction, they should assemble at Shechem and

> set up large stones and cover them with plaster. You shall write on them all the words of this law when you have crossed over. . . . So when you have crossed over the Jordan, you shall set up these stones, about which I am commanding you today, on Mount Ebal, and you shall cover them with plaster. . . . You shall write on the stones all the words of this law very clearly. (Deuteronomy 27:2–4, 8)[6]

The fulfillment of these instructions as recorded in Joshua 8:30–35 suggests that Israelites may have employed a similar means for creating public inscriptions on other occasions, although none has been discovered in the heartland of Israel. However, the likelihood of such a practice is supported by the 1960 discovery of lengthy inscriptions in a script with Aramaic and Ammonite affinities on a plastered wall of a shrine at Deir ʿAlla, in the eastern Jordan River valley, dating to the first half of the eighth century B.C. The 1975 discovery of a few fragmentary texts on plastered walls at the remote Israelite caravanserai/shrine of Kuntillet ʿAjrud in northeast Sinai further illustrates this practice.[7]

Leather was occasionally employed for documents by pre-exilic Israelite scribes. As was the case with papyrus, texts were written in ink on single sheets or on scrolls formed by stitching several sheets together. However, leather was not nearly as common a writing medium in preexilic Israel as it became in the postexilic period.[8] For example, the majority of the Dead Sea Scrolls, from the last two centuries B.C., were written on leather.[9] No text from preexilic Israel has been discovered on leather.

Literacy in Ancient Israel

It may seem odd to discuss Israelite literacy in a study of Israelite inscriptions. Clearly, the evidence of inscriptions indicates that people could write and read. The evidence also indicates that Israelites, like other West Semites, utilized a twenty-two-character alphabet developed by Canaanites about eight hundred years before Jeremiah and Lehi, which made literacy a seemingly simple attainment in contrast to the complex and cumbersome writing systems of the Egyptians, Babylonians, Assyrians, and Hittites; their systems required years to master and essentially limited literacy to professional scribes. However, the extent and degree of literacy among ancient Israelites is an important consideration since it influences our understanding of so many aspects of their lives, such as the accessibility of "scripture" for the average Israelite and how prophets like Jeremiah and Lehi communicated their messages.

While some scholars assert that the majority of ancient Israelites were literate, there is no academic unanimity on this question because there is no way to accurately assess the extent of their literacy. While many Israelites were literate, the majority were probably not fully literate, at least according to our conception of literacy.[10] Literacy requires not only the training to master the skills of reading and writing but also the opportunity to employ and reinforce those skills. The majority of Israelites during the preexilic period were involved in agricultural and pastoral occupations. The political and religious leadership constituted about 5 percent of the total population (the upper class, using modern terminology). Those engaged in administrative and midlevel management positions in the military, palace, or temple, along with those in mercantile activities (traders, shop owners, and large producers), probably constituted about 20–30 percent of the population (the middle class). This means that approximately two-thirds of the Israelite population were in the lower class of their socioeconomic system (not unlike the situation in many less developed countries today). Those Israelites who lived in urban areas, like Jeremiah and Lehi in Jerusalem, undoubtedly developed some degree of literacy. But the majority of the population probably had relatively few opportunities to read and write, decreasing the motivation for literacy.

The Bible and the Book of Mormon consistently depict well-developed writing and reading skills among some Israelites, but they also indicate a significant oral dimension in Israelite society. For instance, the Lord instructed Isaiah to write a prophecy (Isaiah 8:1–2). Lehi and Ezekiel each read from a scroll shown them in vision (1 Nephi 1:11–14; Ezekiel 2:9–10). Nephi indicated that he and his father (and presumably Laban) could read and write (1 Nephi 1:1–3, 16–17; 5:10–16). Jeremiah's scribe Baruch recorded the prophet's teachings more than once (Jeremiah

36:2, 28). However, there is no indication that these or other prophets copied and circulated their teachings for public distribution in written form.[11] The recurring instruction of the Lord to his prophets was to "go speak" to the people (Ezekiel 3:1; cf. Jeremiah 7:2; 36:6; 1 Nephi 1:18).

Moses taught the early Israelites to "keep these words that I am commanding you today in your heart. Recite them to your children and talk about them when you are at home and when you are away, when you lie down and when you rise. Bind them as a sign on your hand, fix them as an emblem on your forehead, and write them on the doorposts of your house and on your gates" (Deuteronomy 6:6–9). This passage underscores the strong oral component of the transmission of knowledge among Israelites ("keep these words . . . in your heart," "recite them"; Exodus 12:25–27 and 17:14 provide other indications of this oral dimension). But the injunction to attach scripture texts to doorposts and gates and to wear them, even if figurative, implies a certain level of literacy (there is no preexilic evidence for the practice of literally "wearing" scripture, such as developed with the wearing of *tefillin*/phylacteries in the Second Temple period).[12]

Among the archaeological evidence for ancient Israelite literacy, ostraca, seals, and seal impressions constitute the bulk of surviving Israelite inscriptions. Seals and bullae were utilized by people in administrative and mercantile positions. Israelite ostraca primarily preserve administrative texts from economic and military contexts. The Mesad Hashavyahu ostracon (discussed below), a rare example of a document from a commoner, preserves a letter dictated to a professional scribe, not written by the sender himself. Thus, the available archaeological evidence demonstrates literacy only among the upper and middle classes.

No evidence has been found that written materials were commonplace among the lower class.

This socioeconomically based disparity in literacy levels is partly a matter of function. Subsistence living does not necessitate developed literacy. Significantly, however, archaeological evidence of literacy is preserved from throughout the land of Israel, not just in the capital or major cities. There were thus literate people dispersed throughout the countryside. Practically speaking, however, the labor, skill, and expense of producing extended religious or literary documents (such as a set of scriptures) placed such works beyond the financial means of most Israelites, in addition to their being beyond the ability of many Israelites to utilize them.[13]

Concluding this brief discussion of Israelite literacy, an important distinction must be made between the ability to write and the ability to read and, furthermore, between the ability to read short, simple texts and longer, more complex texts. Writing reinforces reading skills, but a rudimentary reading skill can be attained without the ability to write. A diverse range of literary skills existed among ancient Israelites. A *tentative* estimate is that about a third of ancient Israelites in Jeremiah's and Lehi's day were fairly to completely literate (i.e., they could read and write on an adequate to an accomplished level); about a third were probably barely to fairly literate (i.e., they were able to read or write to some degree but not necessarily with the same facility); and about a third were completely illiterate to barely literate.[14] This means that the inscriptions reviewed below could not have been read or read very well by some ancient Israelites. Understanding this situation helps to partially explain why the scriptures depict the *public* ministries of prophets like Jeremiah and Lehi as primarily oral in nature.

Major Inscriptions from the Time of Jeremiah and Lehi

The most important Israelite inscriptions from 640 to 586 B.C. will now be reviewed to illustrate the relevant data they preserve.[15] Only representative examples of seals and ostraca from this time period have been included. The descriptions of the documents cited herein are of necessity brief. The reader is invited to pursue the citations provided in appendix 2 and the endnotes for further details and discussion.[16]

Arad Ostraca

Arad (Tel Arad), a Canaanite and then Israelite city, is located about eighteen miles east of Beersheba at the southern border of the kingdom of Judah. The Judahite fortress at Arad, along with a string of similar facilities in the region, played an important role in the defensive system of Judah's southern, Negev frontier from the mid-tenth through the early sixth centuries B.C. A small Israelite temple existed at Arad from the tenth through eighth centuries, but it was never rebuilt following its destruction during the reign of Hezekiah (727–697 B.C.). About two hundred inscriptions were discovered at Arad in excavations carried out from 1962 to 1964, most of them ostraca. Three more ostraca were discovered in 1976. Many of these ostraca are poorly preserved, being broken and/or having faded ink. One hundred and seven of the inscriptions from Arad are written in Hebrew, mainly in ink, although sixteen of them were incised with a stylus on jugs or bowls after the containers had been fired. The bulk of the remaining Arad inscriptions are ostraca written in Aramaic (fifth to fourth century B.C.), with a few later inscriptions in Greek and Arabic. The Hebrew ostraca date mainly from the late eighth to early sixth centuries B.C.[17]

The majority of the Hebrew ostraca from Arad are lists of names and administrative letters to commanders of the fort. Of particular interest here, because they are contemporary with Jeremiah and Lehi, are some ostraca comprising a portion of the archive of Eliashib, Arad's Judahite commander from the later portion of Josiah's reign until about 595 B.C. This correspondence, from stratum VI of the tel, generally consists of orders to Eliashib to provide food supplies (olive oil, wine, bread, and flour) to troops in the region, although at least one ostracon (#24) contains an urgent order at "the word of the king" that troops be sent to Ramat-Negev, a nearby fortress. In addition to ostraca, three stamp seals belonging to Eliashib have been discovered (stratum VII).

Arad ostracon 1:

> To Eliashib: And now, give to the Kittim three *baths*[18] of wine, and write the name of the day. And from the remainder of the first flour you will deliver one measure of flour for them to make bread. You will give (them some) of the wine from the mixing bowls.

This letter preserves instructions to Arad's military commander Eliashib to distribute basic rations to the Kittim. The Kittim were mercenaries, probably Greeks from Cyprus and the Aegean islands, working in the Negev for the kingdom of Judah.[19] A basic administrative accounting system was clearly in place.

Arad ostracon 18:

> To my lord Eliashib: May YHWH inquire after your well-being. And now, give to Shemaryahu a measure (of flour), and to the Kerosite you will give a measure (of flour).[20] And concerning the matter about which you commanded me, it is well. He is staying in the house of YHWH.

The Kerosite in question was probably a member of the clan of Keros, who were Nethinim, or temple servants (see Nehemiah

7:46–47). After giving instructions about rations, this
ostracon reports on a matter known to the sender and
to Eliashib, but not to us.
Someone is staying in one of
the chambers (not the sanctuary proper) of the "house of
YHWH." The phrase "house
of YHWH," or "house of the
Lord," as it is usually rendered in English transla-
tions of the Bible, is the
standard designation for Jehovah's temple in ancient
Israel (e.g., 1 Kings 6:1, 37;
2 Kings 25:9). Whether this
report to Eliashib was intended to indicate the loca-

Arad ostracon 18 (obverse; ca. 600
B.C.; 6.6 x 4.2 cm [= 2.6 x 1.65 in]).
Discovered in 1964 in the Judahite
fortress town of Arad in the Negev.
The last line reads *byt yhwh,* "house of
the Lord." (Israel Museum, Jerusalem)

© Zev Radovan

tion or the status (safety?) of the individual is not discernible,
nor can we tell if the person was at the temple by Eliashib's
order. The Jerusalem temple is presumably the one in question.
Nehemiah 13:4–9 also preserves a report of someone staying
in the Jerusalem temple complex (however, the Eliashib mentioned in this biblical passage is not the same person mentioned in the Arad ostraca).

Lachish Ostraca

Lachish (Tel ed-Duweir) was a prominent Canaanite and
then Judahite city in the Shephelah region of the country, approximately twenty-five miles southwest of Jerusalem and about midway between Ashqelon on the Mediterranean coast and Hebron
in the Judean hill country. Its destruction by the Assyrians in 701

B.C. is recorded in the Bible (2 Kings 18:13–19; 19:8) and is commemorated in bas reliefs that once lined a room in Assyrian king Sennacherib's new palace in Nineveh. Lachish was rebuilt and remained an important Judahite city until its subsequent destruction by the Babylonians, ca. 587 B.C.

An important group of twenty-one ostraca was discovered during excavations at Lachish in the 1930s. Eleven more inscriptions were discovered in renewed excavations in the 1960s to 1980s. Twelve of the first twenty-one Lachish ostraca are letters and two are lists of names. The letters consist mainly of correspondence to the city's military commander, identified as Yaush in ostraca 2, 3, and 6, regarding military, political, and administrative circumstances of the early 580s B.C. As with many of the Arad ostraca, the ink on several of the Lachish ostraca is poorly preserved. Interestingly, ostraca 2, 6, 7, 8, and 18 were all written on sherds from the same pot.[21]

Most of the first group of twenty-one ostraca, those of interest here, were found in a guard room between the outer and inner gate complexes of Lachish, which were destroyed by the Babylonians when Zedekiah was king of Judah. Some earlier scholars dated this group of ostraca to 587–586 B.C., after the Babylonians were already in Judah reconquering the country. However, these texts more likely derive from the time just before the Babylonian invasion of the kingdom of Judah—588 B.C.—after King Zedekiah had broken his vassal treaty with the Babylonians but before the destructive reprisals began. Nebuchadnezzar and the Babylonians arrived in Judah by January 587 B.C., laying siege to Jerusalem for eighteen months before finally destroying the temple and much of the city. Second Kings 25 focuses on the conquest of Jerusalem and the destruction of the temple, but archaeological evidence indicates that the Babylonians also exercised their military might against other significant cities in the kingdom of Judah, including Lachish.

Lachish ostracon 3 (obverse left, top portion of reverse right; 13 x 8 cm [= 5.1 x 3.15 in]). One of the letters discovered in 1935 in a guard room beneath the rubble of a gate tower in the Judahite city of Lachish. This ostracon mentions an unnamed prophet. (Israel Museum, Jerusalem)

Lachish ostracon 3:

Your servant Hoshayahu sends a report to my lord Yaush. May YHWH cause my lord to hear peaceful and good news. And now, please open the ear of (i.e., explain to) your servant concerning the letter which you sent to your servant last night, for your servant has been heartsick since you sent (the letter) to your servant. My lord said, "You do not know how to read a letter!" As YHWH lives, no one has ever attempted (i.e., had) to read a letter to *me!* For I can read any letter which is sent to me, and moreover, I can recite it back in order. Now, your servant has been informed that the captain of the host (i.e., commander), Konyahu the son of Elnatan, has moved south to enter Egypt. He has sent (orders) to retrieve Hodawyahu son of Ahiyahu and his men from here. Furthermore, your servant is sending to my lord the letter (which was in the possession?) of Tobiyahu, the servant of the king, which was sent to Shallum son of Yadda from the prophet, saying, "Beware!"

Hoshayahu, a frustrated subordinate, sent this entertaining letter to his superior officer, Yaush. We do not know where Hoshayahu was stationed, but clearly he did not appreciate a remark made to and about him in a previous letter from Yaush. After protesting his concern and reiterating his abilities, Hoshayahu communicates important information about Judahite troop movements ("Konyahu . . . has moved south to enter Egypt"), which suggests at least a partial coordination of Judahite defensive efforts with Egypt. He then indicates that he has forwarded a letter of warning from an unidentified prophet to someone named Shallum. The specific context of the warning is not known, but given the troubled times the letter was no doubt apropos and may have been political in nature. This unnamed prophet could certainly have been Jeremiah, but this connection, while possible, remains mere speculation. The prophet Urijah, mentioned only in Jeremiah 26:20–23, has also been nominated as "the prophet" in this ostracon; however, this is not possible because of chronological and onomastic differences.[22] Lachish ostracon 16 refers to "]yah, the prophet," but unfortunately the ostracon is broken and the first part of the name is missing (both the names Jeremiah and Urijah end in *-yah(u)* in Hebrew, but so do many other names from this time period). We cannot determine whether this partially named prophet is the same as the unnamed one in ostracon 3.

The comment in Lachish ostracon 3 that Judahite troops had "moved south to enter Egypt" is reminiscent of Jeremiah 26:20–23, which recounts that a prophet named Urijah fled to Egypt, fearing for his life after rebuking King Jehoiakim (609–598 B.C.) and prophesying the destruction of Jerusalem. Judahite troops tracked Urijah down and returned him to Jerusalem, whereupon he was executed (a potential fate for Lehi, Jeremiah, and other prophets as well). Early claims that

Jeremiah 26 and Lachish ostraca 3 document the same event are inaccurate and groundless.[23]

Lachish ostracon 4:

> May YHWH cause m[y lord] to hear good news on this day. And now, everything which my lord sent (me instructions to do), so your servant has done. I have written in the record according to all (the instructions) which you sent to me. And as my lord sent (i.e., asked) concerning the matter of Beth-hrpd: there is no one there. As for Semakyahu, Shemayahu seized him and made him go up (i.e., sent or took him) to the city. Your servant is not able to send the witness there [today]. If (my lord) [cam]e during the morning watch, he would know that we are watching the signal (-fires) of Lachish according to all the signs (code) which my lord has given (us), for we cannot see Azeqah.[24]

In this letter an unnamed subordinate at an unknown site reports to his superior on various matters of concern. He begins by assuring his commander that he has fulfilled his orders. The record that he has made is most likely a column of notations on a sheet of papyrus (the same Hebrew word, *delet,* literally "door," also occurs in Jeremiah 36:23 with this sense).[25] Not only is "the matter of Beth-hrpd" unknown to us, but so also are its location and its pronunciation. Neither do we know who Semakyahu was, nor with what he was charged. The "city" to which Semakyahu has been sent is undoubtedly Jerusalem, to which one always "goes up," as indicated in numerous biblical passages.[26]

The last item in this report presumably refers to a trial run of a signal system that occurred prior to the Babylonian entry into Judah. Some of the first scholars to translate this letter rendered the last phrase as, "we can *no longer* see the signal-fires of Azeqah," suggesting that Azeqah, one of the last three Judahite cities to hold out against the Babylonians, had already fallen, leaving only Lachish and Jerusalem (cf. Jeremiah 34:7). However, the rendition "no longer" was based on a supposed later date for the Lachish letters (587–586 B.C., after the Babylonians were already in Judah), *not* on the text itself. The Hebrew phrase does not mean "no longer"; it means only that the signal could not be seen (perhaps because of the hilly topography of the area or because the signal attempt had "misfired"). Lachish ostracon 4 thus indicates that while movement about the Judahite countryside was generally possible, safety was a concern and trouble was imminent.

Lehi, Ishmael, and their families left Jerusalem several years before these Lachish ostraca were written, while Mulek and those who traveled with him probably left Jerusalem within a year or two of their writing. Hugh Nibley rightly observed the value of the Lachish ostraca in expanding our view of the challenging times in which Lehi, Mulek, and Jeremiah lived: they "give us an eyewitness account of the actual world of Lehi—a tiny peephole, indeed, but an unobstructed one."[27] Thus Nibley often referred to these ostraca when discussing the background of 1 Nephi 1–4. However, some of Nibley's assertions about the Lachish ostraca require qualification or correction. Relying heavily on the initial publication and discussion of the ostraca, he asserted some specific but unsupportable connections between the Bible and these ostraca[28] and made some interpretations that are dated and no longer accepted.[29] Nibley's references to the Lachish ostraca must thus be used cautiously and in conjunction with more up-to-date studies of these valuable documents.

Mesad Hashavyahu Ostracon

Mesad Hashavyahu, a Judahite fort near Yavneh Yam and the Mediterranean coast, was excavated in 1960, resulting in the discovery of four ostraca, three of which are small and insignificant. One, however, contains a letter written by a scribe to an unnamed commander of the fort as dictated by an unnamed farm laborer with a complaint in need of resolution. This ostracon now survives in six pieces (with at least one more piece missing). It dates to the late seventh century, probably to the reign of King Josiah (640–609 B.C.), when Judah regained control of this region by the Mediterranean coast. The personal focus and the social implications of the content of this Mesad Hashavyahu ostracon make it important.

© Zev Radovan

Mesad Hashavyahu ostracon (line drawing; ca. 620s B.C.; 20 x 7.5–16.5 cm [= 7.87 x 2.95–6.5 in]). Discovered in 1960 during the excavation of Mesad Hashavyahu, a Judahite fortress near modern Yavneh Yam. (Israel Museum, Jerusalem)

> May my lord the commander hear the matter of his servant. Your servant is a reaper. Your servant was in Hasar-'Asam. Your servant had reaped and completed (his work) and had stored (the grain) for several days before stopping. When your servant had completed his reaping and it was stored for a few days, Hoshayahu son of Shobay came and took the garment of your servant. When I had finished my reaping, several days ago, he took your servant's garment. All my companions will testify for me, those who were reaping with me in the heat of [the] s[un]. My companions will testify for me, "It is so." I am free from any [guilt. So please return] my garment. And if it does not seem (like an obligation) to the commander to retur[n the garment of your ser]vant, [then show pi]ty on him, and re[turn the garment of] your [ser]vant (anyway, i.e., out of pity). Do not be silent [about this matter].

This interesting letter, the lower portion of which is not well preserved, contains the personal plea of a reaper petitioning a local commander or official for justice. In requesting that the commander intercede on his behalf, the reaper declares his innocence and indicates that witnesses will verify his story. He hopes that if no sense of duty motivates the commander, then pity for the reaper's circumstances will. One assumes that Hoshayahu son of Shobay, the supervisor of a group of farm workers, had a different tale to tell.

This letter's rather rough style suggests that it was dictated by the reaper to a scribe who worked at the local fortress. The message was most likely delivered to the commander as is. The lack of a formal greeting at the beginning (compare the Arad and Lachish letters included above) suggests to some scholars that a scribe may have copied this original draft and added the proper formalities (e.g., an invocation of blessing) before delivery. But the context of this message—a plea from a farm worker to a local official—is such that we would not expect formalities. Compare the fairly similar language in 1 Samuel 26:19: "Now therefore let my lord the king hear the words of his servant."

The reaper's situation as represented on this ostracon is reminiscent of a Mosaic injunction designed to protect those of the lower class of Israelite society, such as day laborers: "If you take your neighbor's cloak in pawn, you shall restore it before the sun goes down; for it may be your neighbor's only clothing to use as cover; in what else shall that person sleep? And if your neighbor cries out to me, I will listen, for I am compassionate" (Exodus 22:26–27; cf. Deuteronomy 24:12–13). The reaper's cloak had been confiscated and not returned to him, despite his claims of having fulfilled his obligations. Although this scripture is not cited as support in the letter, the reaper's request suggests that such a perspective was considered the ideal in his society. And we may assume that the reaper also appealed to a Higher Authority in addition to the local commander.

Neither this particular Mosaic precept nor a reaper's plea for justice is preserved in the Book of Mormon. However, since the Lehites had "the five books of Moses" on the brass plates (1 Nephi 5:11) and lived the law of Moses (e.g., 1 Nephi 4:15–16; 2 Nephi 25:24), and since the Book of Mormon refers to reaping grain (2 Nephi 5:11), as well as to reaping souls (Alma 26:5), one assumes that the Lehites were familiar with the need and the divine injunction to protect day-laboring reapers and other people in similar socioeconomic situations.

Ketef Hinnom Amulets[30]

Ketef Hinnom, or "shoulder of Hinnom," is located on the west side of the Hinnom Valley, which historically formed the western topographic boundary of ancient Jerusalem and served as an area for burials in both the First and Second Temple periods. Two small rolls of inscribed silver foil were discovered in 1979, along with a number of other items dating from the end of the First Temple period through the Second Temple period, in a secondary bone repository beside chamber 25 of burial cave 24 near the modern Scottish Church of St. Andrew. Based on paleographic analysis and

© The Israel Museum, Jerusalem

Reconstruction of a Ketef Hinnom tomb near which two silver amulets were found.

the associated finds, these two inscribed rolls date to about 600 B.C. From wear patterns, each of these silver rolls had apparently been worn on a cord, apparently around someone's neck, as an amulet or charm. When unrolled, one measures 9.7 x 2.7 cm (ca. 3.8 x 1.06 inches) and the other 3.9 x 1.1 cm (ca. 1.54 x 0.43 inches).

The text on these two amulets was incised with a stylus. It is remarkably similar to the Aaronic priestly blessing contained in Numbers 6:24–26, although not completely rendered. Unfortunately, the text, which averages 4–5 letters per line, is not well preserved nor very legible because of wear at the edges of the rolls and wrinkles in the silver. The relationship between the text in Numbers 6 and that preserved on the amulets is as follows:

Numbers 6	Amulet 1 (the larger)	Amulet 2 (the smaller)
	[several lines that are partially to totally illegible]	[several lines that are partially to totally illegible]
	[one who loves] the covenant [. . . m]ercy [. . .] from all . . . [. . .] and from evil [. . .] for YHWH . . .	
24 The Lord bless you and keep you;	May YHWH bless you and keep you.	May YHWH bless you and keep you.
25 the Lord make his face to shine upon you, and be gracious to you;	[May] YHWH [make his fa]ce [shi]ne	May YHWH make his face shine [upon] you and give you peace
26 the Lord lift up his countenance upon you, and give you peace.		[several lines that are partially to totally illegible]

These two small silver rolls are significant for several reasons. First, they preserve the oldest known attestation of a form of a biblical passage in its original language. Thus, as with the brass plates mentioned in the Book of Mormon, these silver rolls indicate that texts which we consider scripture existed and were utilized in ancient Israel before Lehi left Jerusalem. Second, they attest to the Israelite practice of engraving religious texts on metal in the time of Lehi and Jeremiah, although, practically speaking, the brass plates are vastly different in scope from these silver rolls.[31] Finally, they provide evidence of the personalization of a blessing, which according to Numbers 6 was originally pronounced by the priests over the congregation of Israel, in an apparent effort to invoke divine protection against evil influences. The practice of wearing such amulets may be a realization of the figurative instruction in Proverbs 6:20–22: "My child, keep your father's commandment, and do not forsake your mother's teaching. Bind them upon your heart always; tie them around your neck. When you walk, they will lead you; when you lie down, they will watch over you" (cf. Deuteronomy 6:8).

Seals and Bullae

The large quantity of seals and bullae discovered thus far qualifies them as

© Zev Radovan

Ketef Hinnom amulet 2 (ca. 600 b.c.; 3.9 x 1.1 cm [= 1.54 x 0.43 in]). One of two small rolls of silver foil partially preserving a form of Numbers 6:24–25 discovered in1980 during the excavation of a burial chamber near the Church of St. Andrew, Jerusalem. (see photo essay, page 76, for color photo). (Israel Museum, Jerusalem) the best attested type of inscription from ancient Israel. Found individually and in groups, Israelite seals, bullae, and seal impressions on jar handles now number more than seven hundred. These miniature inscriptions provide insights about Israelite society far greater than their size might suggest. Seals were owned and used by upper- and middle-class individuals involved in military, religious, and political administration and in mercantile, scribal, and other occupations. Seals functioned to identify an individual and to authenticate and validate a transaction or command (see comments and references above in "The Media of Inscriptions"). As noted above, since the provenance of most of the seals and bullae is unknown, these objects must be viewed with some skepticism—some are doubtless fakes.

Most Israelite seals belonged to people unknown to us, but a number of seals and bullae from the time of Jeremiah and Lehi may be linked with known biblical personalities.[32] The best example of this is an impression seemingly made by the seal of Jeremiah's scribe, Baruch: "belonging to Berekyahu, son of Neriyahu, the scribe."[33] Although the provenance of the bulla is unknown, it is generally considered authentic and is dated by paleography to the later portion of the seventh century B.C. The text on this bulla is similar to the identifying phrase in Jeremiah 36:32, "Baruch son of Neriah, the scribe," except that Baruch's name on the bulla is a longer, theophoric form of the name preserved in the Bible.[34] A seal with the inscription "belonging to Serayahu, (son of) Neriyahu," likely belonged to Baruch's brother Seraiah, who was an official of King Zedekiah (Jeremiah 51:59).[35] Again, the provenance is unknown.

In 1982, fifty-one bullae were excavated from an Israelite house located on the eastern slope of the Ophel Ridge (Area G), an area that had been destroyed in the Babylonian conquest of Jerusalem. The documents that these bullae originally sealed were destroyed in the resulting fire, but the fire baked and preserved the clay bullae.

One of the seal impressions reads: "belonging to Gemaryahu, [son of] Shaphan." This is likely the Gemariah mentioned in Jeremiah 36:10.[36] A broken bulla from an unknown provenance may have belonged to another son of Shaphan who is mentioned in 2 Kings 22:12 and Jeremiah 26:24: "[belonging to A]hiqam (?), [so]n of Shaphan."[37]

Another bulla that probably derives from a contemporary of Jeremiah and Lehi who is named in the Bible reads:

Seal impression of Baruch, the scribe of Jeremiah the prophet (ca. 600 B.C.; 1.7 x 1.6 cm [= 0.67 x 0.63 in]). The reverse of the bulla (not shown) preserves impressions from papyrus fibers and from the string that had secured a sealed papyrus document. (Israel Museum, Jerusalem)

© Bruce Zuckermann

"belonging to Yerahmeel, son of the king."[38] As recounted in Jeremiah 36:26, Jerahmeel, the son of the king, was one of three officials ordered to arrest Jeremiah and Baruch. (The KJV inaccurately renders this phrase "son of Hammelech," as if Hammelech was a proper name; it is, rather, a transliteration of the Hebrew phrase "son of the king.")[39]

A seal with a similar inscription, "belonging to Malkiyahu, son of the king," is decorated with seven pomegranates and a border of dots.[40] Purchased on the antiquities market by antiquities collector S. Moussaieff, this seal, if it is authentic, probably belonged to the "Malchiah son of the king" mentioned in Jeremiah 38:6 (again, the KJV renders "son of Hammelech" for "son of the king"). The prophet Jeremiah was arrested and placed in "the cistern of Malchiah son of the king" (the KJV renders "cistern" as "dungeon," based on the function of this particular cistern). Some Latter-day Saints have proposed that this seal belonged to Mulek, son of King Zedekiah, who traveled to the Americas as recounted in the Book of Mormon (Helaman 6:10; 8:21).[41] If this is so, the name Mulek functions as a shortened form of the fuller, theophoric form Malkiyahu (compare Baruch and Berekyahu).[42]

Such seals and bullae attest to an active and extensive practice of written communication, documentation, and verification in the days of Jeremiah and Lehi. They help us better understand the bureaucratic activity of their time. Unfortunately, the documents that were secured with such seal impressions have not survived.

The Bible indicates that Jeremiah owned and used a personal seal (Jeremiah 32:10). Given the description of possessions that Lehi left behind in Jerusalem (1 Nephi 2:4; 3:16, 22), it is very likely that Lehi, and perhaps his older sons, owned seals as well, although this is never mentioned in the Book of Mormon.

Inscriptions of Uncertain Date or Authenticity

A set of inscriptions in a cave tomb and on two ostraca are included in this overview of Israelite inscriptions from 640 to 586 B.C. but are designated "uncertain" because of differences of opinion regarding their dating and authenticity.

Khirbet Beit Lei Inscriptions

A tomb cut into a hill near Khirbet Beit Lei, about twenty miles southwest of Jerusalem and five miles east of Lachish, was discovered in 1961. Nine short texts and several drawings (illustrating, among other things, three humans and two ships) were inscribed on the limestone walls of the main chamber in antiquity.[43] The content of these texts is religious, but they have no demonstrable relationship to the burials in the tomb: neither names nor any of the standard burial formulae are contained in these texts. All the inscriptions are very difficult to decipher because of the relatively rough original preparation of the stone's surface, subsequent surface deterioration, and competing scratches on the walls.

Possible dates for these inscriptions range from the late eighth through the early fifth centuries. For example, the original publication and a recent review of this material (including quality photographs and line drawings) conclude that both the design of the burial chamber and the paleography of the inscriptions suggest a date of ca. 700 B.C.[44] That was the time of Hezekiah and Isaiah, not Zedekiah, Jeremiah, and Lehi. Other scholars prefer a date ranging from the early to mid-500s B.C.[45] Still others argue for a postexilic, Persian period date (ca. 400s B.C.) based on certain finds outside the tomb and on certain expressions in the inscriptions.[46] The earlier dating is more likely correct, meaning these inscriptions are too early for consideration in this chapter. However, the main texts are included here since many Latter-day Saints have heard of these inscriptions.

Two differing translations (designated with lowercase "a" and "b") are provided for each of the following three inscriptions to illustrate the significant diversity among scholars on how to render these challenging texts:

Khirbet Beit Lei Inscription A:[47]

> a. Yahveh (is) the God of the whole earth;
> the mountains of Judah belong to him, to the God of Jerusalem. (Naveh)

> b. YHWH, my god, exposed/laid bare his land.
> A terror he led for his own sake to Jerusalem. (Zevit)

Khirbet Beit Lei Inscription B:[48]

> a. The (Mount of) Moriah Thou hast favoured, the dwelling of Yah, Yahveh. (Naveh)

b. The source smote the hand. Absolve (from culpability) the hand, YHWH. (Zevit)

Khirbet Beit Lei Inscription C:[49]

a. [Ya]hveh deliver (us)! (Naveh)

b. Save. Destruction. (Zevit)

Depending on how one transcribes and translates these inscriptions, especially A and B, they may contain moving, positive proclamations about the power of Jehovah or tragic declarations of his power against Judah. It is impossible to determine who wrote these texts, although a prophet or priest may have been responsible. Those who date these inscriptions to the Assyrian invasion of Judah (701 B.C.) or the Babylonian invasions of Judah (590s–580s B.C.) see those troubled times as their historical context.

Some Latter-day Saints have claimed that the Khirbet Beit Lei tomb, in which these inscriptions were found, served as the temporary hiding place of Nephi and his brothers after they fled from Laban (1 Nephi 3:27) and that these texts and pictures were inscribed by Nephi.[50] However, there is no real basis for such a claim. In addition to the obvious challenges of just reading and dating the inscriptions and the linguistic challenge of relating the name Beit Lei with the name Lehi,[51] this burial chamber seems much too distant from Jerusalem to be a reasonable candidate for the brothers' hiding place.

Moussaieff Ostraca

Two interesting ostraca were purchased on the antiquities market by S. Moussaieff. The scholars who recently published these ostraca accept them as genuine, and various laboratory analyses tend to bolster their claim, but a few scholars have expressed concerns regarding their authenticity.[52] Additionally, those who published these ostraca date them paleographically to the latter portion of the seventh century, within the parameters of this survey, but others date them to the eighth century B.C., earlier than the time period dealt with in this chapter.[53] The Moussaieff ostraca are probably authentic, and as such they are valuable resources for our study of ancient Israel. So, they are included here for consideration with the caveat that a few scholars have concerns about their dating and their authenticity.

Moussaieff ostracon 1:

> As Ashyahu the king has commanded you to give to Zekaryahu silver of Tarshish for the house of YHWH, three shekels (so do).

This ostracon contains five short lines of text that record a king's command that three shekels (a measure of weight) of silver be contributed to the temple via a man named Zekaryahu (Zechariah). It may represent a directive or receipt for a donation to the Jerusalem temple. The king's name, Ashyahu, is previously unattested as the name of a Judahite monarch but is understood as a variant of the name Josiah.[54] Tarshish is the name of an unknown location, perhaps in the Mediterranean area, with whose populace Israelites, Phoenicians, and others engaged in mercantile activities, importing luxury goods such as silver and gold (1 Kings 10:22; Isaiah 2:16; 23:1; Jonah 1:3).

Moussaieff ostracon 2:

> May YHWH bless you with peace. And now, may my lord the governor (or commander) hear your maidservant. My husband died (leaving) no sons (or children). So let your hand be with me and give into the hand of your maidservant the inheritance about which you spoke (or promised) to Amasyahu. As for the wheat field in Naamah, you have (already) given (it) to his brother.

This second ostracon contains a plea from a widow to an un-named official regarding a question of inheritance. Amasyahu was probably her deceased husband or a close relative (the husband's brother who had already received the wheat field?). Numbers 27:8–11 indicates that when an Israelite man died with no sons, his inheritance went to his daughters. If the man had neither sons nor daughters, his brother(s) received the inheritance, with the understanding that his widow would be cared for. In this ostra-con the widow requests the use, if not the outright ownership, of land or some other form of inheritance, presumably to (better) provide for her own needs. Her request for official assistance is reminiscent of the reaper's plea on the Mesad Hashavyahu ostra-con. In both letters the person making the request is unnamed, and they may have delivered their scribed request in person. The place name Naamah may refer to the town of the same name not far from Lachish (Joshua 15:41).

Implications of These Israelite Inscriptions

The preceding survey of major Israelite inscriptions from 640 to 586 B.C. has illustrated their value for understanding the intersection of religion, culture, and history during that pivotal time period. These inscriptions generally provide background details in the larger picture of ancient Judah's history, rather than information about major figures from that time period.

Historical Implications

While the content of the Arad ostraca may not seem par-ticularly exciting, they preserve important information about the administration of Judahite border fortresses and forces, including the provisioning of mercenaries. Fortress cities such as Arad played a vital role in defending Judah's southern flank from recurring Edomite incursions at the time of Lehi and

Jeremiah. Edom and the Edomites are mentioned in several Arad ostraca, including 3, 21, 24, and 40, and in such biblical passages as Ezekiel 35:1–5 and Lamentations 4:21–22.

The Lachish ostraca also help illuminate Judahite military administration as well as the preparations made for the Babylonian reprisals that came when King Zedekiah refused to honor his vassal treaty to pay tribute. In them we hear of miscommunication, troop movements, and the seizure of correspondence containing a prophetic warning (#3); of the apprehension of a witness and of a system of signal fires (#4); of a request for supplies (#5); of the communication of disheartening news, which tended "to slacken your hands" (#6; cf. Jeremiah 38:4); and so on. This was a trying time for Judahites, just prior to destruction and suffering that, according to the prophets, they brought on themselves through their lack of loyalty to Jehovah (see, e.g., Jeremiah 25:8–10). The seizure of a witness (#4) and of a letter (#3) illustrates the tension in Judah that developed from Zedekiah's decision to terminate his vassal payments to Babylonia. Some Judahites, including Jeremiah, did not think rebellion against Babylon was the wiser course of action (e.g., Jeremiah 27:12–17). History certainly demonstrates that Zedekiah's choice was disastrous.

Social and Cultural Implications

Socioeconomic Justice. The pleas of the reaper (Mesad Hashavyahu ostracon) and of the widow (Moussaieff ostracon 2) demonstrate the ongoing need for social justice and economic assistance among the common Judahites of Jeremiah and Lehi's day. Dealing with such petitions was a regular requirement for local and regional officials. Although neither plea cites biblical authority or precedent, both texts have affinities with specific biblical passages, as noted above. Mosaic law contained injunctions

that the needs of widows, orphans, and the poor be met merci-
fully and fairly (e.g., Exodus 22:22–23; 23:6; Leviticus 19:10, 15;
Deuteronomy 24:19–21). We are left to wonder what response the
widow and reaper received to their petitions. One can only hope
that the officials to whom they appealed were like Helaman, son
of Helaman, who "did fill the judgment-seat with justice and
equity" (Helaman 3:20, 27).

Letters. Several of the ostraca cited above illustrate basic
Israelite epistolary (letter-writing) conventions ca. 600 B.C., which
varied somewhat depending on such factors as the formality of
the communication. The salutation, for example, usually identified the recipient by name (e.g., Arad, Lachish) or title (e.g.,
Lachish, Mesad Hashavyahu), sometimes invoked a blessing on
the recipient (e.g., Lachish, Arad), and sometimes included the
name of the sender (e.g., Lachish). The transition from the salutation to the body of the letter was often marked by the expression
and now (e.g., Lachish, Arad). Also, the person of inferior status
regularly referred to him- or herself by emphasizing the relationship "your servant" when writing to someone of superior status
(e.g., Lachish, Mesad Hashavyahu, Moussaieff Ostracon 2).

Only a few of these epistolary conventions are evident in letters or portions of letters quoted in the Bible, mainly the transition marker *and now.* The salutations are not generally preserved
because the sender and recipient are identified in the biblical narrative (e.g., 2 Kings 5:6; 10:2–3; 2 Chronicles 2:10–15; Jeremiah
29:4–23, 26–28). Other literary considerations may also have
influenced the form of the biblically preserved letters.[55]

The Book of Mormon contains several quoted letters, but
these are longer than the letters preserved on Israelite ostraca
or in the Hebrew Bible (e.g., Alma 54:4–14, 15–24; Alma 56–58;
3 Nephi 3:1–10), and they may also have been affected by their
inclusion in a larger literary text. While the epistolary data from

ancient Israel and from the Book of Mormon is rather limited, some differences in practice are clearly discernible.[56] For example, the letters quoted in the Book of Mormon do not contain an invocation of blessing upon even nonadversarial recipients (e.g., Alma 56:2; 61:1–2; 3 Nephi 3:1–2). Furthermore, they often conclude with the sender's name (e.g., Alma 54:14, 23–24; 58:41; 3 Nephi 3:10), a practice not attested in ancient Israel. However, the approximately five hundred years between the departure of the Lehites and Mulekites from Jerusalem and the date of the first letter quoted in the Book of Mormon allow time for many cultural changes, including epistolary ones.

Seals. The large number of seals and seal impressions surviving from 640 to 586 B.C. serves to demonstrate the significant amount of commerce and bureaucracy that existed in ancient Judah, despite the fact that the majority of the population did not own seals. The discovery of seals and bullae from people mentioned in the Bible, such as Baruch, is an exciting development that helps to bring these individuals to life.

Documents and containers were sealed to indicate identity, to give authorization, and to provide tamperproof protection. In Arad ostracon 17 a certain Nahum is instructed to send a quantity of olive oil and "seal it with your seal." In concluding a real estate transaction with his cousin, Jeremiah says, "I signed the deed, sealed it, got witnesses, and weighed the money on scales" (Jeremiah 32:10; cf. vv. 9–14). The use of seals is further attested elsewhere in the Bible (e.g., 1 Kings 21:7–8; Esther 8:8–10).[57] Again, the indication that Lehi's family had "exceeding great" property (1 Nephi 3:24–25) suggests a social and economic attainment that would have necessitated the possession and use of a seal by Lehi, although this is not mentioned in Nephi's brief account.

Religious Implications

A few texts from this period preserve specific references to religious features, such as a prophet (Lachish ostraca 3, 16) and the temple (Arad ostracon 18, Moussaieff ostracon 1). Other texts are wholly religious in nature, like the two versions of the Aaronic priestly blessing (Ketef Hinnom silver amulets), and the Khirbet Beit Lei inscriptions (although these probably do not derive from 640 to 586 B.C.).

Even the "nonreligious" Israelite inscriptions from 640 to 586 B.C. indicate a general orientation to Israelite worship at that time. For example, many of the compound personal names from the ostraca and seals have YHWH as one of their components (e.g., Berekyahu, Semakyahu).[58] Also, the salutations in several letters from this period invoke a blessing from YHWH, but from no other deity, on the recipient (e.g., Arad ostracon 18; Lachish ostraca 3, 4; Moussaieff ostracon 2).

Indeed, after reviewing the preexilic evidence, one scholar observed that "in every respect the inscriptions suggest an overwhelmingly Yahwistic society in the heartland of Israelite settlement, especially in Judah. If we had only the inscriptional evidence, it is not likely that we would ever imagine that there existed a significant amount of polytheistic practice in Israel during the period in question."[59] This situation must be understood in relation to prophetic accusations against the Judahites. Jeremiah prophesied, for example, that "the Chaldeans [= Babylonians] who are fighting against this city shall come, set it on fire, and burn it, with the houses on whose roofs offerings have been made to Baal and libations have been poured out to other gods, to provoke me to anger" (Jeremiah 32:29; cf. 11:13, 17; etc.). Since Jehovah/YHWH was the national deity of Judah, it is no surprise to encounter his name regularly in inscriptions. However, the almost complete lack of evidence therein for the worship of other gods from 640 to 586 B.C. is remarkable if one imagines the majority of the inhabitants to have worshiped other deities in addition to Jehovah. Perhaps the prophetic claims are better understood as targeting a certain segment of Judahite society, but not the society as a whole, or as targeting a trend that had reached spiritually but not statistically epidemic proportions. Otherwise one would expect more evidence of the worship of other deities in inscriptions from the period of Jeremiah and Lehi.

In addition to the worship of deities other than Jehovah and to the illegitimate forms of Jehovah worship which the Bible recounts, there was a broader range of sinful activity that incurred the divine rebuke of many Judahites. Nephi clearly indicates that Lehi "truly testified of their wickedness and their abominations" (1 Nephi 1:19; cf. vv 7–18). Furthermore, those who "steal, murder, commit adultery, [and] swear falsely" were not just those who "make offerings to Baal, and go after other gods" (Jeremiah 7:9), but they represented all segments of Judahite society (cf. Jeremiah 23:14).

In conjunction with this depiction of divinely unacceptable activities that are attested in the Bible and 1 Nephi, but not in the inscriptions, one wonders about the number of, and motivation for, Judahites who wore amulets such as those discovered at Ketef Hinnom (how many Judahites understood passages such as Deuteronomy 6:8 and Proverbs 6:20–22 literally?). While some Judahites may have worn amulets to reinforce their focus on a divine perspective, others no doubt regarded them as charms with inherent magical and protective powers because the divine name YHWH was contained thereon.

Finally, the warning from the unnamed "prophet, saying, Beware!" mentioned in Lachish ostracon 3, presumably from a legitimate prophet of Jehovah, reminds us of those passages of scripture that indicate that at this time the Lord sent "many prophets, prophesying unto the people that they must repent, or the great city Jerusalem must be destroyed" (1 Nephi 1:4; cf. Jeremiah 25:2–6; 26:1–6).

Conclusion

Although Lehi, Sariah, Ishmael, and their families left Jerusalem several years before the Babylonians arrived early in 587 B.C., they had been in the Jerusalem area a decade earlier when the Babylonians besieged the city for three months and removed the Judahite king Jehoiachin into captivity, replacing him with his uncle Zedekiah.[60] The "rumors of war" such as fill the Lachish ostraca were not foreign to these families. After these families arrived in the Americas, the Lord indicated to Lehi through a vision that Jerusalem had been destroyed (2 Nephi 1:4). Jeremiah, on the other hand, was called to remain in Jerusalem to witness firsthand the prophesied destruction by the Babylonians.

Although Israelite inscriptions from 640 to 586 B.C. preserve no texts from Jeremiah or Lehi nor specifically mention them, these inscriptions do have much to offer for our study of that crucial time period. They augment the Bible and allow us to better peer across the historical and cultural divide that separates us from the world of ancient Judah. The patient student of ancient Israel's history and culture will be rewarded with many pleasures and insights from further studying these texts. The inscriptions that have been unearthed in the past century generate hope that even more exciting discoveries lie in the future.

Appendix 1: Selective Outline of Preexilic Inscriptions from Ancient Israel[61]

(Augmented with a few other inscriptions of importance from the region)

Inscriptions	Approximate Date B.C.	Remarks
Izbet Sartah ostracon	mid-12th century	Canaanite or Israelite?
Gezer calendar	mid-10th century	
Moabite/Mesha inscription	mid-9th century	Dhiban, Jordan; Moabite
Tel Dan stela fragments	mid-9th century	in Aramaic
Kuntillet ʿAjrud inscriptions	late 9th–early 8th centuries	
Samaria ostraca	early–mid-8th century	
Deir ʿAlla inscriptions	mid-8th century	Jordan; in a dialect related to Ammonite and Aramaic
ivory pomegranate inscription	late 8th century	antiquities market; probably from Jerusalem
Ein Gedi cave inscription	late 8th–early 7th centuries	
Khirbet el-Qom tomb inscriptions	late 8th–early 7th centuries	
Siloam Tunnel inscription	late 8th century	Jerusalem
Silwan Tomb inscription	late 8th century	Jerusalem
Ophel and some Arad ostraca	late 8th century	
Wadi Murabbaʿat papyrus 17	early 7th century	
Moussaieff ostraca	mid–late 7th century	antiquities market
Mesad Hashavyahu (Yavneh Yam) ostraca	late 7th century	
Ketef Hinnom silver amulets	late 7th century	Jerusalem
Ophel ostracon	late 7th–early 6th centuries	Jerusalem
some Arad ostraca	late 7th–early 6th centuries (mainly)	
Lachish ostraca	early 6th century	
seals and bullae	8th–6th centuries	from various sites in Israel and Judah, plus the antiquities market
Khirbet Beit Lei inscriptions	8th–early 6th centuries	

Appendix 2: Main Resources for Ancient Israelite Inscriptions in Translation

The following list provides citations for recent English translations of the inscriptions mentioned in this article, arranged in order of publication. Most of these works provide helpful discussions and references to the original publication of the inscriptions. Some of them include the Hebrew text as well as an English translation.

William W. Hallo and K. Lawson Younger, eds., *The Context of Scripture,* vol. 2, *Monumental Inscriptions from the Biblical World* (Boston: Brill, 2000), and vol. 3, *Archival Documents from the Biblical World* (2002); Sandra L. Gogel, *A Grammar of Epigraphic Hebrew* (Atlanta: Scholars, 1998); James M. Lindenberger, *Ancient Aramaic and Hebrew Letters* (Atlanta: Scholars, 1994); Klaas A. D. Smelik, *Writings from Ancient Israel* (Louisville: Westminster, 1991); Dennis Pardee et al., *Handbook of Ancient Hebrew Letters* (Chico, Calif.: Scholars, 1982); Nahman Avigad, "Hebrew Epigraphic Sources," in *The Age of the Monarchies: Political History,* vol. 4, pt. 1, ed. Abraham Malamat (Jerusalem: Massada, 1979), 20–43; John C. L. Gibson, *Textbook of Syrian Semitic Inscriptions,* vol. 1, *Hebrew and Moabite Inscriptions,* 2nd ed. (Oxford: Clarendon, 1973); James B. Pritchard, ed., *Ancient Near Eastern Texts Relating to the Old Testament,* 3rd ed. with supplement (Princeton: Princeton University Press, 1969).

See these important compilations in languages other than English: Johannes Renz and Wolfgang Röllig, *Handbuch der althebräischen Epigraphik,* 3 vols. (Darmstadt: Wissenschaftliche Buchgesellschaft, 1995); Shmuel Ahituv, *Handbook of Ancient Hebrew Inscriptions* [in Hebrew] (Jerusalem: Mossad Byalik, 1992); Graham I. Davies, *Ancient Hebrew Inscriptions: Corpus and Concordance* (transcriptions only) (New York: Cambridge

University Press, 1991); André Lemaire, *Inscriptions hébraïques,* vol. 1, *Les ostraca* (Paris: Cerf, 1977).

See also the helpful English discussions of various Israelite inscriptions, without translated texts, under the appropriate entries in Eric M. Meyers, ed., *The Oxford Encyclopedia of Archaeology in the Near East,* 5 vols. (New York: Oxford, 1997); Ephraim Stern et al., eds., *The New Encyclopedia of Archaeological Excavations in the Holy Land,* 4 vols. (Jerusalem: Israel Exploration Society and Carta, 1993); and David Noel Freedman et al., eds., *Anchor Bible Dictionary,* 5 vols. (Garden City, N.Y.: Doubleday, 1992).

NOTES

1. Tomb inscriptions include those from Silwan and Khirbet el-Qom. Inscriptions of a religious nature on unquarried stone include those at Khirbet Beit Lei and the Ein Gedi Cave. The Siloam Tunnel inscription is a rare example of an Israelite "monumental" inscription, although on a very small scale.

2. Amihai Mazar, *Archaeology of the Land of the Bible, 10,000–586 B.C.E.* (New York: Doubleday, 1990), 515, cites the remains of only four monumental inscriptions from preexilic Israel: the Siloam Tunnel inscription (complete, but not a stela), two small fragments from Jerusalem, and one small fragment from Samaria. Three pieces from a broken ninth-century B.C. Aramaic inscription discovered at Tel Dan in northern Israel and one fragment of a Philistine temple inscription from Tel Miqne are not technically *Israelite* inscriptions but share linguistic and literary similarities. The existence of a fifteen-line inscription from Jerusalem, presumably dating to the late 800s B.C., was announced in the press in January 2003. Unfortunately, the inscription was not found *in situ* but was purchased on the antiquities market, immediately raising concerns about its authenticity. The text of the inscription recounts efforts to renovate the Lord's temple in Jerusalem and is now commonly referred to as the Jehoash Inscription or the Temple Inscription. This small stela

is now considered to be a forgery by the Israel Antiquities Authority and by many scholars, although some are not convinced of this. See, for example, Frank M. Cross, "Notes on the Forged Plaque Recording Repairs to the Temple," *Israel Exploration Journal* 53/1 (2003): 119–23; Israel Eph'al, "The 'Jehoash Inscription': A Forgery," *Israel Exploration Journal* 53/1 (2003): 124–28; Hershel Shanks, "Assessing the Jehoash Inscription," *Biblical Archaeology Review* 29/3 (2003): 26–30; "What about the Jehoash Inscription?" *Biblical Archaeology Review* 29/5 (2003): 38–39, 83; and the IAA's "Summary Report of the Examining Committees for the James Ossuary and the Yehoash Inscription," *Biblical Archaeology Review* 29/5 (2003): 27–31.

3. For a general introduction to seals, with further references, see Dana M. Pike, "Seals and Sealing among Ancient and Latter-day Israelites," in *Thy People Shall Be My People and Thy God My God* (Salt Lake City: Deseret Book, 1994), 101–17. The standard scholarly reference for Israelite stamp seals is now Nahman Avigad and Benjamin Sass, *Corpus of West Semitic Stamp Seals* (Jerusalem: Israel Academy of Sciences and Humanities, The Israel Exploration Society, and The Institute of Archaeology, The Hebrew University of Jerusalem, 1997).

4. See, for example, the comments about the large number of un-provenanced seals and bullae by Hershel Shanks, "The Mystery of the Bullae," *Biblical Archaeology Review* 29/1 (2003): 6. Curiously, Shanks does not even mention the forgery dilemma. Christopher A. Rollston, in his presentation "Epigraphic Fakes and Frauds: The Anatomy of a Forgery" at the 2002 Society of Biblical Literature annual meeting in Toronto, Canada, provided strong evidence that some seals and bullae are probably forgeries.

5. Regarding writing on metal plates in antiquity, see, for example, H. Curtis Wright, "Ancient Burials of Metal Documents in Stone Boxes," in *By Study and Also by Faith: Essays in Honor of Hugh W. Nibley,* ed. John M. Lundquist and Stephen D. Ricks (Salt Lake City: Deseret Book and FARMS, 1990), 2:273–334; Paul R. Cheesman, "External Evidences of the Book of Mormon," in *By Study and Also*

by Faith, 2:78–84; William J. Hamblin, "Sacred Writings on Bronze Plates in the Ancient Mediterranean" (FARMS paper, 1994); John L. Sorenson, "Metals and Metallurgy Relating to the Book of Mormon Text" (FARMS paper, 1992); John A. Tvedtnes, *The Book of Mormon and Other Hidden Books: "Out of Darkness unto Light"* (Provo, Utah: FARMS, 2000), 41–57.

6. This and all biblical quotations in this article are from the New Revised Standard Version.

7. For a thorough study of the Deir ʿAlla texts, which refer to a seer named Balaam (see Numbers 22–24), see Jo Ann Hackett, *The Balaam Text from Deir ʿAllā* (Chico, Calif.: Scholars, 1980). For a recent treatment of the Kuntillet ʿAjrud inscriptions, see Ziony Zevit, *The Religions of Ancient Israel: A Synthesis of Parallactic Approaches* (New York: Continuum, 2001), 370–405. See also Lawrence E. Stager, "The Shechem Temple where Abimelech Massacred a Thousand," *Biblical Archaeology Review* 29/4 (2003): 33, who suggests that the large, uninscribed stela at ancient Shechem (Tell Balata) had once contained an inscription on a coating of plaster that has not survived.

8. Various strands of evidence indicate that papyrus was much more common than leather as a writing medium in preexilic Israel. See, for example, Meir Bar-Ilan, "Papyrus," in *The Oxford Encyclopedia of Archaeology in the Near East,* ed. Eric M. Meyers (New York: Oxford University Press, 1997), 4:246; Peter T. Daniels, "Writing Materials," in *Oxford Encyclopedia of Archaeology,* 5:360–61; and Menahem Haran, "Book-Scrolls in Israel in Pre-Exilic Times," *Journal of Jewish Studies* 33/1–2 (1982): 161–73.

9. For a general introduction to the Dead Sea Scrolls, see, for example, Donald W. Parry and Dana M. Pike, eds., *LDS Perspectives on the Dead Sea Scrolls* (Provo, Utah: FARMS, 1997). To read these texts in translation, see, for example, Géza Vermès, *The Complete Dead Sea Scrolls in English* (New York: Penguin, 1998).

10. See Susan Niditch, *Oral World and Written Word: Ancient Israelite Literature* (Louisville, Ky.: Westminster John Knox, 1996), 39–40, for examples of the diversity of opinions on ancient literacy. For

other recent treatments of Israelite literacy, see, for example, Richard S. Hess, "Literacy in Iron Age Israel," in *Windows into Old Testament History*, ed. V. Philips Long et al. (Grand Rapids: Eerdmans, 2002), 82–102; James L. Crenshaw, *Education in Ancient Israel: Across the Deadening Silence* (New York: Doubleday, 1998), especially chapter 1; Aaron Demsky, "Literacy," in *Oxford Encyclopedia of Archaeology*, 3:362–69; Alan R. Millard, "Literacy, Ancient Israelite," in *Anchor Bible Dictionary*, ed. David Noel Freedman (Doubleday: New York, 1992), 4:337–40.

11. Israelite prophets *may* well have circulated their teachings in written form. The point is that we do not have evidence for this practice. What is preserved are episodes such as that recounted in Jeremiah 36:1–8 in which the Lord commanded Jeremiah to write the Lord's words, after which Jeremiah's scribe, Baruch, was sent to the Temple Mount to read the text for other Israelites to hear. The Book of Mormon recounts that the multitude that assembled to hear King Benjamin was so large that his oral teachings were transcribed and "sent forth among those that were not under the sound of his voice" (Mosiah 2:8). But this could mean either that scribes went about reading Benjamin's teachings or that numerous written texts were made available for private study. I think the former option is the more likely one.

12. As Millard observes in "Literacy: Ancient Israel," 4:337, "from the book of Exodus onward [in the Old Testament], writing, books, and reading are mentioned frequently and without comment." Examples include Deuteronomy 24:1–3; Joshua 24:26; 1 Samuel 10:25; 2 Samuel 11:14; 2 Kings 5:5–7; 10:1; 22:8–10; and Jeremiah 36. But again, these illustrations support literacy among the upper and middle classes, not among the lower class of producers.

On the Jewish practices of wearing phylacteries and attaching a mezuzah to a doorpost, see, for example, R. J. Zwi Werblowsky and Geoffrey Wigoder, eds., *The Oxford Dictionary of the Jewish Religion* (New York: Oxford University, 1997), s.v. "mezuzah," and "tefillin."

13. The fact that the 1QIsaiah[a] scroll (copied ca. 125–100 B.C.)

found in Qumran Cave 1 is ca. 24 feet long illustrates the practical challenge for anyone attempting to produce, collect, and store scripture "books" on papyrus or leather prior to the invention of the codex in the early Christian era (metal plates were more compact, of course, but could be heavy). Evidence such as that from Qumran suggests that in most cases groups of people, not individuals, possessed caches of scrolls. It would have been quite anomalous in ancient Israel if the brass plates were in Laban's *individual* possession. This collection of plates was probably a resource for an extended family or portion of a community (1 Nephi 3:2–3, 12; 4:20–26).

14. The tentative nature of the broad categories of literacy in ancient Israel provided here cannot be sufficiently emphasized. There is no "hard evidence" on this matter. Likewise, comparisons of literacy rates between ancient and modern societies are fraught with challenges. However, one example of the variety of literary skills in a modern society may prove instructive. The following data and quotations derive from the answers given to "Frequently Asked Questions" on the website for the National Institute for Literacy (www.nifl.gov/nifl/faqs.html). "The [United States] Workforce Investment Act of 1998 defines literacy as 'an individual's ability to read, write, speak in English, compute and solve problems at levels of proficiency necessary to function on the job, in the family of the individual and in society.'" According to the 1992 National Adult Literacy Survey, about 50 percent of the adult population of the United States had only level 1 or level 2 literacy (out of five levels, 5 being the most literate; data from the 2002 survey are not yet available). "Literacy experts believe that adults with skills at Levels 1 and 2 lack a sufficient foundation of basic skills to function successfully in our society." Thus, about half of the adult population in the United States is comprised of people "with low literacy skills who lack the foundation they need to find and keep decent jobs, support their children's education, and participate actively in civic life." The degree of partial literacy or illiteracy is even greater in less developed modern societies and in ancient societies.

15. The translations that follow are mine, based on published photographs and transcriptions, and are intended to be quite literal in order to preserve the "flavor" of the Hebrew originals. Minor restorations in the texts are not noted, while more significant ones are included in square brackets: [ ]. Words included in parentheses, ( ), are provided to help make a smoother translation. Line numbers have not been indicated.

16. Rather than repeatedly citing basic references in the following notes, I have listed the most common and recent English translations of the inscriptions mentioned in this article in appendix 2 (pages 230–31), arranged by date of publication.

17. The major English publication of the Arad ostraca is Yohanan Aharoni, *Arad Inscriptions,* rev. and enlarged by Anson Rainey, trans. Judith Ben-Or (Jerusalem: Israel Exploration Society, 1981).

18. A *bath* is a measure of volume of about 20–30 liters.

19. Although the term Kittim designates various groups during the Second Temple period, it generally refers to Cyprus and the Aegean isles in the Old Testament (see, e.g., Jeremiah 2:10; Ezekiel 27:6).

20. Although it is not apparent from the translation, two different symbols are used in this message to indicate the type and size of the measure of flour that was to be distributed. The symbol in the second instance (line 6) is the same symbol found in Arad ostracon 1 (see above) and is generally interpreted to represent a *homer,* a unit of dry measure of about 150–75 liters. The first symbol in ostracon 18 (line 5) may represent a *letech,* another unit of dry measure, equal to about half a homer.

21. The original publication of the first batch of Lachish ostraca in Harry Torczyner et al., *Lachish (Tell ed-Duweir),* vol. 1, *The Lachish Letters* (New York: Oxford University Press, 1938), provides general information on their discovery and contents, along with photographs and translations. Many of the textual readings and the assertions about their historical context need revising in light of later data and interpretation. See the more recent studies cited in appendix 2, pages 230–31.

22.   In the original publication of the first eighteen Lachish ostraca, Torczyner, *Lachish Letters,* 64–72, developed an elaborate theory to demonstrate that the unnamed "prophet" referred to in Lachish ostracon 3 must be the prophet Urijah mentioned in Jeremiah 26. Despite his assertion that his theory "seems now proved" (p. 72), his attempts to mitigate the differences between the names and dates in these two texts have not been accepted by modern scholars. Latter-day Saint scholar Hugh Nibley, *The Prophetic Book of Mormon* (Salt Lake City: Deseret Book and FARMS, 1989), 382–83, followed Torczyner in declaring "the prophet" of Lachish ostracon 3 to be the Urijah attested in Jeremiah 26, but, again, there is no real basis for this connection, and there are a number of assumptions of scribal error required for this to work.

23.   See the previous note.

24.   The translation "If (my lord) [cam]e during the morning watch" represents a general consensus on how to interpret this challenging line. See Dennis Pardee's alternative rendition in William W. Hallo and K. Lawson Younger, eds., *The Context of Scripture,* vol. 3, *Archival Documents from the Biblical World* (Boston: Brill, 2002), 3:80.

25.   Many scholars, beginning with Torczyner, *Lachish Letters,* 17 and 80, have suggested the term *delet* in Lachish ostracon 4, line 3, refers to a sheet of papyrus. R. Lansing Hicks, "DELET AND MEGILLĀH: A Fresh Approach to Jeremiah xxxvi," *Vetus Testamentum* 33/1 (1983): 52–53, asserted that the Lachish *delet* was a waxed writing board. Nibley, *Prophetic Book of Mormon,* 384 and 403 n. 7, speculated that the Hebrew word *delet* on Lachish ostracon 4 referred to a metal plate. Since the word *delet* used in relation to a writing medium in ancient Israel occurs only here and in Jeremiah 36:23—where it clearly refers to something that was cut and burned, presumably papyrus—the suggestion that it here refers to a metal plate is without any real support.

26.   See, for example, 1 Kings 12:27; 2 Kings 18:17; Ezra 1:3, 5; Matthew 20:17; John 2:12; Acts 15:2; 25:1.

27. Hugh Nibley, *Lehi in the Desert, The World of the Jaredites, There Were Jaredites* (Salt Lake City: Deseret Book and FARMS, 1988), 5.

28. Nibley frequently declared as fact claims and assumptions that, while possible, go beyond any actual evidence. For example, he specifically claimed that Lachish ostracon 6 refers to Jeremiah, whose name is not mentioned in any Lachish ostraca; see, for example, Nibley, *Lehi in the Desert*, 40: "Lachish letter No. 6, in denouncing the prophet Jeremiah for spreading defeatism both in the country and in the city, shows . . ."; *Prophetic Book of Mormon*, 120 n. 68: "Jeremiah seems to have been the leader of the opposition to the government party, to judge by the Lachish Letters"; *Prophetic Book of Mormon*, 384: "From the Lachish Letters we learn that Jeremiah himself made use of other writings circulating at that time, including the Lachish Letters themselves." Furthermore, Nibley's claim, *Prophetic Book of Mormon*, 385, again following Torczyner, that "Jeremiah 38:4, in fact, is a direct quotation from Letter 6," is false. The relevant words in Jeremiah 38:4 are *mrp> >t ydy >nšy hmlḥmh,* literally "he [Jeremiah] is slackening the hands of the men of war" (i.e., he is discouraging them). The relevant words in Lachish ostracon 6, lines 6–7, are *l> tbm lrpt ydyk[. . . wlhš]qṭ ydy h>[nšm . . .],* literally "[someone's words] are not good, slackening your hands and making quiet the hands of the m[en . . .]." A familiar idiom is employed in both passages, but this is not a quotation. Even if the wording were the same, how would one prove such a claim? Various combinations of the verb *rph,* "to slacken, loosen" (*rp>* in Jeremiah 38:4 is an alternate form), and the noun *yad,* "hand," are preserved in the Hebrew Bible/Old Testament, including 2 Samuel 4:1; Isaiah 13:7; 35:3; Jeremiah 6:24; 50:43; Ezekiel 21:7 (21:12 in Hebrew).

29. As an example of a dated assertion, Nibley, *Prophetic Book of Mormon*, 381, accepted the unfounded reading of Lachish ostracon 4 that "we can *no longer* see the signal-fires of Azeqah" and thus inaccurately claimed that this supports Jeremiah 34:7, that the city Azeqah had fallen, leaving only Lachish and Jerusalem when the ostraca were written (cf. the discussion above). Likewise, Nibley's statement in *An Approach to the Book of Mormon*, 3rd ed. (Salt Lake

City: Deseret Book and FARMS, 1988), 96 (cf. *Lehi in the Desert,* 5), that the Lachish ostraca were "written at the very time of the fall of Jerusalem," by which he presumably means 586 B.C., is inaccurate according to our current understanding (see discussion above). Note that in *Prophetic Book of Mormon,* 387, Nibley stated that "the Lachish Letters . . . date to 589–588 B.C."

30. In addition to the references in appendix 2, pages 230–31, see the summary report of the discovery of these amulets and other artifacts by Gabriel Barkay, "Excavations at Ketef Hinnom in Jerusalem," in *Ancient Jerusalem Revealed,* ed. Hillel Geva, reprinted and expanded ed. (Jerusalem: Israel Exploration Society, 2000), 85–106. Pages 102–5 deal with the amulets themselves.

31. William J. Adams Jr. published two short notes on these two silver amulets, rightly noting the support they offer for the use of metal as a medium for scripture texts in the time of Lehi. Unfortunately, Adams inaccurately refers to these silver rolls as "plates" a total of five times in these two notes. See "Lehi's Jerusalem and Writing on Silver Plates," *Journal of Book of Mormon Studies* 3/1 (1994): 204–6; and "More on the Silver Plates from Lehi's Jerusalem," *Journal of Book of Mormon Studies* 4/2 (1995): 136–37. These were reprinted in *Pressing Forward with the Book of Mormon: The FARMS Updates of the 1990s,* ed. John W. Welch and Melvin J. Thorne (Provo, Utah: FARMS, 1999), 23–28.

32. The linking of actual seals or impressions with biblically attested persons is an assumption based on probability. If a seal or impression contains a name + patronym combination that is also attested in the Bible and if the seal or impression is dated to about the time of the person mentioned in the Bible, then a connection between the seal or impression and the biblical person is *assumed,* but it generally cannot be proven.

33. Avigad and Sass, *Corpus of West Semitic Stamp Seals,* 175 #417.

34. A theophoric personal name is one that contains a divine name or title, in this case the suffixed -*yahu,* an abbreviated form of YHWH/Yahweh/Jehovah, in Berekyahu. Abbreviated forms of the

divine name YHWH in Israelite personal names are usually rendered in English Bibles as Jo-/Jeho- (from *yo-* and *yeho-;* e.g., Jonathan, Jehoram) and -iah/-jah (from *-yah* and *-yahu;* e.g., Neriah, Jeremiah, Elijah). The shorter form "Baruch" preserved in the Masoretic Text is a hypocoristicon of the theophoric form Berekyahu. On the difference in vocalization between Baruch and Berekyahu, compare the name of the Levitical porter/gatekeeper Shelemiah (1 Chronicles 26:1–2, 12–14) with the name Shallum (1 Chronicles 9:17–19), generally considered to belong to the same person. On Israelite names in general, see the LDS Bible Dictionary, s.v., "Names of persons"; and Dana M. Pike, "Names," in *HarperCollins Bible Dictionary,* ed. Paul J. Achtemeier, rev. ed. (San Francisco: HarperSanFrancisco, 1996), 733–34. See also Dana M. Pike, "Names, Hypocoristic," in *Anchor Bible Dictionary,* 4:1017–18, and "Names, Theophoric," in *Anchor Bible Dictionary,* 4:1018–19.

35. Avigad and Sass, *Corpus of West Semitic Stamp Seals,* 163 #390.

36. Ibid., 191 #470.

37. Ibid., 181 #431. Extending the inscriptional evidence of this family is a seal that is inscribed with the words "belonging to Asalyahu son of Meshullam," which probably belonged to Azaliah, the father of Shaphan, mentioned in 2 Kings 22:3.

38. Avigad and Sass, *Corpus of West Semitic Stamp Seals,* 175 #414.

39. On the debate over the title "son of the king," which may have served as a title for officials who were not sired by the king but were probably part of the broader royal family, see, for example, Nahman Avigad, *Hebrew Bullae from the Time of Jeremiah: Remnants of a Burnt Archive* (Jerusalem: Israel Exploration Society, 1986), 27–28; and Jeffrey R. Chadwick, "Has the Seal of Mulek Been Found?" forthcoming in *Journal of Book of Mormon Studies* 12/2 (2003).

40. Avigad and Sass, *Corpus of West Semitic Stamp Seals,* 55 #15.

41. See the forthcoming study by Chadwick, "Has the Seal of Mulek Been Found?"

42. Two further examples of individuals named on a seal and a bulla who may also be mentioned in the Bible are included here. A beautiful seal from about 600 B.C. found at Tel en-Nasbeh, ancient Mizpah, has a carving of a cock beneath two registers of text: "belonging to

Ya'azanyahu, servant of the king." Avigad and Sass, *Corpus of West Semitic Stamp Seals,* 52 #8. The Hebrew word ʿebed, "slave, servant," functions as a title for an official when used in this context and does not refer to an actual slave. The latter did not own seals. Perhaps this seal belonged to the Jaazaniah mentioned in 2 Kings 25:23 or Jeremiah 40:8. A bulla from Lachish that also dates to the early 500s B.C. reads: "belonging to Gedalyahu, the royal steward." Avigad and Sass, *Corpus of West Semitic Stamp Seals,* 172 #405. The title "royal steward" (literally, "one who is over the house" of the king) is well attested in the Bible; see, for example, 1 Kings 18:3; 2 Kings 18:18, 37; Isaiah 22:15. It is possible that this impression was made by a seal belonging to Gedaliah son of Ahikam, who was installed as governor of Judah by the Babylonians after they removed King Zedekiah from the throne in 586 B.C. (2 Kings 25:22; Jeremiah 40–41).

43. The pictures were incised at the same time as the texts, but scholarly interpretation of them varies, just as with the reading of the texts. One of the human figures appears to be playing a lyre and one, wearing an odd headdress and robe, has his arms raised in prayer.

44. Joseph Naveh, "Old Hebrew Inscriptions in a Burial Cave," *Israel Exploration Journal* 13 (1963): 74–92; Zevit, *Religions of Ancient Israel,* 405–38, 692–93.

45. For example, Klaas A. D. Smelik, *Writings from Ancient Israel* (Louisville: Westminster, 1991), 165, dates these inscriptions to "the end of the monarchy." Frank M. Cross Jr., "The Cave Inscriptions from Khirbet Beit Lei," in *Near Eastern Archaeology in the Twentieth Century,* ed. James A. Sanders (Garden City, N.Y.: Doubleday, 1970), 304, asserts that these inscriptions "are safely dated to the sixth century," the 500s B.C. This broad dating encompasses the late preexilic, the exilic, and even the early postexilic periods.

46. Examples of presumed postexilic features include phrasing that occurs in the Bible only in postexilic books such as Chronicles; the shorter, Aramaic form of Judah = *Yehud,* according to one rendition of Khirbet Beit Lei inscription A; and curses, perhaps aimed at tomb robbers, pertinent if the burial really dates to the Persian

period. See further the discussion of John C. L. Gibson, *Textbook of Syrian Semitic Inscriptions,* vol. 1, *Hebrew and Moabite Inscriptions,* 2nd ed. (Oxford: Clarendon, 1973), 57; and Smelik, *Writings from Ancient Israel,* 165–66.

47. Naveh, "Old Hebrew Inscriptions in a Burial Cave," 84; Zevit, *Religions of Ancient Israel,* 424. Zevit conveniently provides a comparison of several published translations, including Naveh's, as well as his own rendition (pp. 417–24). Note that Zevit provides a different enumeration of these inscriptions. Thus, Khirbet Beit Lei inscription A is designated "Stop 5, upper inscription," by him. See various other transcriptions and translations compared and contrasted in Johannes Renz and Wolfgang Röllig, *Handbuch der althebräischen Epigraphik* (Darmstadt: Wissenschaftliche Buchgesellschaft, 1995), 1:245–48.

48. Naveh, "Old Hebrew Inscriptions in a Burial Cave," 86; Zevit, *Religions of Ancient Israel,* 426.

49. Naveh, "Old Hebrew Inscriptions in a Burial Cave," 86; Zevit, *Religions of Ancient Israel,* 430.

50. For a review of such claims, see LaMar C. Berrett, "The So-Called Lehi Cave," *Journal of Book of Mormon Studies* 8/1 (1999): 64–66, 79. See the comments of Hershel Shanks, "Is the Mormon Figure Lehi Connected with a Prophetic Inscription near Jerusalem?" *Biblical Archaeology Review* 14/6 (1988): 19.

51. See Paul Y. Hoskisson, "Lehi and Sariah," *Journal of Book of Mormon Studies* 9/1 (2000): 30–31, and the responses to Hoskisson's note by Jeffrey R. Chadwick, Dana M. Pike, and John A. Tvedtnes, plus a final response from Hoskisson (pp. 32–39).

52. Pierre Boudreuil, Felice Israel, and Dennis Pardee, "King's Command and Widow's Plea: Two New Hebrew Ostraca of the Biblical Period," *Near Eastern Archaeology* 61/1 (1998): 2–13, is the English version of the original French publication of these texts. See further Hershel Shanks, "Three Shekels for the Lord," *Biblical Archaeology Review* 23/6 (1997): 28–32. Concerns about authenticity have been raised by Israel Eph'al and Joseph Naveh, "Remarks on the Recently Published Moussaieff Ostraca," *Israel Exploration Journal* 48/3–4 (1998): 269–73; and Angelika Berlejung and Andreas

Schüle, "Erwägungen zu den neuen Ostraka aus der Sammlung Moussaïeff," *Zeitschrift für Althebraistik* 11/1 (1998): 68–73. Pardee briefly rebuts these concerns and provides additional bibliography in Hallo and Younger, *Context of Scripture,* 3:86–87. See also the recent comments by Hershel Shanks, "The 'Three Shekels' and 'Widow's Plea' Ostraca: Real or Fake?" *Biblical Archaeology Review* 29/3 (2003): 40–44.

53. Shanks, "Three Shekels for the Lord," 31, indicates that regarding Moussaieff ostracon 1, Israeli scholar Ada Yardeni agrees with Boudreuil, Israel, and Pardee that the paleography dates it to the late seventh century B.C. But he also reports, based on personal communication, that Frank M. Cross and P. Kyle McCarter "date the handwriting more than a century earlier."

54. It is presumed by those who date this ostracon to the late seventh century B.C. that the name Ashyahu represents a variation of the name Josiah. Both names consist of a form of the verb *ʾwsh* + *yah(u)*. Another option is that the name Ashyahu represents the inversion of the two elements of the name Joash. Such inversion is represented in the Bible, for example, in the name Jehoiachin/Coniah. However, both Israelite kings named Joash ruled in the ninth century, earlier than the generally accepted dating of this ostracon.

55. See the convenient discussion of letters/epistles in the Old Testament in Dennis Pardee et al., *Handbook of Ancient Hebrew Letters* (Chico, Calif.: Scholars, 1982), 169–82.

56. This brief survey of letters of communication cannot deal with the different purposes for which letters were written, the relationship of the correspondents, or other factors that affected to some degree the length and style of a letter in both these cultures. For a convenient discussion of such factors in relation to letters in ancient Hebrew, see Pardee et al., *Handbook of Ancient Hebrew Letters,* 153–64. Nor does this brief survey deal with fragments of letters or references to letters (as opposed to quotations) in the text of scripture.

57. See further Pike, "Seals and Sealing," 103–14.

58. See note 34, above.

59. Jeffrey H. Tigay, *You Shall Have No Other Gods: Israelite Religion in the Light of Hebrew Inscription* (Atlanta: Scholars, 1986), 36.

60. See David Rolph Seely, "Chronology, Book of Mormon," in *Book of Mormon Reference Companion,* ed. Dennis L. Largey et al. (Salt Lake City: Deseret Book, 2003), 197–99. For an alternative perspective on the chronology of this time period in connection with Lehi and Zedekiah, see Jeffrey R. Chadwick, "Lehi's House at Jerusalem and the Land of His Inheritance," in this volume, pages 81–130.

61. A more complete but already somewhat dated list of Israelite inscriptions is found in Sandra L. Gogel, *A Grammar of Epigraphic Hebrew* (Atlanta: Scholars, 1998), 23–25.

Chapter 8

Nephi's Written Language and the Standard Biblical Hebrew of 600 b.c.

William James Adams Jr.

It is evident to all who read the King James Version of the Bible that the English language has changed considerably over the last three centuries. And so it was with the Hebrew of the biblical era. Comparison of the Hebrew of the Bible with the Hebrew found in Judea in extrabiblical Hebrew epigraphical sources (such as inscriptions, writing on pottery shards, etc.) reveals a few interesting features of Hebrew usage that appear to have changed between 1000 b.c. and a.d. 100.[1] Where on this spectrum of linguistic change was the Hebrew that Lehi and Nephi would have written in the Jerusalem of their day?

This question can be answered, in part, by examining the books of the Old Testament that come from that time, particularly 2 Kings, Jeremiah, and Ezekiel. In addition, the epigraphical sources of that period include the Cave of Lei inscriptions, the Hashavyahu Letter, the Arad Letters, and the Lachish Letters.[2] Broadly speaking, the dialect used in these writings is called Standard Biblical Hebrew. More specifically, since the Hebrew texts I will focus on were produced toward the end of this period, I will refer to the dialect as Standard Biblical Hebrew–Late.

This study will identify four elements of Hebrew style and then will examine whether any of those four distinctive features of Standard Biblical Hebrew–Late can be discerned in the English translation of 1 Nephi 1–7, 11–18 and 2 Nephi 25–33 to determine how close to Standard Biblical Hebrew–Late dialect Nephi wrote. This sample of texts from the Book of Mormon covers the span of Nephi's writings and includes different genres, similar to those noted in the right column of table 1. Since quoted speech has not been studied well in Biblical Hebrew, I will not include examples of speeches in this study. Additionally, several devices used solely to render a reasonable English translation will not be considered, such as the infinitive verb *to pass* in the clause *and it came to pass* (since the clause is a translation of a single finite verb in Hebrew) and the word *of* in construct noun phrases (for which see below).

Relativization

A *relative clause* is a subordinate clause that adds information about a noun in the main clause. An example is found in the sentence you have just read. The main clause is "A relative clause is a subordinate clause." The added information that further explains the noun clause is "that adds information about a noun in the main clause." In general, relative clauses in English tend to be introduced by relative pronouns like *which, who,* and *that.* The process that languages use to create relative clauses is called *relativization.* In linguistics, this topic is widely studied.[3] A look at relativization in Hebrew and in the Book of Mormon is revealing.

Relativization is a feature that changed over time in Biblical Hebrew. For example, the percentage of all clauses that

Table 1. The Extrabiblical Hebrew Sources

Diachronic Dialect[4]	Texts[5]	Date[6]	Number of Clauses	Predominant Genre (or Discourse)[7]
Archaic Biblical Hebrew	Gezer Calendar	925 B.C.	8	Description
	Kuntillet ʿAjrud	900	10	Blessing
Standard Biblical Hebrew–Early	Mesha Stone	850	52	Narrative
Standard Biblical Hebrew–Middle	Samaria Ostracon	786	3	Exhortation
	Murabbaʿat Letter	750	4	Exhortation
	Siloam Inscription	700	9	Narrative
	Royal Steward	700	6	Blessing
	Khirbet el-Kom	700	5	Blessing
Standard Biblical Hebrew–Late	Cave of Lei	650	4	Blessing
	Hashavyahu Letter	620	20	Narrative
	Arad Letters	583	63	Exhortation
	Lachish Letters	576	55	Exhortation
Late Biblical Hebrew	Habakkuk Commentary	100	103	Narrative
	Manual of Discipline	100	490	Exhortation
Mishnaic Hebrew	Bar Kokhba Letters	A.D. 100	32	Exhortation

Table 2. Diachronic Changes in the Hebrew Language of Judea as Attested in the Sources

Dialect	Percentage of Clauses That Are Relative	Development of Prepositions	Development of Construct Noun Phrases	Percent of Clauses with Infinitive Verbs
Archaic Biblical Hebrew	0%	Prefix prepositions only attested	Only two nouns in a chain, a proper noun may be the last noun	0%
Standard Biblical Hebrew–Early	10%	Prefixes continue plus new freestanding prepositions are attested that are derived from nouns	Three nouns are joined, of which the first may be plural; all may be preceded by a prepositional prefix, and the last noun may be genitive or definite	0%
Standard Biblical Hebrew–Middle	16%	More new prepositions derived from nouns are attested	The same	6%
Standard Biblical Hebrew–Late	18%	More new prepositions derived from nouns are attested	The same	9%
Late Biblical Hebrew	30%	More new prepositions are attested that are derived from body parts and combining prefixes with freestanding prepositions	Five nouns can be constructed in a chain; the last noun may be plural	29%
Mishnaic Hebrew	35%	More new prepositions are attested that are derived from body parts, prefixes plus proclitic / -m /, and a combination of two prefixes	No new innovations observed	0%

were relative gradually rose from none in Archaic Biblical Hebrew until, by the time of Nephi (600 B.C.), about 18 percent of all clauses were relative clauses (see table 2).

An example from 1 Nephi 1:6 will illustrate how an analysis of relativization is accomplished. The first step is to rearrange the verse so that each line is a clause and then determine which of those lines are relative.

Clause	Is it relative?
And it came to pass	no
as he prayed unto the Lord,	no
there came a pillar of fire	no
and [it] dwelt upon a rock before him:	no
and he saw	no
and [he] heard much;	no
and because of the things *which* he saw	yes
and [*which* he] heard	yes
he did quake	no
and [he did] tremble exceedingly.	no

This verse contains ten clauses, two of which, or 20 percent, are relative. The 20 percent figure is close to the 18 percent average of the Standard Biblical Hebrew–Late dialect. A similar tally of all the clauses in the twenty-four-chapter sample from the written words of Nephi indicates that 17 percent of his clauses are relative clauses (see table 3). Thus, in this feature, the translation of Nephi reflects the language of the Standard Biblical Hebrew–Late dialect.

As can be seen, 1 Nephi reflects the written Hebrew of about 600 B.C., which is referred to as Standard Biblical Hebrew–Late. The dialect of Mormon seems to develop from this dialect and to reflect only features of the Late Biblical Hebrew dialect of Judea. This is not surprising since written

Table 3. Summary of Occurrences of the Features Investigated in the Sample from Nephi and in Mormon 1–4

Feature	Nephi	Mormon 1–4
Relativization	17% of all clauses (n = 2,462)	30% of all clauses (n = 381)
Construct Noun Phrases	All of the features attested for the Standard Biblical Hebrew–Late dialect appear in the translation of Nephi.	The additional features attested in the Late Biblical Hebrew dialect appear in the translation of Mormon 1–4.
Infinitive Verbs	5% of all clauses have infinitives. They are used at points of pivot in narrative.	10% of all clauses have infinitives. They still are used mostly at points of pivot in narrative.
Prepositions	The most frequent prepositions are the less wordy or shorter prepositions. The more wordy or longer prepositions are just coming into use.	The less wordy or shorter prepositions are less frequent, indicating that the more wordy or longer prepositions are becoming more used and infringing on the frequency of the less wordy prepositions.

languages reflect usages older than the current spoken language. This observation would indicate that though Nephi wrote Standard Biblical Hebrew–Late, he and his people were already speaking a form of Late Biblical Hebrew. This spoken language eventually became the written language in the biblical books of Ezra, Nehemiah, Esther, and Chronicles, in the Dead Sea Scrolls, and in Mormon.

Participial Modifiers

Another interesting development in Hebrew at the time of Lehi, one that is first attested in the Standard Biblical Hebrew–Late dialect, is the use of the Hebrew letter *hey* (ה) followed by a participle. Most relative clauses up to this time in the history of the Hebrew language add information only about the nouns at the end of main clauses (in other words, objects of verbs or objects of prepositions). But beginning in late biblical times, the construction *hey + participle,* though rare, was developed to modify nouns that occur earlier in the main clause (such as subjects). Such a rare construction can be seen in 1 Nephi 2:14, which reads, "my father did speak unto them in the valley of Lemuel, with power, being filled with the Spirit." The relative clause "being filled with the Spirit" adds information about the subject, "my father," and not about the other, later nouns (*valley* and *Lemuel*) or pronoun (*them*) in the main clause. In translating this sentence back into Hebrew, I would use a *hey + participle* construction.

Construct Noun Phrases

Most languages have devices for joining nouns together. For example, in English one can put "man" and "book" together as "the man's book." In Hebrew the phrase is turned around to read "the book of the man." Another English example would be "We improvised a garbage can lid handle." The Biblical Hebrew word order would be "handle lid can garbage," which would be translated smoothly as "a handle for the lid of the can for garbage." (The words *for* and *of* are not there in the Hebrew but are devices to create a reasonable English translation.) Nouns so conjoined in Hebrew are called construct noun phrases. In the epigraphical sources used in this study (see table 1), the number of nouns that could be constructed together continually increases so that by the time of the Dead Sea Scrolls used in this study (about 100 B.C.; see table 1), as many as five nouns could be so linked. At the time of Nephi, construct noun phrases could (1) have as many as three nouns, (2) with the last noun being definite, proper, or genitive, and (3) be preceded by prepositions (see tables 2 and 3).

These possibilities can be seen in the following examples: 1 Nephi 3:16 reads "to the land of our father's inheritance." In Hebrew the word order would be "to the land of inheritance of our father." The whole phrase begins with a preposition *to;* it includes three nouns ("land," "inheritance," and "father") in the phrase, and the last noun has a genitive pronoun, "our." Another example is 2 Nephi 25:19, which reads "according to . . . the word of the angel of God." The Hebrew word order would be "according to word of angel of God." This example has three nouns, begins with a preposition, and ends with a proper noun. Thus, the translation of Nephi reflects the elements expected for constructing nouns together in the Standard Biblical Hebrew–Late dialect.

Infinitive Verbs

Infinitives were just beginning to appear in the Hebrew of the epigraphical sources by the time of Nephi (see table 2). Only about 6 percent of verbs in those texts are infinitives. The function of infinitives, reflected in Nephi's writing, is to join several sentences into one. For example, 1 Nephi 1:18 reads, "Behold he went forth among the people, and [he] began *to prophesy* and *to declare* unto them." In the older levels of Biblical Hebrew this example would read "and he went forth among the people, and he began, and he prophesied, and he declared unto them." But with the use of infinitives, the last two independent clauses from the older Hebrew are expressed as part of the second independent clause in 1 Nephi 1:18. Counts in 1 and 2 Nephi indicate that 5 percent (see table 3) of the verbs are infinitives, which is close to the 6 percent found in the Hebrew epigraphical sources of this era.

Infinitive verbs, which are noted in the far right column of table 2, appear most frequently in the text with decision making. Since the primary source for Late Biblical Hebrew is the Dead Sea Scrolls *Manual of Discipline,* which encourages righteous decision making, it is not surprising to see such a high percentage of infinitive verbs. The Bar Kokhba Letters, in Mishnaic Hebrew, issue instructions, but since there are no responses to these instructions recorded, there are no infinitive verbs.

It is also interesting that infinitive verbs in Standard Biblical Hebrew–Late tend to come in pairs and to denote a point of pivot in narrative (or, in other words, a change in behavior). Similarly, two infinitives appear in 1 Nephi 1:18: "behold he went forth among the people, and began *to prophesy* and *to declare.*" Another example is found in 1 Nephi 3:14: "*to be*" and "*to return.*"

Prepositions

The use of prepositions is another feature of Biblical Hebrew that changed with time (see table 2). This is true of English also. Consider the following translations of Mark 9:2 in various periods of English:[8]

Source	Translation		
West Saxon Gospels (about A.D. 1000)	and lædde hig on-sundron	on	ænne heahne munt
Wycliffe version (about 1382)	and ledde hem asydis	in to	an hizh hill
King James Version (1611)	and leadeth them	up into	an high mountain apart

As can be seen, the prepositions preceding "an high mountain" became increasingly more wordy or lengthy.

In the earliest inscriptions of Biblical Hebrew, only four prefixes are used for prepositions in a way that would be most similar to the West Saxon Gospels example above. But by A.D. 100 the Hebrew language had developed a long list of freestanding prepositions, some of which were formed by conjoining prepositions, such as "up into" in the King James example above. In this developmental respect, the Standard Biblical Hebrew–Late of Nephi's time would be on a par with the example from Wycliffe.

The most frequent preposition in Nephi is *of.* However, in almost all incidences, *of* is an English device for translating the Hebrew grammatical feature called a "construct noun phrase" and will not be counted here. One verse in which *of* is not a translation of a construct noun phrase is found in 1 Nephi 3:12. Here, *of* has the sense of "from," which could be translated by the Hebrew prefix preposition *m-*.

The most frequently used prepositions in the sample from Nephi are listed in table 4. Those of greatest frequency are the prepositions that are less wordy or shorter, though some of the more wordy or longer prepositions are also used. In this aspect,

Table 4. Percentage of Words That Are Prepositions in the Sample from Nephi Compared to Percentages in Mormon 1–4

Preposition	Percents in Nephi (n = 21,411)	Percents in Mormon 1–4 (n = 3,721)
unto	1.39%	.60%
in	.80%	.40%
with	.53%	.48%
into	.24%	.13%
because of	.24%	.39%
according to	.15%	.15%
before	.14%	.29%
concerning	.13%	.17%
throughout	0	.11%

it appears that Nephi chose from a pool of simple prepositions, comparable to that which was available to writers of the Standard Biblical Hebrew–Late dialect.

In table 4, the prepositions above the dotted line are the less wordy or shorter prepositions, and the prepositions below the dotted line are the more wordy or longer prepositions. Since the less wordy or shorter prepositions in Mormon 1–4 tend to be used less frequently, we can assume that they are being replaced by more wordy or longer prepositions since the more wordy or longer prepositions are used almost twice as frequently in Mormon 1–4 as compared to the sample from Nephi.

Changed Features in the Language of Mormon

From Mormon 9:33 it is clear that the Hebrew language used by the Nephites changed over the centuries: "The Hebrew hath been altered by us also." Although it exceeds the purposes of this study, it is worth mentioning that in certain respects the Hebrew of the Nephites changed over time in the New World in a fashion similar to the Hebrew in the Old World. For example, in the Old World after Lehi's time, the usage of relative clauses in Hebrew increased to 35 percent of all clauses by the time of the Bar Kokhba letters of A.D. 100 (tables 1 and 2). Counts in Mormon 1–4 reveal that 30 percent of clauses are relative (table 3). Likewise, the previously most frequent prepositions were "in," "unto," "with," and "into," but they are considerably less frequent in Mormon. The increased use of the more wordy prepositions suggests that the Hebrew of Mormon reflects the Late Biblical Hebrew dialect. For further data along these lines, see table 4.

Conclusion

In the history of most languages, change is to be expected. In the Book of Mormon, the Mulekites had allowed their

Hebrew language to become "corrupted" (Omni 1:17; written about 270 B.C.). Likewise, the language of Italy during the Roman Empire was Latin, which became the official language of church, government, science, and letters during the Middle Ages. In the meantime, the language of the people of Italy continued to change. As a result, Italians today must learn Latin as a foreign language. The same is true of modern Israelis who speak modern Hebrew but need to learn biblical Hebrew.

Amid such changes, however, measurements may be taken. Based on this examination of four language features that are known to have changed over time in Hebrew usage in Judea, the English translation of the writings of Nephi manifests usages of a Hebrew writer in 600 B.C. This corroborates the statement made by Nephi in 1 Nephi 1:2 (written about 580 B.C.) that he makes "a record in the language of my father." This statement has been variously interpreted, but from the research reported in this study, it appears that Nephi wrote in the standard written Hebrew used in Judea around 600 B.C.

Notes

1. William J. Adams Jr., "An Investigation into the Diachronic Distribution of Morphological Forms and Semantic Features of Extra-Biblical Hebrew Sources" (Ph.D. diss., University of Utah Middle East Center, 1987).

2. See further the article by Dana Pike, "Israelite Inscriptions from the Time of Lehi and Jeremiah," in this volume, pages 193–244.

3. See, for example, Bernard Comrie, *Language Universals and Linguistic Typology: Syntax and Morphology* (Chicago: University of Chicago Press, 1981), 131–57; 2nd ed. (London: Blackwell, 1989), 138–64.

4. The titles of these diachronic dialects listed in table 1 follow Eduard Kutscher, *A History of the Hebrew Language,* ed. Raphael Kutscher (Jerusalem: Magnes, 1982), 12, although I made distinctions within Standard Biblical Hebrew that he does not and added

the Mishnaic Hebrew dialect. If a source covers a range of dates (such as seventh century B.C.), the date in the table above represents the mean (such as 650 B.C. for the seventh century). The Hebrew linguistic character of the three texts above the dotted line is debated. The double line represents the time of the Babylonian conquest.

5. The references for the texts are Francis I. Andersen, "Moabite Syntax," *Orientalia* 35 (1966): 81–120; Nahman Avigad, "The Epitaph of a Royal Steward from Siloam Village," *Israel Exploration Journal* 3 (1953): 137–43; Millar Burrows, *The Dead Sea Scrolls of St. Mark's Monastery,* 2 vols. (New Haven, Conn.: American School of Oriental Research, 1950–51); Frank M. Cross Jr. and David N. Freedman, *Early Hebrew Orthography: A Study of Epigraphic Evidence* (New Haven, Conn.: American Oriental Society, 1952); Graham I. Davies, *Ancient Hebrew Inscriptions: Corpus and Concordance* (Cambridge: Cambridge University Press, 1991); William G. Dever, "Iron Age Epigraphic Material from the Area of Khirbet el-Kôm," *Hebrew Union College Annual* 40 (1969–70): 139–89; Ruth Hestrin et al., *Inscriptions Reveal: Documents from the Time of the Bible, the Mishna and the Talmud* (Jerusalem: Israel Museum, Catalog 100, 1973); Zeev Meshel, *Kuntillet 'Ajrud: A Religious Centre from the Time of the Judaean Monarchy on the Border of Sinai* [in Hebrew] (Jerusalem: Israel Museum, Catalog 175, 1978); J. Naveh, "Old Hebrew Inscriptions in a Burial Cave," *Israel Exploration Journal* 13 (1963): 74–92; Dennis Pardee et al., *Handbook of Ancient Hebrew Letters: A Study Edition* (Chico, Calif.: Scholars, 1982); and Stanislav Segert, "Die Sprache der moabitischen Königsinschrift," *Archiv Orientální* 29 (1961): 197–267.

6. For the dates, see the sources in note 4 above.

7. The definitions of the discourse structure follow Robert E. Longacre, *The Grammar of Discourse,* 2nd ed. (New York: Plenum, 1983).

8. From Martyn Wakelin, *The Archaeology of English* (Totowa, N.J.: Barnes and Noble, 1988), 15–16.

Chapter 9

LEHI AND EGYPT

John S. Thompson

The Book of Mormon declares that Lehi and members of his family, faithful Israelites living near Jerusalem about 600 B.C., learned the Egyptian language and then used this knowledge to read holy scriptures and keep personal records.[1] It also makes it clear that these faithful Israelites called their children and places in their promised land by Egyptian names.[2] Such propositions would likely have been scorned in Joseph Smith's day; doctors of theology in the early 1800s would have based their views of Egyptian-Israelite relations primarily upon the Israelites' seeming disdain for Egyptian culture as reflected in the Bible. However, as Hugh Nibley pointed out a few decades ago, the abundance of archaeological and literary records then coming forth from the Near East was causing scholars to rethink the nature of Egyptian-Israelite cultural relations, bringing their ideas closer to the Book of Mormon's portrayal.[3]

More recent finds continue to alter or at least sharpen our views as to the conditions in and around Jerusalem during the latter half of the seventh century. What follows summarizes the present state of understanding among the scholars. First, I will review the current understanding of Egyptian interactions with the land of Canaan to show that Egyptian political and cultural influence was at a high point in Lehi's day, and I will discuss the nature of those interactions in order to explore the degree of Egyptian cultural assimilation by Syro-Palestinians. Second, I will review the scholars' views on some of the specific epigraphic evidence that has been recently uncovered, suggesting that Lehi would indeed have had opportunities to learn Egyptian near his home in Jerusalem and to use it not only to read Egyptian but to keep records and teach his posterity. As the prevalence of Egyptian influence in and around Lehi's Jerusalem is made apparent, it becomes clear that the Book of Mormon has indicated all along what the scholars are increasingly coming to understand.

Egypt and Israel

When the current view of Egyptian political interaction with the land of Canaan during the decades surrounding Lehi's day is placed within its broader context of Egyptian-Israelite history, we discover that Egyptian political domination over the area was at a high point at that time. During the early New Kingdom period of Egyptian history (particularly the Eighteenth and Nineteenth Dynasties, about 1539–1190 B.C.), Egypt had a strong imperial presence in the land of Canaan; however, subsequent dynasties leading up to Lehi's day were times of political disunity and comparative weakness in Egypt as foreigners ruled the land.

Under Ramses XI, in the eleventh century B.C., the Twentieth Dynasty collapsed and the political structure of Egypt was divided. Northern Egypt came under the rule of Egyptianized Libyans (the Twenty-first Dynasty), centered at Tanis.[4] However, southern Egypt was controlled for the most part by high priests of Amun at Thebes. Mainly due to the constant internal conflicts caused by this division, the pharaohs of the Twenty-first Dynasty could not maintain any consistent political control over the Levant.[5] However, they did attempt from time to time to exert their influence in that area. For example, a successful campaign against the city of Gezer in Palestine eventually led to a diplomatic marriage between King Solomon and an Egyptian princess.[6] But in spite of small victories such as this, Egyptian political weakness in the region was evident.[7] Consequently, less Egyptian material culture is found in Israel during this time than during the earlier New Kingdom period; however, economic and cultural contact was maintained with Canaan and other parts of Asia through commerce with the Mediterranean coastal states such as Phoenicia.[8]

At the beginning of the Twenty-second (Bubastid) Dynasty (1069–945 B.C.), Sheshonq (the biblical Shishak) sought to resurrect the early Ramesside glories of Egypt by unifying the land and expanding its borders.[9] However, in the wake of major internal Theban rebellions during the ninth century (bringing about the existence of the Twenty-third Dynasty in southern Egypt) and divisions within the Bubastid family itself, this dynasty eventually proved incapable of controlling foreign lands. Ironically, "despite its political weakness," Donald Redford observes, "Egypt remained a repository and a source of wealth . . . [and] the inhabitants of western Asia welcomed trade in the exotic products Egypt had to offer."[10] It was during this time that contemporary Hebrew glyphic art employing the winged scarab, an icon strongly associated with Bubastid land around Sile, began to appear in Caanan.[11]

During the Twenty-fifth (Kushite or Nubian) Dynasty and the subsequent decades surrounding Lehi's time, political and cultural relations between Egypt and Israel reached a new high. Because they were initially able to unite Egypt and obtain a relative stability at home, the Kushite rulers adopted a more rigorous political policy in Syro-Palestine than their Libyan predecessors. However, this expansion of influence caused the Egyptians to bump up against the Assyrians, who were growing from the east. Egypt and Israel, among others, soon became allies to combat this new imperial force. Several attempts by Egypt to resist Assyrian invasion eventually led to its fragmentation. Assyrian overlords were installed over northern Egypt, and in time the Kushite rulers withdrew back into Nubia, marking the end of their dominance over Egypt.

Historian John Taylor states that "the bloodshed and destruction that followed from the Kushite opposition to Assyria proved to be a cloud with a silver lining: it emphasized the necessity for military and civil cooperation by the rulers of the [Egyptian] principalities."[12] This cooperation enabled the Pharaoh Psammetichus I (Psamtik I) to unify all of Egypt. He drew upon mercenaries from surrounding nations, including Israel, for unification purposes as well as for defense against further conflicts with Assyria, and he maintained trade links with the Levant—primarily Phoenicia—and with Greece in order to strengthen his country economically. This, of course, encouraged Egyptian cultural influence in the land of Canaan.

Psammetichus quickly gained independence from Assyria, which had turned its attention to internal conflict and to its eastern and southern neighbor nations, which were growing in power. Once free from Assyrian rule, the Twenty-sixth Dynasty pharaohs continued to play an active role in the politics of the Levant. In fact, as Assyria began to weaken and withdraw from Egypt and Syro-Palestine, Psammetichus quickly filled the void.[13]

Psammetichus's son, Necho II, continued his father's political ambitions in the Levant, sending campaigns east of the Euphrates against the Chaldean armies. En route Necho II defeated and killed King Josiah in 609 B.C. at Megiddo and set up the Egyptian border near the Euphrates; after dealing with the Chaldeans, he returned to establish hegemony over Israel. In the interim, Josiah's son Jehoahaz had ascended the throne for a three-month reign. However, because of his anti-Egyptian sentiments—and probably also through the schemings of his older brother, Eliakim/Jehoiakim, who should have been the heir—Jehoahaz was exiled by Necho II to Egypt, where he died. Necho II placed Jehoiakim on the throne. Not only was the king of Judah installed by Pharaoh, but other officials seem to have been installed as well. Biblical scholar Ephraim Stern, basing his remarks principally upon more recent archaeological evidence, declares, "Through the years from Josiah to the coming of the Babylonians, Egyptian officials ruled both in Philistia and Judah."[14] The exiling of Jehoahaz, the subsequent appointment of Jehoiakim, and the seeming appointment of other officers in the land of Judah by Pharaoh all suggest Egypt's very strong political presence in Israel in the decade prior to Lehi's departure from Jerusalem. This dominance, however, did not last long, for in 605 B.C. the Chaldeans defeated the Egyptians at Carchemish and pushed them back to their own land. Later, Psammetichus II, Necho II's successor, arranged a revolt against the Babylonians with the aid of Zedekiah, then king of Judah, but the Babylonians prevailed and eventually razed the cities of Judah and Palestine to the ground.[15]

As the above historical outline demonstrates, the alliances of Egypt with Israel during the late Twenty-fifth and early Twenty-sixth Dynasties and the subsequent political desires of the Twenty-sixth Dynasty for imperial expansion[16] caused

Egypt's political influence in Israel to reach unprecedented heights. Such was the immediate contemporary political situation in which Lehi and his family existed. This strong political influence surrounding Lehi's day surely would have emphasized those Egyptian cultural features that were already embedded in Canaan during the New Kingdom empire—and even those embedded in subsequent times of political weakness as noted above. But more importantly, this political ambience provided a climate in which contemporary Egyptian cultural influence would flourish.

Gregory D. Mumford, in examining the heretofore largely ignored archaeological picture of Egyptian artifacts in southwestern Asia from 1550 to 525 B.C., has shown that Egyptian cultural influences in Syro-Palestine seem to peak four times in nineteen time divisions—namely, in 1450–1400 B.C. (Eighteenth Dynasty time period), 1250–1150 B.C. (Nineteenth Dynasty time period), 925–850 B.C. (Twenty-second [Bubastid] Dynasty time period), and 750–600 B.C. (Twenty-fifth and Twenty-sixth Dynasty time periods).[17] In addition, Ephraim Stern has recently demonstrated that Egyptian material culture in Israel from the reign of Psammetichus I to that of Psammetichus II (ca. 664–589 B.C.) was plentiful, attesting to the close political interactions that Egypt had with Israel as Assyria dwindled in strength.[18] Thus, as seen above, the more recent historical and archaeological studies demonstrate and emphasize even more that Egyptian political and cultural influence in Canaan was at one of its peaks in the immediate decades leading up to Lehi's time.

While this certainly seems to be an environment that would justify the numerous Egyptian manifestations found in the Book of Mormon, trying to understand the actual nature of the cultural influence of Egypt upon Israel is problematic.

One of the principal questions scholars have debated is whether Egyptian cultural manifestations in other lands suggest that Egypt typically established itself as a direct ruling empire or whether it simply controlled the area politically or economically from afar, using vassal-treaty agreements with Egyptianized or non-Egyptianized local elites ruling under the auspices of Egypt.[19]

Direct rule would imply the annexing of conquered territory and the establishing of Egyptian settlements within their boundaries—not only military garrisons but also civilian settlements, where Egyptian administrators would be permanently stationed in order to impose laws, collect taxes, and so forth (similar to those seen in Egypt's expansion into Nubia).[20] This degree of infiltration would provide strong cultural influences, for the Egyptians themselves would build and settle these sites, bringing with them their culture and ideologies in both domestic and workplace settings.

On the other hand, if Egypt used the local elite to rule conquered territory, then the cultural influence would seemingly be less than that under direct rule; however, it would likely still be present, especially if these local leaders adopted, to one degree or another, the culture of their overlords. The cultural assimilation of things Egyptian by an Egyptianized local elite would most likely be reflected in prestige goods that locals acquired from Egypt or through comparatively minor borrowing of Egyptian features of art and architecture adapted or synthesized into the local culture. This view of Egyptian imperialism, which has become the more popular view defended in recent years,[21] should be of continuing interest to Latter-day Saint audiences, for it suggests that many of the Egyptian artifacts in Syro-Palestine that have shown up in the current archaeological record reflect real assimilation of Egyptian culture by upper-class natives rather than, or in addition to,

Egyptian occupation of the land. Laban and Lehi would certainly qualify among the elite of Jerusalem, as evidenced by references to their position and wealth (see 1 Nephi 3:22–25, 31; 4:20–22).

Egyptian Writing in Israel

Some of the specific cultural artifacts that have recently been uncovered in and around the land of Judah provide good evidence that Lehi would indeed have had opportunities to learn Egyptian near his home in Jerusalem. Archaeologists in Canaan are unearthing a growing body of artifacts that feature Egyptian writing on them.[22] The nature of some of these artifacts, as postulated by the scholars, suggests an adoption by Syro-Palestinian locals of Egyptian script for accounting purposes.[23] Still other artifacts suggest the presence of Egyptian scribes in the area.[24] Due to its prominence, Orly Goldwasser states that Egyptian writing was the more progressive form of Egyptian cultural influence attested in Israel in the eighth and seventh centuries.[25]

The kind of Egyptian script being employed on those artifacts dating around the time of Lehi is hieratic,[26] but since Demotic was the script of the day in northern Egypt and "abnormal hieratic" was predominant in southern Egypt, the normal hieratic tradition in Canaan must have been adopted from an earlier time—possibly, Goldwasser suggests, during the reigns of David and Solomon or even earlier in the tenth century B.C.—and was in continued use in Israel.[27] This last point may have some bearing upon the script that Lehi and Nephi used when making their records. It has generally been assumed that Demotic was the script of choice for Lehi and Nephi, for it is the most compact of the Egyptian characters and was the most predominant in Egypt at this time; however, the archaeological record to date reveals that hieratic was the more commonly used Egyptian script in Israel.[28]

This use of hieratic script in Canaan has led Goldwasser to postulate further that during the height of the New Kingdom's cultural influence in Canaan, many scribes and teachers made their way into the Levant to set up businesses. However, "after the decline of the Egyptian Empire . . . many Egyptians, or Egyptian-trained Canaanite scribes lost their means of existence, and may have offered their scribal and administrative knowledge to the new powers rising in the area, first the Philistines and then the Israelites. . . . We would like to suggest that these Egyptian or Egyptian-trained scribes, cut off from their homeland, well acquainted with Egyptian decorum as well as the Canaanite language, educated local scribes, who in their turn passed on their knowledge to their successors."[29] Such a view, bolstered by the Egyptian title "scribe" appearing in hieratic on an artifact from Lachish,[30] suggests the possibility that by Lehi's day, scribes having a knowledge of Egyptian had existed in the area for quite some time and had maintained a tradition of writing Egyptian.[31] The fact that an Egyptian scribal tradition existed locally could imply that Lehi learned Egyptian from a local scribe or even from his own father, just as Lehi presumably taught Nephi (see 1 Nephi 1:1–2).[32]

Conclusions

At the very beginning of the small plates, Nephi informs the reader: "Yea, I make a record in the language of my father, which consists of the learning of the Jews and the language of the Egyptians" (1 Nephi 1:2). Various interpretations have been given concerning this verse, and the accepted understanding is that Nephi's record was written using at least an Egyptian-based script.[33] It is also possible that Nephi is here

informing the reader that he is making a record using his father's system of writing ("the language of my father") and that
this system, as he goes on to tell us, consists of Jewish learning
and Egyptian language.[34] This would further imply that Lehi's
own personal record, which Nephi had previously copied onto
his large plates and was now about to abridge onto his small
plates (see 1 Nephi 1:16–17; 10:1; 19:1),[35] may also have been
written using Egyptian.[36]

Using aspects of Egyptian language for record keeping
among Lehi's posterity continued all the way to the days of
Mormon and Moroni. By that time, however, Mormon informs us that the language had been "altered"—presumably
the spelling, syntax, and grammar changed according to
speech patterns, as Mormon tells us, but it is also likely that
the script/characters employed were also altered over time so
that it could be read only by the Nephites (Mormon 9:32, 34).[37]
Still, reason dictates that when Lehi and Nephi initially wrote
their records, they used aspects of the Egyptian language that
would have been recognizable to the Egyptians of their day.[38]

Of course, every detail concerning the nature and extent of
Egyptian cultural influence in Israel, particularly writing, has
not yet come forth; for instance, long historical Israelite narratives in Egyptian are not currently attested. Consequently,
the relationship between Egypt and Israel and the cultural
influence that Egypt had upon Lehi's world deserves greater
exploration in the coming years, especially as new archaeological and textual finds continue to change our views as to
what occurred during this time period. For now, however, the
evidence attests to a solidly established relationship between
Egypt and Israel. Egyptian political and cultural influence in
Israel surrounding the time of Lehi was at a peak, Egyptian
language was being employed for record-keeping purposes,

and the possibility of an Egyptian scribal tradition existing in the area of Jerusalem gives plausibility to the Book of Mormon's claim that Lehi and his posterity learned and used Egyptian for record-keeping purposes. The authenticity of the Book of Mormon continues to be sustained as the picture of Lehi's Jerusalem becomes clearer.

NOTES

1. In the opening verses of that portion of the abridged large plates of Nephi of which we have a translation, Mormon informs us that Lehi was taught "in the language of the Egyptians" (Mosiah 1:4). We also learn in this passage that at least a part, if not all, of the brass plates that Laban possessed and Lehi later obtained were written in Egyptian, for Lehi had to use his knowledge of the Egyptian language to read them. The opening verses of the small plates of Nephi seem to imply that Lehi's children were taught Egyptian and used this knowledge to keep a record (see 1 Nephi 1:1–2).

2. Many of the proper names mentioned in the Book of Mormon—including Nephi, Sam, Paanchi, Pahoran, Ammon, and Sidon—may have Egyptian origins. See Hugh Nibley, *Lehi in the Desert, The World of the Jaredites, There Were Jaredites* (Salt Lake City: Deseret Book and FARMS, 1988), 25–42; John Gee, "Four Suggestions on the Origin of the Name Nephi," in *Pressing Forward with the Book of Mormon,* ed. John W. Welch and Melvin J. Thorne (Provo, Utah: FARMS, 1999), 1–5; Paul Y. Hoskisson, "What's in a Name? Nephi," *Journal of Book of Mormon Studies* 9/2 (2000): 64–65.

3. Nibley, *Lehi in the Desert,* 6–13.

4. The major work on this period and subsequent dynasties (22nd–25th) remains Kenneth A. Kitchen, *The Third Intermediate Period in Egypt (1100–650 B.C.),* 2nd ed. (Warminster: Aris and Phillips, 1986).

5. See the cogent comments of Anthony Leahy, "The Libyan Period in Egypt: An Essay in Interpretation," *Libyan Studies* 16 (1985): 51–65.

6. Kitchen argues that this was a beneficial move for both Egypt and Israel by removing the Philistines in this city and was not motivated by any Egyptian desire to control the area including Jerusalem; see his *Third Intermediate Period,* 281–82.

7. Again, see Leahy, "The Libyan Period in Egypt," for why it was weak.

8. Jean Leclant, *The Role of the Phoenicians in the Interaction of Mediterranean Civilizations,* ed. William A. Ward (Beirut: American University of Beirut, 1968), 9–31.

9. See Donald B. Redford, *Egypt, Canaan, and Israel in Ancient Times* (Princeton: Princeton University Press, 1992), 314–15.

10. Ibid., 336–37.

11. Anson F. Rainey, "Wine from the Royal Vineyards," *Bulletin of the American Schools of Oriental Research* 245 (1982): 57–62; A. D. Tushingham, "A Royal Israelite Seal(?) and the Royal Jar Handle Stamps (Part One)," *Bulletin of the American Schools of Oriental Research* 200 (1970): 71–78 .

12. John Taylor, "The Third Intermediate Period," in *The Oxford History of Ancient Egypt,* ed. Ian Shaw (Oxford: Oxford University Press, 2000), 359.

13. See A. Kirk Grayson, *Assyrian and Babylonian Chronicles* (Locust Valley, N.Y.: Augustin, 1975), 90–96.

14. Ephraim Stern, *Archaeology of the Land of the Bible* (New York: Doubleday, 2001), 2:229. Conversely, Anthony Spalinger, "Egypt and Babylonia: A Survey (c. 620 B.C.–550 B.C.)," *Studien zur Altägyptischen Kultur* 5 (1977): 227–30, argues that Egypt maintained two different policies toward Judah and the surrounding Philistine cities respectively: Judah remained relatively free and autonomous even after Josiah's defeat at Megiddo, while Egypt maintained strong control over the Philistine cities.

15. Abraham Malamat, "The Twilight of Judah: In the Egyptian-Babylonian Maelstrom," *Supplements to Vetus Testamentum,* vol. 28 (Leiden: Brill, 1975), 123–45, provides nice detail about the final years of the kingdom of Judah, including its political fluctuations as

it changed loyalties six times between Egypt and Babylon between 609 and 587 B.C.

16. Conversely, Donald B. Redford, "The Relations between Egypt and Israel from El-Amarna to the Babylonian Conquest," in *Biblical Archaeology Today* (Jerusalem: Israel Exploration Society, 1985), 196, believes that Egypt's interest in the Levant at this time was chiefly concerned with simply maintaining the route through the Philistine plain and was not for the purpose of imperial expansion or control.

17. Gregory D. Mumford, "International Relations between Egypt, Sinai, and Syria-Palestine during the Late Bronze Age to Early Persian Period (Dynasties 18–26: c. 1550–525 B.C.): A Spatial and Temporal Analysis of the Distribution and Proportions of Egyptian(izing) Artifacts and Pottery in Sinai and Selected Sites in Syria-Palestine" (Ph.D. diss., University of Toronto, 1998).

18. Stern, *Archaeology*, esp. chap. 8, "Egyptians in Palestine in the 7th Century BCE," 228–35.

19. Recent studies that specifically discuss Egyptian imperialism in relation to Israel include Carolyn R. Higginbotham, *Egyptianization and Elite Emulation in Ramesside Palestine: Governance and Accommodation on the Imperial Periphery* (Leiden: Brill, 2000); Bernd U. Schipper, *Israel und Ägypten in der Königszeit: Die kulturellen Kontakte von Salomo bis zum Fall Jerusalems* (Göttingen: Vandenhoeck and Ruprecht, 1999); A. B. Knapp, "Independence and Imperialism: Politico-economic Structures in the Bronze Age Levant," in *Archaeology,* Annales, *and Ethnohistory,* ed. A. Bernard Knapp (Cambridge: Cambridge University Press, 1992); William G. Dever, "The Late Bronze–Early Iron I Horizon in Syria-Palestine: Egyptians, Canaanites, 'Sea Peoples,' and Proto-Israelites," in *The Crisis Years: The 12th Century B.C.: From beyond the Danube to the Tigris,* ed. William A. Ward and Martha S. Joukowsky (Dubuque, Iowa: Kendall/Hunt, 1992), 99–110; Itamar Singer, "The Political Status of Megiddo VIIA," *Tel Aviv* 15–16 (1988–89): 101–12; Redford, "Relations between Egypt and Israel," 192–205; E. D. Oren, "Governors' Residences in Canaan under the New Kingdom: A Case Study of Egyptian Administration," *Society for the Study of*

Egyptian Antiquities Journal 14 (1984): 37–56; James A. Weinstein, "The Egyptian Empire in Palestine: A Reassessment," *Bulletin of the American Schools of Oriental Research* 241 (1981): 1–28. Other studies of Egyptian imperialism include Ellen F. Morris, "The Architecture of Imperialism: An Investigation into the Role of Fortresses and Administrative Headquarters in New Kingdom Foreign Policy" (Ph.D. diss., University of Pennsylvania, 2001); José M. Galán, "Victory and Border: Terminology Related to Egyptian Imperialism in the XVIIIth Dynasty" (Ph.D. diss., Johns Hopkins University Press, 1993); E. L. Bleiberg, "Aspects of the Political, Religious, and Economic Basis of Ancient Egyptian Imperialism during the New Kingdom" (Ph.D. diss., University of Toronto, 1984); Paul J. Frandsen, "Egyptian Imperialism," in *Power and Propaganda: A Symposium on Ancient Empires,* ed. Mogens T. Larsen (Copenhagen: Akademisk Forlag, 1979), 167–92; B. J. Kemp, "Imperialism and Empire in New Kingdom Egypt (c. 1575–1087 B.C.)," in *Imperialism in the Ancient World,* ed. P. D. A. Garnsey and C. R. Whittaker (Cambridge: Cambridge University Press, 1978), 7–57; David Lorton, *The Juridical Terminology of International Relations in Egyptian Texts through Dyn. XVIII* (Baltimore: Johns Hopkins University Press, 1974).

20. See R. G. Morkot, "Politics, Economics, and Ideology: Egyptian Imperialism in Nubia," *Wepwawet* 3 (1987): 29–49; Stuart T. Smith, *Askut in Nubia: The Economics and Ideology of Egyptian Imperialism in the Second Millennium B.C.* (New York: Kegan Paul, 1995).

21. See in particular Higginbotham, *Egyptianization and Elite Emulation;* and Morris, "The Architecture of Imperialism."

22. For further information on the kingdom of Judah's connections with scribal traditions in Egypt, see Aaron P. Schade, "The Kingdom of Judah: Politics, Prophets, and Scribes in the Late Pre-exilic Period," in this volume, pages 299–336.

23. Shlomo Yeiven, "An Ostracon from Tel Arad Exhibiting a Combination of Two Scripts," *Journal of Egyptian Archaeology* 55 (1969): 98–102; Yohanan Aharoni, "The Use of Hieratic Numerals in

Hebrew Ostraca and the Shekel Weights," *Bulletin of the American Schools of Oriental Research* 184 (1966): 13–19.

24. Orly Goldwasser, "An Egyptian Scribe from Lachish and the Hieratic Tradition of the Hebrew Kingdoms," *Tel Aviv* 18 (1991): 248–53.

25. Ibid., 251.

26. While it is difficult to tell the difference between hieratic and Demotic numerals, the accompanying text on some of these artifacts containing numerals is clearly hieratic, suggesting that the numerals should also be considered hieratic and not Demotic.

27. For studies on Egyptian script of this period, see Michel Malinine, *Choix des textes juridiques en hiératique anormal et en démotique* (vol. 1, Paris: Champion, 1953; vol. 2, Cairo, IFAO, 1983).

28. In addition to the above, see Shlomo Yeivin, "A Hieratic Ostracon from Tel Arad," *Israel Exploration Journal* 16/3 (1966): 153–59. This lends further support to the possibilities raised by John Gee in his "Two Notes on Egyptian Script," in *Pressing Forward,* 244–47.

29. Goldwasser, "An Egyptian Scribe," 251–52.

30. Ibid., 248.

31. See also John A. Tvedtnes and Stephen D. Ricks, "Semitic Texts Written in Egyptian Characters," in *Pressing Forward,* 237–43.

32. Aharoni, "Use of Hieratic Numerals," 19, further remarks that the evidence shows that the use of Egyptian for record keeping was practiced in both Israel in the north and Judah in the south. This is an important insight as it relates to the plates of brass. It has been suggested that these plates were an official document of the northern kingdom of Israel prior to making their way to Jerusalem. See Sidney B. Sperry, "Some Problems of Interest Relating to the Brass Plates," *Journal of Book of Mormon Studies* 4/1 (1995): 185–91; Robert L. Millet, *The Power of the Word: Saving Doctrines from the Book of Mormon* (Salt Lake City: Deseret Book, 1994), 20–46.

33. The majority of scholars believe that Nephi's small plates were written using Hebrew vocabulary, syntax, and grammar but some form of Egyptian script. For example, see John A. Tvedtnes, *The Most Correct Book: Insights from a Book of Mormon Scholar* (Salt Lake City: Cornerstone, 1999), 22–24. Other scholars posit that the

Egyptian language (script, grammar, and vocabulary) was fully employed by Nephi; for example, see Nibley, *Lehi in the Desert,* 16–17.

34. It is wholly possible to interpret "the language of my father" as a unique language system that Lehi used when writing—a sort of personal shorthand. If Lehi as a scribe used or developed a modified language system that employed both Jewish learning and Egyptian language, then it can be said that he was using a "language" to write his records, even though it is not a language that he spoke or typically wrote. This does not mean that the characters, grammar, syntax, or vocabulary that Lehi employed in his writing system were unique to him but simply that he used aspects of the Egyptian language in a unique way with the learning of the Jews. It is also important to note that Nephi states that he is making a record *in* the language of his father as opposed to making a record *of* the language of his father. In both Semitic and Egyptian languages, the word or character typically translated as "in" can also convey the idea of "with" or "by means of." Thus Nephi seems to be stating, at least in this verse, that he is making a record with or by means of his father's language or writing system and not that he is simply making a record of his father's words, as suggested elsewhere. See Nibley, *Lehi in the Desert,* 14.

35. S. Kent Brown, "Nephi's Use of Lehi's Record," in *Rediscovering the Book of Mormon,* ed. John L. Sorenson and Melvin J. Thorne (Salt Lake City: Deseret Book and FARMS, 1991), 3–4, quotes 1 Nephi 1:16–17 and assumes that Nephi abridged his father's record and then recorded the abridgment on the large plates and quoted portions of it on the small plates; however, there is nothing in the text to indicate that the large plates contained Lehi's record in an abridged form. Rather, it may be that the large plates contained a full copy. The phrases "I *make* an abridgement" and "after I have abridged the record of my father then will I . . ." in 1 Nephi 1:17 do not seem to convey any completion of an abridgment up to that time. Since the large plates were created and engraved with Lehi's record prior to the creation of the small plates (see 1 Nephi 19:1–3; cf. 2 Nephi 5:30–31), Nephi would have referred to these plates, as well as the

abridgment (if it were done at that time), as a completed action, describing it with the past tense. Conversely, note his use of the various past tenses when referring to the small plates, which obviously were made prior to his engraving upon them (1 Nephi 1:17: "upon plates which I *have made*"), and also to the large plates and Lehi's record, which was recorded on them (1 Nephi 19:1: "upon the plates which I *made* I *did engraven* the record of my father"). Since an abridgment of Lehi's record does not seem to have been made until after the small plates were made, it is more likely that Nephi simply copied his father's record in full on the large plates (1 Nephi 19:1) and then abridged his father's record for the purpose of recording the "most precious things" on the small plates. See also David E. Sloan, "The Book of Lehi and the Plates of Lehi," in *Pressing Forward,* 59–62.

36. Nibley assumes that Lehi's personal record was written in Egyptian but provides no basis for this assumption. He asserts that Lehi's "language" in 1 Nephi 1:2 refers to Lehi's words as arranged in a speech (as it is used in 1 Nephi 1:15) and not to an actual spoken or written system of communication. Nibley, *Lehi in the Desert,* 14. He also concludes that the phrase "which consists of the learning of the Jews and the language of the Egyptians" modifies Nephi's "record" as opposed to Lehi's "language." Ibid. These two points remove any positive connections between Egyptian language and Lehi's personal record. However, if Lehi's "language" is interpreted as a unique writing system that Lehi employed, as discussed in note 33 above, then it can be concluded that Lehi used Egyptian to some extent in his own personal writings.

37. Moroni referred to the script that he used, calling it "reformed Egyptian" (Mormon 9:32).

38. Assuming that Mormon simply inserted Nephi's small plates intact into the compilation of gold plates that Joseph Smith later received—a point that can be argued from Words of Mormon 1:6, in which Mormon states that he "shall take these [small] plates . . . and *put* them with the remainder of my record" (note that he does not mention "copying" or "abridging" these plates)—then the plates that Joseph Smith received may have been written using two different

scripts. One—containing regular, identifiable features of the Egyptian language contemporary to Lehi—would have been used by Nephi on the small plates. The rest of the record (Mormon and Moroni's abridgment of Nephi's large plates and the plates of Ether) would have been written using the altered script of Mormon's day. A variant reading of the Charles Anthon incident also supports this conclusion. According to Joseph Smith—History 1:64, Martin Harris went to see Anthon with at least two texts—a copy of a text with a translation and a copy of a text that had not yet been translated. For other possibilities, see John L. Sorenson, "The Book of Mormon as a Mesoamerican Record," in *Book of Mormon Authorship Revisited: The Evidence for Ancient Origins,* ed. Noel B. Reynolds (Provo, Utah: FARMS, 1997), 414–17, 453–55, 496–98. Harris informs us that Anthon declared the translation from the first copied selection better than any other translation he had seen "from the Egyptian." Though Anthon was likely not able to truly check the accuracy of translation, as he pretended (the ability to translate Egyptian was a brand-new scholarly ability in Europe that had not quite made its way to America at this time), it is very likely that he was familiar with the look of Egyptian script. His remark to Martin Harris clearly identifies the source of the translation as being "from the Egyptian"; however, when he was shown the second copied selection, Anthon declared the characters in it to be from a mixed variety of languages, suggesting that perhaps he was trying to ascertain their origins but could not be sure. So perhaps Joseph provided Martin Harris with a text from the small plates of Nephi, which was written using Egyptian script, and a text from Mormon's abridgment of the large plates, which would have been written in an "altered" script.

Chapter 10

EGYPTIAN SOCIETY DURING THE TWENTY-SIXTH DYNASTY

John Gee

Egypt in the late seventh and early sixth centuries B.C. is often considered the last high point of pharaonic civilization.[1] Called the Saite (pronounced say-ite) renaissance because the country's capital was at Sais in the Delta, the period of the Egyptian Twenty-sixth Dynasty is noted for its magnificent artwork and its attempt to capture the grandeur of the Egyptian Old and Middle Kingdoms.[2] The Saite period is most noted for its archaizing and canonizing tendencies. The artwork and inscriptions were archaizing because the scribes of that period tried to copy materials from more than a thousand years before, though in the artwork, the canon of proportions of the human figure was altered because the earlier canons had been lost,[3] and some of the vernacular language inevitably appears in the inscriptions.[4] Canonization appears when practices that earlier had been variable now became standardized. For example, before the Saite period, it seems not to have mattered which organ went in which canopic jar,[5] and the Book of the Dead had little regularity in either the selection of the chapters or their ordering,[6] but beginning in the Saite period, both were standardized. Though the Book of Mormon gives evidence of Israelite cultural contact with

Egypt (1 Nephi 1:2; Mosiah 1:2–4; Mormon 9:32–33), it provides no evidence whether Lehi or any of his family members had ever actually been to Egypt. What follows is a brief overview of Saite history and society that allows the reader to draw parallels with scriptures and determine their relevance.[7]

History[8]

The Saite period was generally one of peace and prosperity for Egypt.[9] After the Assyrian conquest of Egypt drove out the Twenty-fifth Dynasty invaders from Nubia, Psammetichus I (664–610 B.C.) was appointed by Assurbanipal to govern Egypt. When his Assyrian master left, however, Psammetichus (also known as Psamtik) allied himself with the Lydian king, Gyges, and revolted from the Assyrians. Psammetichus instituted a number of reforms, both economic and political, and lived to help bring about the downfall of the Assyrians. Under Psammetichus's son, Necho II (610–595 B.C.), Egypt's major foreign opponent was Babylon, and when Josiah, king of Judah, tried to interfere with Egyptian strategy, he was then an enemy as well. After killing Josiah in battle and removing Jehoahaz (who had been chosen by the inhabitants of Judah and who had reigned only three months), Necho II saw to it that the succeeding king of Judah, Eliakim (who was renamed Jehoiakim), was allied with him (2 Kings 23:29–35). Necho II's son, Psammetichus II (595–589 B.C.), was most noted for his invasion of Nubia in his third regnal year (593 B.C.) with the aid of Greek mercenaries who left the first dated Greek graffito in Egypt on the leg of a statue of Ramses II at Abu Simbel.[10] Apries (589–570 B.C.) also opposed the Chaldeans from Babylon and allied himself with Zedekiah of Judah. Unable to control his army, Apries lost his life when his mercenary troops turned on him and elected a successor, Amasis (570–526 B.C.), probably the same capable Egyptian general who had defeated the Nubians twenty-three years earlier and burned their king.[11] Amasis was able to repel the Babylonians and secure the Egyptian borders. His short-lived successor, Psammetichus III, died trying to hold off the Persian invasion under Cambyses in 525 B.C.[12]

Society

From several ancient sources, it is clear that the basis of Egyptian society was the family, and even Egyptian society on a larger scale imitated the institutions of the home.[13] The home began with a marriage between husband and wife that involved an oath[14] made in the presence of a religious official.[15] The marriage was seen as a partnership.[16] Ninety-one percent of the Egyptians lived in families of some sort,[17] and of those who lived alone, most were older and "were probably most often the sole survivors of their families, living alone because they had been unable to marry or their marriages had ended."[18] This was true of both urban and rural areas, with the major difference being that rural families were more likely to contain extended families living together.[19] The average household contained about five people.[20]

At the age of twelve, women began to marry.[21] Men came of age when they turned fourteen years old.[22] Both men and women were liable for taxes, though the tax rates for women were less than those for men.[23] By age twenty, sixty percent of women were married, and virtually all would have been married by the age of thirty.[24] Sixty percent of adult women from ages fifteen to fifty were married at any given time.[25] Men seemed to marry a little later, starting in the late teens,[26] following the proverb: "Take a wife when you are twenty years old so you can have children while you are still young."[27] About half the men were married by the age of twenty-five, and virtually all would have been married by their early fifties.[28] On the average, husbands were seven and a half years older than their wives.[29] "Long-term stable marriages

are ubiquitous,"[30] but broken homes, usually caused from divorce or death of a spouse, were also known.[31] In case of divorce,
the children usually remained with the father.[32] The death of a
spouse was a very real possibility since "if a man aged 25 married a woman aged 15, . . . [there was] better than one chance in
four that one or both spouses [would] die within ten years."[33]
Widowers remarried more often than widows, and divorced men
remarried more often than divorced women;[34] all told, men were
twice as likely as women to remarry after divorce or the death of a
spouse.[35] An Egyptian proverb reveals a cultural basis to this phenomenon: "Do not marry a woman whose husband is alive, lest
you make an enemy for yourself."[36] Marriage within the same village was encouraged: "Do not let your son take for himself a wife
of another village, lest he be taken from you."[37] Illegitimacy was
relatively low (about three to five percent of births),[38] but mortality rates for children were high. One-third of all females born
would not live through their first year; over half would not reach
the age of ten, and only a third would reach the ripe old age of
thirty.[39] Slightly under one-third of all males born would die in
the first year, about half would attain their coming of age at fourteen, and less than one-third would reach the age of forty.[40] The
mortality rate is also reflected in such popular names as *ḏd-ptḥ-
iw=f-ꜥnḫ* (pronounced by the Greeks Teephthaphonuchos) "Ptah
said 'He will live,'"[41] and *ḏd-bꜣst.t-iw=s-ꜥnḫ* "Bastet said 'She will
live.'"[42] Burials of the rich were characteristically in rock-hewn
chapels, above-ground tomb chapels, or deep-shaft tombs with
oversized anthropoid coffins,[43] and burials of the poor were simply in the ground, sometimes with a clay coffin and sometimes
with nothing.[44]

We also know something about the governmental hierarchy
at this time. The pharaoh ruled all of Egypt from Sais, but the
main government functioned from Memphis.[45] Under the pharaoh were the vizier, and then the harbor master, followed by

the chief of the Ma, a Lybian title.[46] Also under the vizier were the generals who commanded the army and navy, which also doubled as police forces.[47] Native Egyptians in previous centuries having been frozen out of the possibility of rising through the ranks of the army,[48] the Egyptian army was generally mercenary, mostly Greek.[49] The Egyptians also had a navy.[50]

The priestly hierarchy was dependent on the particular temple with which it was associated. The three major grades of priests were (1) the *it-nṯr,* or god's father; (2) the *ḥm-nṯr,* or prophet; and (3) the *wꜥb,* or priest.[51] The lower ranks of priests seem to have been lay workers in the temple, who were organized into four groups, called phyles. Each phyle served one month and then took three months off, during which time the priests had another job. To advance in the priestly ranks, one had to have the approval of the king or his representative,[52] as well as an initiation.[53] Associations of priests had an overseer (*mr-šn, lesonis*) who "functioned as a temple president"[54] and who worked through an agent (*rd*).[55]

Literacy

Education was a family affair. Knowledge of reading and writing was passed down from father to son.[56] Education in writing was done by copying models,[57] often of didactic content.[58] Additional education was provided by senior officials mentoring junior ones (usually immediate family members)[59] through correspondence and memoranda.[60] Temple libraries loaned out books and made copies of particular rolls for the benefit of others.[61]

Literacy rates for ancient Egypt are normally estimated to be below one percent of the population,[62] although more recent evidence indicates that over half the population may have been literate.[63] Egypt also exported some scribes, since they are attested as far away as Nimrud in the Assyrian empire.[64]

As literate members of society,[65] priests served as public notaries and experts on law as well. The legal codes were kept in temple archives.[66] Priests served as judges,[67] and judgment took place at the gate of the temple.[68] Priests who were in the courtyard of the temple served as witnesses to documents, often including their priestly titles in their signatures.[69]

A variety of scripts were employed in Egypt at Lehi's time: (1) Hieroglyphs were still employed in stone.[70] (2) Hieratic was still used on papyrus[71] but (3) was also used on stone, which is both harder to carve and to read.[72] (4) A cursive form of hieratic called either late Theban cursive or abnormal hieratic was used in the south part of the country but was being phased out at this time,[73] being replaced through "the reforms of Psammetichus"[74] by (5) Demotic,[75] a different variety of cursive hieratic that developed in the north at a time when the two ends of the country had been politically separate; since the Saites who reunited Egypt came from the north of the country, the business script of their area became the standard for the country. Additionally, (6) some religious manuscripts used a script called linear hieroglyphs that was midway between hieroglyphs and hieratic. (7) There is at least one example of a historical text of this time period consisting of a Semitic language being written in a Demotic script, as well as quotations from one of the psalms of the Hebrew Bible.[76] Egyptian scripts are noted for various playful writings,[77] as well as for plays on words.[78] Sometimes even the Egyptians themselves could not read their own writing correctly.[79]

A typical temple library from the Saite period would likely have the following types of books in it: king-lists, annals, chronicles, prophecies, books of nomes (books describing the sacred places and deities local to a given area), medical texts, wisdom literature, hemerologies (books of lucky and unlucky days), oneiromancies (books for the interpretation of dreams), astronomy texts, lexical texts, ritual rolls (containing festival procedures and temple liturgies), hymns, lists of religious utensils, calendars, construction manuals, painting and sculpture manuals, inventories, property list instructions, oracle texts, priestly correspondence, temple day books, and account texts.[80] The Saite period is not particularly noted for its literary productions, although some stories known from Ptolemaic and Roman copies are thought to have been composed in the Saite period.[81]

Economy

The Egyptian economy in ancient times was based primarily on the abundance of the Nile and on farming. Egypt also served as a conduit for goods from locations further south in Africa,[82] to the Aegean, Greece, Phoenicia, and the Levant (see Isaiah 45:14),[83] not to mention within Egypt itself.[84]

Although private farms probably existed, we know the most about the farms connected with temple land endowments. Kings, and for some reason especially Saite kings, donated parcels of land to temples to furnish endowments to fund the positions of priests and run the temple.[85] The temple or individual priests would lease the land for a year to tenant farmers who would return between one-fourth to one-half (usually one-third) of the crop for the opportunity to work the land and feed their own families.[86] The resulting economic endowments often provided an immense amount of wealth to those individuals who held the corresponding priestly offices or priesthoods.[87] These priesthoods were generally passed from father to son, with attendant quarreling among the sons over the rights to inherit the priesthood and its attendant endowment.[88] Priests tried to accrue several priesthoods because that increased their income.[89]

Information on prices during Saite times is harder to obtain. Rental agreements on land specify only the percentage of the harvest for rent and do not record the amount paid. Legal agreements only rarely give prices. We know that a marriage dowry was usually about two deben of silver and fifty khar (sacks) of emmer[90] and that the penalty for defaulting on the sale of a cow was five kite (half a deben).[91] Prices are available from other time periods, notably Ramesside (1295–1069 B.C.)[92] and Ptolemaic (332–32 B.C.),[93] but they show too much variation within individual time periods to provide much of a reliable guide to Saite times. Marketplaces are also poorly attested at this time. Although we know of marketplace activities from the Old Kingdom showing the sale of fruits and produce, no contemporary scenes are attested from the Saite period. The marketplaces themselves are largely unexcavated, either lying under the floodplain or being swallowed up by the eastward drift of the Nile river that washed away the previous settlements.[94]

Religion

Egyptian religion centered on the temple. The activity of the priests in the temples included both daily and periodic rituals. One of the daily rituals was the care of the cult statue.[95] Offerings were prepared before dawn, and all the offerings, as well as the priests, were purified with soap, water, and incense. All the offerings were brought to the offering table. After lighting a lamp, the priest entered the temple proper which, having no windows, was dark. Then the priest entered the holy of holies,[96] the seal was broken,[97] and the bolt was drawn back on the door of the shrine.[98] The statue was taken out,[99] washed,[100] censed,[101] clothed,[102] anointed,[103] presented with the offerings,[104] and returned to its shrine. Finally, the door was closed, bolted, and resealed, and the priest swept his footprints away as he left. Another of the daily rituals was the execration ritual. A wax figure of an enemy was spat upon, trampled under the left foot, pierced, bound, chopped in pieces, and cast into the fire.[105]

Periodic rituals included a large number of festivals[106] and the consultation of oracles. For example, on the eleventh month of the year, the statue of the goddess Hathor "left her temple at Dendera and sailed upstream to meet Horus at Edfu. . . . En route, the goddess went ashore at several places, including Thebes, to visit the resident gods and goddesses. Throngs of pilgrims streamed to one of these towns or to Edfu, and official deputies were sent from Elephantine, Hierakonpolis, and Kom Mer, and perhaps other places as well."[107] This festival of Reunion (*ḥb n sḫn*)[108] was depicted on both the temples of Edfu and Dendera.[109] During such festivals—the only time the image of the god left the holy of holies and became accessible to the common folk—oracles occurred.[110] Oracles were the most important source of revelatory guidance on such things as whether a child would live[111] since normally seeing the god was a privilege only of the prophets and not even of the priests.

Egypt and Judah

The kingdom of Judah during the late seventh century shared much in common with her superpower neighbor to the south in culture, religion (see Jeremiah 7:17–20; 44:15–28), and foreign policy, but many of these things were not in Judah's best interests, however much they may have been in Egypt's. Despite warnings to the contrary, Judah allied herself with Egypt and, lacking the other country's natural defenses and military assistance, succumbed to the Babylonian onslaught. The natural defense afforded by the extensive high deserts to either side of the Nile was just one of the many differences between Judah and Egypt. Other differences include Egypt's use of a continuous water source from the Nile and its annual rejuvenating inundation as opposed to Judah's lack of rainfall (less than 100 millimeters annually) that made farming a marginal endeavor relying on the blessing of sufficient rain in order to produce a crop to sustain the populace. Although many of the demographic features of Saite Egyptian society might be shared with preexilic Judahite society, care should be exercised in concluding that anything that was true of Saite Egypt was necessarily true of Judah.

Saite period Egyptian society bears some similarities to earlier and later periods of Egyptian history. Its distinguishing characteristics include being the highpoint of archaism, systemization, and canonization and the use of a greater number of native scripts. In many ways, Egypt continued "eating and drinking, marrying and giving in marriage," much as it always had, "as in the days of Noe" (Matthew 24:37–38). At the beginning of the Saite period in 664, the Egyptians and the Jews were allies with a similar point of view; at the end of the Saite period, however, the opposite was the case. In between these dates, Lehi and his party departed Jerusalem, avoiding Egypt, but carrying with them certain memories and cultural influences common to both spheres.

NOTES

1. This is perhaps unfair to the Greco-Roman period but is indicative of the bias of most Egyptologists; see Robert K. Ritner, "Implicit Models of Cross-Cultural Interaction: A Question of Noses, Soap, and Prejudice," in *Life in a Multi-Cultural Society: Egypt from Cambyses to Constantine and Beyond,* ed. Janet H. Johnson (Chicago: Oriental Institute, 1992), 284–86.

2. Jaromir Malek, *Egyptian Art* (London: Phaidon, 1999), 355, 363–74; Gay Robins, *The Art of Ancient Egypt* (Cambridge: Harvard University Press, 1997), 210–29; W. Stevenson Smith and William Kelly Simpson, *The Art and Architecture of Ancient Egypt,* 3rd ed. (New Haven: Yale University Press, 1998), 232, 239 (2nd ed., 395, 408).

3. Gay Robins, *Proportion and Style in Ancient Egyptian Art* (Austin: University of Texas Press, 1994), 160–81.

4. See Peter Der Manuelian, *Living in the Past: Studies in Archaism of the Egyptian Twenty-sixth Dynasty* (London: Kegan Paul International, 1994).

5. See Alan H. Gardiner, *Ancient Egyptian Onomastica* (Oxford: Oxford University Press, 1947), 2:245–49.

6. For which, see Günther Lapp, *The Papyrus of Nu* (London: British Museum, 1997), 36–49; Malcolm Mosher, "Theban and Memphite Book of the Dead Traditions in the Late Period," *Journal of the American Research Center in Egypt* 29 (1992): 143–72.

7. I have tried, insofar as possible, to cite sources from the Saite period. Sources from other periods have been used if there has been no compelling reason not to.

8. Summaries of historical information are readily available in, for example, Alan B. Lloyd, "The Late Period (664–332 B.C.)," in *The Oxford History of Ancient Egypt*, ed. Ian Shaw (Oxford: Oxford University Press, 2000), 369–83; Nicolas Grimal, *A History of Ancient Egypt*, trans. Ian Shaw (Oxford: Blackwell, 1992), 354–66.

9. For specific dates, events, and people of this period, see Robert F. Smith, "Book of Mormon Event Structure: The Ancient Near East," *Journal of Book of Mormon Studies* 5/2 (1996): 110–28.

10. The inscription reads: "When king Psammetichus came to Elephantine, this was written by those who went on by boat with Psammetichus, son of Theocles; they came beyond Kerkis, as far as the river allowed; Potasimto commanded the foreigners and Amasis, the Egyptians. Archon, son of Amoibichos and Pelekos, son of Eudamos wrote this." *Supplementum Epigraphicum Graecum* (Amsterdam: Gieben, 1923–), 16:863; P. W. Pestman, *The New Papyrological Primer*, 2nd ed. (Leiden: Brill, 1994), 7. For Egyptian records of the expedition, see Der Manuelian, *Living in the Past*, 333–71. The expedition brought back 4,200 prisoners, and the Nubian king was burned. Another view of this campaign appears in Herodotus, *Histories* 2.30.

11. See the sources in the previous note.

12. For which, see Eugene Cruz-Uribe, "The Invasion of Egypt by Cambyses," *Transeuphratène* 25 (2003): 9–60.

13. Eugene Cruz-Uribe, "A Model for the Political Structure of Ancient Egypt," in *For His Ka: Essays Offered in Memory of Klaus Baer,* ed. David P. Silverman (Chicago: Oriental Institute, 1994), 45–53; Dorothy J. Crawford, "The Good Official of Ptolemaic Egypt," in *Das ptolemäische Ägypten: Akten des internationalen Symposiums 27–29. September 1976 in Berlin* (Mainz am Rhein: von Zabern, 1978), 200.

14. John Gee, "Notes on Egyptian Marriage: P. BM 10416 Reconsidered," *Bulletin of the Egyptological Seminar* 15 (2001): 19–22, 25.

15. All the marriage documents that we have were written by scribes, who filled a religious office in Egypt; Sven P. Vleeming, "Some Notes on Demotic Scribal Training in the Ptolemaic Period," in *Proceedings of the 20th International Congress of Papyrologists,* ed. Adam Bülow-Jacobsen (Copenhagen: Carsten Niebuhr Institute of Near Eastern Studies, 1994), 185; Erich Lüddeckens, *Ägyptische Eheverträge* (Wiesbaden: Harrassowitz, 1960), 248. For the role of the scribe in the marriage documents, see ibid., 247–53.

16. Eugene Cruz-Uribe, *Saite and Persian Demotic Cattle Documents: A Study in Legal Forms and Principles in Ancient Egypt* (Chico, Calif.: Scholars, 1985), 92.

17. From Roger S. Bagnall and Bruce W. Frier, *The Demography of Roman Egypt* (Cambridge: Cambridge University Press, 1994), 60, table 3.1, and 67, table 3.2. While information in this source is taken from censuses of Roman Egypt, it is likely indicative of Saite Egypt as well, with one possible exception. In the Roman period, as single men aged twenty to twenty-four outnumbered single women in the age range of fifteen to nineteen by about forty percent, there was "an appreciable 'surplusage' of younger males unable to marry and begin a family of their own." Bagnall and Frier, *Demography of Roman Egypt,* 121. The change in the ratio of males to females is likely to have taken place in the Ptolemaic and Roman periods with the importing of large numbers of soldiers (males) serving in the army who were brought into Egypt—there they settled without bringing in any significant number of additional females.

18. Bagnall and Frier, *Demography of Roman Egypt,* 60.

19. Ibid., 67.

20. Ibid., 67–68. This, like many of the other statistics from the Roman period, may not be entirely accurate for the Saite period.

21. Ibid., 112. Suggestions that the early age for Egyptian women marrying was based on Aristotle's political theories seem unlikely; Sarah B. Pomeroy, "Family History in Ptolemaic Egypt," in *Proceedings of the 20th International Congress of Papyrologists*, 595, but see 597.

22. Raphael Taubenschlag, *The Law of Greco-Roman Egypt in the Light of the Papyri 332 B.C.–640 A.D.*, 2nd ed. (Warsaw: Państwowe Wydawnictwo Naukowe, 1955), 167, 178; Pestman, *New Papyrological Primer*, 151.

23. Pomeroy, "Family History in Ptolemaic Egypt," 594.

24. Bagnall and Frier, *Demography of Roman Egypt*, 113.

25. Ibid., 115.

26. Ibid., 116.

27. P. Onch. 11/7, in S. R. K. Glanville, *Catalogue of the Demotic Papyri in the British Museum, Volume II, The Instructions of ꜥOnchsheshonqy* (London: British Museum, 1955), pl. 11.

28. Bagnall and Frier, *Demography of Roman Egypt*, 116.

29. Ibid., 118–19.

30. Ibid., 122.

31. Ibid., 123–24; Wilhelm Spiegelberg, *Demotische Papyri* (Heidelberg: Winter, 1923), 1–19; P. W. Pestman, *Marriage and Matrimonial Property in Ancient Egypt* (Leiden: Brill, 1961), 71–75.

32. Bagnall and Frier, *Demography of Roman Egypt*, 124–25.

33. Ibid., 123.

34. Ibid., 126–27.

35. Ibid., 126.

36. P. Onch. 8/12, in Glanville, *Instructions of ꜥOnchsheshonqy*, pl. 8.

37. P. Onch. 15/15, in Glanville, *Instructions of ꜥOnchsheshonqy*, pl. 15.

38. Bagnall and Frier, *Demography of Roman Egypt*, 155.

39. Ibid., 77.

40. Ibid., 100.

41. Erich Lüddeckens, Heinz-Josef Thissen, W. Brunsch, Günter Vittmann, Karl-Th. Zauzich, *Demotisches Namenbuch* (Wiesbaden:

Reichert, 1980–2000), 17:1365; Jan Quaegebeur, "Considérations sur le nom propre égyptien Teëphthaphônukhos," *Orientalia Lovaniensia Periodica* 4 (1973): 85–100. For the problems with the pronunciation, see Jan Quaegebeur, "The Study of Egyptian Proper Names in Greek Transcription," *Onoma* 18 (1974): 403–20.

42. Lüddeckens et al., *Demotisches Namenbuch,* 17:1364. Other similar names occurring at the time are *ḏd-imn-iw=f-ꜥnḫ* "Amun said 'He will live'" (ibid., 1362), *ḏd-in-ḥr-iw=f-ꜥnḫ* "Onuris said 'He will live'" (ibid.), *ḏd-is.t-iw=f-ꜥnḫ* "Isis said 'He will live'" (ibid.), *ḏd-wp-wꜣ.wt-iw=f-ꜥnḫ* "Wepwawet said 'He will live'" (ibid., 1363), *ḏd-wsir-iw=f-ꜥnḫ* "Osiris said 'He will live'" (ibid.), *ḏd-bꜣst.t-iw=f-ꜥnḫ* "Bastet said 'He will live'" (ibid., 1364), *ḏd-mw.t-iw=f-ꜥnḫ* "Mut said 'He will live'" (ibid., 1365), *ḏd-mnṯ-iw=f-ꜥnḫ* (Gr. Kamentebonch) "Montu said 'He will live'" (ibid., 1366), *ḏd-ḥr-iw=f-ꜥnḫ* "Horus said 'He will live'" (ibid., 1370), *ḏd-ḥr-bn-iw=f-th.ṯ=f* "Horus said, 'He will not be harmed'" (ibid.), *ḏd-ḫnsw-iw=f-ꜥnḫ* (Gr. Chensephonuchos) "Khonsu said 'He will live'" (ibid., 1374–75), *ḏd-tꜣ-wry-iw=s-ꜥnḫ* "Thoeris said 'She will live'" (ibid., 1375), and *ḏd-ḏḥwty-iw=f-ꜥnḫ* "Thoth said 'He will live'" (ibid., 1376).

43. A. Jeffrey Spencer, *Death in Ancient Egypt* (Harmondsworth: Penguin, 1982), 106–8, 185–92, 230–31, 240–41.

44. Gustave Jéquier, *Deux pyramides du moyen empire* (Cairo: IFAO, 1933), 49; A. Niwinski, "Sarg NR-SpZt," in *Lexikon der Ägyptologie,* ed. Wolfgang Helck and Eberhard Otto (Wiesbaden: Harrassowitz, 1975–90), 5:456; Bezalel Porten and John Gee, "Aramaic Funerary Practices in Egypt," in *The World of the Aramaeans II,* ed. P. M. Michèle Daviau, John W. Wevers, and Michael Weigl (Sheffield: Sheffield Academic Press, 2001), 270–71.

45. Alan B. Lloyd, "The Late Period, 664–323 B.C.," in *Ancient Egypt: A Social History* (Cambridge: Cambridge University Press, 1983), 332.

46. Robert K. Ritner, "The End of the Libyan Anarchy in Egypt: P. Rylands IX. cols. 11–12," *Enchoria* 17 (1990): 105–8.

47. Lloyd, "Late Period, 664–323 B.C.," 333.

48. Lloyd, "Late Period, 664–323 B.C.," 309, notes that "most, if not all, of the warrior class originated from Libyan mercenaries who

had settled in Egypt during the New Kingdom or had subsequently infiltrated the country where they were probably permitted to take up residence on condition that they provided military service to the Crown when called upon to do so." See also Lloyd, "Late Period (664–332 B.C.)," 372.

49. Lloyd, "Late Period (664–332 B.C.)," 372–73; Lloyd, "Late Period, 664–323 B.C.," 284; Erik Hornung, *History of Ancient Egypt* (Ithaca, N.Y.: Cornell University Press, 1999), 139; Grimal, *History of Ancient Egypt,* 354–55.

50. See John C. Darnell, "The *Kbn.wt* Vessels of the Late Period," in *Life in a Multi-Cultural Society,* 67–89; Grimal, *History of Ancient Egypt,* 361–63.

51. Gardiner, *Ancient Egyptian Onomastica,* 1:30*–31*, 47*–55*; Lloyd, "Late Period, 664–323 B.C.," 306–7.

52. P. Berlin 13540, in George R. Hughes, "The So-called Pherendates Correspondence," in *Grammatika Demotika* (Würzburg: Zauzich, 1984), 78; Lloyd, "Late Period, 664–323 B.C.," 303.

53. See Jean-Marie Kruchten, *Les annales des prêtres de Karnak (XXI–XXIIIèmes dynasties) et autres textes contemporains relatifs a l'initiation des prêtres d'Amon* (Louvain: Departement Oriëntalistiek, 1989).

54. Lloyd, "Late Period, 664–323 B.C.," 306.

55. See Heinz-Josef Thissen, *Die demotischen Graffiti von Medinet Habu: Zeugnisse zu Tempel und Kult im ptolemäischen Ägypten* (Sommerhausen: Zauzich, 1989), 43–44; Jean-Marie Kruchten, *Le grand texte oraculaire de Djéhoutymose* (Brussels: Fondation Égyptologique Reine Élisabeth, 1986), 152–54.

56. Vleeming, "Demotic Scribal Training," 186. For the relevance of Vleeming's article to the Saite period, see ibid., 185: "The premise from which I start is that the scribal tradition among demotic notary scribes was a continuous one from the Saite into the Roman period."

57. Georges Posener, "Quatre tablettes scolaires de basse époque (Aménémopé et Hardjédef)," *Revue d'Égyptologie* 18 (1966): 45–65; Georges Posener, "Une nouvelle tablette d'Aménémopé," *Revue d'Egyptologie* 25 (1973): 251–52; Crawford, "Good Official of Ptolemaic Egypt," 197. For later examples, see Edda Bresciani, Sergio

Pernigotti, and Maria C. Betrò, *Ostraka demotici da Narmuti I* (Pisa, Italy: Giardini Editori e Stampatori, 1983).

58. Posener, "Quatre tablettes scolaires de basse époque," 45–65; Posener, "Une nouvelle tablette d'Aménémopé," 251–52; Crawford, "Good Official of Ptolemaic Egypt," 197.

59. Vleeming, "Demotic Scribal Training," 186.

60. Crawford, "Good Official of Ptolemaic Egypt," 196–97.

61. Karl-Th. Zauzich, "P. Carlsberg 21 und 22: Zwei Briefe von Bücherfreunden," in *A Miscellany of Demotic Texts and Studies,* The Carlsberg Papyri 3, ed. Paul J. Frandsen and Kim Ryholt (Copenhagen: Carsten Niebuhr Institute of Near Eastern Studies, 2000), 53–57.

62. John Baines and C. J. Eyre, "Four Notes on Literacy," *Göttinger Miszellen* 61 (1983): 65–96; John Baines, "Literacy and Ancient Egyptian Society," *Man* 18 (1983): 572–99.

63. H. S. Smith, "The Saqqara Papyri: Oracle Questions, Pleas and Letters," in *Acts of the Seventh International Conference of Demotic Studies* (Copenhagen: Carsten Niebuhr Institute of Near Eastern Studies, 2002), 373–75.

64. ND 10048, line 19, in J. V. Kinnier Wilson, *The Nimrud Wine Lists* (London: British School of Archaeology in Iraq, 1972), pl. 20.

65. Vleeming, "Demotic Scribal Training," 186; Smith, "Saqqara Papyri," 374.

66. Bernadette Menu, "Les juges égyptiens sous les dernières dynasties indigènes," in *Acta Demotica = Egitto e Vicino Oriente* 17 (1994): 218–19; Vleeming, "Demotic Scribal Training," 185–86.

67. Menu, "Les juges égyptiens sous les dernières dynasties indigènes," 218–19.

68. Jan Quaegebeur, "La justice à la porte des temples et le toponyme Premit," in *Individu, société et spiritualité dans l'Égypte pharaonique et copte. Mélanges égyptologiques offerts au Professeur Aristide Théodoridès,* ed. Christian Cannuyer and Jean-Marie Kruchten (Brussels: Association Montoise d'Égyptologie, 1993), 201–20; Menu, "Les juges égyptiens sous les dernières dynasties indigènes," 219–20.

69. Vleeming, "Demotic Scribal Training," 185–86.

70. Mark Depauw, *A Companion to Demotic Studies* (Brussels: Fondation Égyptologique Reine Élisabeth, 1997), 28–31.

71. Ursula Verhoeven, *Untersuchungen zur Späthieratischen Buchschrift* (Louvain: Peeters, 2001), 16–21; Depauw, *Companion to Demotic Studies,* 31–32.

72. John Gee, "Two Notes on Egyptian Script," *Journal of Book of Mormon Studies* 5/1 (1996): 164–65, 174–76.

73. Michel Malinine, *Choix des textes juridiques en hiératique anormal et en démotique* (vol. 1: Paris: Champion, 1953; vol. 2: Cairo, IFAO, 1983), 1:iv–xvi; Gee, "Two Notes on Egyptian Script," 162–64, 166–74. To the literature cited there, add Günter Vittmann, "Ein kursivhieratisches Wörterbuch," in *Aspects of Demotic Lexicography,* ed. Sven P. Vleeming (Louvain: Peeters, 1987), 149–51; Depauw, *Companion to Demotic Studies,* 22.

74. Ritner, "End of the Libyan Anarchy in Egypt," 102.

75. For an overview, see Depauw, *Companion to Demotic Studies,* 22–23.

76. For bibliography, see John Gee, "La Trahison des Clercs: On the Language and Translation of the Book of Mormon," *Review of Books on the Book of Mormon* 6/1 (1994): 96–97 n. 147, to which now add Depauw, *Companion to Demotic Studies,* 39–41, and for historical aspects, Grant Frame, *Babylonia 689–627 B.C.: A Political History* (Leiden: Nederlands Historisch-Archaeologisch Instituut te Istanbul, 1992), 19–20, 96 n. 157, 109, 131 n. 1, 137, 140, 154–55, 239 n. 150.

77. Michel Malinine, "Jeux d'écriture en démotique," *Revue d'Égyptologie* 19 (1967): 163–66; P. W. Pestman, "Jeux de déterminatifs en démotique," *Revue d'Égyptologie* 25 (1973): 21–34.

78. Janet H. Johnson and Robert K. Ritner, "Multiple Meaning and Ambiguity in the 'Demotic Chronicle,'" in *Studies in Egyptology Presented to Miriam Lichtheim,* ed. Sarah Israelit-Groll (Jerusalem: Magnes, 1990), 1:494–506.

79. P. W. Pestman, "A Comforting Thought for Demotists? Errors of Scribes in the 'Archive of the Theban Choachytes,'" in *Studie in onore di Edda Bresciani,* ed. S. F. Bondì, S. Pernigotti, F. Serra, and A. Vivian (Pisa: Giardini Editori e Stampatori, 1985), 413–22.

80. The list is slightly modified from Donald B. Redford, *Pharaonic King-Lists, Annals and Day-Books: A Contribution to the Study*

of the Egyptian Sense of History (Mississauga, Canada: Benben, 1986), 215–23.

81. Georges Posener, *Le Papyrus Vandier* (Cairo: IFAO, 1985); Ariel Shisha-Halevy, "Papyrus Vandier *Recto:* An Early Demotic Literary Text?" *Journal of the American Oriental Society* 109/3 (1989): 421–22; Kim Ryholt, *The Story of Petese Son of Petetum and Seventy Other Good and Bad Stories* (Copenhagen: Carsten Niebuhr Institute of Near Eastern Studies, 1999), 88–89; Kim Ryholt, "A New Version of the Introduction to the Teachings of 'Onch-Sheshonqy (P. Carlsber 304 + PSI inv. D 5 + P. CtYBR 4512 + P. Berlin P 30489)," in *A Miscellany of Demotic Texts,* 119–20.

82. Indicative (although it applies to the Ptolemaic period) is François Daumas, "Les textes géographiques du trésor D' du temple de Dendara," in *State and Temple Economy in the Ancient Near East* (Louvain: Departement Oriëntalistiek, 1979), 2:689–705.

83. Lloyd, "Late Period (664–332 B.C.)," 374–76; Grimal, *History of Ancient Egypt,* 355.

84. George R. Hughes, "Are There Two Demotic Writings of šw?" *Mitteilungen des Deutschen Archäologischen Instituts Abteilung Kairo* 14 (1956): 80–88.

85. The basic work is Dimitri Meeks, "Les donations aux temples dans l'Égypte du Ier millénaire avant J.-C.," in *State and Temple Economy in the Ancient Near East,* 2:605–87. Of the actual donation stele, by my count thirty-five percent come from the Saite period.

86. George R. Hughes, *Saite Demotic Land Leases* (Chicago: University of Chicago Press, 1952), 3–5, 74–75; for the rates, see the individual documents published in ibid., 9–10, 18, 28–29, 51–52, 68–69.

87. Such financial excesses may stand in part behind the Book of Mormon condemnation of "priestcraft." In addition, the association of the term *priesthood* with the idea of "priestly office" may account for the Book of Mormon usage that similarly connects the term *priesthood* with the office of the high priest. Thus, the text speaks of the fact that "Alma delivered up the judgment-seat to Nephihah, and confined himself wholly *to the high priesthood of the holy order of God,* to the testimony of the word, according to the spirit of revelation and prophecy" (Alma 4:20), while at the same time explaining: "Now

Alma did not grant unto [Nephihah] *the office of being high priest over the church,* but he retained the office of high priest unto himself; but he delivered the judgment-seat unto Nephihah" (Alma 4:17–18). Thus the phrase *the office of . . . high priest over the church* is equivalent here to the phrase *high priesthood of the holy order of God.*

88. To list the most famous examples: P. Rylands IX; see F. Ll. Griffith, *Catalogue of the Demotic Papyri in the John Rylands Library Manchester* (Manchester: Manchester University Press, 1909), 1:pl. XXIII–XLVII; 2: pls. 21–42; 3:60–112; Günter Vittmann, *Der demotische Papyrus Rylands 9,* 2 vols. (Wiesbaden: Harrassowitz, 1998). For the Battle over the Prebend of Amon, see Wilhelm Spiegelberg, *Der Sagenkreis des Königs Petubastis* (Leipzig: Hinrichs, 1910); Bruno H. Stricker, "De strijd om de praebende van Amon," *Oudheidkundige mededeelingen uit het Rijksmuseum van Oudheden te Leiden* 29 (1948): 71–83; Friedhelm Hoffmann, "Die Länge des P. Spiegelberg," in *Acta Demotica = Egitto e Vicino Oriente* 17 (1994): 145–55; Friedhelm Hoffmann, "Der Anfang des Papyrus Spiegelberg—Ein Versuch zur Wiederherstellung," in *Hundred-Gated Thebes,* ed. Sven P. Vleeming (Leiden: Brill, 1995), 43–60; Depauw, *Companion to Demotic Studies,* 88.

89. Janet H. Johnson, "The Role of the Egyptian Priesthood in Ptolemaic Egypt," in *Egyptological Studies in Honor of Richard A. Parker,* ed. Leonard H. Lesko (Hanover: University Press of New England, 1986), 78–79.

90. Lüddeckens, *Ägyptische Eheverträge,* 12–17.

91. Cruz-Uribe, *Saite and Persian Demotic Cattle Documents,* 17–18, 19–20, 26–27, 31; for half price for half a cow, see ibid., 15.

92. Jac J. Janssen, *Commodity Prices from the Ramesside Period* (Leiden: Brill, 1975).

93. Perhaps the best source is Lüddeckens, *Ägyptische Eheverträge,* 288–304.

94. Karl W. Butzer, *Early Hydraulic Civilization in Egypt: A Study in Cultural Ecology* (Chicago: University of Chicago Press, 1976), 34–36 and chart on p. 15.

95. This section relies extensively on six documents: (1) The ritual for the daily cult of Amon (Third Intermediate Period), P. Berlin 3055, in Adolf Erman, *Hieratische Papyrus aus den Königlichen Museen zu Berlin*

(Leipzig: Hinrichs, 1901), 1:Taf. I–XXXVII; (2) the ritual for the daily cult of Mut (Third Intermediate Period), P. Berlin 3014+3053, in Erman, *Hieratische Papyrus,* 1:Taf. 38–66; (3) the daily cult ritual of the temple of Horus at Edfu (Ptolemaic Period), in Maurice Alliot, *Le culte d'Horus à Edfou au temps des Ptolémées,* 2 vols. (Cairo: IFAO, 1949–54); (4) P. Bremner Rhind (Ptolemaic Period), in Raymond O. Faulkner, *The Papyrus Bremner-Rhind (British Museum No. 10188)* (Brussels: Fondation Égyptologique Reine Élisabeth, 1933); (5–6) the Abydos execration ritual in P. Louvre 3129 and P. BM 10252, both in Siegfried Schott, *Urkunden mythologischen Inhalts* (Leipzig: Hinrichs, 1929–1939), VI 4–59.

96. P. Berlin 3055 2/4–3/3, in Erman, *Hieratische Papyrus,* 1:Taf. II–III; P. Berlin 3014 1/5–2/6, in ibid., 1:Taf. 38–39.

97. P. Berlin 3055 3/3–8, in Erman, *Hieratische Papyrus,* 1:Taf. III; P. Berlin 3014 2/6–10, in ibid., 1:Taf. 39.

98. P. Berlin 3055 3/8–4/6, in Erman, *Hieratische Papyrus,* 1:Taf. III-IV; P. Berlin 3014 2/10–3/10, in ibid., 1:Taf. 39–40.

99. P. Berlin 3055 26/2–10, in Erman, *Hieratische Papyrus,* 1:Taf. XXVI; P. Berlin 3053 21/2–22/6, in ibid., 1:Taf. 54–55.

100. P. Berlin 3055 26/9–27/7, in Erman, *Hieratische Papyrus,* 1:Taf. XXVI–XXVII.

101. P. Berlin 3055 27/7–10, in Erman, *Hieratische Papyrus,* 1:Taf. XXVII.

102. P. Berlin 3055 27/10–30/8, in Erman, *Hieratische Papyrus,* 1:Taf. XXVII–XXX.

103. P. Berlin 3055 30/8–32/8, in Erman, *Hieratische Papyrus,* 1:Taf. XXX–XXXII.

104. P. Berlin 3055 37/6–8, in Erman, *Hieratische Papyrus,* 1:Taf. XXXVII.

105. *Schott, Urkunden mythologischen Inhalts,* VI 5, 37–53; P. Bremner Rhind 22/2–23/16, in Faulkner, *Papyrus Bremner-Rhind,* 42–47. For these actions in their larger ancient Egyptian context, see Erik Hornung, *Das Amduat: Die Schrift des verborgenen Raumes* (Wiesbaden: Harrassowitz, 1963), 1:12, 15, 21, 28, 105, 120, 124–26, 163–65, 188–90; 2:26, 29–30, 48, 132–34, 158–59, 180–82; Erik Hornung, *Altägyptische Höllenvorstellungen* (Berlin: Akademie, 1968), 17–29; Anthony Leahy,

"Death by Fire in Ancient Egypt," *Journal of the Economic and Social History of the Orient* 27 (1984): 199–206; Georges Posener, *Le Papyrus Vandier* (Cairo: IFAO, 1985), 32–33, 75–77; Anthony Leahy, "A Protective Measure at Abydos in the Thirteenth Dynasty," *Journal of Egyptian Archaeology* 75 (1989): 43, 45 n. n; Erik Hornung, *Die Unterweltsbücher der Ägypter* (Zürich: Artemis, 1989), 61, 65, 70–71, 73, 77, 82–83, 88, 102–3, 112, 116–17, 119–21, 127, 130–32, 134–35, 142–43, 149, 154–55, 159–60, 164–65, 168–69, 174–75, 179–81, 183–84, 186–87, 191–92, 206–7, 227, 254–55, 268, 270–73, 278–79, 282–83, 299–301, 314–15, 361, 404–5, 407, 454–55, 459, 477, 490–91; Harco Willems, "Crime, Cult and Capital Punishment (Moʿalla Inscription 8)," *Journal of Egyptian Archaeology* 76 (1990): 37, 40–41, 46–47, 49–51; Scott Morschauser, *Threat-Formulae in Ancient Egypt: A Study of the History, Structure and Use of Threats and Curses in Ancient Egypt* (Baltimore: Halgo, 1991), 81, 96–109, 115, 132–33, 135; Erik Hornung, *Idea into Image: Essays on Ancient Egyptian Thought,* trans. Elizabeth Bredeck (New York: Timken, 1992), 99–102; Robert K. Ritner, *The Mechanics of Ancient Egyptian Magical Practice* (Chicago: Oriental Institute, 1993), 82–88, 113–36, 142–44, 157–59, 163–71; Lorelei H. Corcoran, *Portrait Mummies from Roman Egypt (I–IV Centuries A.D.) with a Catalog of Portrait Mummies in Egyptian Museums* (Chicago: Oriental Institute, 1995), 53–55.

106. For the festivals, see Sherif el-Sabban, *Temple Festival Calendars of Ancient Egypt* (Liverpool: Liverpool University Press, 2000).

107. Ragnhild B. Finnestad, "Temples of the Ptolemaic and Roman Periods: Ancient Traditions in New Contexts," in *Temples of Ancient Egypt,* ed. Byron E. Shafer (Ithaca, N.Y.: Cornell University Press, 1997), 225–26.

108. On the festival in general, see Maurice Alliot, *Le culte d'Horus à Edfou au temps des Ptolémées* (Cairo: IFAO, 1954), 2:453–58; Hartwig Altenmüller, "Die Fahrt der Hathor nach Edfu und die »Heilige Hochzeit«," *Egyptian Religion: The Last Thousand Years: Studies Dedicated to the Memory of Jan Quaegebeur,* ed. Willy Clarysse, Antoon Schoors, and Harco Willems (Louvain: Peeters, 1998), 2:753–65.

109. Finnestad, "Temples of the Ptolemaic and Roman Periods," 221.

110. See Jaroslav Černý, "Le culte d'Amenophis Iᵉʳ chez les ouvriers

de la nécropole thébaine," *Bulletin de l'Institut français d'archéologie orientale* 27 (1927): 159–203, pls. I–IX; Jaroslav Černý, "Une expression désignant la réponse négative d'un oracle," *Bulletin de l'Institut français d'archéologie orientale* 30 (1931): 491–96; Jaroslav Černý, "Questions adressées aux oracles," *Bulletin de l'Institut français d'archéologie orientale* 35 (1935): 41–58, pls. I–IV; Jaroslav Černý, "Le tirage au sort," *Bulletin de l'Institut français d'archéologie orientale* 40 (1941): 135–41; Jaroslav Černý, "Nouvelle série de questions adressées aux oracles," *Bulletin de l'Institut français d'archéologie orientale* 41 (1942): 13–24, pls. I–III; Jaroslav Černý, "Egyptian Oracles," in Richard A. Parker, *A Saite Oracle Papyrus from Thebes* (Providence, R.I.: Brown University Press, 1962), 35–48; Jean-Marie Kruchten, "Un instrument politique original: la «belle fête de *pḥ-nṯr*» des rois-pretres de la XXIe dynastie," *Bulletin de la Société Française d'Égyptologie* 103 (June 1985): 6–26; John Baines, "Practical Religion and Piety," *Journal of Egyptian Archaeology* 73 (1987): 88–93; Alexandra von Lieven, "Divination in Ägypten," *Altorientalische Forschungen* 26 (1999): 77–126; Karl-Th. Zauzich, "Die demotischen Orakelfragen—eine Zwischenbilanz," in *A Miscellany of Demotic Texts,* 1–25; Ritner, *Mechanics of Ancient Egyptian Magical Practice,* 214–20; Kruchten, *Le grand texte oracular de Djéhoutymose,* 63–65, 328–32; Janet H. Johnson, "Louvre E 3229: A Demotic Magical Text," *Enchoria* 7 (1977): 90–91; Teresa R. Moore, "The Good God Amenhotep: The Deified King as a Focus of Popular Religion during the Egyptian New Kingdom" (Ph.D. diss., University of California, Berkeley, 1994), 346; A. G. McDowell, *Jurisdiction in the Workmen's Community of Deir el-Medîna* (Leiden: Nederlands Instituut voor het Nabije Oosten, 1990), 107–41, 255–59; Siegfried Morenz, *Egyptian Religion,* trans. Ann E. Keep (Ithaca, N.Y.: Cornell University Press, 1973), 107; John Gee, "The Earliest Example of the *pḥ-nṯr*?" *Göttinger Miszellen* 194 (2003): 25–27.

111. Parker, *A Saite Oracle Papyrus from Thebes,* 43; Zauzich, "Die demotischen Orakelfragen," 1–25.

Chapter 11

THE KINGDOM OF JUDAH: POLITICS, PROPHETS, AND SCRIBES IN THE LATE PREEXILIC PERIOD

Aaron P. Schade

The purpose of this chapter is to define the general condition of the kingdom of Judah on the eve of her destruction in 586 B.C.[1] This will be done within the context of the social and political climate of the day and in relation to foreign interactions between Judah and her neighbors. An examination of both internal and external affairs will more clearly portray the final days of the kingdom of Judah and afford a historical context for the prophetic messages and opposition that prophets such as Jeremiah and Lehi encountered there. Contemporaneous individuals, places, and events, coming from both biblical and extrabiblical sources, will be discussed, along with early accounts of Lehi's ministry in Jerusalem as contained in the Book of Mormon.

One may wonder how the Book of Mormon can contribute to this type of study. The historical content of the Book of Mormon actually becomes an invaluable tool in the study of preexilic Judah as it sheds light on typically enigmatic and problematic areas of understanding. Throughout this chapter various cultural and social aspects that are portrayed in the Book of Mormon will be viewed in conjunction with what is known in current scholarship in relation to the respective topics. These topics include political and social attitudes, persecutions of prophets, and scribal traditions in Judah in the late preexilic period.

Historical Overview

In order to more fully comprehend the social and political atmosphere in which prophets such as Lehi and Jeremiah ministered, it is necessary to define the effects of the reign of Josiah (one of the most righteous kings in Judah's history). This will thus act as a starting point for the discussion of the kingdom of Judah in the days preceding her destruction.

Josiah ruled as king of Judah from 640 to 609 B.C.[2] He came to the throne at the age of eight following the murder of his father Amon (2 Kings 21:23–24; 22:1), and the affairs of the kingdom were probably run by others in the royal court until he became of age. It should be remembered that the previous years had been difficult for Judah and that parts of the country had been razed by the Assyrians only decades earlier. Though it had not suffered the fate of the kingdom of Israel in 722 at the hands of the Assyrians, in 701 Sennacherib had invaded the region, destroying many of the kingdom's cities and deporting thousands along the way.[3] Though the effects of this invasion had been felt for decades, by the end of Josiah's reign some of these cities were rebuilt and reoccupied. By the beginning of his kingship, Assyria's grip on Judah had weakened, and Josiah witnessed a relative degree of freedom that afforded him and the kingdom of Judah some political and economic success in this period.[4]

The kingdom's political success was built on the back of a religious revitalization instigated by Josiah. Josiah's famous religious reform began around 628/627 B.C.[5] This was the approximate time of a Babylonian revolt against Assyria, under whom Judah was still a vassal.[6] This was also a time in which civil conflict brewing in Assyria would eventually lead to a civil war there a few years later. The eye of the Assyrians was thus cast away from Josiah and toward affairs closer to home. This Assyrian absence gave Josiah some room to maneuver.

One of the significant events that sparked Josiah's religious revival (according to the king's account) included the finding of "the book of the law" in the temple (2 Kings 22:8),[7] giving way to Josiah's reforms.[8] Josiah implemented a policy of centralized temple worship confined to the Jerusalem temple and overthrew idolatrous practices throughout the kingdom. A description of his reform states:

> Hezekiah's policy may have been consistent, and consistently less fanatical than Josiah's. No report indicates that Hezekiah centralized the rural priests in the capital (2 Chron. 31.15–20). Conversely, Josiah executed the priests of Samaria (2 Kgs 23.20), and herded those of Judah into the temple (2 Kgs 23.8–9). Josiah seems to have taken the business of centralization a good deal more seriously than Hezekiah. Unlike Hezekiah, he allegedly suppressed all worship outside the temple, not just sacrifice outside Jerusalem and the state forts.[9]

Josiah valiantly attempted to abolish idolatry during his religious reforms, but by the time of the ministries of Jeremiah and Lehi, idolatrous practices had again begun to permeate Judean mentality. The reliance on the God who had delivered their ancestors out of Egypt (which Josiah had attempted to reinstate among his people) had disappeared. The Lord described their obstinate nature and mentality with these words and warning:

> Stop before your feet are bare and your throat is parched. But you said, "No; I am desperate. I love foreign gods and I must go after them." As a thief is ashamed when he is found out, so the people of Israel feel ashamed, they, their kings,

their princes, their priests, and their prophets, who say to a block of wood, "You are our father" and cry "Mother" to a stone. On me they have turned their backs and averted their faces from me. Yet in their time of trouble they say, "Rise up and save us!" Where are the gods you made for yourselves? In your time of trouble let them arise and save you. For you, Judah, have as many gods as you have towns. (Jeremiah 2:25–28 Revised English Bible)

Thus many were turning to idolatry for religious consolation.[10] The Lord lamented, "I planted you as a choice red vine, a wholly pure strain, yet now you are turned into a vine that has reverted to its wild state!" (Jeremiah 2:21 REB).[11] Despite Josiah's efforts, the hearts of the people failed to turn toward the Lord, and idolatrous attitudes would again show their face in the kingdom of Judah.

Josiah was also able to expand the realms of his domain.[12] His expansionist efforts were fueled by his religious reforms: "Josiah was able to launch his annexation policy only after initiating his reform (around 628 B.C.; cf. II Chron. xxxiv 6), and he seems to have gained control solely over the former Assyrian province of *Samerina* and to have established a corridor reaching the coast in the northern Shephelah."[13] In the days of Manasseh the Assyrians had opened extensive markets into Judah, many of which may have been located on or near Judah's borders.[14] Now, with Assyrian influence diminishing within his borders, Josiah was able to take full advantage of the established commercial activity. He broke up lineage compounds within the kingdom and established state trade within his borders.

In the late seventh century, the clans having been demolished, nothing but the nominal sovereignty of Assyria impeded royal plans for expansion. A certain amount of retribalization had no doubt occurred. Against these, even while embracing the ideology of the lineages, Josiah directed his reforms—and against any cultural elements that reinforced symbolically the cohesion of the lineage against the state. The state's relations with the nuclear family and more specifically with its adult male heads were direct, now unmediated—precisely individual.[15]

Josiah pursued religious reforms, economic recovery, and expansion that would forever mark him as one of the greatest and most righteous kings Judah had ever seen. His untimely death brought serious consequences and retrogression in the kingdom of Judah.

Josiah was killed by Pharaoh Necho II at Meggido in 609 B.C. This occurred as the Egyptians were marching north to assist their ally (Assur-uballit II of Assyria) who was falling to the Babylonians and the Medes in western Mesopotamia.[16] "His sudden death and the hasty departure of Necho from the land left a vacuum, which was well used by the supporters of Jehoahaz, who crowned him in place of his father."[17] During the next four years (609–605 B.C.), Judah was under Egyptian domination until the Babylonian victory at Carchemish in 605. After Jehoahaz's[18] short three-month reign in 609, he was imprisoned in Necho's headquarters in Riblah. Egypt then set Jehoiakim,[19] brother of Jehoahaz, upon the throne, and he reigned for the next eleven years in Judah (609–598 B.C.; 2 Kings 23:33–34).

Jehoiakim becomes a pivotal figure in the study of the early history of the Book of Mormon, as he reigns almost to the beginning of Lehi's ministry in Jerusalem. During his reign the Babylonians defeated the Egyptians at Carchemish (605 B.C.), up until which time Judah had been an Egyptian vassal.[20] Nebuchadnezzar (605–562) succeeded his father (Nabopolassar) shortly thereafter (605), and in that year Nebuchadnezzar and the Babylonians invaded the area of Palestine. Judah then became a part of their domain sometime around 604/603.[21] Concerning this period, Abraham Malamat commented: "With the decline of the mighty empire of Assyria, toward the end of the seventh century BC and the striking victories of the young Nebuchadnezzar in the summer of 605 BC, a most reluctant Judah was swept into the ensuing confrontation that erupted between the Neo-Babylonian empire and Egypt," and "The small state of Judah, located at the particularly sensitive crossroads linking Asia and Africa, was influenced more than ever before by the international power system, now that the kingdom's actual existence was at stake."[22] This would eventually create severe tension among various factions (pro-Babylonian vs. pro-Egyptian) within the kingdom of Judah.

Following a stalemate battle between Egypt and Babylon (winter of 601/600), Jehoiakim decided to revolt against Babylon. This was probably encouraged by Egypt, who was nudging Judah to defect to the Egyptian camp.[23] For the next two years the Babylonians recuperated and eventually took action against Jehoiakim in 598 (at which time he died).[24]

Following the death of Jehoiakim, his son Jehoiachin reigned for just over three months before he was deposed by Nebuchadnezzar (597). Thousands[25] (including his officials) were exiled with him to Babylon.[26] This deportation would take a terrible toll on the kingdom, leaving doubts and uncertainty among the people and leadership.[27] It is probably not a historical coincidence that amid this time of deportation and chaos Lehi began his official ministry, as guidance and direction were desperately needed (1 Nephi 1:4).

"King Nebuchadnezzar of Babylon advanced against the city [Jerusalem], while his troops were besieging it. Thereupon King Jehoiachin of Judah surrendered to the king of Babylon, along with his mother, his courtiers, his commanders and his officers. . . . He [the king of Babylon] carried away all Jerusalem, and all the commanders, and all the warriors . . . and he carried away Jehoiachin to Babylon; and the king's mother, the king's wives, his officials, and the chief men of the land, he took into captivity from Jerusalem to Babylon" (2 Kings 24:11–12, 14–15).[28]

Jehoiachin's uncle, Zedekiah (also known as Mattaniah), was pronounced the new crown prince of Judah in 597 B.C.[29] He reigned until the kingdom fell to the Babylonians in 586. In 587 the final siege of Jerusalem began, and by this time most of the kingdom of Judah had fallen.[30] Though the Egyptians moved forward to aid Zedekiah, they retreated and "Judah found herself in a highly vulnerable position. From both a diplomatic and military point of view, Judah was left in the lurch and had to face the Babylonian might alone—'all her friends have dealt treacherously with her' (Lam. 1.2)."[31] The Babylonians eventually breached the walls of Jerusalem in 586 B.C. Zedekiah escaped, but the Babylonians captured him near Jericho and took him to Riblah where they killed his sons and princes in front of him, put out his eyes, and threw him in prison in Babylon until he died there (Jeremiah 52:10–11).[32]

Judah had faced many difficulties leading up to her destruction, and the final years of her existence have been summarized as follows:

> In the last two decades of its existence, the rapid pace of the international scene demanded of the Judean rulers exceedingly skilful manoeuvring in order to cope with kaleidoscopic situations. A series of no less than six critical turning points in Judah's foreign policy can be discerned, marking drastic shifts in loyalty from one major camp to the other—all within these twenty years. In other words, the political orientation of Judah alternated radically at an average frequency of every three years. In reacting to external temptations, the little kingdom eventually succumbed not only to international intrigues, but to her own risky policies as well.[33]

Such was the social and political climate of this late preexilic period in Judah's history, in which Lehi and Jeremiah commenced their ministries.

Many Prophets and Their Messages[34]

After examining the external, political circumstances leading up to the time of Judah's destruction, we can turn our attention to more internal affairs. This includes prophetic messages that swayed people's political orientation and allegiances. Prophets were viewed as predictors and were looked to for answers in political binds. In the case of Judah, the people had to wade through the rhetoric of sycophants and "false prophets" while trying to endure the usually unflattering words of the "true prophets." To the dismay of Judah, in the end, popularity lost out to reality and destruction ensued.

In the final days of Judah, many prophets prophesied among the people (1 Nephi 1:4 and Jeremiah 25:4). This was in accordance with the Lord's efforts to lead his people into the paths of repentance. Amos 3:7 states, "Surely the Lord God will do nothing, but he revealeth his secret unto his servants the prophets." In God's work, blessings and consequences of disobedience are always clearly defined, and ample opportunities to repent are always extended. A few of the prophets preaching such a message in Jerusalem at this time included Jeremiah and Lehi.

The life of the prophet Jeremiah began in the reign of Josiah and ended at a time postdating the Babylonian conquest of Jerusalem in 586 B.C. when he was taken against his will to Egypt (Jeremiah 43:5–7). The opening verses of the book bearing Jeremiah's name begin: "The words of Jeremiah the son of Hilkiah, of the priests that were in Anathoth in the land of Benjamin: To whom the word of the Lord came in the days of

Josiah the son of Amon king of Judah, in the thirteenth year of his reign" (Jeremiah 1:1–2). These verses describe Jeremiah's priestly heritage and situate him within the reign of Josiah. The Lord declared to Jeremiah, "Before I formed thee in the belly I knew thee; and before thou camest forth out of the womb I sanctified thee, and I ordained thee a prophet unto the nations" (Jeremiah 1:5).

Lehi (the first prophet of the Book of Mormon) resided in Jerusalem with his family sometime around 600 B.C. The first mention of a concrete historical reference is "in the commencement of the first year of the reign of Zedekiah, king of Judah . . . and in that same year there came many prophets, prophesying unto the people that they must repent, or the great city Jerusalem must be destroyed" (1 Nephi 1:4). This would have been just after King Jehoiachin was exiled to Babylon, Jerusalem had suffered its first capture at the hands of the Babylonians, and Zedekiah had been installed by Nebuchadnezzar, king of Babylon (i.e., 597 B.C.).[35] When Lehi was called as a prophet "he was carried away in a vision" (1 Nephi 1:8) and after seeing much he was given a book to read (1 Nephi 1:11).[36] Such miraculous revelations and events marked the beginning of these prophets' ministries, but in the heat of international politics, the people seemed to close their eyes to the messages of deliverance the Lord was trying to send them through his chosen servants.

The Lord does not work by surprises, and this leads us to what the prophets were teaching. The Lord spoke to Jeremiah:

> And thou shalt say unto them, Thus saith the Lord; If ye will not hearken to me, to walk in my law, which I have set before you, To hearken to the words of my servants the prophets, whom I sent unto you, both rising up early, and sending them, but ye have not hearkened; Then will I make

this house like Shiloh, and will make this city a curse to all the nations of the earth. (Jeremiah 26:4–6)

Lehi's calling from the Lord to minister among the people came in the form of a revelation[37] in which he was commanded to read a book; the following is part of what he read: "Wo, wo, unto Jerusalem, for I have seen thine abominations! Yea, and many things did my father read concerning Jerusalem—that it should be destroyed, and the inhabitants thereof; many should perish by the sword, and many should be carried away captive into Babylon" (1 Nephi 1:13). Lehi then proceeded to prophesy among the people (1 Nephi 1:18). The message of the previously cited prophets was simple: repent and follow the prophets or be destroyed.

Beyond repentance, Jeremiah was also teaching that Judah was to submit to the Babylonians because they were not going to defeat them (Jeremiah 34:1–9; 36:29). "Jeremiah, who regarded Nebuchadnezzar as 'God's chosen rod' (of chastisement) realized that the opportune moment had passed: now only voluntary submission to the Babylonians could save Judah; it was the choice between 'the way of life and the way of death' (Jer. 21.8–9)."[38] To make things more difficult for the people, at this time when "true prophets" of God were receiving divine direction to warn the people of Judah to repent, as well as to surrender themselves peacefully over to the Babylonians, others were preaching the safety and impregnability of Judah. One such "false prophet" who was attempting to dissuade the people from submission was Hananiah.[39] When the prophet Jeremiah had placed a wooden yoke around his neck (symbolic of captivity), Hananiah took it and broke it in front of the people as he "falsely" prophesied safety from the assaults of the Babylonians. Jeremiah was then instructed of the Lord to "Go and tell Hananiah, saying, Thus saith the Lord; Thou hast broken the yokes of wood; but thou shalt make for them yokes of iron. . . . Then said the prophet Jeremiah unto Hananiah the prophet, Hear now, Hananiah; The Lord hath not sent thee; but thou makest this people to trust in a lie" (Jeremiah 28:13, 15). Encouraged by such false prophets and prophecies, many in Jerusalem seemed to believe (because of the miraculous delivery the city had experienced when faced with the Assyrian onslaught of 701 B.C. [2 Kings 18–19; Isaiah 36–37] and probably to some degree when Judah was spared in 722 when Israel was conquered) that Jerusalem truly was indestructible and still under the protection of the Lord. In order to counter such false deliveries Jeremiah desperately and compassionately pled with his people:

> Why will ye die, thou and thy people, by the sword, by the famine, and by the pestilence, as the Lord hath spoken against the nation that will not serve the king of Babylon? Therefore hearken not unto the words of the prophets that speak unto you saying, Ye shall not serve the king of Babylon: for they prophesy a lie unto you. For I have not sent them, saith the Lord, yet they prophesy a lie in my name; that I might drive you out, and that ye might perish, ye, and the prophets that prophesy unto you. (Jeremiah 27:13–15)[40]

However, Jeremiah's preaching was to no avail. "Like Isaiah in his day, or Ezekiel his younger contemporary, Jeremiah strove to smash the popular image of Egypt, which had led to a false sense of security among the Judean leadership and spread a spurious hope of military support (cf., e.g., Egypt as 'a staff of reed to the house of Israel . . . and when they leaned upon thee thou didst break,' in Ezek. xxix 7–8)."[41] "Instead of turning to powerful Babylon, the Judeans toyed with false hopes created by the misleading image of Egypt that led to Judah's hazardous gamble on her."[42] It was in this climate of overconfidence and misconstrued righteousness, with the expectation to qualify for the deliverance of the Lord, that prophets such as Jeremiah and Lehi ministered. It appears that even Lehi—and possibly Jeremiah (Jeremiah 11:21)—encountered such attitudes within their own families. The attitude of Laman and Lemuel (two of Lehi's sons) is portrayed:

> Now this he spake because of the stiffneckedness of Laman and Lemuel; for behold they did murmur in many things against their father, because he was a visionary man, and had led them out of the land of Jerusalem, to leave the land of their inheritance, and their gold, and their silver, and their precious things, to perish in the wilderness. And this they said he had done because of the foolish imaginations of his heart. And thus Laman and Lemuel, being the eldest, did murmur against their father. And they did murmur because they knew not the dealings of that God who had created them. Neither did they believe that Jerusalem, that great city, could be destroyed according to the words of the prophets. And they were like unto the Jews who were at Jerusalem, who sought to take away the life of my father. (1 Nephi 2:11–13; see also 1 Nephi 17:43–45)

Such was the mentality and attitude of the people in Jerusalem on the eve of its destruction.

Opposition to These Prophets

As alluded to earlier, the prophets' messages tended to create factions among the people. The messages of the prophets were generally not cordially received. Many prophets do not win popularity contests, nor is the word of God that they preach dependent on it. Thus these prophets encountered stiff opposition in all its forms in the course of their declarations. The following describes the specific difficulties that Lehi's prophetic pronouncements brought upon him, as recorded by his son Nephi:

Therefore, I would that ye should know, that after the Lord had shown so many marvelous things unto my father, Lehi, yea, concerning the destruction of Jerusalem, behold he went forth among the people, and began to prophesy and to declare unto them concerning the things which he had both seen and heard. And it came to pass that the Jews did mock him because of the things which he testified of them; for he truly testified of their wickedness and their abominations; and he testified that the things which he saw and heard, and also the things which he read in the book, manifested plainly of the coming of a Messiah, and also the redemption of the world. And when the Jews heard these things they were angry with him; yea, even as with the prophets of old, whom they had cast out, and stoned, and slain; and they also sought his life, that they might take it away. (1 Nephi 1:18–20)[43]

Lehi's life was not the only one in jeopardy. Probably early in the reign of Jehoiakim (609–598),[44] an important event occurred involving one Urijah (Jeremiah 26:20–23). Urijah (ca. 609) had prophesied against Jerusalem (just as Jeremiah had done and Lehi would do), thus infuriating the king and his officials. Fearing for his life, Urijah fled to Egypt. He was pursued by a posse of the king headed by Elnatan[45] and was captured and returned to Jerusalem, where he was executed and disrespectfully cast into a grave. A similar pursuit is related in Lachish ostracon 3.13–18.[46] A commander named Konyahu, son of Elnatan, had gone down into Egypt; this letter seems to be describing the need for more men for an organized posse or a deputized search team.[47] As discussed by Dana Pike, chronological considerations make it impossible to render the events in Lachish and the ones in Jeremiah 26 as one and the same.[48] However, it is highly plausible that these two texts are referring to episodes of a similar nature. The individuals mentioned in Lachish ostracon 3 could very well have been pursuing a prophet who was prophesying against the city and had fled to Egypt. The conclusion of Lachish ostracon 3 lends more credence to the possibility of contextual similarities with the conclusion of Jeremiah 26. Lachish ostracon 3.19–21 describes a letter received from the prophet, which began "Beware." This letter was to be sent to Jerusalem reporting that Konyahu and others (whom he commissioned at Lachish) had gone to Egypt, possibly seeking the capture or extradition of the prophet (or another of "similar persuasion"),[49] who was weakening the hands of the people through his proclamations and warnings to "Beware" of destruction.[50] The historical alignment of the events comprising the end of Jeremiah 26 (Urijah) and the Lachish record is also complementary. Judah under Jehoiakim had been an Egyptian vassal. This explains why his posse was free to enter Egyptian borders in pursuit of Urijah.[51] The later Lachish event also finds historical confirmation in that Zedekiah gained the support of Apries (589–570 B.C.) in his break with Nebuchadnezzar.[52] Judah again had Egyptian support and would have had clearance to pursue a wanted individual or fugitive into Egypt. These two disparate episodes suggest a zero-tolerance attitude by the royal officials toward the perceived pro-Babylonian messages of the prophets.[53]

As just alluded to, Jeremiah faced intense opposition within Jerusalem. His words elicited such a response from the people: "Now it came to pass, when Jeremiah had made an end of speaking all that the Lord had commanded him to speak unto all the people, that the priests and the prophets and all the people took him, saying, Thou shalt surely die" (Jeremiah 26:8). Jeremiah was also imprisoned on multiple occasions. One of these incarcerations, as well as the recalcitrant nature of the people, is described by Nephi: "For behold, the Spirit of the Lord ceaseth soon to strive with them; for behold, they have rejected the prophets, and Jeremiah have they cast into prison. And they have sought to take away the life of my father, insomuch that they have driven him out of the land" (1 Nephi 7:14).

On the eve of the Babylonian destruction, Jerusalem was an intense hotbed of prophetic persecution. Concerning the disregard for prophetic utterances in relation to submitting to Babylon and not trusting Egypt we read:

> The Judean leadership failed to grasp the shift in balance of power, and continued to cling to the dubious image of a strong Egypt which would rush to the aid of its allies in time of need. . . .
>
> In this light, we can appreciate all the more the deep foresight and realistic historical perspective of the prophetic circles in Judah, who had a genuine understanding of the international scene at that time. The great prophets of the day, Jeremiah and Ezekiel (or Uriah, the son of Shemaiah from Kiriath-jearim, who prophesied "in words like those of Jeremiah," Jer. 26.20) were entirely free of the "establishment" line of thought, unlike the false prophets, and were thus able to grasp the situation in more realistic terms. Therefore, theirs was a sober and unbiased appreciation of the situation, for the long-range benefit of the nation, as opposed to the immediate, feasible interests so typical of the establishment and its supporters, the false prophets, such as Hananiah. . . .
>
> In modern terms, these prophets served—*with due recognition of their far more profound motives*—as analysts and commentators, quite independent of official policy and general consensus. In doing so, they played an active role in the acute issue of foreign political orientation, which had gradually intensified the polarity between the pro-Egyptian and pro-Babylonian factions. This polarity crossed lines—from the royal court onward, through state officials and priestly circles down to the masses. Likewise,

political orientation and ideology proved the main bone of contention between the true and false prophets.[54]

The factions created between pro-Babylonian and pro-Egyptian attitudes (which were exacerbated between the teachings of true and false prophets) proved fatal to the kingdom. Such divisions are discerned in Jeremiah 26 when, after no small debate among the people and leaders, it was decided to spare Jeremiah's life. Later in the same chapter Urijah was killed for preaching in the same fashion. These factions stemmed from a desire to combat Assyria at the side of Egypt rather than to submit to the Babylonians, as counseled by the true prophets of the Lord (false prophets such as Hananiah preached an anti-Babylonian message—the people were not to submit, and victory would follow). Egypt was a logical choice for an ally because Jewish colonies had been established there for years.[55] These ties made it easier to side with a power that was weaker and less threatening than the Babylonians who were at the doorstep. Such conflicting attitudes between the people and the local leadership throughout the final days of Judah's existence would bring Judah into a compromising situation from which she would not be able to escape. It was in this political and social climate that prophets such as Jeremiah and Lehi were attempting to persuade people to hearken to the Lord and be spared.

In the midst of such a volatile situation and impending destruction, the Lord commanded Lehi to take his family and leave Jerusalem. This probably came as no surprise to Lehi (especially when the Lord explained the purpose for the departure). It is possible that Lehi had witnessed the events that had transpired in the life of Urijah.[56] He was well aware of the danger and threats on his life, but so was the Lord. God had a specific agenda for Lehi and his family, one that required preserving his life.

> For behold, it came to pass that the Lord spake unto my father, yea, even in a dream, and said unto him: Blessed art thou Lehi, because of the things which thou hast done; and because thou hast been faithful and declared unto this people the things which I commanded thee, behold, they seek to take away thy life. And it came to pass that the Lord commanded my father, even in a dream, that he should take his family and depart into the wilderness. And it came to pass that he was obedient unto the word of the Lord, wherefore he did as the Lord commanded him. (1 Nephi 2:1–3; see 1 Nephi 3:17–18)

Lehi was obedient to the Lord in taking his family out of Jerusalem, thus preserving their lives. He took them out of the hotbed of prophetic persecutions and into the Judean wilderness. Significantly, the Lord inspired Lehi and his family to flee southward, in a path that would have led them through modern-day Saudi Arabia and into Oman.[57] The first place that a posse in search of them would have looked was in Egypt, where Semites had been fleeing in times of famine and danger for over thirteen hundred years and where Jewish settlements were well established in this period of time.

The Kingdom of Judah's Connections with Egyptian Scribal Traditions

Judeo-Egyptian interconnections required a formal means of communication. This would have included scribal activity between the two states. While the role of the Egyptian scribal tradition in late preexilic Judah remains unclear, the Egyptian scribal community in Canaan is rather well established until the late Nineteenth or early Twentieth Dynasty (ca. early twelfth century B.C.). Hieratic ostraca from this early time "provide clear evidence" of Egyptian scribal activities in city-states such as Tell el-Far'ah, Tel Sera', and Lachish.[58] After that time there is a lacuna in the Egyptian scribal traditions in Canaan. However, indications of a continuation of such a tradition into the late preexilic period in Judah is indicated by the existence of hieratic numerals and signs in the Hebrew epigraphic material, and their presence raises many questions as to the scribal traditions and practices of the times. With no definitive answer as to why this seemingly unusual practice occurs in this period and region (in which a large void lies in the understanding of the Egyptian scribal tradition in Judah), Orly Goldwasser states a possible hypothesis:

> It might be suggested, as a working hypothesis, that this peculiar and isolated variation of hieratic developed locally from the Egyptian scribal tradition in Canaan itself. . . . We would like to suggest that these Egyptian or Egyptian-trained scribes, cut off from their homeland, well acquainted with Egyptian decorum as well as the Canaanite language, educated local scribes, who in their turn passed on their knowledge to their successors. After three or four centuries of such evolution, most of the Egyptian terms were assimilated into the local language, and the numerals remained the only definitive testimony for the Egyptian archetype.[59]

The Book of Mormon confirms that the Egyptian scribal tradition in Judah extended into the late seventh century. Archaeological evidence suggests that an extensive Egyptian community resided in Lachish up until the conquest of Sennacherib (ca. 701 B.C.). Human skulls (695 to be exact) from a mass grave in Lachish were examined, and "curiously, the crania indicate a close racial resemblance to the population of Egypt at that time." Also, "They show, further, that the population of Lachish was probably derived principally from Upper Egypt. . . . If so, this indeed is a conclusion of far-reaching implications."[60] This evidence not only establishes an Egyptian presence, but would also suggest an Egyptian scribal tradition within Judah's borders almost into the sixth century. Other evidence also suggests an Egyptian presence in Judah's borders at this time. Na'aman suggests that the site of Meṣad Ḥashavyahu was built by Egyptians (based among other things on the merits of its architecture and layout, which are at variance with others in the region) and opines that the context of the famous ostracon found on that site (generally dated to the reign of Josiah) should be viewed in light of an Egyptian backdrop.[61] Na'aman further suggests that the hieratic writing of numerals found at Arad suggests an Egyptian domination over that site. He also believes that the building of the site of Kadesh-barnea (where hieratic numerals have also turned up) was originally initiated by the Assyrians and controlled by the Egyptians in its last phase (prior to its destruction in ca. 604):

> In my opinion, Egyptian control of the site during the last phase of the fortress' existence is hinted at by the presence of ostraca in hieratic writing, bearing various figures (from 1 to 10,000) and dimension units commonly in use in the area at the time. These may have been used by pupils of Semitic origin, for practice in the Egyptian method of record-keeping then in force; this would explain the few Semitic words appearing on the ostraca.[62]

Though Na'aman may have overstated Egypt's formal presence in the region, their interest and affairs are clearly felt in the archaeological and epigraphic evidence at hand within Judah's borders almost into the sixth century (the approximate time of Lehi's ministry). The employment of Egyptian in the Book of Mormon in this time period is consistent with other findings of modern scholarship, and the Book of Mormon begins to confirm such evidence.[63]

Though conclusive evidence cannot be offered that such an Egyptian scribal tradition in the late preexilic period in Judah existed, the presence of the Egyptian language within Judah's borders at this time is in harmony with what is suggested by other evidence. This makes sense, as there would have been bilingual individuals trained in both Hebrew and Egyptian, just as individuals had been bilingual in the major empires of the ancient Near East. That is not to say bilingualism functioned on a large scale (though it could have), but that it did operate among trained scribes is witnessed in the Egyptian remnants and vestiges extant in the Hebrew epigraphic material, as well as in the Book of Mormon.[64]

Concerning the language (which is discussed elsewhere in this volume) and writing techniques of the Book of Mormon, Daniel Peterson has concluded that "most who have studied the subject conclude that this signifies writing the Hebrew language in modified Egyptian characters."[65] It would seem that space limitations would have caused the writers of the plates to move away from an alphabetically based system (and hence from one script to another) to a system logographic in nature. This would have created more writing space and would have necessitated bilingual abilities on the part of these authors (both of Hebrew and Egyptian).[66] That the Nephite authors were capable of dealing with language acquisition and linguistic shifts is witnessed in Mormon 9:32–33, and there are numerous ancient Near Eastern examples of alterations in linguistic dialects and families.[67] In the case of script-switching between two alphabetic languages or dialects, this is witnessed between Phoenician and Aramaic (Arslan Tash).[68]

In relation to the orthography of this reformed Egyptian, John Gee has discussed an "abnormal hieratic" in use in southern Egypt in the Twenty-fifth and Twenty-sixth Dynasties (727–

548 B.C.)[69] that might be more plausible than the suggestion of Demotic.[70] Paleography is a difficult issue since the Nephites had altered the language and since the relevant scripts originated from a single source (Middle Egyptian), wherein at some point in time overlapping similarities occurred in the appearance of random characters. This results in the script resembling both Egyptian logograms and Hebrew characters. This is indeed an issue to be dealt with when examining the few copies of the original characters in our possession today. Other questions come into play: Did the Nephites revert back to a paleo-Hebrew script in writing good Hebrew names (as is witnessed elsewhere in the ancient Near East), or did they use a makeshift system based on Egyptian (or some combination of both)?[71] Was *matres lectiones* abandoned or preserved? Do the characters represent earlier or later developments in the language (or some combination of both)?[72] Whatever the case may be, the Book of Mormon claims that Lehi and his family were familiar with a dialect of the Egyptian language.

Other Scribal Activity: Laban's Records and Writing on Metal Plates

Laban possessed the records that Nephi obtained. It is difficult to ascertain exactly who Laban was, as the sources say little about him. What we do know, however, answers some vital questions as to why he possessed the records. Laban "was a descendant of Joseph, wherefore he and his fathers had kept the records" (1 Nephi 5:16). The "wherefore" in this statement appears to be an explanation of an almost implicit, matter-of-fact concept. Biblical and extrabiblical findings also help clarify such a scribal axiom:

> It is of interest to note that the above biblical passages [Joshua 18:6, 9; Judges 5:14; 8:14] mention members of the

tribes of Joseph (Joshua the Ephraimite, the leaders of Machir
and Gideon of Menasseh). Our abecedary found in the foot-
hills of Ephraim, some 40 kms. due west of Shiloh—in addition to the palaeographically similar Raddana handle, found
at the southern border of Ephraim—indicates a wide distribution and use of writing during the period of the Judges, at least
among the tribes of Joseph.[73]

In an early period of Israel's history, a tradition of writing began within the tribe of Joseph. It is thus not surprising (even
centuries later) to find Laban, a descendant of Joseph, in possession of written records—especially if the skill of writing with
all its conventions was diligently preserved within the lineage,
as was the case with Nephi (1 Nephi 1:1–2) and King Benjamin
(Mosiah 1:2–4) centuries later. Thus Laban's plates found their
continuance in the lineage of Joseph through Lehi and his family, and eventually Joseph Smith—another descendant of Joseph
(2 Nephi 3:11–12)—translated the Nephite writings.

Scribal activity had increased in the late preexilic period
in Judah. The time of Hezekiah has been defined as a critical
period for literary activity in ancient Israel:

> At this time, there was a surge in the population of Jerusalem,
> partially due to disenfranchised people coming into Jerusalem
> from the northern kingdom. In addition, Hezekiah appar-
> ently encouraged the collection and editing of various literary
> materials (cf. Prov 25:1); this literary activity was undoubtedly
> prompted by the destruction of the northern kingdom, and
> perhaps also the crisis surrounding Sennacherib's invasion.[74]

Laban's possession of a scriptural record is thus not surprising.
The content of the brass plates became a significant contribution to the spiritual growth of the descendants of Lehi and
his family (as well as of the many lives the Nephite record has
influenced in our day).[75] For the Lehites, having that record

made the difference between spiritual survival and spiritual death (1 Nephi 4:15–16).

The imperative nature of conveying and preserving God's word in Lehi's world is vividly demonstrated in an incident reported in the book of Jeremiah:

> In the fourth year of Jehoiakim son of Josiah, king of Judah, this word came to Jeremiah from the Lord: Take a scroll and write on it all the words I have spoken to you about Jerusalem, Judah, and all the nations, from the day that I first spoke to you during the reign of Josiah down to the present day. Perhaps the house of Judah will be warned of all the disaster I am planning to inflict on them, and everyone will abandon his evil conduct; then I shall forgive their wrongdoing and their sin. Jeremiah summoned Baruch son of Neriah, and Baruch wrote on the scroll at Jeremiah's dictation everything the Lord had said to him. (Jeremiah 36:1–4 REB)

When the unpleasant content of these writings was brought to the attention of the king and all his officials, they were promptly destroyed. Jeremiah then redictated the content of the scroll "and much else was added to the same effect" (Jeremiah 36:32 REB). Perhaps because of the ease with which materials such as parchment or ostraca were destroyed, records began to be kept on metallic plates or scrolls whenever this was a viable option. Such metal documents would have been more difficult to destroy and more likely to endure the elements of nature and time. They also reflected the value and preciousness of the content of the text.[76] Several of the metallic ancient Near Eastern writings in existence today appear in religious or covenantal contexts or contain the mandates of the king.

Indeed, by the time of Lehi's ministry in Jerusalem, the inscribing of metal objects was already an established practice in the ancient Near East. The employment of metallic mediums for inscriptions had been in use for centuries. From ca. 1900 B.C. four separate pseudohieroglyphic syllabic texts (Proto-Byblian) were inscribed on bronze copper spatulate tablets.[77] This antedates a purely consonantal alphabet in the ancient Near East. In the past century and a half, inscriptions in various languages have been discovered on metallic objects throughout the region. In the period of the early Hittite "Great Kings" there is the "Treaty of Tudhaliya" from Hattusha, which was written on a bronze tablet. A cuneiform inscription on a bronze blade dating to the fourteenth-thirteenth century was excavated in the Tabor valley.[78] There are over fifty bronze inscribed Phoenician arrowheads that date from as early as the early eleventh to the tenth century B.C., as well as eleventh-tenth–century cuneiform bronze arrowheads from Luristan and western Iran—very similar to the Phoenician arrowheads.[79] Furthermore, numerous inscriptions on bronze tablets have been found in South Arabia and Yemen,[80] and a document from ca. A.D. 426 purports that metal plates were used in the time of Noah.[81] Needless to say, other inscriptions in various Near Eastern languages and dialects are inscribed on mediums such as gold, silver, and bronze, as well as on objects such as pendants, bowls, bottles, and plaques. At the very least, they demonstrate the relatively early adoption of the practice of inscribing metals. In describing an eleventh-century B.C. Phoenician inscription on a bronze spatula and an eighth- or ninth-century cuneiform patent issued by a Median king that was inscribed on a flat copper object, W. F. Albright maintained, "while this object is not identical with the Byblian ones in shape, there can be little doubt that they go back to some common source and that the custom of inscribing certain formulaic inscriptions on flat copper objects of cultic provenience was older and more widespread than has hitherto been guessed."[82] This statement was made some sixty years ago, and even today "more than 100 examples of ancient writing on metal plates have been discovered, including [a] gold plate of Darius, buried in a stone box in 516–515 B.C."[83] It seems that inscribing on metal plates may be more consistent and uniform with ancient Near Eastern traditions than has been previously believed.[84]

In summary, the scribal activity described in the Book of Mormon reflects an Egyptian scribal tradition in preexilic Judah that archaeological, palaeographic, and anthropological evidence currently suggests. Writing in an Egyptian dialect, a tradition of writing within the lineage of Joseph, and the inscribing of metallic plates is consistent with the findings and interpretations of the evidence in current scholarship in relation to scribal activity in the kingdom at this time. These elements of scribal activity also reflect aspects of Egyptian interconnections with the kingdom of Judah.

Conclusion

The items discussed in this chapter portray some of the circumstances, challenges, attitudes, and difficulties that prophets such as Lehi and Jeremiah faced. Other issues relevant to Book of Mormon contributions to the study of this time period include confirming the persecution of the prophets in Jerusalem on the eve of its destruction (which is rather telling) and attitudes of the indestructibility of Jerusalem among its people. An important contribution the Book of Mormon makes—in light of current scholarship discussed in this chapter—relates to establishing an Egyptian scribal tradition in the sixth century in Judah. This is significant as scholars are searching for ways to explain the appearance of such a tradition.

In conclusion, it is miraculous in itself that Nephi was able to obtain the plates (that his people's faith might be preserved) in this turbulent time, and he recognized the Lord's hand in this endeavor. These scriptures were instrumental in perpetuating the faith of many throughout the course of the Book of Mormon's history, and the testimonies of the Book of Mormon prophets have resulted in the blossoming of the faith of millions today. The chain of events that transpired from Lehi's ministry in Jerusalem—including his dreams, obtaining the plates, transporting them to the American continent, the rise and fall of civilizations, and the eventual transmission and translation by the Prophet Joseph Smith—leaves no doubt that the Book of Mormon truly is part of a "marvelous work and a wonder" (2 Nephi 25:17; 27:26).

Notes

1. For a discussion on this date as opposed to 587, see Gershon Galil, *The Chronology of the Kings of Israel and Judah* (Leiden: Brill, 1996), 108–18; and Abraham Malamat, "The Kingdom of Judah between Egypt and Babylon: A Small State within a Great Power Confrontation," in *Text and Context: Old Testament and Semitic Studies for F. C. Fensham,* ed. W. Claassen (Sheffield: Sheffield Academic Press, 1988), 117–29.

2. Some believe that Josiah's coronation occurred in 639 B.C. See for example Nadav Na'aman, "The Kingdom of Judah under Josiah," *Tel Aviv* 18 (1991): 3.

3. The siege of Lachish (a city in the kingdom of Judah) is famously displayed on Assyrian bas reliefs from Nineveh. The depiction shows Assyrian battering rams and archers coming against the city. Second Kings 18:3–19:37; 2 Chronicles 32:1–22; and Isaiah 36–37 describe the Assyrian invasion of Judah and Jerusalem. Second Kings 19:35 claims a victory over the Assyrian army, but Sennacherib reports to the contrary that he seized thousands of people as booty (an obvious exaggeration). The Bible is silent on this deportation, and with the Assyrians' propensity to exaggerate it is difficult to assess the true figure.

4. "Some scholars have claimed that the Assyrian domination of Palestine collapsed several years before the death of Ashurbanipal in 631

B.C.E. [and thus before Josiah's reign], and that, at the time of Josiah's rise to power, the Assyrian presence had become so weak as to be scarcely noticeable, enabling Josiah to operate for many years in the vacuum thus created." Na'aman, "Kingdom of Judah under Josiah," 34.

5. The accounts of Josiah's reform as contained in 2 Kings 22–23 and 2 Chronicles 34–35 seem to have different agendas, and the chronology and sequence of the reform are at variance with one another. For a brief discussion on this, see George E. Mendenhall, *Ancient Israel's Faith and History: An Introduction to the Bible in Context,* ed. Gary A. Herion (Louisville, Ky.: Westminster John Knox, 2001), 166–72.

6. This is the time we first encounter Jeremiah (Jeremiah 1:1–2).

7. Second Kings 23:2 also refers to this as "the book of the covenant."

8. This scroll contained elements of the law as found in the book of Deuteronomy and offered direction and instruction in Josiah's implementation of the reform. As a result of the similarities, there is much debate as to when the book of Deuteronomy was written.

9. Baruch Halpern, "Jerusalem and the Lineages in the Seventh Century BCE: Kinship and the Rise of Individual Moral Liability," in *Law and Ideology in Monarchic Israel,* ed. Baruch Halpern and Deborah W. Hobson (Sheffield: JSOT, 1991), 68.

10. For a study of the distribution of religious icons (Judean pillar figurines) in the kingdom of Judah in this period, see Raz Kletter, "Pots and Polities: Material Remains of Late Iron Age Judah in Relation to Its Political Borders," *Bulletin of the American Schools of Oriental Research* 314 (1999): 19–54.

11. This language is reminiscent of the language found in Jacob 5 in the Book of Mormon.

12. The extent to which this expansion occurred is still under debate, and a definitive conclusion has yet to be reached.

13. See Abraham Malamat, "The Twilight of Judah: In the Egyptian-Babylonian Maelstrom," *Supplements to Vetus Testamentum,* vol. 28 (Leiden: Brill, 1975), 125. As previously stated, Assyria was battling a Babylonian revolt at this time, which contributed to Josiah's successful

efforts of expansion. The other superpower in the region (Egypt) was busy aiding Assyria, and they were also attempting to secure the maritime transportation routes on the coastal region (thus being far enough away from the mountains in Judah to enable Josiah some room to operate). "This state of affairs gave Josiah considerable freedom of action in the internal regions of the country, and there can be no doubt that he exploited this freedom to gather strength, to unify and crystallise his kingdom (the cultic reform played a major role in these trends), and, to a certain extent, even to expand his borders." Na'aman, "Kingdom of Judah under Josiah," 40–41.

14. Halpern, "Jerusalem and the Lineages," 63. Finkelstein has commented: "Manasseh's realpolitik in his relations with Assyria enabled him to profit from the geopolitical conditions of the early seventh century BCE. It is reasonable to assume that, despite the tribute that had to be paid to Assyria, Judah under Manasseh started an economic revival, mainly because of its activity in the south, in the Beer-sheba sector of the Arabian trade routes. It is conceivable that the Assyrians encouraged this revival, in order to maintain the economic strength of the Judahite buffer state. It is worth noting in this connection that a text reporting tribute given by south Levantine states to Esarhaddon or Ashurbanipal indicates that Judah's tribute was smaller than that paid by Ammon and Moab." Israel Finkelstein, "The Archaeology of the Days of Manasseh," in *Scripture and Other Artifacts: Essays on the Bible and Archaeology in Honor of Philip F. King*, ed. Michael D. Coogan, J. Cheryl Exum, and Lawrence E. Stager (Louisville, Ky.: Westminster John Knox, 1994), 180–81.

15. Halpern, "Jerusalem and the Lineages," 76–77. Mendenhall, *Faith and History*, 172, states that Josiah's religious reforms "were actually little more than a typical exploitation of religious tradition to consolidate political control."

16. The circumstances surrounding Josiah's death are highly problematic and speculative. Put simply, it is not known why he was there at Megiddo or exactly what course of events led to his death. Theories range from Josiah's attempts at blocking Egypt's advance

to confront Babylon (thus aiding Assyria) to Josiah being summoned there by Egypt, after which, for some reason they decided to execute him. See Abraham Malamat, *History of Biblical Israel: Major Problems and Minor Issues* (Leiden: Brill, 2001), 293–97, for a discussion of a few of these theories.

17. Gershon Galil, "The Babylonian Calendar and the Chronology of the Last Kings of Judah," *Biblica* 72 (1991): 376.

18. Jehoahaz is also known as Shallum (see 2 Kings 23:30; 1 Chronicles 3:15; 2 Chronicles 36:1; Jeremiah 22:11).

19. Jehoiakim was originally called Eliakim (see 2 Kings 23:34; 2 Chronicles 36:4).

20. Second Kings 23:35 states that Jehoiakim imposed a tax on his people to collect the tribute he paid to Egypt.

21. Jeremiah 36:9 describes a fast that was proclaimed in Jerusalem and a council that deliberated during this time. Galil, "Babylonian Calendar," 376, opines that Jehoiakim may have gathered this council to discuss surrendering to the Babylonians.

22. Malamat, "Kingdom of Judah," 118, 119.

23. Ibid., 124.

24. Galil, "Babylonian Calendar," 377, attempts to lower the chronology of Zedekiah's coronation by a year (thus affecting this date); however, it appears that Jehoiakim's death occurred toward the end of 598.

25. The exact number has been debated. See Malamat, "Twilight of Judah," 132–34.

26. This may also have been the time Ezekiel was taken into Babylonian captivity. See Mendenhall, *Faith and History,* 186.

27. "Nebuchadnezzar's policy of deportation and 'heavy tribute' ultimately proved shortsighted. The very foundations of the kingdom were undermined; social and economic chaos, as well as psychic and spiritual distress prevailed, as can be discerned in the prophets' words." Malamat, "Kingdom of Judah," 125.

28. This translation is taken from Tsvi Schneider, "Six Biblical Signatures: Seals and Seal Impressions of Six Biblical Personages

Recovered," *Biblical Archaeology Review* 17/4 (1991): 32. Schneider also refers to the seal of a biblical figure about whom little is known and opines that this Azariah (the high priest) went into exile in 597 with Jehoiachin (ibid.). Again, it is probably no coincidence that Lehi received his vision (which presumably opened his ministry) about this time when high profile characters in the kingdom had been deported and questions concerning the state of the nation and what action to take were at an all-time high.

29. For a discussion on the chronology of these kings in relation to the Babylonian calendar, see Galil, "Babylonian Calendar," 367–78.

30. Subsequently, the archaeological excavations throughout Judah reveal utter destruction from Timnah in the west to Ein Gedi in the east, and from Jerusalem in the north to Lachish in the south. See Malamat, "Kingdom of Judah," 117–18.

31. Ibid., 126.

32. Jehoiachin's fate seems to have been somewhat different. Babylonian ration lists dating to ca. 592 cite Jehoiachin and his sons as recipients of monthly allocations of oil. Second Kings 25:27–30 states that Jehoiachin was later released from prison by Nebuchadnezzar's successor and was treated with kindness (receiving rations for sustenance). See Antony Kamm, *The Israelites: An Introduction* (London: Routledge, 1999), 104.

33. Malamat, "Kingdom of Judah," 119–20.

34. For a recent treatment of prophetic activity in Judah and its environs (including the Neo-Babylonian empire) as contained in extrabiblical sources, see Martti Nissinen, *Prophets and Prophecy in the Ancient Near East* (Atlanta: Society of Biblical Literature, 2003).

35. William L. Holladay, *Jeremiah 2: A Commentary on the Book of the Prophet Jeremiah Chapters 26–52,* ed. Paul D. Hanson (Minneapolis: Fortress, 1989), 31; Nicolas Grimal, *A History of Ancient Egypt* (Oxford: Blackwell, 1992), 361; and Erik Hornung, *A History of Ancient Egypt: An Introduction* (Ithaca: Cornell University Press, 1999), 140. It is no wonder some of Nephi's earliest words included, "having seen many afflictions in the course of my days" (1 Nephi 1:1).

36. Isaiah also began his ministry with a vision (Isaiah 6:1–8) and John was instructed (similarly to Lehi) within his vision to eat a book (Revelation 10:9–10). See also Ezekiel chapters 1–3. Other prophets, including Joseph Smith, also began their ministries with visions.

37. See John W. Welch, "The Calling of Lehi as a Prophet in the World of Jerusalem," in this volume, pages 421–48.

38. Malamat, "Kingdom of Judah," 123.

39. Hananiah was not the only false prophet Jeremiah encountered. There was also Zedekiah son of Maaseiah, and others (Ahab son of Kolaiah and Shemaiah) who were falsely prophesying in Babylon (Jeremiah 29:21–32).

40. A problem that Jeremiah's preaching created was that he was viewed as being politically pro-Babylonian. He was actually pro-Judah and was attempting to save his people by following the direction of the Lord (though the people were unable to discern this).

41. Malamat, "Twilight of Judah," 129.

42. Malamat, "Kingdom of Judah," 128.

43. See also Jeremiah 26:1–15 for an incident in Jeremiah's life.

44. Because Jeremiah 26 begins with the beginning of Jehoiakim's reign, Holladay argues that Urijah was executed in the early part of Jehoiakim's reign. Holladay, *Jeremiah 2,* 103.

45. The Septuagint (LXX) does not contain Elnatan's name. If his name was a later editorial addition, it is possible that this was done to preserve his lineage. If this is the case, it may form a familial, military, or authoritative lineage in light of Lachish ostracon 3. If this was the intention of later editors, it seems to imply a prior knowledge of the relationship between Elnatan and Konyahu. The coincidence of the Masoretes or a later redactor choosing a name that fits so conveniently with extrabiblical sources seems miniscule.

46. For a translation of this text and a discussion of these events, see Dana M. Pike, "Israelite Inscriptions from the Time of Jeremiah and Lehi," in this volume, pages 193–244.

47. It is not implausible that the Elnatan of Jeremiah 26 and the Konyahu son of Elnatan in Lachish ostracon 3.15 would equate to

a father/son relationship. Various administrative, secular, and religious posts were inherited by family members throughout the ancient Near East. Examples of this can be seen in the Tobiah family, where Seraiah's (2 Kings 25:18) grandson Jeshua was high priest at the time of the return from captivity, as well as in Egyptian wisdom literature and stelae. See Benjamin Mazar, "The Tobiads," *Israel Exploration Journal* 7 (1957): 234–35. See "The Teaching for Merikare," in Raymond O. Faulkner, trans., *The Literature of Ancient Egypt: An Anthology of Stories, Instructions, and Poetry,* ed. William Kelly Simpson (New Haven: Yale University Press, 1973), 183. In the stele of Senwosret-Senbu, BM 557, a son bearing his father's name also holds the same title of "overseer of the treasury." Inherited offices also occurred in Assyrian administrative positions.

48. See especially Pike, "Israelite Inscriptions," 237 n. 22 above.

49. In describing the unnamed prophet mentioned in Lachish ostracon 3, Parker assigns "Jeremiah or another of similar persuasion" as potential candidates. See Simon B. Parker, "The Lachish Letters and Official Reactions to Prophecies," in *Uncovering Ancient Stones: Essays in Memory of H. Neil Richardson,* ed. Lewis M. Hopfe (Winona Lake, Ind.: Eisenbrauns, 1994), 76.

50. I use the words "weakening the hands" of the people deliberately here in light of Lachish ostracon 6 and Jeremiah 38:4. I do this to again connect the possibility of contextual similarities between Lachish ostracon 3 and Jeremiah 26 (which states that Urijah "prophesied against the city and against this land according to all the words of Jeremiah," Jeremiah 26:20). In this volume, Pike, "Israelite Inscriptions," 238 n. 28 above, cautions against identifying Jeremiah as the referent in Lachish ostracon 6. Concerning the similar phraseology between the two, he states that this is not a direct quotation and that these terms are used elsewhere in the Bible. He is right: this is not a direct quotation; however, it is a recollection of the event. Both Lachish ostracon 3/Jeremiah 26 and Lachish ostracon 6/Jeremiah 38 appear to be describing confrontations between religious and political orientations. The prophets prophesy contrary to the propaganda of the government officials, and

they in turn seek to incarcerate and punish them. In light of the context of Jeremiah 38:1–4 (which describes Jerusalem's destruction and the abduction of Jeremiah as a result of these proclamations), the similar phraseology in Lachish ostracon 6 argues in favor of connecting the two episodes. Furthermore, two seals were found at Lachish bearing the names of Shephatyahu and one "Gedalyah, royal steward." See Sandra L. Gogel, *A Grammar of Epigraphic Hebrew* (Atlanta: Scholars Press, 1998), 487, seals 5 and 6. This places individuals by these names (both possessing seals) in both the biblical and extrabiblical texts. As officials, it would not have been unusual for their seals to be located in fortresses outside of Jerusalem for the sake of private and secured communications. In regard to Lachish, they would have carried on written correspondence with them. They may also have been required to visit Lachish on occasion (see Lachish ostracon 4.7–13 and the difference between sending the Kittim and Elyashib being ordered to go in person in Arad ostraca 2 and 3). Thus in both cases the messages of destruction were proclaimed, officials of the kings were sent after them, and the prophets were either detained or executed for the disheartening words they were proclaiming against the kingdom. Though there is no definitive proof that this actually was the prophet Jeremiah mentioned in the Lachish ostracon 6, the gap of uncertainty may not be as wide as Pike implies.

51. Holladay, *Jeremiah 2,* 109.

52. Hornung, *History of Ancient Egypt,* 141.

53. The context of Jeremiah 38:4–5 is unclear as to whether Zedekiah actually supported the abduction of Jeremiah. He states that he could not stop them even if he wanted to, or at least punish them if they did. This passive allowance on the part of Zedekiah may have been inspired by the fear of offending his cabinet and whatever consequences that might have brought. An interesting comment has been made insinuating Zedekiah's lack of power among his people, "The new king and last monarch of Judah, Zedekiah, summoned, or was forced to summon, an anti-Babylonian conference of delegates of petty kingdoms in Jerusalem in the year 594/593 BC, thus rebelling

against the power which had enthroned him, a step in conflict with his own personal interest." See Malamat, "Kingdom of Judah," 125. This conference was held amidst "false prophets" predicting victory over the Babylonians. Nebuchadnezzar was suppressing a revolt in his country, and Psammetichus II had recently taken the throne in Egypt and was possibly encouraging such a revolt. It is thus possible that Zedekiah agreed to detain Jeremiah upon observing the determination of his officers and recalling the precedent established by Jehoiakim. These items seem to suggest that Zedekiah did not have much influence among his people.

54. Malamat, "Kingdom of Judah," 122–24.

55. Jewish residences in Egypt are listed in Jeremiah 44:1—Migdol, Tahpanhes, Noph, and Pathros. The exact location of Migdol is uncertain. Exodus 14:2 gives an approximate location in the eastern Delta region of Lower Egypt. Ezekiel 29:10 places it on the extreme borders of Egypt. Some suggested sites include Tell el-Her and Tell el-Maskhuta. See *The Anchor Bible Dictionary* (New York: Doubleday, 1992), s.v. "Migdol." Noph was the Egyptian city of Memphis. The New Kingdom Memphis had housed a community of Canaanite merchants and mercenaries and also received a wave of exiles who were fleeing the Babylonians (ibid., s.v. "Memphis"). Pathros was a subsection comprising Upper Egypt, probably somewhere between Memphis/Cairo and Aswan. It was on its southern border that a military installation from Judah was established (ibid., s.v. "Pathros"). Tahpanhes was an outpost in the Eastern Delta bordering Sinai. It is presumed to be the location of Tell ed-Defenna/Dafna, 8 km west of el-Qantara and 24 km southwest of Pelusium/Tell el-Farama (ibid., s.v. "Tahpanhes"). It was to Tahpanhes that Jeremiah was taken toward the end of his life (Jeremiah 43:5–7). For an interesting and positive outlook on Egypt in the eyes of the Israelites, see Mordechai Cogan, "The Other Egypt: A Welcome Asylum," in *Texts, Temples, and Traditions: A Tribute to Menahem Haran,* ed. Michael V. Fox et al. (Winona Lake, Ind.: Eisenbrauns, 1996), 65–70.

56. See John W. Welch, "The Trial of Jeremiah: A Legal Legacy from Lehi's Jerusalem," in this volume, pages 337–56.

57. See S. Kent Brown, "Jerusalem Connections to Arabia in 600 B.C.," in this volume, pages 625–46.

58. Orly Goldwasser, "Hieratic Inscriptions from Tel Seraᶜ in Southern Canaan," *Tel Aviv* 11 (1984): 86–87.

59. Ibid., 251–52.

60. David Ussishkin, *The Conquest of Lachish by Sennacherib* (Tel Aviv: Institute of Archaeology, 1982), 56–57.

61. Na'aman, "Kingdom of Judah under Josiah," 46–49. See also Nili S. Fox, *In the Service of the King: Officialdom in Ancient Israel and Judah* (Cincinnati: Hebrew Union College Press, 2000), 245 n. 195, for a summary of other prominent scholars who believed that the site was under Egyptian control in one form or another at this time. I have conducted a literary analysis on the inscription and have found particular affinities and similarities of style to that found in Egyptian writings from a similar genre. Though there is some degree of biblical law reflected in the text, it is in more general terms than is usually ascribed.

62. Na'aman, "Kingdom of Judah under Josiah," 48.

63. This being said, I am not necessarily in agreement with all of Na'aman's conclusions, but Egyptian occupation at this time seems viable.

64. For further discussion on Lehi's use of Egyptian, see John S. Thompson, "Lehi and Egypt," in this volume, pages 259–76.

65. Daniel Peterson, "Mounting Evidence for the Book of Mormon," *Ensign,* January 2000, 19.

66. Bilingual inscriptions are not uncommon in the region. As early as the first half of the second millennium and beyond, one can find examples of Middle Egyptian-Hittite, Hittite-Akkadian, Phoenician-Luwian (Hittite hieroglyphic), and Aramaic-Assyrian, to name a few. There are also bilingual and polyglot dictionaries. Joseph in Egypt also appears to have been bilingual (Genesis 42:21–23) and in a

hieroglyphic Luwian inscription set up by Yariris, he claimed to read twelve languages.

67. This is witnessed in Semitic glosses in Egyptian Second Intermediate texts, the Canaanite glosses in Amarna Akkadian, and the Deir ʿAlla text, which is still under debate as to exactly how to classify it, as it possesses characteristics of both Hebrew and Aramaic. A recently discovered incense altar in Moab may also be added to the list, as it is at variance with what is expected in the Moabite language.

68. There are also instances of Aramaic texts written in Demotic.

69. John Gee, "Two Notes on Egyptian Script," *Journal of Book of Mormon Studies* 5/1 (1996): 162–76. Gee also cites in his note 20 an example of an Egyptian (Demotic) inscription on metal; he refers to Adel Farid, "Sieben Metallgefäße mit demotischen Inschriften aus Kairo und Paris," *Revue d'Égyptologie* 45 (1994): 117–32 and plates XIII–XVII.

70. See John Gee, "Egyptian Society during the Twenty-sixth Dynasty, in this volume, pages 277–98.

71. There is at least one example where a name is purported to have been discovered that employs two biliteral Egyptian signs; however, certainty of this interpretation is lacking.

72. A recent study on the hieratic characters in the extant Hebrew corpus comments on the paleographic divergences with the hieratic found in Egypt and speaks of an "Israelitization" of the hieratic system. Fox, *In the Service of the King,* 279. This is interesting in light of the shifting nature of the language in the Nephite record and leads one to wonder if such changes were beginning to be witnessed in Jerusalem before Lehi and his family left.

73. Aaron Demsky, "A Proto-Canaanite Abecedary Dating from the Period of the Judges and Its Implications for the History of the Alphabet," *Tel Aviv* 4 (1977): 24.

74. William Schniedewind and Daniel Sivan, "The Elijah-Elisha Narratives: A Test Case for the Northern Dialect of Hebrew," *Jewish Quarterly Review* 87/3–4 (1997): 337.

75. The plates contained the five books of Moses, a record of the Jews from the beginning to the reign of Zedekiah (including the prophecies of Jeremiah), and a genealogy of the fathers (1 Nephi 5:11–16).

76. This is witnessed in the name of the Mandaean book of scripture (*ginza rabba*), "the great treasure," as well as in the Latter-day Saint scripture the Pearl of Great Price.

77. George E. Mendenhall, *The Syllabic Inscriptions from Byblos* (Beirut: American University of Beirut, 1985), ix. Mendenhall actually dated them from as early as the twenty-fourth century, though this seems too early in light of other epigraphic evidence.

78. M. Dietrich and O. Loretz Münster, "The Cuneiform Alphabets of Ugarit," *Ugarit-Forschungen* 21 (1989): 109.

79. Benjamin Sass, "Inscribed Babylonian Arrowheads of the Turn of the Second Millennium and Their Phoenician Counterparts," *Ugarit-Forschungen* 21 (1989): 349. It may be argued that these inscriptions are relatively short; however, it is interesting that so many occur during times in which so little has actually been discovered at the respective times and regions. The Proto-Byblian compositions are lengthy texts, and the Phoenician arrowheads constitute the only surviving remnants of the final stages of the development from a pictographic to a linear alphabetic script (i.e., Proto-Canaanite > Northwest Semitic dialects). These arrowheads represent the earliest Phoenician material, and not until the tenth century do the earliest and lengthier Phoenician, Aramaic, Hebrew, and Moabite inscriptions occur on any medium.

80. Mohammed Maraqten and Yusuf Abdallah, "A Recently Discovered Inscribed Sabean Bronze Plaque from Maḥram Bilqīs near Mārib Yemen," *Journal of Near Eastern Studies* 61/1 (2002): 49–53.

81. For later findings, see John A. Tvedtnes, "Hiding the Secret Plans," *Insights* 22/8 (2002): 2. See generally H. Curtis Wright, "Ancient Burials of Metal Documents in Stone Boxes," in *By Study and Also by Faith: Essays in Honor of Hugh W. Nibley,* ed. John M.

Lundquist and Stephen D. Ricks (Salt Lake City: Deseret Book and FARMS, 1990), 2:273–334.

82. William F. Albright, "The Copper Spatula of Byblus and Proverbs 18:18," *Bulletin of the American Schools of Oriental Research* 90 (1943): 37.

83. Peterson, "Mounting Evidence," 18.

84. For a discussion on silver rolls containing apparent biblical passages from ca. 600, see Pike, "Israelite Inscriptions," in this volume, pages 213–15; and William J. Adams Jr., "Lehi's Jerusalem and Writing on Metal Plates," *Journal of Book of Mormon Studies* 3/1 (1994): 204–6.

Chapter 12

The Trial of Jeremiah: A Legal Legacy from Lehi's Jerusalem

John W. Welch

Early in the reign of King Jehoiakim (the son of King Josiah), the prophet Jeremiah found himself in legal difficulty at the temple in Jerusalem. This public encounter and perilously close call with the law have become an unforgettable feature in the cultural and religious landscape of Lehi's world. Gauging by the number of points of contact between the Book of Mormon and the account of the trial of Jeremiah found in Jeremiah 26, this lawsuit and its contemporary points of jurisprudence were influential both in the life of Lehi and also in the legacy he left his posterity. Some of those contacts were broad, cultural phenomena; other points were more direct, conscious reactions. Several legal elements manifested in or relevant to this proceeding remained pertinent in Nephite jurisprudence for many centuries to come. Reliving Jeremiah's courageous denunciation of the political potentates of his day affords readers over twenty-six hundred years later a significant glimpse into the social and legal dynamics of Lehi's day.

Several factors indicate that Lehi and Nephi probably knew of Jeremiah's temple sermon and the legal complications that his remarks sparked. It is even possible that Lehi was present on that occasion and witnessed the arrest of Jeremiah and the ensuing legal fracas. The trial of Jeremiah, which is the earliest autobiographical information recorded in the book of Jeremiah, occurred around 609 B.C., in the first year of the reign of King Jehoiakim. Lehi would have been around forty or forty-five years old at the time, making him a close contemporary of Jeremiah.[1] Jerusalem was a small city;[2] therefore, Lehi and the other men functioning concurrently in the circle of prophets in Jerusalem would undoubtedly have known each other fairly well.[3] Jeremiah himself refers to other prophets who had stepped forward to criticize the wickedness that prevailed among the Jews in Jerusalem at that time (Jeremiah 26:5), so it is clear that Jeremiah did not operate alone. Nephi similarly attests that only a few years after that time "there came many prophets, prophesying unto the people that they must repent, or the great city Jerusalem must be destroyed," with Lehi delivering the same message (1 Nephi 1:4, 13).

In addition to his personal familiarity with Jeremiah (see 1 Nephi 7:14), Lehi may have had a written account of the trial of Jeremiah on the plates of brass, for they included "many prophecies which have been spoken by the mouth of Jeremiah" (1 Nephi 5:13). Although one cannot be sure which passages were contained on the plates of brass, Jeremiah's discourse in which he delivered the word of the Lord prophesying the destruction of the temple and the cursing of the city (Jeremiah 26:3–6) would have been among his earliest prophecies and thus among the most likely passages from this prominent prophet to have been found by Lehi on those hard-won plates. The trial of Jeremiah, of course, was not the only legal text found on the plates of brass. Also included were five books of Moses, which contained the Ten Commandments and other legal materials and precedents. All these legal sources contributed to the legal legacy transported by Lehi from Jerusalem to the New World, but this study focuses on the trial of Jeremiah in particular because it can be dated with certainty to the world of Lehi's Jerusalem. Words and phrases, in addition to the overall pattern of legal concerns and procedures in the trial of Jeremiah, are echoed much later in the Book of Mormon, further indicating that Lehi and his posterity were familiar with this pivotal episode in Jeremiah's life.

Jeremiah's Message and Offense

Shortly after the catastrophic death of King Josiah in 609 B.C., Jeremiah positioned himself prominently in the court of the temple at Jerusalem in order to deliver his message to everyone who came in and out of that holy place. As directed by God (Jeremiah 26:2), he called the people of Jerusalem to repentance, their wickedness having well been the cause of God's disapproval that led to the debacle at Megiddo.

Jeremiah's aggressiveness may remind Book of Mormon readers of the boldness of the prophet Abinadi, who entered the temple city of Nephi to deliver a similar message of repentance or doom to the people of King Noah in the land of Nephi (Mosiah 11:20; 12:1).[4] Besides affording these prophets the opportunity to speak to large crowds of influential people, the temple location of Jeremiah's prophetic reprimand also made his words that much more provocative.[5] Predictions of doom and destruction made in private, outside the hearing of most people, and distant from the Holy Presence could probably have been tolerated in most cases; but the authorities administering the temple could not tolerate such direct effrontery to the house of the Lord.

New Testament readers will readily recall that Jesus likewise caused offense when he disrupted the business of the money changers and predicted the destruction of the Temple of Herod while standing squarely in the temple precinct (Mark 11:15–18; 14:58). Interestingly, Jesus himself was compared by some people in his own day with the prophet Jeremiah (Matthew 16:14) and was quoting Jeremiah 7:11 ("Is this house, which is called by my name, become a den of robbers in your eyes?") when he denounced the temple administrators for turning the house of God into a den of thieves (Mark 11:17). The fact that significant similarities exist between the report of the trial of Jeremiah and the way in which the trial of Jesus is told in the New Testament Gospels shows that the trial of Jeremiah retained a prominent place in Jewish memory for several centuries in the Old World,[6] making it all the more plausible that this legal encounter was vividly remembered in the New World as well. For instance, perhaps recalling the problems encountered by Jeremiah and Abinadi and thus attempting to avoid overly provoking the people in the city of Zarahemla to anger, Nephi, son of Helaman, did not go into the temple precinct but instead prayed from his own tower, from which he ended up delivering his message of prophetic warning and rebuke while more safely positioned on his own property (Helaman 7:10).

Jeremiah was instructed by the Lord to deliver a certain message word for word—"diminish not a word" (Jeremiah 26:2). The ability and duty of official messengers and legal agents in the ancient world to deliver the words of their patron perfectly verbatim is well attested in many literary sources from this time. For example, verbatim messages are common in the conduct of messengers in the Homeric epics.[7] Similarly, in Lehi's world, messengers did not have authority to add to or subtract from the message that they were to deliver, and accordingly Jeremiah makes a point of affirming that he delivered every word with which he had been entrusted, "all that the Lord had commanded him to speak" (Jeremiah 26:8). The Hebrew legal system, which depended primarily on verbal communication and oral testimony rather than on written documentation, placed particularly high value on the accuracy and faithfulness of such deliveries by messengers, spokesmen, witnesses, and officials.

In reading King Benjamin's speech and other texts in the Book of Mormon, one senses that the same principle continued to operate in Nephite legal religious practice. In Mosiah 3:23, for example, Benjamin certified that he had faithfully and precisely delivered the words given to him by the angel of the Lord: "And now I have spoken the words which the Lord God hath commanded me."[8] Similar certifications of messengers are found in Mosiah 11:20 and 12:1.

The substance of Jeremiah's complaint against the people was that they had not conducted themselves according to the laws that God had set before them (Jeremiah 26:4) and that they had not obeyed the words of the prophets that God kept sending to them (Jeremiah 26:5). Significantly, Jeremiah required obedience to both the law and the prophets: "If ye will not hearken to me, to walk in my law, which I have set before you, To hearken to the words of my servants the prophets, whom I sent unto you, . . . then will I . . . make this city a curse to all the nations of the earth" (Jeremiah 26:4–6). For Jeremiah, these two sources of divine direction are not mutually exclusive. Typically, modern scholarship has segregated these two domains as wholly separate spheres of operation, but the warning and indictment given by Jeremiah sees legal and prophetic mandates going hand in hand.[9]

In a similar way, the Book of Mormon prophets find themselves in strong support of both the law and the prophets, a dualistic position tracing back to the words of the prophet Jeremiah. Despite knowing the "deadness of the law" without its proper spiritual context (2 Nephi 25:27), the Nephites were strict to obey the law of Moses (2 Nephi 5:10; Jarom 1:5; Alma 30:3; 3 Nephi 1:24–25) until it was fulfilled through the death and resurrection of Jesus Christ (3 Nephi 9:17). At the same time, the Nephites perpetually venerated and utilized the writings of Isaiah and all the other holy prophets.[10]

Unfortunately, Jeremiah is not specific about which prophets or which laws the people had ignored. It would, of course, be extremely significant to know which laws (he uses here the word *torot,* the plural of *torah*) he had in mind. One may assume that he made reference to the laws of Deuteronomy, but other bodies of written or customary law are also possible. At a minimum, Jeremiah's accusation provides evidence that laws were known, were used as standards of behavior, and could provide the basis for legal prosecution at the time of Lehi.

The threat from the Lord lodged by Jeremiah against the people in Jerusalem took the form of a simile curse: "I will make this house like Shiloh" (Jeremiah 26:6).[11] This curse alludes to the destruction of the shrine at Shiloh that resulted in the loss of the ark of the covenant in the disastrous battle of Ebenezer around 1050 B.C. when the Philistines dealt a severe military blow to the Israelites.[12] The point of Jeremiah's curse, of course, was that even the tabernacle and the ark had not protected the Israelites at Shiloh, and similarly the temple at Jerusalem would not protect the kingdom of Judah unless its people would repent and remain righteous.

Jeremiah's use of simile curses and other symbolic speech-acts seems to have remained strong in the Nephite memory. The form of his judgmental simile curse, as well as its content and context, aligns well with the simile curse issued by Abinadi when he cursed King Noah to the effect that his life would "be valued even as a garment in a hot furnace" (Mosiah 12:3). Not only is the comparative form the same in both of these curses, but the essence of Abinadi's curse was also grounded, like Jeremiah's, in the warning that even the temple in the city of Nephi would not shelter the people as long as they retained their wicked ways. In addition, simile curses appear elsewhere in the Book of Mormon.[13]

Jeremiah also prophesied that the city of Jerusalem would become "a curse to all the nations of the earth" (Jeremiah 26:6). In other words, people in anger or distress would speak the name of Jerusalem in disparaging and denigrating ways in connection with oaths and cursing. The shame and dishonor of having one's name ridiculed and associated with evil and malediction was deeply offensive and insulting to ancient people.[14]

Reflecting not only this general sentiment but also the particular words of Jeremiah, the Book of Mormon also predicts that people who would reject the Holy One of Israel would become a "hiss and a byword and be hated among all nations" (1 Nephi 19:14; and conforming to Seidel's law of ancient Israelite rhetoric, this two-part imprecation is quoted in reverse order in 3 Nephi 16:9).[15]

The Indictment of Jeremiah by His Accusers

Legal action against Jeremiah was then initiated by the priests, prophets, and all the people who heard him (Jeremiah 26:8).[16] They had witnessed his language and conduct. Under Israelite law, anyone who heard or knew of a violation of the law was under an obligation to take action to prosecute and punish the offender: "If a soul sin, and hear the voice of swearing, and is a witness, whether he hath seen or known of it; if he do not utter it, then he shall bear his iniquity" (Leviticus 5:1). An example of the operation of this legal duty is found in the trial of the blasphemer in Leviticus 24:14; when "all that heard" the blasphemy brought the blasphemer before Moses, he sought the will of the Lord in the matter, pronounced the verdict, and turned the offender over to all those who had heard the blasphemy to take him outside the camp and stone him. Accordingly, in commencing the trial of Jeremiah, the priests, prophets, and presumably all the people seized him, thronging about him in a moblike action.[17] Perhaps he was about to be lynched, exactly as would later just about happen to the apostle Paul, who was also seized at the temple of Jerusalem for the offense of bringing Gentiles inside the inner court of the temple, thus allegedly "pollut[ing] this holy place" (Acts 21:28–31).

Reflecting this typical Israelite practice, groups of people in the Book of Mormon were frequently the initiators of legal actions. The people seized Abinadi and took him to King Noah (Mosiah 12:9). The people apprehended Nehor and took him to Alma (Alma 1:10). Later, in Zarahemla, Nephi's political opponents ask the people, "why do ye not seize upon this man and bring him forth, that he may be condemned according to the crime which he has done?" (Helaman 8:1), suggesting that even these Gadianton affiliates recognized that not only prudence but also long-standing legal tradition required them to wait until the people took action before they could initiate legal charges against Nephi.

The people accused Jeremiah with the phrase, "for this you must die" or, as in the KJV, "thou shalt surely die" (Jeremiah 26:8).[18] The Hebrew expression used here is *mot tamut*, "die a death," and is related to the legal formula *mot yumat,* which is often used in legal contexts—for example, throughout the Code of the Covenant in Exodus 21–23—to describe offenses for which a person is subject to the death penalty or is worthy of death.[19]

Apparently the same formulation was invoked by King Noah in stating the charge of blasphemy against Abinadi: "We have found an accusation against thee, and thou art *worthy of death*" (Mosiah 17:7).

The Seating of the Judges

Before matters could develop very far in the trial of Jeremiah, however, certain princes or officials (*sarim*) from the palace arrived (Jeremiah 26:10). It is unclear whether they heard the commotion and came on their own accord or if they were summoned by Jeremiah's friends or other concerned citizens.[20] Either way, their strong intervention in the case must have confronted and annoyed the priests and religious leaders associated with the temple, whose interests had been threatened by Jeremiah.[21] Interestingly, the officials assumed full jurisdiction over the proceeding and, as far as the narrative in the book of Jeremiah discloses, the concerns and allegations of the accusers were given little attention.

This culture of factional interests competing against each other continues in the culture of the Book of Mormon, where the interests of the palace and the temple, not surprisingly, often collided. Thus, perhaps consciously following Jeremiah's very example, the priest Jacob went to his temple in the city of Nephi (Jacob 2:2) to rebuke especially the royal faction who had begun "to excuse themselves in committing whoredoms" by citing the precedents of Kings David and Solomon (Jacob 2:23). Often in the books of Helaman and 3 Nephi, civic leadership was at odds with religious leaders, and righteous religious groups frequently found themselves in the minority.[22] Whether consciously designed or unconsciously developed, the competition between these elements in Nephite government created a type of balance of power, preserving the expectation manifested in the trial of Jeremiah that one segment of government would keep the other in check.

It is unclear, however, what authority was held by the officials who came in and took charge. In an effort to sort out this uncertainty and confusion, one may turn to the account of the legal reforms of Jehoshaphat in 2 Chronicles 17 and 19. Although those reforms are attributed to King Jehoshaphat, who was a contemporary of Elijah three hundred years before the time of Jeremiah, scholars often argue that the judicial system reported in this text reflects more accurately the courts at the time of the Chronicler (shortly after the time of Jeremiah and Lehi) rather than the system in operation in the early monarchy. Be that as it may, the purported reforms of Jehoshaphat offer important clues about the law courts as they would have existed in preexilic Israel generally.[23]

At the outset of his reforms, King Jehoshaphat ordered five of his princes or officials (*sarim*) to go into the cities of Judah to teach, taking with them "the book of the law of the Lord" (2 Chronicles 17:7–9). After the death of Ahab, Jehoshaphat was rebuked by Jehu, the seer, for having helped the ungodly Ahab; in response, the king "set judges in the land throughout all the fenced [walled] cities of Judah, city by city" (2 Chronicles 19:5). He instructed these judges to judge righteously and to warn the people not to break the law of the Lord. Moreover, in Jerusalem a more elaborate court system was established, with the Levites, priests, and the chief of the fathers of Israel being appointed as judges (2 Chronicles 19:8). Amariah, the chief priest, was given stewardship over "all matters of the Lord" or sacral concerns, while Zebadiah, the leading chief, was given jurisdiction over "all the king's matters" (2 Chronicles 19:11). Interestingly, however, the *sarim* were not mentioned specifically in 2 Chronicles 19, although it may be understood that the terms "chief of the fathers of Israel" and "ruler of the house of Judah" were synonymous with these "officials" or "princes."

That being the case, the *sarim,* who arrived at the temple and who took issue with the priests and the prophets who were accusing Jeremiah, technically may only have had jurisdiction over the civic matters of the king, whereas one would have expected that a charge of false prophecy would have arisen as a religious concern, a "matter of the Lord." Nevertheless, in Jeremiah's day (and in the ancient world generally), jurisdictional lines were not always sharply divided. Although a charge of false prophecy might technically be a matter of sacred concern, if the oracle impinged upon the king or his royal administration (as certainly was the case with Jeremiah's broad censure of all the people, together with his cursing of the city of Jerusalem), then the matter could easily evolve into a concern worthy of royal cognizance.

Indicating the likely operation and persistent endurance of this divided judiciary in Jerusalem in Lehi's day, a similar jurisdictional situation arises 450 years later in the trial of Abinadi (see Mosiah 12–17), where the interests of King Noah and the concerns of his priests were alternately raised against that prophet, who, like Jeremiah, had also chastised the people and cursed the king and his regime. In Abinadi's case, however, the royal and priestly interests were allied together against the prophet, whereas in Jeremiah 26 the royal officials opposed the priests and prophets who had commenced action against Jeremiah.

Excavation of the city gate at Beersheba (Tell es-Saba‹), showing the benches where men gathered to conduct business and the city elders held trials.

The officials took their seats in the New Gate of the house of the Lord.[24] Doing "justice 'at the gate'" was idiomatic in ancient Israel.[25] When he purchased Naomi's property and with that acquisition assumed the liabilities associated with raising up seed to Elimelech, Boaz convened a court of ten elders at the town gate (Ruth 4:1–2). Archaeology demonstrates that seats were placed within the gates of the walled cities of Israel.[26] The gates were quintessential public places controlled by guards and central to general traffic, making them ideal places for public legal proceedings. Jeremiah's account makes particular reference to the fact that the officials "sat down in the entry of the new gate" (Jeremiah 26:10) on their judgment seats.

No physical feature of the Nephite justice system is more prominent than is the governmental judgment seat, which is mentioned forty-seven times in the Book of Mormon during the period of the reign of the judges.[27] While the high priests of Noah in the city of Nephi had seats that were "set apart" specifically for them in their temple (Mosiah 11:11), the Nephite records do not indicate where the judgment seats were located in Zarahemla. But the tradition of having a place of judgment with seats that imbued officials with the cloak of judicial authority was clearly a part of Lehi's world in Jerusalem that seems to have carried over into the Nephite legal system.

Before these seated officials, the prophets and priests pressed their charge against Jeremiah, accusing him of having "prophesied against this city" (Jeremiah 26:11). Typical of ancient jurisprudence, the alleged crime was not particularly well defined. Modern lawyers would want to define the criminal charge more specifically: Was the problem treason or false prophecy? In all likelihood, it was both. Any prophet who prophesied falsely could be subjected to the death penalty under the legal rules reflected in Deuteronomy 18:20, but it is unlikely that common people would have become very agitated over an alleged false prophecy unless it affected something very important, such as the temple, the king, or the core values of the nation.[28]

Accordingly, Abinadi's charges against King Noah (Mosiah 12:3), Alma's castigation of the people in Ammonihah (Alma 9:12–24), or Stephen's declamation against the law of Moses (Acts 7:47–53) were not only socially offensive to their audiences but became the impetus for legal actions precisely because they were inimical to such crucial and central institutions.

Jeremiah's Defense

No lawyers or advocates, of course, were used in ancient Israelite courts. Jeremiah, like the Nephite prophets Jacob, Abinadi, and Alma, was given the chance to defend himself (Jeremiah 26:12–15). He testified that he spoke in the name of the Lord. He submitted to the will of the officials, telling them that he was willing to have them do what they thought was "good and meet [proper]" (Jeremiah 26:14). The words used by Jeremiah seem to indicate his acceptance of the jurisdiction of these officials.[29] Since Jeremiah, of course, would rather have the officials as his judges than have the priests and people carry out their own version of justice, his preference to come under the jurisdiction of the princes is understandable.

Similar language was used by the people in Mosiah 12:16, as they willingly turned Abinadi over to the jurisdiction of King Noah, saying, "Do with him as seemeth thee good." Evidently this phrase reflects some kind of formality in ancient Israelite law, for otherwise this would be an odd thing for the people to say to their king. One would think that a king could do whatever he wanted in any event. Whenever a lawsuit had begun in the hands of one group of people, however, it would be important for that group to relinquish their jurisdictional interest in the case as they formally turned the matter over to someone else.

Jeremiah, like Abinadi, defended himself most effectively by raising the specter of "innocent blood," the shedding of which would bring divine judgment upon the judges, the city, and all the people (Jeremiah 26:15). God was seen in Jeremiah's world as a redeemer, and in this capacity he was seen theologically as carrying out the ancient legal duties borne by the avenger or redeemer of blood. Members of a murder victim's family were obligated to avenge that death and to seek blood for blood (see Genesis 9:5–6; Numbers 35:19, 21). Cities of refuge were established to harbor those who had shed blood accidentally, unintentionally, or involuntarily, but anyone who consciously shed innocent blood was given no place to hide, especially from divine judgment. In the same way, Jeremiah argued that if these judges and officials, who ruled over the city, acted wrongly, their misconduct would be answered with a collective curse of divine judgment upon the entire city. Likewise, because the people had initiated the action against Jeremiah, the entire populace could be held liable under the legal principle of collective responsibility that still had force and effect in Jeremiah's day even though a more distinct sense of personal accountability was also emerging in biblical thought at this time (Deuteronomy 24:16; Jeremiah 31:29–30; Ezekiel 18).[30]

Consistent with the underlying rationales implicit in Jeremiah's legal defense, similar conceptual forces remained operative in Nephite jurisprudence for several ensuing centuries. The fear of shedding innocent blood arises on several occasions: Abinadi warned Noah that "if ye slay me ye will shed innocent blood" (Mosiah 17:10); Alma argued that Gideon's blood "would come upon us for vengeance" (Alma 1:13)—that is, would bring condemnation not only upon Alma but also upon all his people if they were not to reach a proper verdict and execute Gideon's slayer, Nehor. Alma assured Amulek that the "blood of the innocent shall stand as a witness against [their slayers], yea, and cry mightily against them at the last day" (Alma 14:11). It is understood in these texts that the entire populace would suffer from the miscarriage of justice by the leaders of the land; nevertheless, the doctrines of the Book of Mormon (for example, Alma 34:11) and the teachings of Lehi in particular (for example, 2 Nephi 1:5–22) stand at an important juncture in the transition from a legal system based primarily on corporate responsibility to a theology and ideology grounded more on individual responsibility.

Judicial Verdict

The officials seated in the trial of Jeremiah reached their decision and announced their verdict fairly quickly, finding Jeremiah innocent without much difficulty, having decided that he had indeed spoken in the name of the Lord (Jeremiah 26:16). In particular, older members of the panel of judges remembered and cited as precedent the case of Micah the Morasthite, who had prophesied against Jerusalem in the days of Hezekiah. Micah had said that Zion would become a plowed field, Jerusalem would be left as heaps of rubble, and the temple site would revert to a wooded ridge as the high places of a forest (Micah 3:12); in other words, the holy city would become an unoccupied, obliterated site filled only with trees, either natural or perhaps involving pagan worship.

These warnings, also expressed in the form of a simile curse, echo again the literary form that was used so provocatively by the Book of Mormon prophet Abinadi. The threat that Jerusalem would be piled up in "heaps" may also be an indirect allusion to Deuteronomy 13:16, where the law of the apostate city provides that after a city has been warned and does not repent of its apostasy, it will be destroyed by the sword and the city shall remain a ruin forever. The powerful effect of this formulation of divine judgment in Jeremiah 26:18 may well indicate that the elders in Jeremiah's day were conscious of the law of the apostate city in Deuteronomy 13:12–18, giving further legal emphasis to the prophetic warnings of Micah in the days of Hezekiah. The fate of an apostate city—that it would become a "heap" or rubble—was suitably remembered by Alma and associated with the complete destruction of the apostate inhabitants and buildings of the city of Ammonihah: "Yea, every living soul of the Ammonihahites was destroyed, and also their great city, which they said God could not destroy, because of its greatness. But behold, in one day it was left desolate; and the carcases were mangled by dogs and wild beasts of the wilderness. Nevertheless, after many days their dead bodies were heaped up upon the face of the earth, and they were covered with a shallow covering" (Alma 16:9–11).[31]

The elders at the trial of Jeremiah encouraged the people at the gate to be like their predecessors, who had listened to Micah and who had repented and sought to please Jehovah (Jeremiah 26:19). Jeremiah was released, but apparently the case was a close one even after the arguments and wisdom of the older men had been presented. One of the officials in particular, Ahikam, favored the release of Jeremiah; without his support, the text speculates that Jeremiah probably would have been executed (Jeremiah 26:24). Presumably he would have been turned over to the people to be put to death, following the traditional legal practice in which those who had heard and witnessed the misconduct would carry out the execution (Leviticus 24:14).

Conclusion

The trial of Jeremiah was an important part of the cultural landscape in the world of Jerusalem in the late seventh century. Not only did this procedure impress itself deeply on Nephite judicial procedure for years to come, but the specter of Jeremiah's trial must have hung ominously over Lehi himself, for Lehi and his fellow prophets would certainly have been well aware of Jeremiah's narrow escape. When asked to deliver essentially the same message as Jeremiah had already delivered (1 Nephi 1:13–18), Lehi could well have expected to receive a similarly hostile and life-threatening reception.[32] Only with great courage could he have gone forward, delivering his message while knowing full well that serious legal ramifications would almost certainly follow.

NOTES

1. Although it is unknown exactly when Lehi was born, it is clear that he would have been middle-aged or older during this time. See

John W. Welch, "Longevity of Book of Mormon People and the 'Age of Man,'" *Journal of Collegium Aesculapium* 3 (1985): 34–45. See also John L. Sorenson, "The Composition of Lehi's Family," in *By Study and Also by Faith: Essays in Honor of Hugh W. Nibley,* ed. John M. Lundquist and Stephen D. Ricks (Salt Lake City: Deseret Book and FARMS, 1990), 34–45.

2. Roland de Vaux, *Ancient Israel* (New York: McGraw-Hill, 1965), 1:229–31. See Philip J. King, "Jerusalem," in *Anchor Bible Dictionary,* ed. David Noel Freedman (New York: Doubleday, 1992), 3:753.

3. On the grounds "for thinking that guilds of professional prophets" functioned at this time, see E. W. Heaton, *The Hebrew Kingdoms* (Oxford: Oxford University Press, 1968), 231–37.

4. The specific details of the legal trials in the Book of Mormon have been examined in the course materials I have used for several years in teaching law in the ancient Near East, Bible, and Book of Mormon at the J. Reuben Clark Law School at Brigham Young University. The publication of those materials is forthcoming.

5. Robert P. Carroll, *Jeremiah: A Commentary* (London: SCM, 1986), 515–16.

6. John W. Welch and John F. Hall, *Charting the New Testament* (Provo, Utah: FARMS, 2002), chart 10-16, based on Bernard S. Jackson, "The Trials of Jesus and Jeremiah," *BYU Studies* 32/4 (1992): 63–77.

7. For example, *Iliad,* 2.11–40, 181–210. Discussed in E. Theodore Mullen Jr., *The Divine Council in Canaanite and Early Hebrew Literature* (Chico, Calif.: Scholars, 1980), 209–10; John W. Welch, "The Calling of Lehi as a Prophet in the World of Jerusalem," in this volume, pages 421–48.

8. See also 1 Nephi 8:36; Mosiah 18:1; 25:21; Alma 6:8; Helaman 10:4; and 3 Nephi 11:40.

9. For a demonstration that the dual agency of Moses as lawgiver and prophet strongly connects these two domains, especially in Deuteronomy 34:10–12, see Stephen B. Chapman, *The Law and the Prophets* (Tübingen: Mohr, 2000), 125–31.

10. See, for example, 1 Nephi 15:20; 19:23; 2 Nephi 11:2, 8; Mosiah 14; and 3 Nephi 23:1.

11. On simile curses in general, see Mark J. Morrise, "Simile Curses in the Ancient Near East, Old Testament, and Book of Mormon," *Journal of Book of Mormon Studies* 2/1 (1993): 124–38.

12. John Bright, *Jeremiah* (Garden City, N.Y.: Doubleday, 1979), 170.

13. Donald W. Parry, "Hebraisms and Other Ancient Peculiarities in the Book of Mormon," in *Echoes and Evidences of the Book of Mormon,* ed. Donald W. Parry, Daniel C. Peterson, and John W. Welch (Provo, Utah: FARMS, 2002), 156–59.

14. Herbert C. Brichto, *The Problem of "Curse" in the Hebrew Bible* (Philadelphia: Society of Biblical Literature, 1963), 4–13; Lyn M. Bechtel, "Shame as a Sanction of Social Control in Biblical Israel: Judicial, Political, and Social Shaming," *Journal for the Study of the Old Testament* 49 (1991): 47–76; Paul Keim, "Mundane Malediction and Sacral Sanction in Biblical Law," unpublished paper presented in 1994 to the Biblical Law Group of the Society of Biblical Literature, 15–16.

15. Moses Seidel, "Parallels between Isaiah and Psalms (in Hebrew)," *Sinai* 38 (1955–56): 149–72, 272–80, 335–55. For a discussion of some other quotations in reverse order, see David Bokovoy, "Inverted Quotations in the Book of Mormon," *Insights* 13/9 (2000): 2.

16. Bright, *Jeremiah,* 170.

17. Ibid.

18. See also verse 11, in which "the priests and the prophets" declare to "the princes and to all the people, saying, This man is worthy to die; for he hath prophesied against this city, as ye have heard with your ears." The Hebrew for "worthy to die" is *mishpat mawet,* literally meaning "judgment of death." See William McKane, *A Critical and Exegetical Commentary on Jeremiah* (Edinburgh: Clark, 1996), 2:678.

19. Bright, *Jeremiah,* 170; Carroll, *Jeremiah,* 512.

20. Bright, *Jeremiah,* 170; McKane, *Commentary on Jeremiah,* 2:680.

21. Discussed in Carroll, *Jeremiah,* 516.

22. See, for example, the conflicts in Helaman 6 and 16; 3 Nephi 1 and 7. Relationships between royalty and the temple were undoubtedly complex and changing. During some administrations, such as in the days of Solomon or Alma, the political and religious institutions

were aligned; during others, however, they conflicted. Their separate domains made such tension always possible.

23.   Robert R. Wilson, "Israel's Judicial System in the Preexilic Period," *Jewish Quarterly Review* 74/2 (1983): 229–48, esp. 244–45.

24.   McKane, *Commentary on Jeremiah,* 2:678; Carroll, *Jeremiah,* 513.

25.   De Vaux, *Ancient Israel,* 1:152–53, 155.

26.   Ephraim Stern, "How Bad Was Ahab?" *Biblical Archaeology Review* 19/2 (1993): 18–29.

27.   See, for example, Alma 1:2; 4:17–18, 20; 30:33; 50:37, 39; and 62:2, 8.

28.   Bright, *Jeremiah,* 172.

29.   Carroll, *Jeremiah,* 517.

30.   Joel S. Kaminsky, *Corporate Responsibility in the Hebrew Bible* (Sheffield: Sheffield Academic Press, 1995), 116–78.

31.   See further discussion by John W. Welch, "The Destruction of Ammonihah and the Law of Apostate Cities," in *Reexploring the Book of Mormon,* ed. John W. Welch (Salt Lake City: Deseret Book, 1992), 176–79.

32.   See, for example, Jeremiah 26:20–23, which records the account of the prophet Urijah. He fled to Egypt after delivering his message but was found and returned to Jerusalem by King Jehoiakim, who put him to death; see also McKane, *Commentary on Jeremiah,* 2:669–77.

Chapter 13

Lehi and Jeremiah: Prophets, Priests, and Patriarchs

David Rolph Seely and Jo Ann H. Seely

"For it came to pass in the commencement of the first year of the reign of Zedekiah, king of Judah, . . . there came many prophets, prophesying unto the people that they must repent, or the great city Jerusalem must be destroyed" (1 Nephi 1:4). Thus Nephi begins his record with the call of his father Lehi to become a prophet and to join the other prophets in Jerusalem prophesying the imminent destruction of Jerusalem.[1] Jeremiah was one of these prophets. Lehi in his brief ministry in Jerusalem[2] would deliver the same message that Jeremiah had delivered for almost thirty years before Lehi's call, and he would suffer the same rejection and persecution. Their respective lives and records, preserved in the Book of Mormon and the Bible, richly complement each other. Lehi and Jeremiah are first and foremost prophets. They lived and ministered to their people in a pivotal time in the history of Israel. Their records are timely in that they illustrate the perils of the period that led to the disaster of Babylonian conquest and exile for Israel and the departure of Lehi's family for the promised land. At the same time their

Jeremiah, by Michaelangelo. Detail from the Sistine Chapel.

Detail of *Lehi Preaching in Jerusalem,* by Del Parson.

messages are timeless. Lehi and Jeremiah testified of Christ through their deeds and through their words, and both looked forward to the restoration.

Lehi and Jeremiah are an interesting study in contrast. Both were prophets, but Lehi was called to leave Jerusalem and deliver his family from destruction, while Jeremiah was called to stay and witness the destruction and exile of his people. Both were priests—Lehi after the order of Melchizedek and Jeremiah a member of a distinguished Aaronid family. Both were patriarchs—Lehi of a family that would become a people divided among themselves for centuries and Jeremiah of a people who were already divided, taken into exile where they would face the challenge of maintaining their identity.

A brief review of their backgrounds and missions may foster a greater appreciation for these prophets and help illuminate the message they proclaimed. We can learn from the book of Jeremiah what it was like to live in Jerusalem at the time of Lehi, and we get a sober view of what would have happened to Lehi and his family had they not been warned by the Lord to flee.

Lehi was a wealthy family man who was well educated, as evidenced by the instruction he gave his children (see 1 Nephi 1:1–2). Because Lehi was familiar with the language of the Egyptians and with desert life, many have suggested he was a merchant.[3] He was married to Sariah, and they had four sons and an unspecified number of daughters. Two more sons were born in the wilderness as they traveled. Jeremiah, on the other hand, was a priest and was commanded not to marry or have children because the deplorable situation in Jerusalem would only result in the deaths of those children. Although Lehi found many challenges in his own family, Jeremiah would face a terrible loneliness in his prophetic calling (see Jeremiah 16:1–4).

Both men came to their people prophesying the destruction of Jerusalem because the people had broken the covenant, and both would contribute to an understanding of the covenant tradition in the future. Lehi and his family would inherit a new promised land in the Americas, given by covenant (see 2 Nephi 1:9); Jeremiah would look to the future when the Lord would give to his children "a new covenant" (Jeremiah 31:31–33).

The lives of these two men are symbolic of different aspects of Israel's relationship with the Lord. Jeremiah's life was a symbol of the justice of God and the impending destruction of Jerusalem. He was commanded not to marry and not to have children, lest they die grievous deaths (see Jeremiah 16:1–4), and he was commanded not to mourn for the people because the Lord had taken away his "lovingkindness and mercies" (Jeremiah 16:5–7). Neither was he allowed to participate in the house of feasting and joy because the day was upon Judah when gladness would cease (see Jeremiah 16:8–9). And yet Jeremiah experienced the mercies of the Lord as his life and that of his scribe Baruch were spared. Jeremiah sought solace and comfort in his relationship with the Lord and prophesied the return and restoration of his people (see Jeremiah 30–31).

Lehi's life illustrated the "tender mercies of the Lord" (1 Nephi 1:20; 2 Nephi 1:2). He was commanded to deliver his family from destruction, to leave Jerusalem, and to inherit another promised land. His family was chosen to be a remnant of the house of Israel that would be preserved from destruction (see 2 Nephi 3:5). And yet Lehi underwent severe trials in the wilderness and experienced the justice of God as he witnessed the apostasy of his sons and looked into the future and saw the terrible destructions of his people. Both prophets rejoiced in their visions of the coming of the Messiah. Jeremiah saw him in terms of justice: he "shall execute judgment and justice in the earth" (Jeremiah 23:5). Lehi saw him coming in mercy and justice (see 2 Nephi 2:8, 12).

Jeremiah, in his ministry, longed to flee into the wilderness: "Oh that I had in the wilderness a lodging place of wayfaring men; that I might leave my people, and go from them! for they be all adulterers, an assembly of treacherous men" (Jeremiah 9:2). On one occasion in his tent in the wilderness, Lehi began to murmur against the Lord because of his afflictions (see 1 Nephi 16:20), and his family forever remembered Jerusalem with nostalgia.[4]

Historical Setting

Jeremiah and Lehi were both descendants of Israel. Jeremiah was from the tribe of Levi through Aaron (see Jeremiah 1:1) and was descended from the priestly family of Abiathar. Abiathar, one of the two high priests that served under David, had supported the rebellion of David's son Adonijah; consequently, Solomon exiled Abiathar to the little town of Anathoth, two and a half miles to the northeast of Jerusalem (see 1 Kings 2:26–27). Centuries later Jeremiah was born and lived in Anathoth but spent much of his ministry in Jerusalem.

Lehi descended from the tribe of Joseph through Manasseh (see Alma 10:3), which had been assigned territory in the north when Israel entered the promised land. Nephi tells us that Lehi had lived his entire life at Jerusalem until he was called by the Lord to flee into the wilderness (see 1 Nephi 1:4). We do not know when or under what circumstances Lehi's ancestors left the land of their inheritance in Manasseh and moved to Jerusalem, but several times in the Old Testament mention is made of members of different tribes residing in Jerusalem. At the time of Asa (898 B.C.; see 2 Chronicles 15:9) and later during the days of Hezekiah (715–687 B.C.; see 2 Chronicles 30:25), there is mention of descendants of Manasseh in Jerusalem. Perhaps they had moved there to participate in the religious reforms of these two kings, or perhaps the latter group had fled from the destruction of the northern kingdom in 722 B.C. Archaeological evidence suggests that Jerusalem grew dramatically during the reign of Hezekiah, probably because of the influx of refugees from the north. This growth in population was accommodated with the construction of two new residential and commercial quarters in Jerusalem called the Mishneh (where Huldah resided; see 2 Kings 22:14) and Makhtesh (see Zephaniah 1:10).[5]

David established the capital of the united kingdom in Jerusalem around 1000 B.C., and his son Solomon built the temple there. In 922 B.C., at the beginning of the reign of Solomon's son Rehoboam, the kingdoms divided between the ten northern tribes and the two southern tribes. In 722 B.C. the northern kingdom of Israel was destroyed and the ten tribes were taken into captivity by Assyria. Although many cities in the southern kingdom were destroyed by the Assyrians in 701 B.C. (see 2 Kings 18:13), Jerusalem was miraculously preserved because the people repented under the direction of the prophet Isaiah and the righteous king Hezekiah (715–687 B.C.; see 2 Kings 18–19; Isaiah 36–37). Hezekiah was followed by Manasseh, known in 2 Kings as the most wicked of all the kings of Judah. He established idolatrous worship throughout the land, even in the temple, and shed much innocent blood (see 2 Kings 21). We do not know exactly the dates of the births of Jeremiah or Lehi, but it is very likely that they were born either during or immediately after the reign of the wicked king Manasseh (687–642 B.C.) and that they were very close to the same age. Jeremiah was called to be a prophet as a young man in 627 B.C. (see Jeremiah 1:6).[6] Lehi was called to be a prophet in 597 B.C., already a man with grown sons and daughters.

Jeremiah and Lehi lived their early years during the reign of King Josiah, known as one of the most righteous of Judah's kings. He came to the throne at a young age and was instrumental in cleansing the temple and reestablishing the covenant. Both Lehi and Jeremiah must have been encouraged by the repentance of the people. As the Assyrian Empire was beginning to weaken, there were great hopes of nationalism, but Josiah was tragically killed at Megiddo in 609 B.C., after which two decades of tumult began. Josiah was replaced by Jehoahaz, who was shortly taken into exile to Egypt and replaced by his brother Jehoiakim (609–587 B.C.). At the Battle of Carchemish in 605 B.C., Babylon decisively defeated Assyria. Jehoiakim rebelled against Babylon, which led to the exile of a select group of Jews to Babylon in 598 B.C. Jehoiakim died and was replaced by his son Jehoiachin, who was promptly exiled to Babylon after ruling only three months. The Babylonians next put Zedekiah, a son of Josiah, on the throne. All of these events combined to shape the world of Jeremiah and Lehi in which the beginning of the Book of Mormon takes place.

The Jerusalem of their time was a city of about 125 acres and a population of between 25,000 to 30,000 people.[7] It had expanded beyond the original Jebusite city that David conquered to include the temple and its surroundings built by Solomon, the citadel with the palaces, as well as the quarters called the Mishneh and Makhtesh. The city walls had been expanded and repaired by Uzziah, Hezekiah, and Manasseh to encompass much of the hill to the west of the city. Jeremiah, who lived in a village outside of Jerusalem, spent much of his time in and around the temple precincts because of his duties as prophet and priest. Lehi may have lived in one of the new quarters of Jerusalem or even outside the city.[8]

Lehi and his family certainly knew of the prophet Jeremiah. Some of his prophecies up to the time of Zedekiah had already been copied onto the brass plates (see 1 Nephi 5:13). Furthermore, Nephi made note of Jeremiah's incarceration (see 1 Nephi 7:14). These observations raise an important question of whether Lehi and his family departed early in the reign of King Zedekiah, perhaps within the first year of his reign (597–596 B.C.), or whether the party left Jerusalem just before the final Babylonian siege some ten years later. Randall Spackman has brought forward reasons for the later dating that are based largely on Nephi's reference to the imprisonment of Jeremiah (see 1 Nephi 7:14) and the fact that, according to Jeremiah's book, he went to prison in the tenth year of Zedekiah's rule, only months before the Babylonians captured the city (see Jeremiah 32:1–2; 37:15–16, 21; 38:6–13, 28).[9] The book of Jeremiah is silent about Jeremiah's activities during the first year of Zedekiah's reign. If Jeremiah was imprisoned at that time, as suggested by the Book of Mormon (see 1 Nephi 7:14), we would not expect to find a reference to this imprisonment in the Bible. But two passages in Jeremiah's book may refer to earlier imprisonments. In 605 B.C. Jeremiah declared "I am shut up," referring to the fact that he was restricted from going into the temple area (Jeremiah 36:5). The Hebrew word he used (ʿatsur) is ambiguous. It can mean "imprisoned" or "in custody." In fact, it is the word in Jeremiah 33:1 that refers to his imprisonment. Later, in 601 B.C., Jeremiah was punished by being put in "the stocks" (Jeremiah 20:1–6). The Hebrew word used here is also not clear; some translations take it as meaning "imprisoned." Hence, Jeremiah's celebrated imprisonment just before the city fell to the Babylonians in 587 B.C. was not the only instance in which the prophet had been officially restrained.[10]

Lehi and Jeremiah may have known each other, and it may well have been through the priesthood that they shared association. We may assume that those commissioned by the Lord to prophesy in Jerusalem were acquainted with each other. Orders of the prophets known as the "sons of the prophets" were known in ancient Israel from the time of Saul and Samuel (see 1 Samuel 10:5; 19:20) and at the time of Elijah (see 1 Kings 18:4) and Elisha (see 2 Kings 2:3; 3:11; 4:1, 38; 6:1–2). (False prophets were also apparently organized [see 1 Kings 22:6; 2 Kings 23:2; Jeremiah 26: 7–8].) It is possible that a group of legitimate prophets also existed in Jerusalem shortly before the exile. Joseph Smith taught that all the prophets, presumably including Jeremiah, had the Melchizedek Priesthood.[11] Lehi and his family certainly had the Melchizedek Priesthood, as evidenced by Alma 13, which describes the Nephite priesthood as Melchizedek. It is likely that Lehi and Jeremiah were part of a Melchizedek Priesthood community in Jerusalem, and it is not unlikely that one even received his priesthood authority from the other.

The Records

Lehi kept a record, although we only know it through the writings of his sons. Nephi used his father's record in his own account on the large plates and the small plates.[12] In the small plates, Nephi and Jacob give us portions from the record of Lehi interspersed in their own writings (see 1 Nephi 1–2 Nephi 4; Jacob 2:23–24; 3:5). Nephi tells us he did not make a "full account of the things which [his] father hath written, for he hath written many things which he saw in visions and in dreams; and he also hath written many things which he prophesied and spake unto his children" but that he made an "abridgment of the record of [his] father" (1 Nephi 1:16–17).

A collection of the writings of Jeremiah was preserved on the brass plates and another passed down—now found in the Old Testament. The Book of Mormon records that the brass plates contained "the prophecies of the holy prophets, from the beginning, even down to the commencement of the reign of Zedekiah; and also many prophecies which have been spoken by the mouth of Jeremiah" (1 Nephi 5:13).[13] Although we do not know the process by which the keeper of the brass plates acquired and wrote the prophecies on the plates, the book of Jeremiah is the only book in the entire Bible that tells us how it originated.

In 605 B.C. the Lord commanded Jeremiah to recite to his scribe Baruch all the words of the Lord from the time of Josiah down to that moment (see Jeremiah 36:1–4). Jeremiah then commanded Baruch to take this scroll and read it to the people in the precincts of the temple (see Jeremiah 36:8). This Baruch did, but, when King Jehoiakim heard about it, he ordered Baruch to deliver the scroll to the king. Jehoiakim had a servant read the scroll to him, and as he heard the words of the Lord read to him, he took his knife and cut the scroll in pieces and burned it (see Jeremiah 36:20–26). The Lord then commanded Jeremiah to take a fresh scroll and give it to Baruch and to dictate again the prophecies. Baruch wrote down all of the prophecies that had been lost, together with many similar words (see Jeremiah 36:32).

From this account we learn many significant things about the book of Jeremiah, and several possibilities emerge as to how Jeremiah's writings were preserved on the brass plates. First, it seems clear that Jeremiah maintained the prophecies in his memory for a long time. Jehoiakim's destruction of the scroll of Jeremiah may have provided the impetus for the keeper of the record on the brass plates to acquire a copy of the prophecies of Jeremiah. The keeper of the brass plates could have had Jeremiah dictate the prophecies directly to him to be recorded on the plates; possibly Baruch loaned him the scroll; or perhaps the keeper of the brass plates copied the record from the second scroll as a backup in case the scroll was again destroyed. It is interesting that the Book of Mormon does not specify that the prophecies of Jeremiah up to the time of Zedekiah were preserved. Perhaps this is an indication that the sayings of Jeremiah were copied onto the brass plates in conjunction with the attempt to destroy the prophecies of Jeremiah during the reign of King Jehoiakim (see Jeremiah 36).

Prophetic Calling

Both prophets began their records with an account of their call. Jeremiah was called in his youth. In 627 B.C. the word of the Lord came to Jeremiah and called him to be a prophet to the nations, delivering messages of destruction—"to destroy, and to throw down"—and of restoration—"to build, and to plant" (Jeremiah 1:10). The Lord revealed to him, "Before I formed thee in the belly I knew thee; and before thou camest forth out of the womb I sanctified thee, and I ordained thee a prophet unto the nations" (Jeremiah 1:5). Jeremiah was overwhelmed and replied in language rather like that of Enoch and Moses, "Ah, Lord God! behold, I cannot speak: for I am a child" (Jeremiah 1:6). The Lord commanded him to "be not afraid" (Jeremiah 1:7) to go where he was sent and to deliver the message, which was given symbolically to Jeremiah by the touch of the Lord's hand to his mouth (see Jeremiah 1:7–10). The Lord reassured him that "I have made thee this day a defenced city, and an iron pillar" against the kings, princes, priests, and people, and "they shall not prevail against thee; for I am with thee" (Jeremiah 1:18–19; see also 1:11–17). His entire life's mission consisted of delivering the word of the Lord and witnessing the calamities that befell those who would not respond.

Lehi, on the other hand, received his visionary call as a mature man, while praying "with all his heart, in behalf of his people" (1 Nephi 1:5)—behavior already suggesting prophetic stature. Because we do not have his complete record, we cannot be certain that this is the first time he received divine instruction, but it is the first vision that we have record of, and it is reminiscent of the vision in Isaiah 6, where that prophet saw the Lord upon his throne at the time he received his prophetic call (see Isaiah 6:1–13). Lehi recorded that "he thought he saw God sitting upon his throne" with the angels singing and praising God. He then saw one whose "luster was above that of the sun at noon-day" and "twelve others following him" (1 Nephi 1:8–10). Lehi was also given a book to read, from which he learned of the abominations and destruction of Jerusalem and that many would perish and many would be taken to Babylon in captivity. He did not respond with fear but with rejoicing because the Lord is "merciful, thou wilt not suffer those who come unto thee that they shall perish!" In fact, "his whole heart was filled, because of the things which he had seen, yea, which the Lord had shown unto him" (1 Nephi 1:14–15). Lehi then "went forth among the people, and began to prophesy and to declare unto them concerning the things which he had both seen and heard" (1 Nephi 1:18).

Types of Moses and Types of Christ

Although Jeremiah and Lehi were both prophets and both delivered similar messages, their lives were quite different. Each of their ministries manifested the will of the Lord and testified of the Savior, but in very different ways.

Lehi and his family would relive the exodus.[14] Lehi received his call when he went before the Lord in the tradition of Moses as mediator for his people (see Exodus 32:30–32), praying "in behalf of his people" (1 Nephi 1:5). The Lord appeared to him just as he appeared to the children of Israel in the wilderness— as a "pillar of fire" (1 Nephi 1:6). Lehi became like Moses as he gathered his children, delivered them from the apostate and idolatrous world of Jerusalem, and led them into the wilderness. There they were tested and tried, as were the children of Israel. At the same time they were guided and protected by the Lord. Nevertheless, his family, like the children of Israel, responded by murmuring. Just as Moses suffered from the hardheartedness, stiffneckedness, and rebellion of the children of Israel, at one point including members of his own family, Aaron and Miriam, so did Lehi suffer from the rebellion of his own children. Furthermore, the children of Israel rebelled against Moses and sought to kill him; Laman and Lemuel, along with the children of Ishmael, rebelled against Lehi and attempted to kill him (see 1 Nephi 16:13; 17:44).

Whereas Moses led his people to Sinai, where they received the law on tablets of stone and built the ark and the tabernacle, Lehi led his people into the desert with the law safely preserved on plates of brass. After many trials the children of Israel entered Canaan, a land of milk and honey, under the direction of Joshua. Lehi led his family to the promised land—a land of great abundance given to them by covenant (see 1 Nephi 18:24–25)—with the same conditions given to the children of Israel as they entered Canaan: if they were righteous, they would prosper; if they were wicked, they would be destroyed (see 2 Nephi 1:20).

Moses, before he was taken away from his people,[15] gathered the children of Israel and pronounced a series of blessings and curses upon their heads and prophesied that in the future the children of Israel would be scattered by their enemies and then gathered (see Deuteronomy 27–30). Likewise, Lehi, on his deathbed, gathered his posterity around him and pronounced upon them conditional blessings and curses. Lehi saw his seed both blessed and cursed, depending on their acceptance of the Holy One of Israel, and their eventual destruction, scattering, and gathering (see 2 Nephi 1:1–4:12).

Lehi would be remembered by his descendants as the deliverer and the founder of their community (see Mosiah 7:19–20), and the divine deliverance of Lehi and his family was understood as a type and a shadow of the divine deliverance from sin and death that would be provided in the future by the atonement (see Alma 36:28–29). Lehi was a patriarch over a family that would build, plant, and establish a covenant community that would last for more than a thousand years. They would write a book that would contain the fulness of the gospel and would be one of the keystones of the restoration. This book would be restored in the latter days to bring Lehi's descendants back to a knowledge of the covenants and to Christ.

The course of Jeremiah's life tragically turned out to be a reversal of the exodus. Whereas Moses led his people away from idolatrous Egypt and presided over a people that wandered in the wilderness for forty years until they had purified themselves to enter the promised land, Jeremiah ministered for forty years (627–587 B.C.) to a people who became increasingly wicked until they were expelled from the promised land. Jeremiah was a prophet whose mission can be seen as opposite to that of Moses.[16] Moses openly contested the gods of Pharaoh and demonstrated the power of God to deliver his people at the Red Sea. Jeremiah called the people to repent of their worship of idols but openly urged them to surrender and taught them that it was the Lord's will for them to submit to wicked and idolatrous Babylon. Although Moses heroically interceded for his people at Sinai, Jeremiah was commanded not to intercede for his people (see Jeremiah 7:16–20; 15:1–4). Moses was the intermediary who established the covenant with Israel at Sinai and brought to his people the law inscribed on stone. Jeremiah looked forward to the establishment of the new covenant when the law would be written on the fleshy tablets of the heart (see Jeremiah 31:31–34). Moses left his people at Nebo on the threshold of the promised land; Jeremiah was forced by his friends to leave the promised land and, crossing the wilderness, to enter Egypt. His final words were prophecies foretelling the destruction of those from Judah who would return to Egypt and resume the practice of idolatry (see Jeremiah 44).

An overlooked role of Jeremiah's life was that he presided over the exile from afar. Many of the righteous among Israel were exiled to Babylon, and Jeremiah, although he had no direct descendants that we know of, was a patriarch over Israel in exile. He wrote a letter to the exiles urging them to build and to plant (see Jeremiah 29:5) and to raise their families where they were. Jeremiah advised his contemporaries to submit to Babylon, for the Lord was in charge. He told them that Israel would only be restored and gathered in the time of the Lord. The children of Israel emerged from the exile strengthened against idolatry. Jeremiah was remembered by his people as providing the model of living in the exile, of patiently submitting to the political rule of other powerful nations until the Lord again would gather and restore them to their homeland. In a sense, Jeremiah was the father of the Jews in exile. The model authored by Jeremiah has been followed by the Jews until the twentieth century, when they again established a homeland in Israel and began to exercise political independence.

"The Manner of Prophesying"

There was a sophisticated tradition or style of prophecy among the ancient Israelites called by Nephi "the manner of prophesying among the Jews" (2 Nephi 25:1). The word of the Lord was communicated to the prophets through dreams, visions, or sometimes through the spoken word. It was often presented in poetry, replete with dramatic and vivid imagery and symbols. Sometimes the prophets communicated the word of the Lord orally, sometimes in writing, and sometimes through symbolic acts. Jeremiah and Lehi are both prime examples of prophets within this tradition. They were both visionary men whose lives and prophecies were full of graphic symbols and images.

Many of Lehi's divine communications came through dreams and visions. At the outset of his ministry he saw God on his throne and the coming of the Savior, and he read a book containing the abominations of his people. He then saw the marvelous vision of the tree of life that represented the quest for eternal life (see 1 Nephi 8). In this vision Lehi saw his family following a path, holding to a rod of iron, and moving through the mist of darkness toward the tree of life to partake of the fruit. Laman and Lemuel would not partake of the fruit, and Lehi used his account of this vision to exhort his sons to hearken to his words and seek the mercy of the Lord. Nephi, desiring to "see, and hear, and know of these things," prayed to the Lord for help in understanding. In response, he was told that "the mysteries of God shall be unfolded . . . by the power of the Holy Ghost" (1 Nephi 10:17, 19). Laman and Lemuel were not able to understand the symbolism of Lehi's vision and complained, "We cannot understand the words which our father hath spoken," and Nephi asked them, "Have ye inquired of the Lord?" (1 Nephi 15:7, 8). On another occasion in the wilderness, Lehi named the river Laman and the valley Lemuel in a dramatic attempt to teach his sons through symbolic acts.

Jeremiah too had visions—frequently they were occasions when the Lord used ordinary objects such as an almond rod (see Jeremiah 1:11–12), a seething pot (see Jeremiah 1:13–14), a basket of figs (see Jeremiah 24), and a cup of wrath (see Jeremiah 25:15–38) to teach divine truths. Throughout his ministry Jeremiah was called upon to perform a series of dramatic symbolic acts to teach his people: burying a linen girdle as a symbol of the exile (see Jeremiah 13), watching a potter at work as a symbol of the destruction and restoration of Israel (see Jeremiah 18), breaking an earthen flask as a symbol of destruction (see Jeremiah 19), wearing a yoke as a symbol of captivity (see Jeremiah 27:2–28:17), purchasing land in Anathoth as a symbol of return and restoration (see Jeremiah 32:6–44), and bringing the Rechabites before the king as an example of a people faithful to their covenants.

Message: Repent or Be Destroyed

The prophecies of Jeremiah and Lehi have four common and central themes: repentance and the impending destruction and exile by the Babylonians; the coming of the Messiah; the future scattering and gathering of Israel; and the eventual restoration of the gospel in the latter days.

In the years preceding Lehi's departure from Jerusalem, King Josiah had cleansed the temple and renewed the covenant between the Lord and his people. What should have been the best of times, however, had become the worst of times. Lehi testified to Jerusalem of her "wickedness and . . . abominations" (1 Nephi 1:19), and Jeremiah spelled out what they were. At the beginning of the reign of Jehoiakim (609 B.C.), Jeremiah delivered a powerful sermon at the temple (see Jeremiah 7; 26). He warned his people that the temple would not save them from destruction if they did not repent. Although the sacrificial system of the law of Moses was faithfully being carried out at the temple, it masked the hypocrisy of the people who broke the Ten Commandments and worshipped idols. Jeremiah accused his people of stealing, murder, swearing falsely, all manner of idolatry (see Jeremiah 7:9), and of oppressing the stranger, the fatherless, and the widows (see Jeremiah 7:6). The people, on the other hand, trusted that the temple made them invincible. They probably looked back to the reign of Hezekiah when they were delivered from the Assyrian destruction in 701 B.C. by the miraculous destruction of the Assyrian army (see 2 Kings 19).[17] The people thought that the Lord would deliver them from the Babylonians. This attitude is reflected in the Book of Mormon by Laman and Lemuel, who never did "believe that Jerusalem, that great city, could be destroyed" (1 Nephi 2:13; see also Helaman 8:21).

Both men were persecuted for their prophecies, and the Jews sought their lives. Jeremiah was repeatedly arrested, tried, and eventually put into a pit. Lehi's life was threatened in Jerusalem, and in the wilderness he had to face the murmuring and the persecution of his own sons (see 1 Nephi 2:13). That the threat to their lives was real is illustrated by the story in the book of Jeremiah of the prophet Urijah, the son of Shemaiah, who prophesied against Jerusalem during the reign of King Jehoiakim according to all the words of Jeremiah. When the king heard his words, he sought his life; Urijah fled to Egypt but was forcefully extradited and taken back to Jerusalem, where the king had him executed with a sword and thrown into a common grave (see Jeremiah 26:20–23).

Lehi was able to escape the destruction of Jerusalem that he witnessed in vision (see 2 Nephi 1:4). Jeremiah witnessed with his own eyes the disaster that he had attempted for forty years to avoid—the destruction of his people and the exile of the remainder. Jeremiah's record contains a sobering description of what would have happened to Lehi's family had they remained in Jerusalem. Jeremiah describes the Babylonian siege that lasted two and a half years and tells us that famine ravaged the city; when the city fell, many were slain, the temple was sacked and burned, and most of the survivors were taken into exile (see Jeremiah 39; 52). In the book of Lamentations Jeremiah describes young and old, virgins and young men, lying dead in the streets (see Lamentations 2:21); the famine became so intense that "pitiful women" cooked and ate "their own children" (Lamentations 4:10).

Message: Coming of Christ

Both prophets saw and prophesied the coming of the Messiah. Lehi saw a vision in which he read from a book things that "manifested plainly of the coming of a Messiah, and also the redemption of the world" (1 Nephi 1:19). Lehi further described a detailed dream in which he saw the coming of John the Baptist, John's baptism of the Messiah, and the ministry of the Savior, his rejection and crucifixion on earth, and his resurrection (see 1 Nephi 10:4–11). Most important, Lehi, in a masterful sermon directed to his son Jacob, taught the doctrine of the fall and the atonement and how the plan makes eternal life possible (see 2 Nephi 2).

The prophet Nephi (son of Helaman) taught his people that many Old Testament prophets, including Jeremiah, had seen the day of the coming of the Messiah and the redemption that he would bring (see Helaman 8:20, 22–23). The writings of Jeremiah in the Bible indeed contain two such prophecies about the coming of the Messiah (see Jeremiah 23:1–8; 33:15–18)—perhaps there were more on the brass plates that are no longer preserved in the Bible. Both prophecies foresaw the day when God will "raise unto David a righteous Branch, and a King" who will "reign and prosper, and shall execute judgment and justice in the earth" (Jeremiah 23:5; see also 33:15). Interpreters have variously seen these prophecies as pointing to either the first or the second comings of Christ or both.

Message: Scattering and Restoration

Jeremiah and Lehi are central to the restoration. Not only did they see and prophesy the events of the restoration, but their records played a significant role in the reestablishment of the covenant in the fulness of times. In 1823 Moroni appeared to Joseph Smith and read to him a series of Old Testament prophecies to be fulfilled in the restoration. Among these prophecies were Malachi 3–4; Isaiah 11; Acts 3:22–23; Joel 2:28–32 (see JS—H 1:36–41). Oliver Cowdery recorded that Moroni also had read a series of passages from Jeremiah including 16:16; 30:18–21; 31:1, 6, 8, 27–28, 32–33; 50:4–5.[18] In these passages Jeremiah saw the day when the "hunters" and "fishers" would be sent forth to gather Israel (Jeremiah 16:16); when God would gather Israel to be his people (see Jeremiah 31:1); when "the watchmen upon the mount Ephraim shall cry, Arise ye, and let us go up to Zion unto the Lord our God" (Jeremiah 31:6); when the Lord would "sow" again the land with the seed of the house of Israel and Judah, who would then build and plant (Jeremiah 31:27–28); and when the Lord would "make a new covenant with the house of Israel, and with the house of Judah" (Jeremiah 31:31)—in the words of the Lord, "Not according to the covenant that I made with their fathers" in Egypt, which was written in stone, but a "law in their inward parts, and write it in their hearts" (Jeremiah 31:32, 33).[19]

Lehi delivered to his family a prophecy given by the Lord to Joseph of Egypt that a "righteous branch" of the house of Israel, not the Messiah (2 Nephi 3:5), would be broken off, and in the future a choice seer would be raised out of this lineage (see 2 Nephi 3:6), who would bring many to the knowledge of the covenants made with the fathers (see 2 Nephi 3:7). He continued that the descendants of Judah and the descendants of Joseph would both write records that would "grow together, unto the confounding of false doctrines and laying down of contentions, and establishing peace among the fruit of thy loins, and bringing them to the knowledge of their fathers in the latter days, and also to the knowledge of my covenants, saith the Lord" (2 Nephi 3:12).

Lehi and Jeremiah both participated in the fulfillment of these prophecies. Lehi, a descendant of Joseph, founded the people that would author the Book of Mormon. In 1827 Moroni delivered the gold plates, containing a record of Lehi's descendants, to Joseph Smith, fulfilling the prophecy of Joseph of Egypt. For Joseph Smith was "a choice seer" from the loins of Joseph (2 Nephi 3:7) with the power to bring forth the word of the Lord to Lehi's seed (see 2 Nephi 3:11). He was named after Joseph of old and after his father Joseph (see 2 Nephi 3:15). The Book of Mormon would be an instrument in the hand of the Lord to bring his children to Christ through the restoration and to bring about the gathering of Israel and Judah in the latter days.

Jeremiah died in obscurity in Egypt, but his words were passed down through the ages in the Bible, the writings of the Jews. In 1830 the Book of Mormon was published, and with the publication of the Book of Mormon the records of these two peoples were joined, fulfilling the prophecy of Joseph of Egypt that these records "shall grow together" to bring many to the knowledge of the covenants (see 2 Nephi 3:12). Although the will of the Lord was manifested very differently in their lives and writings, Lehi and Jeremiah in their prophetic callings proclaimed to all their witness of Christ.

NOTES

This article was originally published in the *Journal of Book of Mormon Studies* 8/2 (1999): 24–35; it has been revised slightly.

1. Besides Jeremiah and Lehi, from this period we know of the prophetess Huldah and the prophets Zephaniah, Habakkuk, and Urijah of Kirjath-jearim (see Jeremiah 26) in Judah, and Ezekiel and Daniel in exile.

2. Some interpret the Book of Mormon evidence that Lehi left Jerusalem within a very short period after his call. Others have argued that he may have prophesied for ten years in Jerusalem before he left. See Randall P. Spackman, "The Jewish/Nephite Lunar Calendar," *Journal of Book of Mormon Studies* 7/1 (1998): 57.

3. See Hugh W. Nibley, *Lehi in the Desert, The World of the Jaredites, There Were Jaredites* (Salt Lake City: Deseret Book and FARMS, 1988), 34–42. See also John A. Tvedtnes, "Was Lehi a Caravaneer?" in *The Most Correct Book: Insights from a Book of Mormon Scholar* (Salt Lake City: Cornerstone, 1999), 77–98.

4. S. Kent Brown, "What Is Isaiah Doing in First Nephi? Or, How Did Lehi's Family Fare so Far from Home," in *From Jerusalem to Zarahemla* (Provo, Utah: BYU Religious Studies Center, 1998), 12–17.

5. Nahman Avigad, *Discovering Jerusalem* (Nashville: Nelson, 1983), 54.

6. Some scholars believe this date represents the birth of Jeremiah, who was called from the womb—in which case he would be almost thirty when the Book of Mormon opens, younger than Lehi.

7. Magen Broshi, "Estimating the Population of Ancient Jerusalem," *Biblical Archaeology Review* 4/2 (1978): 12.

8. When Nephi and his brothers were sent back to Jerusalem to obtain the brass plates, they found it necessary to "go down to the land of our father's inheritance" (1 Nephi 3:16) in order to retrieve their property and "up again unto the house of Laban" (1 Nephi 3:23) to bargain with Laban for the plates (see 1 Nephi 3:22–24). Some Latter-day Saint scholars believe this language indicates Lehi and his family lived "outside" of Jerusalem. Nibley, *Lehi in the Desert*, 7 n. 12. See also Lynn

M. Hilton and Hope Hilton, *In Search of Lehi's Trail* (Salt Lake City: Deseret Book, 1996), 34–35.

9. Randall P. Spackman, "Introduction to Book of Mormon Chronology: The Principal Prophecies, Calendars, and Dates" (Provo, Utah: FARMS, 1993), 6–14; and "Jewish/Nephite Lunar Calendar," 57–59.

10. See W. L. Holladay, *Jeremiah* (Philadelphia: Fortress, 1986), 1:1–10, for a chronology of events in Jeremiah's prophetic career.

11. See *Teachings of the Prophet Joseph Smith,* sel. Joseph Fielding Smith (Salt Lake City: Deseret Book, 1976), 180–81.

12. The translation of Mormon's abridgment of the large plates for the period from Lehi to Mosiah was part of the 116 pages lost by Martin Harris (*History of the Church,* 1:20–28; D&C 3, 10). For a discussion of Lehi's record, see S. Kent Brown, "Recovering the Missing Record of Lehi," in *From Jerusalem to Zarahemla,* 28–54.

13. The writings of several prophets that are preserved on the brass plates are not found in the Old Testament: Zenos, Zenock, Neum, and Ezias (see 1 Nephi 19:10; Helaman 8:19–20).

14. Important articles discussing the exodus typology in the Book of Mormon include George S. Tate, "The Typology of the Exodus Pattern in the Book of Mormon," in *Literature of Belief: Sacred Scripture and Religious Experience,* ed. Neal E. Lambert (Provo, Utah: BYU Religious Studies Center, 1981), 245–62; S. Kent Brown, "The Exodus Pattern in the Book of Mormon," in *From Jerusalem to Zarahemla,* 75–98.

15. Although the biblical text implies that Moses died, the Book of Mormon makes it clear that he was actually translated (see Alma 45:19).

16. Some scholars have even called him an "anti-Moses." See, for example, Luis A. Schokel, "Jeremías como anti-Moisés," in *De la Torah au Messie, Mélanges Henri Cazelles,* ed. M. Carrez, J. Doré, and P. Grelot (Paris: Desclée, 1981), 245–54.

17. See Jeffrey R. Chadwick, "Lehi's House at Jerusalem and the Land of His Inheritance," in this volume, pages 81–130.

18. Oliver Cowdery's report is found in the *Messenger and Advocate* 1/5 (1835): 78–80; 1/7 (1935): 108–12; and 1/10 (1835): 156–59.

A convenient list and important discussion of these passages can be found in Kent P. Jackson, "The Appearance of Moroni to Joseph Smith (JS—H 27–49)," in *Studies in Scripture: Volume Two: The Pearl of Great Price,* ed. Robert L. Millet and Kent P. Jackson (Salt Lake City: Randall Book, 1985), 339–66.

   19. See *Teachings of the Prophet Joseph Smith,* 14–15.

Chapter 14

Sacred History, Covenants, and the Messiah: The Religious Background of the World of Lehi

David Rolph Seely

Lehi and his family were shaped by their ancient heritage preserved to some extent for us today in the Old Testament. A knowledge of the religious background of Lehi and his family can help us to understand many aspects of the Book of Mormon. In particular, the title page of the Book of Mormon, probably written by Moroni, describes the contents of the Book of Mormon and identifies the three intended purposes of the Book of Mormon to the readers in the latter days. These three purposes are:

1. "To show unto the remnant of the House of Israel what great things the Lord hath done for their fathers";

2. "And that they may know the covenants of the Lord, that they are not cast off forever";

3. "And also to the convincing of the Jew and Gentile that Jesus is the Christ, the Eternal God, manifesting himself unto all nations."

This study approaches the religious background of Lehi's world and its impact on the Book of Mormon by discussing these three subjects: the great things contained in sacred history, the covenants of the Lord, and the significance of Jesus as the Christ.

The religious heritage of Lehi and his family was transmitted both orally and in written form. While the stories of the past about Adam and Eve, Abraham, and Moses were passed from parents to children, the key to understanding the religious background and tradition of Lehi and his world is to be found in the plates of brass, which contained the written form of the ancient religious traditions. In this record we can see the importance of the three purposes of the Book of Mormon.

Nephi described the contents of the brass plates as containing four kinds of material: law, history, writings of the prophets, and genealogy. Nephi noted that the record would be important for his people in that it contained the law (1 Nephi 4:16) in the "five books of Moses" (1 Nephi 5:11) that would be of "great worth unto us, insomuch that we could preserve the commandments of the Lord unto our children" (1 Nephi 5:21). The law was the heart of the biblical covenants made with Abraham and Moses and foreshadowed the "new covenant" that Jesus Christ would bring.

In addition, the plates of brass contained a history of Israel, "a record of the Jews from the beginning [including the creation and the account of Adam and Eve], even down to the commencement of the reign of Zedekiah" (1 Nephi 5:12). From this record the Nephites would be able to remember and teach the "great things" that the Lord had done for their fathers from Adam and Eve to Abraham and Moses all the way to the present.

The brass plates also preserved "the prophecies of the holy prophets, from the beginning, even down to the commencement of the reign of Zedekiah" (1 Nephi 5:13). From the plates of brass, Nephi, Jacob, Abinadi, and other Book of Mormon prophets would have had access to the words of Isaiah, Zenos, Zenock, Neum, and others. The most important prophecies were those of the coming of the Messiah since the Book of Mormon peoples lived before Christ and had to rely on inspired views of the future in order to understand the nature and reality of Jesus Christ and the atonement.

Finally, Lehi was delighted to find that his family genealogy tracing his lineage back to Joseph was also preserved on this record (1 Nephi 5:14); this helped them to understand their place in the Abrahamic covenant through the promises and covenants of the birthright son, Joseph. In addition, Nephi noted that the language of his fathers would be preserved through this record (1 Nephi 3:19).

While there is much we do not know about the brass plates—their origin, transmission, and exact contents[1]—we do know enough to be able to appreciate the importance of a written record to a religious community and to see the significance of sacred history, prophecies, and expectations concerning the coming of Christ. These three elements were part of Lehi's Jerusalem, growing out of his rich Israelite heritage.

Sacred History as a Record of the Great Things the Lord Has Done for the Fathers

Which is to show unto the remnant of the House of Israel what great things the Lord hath done for their fathers (Title Page)

The sacred history (a history that acknowledges the participation of God in the affairs of humans) contained in the Bible preserves the record of the great things the Lord has done for his children throughout history. The covenant people at the time of Lehi understood that their relationship was with a God who could and would intervene in history on their behalf. The central events that defined Israel—as judged by the Old Testament—are the creation, the calling of Abraham out of the world by covenant, the exodus and crossing of the Red Sea, and the conquest of the promised land. Lehi and his family secured the plates of brass as a record of these events in order to better help them remember their sacred history. The Book of Mormon carries on this tradition of measuring Israel's relationship with God by recording the great things God had done in the past for their fathers and in the present for them. The Book of Mormon prophets exhort future readers to remember all these great things.

From the beginning of time, records were kept of the relationship between God and his children. Adam kept a record by the spirit of inspiration, and Adam and Eve taught their children to read and write (Moses 6:5–6) and taught them the gospel (Moses 6:56–58). The most important teaching was "that all men, everywhere, must repent," and this must have included the knowledge of the coming of the Only Begotten to atone for the sins of the world—that God would intervene in the course of history and redeem his children from the fall. Abraham also had access to and created sacred records. Specifically, he referred to a "chronology running back from myself to the beginning of the creation" (Abraham 1:28). The Pearl of Great Price preserves a book that he left to his posterity.

Moses came and established the Mosaic covenant with the people. According to the Book of Moses, he received a vision of the creation, the fall and the atonement, and the record of Enoch. According to tradition, the books from Genesis to Deuteronomy were authored by Moses, and Nephi mentions that the five books of Moses were found on the brass plates.

Sacred History

Before the Lord gave the covenant on Mount Sinai, he rehearsed for his people his role in delivering them from Egypt, "Ye have seen what I did unto the Egyptians, and how I bare you on eagles' wings, and brought you unto myself" (Exodus 19:4). This set the pattern in the Bible that the covenant obligations were to be preceded by a recital of the great things the Lord had done for his people. The purpose of this reminder was to prompt Israel about her obligation to the Lord and to inspire the Israelites to be obedient to their covenants.

Another example is found in the book of Deuteronomy, which is a restatement at Mount Nebo of the covenant given at Sinai. The first four chapters of Deuteronomy review the specific ways in which the Lord intervened on behalf of the children of Israel during the exodus from Egypt through the wilderness to Mount Nebo and on the plains of Moab. The law is then rehearsed in the ensuing chapters. The book of Deuteronomy identifies the significance of the exodus in sacred history: "For ask now of the days that are past, which were before thee, since the day that God created man upon the earth, and ask from the one side of heaven unto the other, whether there hath been any such thing as this great thing is, or hath been heard like it?" (Deuteronomy 4:32).

At Shechem Joshua led the people in a ceremony of covenant renewal in which he reminded the people of a series of important events beginning with the call of Abraham: "And I took your father Abraham from the other side of the flood [Euphrates], and led him throughout all the land of Canaan, and multiplied his seed, and gave him Isaac" (Joshua 24:3). Joshua also reminded the people how the Lord through Moses and Aaron had delivered them from Egypt and how the Lord delivered the land of Canaan to them through their faithfulness

and the victory over their enemies. The function of this historical prologue is stated: "Now therefore fear the Lord, and serve
him in sincerity and in truth: and put away the gods which your
fathers served on the other side of the flood [the Euphrates], and
in Egypt; and serve ye the Lord" (Joshua 24:14).

The most complete recounting of Israel's sacred history is
found in Ezra's ceremony of covenant renewal with the exiles
returned from Babylon (Nehemiah 9:6–38). In this ceremony
Ezra recounted the history of Israel and included such events
and people as the creation, Abraham, Moses, the conquest, the
period of the judges, the ensuing years in which the Lord sent
prophets to his disobedient children to warn them of impending destruction, and the return and reestablishment of the
covenant.

Remembering in the Old Testament

Throughout the Old Testament, the Lord implored his children to "remember" him and to measure their relationship with
him through the events of the past.[2] The defining event of the
Old Testament world was the deliverance from bondage in Egypt
and from death at the Red Sea and the deliverance through the
wilderness to the promised land. "Thou in thy mercy hast led
forth the people which thou has redeemed: thou hast guided
them in thy strength unto thy holy habitation" (Exodus 15:12).
"And thou shalt remember all the way which the Lord thy God
led thee these forty years in the wilderness" (Deuteronomy
8:2). "Remember the days of old, consider the years of many
generations" (Deuteronomy 32:7). "Remember these, O Jacob and
Israel; for thou art my servant: I have formed thee; thou art my
servant: O Israel, thou shalt not be forgotten of me" (Isaiah 44:21).
Regarding the sabbath: "And remember that thou wast a servant
in the land of Egypt, and that the Lord thy God brought thee out

thence through a mighty hand and by a stretched out arm: therefore the Lord thy God commanded thee to keep the sabbath day" (Deuteronomy 5:15; cf. 15:15; 16:3, 12; 24:18).

Through the law of Moses, the Lord provided the children of Israel a host of different ways of remembering him through sacrifices and offerings, holy days, festivals, and laws of cleanliness and uncleanliness: on the Sabbath Israel was to remember the creation (Exodus 20:8–11) and the deliverance from bondage at the exodus (Deuteronomy 5:12–15). Passover (Exodus 12) was a celebration to remember the night the Lord delivered them from Egypt. In addition, the Lord commanded Israel to erect a series of memorials of stone to commemorate his great acts: the pile of stones to recall the miraculous crossing of the Jordan (Joshua 4:9) and the stone pillar at Shechem to remember the covenant (Joshua 24:27). The Lord commanded Israel to remember him and his words as they sat, walked, lay down, and rose up; he also commanded Israel to bind the words of the Lord on their hand, between their eyes, and on their doors (Deuteronomy 6:7–9), which led to the tradition of the *tefillin* and *mezuzah*. Most important, the records of the events and the laws were preserved, and the Lord commanded the children of Israel to review the events and laws by reading the records and to participate in a process of covenant renewal (Deuteronomy 31:10–11).

Remembering in the Book of Mormon

The Book of Mormon continues this tradition brought with Lehi from the world of Jerusalem. From the beginning, Book of Mormon prophets exhorted their people to remember the great things the Lord had done for their fathers in the past.[3] Lehi reminded his descendants that they were blessed with the knowledge of the creation (2 Nephi 1:10). Many prophets reminded the people of their ancestor Abraham and the covenants the

Lord made with him (2 Nephi 8:2; 27:33; Jacob 4:5; Alma 5:24; 7:25; 13:15; Helaman 3:30; 8:16–17). Lehi and Moroni rehearsed to their people the important role Joseph played in their history (2 Nephi 3; Alma 46:23–24). But the most important event of the past for the Book of Mormon peoples—just as for their Old Testament counterparts—was the exodus, including the divine intervention in the deliverance from Egypt; the dramatic miracle at the Red Sea; guidance, sustenance, and protection in the wilderness; and the eventual conquest of the land of Canaan. Several Latter-day Saint scholars have studied at some length the nature of the typology of the exodus throughout the Book of Mormon.[4]

At the beginning of his record, Nephi identified the theme of his work on the small plates: "The tender mercies of the Lord are over all those whom he hath chosen, because of their faith, to make them mighty even unto the power of deliverance" (1 Nephi 1:20; cf. 1 Nephi 1:14; 2 Nephi 1:2–3; 2:8, 12; 4:26; 9:8, 19; 11:5; 24:1). In light of this theme and together with his faith that the Lord gives no commandments "save he shall prepare a way for them that they may accomplish the thing which he commandeth them" (1 Nephi 3:7), Nephi quickly identified the Lord's deliverance of Lehi and his family from Jerusalem into the wilderness and the journey to the promised land as an experience parallel to that of the exodus. He likened their situation in the wilderness to that at the time of Moses, complete with murmuring, hunger, thirst, affliction, death, and the need for direction. Nephi sought to inspire faith in their attempt to get the plates of brass from Laban when he exhorted his brothers, "Therefore let us go up; let us be strong like unto Moses; for he truly spake unto the waters of the Red Sea and they divided hither and thither, and our fathers came through, out of captivity, on dry ground, and the armies of Pharaoh did follow and were drowned in the waters of the Red Sea. . . . Let us go up; the Lord is able to deliver us, even as our fathers, and to destroy Laban, even as the Egyptians" (1 Nephi 4:2–3).

In this case the power of remembering the great things the Lord had done for their fathers can be seen from these events. And those who remember these events can thus derive the faith and the strength to accomplish the Lord's will. Later Nephi chastised his brothers for forgetting "what great things the Lord hath done for us, in delivering us out of the hands of Laban, and also that we should obtain the record" (1 Nephi 7:11).

In the Book of Mormon, the Lord's deliverance of Lehi and his family from destruction at Jerusalem became for them the pivotal event in their own history.[5] Their consciousness of sacred history expanded to include the exodus as well as their own personal deliverance from destruction. Nephi rebuked his brothers because they had forgotten that they had seen an angel (1 Nephi 7:10). Additionally, they had forgotten "that the Lord is able to do all things according to his will" (1 Nephi 7:12). On his deathbed, Lehi spoke to his family "and rehearsed unto them, how great things the Lord had done for them in bringing them out of the land of Jerusalem" (2 Nephi 1:1), attributing the divine intervention on their behalf to the "mercies of God" (2 Nephi 1:2). Later Book of Mormon prophets continued this tradition: King Benjamin (Mosiah 7:19), Alma (Alma 36:28), and Nephi$_2$ (Helaman 8:11). The exodus typology continued to be applied to other situations. For example, when Alma's people were delivered from Lamanite bondage (Mosiah 24), Alma said, "Yea, and I also remember the captivity of my fathers; for I surely do know that the Lord did deliver them out of bondage, and by this did establish his church. . . . Yea, I have always remembered the captivity of my fathers; and the same God who delivered them out of the hands of the Egyptians did deliver them out of bondage" (Alma 29:11–12).

The most important thing to be remembered in the pages of the Book of Mormon is the coming and mission of the Messiah.

For those who lived before his time, Lehi and Nephi provided visions of the future. Nephi identified prophecies about his death and resurrection from the brass plates (1 Nephi 22:20–21; cf. Deuteronomy 18:15–18) and added to them his own prophecies (1 Nephi 11; 2 Nephi 31). The events of deliverance in the past are all seen as types and shadows of the deliverance made possible through the atonement.

This was dramatically illustrated by Alma the Younger in recounting the story of his conversion to his son Helaman (Alma 36). Many have noted that chapter 36 is a long, complex, and elegant chiasmus centering on Alma's crying out to the Savior for forgiveness and mercy.[6] On either side of the center is an informative passage that shows the development of the concept of remembering in the Book of Mormon. Alma exhorted Helaman, "I would that you should do as I have done, in remembering the captivity of our fathers; for they were in bondage, and none could deliver them except it was the God of Abraham, and the God of Isaac, and the God of Jacob; and he surely did deliver them in their afflictions" (Alma 36:2). At the end of the chapter, Alma further listed the great things that the Lord had done for his fathers and exhorted his son to retain in remembrance that he had delivered

> our fathers out of Egypt, and he has swallowed up the Egyptians in the Red Sea; and he led them by his power into the promised land; yea, and he delivered them out of bondage and captivity from time to time. Yea, and he has also brought our fathers out of the land of Jerusalem; and he has also, by his everlasting power, delivered them out of bondage and captivity, from time to time even down to the present day; and I have always retained in remembrance their captivity; yea, and ye also ought to retain in remembrance, as I have done, their captivity. (Alma 36:28–29)

But Alma taught that in the middle of his conversion, "while I was harrowed up by the memory of my many sins, behold, I remembered also to have heard my father prophesy unto the people concerning the coming of one Jesus Christ . . . to atone for the sins of the world." Therefore, he cried to the Lord Jesus Christ, and he was cleansed and delivered from his sins—that "I could remember my pains no more" (Alma 36:17, 19). In other words, Alma invited all to remember first and foremost the atonement of Jesus Christ as the culmination of the great things the Lord has done for our fathers and for us.

When the Savior appeared to the Nephites, he taught them the gospel and administered the sacrament as a covenantal ordinance—representing the power of the atonement—and admonished his disciples to "always remember me. And if ye do always remember me ye shall have my Spirit to be with you" (3 Nephi 18:7, 11). And thus the Book of Mormon shows unto the remnant of the house of Israel what great things the Lord has done for their fathers (see 1 Nephi 7:11; 2 Nephi 1:1; Mosiah 27:16). Moroni, at the end of his record, concluded by reminding us of the importance of remembering in our quest for spiritual knowledge: "when ye shall read these things, if it be wisdom in God that ye should read them, that ye would remember how merciful the Lord hath been unto the children of men, from the creation of Adam even down until the time that ye shall receive these things" (Moroni 10:3).

The Covenants of the Lord

> And that they may know the covenants of the Lord, that they are not cast off forever (Title Page)

Lehi and his family understood their relationship with God through covenants. They and other righteous people in Lehi's

Jerusalem inherited this foundational religious concept from their noble predecessors. The scriptures contain records of the covenants made with Adam and Eve, Enoch, Noah, Abraham, Isaac, Jacob, Joseph, Moses, and David, as well as of the "new covenant" established by Jesus Christ and restored in the latter days as the "new and everlasting covenant" (D&C 22). Two important covenants are emphasized in the Old Testament that must be explored in order to better understand the religious background of Lehi: the Abrahamic and the Mosaic covenants. In addition, the temple is a focal point of the covenant.

Abrahamic Covenant

The most important of all of the covenants is the Abrahamic covenant—established through the patriarch Abraham sometime around 2000 B.C. As part of the covenant, the Lord commanded Abraham to become like God: "Walk before me, and be thou perfect" (Genesis 17:1). In addition, Abraham continued to worship the Lord through the offering of blood sacrifice in similitude of the future sacrifice of the Lamb of God and instituted the practice of circumcision (Genesis 17). The Abrahamic covenant was accompanied and administered by the Melchizedek Priesthood, which Abraham received from Melchizedek (D&C 84:14). This covenant continues to be the covenant through which the Lord administers the plan of salvation to his children today. The Abrahamic covenant is variously expressed throughout the book of Genesis (Genesis 12:1–7; 15:1–16; 17:1–6; 22:15–18), as well as in the Book of Abraham (Abraham 2), and includes three specific promises that are essential to understanding the Book of Mormon: land, posterity, and blessing.

First, the Lord promised the land of Canaan to Abraham: "Unto thy seed will I give this land" (Genesis 12:7). This was never realized by Abraham himself but would be by his posterity (Genesis 15:16). It is clear that the Abrahamic promise of land represented a much greater blessing than simply the land of Canaan. The patriarchal blessing given to Joseph by his father, Jacob, declared that "Joseph is a fruitful bough, even a fruitful bough by a well; whose branches run over the wall" (Genesis 49:22). This promise was fulfilled by Lehi and his descendants as the Lord led them to the promised land in the New World (1 Nephi 19:24; Jacob 2:25; cf. 1 Nephi 5:14, 16; 2 Nephi 3:4; Alma 10:3) and resulted in the expansion of the covenant lands to include the Americas in the Abrahamic covenant as the inheritance of Joseph. The resurrected Savior taught the Nephites: "And behold, this people will I establish in this land, unto the fulfilling of the covenant which I made with your father Jacob; and it shall be a New Jerusalem" (3 Nephi 20:22).

The Abrahamic promise of land transcends geography. In the Old Testament theology of the land, the promised land belongs to the Lord, "for the land is mine; for ye are strangers and sojourners with me" (Leviticus 25:23). In this sense the covenant promise of land represents an earthly inheritance with a more exalted spiritual promise of a place in the kingdom of God. This is the way the promise of land is understood in the New Testament as an "heir of the world" (Romans 4:13) and a "better country, that is, an heavenly" (Hebrews 11:16). Ultimately the eternal reward for the faithful will be the celestial kingdom, which will be on the earth (D&C 88:14–26; cf. 77:1; 130:7).

The second promise was that of posterity—a posterity as numerous as the stars in the heaven and the sand of the sea (Genesis 22:17). While Abraham for many years did not have any children, eventually he had at least eight sons (Genesis 25:1–9). Related to this promise, the Lord changed the name of the patriarch Abram to Abraham, meaning "father of many nations" (Genesis 17:5), representing the fact that his descendants would spread throughout the earth. Throughout the history of Israel, the people would be blessed with posterity. This promise is prominent in the Book of Mormon. Lehi prophesied that his descendants would "raise up seed unto the Lord in the land of promise" (1 Nephi 7:1). Nephi beheld his seed and the seed of his brethren in the future "even as it were in number as many as the sand of the sea" (1 Nephi 12:1) and prophesied that the seed of Joseph "should never perish as long as the earth should stand" (2 Nephi 25:21).

This promise was also a spiritual one. The Lord promised Abraham that all who would accept the gospel would be "called after thy name, and shall be accounted thy seed" (Abraham 2:10). Thus Abraham was to become the spiritual father of all those who accept Christ. Additionally, inherent in this promise is the assurance given to Abraham and his faithful descendants of eternal increase (D&C 131:1–4; 132:19–25, 30, 55).

The third promise was that of blessing. The Lord promised Abraham and his posterity that they would enjoy the blessings of the earth, be a great nation, and have the blessings of the gospel, the priesthood, and eternal life (Abraham 2:9–11). Most notably, the Lord promised Abraham that his seed would be the means by which the Lord could bless the whole world with the knowledge of Christ and his atonement: "And in thy seed shall all the nations of the earth be blessed" (Genesis 22:18). This blessing was further explained in the Book of Abraham—the Lord clarified that this blessing would be brought about through the priesthood (Abraham 2:9–11). The "seed" of Abraham that would bless the nations would have a twofold fulfillment. This promise also included the coming—through the lineage of Abraham—of the Savior Jesus Christ (Matthew 1:1–17), who would bless all nations through his atonement. This was recognized by Paul in his epistle to the Galatians: "And to thy seed, which is Christ" (Galatians 3:16). Nephi₂ declared, "Abraham saw of his coming, and was filled with gladness and did rejoice" (Helaman 8:17).

The covenant of Abraham was meant to be passed along to Abraham's descendants through Isaac, Jacob, and the twelve tribes of Israel. Jacob, like Abraham, received a covenantal name, "Israel" (Genesis 32:28). Great emphasis was placed in the scriptures on the duty of the seed of Abraham, often called the house or children of Israel, to bless the nations. The Book of Mormon peoples were keenly aware of their role as heirs to the Abrahamic covenant. Nephi referred to the role of the house of Israel in bringing about the salvation of the world in the latter days: "In thy seed shall all the kindreds of the earth be blessed" (1 Nephi 15:18; 22:9). The resurrected Savior repeated this charge to the Nephites at the temple in Bountiful: "The Father having raised me up unto you first, and sent me to bless you in turning away every one of you from his iniquities; and this because ye are the children of the covenant—And after that ye were blessed then fulfilleth the Father the covenant which he made with Abraham, saying: In thy seed shall all the kindreds of the earth be blessed" (3 Nephi 20:26–27).

Abraham and Sarah, as well as their ancestors Adam and Eve, were models for their descendants through their lives of faith and righteousness. Throughout the stories in Genesis, Abraham and Sarah were tested in terms of their faith, obedience, hospitality, loyalty, and willingness to sacrifice everything for the Lord. The final test came when the Lord asked Abraham to sacrifice his son Isaac (Genesis 22). This he did willingly, and the Lord called out to him, "Now I know that thou fearest God, seeing thou hast not withheld thy son, thine only son from me" (Genesis 22:12), and restated for the final time the glorious promises of the covenant (Genesis 22:15–18). In the Book of Mormon Jacob taught that this act of faith was a sign of the atonement: "It was accounted unto Abraham in the wilderness to be obedient unto the commands of God in offering up his son Isaac, which is a similitude of God and his Only Begotten Son" (Jacob 4:5).

Probably because the brass plates were kept by the descendants of Joseph (1 Nephi 5:14; 2 Nephi 3:4), they contain records of the promises the Lord gave to Joseph that are no longer in the Bible (although see those restored in Genesis 50:24–38 JST). On his deathbed Lehi read these promises from the record to his family, and these promises are prominent throughout the Book of Mormon. Lehi revealed to his son Joseph that Joseph of Egypt saw the day of the Lehites and recognized that the Lord had broken off a branch of Israel and that the Messiah would be made manifest to them in the latter days (2 Nephi 3:5). Further, he saw that the Lord would raise up Moses to deliver the children of Israel from Egypt (2 Nephi 3:10, 16–18). And in the latter days the Lord would raise up a prophet and seer—the Prophet Joseph Smith (named after Joseph of old as well as after his father)—from the lineage of Joseph of Egypt, who would bring many to the "knowledge of the covenants" that the Lord had made with their fathers (2 Nephi 3:7–9, 11–15, 18–20). Most important for the Book of Mormon peoples, this prophet would be instrumental in bringing forth their writings (2 Nephi 3:11–12) to lead their descendants, as well as all people, to salvation (2 Nephi 3:19–21). The promises given to Joseph of the preservation of his seed were echoed later by Captain Moroni at the raising of the title of liberty (Alma 46:23–24) and by the Savior (3 Nephi 10:17; 15:12). And the role of the remnant of Joseph in the latter days was seen and taught by Moroni (Ether 13:6–10).

Mosaic Covenant

Moses was called to deliver his people from Egypt and take them to Mount Sinai, where the Lord would give them the higher law. Because of the faithlessness, hardheartedness, and spiritual immaturity of the Israelites, the Lord gave to them the lower law instead—the Mosaic covenant. Whereas the Lord commanded Abraham to "be . . . perfect" (Genesis 17:1), he commanded the children of Israel to "be holy: for I the Lord your God am holy" (Leviticus 19:2). The promises of the Mosaic covenant were the same as of the Abrahamic covenant: land, posterity, and blessing. The conditional nature of the Mosaic covenant was emphasized in that the temporal blessings of prosperity and protection were spelled out in greater detail and were accompanied by an ominous series of corresponding curses. While the goal of the two covenants is essentially the same, the laws were somewhat different. The lower law was to be administered primarily through the Aaronic Priesthood, and the carnal commandments were added to what had been the higher law (Exodus 34:1–2 JST).

The Structure of the Covenant

Based on the pioneering work of George E. Mendenhall and others,[7] biblical scholars have identified a simple underlying structure to a biblical covenant pattern consisting of seven elements. These seven elements are present in the narrative of the giving of the Mosaic covenant at Sinai (Exodus 19–24) and also in the numerous occasions when the covenant is formally renewed in the Bible in Deuteronomy 1–31, Joshua 24, 2 Kings 22–23, and Nehemiah 9–10. A review of these elements can greatly aid in understanding the contents and dynamics of the Mosaic covenant.

1. Preamble. In each example of the giving of a covenant, a preamble acknowledges the divine origin and authority of the covenant, either from God himself or through his prophet. For example, in Exodus the covenant is introduced first through Moses as the Lord's agent: "And Moses went up unto God, and the Lord called unto him out of the mountain, saying, Thus shalt thou say to the house of Jacob . . ." (Exodus 19:3) and then by the Lord himself: "And God spake all these words, saying, I am the Lord thy God . . ." (Exodus 20:1–2). Joshua introduced the covenant simply: "Thus saith the Lord God of Israel . . ." (Joshua 24:2). In terms of the Book of Mormon, Nephi, Lehi, and all the other prophets acknowledged the divine origin of the promise of the land to them and their descendants.

2. *Historical Prologue.* Whenever the Lord reiterates the covenant, he commences by reminding the children of Israel of the "great things" he has done for their fathers and for them. For example, when the Lord gave the covenant on Sinai he began: "Ye have seen what I did unto the Egyptians, and how I bare you on eagles' wings, and brought you unto myself. Now therefore, if ye will obey my voice indeed, and keep my covenant, then ye shall be a peculiar treasure unto me above all people" (Exodus 19:4–5). In this brief statement the Lord reminded Israel of his past intervention on their behalf and reiterated their future obligation—that they were to remain faithful to his covenant.

Joshua at Shechem recounted the divine relationship beginning with the Lord calling Abraham out of the world and then turning to the miraculous events of the exodus and the conquest (Joshua 24:2–18). Ezra, when he officiated at the renewal of the covenant in Jerusalem after the exile, commenced with the creation, then Abraham, the exodus, and the conquest and finally dwelt on the ensuing ingratitude of the children of Israel as demonstrated by their disobedience to the commandments (Nehemiah 9:6–33). In fact, much of the narrative in the Old Testament serves as a historical prologue to the covenant.

This aspect of the covenant is extremely important in the Book of Mormon. As discussed above in the first section of this paper, the Book of Mormon acknowledges the importance of the sacred history on the title page, where it says to remember the "great things the Lord hath done for their fathers." The Book of Mormon writers constantly acknowledged their deliverance from Jerusalem as an event that played out in the typology of the exodus and ultimately recognized that the greatest event of intervention by God on behalf of his children was the atonement—an event to which all other events were types and shadows.

3. *Stipulations.* The heart of the covenant is the law—the commandments—those things the Lord has commanded his children to do or not to do. In the Book of Mormon, this is probably what is meant by the phrase *law of Moses.* The commandments of the law of Moses can be conveniently divided into two categories: ethical commandments—as represented and epitomized by the Ten Commandments and supplemented by a host of religious and civil commandments regarding how to treat others, deal with crime in society, and take care of the poor—and the ritual laws pertaining to festivals, concepts of being clean and unclean, sacrifices, and offerings.[8]

The Book of Mormon peoples constantly reminded us that they were living the law of Moses. Nephi recorded that he and his people "did observe to keep the judgments, and the statutes, and the commandments of the Lord in all things, according to the law of Moses" (2 Nephi 5:10; cf. Jarom 1:5; Alma 30:2–3). While the Book of Mormon peoples lived the law of Moses, they did so with the Melchizedek Priesthood (Alma 5:3; 13:6–11), and this may have had an impact on how they lived the law. They surely continued the practice of blood sacrifice and circumcision required by the covenant of Abraham until the coming of the resurrected

Savior, at which time these practices were fulfilled (3 Nephi 9:19–20; Moroni 8:8).

The Ten Commandments were also inscribed on the plates of brass in the same form that has come down to us in the Bible—Abinadi quoted them to the priests of Noah in essentially the same form as that found in Exodus (Mosiah 13). The Ten Commandments are well documented throughout the Book of Mormon and are central to the preaching of Book of Mormon prophets, who taught that keeping the Ten Commandments was the standard required by the covenant. However, failure to keep them was cited as the reason for the moral decline and destruction of the people.[9] Nephi warned that those who failed to keep the commandments not to murder, lie, steal, envy, commit whoredoms, and take the name of the Lord in vain would perish (2 Nephi 26:32). The breaking of three commandments of the ten—murder, stealing, and adultery—is often cited as the reason for the destruction of the covenant people in the Book of Mormon (Mosiah 2:13; Alma 16:18; 50:21; Helaman 6:23; 7:21–22; 13:22), just as in the teachings of Old Testament prophets (Hosea 4:1–2; Jeremiah 7:9; Ezekiel 18; 22).

In addition to the Ten Commandments, other ethical commandments are given under the law of Moses as found primarily in the Covenant Code in Exodus 21–24, the Holiness Code in Leviticus 19–26, and the legal portion of Deuteronomy 12–26. The Book of Mormon includes references to many of these laws that have been studied at length by Latter-day Saint scholars.[10]

While in the Bible ritual law is described in great detail, the Book of Mormon reveals very little information about these commandments. Lehi and his family offered sacrifices in the wilderness, but there is no mention of the dietary code, of laws of cleanliness and uncleanliness, of the festivals (by name at least) besides the Sabbath, or of the various sacrifices and offerings besides the burnt offering and perhaps the thanks-giving offering. This has led to some speculation that since the Nephites had the Melchizedek Priesthood, perhaps they did not obey each and every aspect of the law as recorded in the Bible. On the other hand, the Nephites had the brass plates with the five books of Moses on them—though we do not know exactly what was on them or in what form the texts were at that time. And since the Book of Mormon is largely a spiritual record and the product of abridgment, perhaps we should not expect to find a detailed account of the ritual laws in its pages.[11]

4. *Witnesses.* As in all ancient cultures, the sealing of cove-nant or treaties is accompanied by a citation of witnesses. In the Bible, Deuteronomy specifies the witness of the covenant of Moses as the "heavens" and the "earth" (Deuteronomy 32:1) and as a hymn to be sung by the people. In the account of Joshua at Shechem, Joshua said, "Ye [the people] are witnesses against yourselves that ye have chosen you the Lord, to serve him. And they said, We are witnesses" (Joshua 24:22). In addition, Joshua erected a stone monument that was accounted as a witness (Joshua 24:26–27). Ezra, at the end of the covenant renewal ceremony, had the people who renewed the covenant enter their names on a list as a witness (Nehemiah 10). Similarly, the Book of Mormon people who obeyed King Benjamin's invitation to renew their covenants with God recorded their names on a list as a witness (Mosiah 6:1).

5. *Provisions for Deposit and Public Reading.* Under the law of Moses, the law was to be safely deposited and publicly read in order to aid in remembrance. According to Deuteronomy, the law was deposited in the ark of the covenant and read to the peo-ple every seven years at the Feast of Tabernacles (Deuteronomy 31:10–11). The plates of brass served as the repository of the

covenant for the people in the Book of Mormon. Copies must have been made from this record since Abinadi and others had access to its teachings. The importance of the brass plates to Lehi's descendants is demonstrated by what happened to the Mulekites, who brought no records with them and gradually lost their language and their religious traditions (Omni 1:14, 17).

6. *Blessings and Curses.* While the Abrahamic covenant is spoken of throughout the scriptures with emphasis on the blessings of the covenant, the Mosaic covenant, perhaps because it was given to a people who were spiritually immature—hardhearted and stiffnecked—contains a series of specific blessings and curses. The blessings are found explicitly stated in Deuteronomy 27–28. The blessings include prosperity from the fields and the flocks, posterity, and protection from disease and from enemies (Deuteronomy 28:1–13). The curses are the opposite: famine, poverty, pestilence, and destruction (Deuteronomy 28:15–68).

Legally, the breaking of the covenant would result in the destruction of Israel, but because of his mercy (Isaiah 14:1), the Lord promised that he would preserve a remnant (Isaiah 10:20–22) that would be scattered (Deuteronomy 28:63–65) and eventually gathered (Deuteronomy 30:1–10). This is the basis for the entire discussion in the Book of Mormon in which Lehi, Nephi, and Jacob understood that the destruction of Jerusalem was due to Israel's disobedience. At the same time, ancient prophets recognized that a remnant would be preserved and that in the future the Lord would provide a way to gather scattered Israel. The gathering of Israel is a central concern of nearly all the Book of Mormon prophets.

The Book of Mormon presents a similar situation in which the descendants of Lehi who were to inherit the land through promise would break the covenant and be destroyed and scattered: the Nephites by the Lamanites and the Lamanites eventually by the Gentiles. This mechanism is also at work in the course of the Nephite cycle, where obedience is followed by prosperity, then apostasy, destruction, repentance, and so on.

7. *Oath Ceremony.* When Moses initially made the covenant with the children of Israel at Sinai, he first read the words of the Lord given on Sinai. The people agreed to obey them, and Moses sprinkled the people with the blood of the sacrifices: "Behold the blood of the covenant" (Exodus 24:8). Covenant renewal ceremonies are recorded in the Bible in Deuteronomy 27–28; Joshua 24; 2 Kings 23; and Nehemiah 9–10. In each case the seven elements of covenant are apparent and the people reaffirm their commitment to the covenant. From modern revelation we know that baptism was practiced under the law of Moses in ancient Israel (D&C 84:26–27). Nephi and the other Book of Mormon prophets emphasized that the covenant oath ceremony in the New World was also baptism (2 Nephi 31; Mosiah 18).

Latter-day Saint scholars have studied the speech of King Benjamin and hypothesized that this was a covenant renewal ceremony associated with the Feast of Tabernacles in the Bible. King Benjamin assembled his people in tents, and all seven elements of the covenant can be identified in the narrative demonstrating the biblical dynamics of covenant structure.[12] Stephen D. Ricks identified the following: (1) in the preamble, King Benjamin delivered the words given him by an angel (Mosiah 3:2); (2) the historical prologue included King Benjamin reviewing his selfless service as king (Mosiah 2:19, 21); (3) the stipulations were stated when King Benjamin commanded the people to believe in God, repent of their sins, and seek forgiveness in humility (Mosiah 4:9–10); (4) the witnesses were the people themselves, who were willing to enter into the covenant (Mosiah 5:5) and allow their names to be listed (Mosiah 6:1); (5) blessings and curses were implied—those who accepted the name of Christ were portrayed as sitting at his right hand, while those who did not were consigned to his left and those who transgressed the name of Christ would be blotted out in their hearts (Mosiah 5:8–11); (6) the deposit and public reading occurred when King Benjamin had the words of his speech published and distributed (Mosiah 2:8–9); and (7) the oath ceremony consisted of the people repenting of their sins and having their names recorded on a list (Mosiah 6:1).

The covenant given to Lehi and his descendants is connected to both the Abrahamic and the Mosaic covenants. The covenant is simply stated in the Book of Mormon—apparently assuming that the Lehites knew of the promises and blessings and curses of those earlier covenants. The covenant is first stated to Nephi: "And inasmuch as ye shall keep my commandments, ye shall prosper, and shall be led to a land of promise; yea, even a land which I have prepared for you; yea, a land which is choice above all other lands" (1 Nephi 2:20; cf. 4:14). Lehi restated this promise and added that the land would be consecrated for liberty and the worship of the Lord God of Israel and the inhabitants of the land—if they kept his commandments, they would be protected by the Lord from their enemies (2 Nephi 1:1–12).

The Book of Mormon, the voice from the dust written by the seed of Abraham, dramatically fills the role of the seed of Abraham in blessing the world. Thus this record contains a history of a covenant people in the New World who find their identity in the Abrahamic and Mosaic covenants. Throughout their history they often broke the covenant and suffered the consequences. This record reminds us that the covenants of the Lord are still in effect and that the restoration is going forth to gather covenant Israel for the final time. In addition, the Book of Mormon calls to us—as the seed of Abraham—to valiantly fill our role as heirs to the covenant to bless the nations. In the Book of Mormon many prophets exhorted their contemporaries and us to remember the Abrahamic covenant: Isaiah cried out, "Look unto Abraham, your father" (2 Nephi 8:2//Isaiah 51:2). Nephi specifically identified his work in writing his record to bring souls to the God of Abraham, Isaac, and Jacob (1 Nephi 6:4). Alma and Nephi₂ invited us to "sit down with Abraham, Isaac, and Jacob" (Alma 7:25; cf. 5:24; Helaman 3:30). And Mormon (Mormon 5:20) and Moroni promised that the covenants of Abraham would ultimately be fulfilled (Mormon 9:11; Ether 13:11).

The Temple

The Temple of Solomon is another important part of the religious background of Lehi's world. It was a symbol of the covenant, and many of the symbols and ordinances celebrated were certainly types and shadows of the coming of the Messiah. Thus a brief description of Solomon's temple in Jerusalem may prove useful. In the Old Testament, the temple is called "the house of the Lord" (1 Kings 3:1), which clearly describes the primary symbol of this building—the presence of the Lord in the midst of his people. The presence of God is important in the spiritual history of the covenant people. After the fall and their expulsion from the Garden of Eden, Adam and Eve sought to regain the presence of God through worship, prayer, the building of altars, and the offering of sacrifice in "similitude of the sacrifice of the Only Begotten of the Father" (Moses 5:7).

Abraham and the patriarchs followed this model and erected altars, often at the top of a hill or mountain, to offer prayer and sacrifice. At several sacred places like Shechem,

Bethel, Hebron, and Beersheba, the Lord appeared to them, blessed them, and gave them covenants. At Bethel Jacob saw a dramatic vision of the ladder of heaven with angels ascending and descending. The Lord appeared and made the Abrahamic covenant with him there. At the end of this experience Jacob exclaimed, "This is none other but the house of God, and this is the gate of heaven" (Genesis 28:17)—and he named the place Bethel, which means "the house of God."

Moses led the children of Israel out of Egypt to Mount Sinai, where they were to worship the Lord and enter into his presence. While the spiritually immature children of Israel were not able to receive the higher law at Sinai, they did enter into the Mosaic covenant with the promise that if they were faithful, they would be able to enter into the presence of God. The Lord gave them directions to build the tabernacle complex and the ark of the covenant—concrete and visible symbols of their quest through covenant to enter back into the presence of God. Thus, the tabernacle was an important institution of the law of Moses. The tabernacle would serve as a portable center of worship under the law of Moses until the temple was built in Jerusalem.

Following the conquest, the tabernacle and the ark of the covenant resided in various locations until David conquered the Jebusites and moved them to his capital, Jerusalem. Solomon built and dedicated the temple in about 960 B.C. Throughout the history of Israel, however, the people were not obedient to the commandments but continuously sought to build idols both to Jehovah and to other gods and goddesses of their Canaanite neighbors.

The Lord sent prophets like Hosea, Amos, and Isaiah to warn of the dangers of such practices, but to little avail. King Hezekiah (715–687) sought to reform Israel's religion, as did his grandson Josiah (640–609). Josiah was successful, and the writer of Kings records that he cleansed the land and the temple from idolatrous practices. Most important, Josiah implemented a plan of centralization—probably based on the texts of Deuteronomy 12–26—in which all sacrifice must be offered only at the temple in Jerusalem. This dramatically changed the practice of religion in Israel; from that time forth, all sacrifices and thus all the ordinances and festivals requiring sacrifice had to be observed at Jerusalem. Thus at the time of Lehi, on the eve of the destruction of the temple, Solomon's temple had been cleansed by Josiah and was, according to Kings, being run according to the law of the Lord.[13]

Shortly after Lehi and his family departed from Jerusalem, the temple was destroyed by the armies of Nebuchadnezzar, and many temple vessels were taken to Babylon in 586 B.C. The children of Israel would later return from Babylon in 539 to rebuild the temple—called the Second Temple, or Temple of Zerubbabel—in 515. This temple would stand until it was replaced by that of King Herod at the time of Christ. Herod's temple would be destroyed in A.D. 70 when Jerusalem was destroyed by the Romans and the Jews were scattered from Jerusalem.

The dimensions and furnishings of Solomon's temple are described in 1 Kings 6–7 and 2 Chronicles 3–5. The temple was oriented with the doors facing to the east—which in Jerusalem was away from the city toward the Mount of Olives. A courtyard in front of the building contained a great altar, a bronze basin, and ten portable bronze water basins. The great altar, fifteen feet high and thirty feet square, was a place of sacrifice where the burnt offerings—probably the continuation of the sacrifice given by Adam and Eve in similitude of the Lamb of God—were sacrificed along with the host of other sacrifices of the law of Moses. The brazen sea, fifteen feet in diameter and over seven feet tall, rested

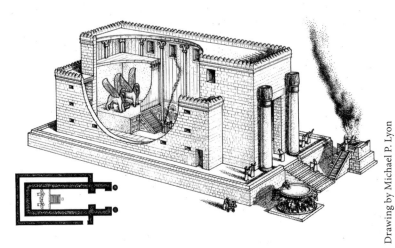

Drawing by Michael P. Lyon

The Temple of Solomon had a large courtyard containing an altar for sacrifices and a great bronze basin that rested on the backs of twelve oxen for the ritual washings of the priests. The temple was divided into three rooms: the porch; the holy place, containing the menorah, the table of shewbread, and the altar of incense; and the holy of holies, with the cherubim on each side of the ark of the covenant.

on the backs of twelve oxen, three facing each of the cardinal directions. Together with the ten smaller bronze basins mounted on wheels, the basin provided water that was used for washing and purification for the priests.

The temple building itself was a rectangular building that measured approximately 150 feet long and 75 feet wide and was divided into three rooms. At either side of the huge entrance doors were two large pillars of bronze called Jachin and Boaz—each twenty-seven feet high. Their function is unknown, though scholars speculate that they were symbols of the covenant—Jachin meaning "he establishes" (cf. Psalm 89:4) and Boaz "in him is strength" (cf. Psalm 21:1).

The first room, called the porch (Heb. ʾulam), was thirty feet square and appears to have been an empty space that served as a transition into the temple. The second room, the holy place (Heb. *hekhal*)—sixty feet long, thirty feet wide, and forty-five feet high—contained several furnishings. First, there were ten large wooden lampstands overlaid with gold—the light of the lamps probably represented the presence of God. They were probably in the form of the seven-armed menorah in the tabernacle that in Jewish tradition symbolized the tree of life. Next were ten tables containing the "shewbread," or "bread of the presence," offered by the people and eaten by the priests as representatives of the Lord. Finally there was a golden incense altar where incense was offered to the Lord, perhaps symbolizing prayer (Psalm 141:2; Revelation 5:8; 8:3).

Between the holy place and the most holy place (Heb. *debir*)—or holy of holies—was a large and beautiful veil decorated with cherubim, understood as creatures guarding the throne of God. The holy of holies was a room with the dimensions of a cube of thirty feet—probably signifying the perfection of God. Inside the holy of holies was the ark of the covenant—a wooden box or chest covered with pure gold that represented both the covenant and the throne of God. Inside the box were the stone tablets, a bowl of manna, and the rod of Aaron. On top of the box was a gold slab—called the mercy seat—and on either side of this slab were two gigantic cherubim fifteen feet high, made of olive wood and covered with gold foil. In the Old Testament God is said to "dwell" or "sit" between the cherubim (Psalm 80:1; 99:1; Isaiah 37:16).

Temple worship consisted of the daily sacrifices and offerings at the temple. The high priest and the other priests officiated and were accompanied by the Levites. Israel gathered at the temple to celebrate the festivals of the year: the three pilgrimage festivals of Passover, Weeks, and Tabernacles, and the Day of Atonement—the only time when the high priest would enter the holy of holies and offer the blood of the sacrifice on the mercy seat to expiate sin (Leviticus 16). The people came to the temple daily to offer and observe the sacrifices and offerings, to sing and pray, and to receive the blessing of the high priest (Numbers 6:22–27).

The basic theology of the temple can easily be derived from the Bible in the dedicatory prayer offered by Solomon in 1 Kings 8 (2 Chronicles 6). Clearly the temple represented the house of the Lord and the dwelling place of God among his people. Solomon declared, "I have surely built thee an house to dwell in, a settled place for thee to abide in for ever" (1 Kings 8:13). In addition, the temple was closely connected with the covenant. Solomon addressed the Lord "who keepest covenant and mercy" and prayed that the Lord would hear the prayers of the faithful and repentant offered toward the temple. Solomon also recognized the blessings and curses connected with the covenant and asked the Lord to justify the righteous and condemn the wicked and to deliver his people from enemies, famine, pestilence, and sickness. Finally Solomon identified the temple as a symbol of missionary work as he prayed that the Lord would acknowledge the prayers of the stranger who came to worship the one and only true God (1 Kings 8:23–53). After the dedication the Lord warned Israel, repeating the conditional nature of the covenant, "But if ye shall at all turn from following me, ye or your children, and will not keep the commandments . . . then will I cut off Israel out of the land which I have given them; and this house, which I have hallowed for my name, will I cast out of my sight" (1 Kings 9:6–7).

There are many other aspects of temple theology found throughout the scriptures, such as visions, angels, the throne theophany, the creation, the Garden of Eden, the tree of life, levels of sacredness, the theology of the high priest as a representative of

Jehovah, and the temple as a place of judgment—many of which also occur in the Book of Mormon.[14]

The Book of Mormon records that Nephi built a temple in the New World after the pattern of the Old: "And I, Nephi, did build a temple; and I did construct it after the manner of the temple of Solomon save it were not built of so many precious things; for they were not to be found upon the land, wherefore, it could not be built like unto Solomon's temple. But the manner of the construction was like unto the temple of Solomon; and the workmanship thereof was exceedingly fine" (2 Nephi 5:16). Nephi built the first temple in the land of Nephi, and further temples were eventually built elsewhere. King Benjamin taught at a temple in Zarahemla (Mosiah 1:18–2:7), Alma and Amulek preached repentance at several temples in the land of Zarahemla (Alma 16:13), and Jesus Christ appeared to the surviving Nephites in the temple at Bountiful (3 Nephi 11:1).

After leaving Jerusalem, Lehi built an altar and offered sacrifice in the wilderness (1 Nephi 2:7; 5:9; 7:22).[15] The writers of the Book of Mormon continually tell us that they practiced the whole of the law of Moses. Because temple worship and practices are never explicitly described in the Book of Mormon, it is difficult to know exactly what Nephite temple worship consisted of. If the Book of Mormon people practiced the law of Moses as described in the Bible, temple worship in the New World was probably very similar to that in the Old. On the other hand, since the Book of Mormon people had the Melchizedek Priesthood, it is possible that the law of Moses as recorded in the Bible was altered in terms of temple worship to better suit their needs.

John W. Welch exhaustively described the history and significance of the temple in the Book of Mormon and the many possible connections that may have existed between the temple and living the law of Moses.[16] He presented evidence that the Nephites practiced a system of sacrifices and offerings and that they celebrated festivals connected with the law of Moses—in particular the Feast of Tabernacles and the Day of Atonement.

Jesus Is the Christ

> And also to the convincing of the Jew and Gentile that Jesus is the Christ, the Eternal God, manifesting himself unto all nations (Title Page)

Because the people in the Old Testament and in the first half of the Book of Mormon lived in a time before the coming of the Savior, their knowledge of his coming, his ministry, and his atoning sacrifice depended on the teachings of the prophets. Throughout history the Lord has sent prophets to his children as custodians of the covenant—to preach repentance to those who were members of the covenant and to invite those who were not to be baptized. Indeed, the Lord has said that he will do nothing except he reveal his "secret [Heb. *sôd*]" to his prophets (Amos 3:7). Prophets such as Enoch, Elijah, Elisha, Hosea, Amos, Isaiah, and Jeremiah all delivered a similar message to the covenant people—repent or face the consequences. They worshipped the Lord, the great Jehovah, who would himself come down to redeem his people. Preexilic Israelite religion pointed those who had eyes to see and ears to hear toward the salvation of this Lord and anointed Messiah.

In addition to their message of repentance, prophets often revealed future events—usually promising either blessings or destruction—in order to help motivate the people to repent. Lehi and his family lived during one of the greatest crises in Israelite history—the disobedience of the people would subsequently lead to their deliverance into the hands of the Babylonians. The

Book of Mormon records, "And in that same year there came many prophets, prophesying unto the people that they must repent, or the great city Jerusalem must be destroyed" (1 Nephi 1:4). Prophets from this period include Zephaniah, Jeremiah, Huldah, Nahum, Habbakuk, and Urijah. The writings of many of these prophets have survived, most notably the prophecies of Jeremiah. Chronicles describes the time period of Zedekiah's reign in precisely the same terms as the Book of Mormon: "And the Lord God of their fathers sent to them by his messengers, rising up betimes, and sending; because he had compassion on his people, and on his dwelling place: But they mocked the messengers of God, and despised his words, and misused his prophets, until the wrath of the Lord arose against his people, till there was no remedy" (2 Chronicles 36:15–16).

At the same time, many false prophets appeared. In particular, the false prophets at the time of Jeremiah predicted that the Babylonian threat would soon end, while Jeremiah preached the word of the Lord to surrender to Babylon. Jeremiah explained the critical factor between true prophets and false prophets: "For who hath stood in the counsel [Heb. *sôd*] of the Lord, and hath perceived and heard his word?" (Jeremiah 23:18). Jeremiah accused the prophets of not having access to the heavenly council and speaking the words and visions from themselves and not from the Lord: "Hearken not unto the words of the prophets that prophesy unto you: they make you vain: that speak a vision of their own heart, and not out of the mouth of the Lord" (Jeremiah 23:16).

The most important future event prophesied by all the true prophets was the coming of the Messiah. A knowledge of the reality of the future coming of the Messiah and of the doctrine of the atonement was essential for the people to practice repentance.

The Book of Moses reveals that the fulness of the gospel of Jesus Christ was taught to the human family from the beginning. Adam and Eve were commanded to offer sacrifice in "similitude of the sacrifice of the Only Begotten of the Father" (Moses 5:7). The Old Testament is full of prophecies and allusions to the coming of the Son of God in the flesh to redeem the world. Abraham offering his son Isaac (Genesis 22) was already anciently understood by the Nephites to be in similitude of the Father offering his Only Begotten Son (Jacob 4:5). In the patriarchal blessing given to Judah, mention is made of the kingship that would reside in Judah and an entity named Shiloh that would come to gather the people (Genesis 49:10–11). The Lord revealed to Moses the coming of a prophet like unto Moses (Deuteronomy 18:15–18)—a prophecy that was understood by Nephi (1 Nephi 22:20–21), and later by Peter, to be a reference to the Savior (Acts 3:22).

The greatest of the messianic prophecies to have survived in the Old Testament are found in the writings of Isaiah, which were preserved on the plates of brass and used by the Nephites in their own writings. Nephi loved these writings, in particular the writings of Isaiah, which he quoted at length in his record (1 Nephi 20–21//Isaiah 48–49; 2 Nephi 12–24//Isaiah 2–14). Abinadi quoted portions of messianic prophecies in Isaiah 52 and all of 53 in his address to the priests of Noah (Mosiah 12, 14). Nephi and others quoted from the messianic prophecies of the Israelite prophets Zenock, Neum, and Zenos (1 Nephi 19:10), which are not found in the Old Testament.

Lehi, and later his son Nephi, were called to be prophets, and their calls match well the biblical tradition associated with the calling of prophets. Latter-day Saint scholars who have studied the call of Lehi have found that it contains many elements in common with accounts of the calls of other Israelite prophets. In particular, the vision of God sitting on his throne surrounded by angels fulfills Jeremiah's primary definition of a prophet—that he has become a member of the Lord's divine council.[17] The message of Lehi and Nephi also corresponded with the messages of other Old Testament prophets—repent or be destroyed. Lehi and Nephi both prophesied of the coming of the Messiah. Lehi received a knowledge of "the coming of a Messiah, and also the redemption of the world" (1 Nephi 1:19) and prophesied "a prophet would the Lord God raise up among the Jews—even a Messiah, or, in other words, a Savior of the world" (1 Nephi 10:4). Nephi saw a vision of the earthly ministry of Jesus in connection with the vision of the tree of life (1 Nephi 11).

The Book of Mormon specifically claims that Lehi and his descendants understood the whole of the law of Moses as pointing toward Christ. Jacob taught: "Behold, my soul delighteth in proving unto my people the truth of the coming of Christ; for, for this end hath the law of Moses been given; and all things which have been given of God from the beginning of the world, unto man, are the typifying of him" (2 Nephi 11:4; cf. 2 Nephi 25:24–25, 27, 30; Alma 25:15; 30:3). King Benjamin further taught, "Yet the Lord God saw that his people were a stiffnecked people, and he appointed unto them a law, even the law of Moses. And many signs, and wonders, and types, and shadows showed he unto them, concerning his coming; and also holy prophets spake unto them concerning his coming" (Mosiah 3:14–15).

Thus some people in Old Testament times as well as in the Book of Mormon had many indications of the coming of the Messiah through the law of Moses. The many sacrifices and offerings commemorated various aspects of the atonement and were fulfilled in Christ (3 Nephi 9:19–20). The feast of Passover looked backward and forward to deliverance through a sacrificial lamb and was fulfilled by Christ at the last supper (Exodus 12; Matthew 26:26–29). Likewise, the high priest entering the holy of holies on the Day of Atonement looked forward to Christ as explained by Hebrews 9–10. And Moses raised the brazen serpent in the wilderness as a type of the "lifting up of Christ" (Numbers 21:6–9; John 3:14; 2 Nephi 25:20). Jacob and Abinadi taught that all the prophets knew and taught of the coming of Christ (Jacob 4:4; Mosiah 13:33). Nephi₂ taught that "Abraham saw of his coming, and was filled with gladness and did rejoice" (Helaman 8:17); he also reported that all the prophets from the time of Abraham prophesied of the coming of the Messiah (Helaman 8:16).

The Book of Mormon thus teaches about Christ from three vantage points. First, it contains prophecies and testimonies uttered by prophets who lived in times before his coming: Zenos, Zenock, Neum, Isaiah, Lehi, Nephi, Jacob, Alma, and Nephi₂. Many of these prophets such as Lehi, Nephi, and Jacob had actually seen the Savior (1 Nephi 1:9; 2:16; Jacob 2:4; 11: 2–3). Most important, these men taught the doctrine of Christ and the atonement in a more complete way. Second, the Book of Mormon contains another witness, besides the biblical record, of the resurrection of the Savior. During his visit he delivered a pure statement of his doctrine and church. Finally, the prophets in the Book of Mormon looked back to the time of Christ, indicating to us how to gain a testimony of him.

The Book of Mormon prophets not only understood the future coming of the Messiah, but they understood that the Messiah would be God in the flesh. Nephi saw a vision of the divine parentage of Jesus Christ in his vision of the condescension of God in connection with the tree of life (1 Nephi 11). Jacob taught that "the Holy One of Israel, should manifest himself to them in the flesh" (2 Nephi 6:9). And Abinadi expounded on the messianic prophecies in Isaiah 52–53, demonstrating how the Messiah would be God coming to earth and would minister as the Father and the Son (Mosiah 12–15).

The prophet Isaiah prophesied, "The Lord hath made bare his holy arm in the eyes of all nations; and all the ends of the earth shall see the salvation of our God" (Isaiah 52:10). Nephi saw the day when the Savior "shall manifest himself unto all nations, both unto the Jews and also unto the Gentiles" (1 Nephi 13:42). Abinadi interpreted the Isaiah passage to refer to the atonement of Jesus Christ—the knowledge of which must go forth to all. Further, all the Book of Mormon prophets taught of the atonement of Jesus Christ. As prophesied by the prophets, Jesus Christ came first to the Jews, then to his lost sheep—the remnant of the Nephites and the other tribes of the house of Israel (3 Nephi 15).

But more important than the simple testimony of the coming of the Messiah, the Book of Mormon teaches us the meaning of the Messiah and his atoning mission. Consider Nephi's vision about Christ and his teaching the condescension of God (1 Nephi 11) and his description of the doctrine of Christ (2 Nephi 31). Remember Alma's dramatic description of the intervention of the Savior into his life and the power of the atonement to make us new persons (Alma 5, 36). And consider Moroni's closing words in the Book of Mormon inviting all to come to Christ: "Come unto Christ, and be perfected in him," that by his grace "ye become holy, without spot" (Moroni 10:32–33).

The Book of Mormon was translated and published by the Prophet Joseph Smith in 1830. The gospel has since gone forth as prophesied by the Book of Mormon prophets. The three anciently stated purposes of the Book of Mormon are being fulfilled. As the Book of Mormon goes forth to the world, many read in its pages of the "great things" the Lord has done for their fathers, including the ancient patriarchs, Moses and the children of Israel, and Lehi and his family, whose deliverance from Jerusalem made the Book of Mormon possible. Further, readers of this book can identify and testify of the "great things" he has done and continues to do for them. Most important, readers can identify the greatest thing the Lord has done for us in the atonement of Jesus Christ.

The fulfillment of the Abrahamic covenant continues as the seed of Abraham goes forth to bless the nations of the earth, teaching the remnant of the house of Israel that the covenants of the Lord are still in force and that they are not cast off forever. And the Book of Mormon adds its testimony of the divinity of Jesus Christ to the testimony of the Bible. An astute observer of the restoration and the going forth of the Book of Mormon can readily see that Jesus the Christ is in the process of "manifesting himself unto all nations" (Title Page).

NOTES

1. See John L. Sorenson, "The 'Brass Plates' and Biblical Scholarship," *Dialogue* 10/4 (1977): 31–39; Robert L. Millet, "The Influence of the Brass Plates on the Teachings of Nephi," in *The Book of Mormon: Second Nephi, The Doctrinal Structure,* ed. Monte S. Nyman and Charles D. Tate Jr. (Provo, Utah: BYU Religious Studies Center, 1989), 207–25; Noel B. Reynolds, "The Brass Plates Version of Genesis," in *By Study and Also by Faith: Essays in Honor of Hugh W. Nibley,* ed. John M. Lundquist and Stephen D. Ricks (Salt Lake City: Deseret Book and FARMS, 1990), 2:136–73; and John W. Welch, "Authorship of the Book of Isaiah in Light of the Book of Mormon," in *Isaiah in the Book of Mormon,* ed. Donald W. Parry and John W. Welch (Provo, Utah: FARMS, 1998), 430–34.

2. An informative and stimulating study of the concept of "remember" in the Bible and in the history of Judaism is found in Yosef Hayim

Yerushalmi, *Zakhor: Jewish History and Jewish Memory* (Seattle: University of Washington Press, 1982).

3. For studies on the concept of remembering in the Book of Mormon, see Louis Midgley, "The Ways of Remembrance," in *Rediscovering the Book of Mormon,* ed. John L. Sorenson and Melvin J. Thorne (Salt Lake City: Deseret Book and FARMS, 1991), 168–76, and "'O Man, Remember, and Perish Not' (Mosiah 4:30)," in *Reexploring the Book of Mormon,* ed. John W. Welch (Salt Lake City: Deseret Book, 1992), 127–29.

4. Several substantial and significant articles trace the typology of the exodus in the Book of Mormon: George S. Tate, "The Typology of the Exodus Pattern in the Book of Mormon," in *Literature of Belief: Sacred Scripture and Religious Experience,* ed. Neal E. Lambert (Provo, Utah: BYU Religious Studies Center, 1981), 245–62; Terrence L. Szink, "Nephi and the Exodus," in *Rediscovering the Book of Mormon,* 38–51; S. Kent Brown, "The Exodus Pattern in the Book of Mormon," *BYU Studies* 30/3 (1990): 111–26.

5. This same acknowledgment is found in the Jaredite narrative as Shule remembers the great things the Lord did for his people in delivering them across the sea (Ether 7:27).

6. John W. Welch, "A Masterpiece: Alma 36," in *Rediscovering the Book of Mormon,* 114–31.

7. George E. Mendenhall, "Covenant Forms in Israelite Tradition," *Biblical Archaeologist* 17/3 (1954): 50–76. See also Dennis J. McCarthy, *Treaty and Covenant* (Rome: Biblical Institute Press, 1978), and Moshe Weinfeld, *"berith,"* in *Theological Dictionary of the Old Testament,* ed. G. Johannes Botterweck and Helmer Ringgren (Grand Rapids, Mich.: Eerdmans, 1975), 2:253–79.

8. An excellent article on the law of Moses in the Book of Mormon is Kent P. Jackson, "Law of Moses," in *Book of Mormon Reference Companion,* ed. Dennis L. Largey et al. (Salt Lake City: Deseret Book, 2003), 504–6.

9. David Rolph Seely, "The Ten Commandments in the Book of Mormon," in *Doctrines of the Book of Mormon, The 1991 Sperry*

Symposium, ed. Bruce A. Van Orden and Brent L. Top (Salt Lake City: Deseret Book, 1992), 166–81.

10. See John W. Welch, Proceedings of the Book of Mormon Law Conference, in *Studia Antiqua* (Summer 2003).

11. For a discussion of this issue, see John W. Welch, "The Temple in the Book of Mormon," in *Temples of the Ancient World,* ed. Donald W. Parry (Salt Lake City: Deseret Book and FARMS, 1994), 297–387.

12. Stephen D. Ricks, "Kingship, Coronation, and Covenant in Mosiah 1–6," in *King Benjamin's Speech,* ed. John W. Welch and Stephen D. Ricks (Provo, Utah: FARMS, 1998), 233–76.

13. The biblical view of Josiah's reforms is found in 2 Kings 22–23. For another point of view see Margaret Barker, "What Did King Josiah Reform?" in this volume, pages 523–42. Barker believes that in the process of reform Josiah and his followers discarded many important aspects of the ancient Israelite temple religion.

14. See Kevin Christensen, "The Temple, the Monarchy, and Wisdom: Lehi's World and the Scholarship of Margaret Barker," in this volume, pages 449–522.

15. For a discussion of the possible significance of these sacrifices see S. Kent Brown, "Why Were Those Sacrifices Offered by Lehi?" in *From Jerusalem to Zarahemla* (Provo, Utah: BYU Religious Studies Center, 1998), 1–8. For a discussion of the fact that Lehi built an altar and offered sacrifice outside of Jerusalem, see David Rolph Seely, "Lehi's Altar and Sacrifice in the Wilderness," *Journal of Book of Mormon Studies* 10/1 (2001): 62–69, 80.

16. Welch, "Temple in the Book of Mormon," 297–379.

17. Blake T. Ostler, "The Throne-Theophany and Prophetic Commission in 1 Nephi: A Form-Critical Analysis," *BYU Studies* 26/4 (1986): 67–95. See also John W. Welch, "The Calling of Lehi as a Prophet in the World of Jerusalem," in this volume, pages 421–48.

Chapter 15

The Calling of Lehi as a Prophet in the World of Jerusalem

John W. Welch

First Nephi 1 reports in very brief but significant terms the essential facts about the call and public ministry of the prophet Lehi. These rich verses reward close examination. While many approaches can be taken to enhance our understanding and appreciation of the inspiration and courageous dedication of this father-prophet,[1] the approach taken in this study seeks to examine several details in the text of 1 Nephi 1, attempting, among other things, to see Lehi's prophetic call in light of his world by inquiring how his words and experiences may have been understood by his contemporaries. In many remarkable respects Lehi had much in common with other prophets of God called in that classic era of ancient Israelite prophecy.

Despite the fact that the text reporting the call of Lehi is very brief,[2] it employs several key words and images that were full of tradition and conveyed much meaning in the world in which Lehi lived. By understanding the significance of these ancient words and phrases, modern readers can appreciate many interesting aspects of Lehi's prophetic call. Especially important is Lehi's vision in which he sees God "sitting upon his throne, surrounded with numberless concourses of angels" (1 Nephi 1:8). It appears that by this experience, which compares closely with the so-called council visions of Old Testament prophets,[3] Lehi became a prophet.

"In the commencement of the first year of the reign of Zedekiah" (1 Nephi 1:4)

The engaging story of Lehi's call is familiar to virtually every person who has ever begun to read the Book of Mormon. It came in the commencement of the first year of the reign of Zedekiah (1 Nephi 1:4),[4] king of Judah, in 597/596 B.C. This was undoubtedly an unforgettably troubling year, for in the first part of December, 598 B.C., Jehoiakim, king of Judah, had died. His son Jehoiachin, who was probably only an adolescent, was made king.[5] Three months and ten days later, on 16 March (2 Adar), 597 B.C., Jerusalem fell, having been besieged by the Babylonians (2 Kings 24:10–16).[6] They deposed King Jehoiachin and deported him to Babylon, along with many of the leading citizens, soldiers, and craftsmen of Jerusalem (Jeremiah 24:1),[7] leaving Jehoiachin's uncle, the mere twenty-one-year-old Zedekiah, on the throne as a puppet king.[8] Therefore, at the time when Lehi became concerned about the welfare of his people, the still-insurgent Jews at Jerusalem already knew well the indomitable military power of the Babylonians and were in a weakened political position with an inexperienced, twenty-one-year-old king at their helm. The situation in Jerusalem was grave and volatile, if not already desperate.

Such circumstances as trouble in the land and the coronation of a new king often precipitated prophetic action in the ancient world. One scholar, for example, has argued from circumstantial evidence in the Old Testament that prophecy played an especially important role at or around the coronation of each new king. He suggests that the distinctive council visions and messenger prophecies of Micaiah (1 Kings 22:1–38), Isaiah (Isaiah 6, 40), Ezekiel (Ezekiel 1–10), and Amos (Amos 7:1–3, 4–6, 7–9; 8:1–3; 9:1), as well as Jeremiah's temple sermon (Jeremiah 26)—which have much in common with 1 Nephi 1—all occurred around the New Year, at "the epiphany and enthronement of Yahweh," the day when the king was typically crowned and the fates or destinies pronounced.[9] If there is any merit to such suggestions, we may understand more clearly the sharply negative reaction which Lehi's public message evoked[10] since it was apparently near the day when the Israelites were celebrating Zedekiah's enthronement, or at least "in the commencement" of the first year of his troubled reign, that many prophets, including Lehi, came forth and spoke out pessimistically against Zedekiah's newly installed regime.

"Many prophets" (1 Nephi 1:4)

Nephi reports that "there came many prophets, prophesying unto the people that they must repent, or the great city Jerusalem must be destroyed" (1 Nephi 1:4). Who were these other prophets and how do their words compare with Lehi's? Prophetic messages of judgment and destruction were in fact common among the so-called classical prophets of Israel who are known to have been active at this time. For example, during Lehi's lifetime, Nahum (ca. 612 B.C.) proclaimed the vengeance of the Lord on his enemies and marked the fall of Nineveh. Zephaniah (who also lived during this time) prophesied that God would sweep the earth completely clean and would stretch his hand over Judah to punish its royal house and to wipe out of Jerusalem all remnants of Baal (Zephaniah 1:2–9). "By the fire of his jealousy the whole land shall be consumed," he prophesied (Zephaniah 1:18). "Gather together, you unruly nation, . . . before the burning anger of the Lord comes upon you," he exhorted (Zephaniah 2:1–2; cf. 3:8).[11] Zephaniah spoke doom against Jerusalem, calling it a tyrant city, filthy and foul (Zephaniah 3:1–8), while he also promised that a poor and afflicted remnant would be preserved by finding refuge in the Lord (Zephaniah 3:11–13; cf. Isaiah 6:13, which also holds out some optimism for the return or repentance of a remnant through the power of the "holy seed") and that the survivors would be rescued and gathered when the proper time would come (Zephaniah 3:19–20). Habakkuk (ca. 609–598 B.C.) prophesied during the reign of Jehoiakim[12] of the destruction of the treacherous and of the overconfident, pronouncing five woes upon extortioners, exploiters, debauchers, and idolaters (Habakkuk 2:5–20), while also offering a prayer to God that he be merciful (Habakkuk 3:2). Jeremiah was also similarly active during and after Lehi's day. And indeed, there were undoubtedly many other prophets who arose during this time for whom we have no names (2 Chronicles 36:15–16).[13] It is significant when placing Lehi among his contemporaries to see that he was not a lone voice delivering the messages of woe, destruction, mercy, and redemption. He likewise prophesied that Jerusalem would be destroyed and that its inhabitants would perish by the sword (1 Nephi 1:13), yet he also praised the mercy of God (1 Nephi 1:14) and looked forward to the "redemption of the world" (1 Nephi 1:19). Although 1 Nephi makes no explicit statement relating Lehi's message to that of his contemporaries, the point is evident: The people in Jerusalem in Lehi's day had been warned expressly and repeatedly.

Nephi also leaves the ill fate of these other prophets unstated. Only a few years earlier, for example, the prophet Urijah had been persecuted, had fled to Egypt, and was subsequently extradited, convicted, and ignominiously executed for preaching the same message that the prophets were again preaching in the first year of the reign of Zedekiah (Jeremiah 26:20–23). Similarly, 2 Chronicles 36:15–16 later explains what had happened to these prophets and why: "And the Lord God of their fathers sent to them by his messengers, . . . because he had compassion on his people, and on his dwelling place: But they mocked the messengers of God, and despised his words, and misused his prophets, until the wrath of the Lord arose against his people, till there was no remedy." The fact that he was willing to deliver that very message entrusted to him by God, knowing full well that precisely the same thing would undoubtedly happen to him as had already happened to others delivering that identical message only a few months or years before, marks Lehi as a man of extraordinary courage, commitment, and devotion to the Lord and to his people, one of the hallmarks of a true prophet of the Lord.

It was also typical at this time for these prophets to work largely by themselves. "They fulfill[ed] their missions . . . alone as individuals,"[14] although this does not imply that they were "detached from the mainstream of Israel's religious tradition."[15] Lehi appears to have worked this way, acting on his own inspiration and initiative,[16] for Nephi's account is silent about any involvement Lehi might have had with his fellow prophets. He may have gone forth and prayed unto the Lord (1 Nephi 1:5) because he was among the prophets who were already actively crying repentance in Jerusalem, but it appears more likely that he was profoundly moved to pray, motivated by the problems in Jerusalem and by the messages of the prophets whom he had just heard.

"Prayed . . . in behalf of his people" (1 Nephi 1:5)

Lehi's first recorded impulse was to pray "in behalf of his people" (1 Nephi 1:5). In so doing, he was in harmony with the spirit of classic Hebrew prophecy that flourished during his day. A prophet who knows with moral certainty what will happen to his people has been characterized as having an "irresistible" need not only to deliver his message, but also "to intercede on behalf of his people."[17] Such attempts by the prophets to try through prayer to offset the impending doom of all their people as a whole community have been identified as one of the notable functions of the classic Israelite prophets during the time of Lehi.[18] Thus, Lehi's action would probably have been viewed by his contemporaries as being in tune with the spirit of prophecy in his day.

"A pillar of fire" (1 Nephi 1:6)

As Lehi prayed, he beheld a pillar of fire dwelling upon a rock in front of him (1 Nephi 1:6). From this pillar Lehi saw and heard many powerful things,[19] but Nephi does not elaborate on who or what Lehi saw in this pillar of fire. Joseph Smith described how God, angels, and spirits appear in fiery manifestations; he taught, for instance, that "spirits can only be revealed in flaming fire and glory."[20] From ancient sources, too, one learns that the appearance of fire, especially a pillar of fire, was a frequent mode of heavenly manifestation, sometimes of God and other times of his messengers or of the holy beings who surrounded him. God appeared to Moses in a burning bush (Exodus 3:2) and on a flaming Mount Sinai (Exodus 19:18); he also appeared over the tabernacle at night in a fire (Numbers 9:15) and over the door of the tabernacle by day in a similar "pillar of a cloud" (Deuteronomy 31:15). On some occasions in the Old Testament, fire was associated with God's messengers, especially those emanating from God's council (discussed further below; see, e.g., Psalm 104:4), whose fiery description can be compared with the appearance of Moroni in Joseph Smith—History 1:30–32; in other ancient accounts, fire was used to combat God's enemies.[21] Thus, we cannot be certain who or what[22] Lehi saw in the pillar of fire that appeared to him. Lehi could have seen God in this pillar, but since Lehi's vision of God himself is reported as the next stage of the vision, it seems more likely to me that what he beheld at this time was a messenger of God whose threatening words and presence, perhaps summoning Lehi, caused Lehi to "quake and tremble exceedingly" (1 Nephi 1:6).

"He thought he saw God sitting upon his throne, surrounded with numberless concourses of angels" (1 Nephi 1:8)

Lehi returned directly to his bed, where the next part of his vision opened. There, most significantly, he beheld "God sitting upon his throne, surrounded with numberless concourses of angels" (1 Nephi 1:8). Such visions of God seated in the midst of his host assembled in heaven appear to have been particularly meaningful for people in Lehi's day.[23] If the prevailing understanding is correct, it was by such a vision that a prophet received his commission, his authorization, his perspective, his knowledge of God, and his information about God's judgments and decrees. Similarly, from the texts of the Book of Mormon one can assume that in connection with his encounter with God and the heavenly council, Lehi likewise received his call to serve as a prophet of God, as the following details further show.

In many other texts from the ancient Near East, God is visualized presiding over and working with his council. Important relationships between this council and God's prophets have been scrutinized in recent years by several scholars.[24] While the members of this council served several functions, such as accompanying their God in battle[25] and giving "praise to his glorious position,"[26] the council's most distinctive purpose was to govern the world by delivering the decrees of God.[27] These decrees were typically issued to messengers or prophets who would deliver them to those affected. In earlier years, the prophets of Israel had delivered their messages primarily to the kings of Israel, but in Lehi's day, they typically directed these edicts, like imperial heralds, to the entire population.[28]

Three main elements common to most accounts of such council visions in the Bible have been identified. They are first, that God was described as surrounded by his numerous host; second, that the discussion of the council was brought to a conclusion by a council leader; and third, that the word of God was then stated to determine the fate of a person or group.[29] The heralds of the council who delivered God's decrees were sometimes deities or angels; at other times they were human prophets, messengers, or apostles who were admitted in a vision into the council, made privy to the judgment of the council, and then dispatched to make their assigned proclamation. From the fact that many ancient Near Eastern accounts show the messenger delivering the identical words he received from the council, it has been concluded that it was apparently important to these people that "the message [be] delivered in precisely the same words that had been given to the divine couriers"[30] and that this gave divine authority and legitimacy to the decrees the prophet or messenger delivered.[31] That council, its decrees, its intimate confidences, and the heavenly principles upon which this council was based were known in Hebrew as the *sôd* (Greek *mysterion*),[32] and knowing the *sôd* conferred great power and wisdom.

This understanding of God, his heavenly council, and the prophet's role as a messenger of that council has been derived from several passages in the Old Testament and in ancient Near Eastern literature. It was apparently fairly well understood in Lehi's day. For example, 1 Kings 22:19–23, as noted earlier, records the experience of the prophet Micaiah, who saw God and his council, heard its deliberation and resolution, and was sent forth with the decree of God:

> And he said, Hear thou therefore the word of the Lord: I saw the Lord sitting on his throne, and all the host of heaven standing by him on his right hand and on his left. And the Lord said, Who shall persuade Ahab, that he may go up and fall at Ramoth-gilead? And one said on this manner, and another said on that manner. And there came forth a spirit, and stood before the Lord, and said, I will persuade him. And the Lord said unto him, . . . thou shalt persuade him, and prevail also: go forth, and do so.

Likewise, Jeremiah 23:18 (contemporaneous with Lehi) asks rhetorically about those who are true prophets: "But who has stood in Yahweh's council [*sôd*] and seen—and heard his word? Who has carefully marked [obeyed] his word?"[33] This passage stresses the importance in Lehi's day for a prophet not only to stand in the council of God, but also to both see and hear what goes on there and then to carry out his assignment meticulously by delivering the precise words of the council's decree, just as Lehi does. To so report and do, it has been concluded, was certification in that day that the prophet was a true messenger of God.[34]

Our understanding of Lehi's mission as a prophet can be increased in this light. As Jeremiah demands of a true prophet, Lehi indeed beheld God and his assembly, saw and heard (1 Nephi 1:18, 19; also 1:6) what transpired there, and then "went forth . . . to declare unto [the people of Jerusalem] concerning the things which he had both seen and heard" (1 Nephi 1:18).

"Angels" (1 Nephi 1:8)

In Lehi's vision, God was surrounded by his numerous host. As described above, it appears that the host was typically viewed in antiquity as serving three functions—namely, praising God, delivering the decrees of the council, and accompanying God in battle. The first two of these functions are quite clearly present in Lehi's vision, and the third may be inferred. First, in 1 Nephi 1:8, the host was "singing and praising their God."[35] Second, Lehi describes the members of the host as angels (literally, "messengers"). In both Hebrew and Greek, the words translated as "angel" or "apostle" can literally mean "messenger," indicating the likely presence here of the messenger function of these individuals in God's council. As in the paradigm above, a conspicuous council leader also came forth in Lehi's vision to deliver a book to him and to send him forth as a messenger. Third, while that was done, twelve others from the council then "went forth upon the face of the earth." Perhaps they were viewed as fulfilling the warrior function often served by these heavenly beings. The vision of Ezekiel appears to have been grounded in a similar manifestation. He saw "six men" come forth, each with "a slaughter weapon in his hand; and one man among them was clothed with linen, with a writer's inkhorn by his side" (Ezekiel 9:2).[36] It is possible that the twelve whom Lehi saw were likewise coming forth to take their battle stations or warning posts, imminently prepared to execute judgment upon Jerusalem, but there is no express indication in 1 Nephi who these twelve were or what they did. They probably should not be thought of as archangels, as understood in later Judaism.[37] Perhaps more relevant is the possibility that the number twelve may have had significance in the minds of Lehi and his contemporaries because multiples of twelve often had judicial and administrative significance in the courts and official bodies of Israel. Later, Lehi would learn more about the coming of the Messiah and his twelve apostles, but in the context of Lehi's vision up to this particular point, these twelve would probably have been thought of as functioning in the role of executing God's judgment, rather than in the other roles they would later fulfill during Jesus' earthly ministry.[38]

"One descending" (1 Nephi 1:9)

The leader of this council was exceptionally glorious ("his luster was above that of the sun at noon-day," 1 Nephi 1:9; cf. Acts 22:6; Joseph Smith—History 1:30), but beyond that he is not specifically identified in the text. It may be that this principal messenger was one of the angels, if the pronoun *one* in 1 Nephi 1:9 refers to "one" of the angels, which would be the closest plural antecedent out of which "one" might have been identified. On the other hand, it seems more likely that the "One descending" was the Holy One of Israel, the Lord himself, who then had left his throne to deliver in person his decree to his messenger the prophet,[39] for as in Amos 3:7 the Lord God himself "reveal[s] his secrets (*sôd*) unto his servants the prophets." Under this understanding, the one who came down[40] to speak to Lehi was the God himself who had been initially seated on his throne, and thus Lehi's exclamation "unto the Lord" at the conclusion of his vision, extolling the highness of his throne (1 Nephi 1:14), should be understood as having been made in a direct personal statement to that God, Christ himself, as he stood right before Lehi (1 Nephi 1:11).[41]

"A book" (1 Nephi 1:11)

The edict delivered to Lehi contained the judgments of God and his council upon the city of Jerusalem.[42] It began with a curse upon the city: "Wo, wo, unto Jerusalem, for I have seen thine abominations!" (1 Nephi 1:13; cf. Ezekiel 2:10).[43] From this decree, Lehi learned many other things about the destruction of Jerusalem by the sword (1 Nephi 1:13; cf. David's vision in 1 Chronicles 21:16); he also read there about the coming of a Messiah and, as others too had prophesied about the eventual recovery of the scattered remnant (cf. Zephaniah 3:19–20), about "the redemption of the world" (1 Nephi 1:19).

It is interesting that Lehi read this information in "a book" (1 Nephi 1:11).[44] The book may have been a scroll, or it could have been composed of tablets. A close analogue to 1 Nephi 1:11 is found in the contemporary writings of Habakkuk, where the Lord spoke to Habakkuk about the preparation of a book that a herald from the Lord's council was to carry forth with speed: "And the Lord answered me, and said, Write the vision, and make it plain upon tables, that he may run that readeth it" (Habakkuk 2:2). Equally, it appears that the unstated instruction to Lehi was that he should deliver his message posthaste.[45] The fact that Lehi was handed a written decree may also reflect the contemporary legal and political practices of his day. Some have theorized that preclassical, nonwritten prophecy flourished in the ninth and tenth centuries B.C. in part because at that time an "oral message was still regarded as an authoritative decree."[46] During Lehi's day, however, written edicts under the Assyrian practice had become the standard legal mode of issuing proclamations and prophets were more concerned with writing, and thus the authoritativeness of Lehi's words in the minds of his listeners was probably enhanced by the fact that he could report that he had read these words in a written decree.

"He did exclaim many things" (1 Nephi 1:14)

Lehi's reaction to this edict was profoundly spiritual. "He was filled with the Spirit of the Lord," and "his soul did rejoice, and his whole heart was filled" (1 Nephi 1:12, 15). He spontaneously and eloquently joined the heavenly host in praising God. By so doing he functionally, if not constitutionally, joined the council as one of its members. Since his words seem to reflect poetic composition similar to exaltations of God's controlling power and wisdom found in ancient Near Eastern literature,[47] it may have been that Lehi, too, sang his words of praise, like other hymns or psalms of praise in his day were sung:

> Great and marvelous are thy works,
> O Lord God Almighty!
> Thy throne is high in the heavens.
>
> and thy power, and goodness, and mercy
> are over all the inhabitants of the earth;
>
> and, because thou art merciful,
> thou wilt not suffer those who come unto thee
> that they shall perish! (1 Nephi 1:14).

"He truly testified" (1 Nephi 1:19)

Lehi next "went forth among the people, and began to prophesy and to declare unto them" what he had "seen and heard" (1 Nephi 1:18). He had little choice but to speak out, in the sense that he, like the other prophets of God, was impelled and constrained by the Spirit. Prophets speak because they must and because they cannot hold back what they know. Lehi probably also knew, like Ezekiel, that if he did not deliver the warning that God had commanded him to speak, then the blood of all the wicked would be required at his hand, but if he warned the wicked, then he would save his own soul (Ezekiel 3:17–19).

His message was one of testimony. "He truly testified of their wickedness and their abominations" (1 Nephi 1:19). Since Lehi had seen the facts in the council and in the book, he could stand as a witness and testify against the people, much as a plaintiff would lodge a complaint or accusation against a defendant or lawbreaker. If he spoke like the other prophets of his day, Lehi's testimony was punctuated with blunt, declarative statements, offering no excuses, rationales, theological justifications, or explanations. He simply declared the message he had been told to give. Thus, like several other prophets at this time who brought so-called prophetic lawsuits against the people of Israel or those in the Book of Mormon,[48] Lehi issued a declarative testimony or affidavit against the wickedness of the people in Jerusalem. In addition, he could also deliver the verdict, as in the formulaic prophetic judgment speeches of other contemporaneous prophets,[49] for the verdict in heaven had already been handed down.

While Lehi's reference to the redemption of the world offered hope to the people of Jerusalem that they would someday be bought back from this foreclosure and that the world would eventually be saved (1 Nephi 1:19), even though it be utterly wasted (cf. Zephaniah 1:2), the reaction to his message was still predictable. The people became angry and tried to kill him. Since they were law-abiding citizens, they probably raised some technical charge of treason or false prophecy against Lehi, as they did against Jeremiah (Jeremiah 26:11), but their underlying motive would more likely be found in the fact that Lehi, like so many prophets, spoke concerning the coming of a Messiah to overthrow the wicked establishment. In the face of this threat, and just as the Lord also promised to protect Jeremiah, the Lord delivered Lehi, for, as Nephi explains, "the tender mercies of the Lord are over all those whom he hath chosen, because of their faith, to make them mighty even unto the power of deliverance" (1 Nephi 1:20). In a dream, Lehi was blessed by the Lord for having faithfully fulfilled the assignment he had been given. He was permitted and commanded to leave his post "and depart into the wilderness" (1 Nephi 2:1–2), so that he could become an instrument "unto the fulfilling of the word of the Lord, that [Israel] should be scattered upon all the face of the earth" (1 Nephi 10:13).

"The mysteries of God" (1 Nephi 2:16)

Not everyone, however, rejected Lehi's message. At least Nephi desired to know the truthfulness of the words of his father. In faith, with great desires and lowliness of heart,[50] and being willing to be obedient and not rebellious, Nephi sought and received a confirmation from God so that he "did believe all the words which had been spoken" by Lehi (1 Nephi 2:16). In a comparable way, the Lord will make known to all his children the truthfulness of the words of his messengers, the prophets.

It is significant to me that Nephi specifically says here that he desired "to know of the mysteries of God" (1 Nephi 2:16). While all are invited to seek and all are promised knowledge (1 Nephi 15:8; Matthew 7:7; Moroni 10:4–5), this is not an open invitation for all men and women to seek "mysteries" beyond the declarative words of the prophets. When Nephi said that he desired to know of the "mysteries," he was most likely referring quite precisely to the information that Lehi had just learned through his visions in 1 Nephi 1.[51] As stated above, the Hebrew word *sôd* basically means "council," but by association, it also came to mean the decree of the council itself.[52] Because the council and its actions were not open to the general public, they were thought of as being very confidential, esoteric, or secret, also "convey[ing] the notion of intimate friendship."[53] Hence, the word *sôd* can also be translated as "mystery": "*Sôd* also came to be used for the secret decision rendered at such councils, and . . . in the Hebrew represented by Prv, Sir, and Qumrân, *sôd* is used simply for secrets or mysteries."[54] Just as Raymond E. Brown has concluded that "the background of such a concept is that of the prophets being introduced into the heavenly assembly and gaining a knowledge of its secret decrees,"[55] so it would appear that Lehi, in just such a way, had attained access on this occasion to the mysteries of God. From this, one can see that while the decrees of the divine council (*sôd*) were confidential and privileged information (and that in this sense they can be called *mysteria*), they were not puzzles or cryptic information. Hence when Nephi has great desires to "know of the mysteries of God" so shortly after Lehi had experienced the *sôd*, it would appear that Nephi is similarly seeking to know the *sôd* and the decrees and glories of that council, just as Lehi had known them and as Jeremiah speaks of them. He is blessed with a visit of the Lord and a belief in "all the words" which Lehi had spoken—the words which Lehi had delivered as he had received them from the Lord (1 Nephi 2:16).

Conclusion

First Nephi chapter 1 can clearly be approached in many ways to better understand and appreciate the call of Lehi as a prophet of God. I have tried to use a variety of information about the gospel and about Lehi's own day to elucidate the possible meanings of his visions in 1 Nephi 1. From this, one can see how Lehi's dedication and inspiration can be confirmed in terms of several universally applicable aspects of prophecy. Under generally applicable definitions of what it means to be a prophet, Lehi certainly qualifies. Hugh B. Brown has defined eleven characteristics that "should distinguish a man who claims to be a prophet." Lehi manifests them all: (1) "He boldly claim[s] that God has spoken to him"; (2) he is "a dignified man [bearing] a dignified message"; (3) he "declare[s] his message without fear"; (4) he bears witness without argument or concession; (5) he "speak[s] in the name of the Lord"; (6) he "predict[s] future events . . . [that] come to pass"; (7) his message pertains to future as well as present generations; (8) he "endure[s] persecution"; (9) he "denounce[s] wickedness fearlessly"; (10) he does "things that no man could do without God's help"; and (11) "his teachings [are] in strict agreement with scripture."[56] Other criteria can be added to this list, for example, (12) that he prophesies of Christ.[57] Each of these characteristics is found in 1 Nephi 1:4–20 and in the life and courageous deeds of the prophet Lehi.[58]

Additionally and equally so, Lehi's prophetic attributes can be understood and confirmed in light of classical Israelite prophecy specific to his own contemporaneous world. Like other prophets in the seventh century, Lehi was steeped in the precise terminology and conception of the divine heavenly council (1 Nephi 1:8) and in its many particular functions and its distinctive images and protocol, which gave meaning and power to his message. Like his many prophetic contemporaries, Lehi also abhorred and testified against the abominations he saw in Jerusalem (1 Nephi 1:19); he and they rejected the arrogant nationalism of many Jews in Jerusalem and spoke instead of a worldwide redemption (1 Nephi 1:19); he spoke out publicly, triggered by events at the commencement of a new king's reign (1 Nephi 1:4); he pleaded with God in behalf of his people (1 Nephi 1:5); he called for simple righteousness, addressing the general population as opposed to the king (1 Nephi 1:18); and he worked essentially alone and was greatly concerned that his prophecies be written down. These were typical characteristics of prophets of this time; they and several others like them are reflected in remarkable detail in the abbreviated account of 1 Nephi 1.

Prophets have been called upon by God to say and do many different things over the centuries. Some have been called like Moses as lawgivers, or like Joshua as military leaders. Abraham served as a paragon of faith, peace, and covenant making, while others like Elijah were outspoken in decrying the wickedness of kings and idolatry.[59] Similarly, Lehi's role among the prophets of God was specifically suited to the needs of the Lord in that day.

He was called as a messenger of the Lord, faithfully delivering God's decree against Jerusalem and obediently following the direction of the Lord during that pivotal period in the history of Jerusalem and of the world as well. By all eternal and historical criteria, Lehi qualifies functionally, archetypally, literarily, spiritually, and scripturally as one of the great prophets of God. His call as a prophet in 1 Nephi 1 gives a foundation of divine authority, revelation, and guidance for everything that follows father Lehi's posterity throughout the Book of Mormon.

Notes

This article first appeared in *The Book of Mormon: First Nephi, The Doctrinal Foundation,* ed. Monte S. Nyman and Charles D. Tate Jr. (Provo, Utah: BYU Religious Studies Center, 1988), 35–54. It has been updated and modified in a few respects.

1. For various approaches, see Hugh Nibley, *Lehi in the Desert, The World of the Jaredites, There Were Jaredites* (Salt Lake City: Deseret Book and FARMS, 1988), 4–13, and Hugh Nibley, *An Approach to the Book of Mormon,* 3rd ed. (Salt Lake City: Deseret Book and FARMS, 1988), 46–54; George Reynolds and Janne M. Sjodahl, *Commentary on the Book of Mormon* (Salt Lake City: Deseret News Press, 1955), 1:7–12; Sidney B. Sperry, *Book of Mormon Compendium* (Salt Lake City: Bookcraft, 1968), 97; S. Kent Brown, "Lehi's Personal Record: Quest for a Missing Source," *BYU Studies* 24/1 (1984): 19–42; Blake T. Ostler, "The Throne-Theophany and Prophetic Commission in 1 Nephi: A Form-Critical Analysis," *BYU Studies* 26/4 (1986): 67–95.

2. First Nephi 1 contains only an abridgment of the record of Lehi (1 Nephi 1:17). Sometimes Nephi appears to paraphrase his father's words, as in 1 Nephi 1:15, "after this manner was the language of my father"; other times he is quoting verbatim, as in 1 Nephi 1:8 (cf. Alma 36:22, also quoting these twenty-one words of Lehi) and 1 Nephi 1:13.

3. I speak of Lehi's vision as a "council vision." I do this for several reasons, primarily because it is similar to the council vi-

sions of Old Testament prophets. Also, the word *concourse* in Joseph Smith's day meant "a moving, flowing or running together; . . . a *concourse* of men," and it is used in this sense in 1 Nephi 8:21; but the word also meant "a meeting; an assembly of men; an assemblage of things," thus indicating that the idea of a council might be more expressly present in Lehi's account than a modern reader is likely to notice. Noah Webster, *American Dictionary of the English Language* (1828). See also Hugh Nibley, *Since Cumorah,* 2nd ed. (Salt Lake City: Deseret Book and FARMS, 1988), 186, describing Lehi's vision as one that takes us "back to a council in heaven as a fitting prologue to a religious history." The term *council,* of course, should not be understood to describe a small group. Like the premortal council in heaven, the council that Lehi beheld was not a small cabinet meeting, but was multitudinous, as is reflected in the fact that the word *concourses* is plural. However, comparisons between Lehi's vision and the "council visions" of his contemporaries or others should not be overstated. Like all comparisons, there will be differences as well as similarities.

4. Events in the ancient world were normally dated by reference to regnal years. A similar reference introduces Isaiah's council vision in Isaiah 6:1, "In the year that king Uzziah died."

5. According to 2 Chronicles 36:9, Jehoiachin was eight years old when he was placed on the throne. According to 2 Kings 24:8, he was eighteen, but since his father Jehoiakim only lived to be thirty-six, the younger age for Jehoiachin seems more likely.

6. A contemporaneous cuneiform tablet records the specific events surrounding this conquest. See D. Winton Thomas, ed., *Documents from Old Testament Times* (Edinburgh: Nelson, 1958), 80. A different account is given in 2 Chronicles 36:5–10, which reports that Jehoiakim was still king when the Babylonians attacked, that Jehoiachin was placed on the throne for three months and ten days and then was brought to Babylon and replaced by Zedekiah.

7. Jeremiah 52:28 numbers them at 3,023. Second Kings 24:14 reports that ten thousand were taken captive, perhaps in a second stage of deportation. See Robert F. Smith, "Book of Mormon Event

Structure: The Ancient Near East," *Journal of Book of Mormon Studies* 5/2 (1996): 121–22; John W. Welch, "They Came from Jerusalem," *Ensign,* September 1976, 27–31.

8.   Zedekiah was apparently placed on the throne on 22 April (10 Nisan) 597 B.C., but his coronation would have taken place either on 1 Tishri, or on 1 Nisan of the following year, and thus it is unclear whether the Book of Mormon phrase "in the commencement of the first year of the reign of Zedekiah" (1 Nephi 1:4; cf. Jeremiah 49:34) refers to the day he began to rule or the day of his coronation. Smith, "Book of Mormon Event Structure," 122.

9.   Edwin C. Kingsbury, "The Prophets and the Council of Yahweh," *Journal of Biblical Literature* 83/3 (1964): 284, pointing especially to parallels in the determination of destiny in the council of the gods following the reenthronement of Marduk in the Babylonian year-rite. Cf. Geo Widengren, *The Ascension of the Apostle and the Heavenly Book (King and Saviour III)* (Leipzig: Harrassowitz, 1950), 10. These sources help us understand reasons why the New Year was an effective time for a prophetic call.

10.   The reaction of the people in Jerusalem was political in the sense that his message indicted and condemned the city, whose inhabitants then collectively sought Lehi's life. This would have involved, in my opinion, several forms of legal and political action, much like the lawsuit brought against Jeremiah and the extradition procedure initiated in the case of Urijah, discussed in Jeremiah 26.

11.   John D. W. Watts's translation of these verses, in *The Books of Joel, Obadiah, Jonah, Nahum, Habakkuk and Zephaniah* (Cambridge: Cambridge University Press, 1975).

12.   John Bright, *Jeremiah* (Garden City, N.Y.: Doubleday, 1965), xxviii. There may have been others. Although they cannot be dated precisely, prophecies such as Joel's predictions of the disastrous "day of the Lord" (Joel 1:15; 2:1, 11, 31; 3:14) and his pleas for repentance also can "most naturally . . . be understood [in] reference to the cataclysmic events of 587 B.C." Leslie C. Allen, *The Books of Joel, Obadiah, Jonah, and Micah* (Grand Rapids, Mich.: Eerdmans, 1976), 24. Obadiah's prophecies, particularly in Obadiah 1:11–14, speaking of an

overthrow of Jerusalem and of God's justice, may also relate to events in Lehi's day. Allen, *Books of Joel,* 129–30. Watts, *Books of Joel,* 13, sees the "Day of the Lord" as the liturgical high day of the great autumn festival (1 Tishri?) from the time of Amos through Joel.

13. This exemplifies the eternal principle that God will warn all nations of his judgments; see Marion G. Romney, in Conference Report, April 1958, 128.

14. Walter S. Wurzburger, "Prophets and Prophecy," in *Encyclopaedia Judaica* 13:1162; see also Eric W. Heaton, *The Hebrew Kingdoms* (London: Oxford University Press, 1968), 237–44. Compare Abinadi, Samuel the Lamanite, John the Baptist, and other such prophets who stand alone in crying out the word of the Lord.

15. Heaton, *Hebrew Kingdoms,* 243.

16. Compare Lehi with the description of the "independent prophets" in ibid., 238–39.

17. Wurzburger, "Prophets and Prophecy," 1169.

18. For example, Jeremiah was told to cease praying on behalf of his people (Jeremiah 14:11). Wurzburger, "Prophets and Prophecy," 1169–71. This prophetic and intercessory function was also served by prophets such as Abraham (Genesis 20:7) and Samuel (1 Samuel 7:5–9), and in the Book of Mormon notably by Enos (Enos 1:9–17).

19. Nephi does not indicate whether this was Lehi's first vision. It seems probable that it was, although a similar vision in Isaiah 6 is thought by some to have come in the midst of Isaiah's work as a prophet, rather than as his first revelatory experience.

20. *Teachings of the Prophet Joseph Smith,* sel. Joseph Fielding Smith (Salt Lake City: Deseret Book, 1976), 325. See also Doctrine and Covenants 29:12, which prophesies that Christ will come "in a pillar of fire" with his Twelve Apostles "to judge the whole house of Israel." Similarly, here the function of the pillar of fire seems to be associated with God's judgment upon Jerusalem. See note 22 below.

21. See Genesis 3:24; 19:24; Exodus 14:24; Numbers 21:27–30; Deuteronomy 9:3; Malachi 4:1. Compare especially Psalm 104:4 with the description of the messengers of Yamm in the Ugaritic Text, André Herdner, ed., *Corpus des tablettes en cunéiformes alphabétiques*

(Paris: Imprimerie Nationale, 1963), 2.I.32–33 (hereafter *CTA*). "A fire, two fires, they appear // He sees a brandished sword!" Cyrus Gordon, *Ugaritic Literature: A Comprehensive Translation of the Poetic and Prose Texts* (Rome: Pontifical Biblical Institute, 1949), 14. Discussed in E. Theodore Mullen Jr., *The Divine Council in Canaanite and Early Hebrew Literature* (Chico, Calif.: Scholars, 1980), 199. It has been concluded that, among the Israelites and the peoples of the ancient Near East, fire was "intimately associated with those divine beings who attend the great gods, and the fire appears to be a sort of weapon." Patrick D. Miller Jr., "Fire in the Mythology of Canaan and Israel," *Catholic Biblical Quarterly* 27/3 (1965): 259.

22. It is possible that the pillar contained things having to do with the destruction of Jerusalem. Amos had prophesied that the fire of God would destroy the walls and palaces of Tyre (Amos 1:4, 10). Perhaps in Lehi's vision the rock upon which the pillar dwelt was symbolic of hard-hearted Jerusalem, or of its walls, or of Jerusalem as the mountain of the Lord. Possibly a flaming sword was involved. The sword of God's justice, which hangs over people threatening their destruction (1 Nephi 15:30; Alma 60:29; Helaman 13:5; 3 Nephi 20:20; Mormon 8:41), may be related to God's destroying fire, since the Hebrew words *lahat* and *lahab* each mean both "flame" and "sword blade" and since God's messengers are not only "accompanied by the imagery of fire" but also frequently come bearing swords. Mullen, *Divine Council,* 199; see Genesis 3:24; Numbers 22:31; Joshua 5:13. If a flaming sword was involved, Lehi's vision may have been similar to one given to King David, when he "saw the angel of the Lord stand between the earth and the heaven, having a drawn sword in his hand stretched out over Jerusalem" (1 Chronicles 21:16). See also Isaiah 29, which prophesied that God would wage a holy war against Jerusalem to visit that city with "the flame [*lahab*] of devouring fire" (Isaiah 29:6). Heavenly armies and council visions generally were connected with this fire motif. Patrick D. Miller Jr., "The Divine Council and the Prophetic Call to War," *Vetus Testamentum* 18/1 (1968): 100–107.

23. Ostler, "Throne-Theophany," 70–83, 90, has demonstrated that Lehi's throne theophany, in addition to being similar to other prophetic

accounts from Lehi's day, also resembles several visions in the later Pseudepigrapha; but one need not go beyond sources from Lehi's day in order to find historical analogues for each aspect of Lehi's vision. For example, Ostler, "Throne-Theophany," 73, 75, looks to the Pseudepigrapha for an instance of a prophet acting as an intercessor on behalf of his people, whereas Jeremiah 14:11; 18:20; and other texts place this prophetic function in preexilic times. He also places more emphasis on the throne and less on the council than appears appropriate. For a discussion of another form of prophetic call that was current in Lehi's day, in which the prophet meets God, is commissioned, objects, is reassured, and is given a sign, see Stephen D. Ricks, "The Narrative Call Pattern in the Prophetic Commission of Enoch (Moses 6)," *BYU Studies* 26/4 (1986): 97–105; and Stephen D. Ricks, "Heavenly Visions and Prophetic Calls in Isaiah 6 (2 Nephi 16), the Book of Mormon, and the Revelation of John," in *Isaiah in the Book of Mormon,* ed. Donald W. Parry and John W. Welch (Provo, Utah: FARMS, 1998), 171–90.

24.   See, for example, Mullen, *Divine Council;* Claus Westermann, *Basic Forms of Prophetic Speech* (Philadelphia: Westminster, 1967), 98–128; Widengren, *Ascension of the Apostle;* Frank M. Cross Jr., "The Council of Yahweh in Second Isaiah," *Journal of Near Eastern Studies* 12/4 (1953): 274–77; Kingsbury, "Prophets and the Council of Yahweh," 279–86; Miller, "Divine Council," 100–107; John S. Holladay Jr., "Assyrian Statecraft and the Prophets of Israel," *Harvard Theological Review* 63 (1970): 29–51; N. L. A. Tidwell, "Wāʾōmar (Zech 3:5) and the Genre of Zechariah's Fourth Vision," *Journal of Biblical Literature* 94/3 (1975): 343–55; Joseph Fielding McConkie, "Premortal Existence, Foreordinations, and Heavenly Councils," in *Apocryphal Writings and the Latter-day Saints,* ed. C. Wilfred Griggs (Provo, Utah: BYU Religious Studies Center, 1986), 173–98. Similar conceptions of the assembly of the gods convened in heaven are found among the Canaanites, the Babylonians, the Greeks, and others in the ancient Near East.

25.   Mullen, *Divine Council,* 181–85; see, for example, Deuteronomy 33:2–3; Psalm 89:6–9.

26.   Mullen, *Divine Council,* 209; see also 145–46, 200.

27. Ibid., 209. Those verdicts were issued by God pursuant to eternal principles, divine laws, and immutable regulations. In the Sumerian Hymns, one frequently encounters terms involving the word *ME*, whose precise meaning cannot be determined but which embraces "world order," "divine command or edict," "divine norms," "secrets, mysteries," "fate or destiny," and "divine powers." Karl Oberhuber, *Der numinose Begriff ME im Sumerischen* (Innsbruck: Leopold-Franzens-Universität, 1963), 3. Rudolf Otto, *Das Heilige* (Munich: Biederstein, 1947), describes the *numina*, or eternal things, which existed before the gods and the world came into being, and Oberhuber, *Der numinose Begriff ME*, 5–8, points out the possible relation between the meaning of *ME* and the *numina*. The *ME*s may be related historically to the principles, decrees, edicts, fates, and powers of the divine council in the Semitic sources. See also Gertrud Farber Flügge, *Der Mythos "Inanna und Enki" unter besonderer Berücksichtigung der Liste der m e* (Rome: Biblical Institute, 1973); Thorkild Jacobsen, *Toward the Image of Tammuz and Other Essays on Mesopotamian History and Culture* (Cambridge: Harvard University Press, 1970), 359–60 n. 20; Yvonne Rosengarten and André Baer, *Sumer et le sacré: Le jeu des "prescriptions" ("m e"), des dieux et des destins* (Paris: Boccard, 1977). I am grateful to Paul Hoskisson for bringing these Mesopotamian materials to my attention. Compare Kingsbury, "Prophets and the Council of Yahweh," 284–85, briefly comparing Israelite prophecies with the Babylonian year-rite determination of destinies; Widengren, *Ascension of the Apostle*, 91. Compare also Alma 42, similarly affirming that God is subject to eternal law.

28. Holladay, "Assyrian Statecraft," 42–46.

29. Mullen, *Divine Council,* 218 n. 180, summarizing Tidwell, "Wāʾōmar." See 1 Kings 22:19–22; Isaiah 6:1–10; 40:1–8; Job 1:6–12; 2:1–6; and Zechariah 1:8–13; 3:1–7; 6:1–8, as discussed by Mullen. He continues: "the council descriptions contained in Psalms 29, 82, 89:6–9, and Deut 32:8–9 cannot be fitted into this outline" (218 n. 180).

30. Mullen, *Divine Council,* 209–10. Cf. Mosiah 3:23, where the angel of God certifies that he has "spoken *the words* which the Lord God hath commanded me." See also Mosiah 11:20; 12:1.

31. "It would seem that the question of the messenger's authority could be answered simply: it is that of the one who sends him." James F. Ross, "The Prophet as Yahweh's Messenger," in *Israel's Prophetic Heritage: Essays in Honor of James Muilenburg,* ed. Bernhard W. Anderson and Walter Harrelson (New York: Harper, 1962), 101. Joseph Smith explained how this authority was conferred: "All the prophets had the Melchizedek Priesthood and were ordained by God himself." *Teachings of the Prophet Joseph Smith,* 181.

32. Also in Hebrew as the ʿedat, or *dor.* See Mullen, *Divine Council,* 118–19; for further sources, especially in relation to the divine council as a background for Psalm 82:6 and John 10:34, see Daniel C. Peterson, "'Ye Are Gods': Psalm 82 and John 10 as Witnesses to the Divine Nature of Humankind," in *The Disciple as Scholar: Essays on Scripture and the Ancient World in Honor of Richard Lloyd Anderson,* ed. Stephen D. Ricks, Donald W. Parry, and Andrew H. Hedges (Provo, Utah: FARMS, 2000), 506–8.

33. Bright's translation, in *Jeremiah,* 148.

34. Mullen, *Divine Council,* 221.

35. This compares with Isaiah's vision of God seated in the presence of the seraphim (literally, "fiery things"), who praised his holiness and glory (Isaiah 6:1–3). See also Ezekiel 1:4–28; *1 Enoch* 14:22. Michael Carter has suggested to me that such singing and circumambulation "surrounding" God may have cosmogonic and cultic significance.

36. The overall character of Ezekiel's vision is "the proclamation of an act of judgement." Walther Zimmerli, *Ezekiel* (Philadelphia: Fortress, 1979), 1:247; thus these six come forth to execute judgment.

37. Since he wrote at a time when the council members typically remained anonymous in deference to the Supreme Deity (see Mullen, *Divine Council,* 178), it is unlikely that Lehi would have thought in terms of the intricate angelology that developed under Babylonian influence during the sixth and fifth centuries, and thus Reynolds and Sjodahl's reference, *Commentary on the Book of Mormon,* 8–9, 11–12,

to the angelic names and personalities found in Daniel, *1 Enoch,* and other Old Testament Pseudepigrapha is probably out of place.

38. Nephi later calls the Twelve "the apostles of the Lamb" (1 Nephi 11:34). Both the Hebrew word *shaliah,* meaning "sent one" or "agent," and the Greek word *apostolos,* "one sent forth," also mean "messenger," and thus Nephi's word is not inapposite to messengers of the heavenly council; see Widengren, *Ascension of the Apostle,* 31–36, 47. See further Joseph Fielding McConkie, "The Doctrine of a Covenant People," in *The Book of Mormon: Third Nephi 9–30, This Is My Gospel,* ed. Monte S. Nyman and Charles D. Tate Jr. (Provo, Utah: BYU Religious Studies Center, 1993), 165–68.

39. Thus it is appropriate that the word *one* was capitalized in the 1981 LDS edition of the Book of Mormon.

40. On God's position in the heavens or on his mountain, see Exodus 19–20; 1 Nephi 11:1; Moses 1; Richard J. Clifford, *The Cosmic Mountain in Canaan and the Old Testament* (Cambridge: Harvard University Press, 1972). On God coming down, compare Ugaritic Text *CTA* 14.II.57–58, which Mullen, *Divine Council,* 179, reconstructs to describe how the council of the gods there, led by ʾEl and Baʿal, "descended" to the earthly meeting place.

41. Marion G. Romney affirmed that this being was Christ the Lord, in Conference Report, October 1970, 28.

42. "This contained the decision of the court. It was the judgment of that great court." Reynolds and Sjodahl, *Commentary on the Book of Mormon,* 9.

43. On the connection between the curse and the announcement of judgment, see Westermann, *Basic Forms of Prophetic Speech,* 190–98.

44. Another appearance of the heavenly book is discussed in Doctrine and Covenants 77:14; see also Widengren, *Ascension of the Apostle,* 25, who connects this book with the book of law that (like the Urim and Thummim) was worn on the king's breast at his coronation (2 Kings 11:12) and was related to the book of life associated with the New Year (cf. Mosiah 5:11; 6:1–2). Widengren, *Ascension of the Apostle,* 10, 38; cf. 1 Nephi 1:4, discussed above. The heavenly book appears often in Mesopotamian, Jewish, Samaritan, Gnostic, and other sources.

45.   The scroll that Ezekiel sees, reads, and eats (Ezekiel 2:9–3:2; cf. Revelation 10:9) is a subsequent development of this motif. Going beyond the prophets like Lehi and Habakkuk a generation before him, Ezekiel not only reads but eats the words he is commanded to deliver. Like Lehi's book, however, Ezekiel's roll spelled out "lamentations, and mourning, and woe" (Ezekiel 2:10).

46.   Mullen, *Divine Council,* 216; see also Westermann, *Basic Forms of Prophetic Speech,* 104.

47.   Compare, for example, the tricolon in Ugaritic Text *CTA* 3.V.38–39, "Your decree, O ʾĒl, is wise, // Your wisdom is eternal, // A life of fortune, your decree," discussed in Mullen, *Divine Council,* 145 (cf. Psalm 29:1–2). David Noel Freedman, *Pottery, Poetry and Prophecy: Studies in Early Hebrew Poetry* (Winona Lake, Ind.: Eisenbrauns, 1980), argues convincingly that poetry was a concomitant of ancient Israelite prophecy.

48.   See Kirsten Nielsen, *Yahweh as Prosecutor and Judge: An Investigation of the Prophetic Lawsuit (Rib-Pattern)* (Sheffield: University of Sheffield, 1978); Antoon Schoors, *I Am God Your Saviour: A Form-Critical Study of the Main Genres in Is. XL–LV* (Leiden: Brill, 1973), 189–245. For an analysis of several such cases in the Book of Mormon, see John W. Welch, "Benjamin's Speech as a Prophetic Lawsuit," in *King Benjamin's Speech: "That Ye May Learn Wisdom,"* ed. John W. Welch and Stephen D. Ricks (Provo, Utah: FARMS, 1998), 225–32.

49.   See Westermann, *Basic Forms of Prophetic Speech,* 169–204. We have too little of Lehi's public statement, however, to know whether his words were couched in terms of a prophetic lawsuit, a prophetic judgment speech, or some other form of prophetic rhetoric.

50.   Compare "At times God does reveal His secrets especially to the humble." "Sir 3,19. . . . It is to the humble that He reveals His secrets (*mystēria-sôdāw*)." Raymond E. Brown, "The Pre-Christian Semitic Concept of 'Mystery,'" *Catholic Biblical Quarterly* 20/4 (1958): 424 and n. 32.

51.   This is not to limit the meaning of the phrase *the mysteries of God* in other contexts. But at the time Nephi inquired of the Lord in 1 Nephi 2:16, it seems that what he was seeking to know was the truth of the things that Lehi had learned in his vision in 1 Nephi 1:6–14.

52. Ross, "Prophet as Yahweh's Messenger," 103. Discussed further in John A. Tvedtnes, "Hebraisms in the Book of Mormon: A Preliminary Survey," *BYU Studies* 11/1 (1970): 59, showing Book of Mormon usages consistent with the semantic range of meaning of the Hebrew *sôd*.

53. R. Brown, "Pre-Christian Semitic Concept of 'Mystery,'" 421; see also 417–21.

54. Ibid., 421.

55. Ibid.

56. Hugh B. Brown, *Eternal Quest* (Salt Lake City: Bookcraft, 1956), 130–31.

57. Both the Book of Mormon (Jacob 4:4; 7:11) and Jewish rabbinic tradition, in Babylonian Talmud *Berakoth* 34b, affirm that all the prophets know of Christ. The Talmud states: "R. Hayya b. Abba . . . said in the name of R. Johanan: All the prophets prophesied only for the days of the Messiah, but as for the world to come, '*Eye hath not seen, oh God, beside Thee.*'"

58. Compare also the similarly defining attributes of a prophet given in Wurzburger, "Prophets and Prophecy," 1151–52, and Truman G. Madsen, *Joseph Smith among the Prophets* (Salt Lake City: Deseret Book, 1965). Wurzburger, "Prophets and Prophecy," 1160–61, also offers a helpful summary of the attributes of classical Israelite prophets as distinguished from prophets in other periods of Israelite history.

59. See generally H. Wheeler Robinson, *Inspiration and Revelation in the Old Testament* (Oxford: Clarendon, 1946).

Chapter 16

THE TEMPLE, THE MONARCHY, AND WISDOM: LEHI'S WORLD AND THE SCHOLARSHIP OF MARGARET BARKER

Kevin Christensen

Starting with *The Older Testament* in 1987, Margaret Barker proposes a new reconstruction of religious life and practice in Jerusalem before the exile.[1] Barker is a revisionist biblical scholar from England. As a revisionist, her views stand apart from the mainstream, though her books have been garnering more and more attention. She claims that a "fundamental misreading of the Old Testament" has been "forced upon us by those who transmitted the text,"[2] meaning those who initiated Josiah's reform and their exilic and postexilic heirs, the group that even conventional scholarship identifies as the Deuteronomists—a school of authors or redactors of the biblical books from Deuteronomy through 2 Kings.[3] Thus, according to Barker, the Deuteronomists have superimposed upon the biblical history—in particular, Deuteronomy through 2 Kings—their own particular theological emphasis both in their selection of material to be preserved and in the theological emphasis and interpretation of the history they tell. Barker directs our attention to "the conflicts of the sixth century B.C. when the traditions of the monarchy were divided as an inheritance amongst several heirs."[4] What makes her work of particular interest to Latter-day Saints is the picture she constructs of First Temple theology and practice based on "the accidents of archaeological discovery and the evidence of pre-Christian texts preserved and transmitted only by Christian hands."[5] That is, based on a wide reading of newly discovered texts and a rereading of familiar texts, she constructs a picture of the religion of preexilic Jerusalem that is strikingly different from the conventional view. Lehi and Nephi offer us another look at the same time and place. How do the pictures compare?

Her model centers on the temple, the monarchy, and the wisdom tradition, all of which were intertwined in the pre-exilic era but were transformed by reforms initiated by Josiah (2 Kings 22–23), and changes continued during the exile by the Deuteronomic school in response to the destruction of the temple and monarchy in 587 B.C.[6] In comparison, the Book of Mormon begins in "the commencement of the first year of the reign of Zedekiah, king of Judah," Nephi's father Lehi "having dwelt at Jerusalem in all his days," when "there came many prophets, prophesying unto the people that they must repent, or the great city Jerusalem must be destroyed" (1 Nephi 1:4). The young Lehi was a contemporary of Josiah, in whose reign the book of the law was rediscovered during a renovation of the temple dated at 621 B.C. (see 2 Kings 22 and 2 Chronicles 34). The clear Deuteronomic influence in the Book of Mormon plausibly follows from Lehi's experience of Josiah's ten-year reforms and whatever version of their texts Nephi obtained from the plates of Laban.[7] No matter which proposed date we take for Lehi's departure from Jerusalem, most of Lehi's mature life in that city would have been after Josiah's death and, hence, during the period when his reform unraveled.

The death of Josiah destabilized everything; the power of Egypt did the rest. The king was quickly replaced. The landed nobility was rendered powerless by high taxes. The administration was changed, even if this happened slowly, as we see from the very different groups of people mentioned in the brief accounts of the book of Jeremiah for the period of Jehoiakim and Zedekiah. Even among the priests things changed. The groups that had collaborated in a happy period were soon back at their old rivalries. The single movement was dead; the many parties at court returned.[8]

The Book of Mormon stands in clear contrast with the efforts of these reformers. After reaching the New World, Nephi soon sets about constructing a temple, accepts de facto kingship, consecrates high priests, and demonstrates in his writings elaborate ties to known and surmised wisdom traditions, all stemming from the pre-Josiah era.[9] In claiming roots in Jerusalem at that specific time, Nephi and Lehi give us a look at the other side of the "formidable barrier"[10] that the exile represents. Barker makes her new reconstruction in light of her wide-ranging review of primary sources, including new information from "the accidents of archaeological discovery and the evidence of pre-Christian texts preserved and transmitted *only by Christian hands.*"[11] How does her view compare with what we see among Lehi and his descendants?

In this study, I show that Lehi's first visions provide a direct connection to Barker's reconstruction of the beliefs and practices of preexilic Israel. I explore in greater detail Barker's reconstruction of the First Temple, the monarchy, and the lost wisdom traditions. Under each of these three themes, I show parallels to the Book of Mormon and then give some concluding observations. Because the parallels occur in radically different settings, without collusion, and because both differ dramatically from the common views, each can provide checks and potential illumination for the other. In order to be significant, any parallels that we find should appear as part of a woven fabric rather than as isolated instances. Any differences should have valid explanations in terms of reasonable historical factors and the nature of available sources. If there is no truth to either account, we should expect the views to have little or nothing in common. If one is accurate and the other false, we should also expect their accounts to have little or nothing in common. If both are accurate, they ought to demonstrate elaborate convergence, which indeed they do.

Connections with Lehi's Visions

In approaching Lehi's accounts of his visions, we should be aware of contradictory tensions within the Old Testament canon regarding the possibility of vision, as Barker explains:

> This can be demonstrated most easily by comparing Exodus 24.10 and Deuteronomy 4.12. The Exodus text describes the events on Mount Sinai; the elders saw the God of Israel on his throne, presumably in a vision. This is a vision of God exactly like that seen by Isaiah (Is. 6), Ezekiel (Ezek. 1) and John (Rev. 4).[12] The Deuteronomy text wants none of this, and emphasises that there was only a voice at Sinai. The presence of the LORD was not a vision to inspire them, but a voice giving commands that had to be obeyed.
>
> This tension between the word and vision was also a tension between new and old, between the law-based religion and the temple-based religion. It can be traced all through the Bible.[13]

Lehi immediately shows himself as a "visionary man," tied to the older traditions:

> And being thus overcome with the Spirit, he was carried away in a vision, even that he saw the heavens open,

and he thought he saw God sitting upon his throne, surrounded with numberless concourses of angels in the attitude of singing and praising their God. And it came to pass
that he saw One descending out of the midst of heaven, and
he beheld that his luster was above that of the sun at noon-
day. And he also saw twelve others following him, and their
brightness did exceed that of the stars in the firmament.
(1 Nephi 1:8–10)

Specific elements in Lehi's initial visions (1 Nephi 1:7–14) include
the anthropomorphic nature of God, the throne, the numberless
angelic hosts, the "One" like the sun at noonday, the twelve others
like "stars," the heavenly book (1 Nephi 1:11), and the judgment
(1 Nephi 1:13). These themes compare with Barker's explanation
that "the pattern of the 'lost' tradition therefore included, as well
as the angels and the great judgement, the stars and the foreign
kings, the kingship of Yahweh, the Holy Ones, exaltation, sonship and wisdom."[14] Lehi's initial report of his vision does not
mention use of the title Holy Ones, nor does it mention sonship.
But Lehi's later discourses to his people in 2 Nephi favor the important title Holy One (see 2 Nephi 1:10; 2:10; 3:2),[15] and we shall
see that Lehi's blessings to his family and the visions of the tree of
life demonstrate many ties to the early wisdom traditions.[16] The
important theme of sonship appears later in temple contexts.[17]

Consider particularly the treatment of the stars and of the
numberless hosts in the vision Lehi received at the time of his call
and factors that lead directly to the three pillars of First Temple
religion: temple, monarchy, and wisdom. According to Barker,

> Both constellations and "host" [of heaven, associated with
> the title Lord of Hosts] had been venerated in Israel, and the
> personified stars rejoiced at the creation (Job 38.7). The stars
> in Gen. 1 are defined as no more than lights to rule over the
> day and night and to determine the seasons, thus reflecting
> the post-exilic community's attitude to them. The stars were

associated with royal figures (Isa. 14.12; Num. 25.17) and, most significant of all, were thought to be *bound* by Yahweh in order to serve him (Job 38.31). Hence the characteristic stance of the later apocalypses, which distinguished them from their Hellenistic counterparts; the stars in no way compelled man to act. The wisdom tradition did concern itself with stars (Wis. 7.17ff), and the Jews were known as astronomers.[18]

Great angelic figures had/were stars: e.g. Num. 24.17, the messianic ruler rises as a star, Isa. 14.12 the king of Babylon is the Day Star, Matt. 2.2 the new star means a new king of the Jews.[19]

In addition to the star passages she cites here, elsewhere in *The Older Testament* Barker explores a number of biblical passages that include these themes; however, the Hebrew has sometimes been corrupted to the point that it no longer reads clearly. She notes enough passages on this theme that have the same kind of textual problems that the situation suggests deliberate hands at work:

A high proportion of the opaque texts of the Old Testament seem to be dealing with the same subject matter, namely angels, stars, and the elements which surface in later apocalyptic, and we have grounds for taking a fresh look at the Old Testament and those who transmitted it.[20]

Remember that Nephi predicts that the Bible texts will suffer in transmission (1 Nephi 13:26)[21] but that other texts will come forth and restore the plain and precious things that had been lost (1 Nephi 13:40). That loss is especially clear regarding Nephi's experience reliving Lehi's vision of the tree of life, which has been recognized as "apocalyptic" in character,[22] Nephi himself making the connection to the future apocalyptic revelation of John explicit (1 Nephi 14:27). Barker, coming from the other direction, connects the book of Revelation back to a largely lost tradition that is well represented in the writings of Lehi's contemporary, Ezekiel:

> The Book of Revelation has many similarities to the prophecies of Ezekiel, not because there was a conscious imitation of the earlier prophet, but because both books were the product of temple priests (Ezek. 1.3) and stood in the same tradition. There is the heavenly throne (4.1–8, cf. Ezek. 1.4–28 [cf. 1 Nephi 1:8; Jacob 4:14; Moroni 9:26]); the sealing of the faithful with the sign of the Lord (7.3, cf. Ezek. 9.4 [cf. Mosiah 5:15]);[23] the enthroned Lamb as the Shepherd (7.17, cf. Ezek. 34.23–24 [cf. 1 Nephi 13:41; Alma 5]); the coals thrown onto the wicked city (8.5, cf. Ezek. 10.2 [cf. 1 Nephi 14:15, 17; 3 Nephi 8:8, 24; 9:3, 8, 9, 11]); eating the scroll (10.10, cf. Ezek. 3.1–3 [cf. 1 Nephi 1:11–12; 8:11–12]); measuring the temple (11.1 and 21.15, cf. Ezek. 40.3 [cf. 2 Nephi 5:16]); the seven angels of wrath (16.1–21, cf. Ezek. 9.1–11 [cf. 3 Nephi 9–10]);[24] the harlot city (18.9, cf. Ezek. 26.17–18 [cf. 1 Nephi 14:17]); the riches of the wicked city (18.12–13, cf. Ezek. 27.1–36 [cf. 1 Nephi 13:5–8]); the fate of Gog (19.17–21 and 20.8, cf. Ezek. 39.1–20 [cf. 1 Nephi 11:34–36]); the vision of Jerusalem (21.9–27, cf. Ezek. 40.1–43.5 [cf. 1 Nephi 13:37; 3 Nephi 21:23]); the river flowing from the temple and the tree of life (22.1–2, cf. Ezek. 47.1–12 [cf. 1 Nephi 8, 11]).[25]

At every point in which Barker shows the relationship between Ezekiel and Revelation, I have noted a reference to the same themes in the Book of Mormon, mostly in 1 Nephi. The most conspicuous theme in Lehi's vision in 1 Nephi 8—the tree of life—appears not as an isolated parallel but as one element amid a constellation of related themes. The same explanation for the relationship that Barker gives holds true—these writers all stand in the same temple tradition.

> It cannot be coincidence that amongst the few scraps of
> information we can glean [from the prophets and Psalms]
> about the first Temple, we discover trees, cherubim, the
> throne of God, a mountain cult, life-giving waters, a serpent,
> and a blurring of the distinction between earth and heaven
> in the sacred space of the sanctuary. The picture we draw
> from the Deuteronomic account alone is very different: there
> is no emphasis upon the supernatural or Eden motifs. The
> ark is a mere box, there is no mention of the divine throne,
> nor of the living waters, the mountain setting nor the role of
> the cherubim. There is no tree of life, no Menorah. In other
> words, it is possible to fit Ezekiel's Eden into the Temple we
> can construct from non-Deuteronomic sources, and it is
> also clear that the myth in which Ezekiel sets his Eden was
> the myth of the old cult. The ancient Temple was Eden, the
> mountain of the gods, in which there was the divine throne,
> and in which judgement took place.[26]

The Book of Mormon contains the tree of life and waters
of life (1 Nephi 8:10; 11:25), the righteous as trees (Jacob 5), the
cherubim (Alma 42:3), the throne (1 Nephi 1:8), the high mountain of God (1 Nephi 11:1; 17:7; 2 Nephi 4:25), and the judgment (1 Nephi 11:34–36; Jacob 5:77). In the accounts of Lehi's
and Nephi's angelic escort (1 Nephi 8:7; 11:11), and later in the
experiences of the people with the Lord at the temple (3 Nephi
11–29), the distinction between heaven and earth disappears almost entirely at several points.[27] Barker looks at existing biblical
texts, especially in Psalms and the Prophets, and their relation
to postexilic noncanonical materials, which, she suggests, is best
explained in terms of survivals from the royal cult.

> But there are other sources [besides Samuel and Kings] which
> give a significantly different view of Solomon's temple and its
> cult, and it is to these we must turn if we are to call up the
> ancient kings. The prophets and psalms are full of colourful
> imagery which may once have been more than mere imagery.

Many later texts are thought to be bizarre growths upon the purity of the old religion when in fact they are memories of the older ways as they really had been.[28]

The process rather has been one of following the Enochic stream to its source [the first Temple], and seeing what other waters have flowed from it.[29]

Observing that this recurrence of First Temple themes extended into the Christian era, Barker remarks:

What gripped the minds and hearts of all sides in these disputes was not the actual temple in Jerusalem, but the ideal, the memory of a temple which was central to the heritage of Israel. It is this ideal, this vision at the heart of the ancient cult which has been lost. How such a thing could have happened is, in itself, an important question. The shadows of the temple fall across the writings of the prophets and the psalms, and from these we have to guess the beliefs which inspired the rituals of the heavenly world which it represented. The writings of the visionaries and the later mystics are also set in this world of the ancient temple. To reconstruct this world we must cast our net wider than just those writings which describe the temple; we must look also at those which are set within it, those in which the golden cherubim on the walls of Solomon's temple become the living creatures of the heavenly sanctuary and the olivewood cherubim overlaid with gold become the chariot throne of God.[30]

Temple

The Book of Mormon does not include passages like those in Leviticus that prescribe sacrificial rituals, like those in Exodus or the *Temple Scroll* that describe the dimensions of the tabernacle or the temple, nor like those in *1 Enoch* with a vision set in the holy of holies. But the text does include extensive temple imagery in the visions and discourses of

Nephi and Lehi and enlightening temple discourses at various temples—including those by Jacob at Nephi's temple, by Limhi and Abinadi at Noah's temple, by Benjamin at Zarahemla, and by the risen Jesus at Bountiful. In many ways these temple discourses reflect the appropriate rituals and, indeed, are best appreciated in the context of the temple.[31] In describing the first temple built by the Nephites, Nephi explains that he "did construct it after the manner of the temple of Solomon save it were not built of so many precious things" and that the workmanship was "exceedingly fine" (2 Nephi 5:16).[32]

For Barker, no feature of preexilic Israelite religion was more prominent than the temple. She explains that "the earthly sanctuary, whether it was the tent or the temple, was thought to reflect a heavenly pattern."[33] Further, she observes,

> one of the keys to any understanding of the temple cult is the realization that the rituals and the personnel were also thought to be the visible manifestation of the heavenly reality. The priests were the angels, the high priest was the representative of the Lord.[34]

A number of Latter-day Saint authors have established that King Benjamin's discourse is a complex ritual text, that during the ritual Benjamin functions as the high priest, and that Abinadi's discourse in Noah's temple shows themes appropriate to Pentecost.[35] Indeed, in 3 Nephi 8–29, the line between ritual and history becomes blurred throughout as Jesus enacts the role of the temple high priest in a most dramatic fashion.

Levels of Sacredness

The most obvious aspect of the temple in Jerusalem involved the levels of sacredness, increasing from the inner court to the holy place and to the holy of holies. According to Mircea Eliade, the three parts of the temple at Jerusalem correspond to the three cosmic regions. The lower court represents the lower regions ("Sheol," the abode of the dead), the holy place represents the earth, and the holy of holies represents heaven. The temple is always the meeting point of heaven, earth, and the world of the dead.[36] Lehi's cosmology saw the world in these three realms (heaven, 1 Nephi 1:8; the earth, 1 Nephi 1:14; and the realm of the dead, 2 Nephi 1:14). King Benjamin, speaking from his temple, also sees the cosmos in terms of heaven, the earth, and the realm of the dead (Mosiah 2:25, 26, 41), with entrance into God's presence as the ultimate joyous state (Mosiah 2:41). Considering 3 Nephi as a whole, we can also find these three distinct levels of sacredness: (1) darkness/separation (3 Nephi 8–10), (2) preparation/initiation (3 Nephi 11:1–17:23; 18:1–37; 19:13; 20:1–28:12), (3) apotheosis/at-one-ment (3 Nephi 17:24; 18:36–39; 19:14, 25–31; 28:10–18).

Creation Themes

Barker explains that "since the temple was a statement about the natural order, it was closely associated with the myth of the creation."[37] All the major temple discourses in the Book of Mormon include significant references to the creation (see Jacob 9:6; Benjamin in Mosiah 2:21, 25; 3:11; 4:9; Abinadi in Mosiah 13:19; 16:3; Jesus in 3 Nephi 9:18; 26:3). Stephen D. Ricks observes that "in Israelite thought, 'the motifs of covenant-renewal, enthronement, and resurrection cannot be kept in isolation from each other.' And with this matrix in mind, it becomes more significant that Benjamin intertwines the themes of dust, kingship, covenant, enthronement, and resurrection throughout his speech."[38] The account of the destruction in 3 Nephi 8–10 alludes to the older myths of creation involving the defeat of hostile forces and uses the Lord's declaration that he is the "light of the world" (3 Nephi 9:18) to introduce a new creation.[39] Further, at one point he discourses on "all things, even from the beginning" (3 Nephi 26:3), which implies a creation narrative. In all these accounts, the Book of Mormon implies creation as an ongoing process, an approach that appears explicitly in the Moses and Abraham accounts in the Pearl of Great Price. According to Barker, the idea of creation containing conflict and opposition, as well as being a continuing process, is older than the Genesis account.[40]

Temple as Eden and Meeting Point of Heaven and Earth

Barker explains that the ancient temple in Jerusalem was furnished so as to represent the Garden of Eden:

> Descriptions of the *temple,* however, do suggest that it was Eden. Ezekiel described a temple built on a high mountain (Ezek. 40.2), whose courtyards were decorated with palm trees (Ezek. 40.31, 34). The interior was decorated with palm trees and cherubim (Ezek. 41.17ff.), and from the temple flowed a river which brought supernatural fertility (Ezek. 47.1–12). Ezekiel did not invent these Eden-like features; each is mentioned elsewhere in the Old Testament. The temple on a high mountain was the theme of Isa. 2.2–4 and Mic. 4.1–3; the righteous were described as the trees of the house of the Lord (Ps. 92.13), a metaphor which would have been pointless had there been no trees there; 1 Kings 6.29 described the palm trees, cherubim and flowers carved on the temple walls; and several prophets looked forward to the day when waters would flow from the temple (e.g. Zech. 14.8; Joel 3.18). Hezekiah had removed a bronze serpent from the temple (2 Kings 18.4),[41] and the seven-branched candlestick, as we shall see presently, was remembered as the tree of life. Ezekiel, it seems, had a vision of a garden sanctuary like those known elsewhere in the ancient Near East, but it was also an accurate description of the temple he had known in Jerusalem.[42]

We do not have formal descriptions of the Book of Mormon temple furnishings. However, references to the fall of Adam and to Eden are explicit in several temple discourses. And the key imagery of the tree of life and the fountain of living waters appears in the visions of Lehi and Nephi. Lehi's discourse to his son Jacob in 2 Nephi 2 includes not only a discussion of Eden and the creation, but also the fall of Adam. Lehi mentions Jacob's own vision, the fallen angels, the atonement of the Messiah, the Holy One, and the coming judgment. These all show affinities with Barker's reconstruction and are apt considering Jacob's later role as a temple priest. Jacob 5 quotes at length the allegory of the olive tree, in which both the righteous and the wicked are described as trees, and which includes "harvest as judgment" themes that are conspicuous in Barker's view. Jeremiah, Nephi$_1$, and Nephi$_2$ allude to the bronze serpent story about Moses (Jeremiah 8:17–19;[43] 2 Nephi 25:20; Helaman 8:14–15). The temporary tents or tabernacles in the Mosiah account of Benjamin's discourse (Mosiah 2:6), besides functioning as reminders of Israel's wandering in the desert, may also bring to mind the palms that decorated the First Temple and also suggest Eden. "The temple was Eden and its rituals will have interacted with this fundamental belief about the creation. The temple itself, like Eden, was between heaven and earth with access to both the divine and material worlds."[44] The 3 Nephi account of Jesus at the temple demonstrates, in a very literal fashion, the access to both the divine and material worlds.

Priests

The Nephites did not have any Aaronic or Levitical priests, but this was in keeping with their descent from Joseph (1 Nephi 5:16)[45] and was evident in their ties to the older temple traditions. According to Barker,

The anointed high priest of the first temple cult was remembered as having been different from the high priest of the second temple cult since the latter was described simply as the priest who "wears many garments," a reference to the eight garments worn by him on Yom Kippur: "And who is the anointed [high priest]? He that is anointed with the oil of unction, but not he that is dedicated with many garments." (m. *Horayoth* 3.4). It was also remembered that the roles of the anointed high priest and the high priest of many garments differed in some respects at Yom Kippur when the rituals of atonement were performed. The anointed high priest, they believed, would be restored to Israel at the end of time, in the last days.[46]

Further, Barker explains,

> Melchizedek was central to the old royal cult. We do not know what the name means, but it is quite clear that this priesthood operated within the mythology of the sons of Elyon, and the triumph of the royal son of God in Jerusalem. We should expect later references to Melchizedek to retain some memory of the cult of Elyon.... The role of the ancient kings was that of the Melchizedek figure in 11QMelch.[47]

The first explicit discussion of priesthood in the Book of Mormon comes from Jacob. He makes associations with the temple and reports the same obligations as does Ezekiel:

> Wherefore I, Jacob, gave unto them these words as I taught them in the temple, having first obtained mine errand from the Lord. For I, Jacob, and my brother Joseph had been consecrated priests and teachers of this people, by the hand of Nephi. And we did magnify our office unto the Lord, taking upon us the responsibility, answering the sins of the people upon our own heads if we did not teach them the word of God with all diligence; wherefore, by laboring with our might their blood might not come upon our garments;

otherwise their blood would come upon our garments, and
we would not be found spotless at the last day. (Jacob 1:17–19;
cf. Ezekiel 3:17–21; 18:21–30; 33:2–20)

Later, Alma explains that the Book of Mormon prophets and
priests operate under the Melchizedek priesthood (Alma 13:1–14).

Fallen Angel Myths

Lehi, Benjamin, and Alma—all high priests—demonstrate
their awareness of an Eden story, but one with several significant
differences from the traditional Genesis account (see 2 Nephi 2;
Mosiah 2–5; Alma 9–13).[48] All emphasize the fallen angels, their
importance, and the atonement "prepared from the foundation
of the world" (Mosiah 4:6, 7). Barker emphasizes that the crucial importance of the fallen angel stories is prominent in the
Enoch literature, virtually absent in the Deuteronomic portions
of the Old Testament, but assumed everywhere in Isaiah and the
New Testament.[49] For example, Barker shows that certain of the
fallen angels were associated with particular maladies:

> There are significant word patterns in [Isaiah] 35.5–6: the
> blind, the deaf, the lame and the dumb are healed in the
> renewal of the creation, but the names of these four are also
> those of four types of angel. . . . How these supernatural be-
> ings were connected to these disabilities is not clear, but it
> is surely no coincidence that Jesus used the curing of these
> four types as his sign. John the Baptist asked if Jesus was
> the one expected (Luke 7.20ff), and the reply was an amal-
> gam of these verses and Isa. 61.1. . . . In the Gospels, the
> defeat of what these creatures represented is seen as a sign
> of the kingdom of God.[50]

The Messiah was expected to demonstrate his power over
these fallen angels. These associations appear consistently in
Book of Mormon prophecies of the coming of the Messiah and

in the depictions of their fulfillment in 3 Nephi. For example, Nephi's vision associates healings and the casting out of devils.

> And he spake unto me again, saying: Look! And I looked, and I beheld the Lamb of God going forth among the children of men. And I beheld multitudes of people who were sick, and who were afflicted with all manner of diseases, and with devils and unclean spirits; and the angel spake and showed all these things unto me. And they were healed by the power of the Lamb of God; and the devils and the unclean spirits were cast out. (1 Nephi 11:31)

The presence of the fallen angel accounts in the Book of Mormon (and in other Latter-day Saint accounts) becomes very important when we look at Barker's reconstruction. She explains:

> There was a whole spectrum of ideas as to the nature of sin and evil. . . . At one end, sin was disobedience, an individual's transgression of one of the laws, and at the other sin was also disobedience, but the disobedience of the angels who misused their divine knowledge and brought calamity to the earth as a result. Somewhere between these two extremes, we can place the two spirits at work to influence man's actions, a position which seems to be a compromise between the "external influences" view of 1 Enoch, and the "intentional disobedience" view of later Judaism. Looking at these two extremes, we should expect to find the latter within a system which gave prominence to the role of the heavenly powers. If these two systems both developed from Israel's more ancient religion, it should be possible to find in the Old Testament evidence for the roots of both, or else to find evidence in the "intertestamental" period for the origin of one or the other. If the post-exilic period was the time when the era of the Law was becoming established, and the era of the angel mythology being eclipsed, it is there that we should expect to find

evidence of both, and perhaps some relationship between them, at the time when both systems were current.[51]

The emphasis in the Book of Mormon on the fallen angel stories as part of the explanation of evil is central, and Lehi's fusion of them with the Genesis Eden story in 2 Nephi 2 fits nicely into Barker's suggestion of a time when both systems were current, though it does so just before the exile. She sees the Adam story as exilic.

> And I, Lehi, according to the things which I have read, must needs suppose that an angel of God, according to that which is written, had fallen from heaven; wherefore, he became a devil, having sought that which was evil before God. And because he had fallen from heaven, and had become miserable forever, he sought also the misery of all mankind. Wherefore, he said unto Eve, yea, even that old serpent, who is the devil, who is the father of all lies, wherefore he said: Partake of the forbidden fruit, and ye shall not die, but ye shall be as God, knowing good and evil. (2 Nephi 2:17–18; cf. 2 Nephi 9; Alma 12:22–36)

In the Book of Mormon and other Latter-day Saint scriptures, human sin does not explain the origin of evil. However, the presence of evil beings provides a context in which humans can choose between good and evil and in which the fall of mankind is not a catastrophe, but our entrance into a place of probation and testing, where there is opposition in all things. Barker's explanation of the older view also resonates with Lehi's teachings: "There *was* a mythology in which heavenly beings were held responsible for the origin of evil. A movement which sought to remove these beings also lost the benefit of their mythology and its explanation of evil."[52]

Barker remarks, "It has been suggested that the fallen angel themes of 1 Enoch were in fact an attack upon the corrupt priesthood of the second temple period."[53] Similarly, the account of Amulon's wicked priests shows the use of allusions to the fallen angel myth to interpret that story.[54] The arch sin of the fallen angels in the Enoch accounts was pride, and in consequence of their fall, they spread a corrupt form of wisdom. In the Enoch accounts, the fallen angels intermarried with human women, and their offspring were destroyed in the time of Noah.[55] In the Book of Mormon, Amulon's priests are described from the beginning as proud (Mosiah 11:5–13); they also pervert sacred knowledge for gain (Mosiah 11:5–6; 12:28–29) and take wives they should not have (Mosiah 20:1–5). Amulon's priests teach the Lamanites to be cunning and wise "as to the wisdom of the world" (Mosiah 24:7; see 23:31–35; 24:1–7). Finally, their descendants from the union with the stolen wives become "hardened" and meet with destruction (Alma 25:4, 7–9).

With respect to the Genesis 2–3 account and Lehi's version of the Garden story, we should compare and contrast Barker's reading of the evidence from this period with that of Bruce Pritchett.[56] Where Barker says that "there is neither reference nor allusion to this passage in any other part of the Old Testament,"[57] Pritchett argues that "though there are numerous biblical passages that mention Adam, Eden, or various doctrinal points deriving from the Paradise narrative, four biblical passages refer to the fall account in ways that particularly illuminate Lehi's doctrine: Psalm 82:7, Hosea 6:7, Job 31:33, and Ezekiel 28:11–19."[58] Once past that initial disagreement about preexilic references to Adam, the views that Barker and Pritchett present converge beautifully. For example, Barker convincingly argues that the connections between Ezekiel 28 and Isaiah 14 are closer than those between Ezekiel and Genesis 2–3:

> We can deduce more about the older Temple from other texts. Jer. 17.12, Isa. 6. and Ps. 11.4 all link the sanctuary to

the glorious throne in heaven. Isa. 6 and Dan. 9 link the sanctuary to the host of heaven, and Daniel, even at that late date, links it specifically to the heavenly power struggle, i.e. to the myth of Isa. 14 and Ezek. 28. In the Temple there was also a bronze serpent (2 Kings 18.4).[59]

Again, the themes that Barker ties to the First Temple appear conspicuously in the Book of Mormon, with the same associations. Barker sees the fallen angel stories as primary and the Genesis story as a later derivative in which "we can detect the earlier myth, but the whole structure has been brilliantly realigned so as to make human disobedience and the hankering after divine wisdom replace divine disobedience and the corruption of wisdom."[60] Pritchett, though he did not refer to Barker's then recently published studies, agrees that the existing Genesis account is a late redaction and variant of earlier themes and, in discussing Lehi's version, refers to many of the same passages that she does. Consequently, Pritchett encounters the essential themes of the fallen angel stories:

> Whether those receiving judgment were gods or humans themselves, the important point is that Psalm 82 shows a belief that God's sentence involved losing immortality, which Psalm 82:7 illustrates with two parallel images: Adam's loss of immortality and the *sārîm*'s loss of immortality. Since this punishment comes as a result of sin (failure to judge righteously or defend the helpless, Psalm 82:2–4), it can be reasonably inferred that at the time of this psalm's writing, the ancient Israelites believed that Adam's loss of immortality, as the *sārîm*'s loss of immortality, resulted from some sin and, as suggested by the fact that many translators see here a reference to mankind in general, that mankind universally inherited death from Adam.
>
> The psalm indicates the disobedience of those "said [to be] gods" (Psalm 82:6) by using, in parallelism, two mythological

types of rebellion that run throughout the Old Testament—not only the fall of humans (Genesis 3), but the fall of certain divine beings as well (Genesis 6:1–4; cf. Isaiah 14:12–15). Interestingly enough, Lehi also mentions both these elements in his discourse on the fall (2 Nephi 2:17–27).[61]

For Barker, one of the most important aspects of Enoch accounts of the fallen angel myth is that they provide keys to understand the atonement.

> *1 Enoch* 10 describes the judgement; the four archangels are sent out to bind Azazel and imprison him and then to destroy the fallen angels and their children. They then heal the earth, purify it from all defilement, oppression and sin and inaugurate an era of righteousness and fertility: "And he will proclaim life to the earth that he is giving life to her" (*1 En.* 10:7). *Here, at last, is a text which gives the meaning of atonement; it was the process by which the effects of sin were removed so that the earth could be healed and restored.* It was a rite of re-creation when the Lord came forth from his holy place and established his kingdom.[62]

3 Nephi 9–28 follows the same pattern: a renewal of the creation, the appearance of the Lord, and the establishment of his kingdom.[63] Further, the name of Azazel in the Enoch account has connections to the scapegoat ritual of the Day of Atonement.

> There is a desert demon in Leviticus 16.6–10 with a similar name—Azazel. The ancient ritual of the scapegoat required that a goat be sent into the wilderness to Azazel. The goat carried all the transgressions and sins of Israel into the wilderness, to Azazel (Lev. 16.20–22). The Old Testament tells us nothing more about Azazel, or why he was in the wilderness. He must have been important, as he is the only one apart from God to whom a sacrifice is to be offered, and it was thought appropriate to send sins to him, out in the desert. In Enoch, we find that Asael, the fallen leader of the angels, is imprisoned in the wilderness. Enoch tells us how he got there, and who he really was.[64]

Terrence L. Szink and John W. Welch have explained how King Benjamin actually enacts the Day of Atonement ritual during his discourse, including the scapegoat ritual, "And again, doth a man take an ass which belongeth to his neighbor, and keep him? I say unto you, Nay; he will not even suffer that he shall feed among his flocks, but will drive him away, and cast him out. I say unto you, that even so shall it be among you if ye know not the name by which ye are called" (Mosiah 5:14). Szink and Welch observe that "had Benjamin said that the sinner would be driven out like a goat instead of an ass, these connections with the Day of Atonement would have been more direct. But in fact, the kind of animal used in such settings was not critical among Israel's neighbors in the ancient Near East."[65]

Further Temple Imagery

Certain preexilic furnishings of the temple are neither described nor alluded to in the Book of Mormon, such as the cherubim design for the divine throne and the ark of the covenant in the holy of holies. Whether they were not part of the tradition that Lehi knew because of Josiah's reform or because of reticence on the part of the Book of Mormon authors and editors, we cannot say. In some cases, we may be blinded by our own preconceptions in considering the terminology. For instance, since in the First Temple "Ark and Throne are the same symbol,"[66] Lehi's vision of the throne may imply more than we realize. However, enough First Temple imagery does appear to establish a consistent position.

Bread of the Presence. For example, Barker explains, "The bread of the Presence was twelve loaves set out each sabbath in two rows of six on the golden table. . . . The bread was treated as a grain offering, sprinkled with pure frankincense and later eaten by the priests 'in a holy place' (Lev. 24.5–9)."[67]

If we read the 3 Nephi account from the Israelite expectation, rather than from a Christian view of the sacrament, we can perceive the bread of the Presence there. "And when the disciples had come with bread and wine, he took of the bread and brake and blessed it; and he gave unto the disciples and commanded that they should eat" (3 Nephi 18:3). Note that there are twelve disciples, that the bread is given in remembrance of one who was actually present, and that the word bread occurs exactly twelve times in 3 Nephi.

Tree of Life. Barker observes that the menorah lamp was imagined as a tree of life and that the tree represented the Lord and had associations with the King.

> On the south side of the *hekal* was the great lamp, made of solid gold, which had to be fuelled with pure olive oil (Exod. 27.20). It was made like a seven-branched tree, decorated with almonds and flowers (Exod. 25.31–7). At the top of each branch was a lamp; it was these seven lamps which Zechariah saw in his vision and recognized as the eyes of Yahweh (Zech. 4.10). The sevenfold lamp will prove to be important evidence for understanding the temple cult; the Lord was not singular but plural. In the older cult, the manifold Lord was present in the temple, whereas in the "reformed" worship the Lord was One (Deut. 6.4), and only his Name was in the temple (Deut. 12.11). . . . [T]he lamp represented the Lord and . . . the lamp represented the tree of life.[68]

Several studies have shown how central the tree of life is in the Book of Mormon.[69] Lehi's vision leads to Nephi's vision of the tree of life (1 Nephi 11:2–3).[70] And the interpretation of the vision is consistent with the time and place of its origin.[71] "As early as Zechariah and as late as Josephus, the lamp was linked to the angelic tradition extant now in the extra-canonical apocalypses. Both the lamp and the apocalypses were forbidden."[72]

Lehi's and Nephi's visions have been linked with the apocalyptic genre. Barker has insisted that the apocalypses point back to the preexilic tradition.[73] She also discusses how "Wisdom, which was the feminine aspect of the Lord, was also described as a tree of life (Prov. 3.18)."[74] Daniel C. Peterson's essay on "Nephi and His Asherah" shows how these same associations underlie Nephi's vision of the tree of life.[75]

Fountain of Living Waters. Barker writes that "in the traditions of the ancient Near East there is 'a garden of paradise' where a gardener supervises the Tree of Life growing at the Water of Life. . . . The Testament of Judah describes the Messiah as, 'This Branch of God Most High, And this fountain giving life unto all' (Test. Jud. 24.4). Note that the royal figure is both Tree and Fountain."[76] Accordingly, in the Book of Mormon, in answer to a question about the meaning of the tree of life (1 Nephi 11:9–11), Nephi is granted a vision of "the Lamb of God, yea, even the Son of the Eternal Father" (1 Nephi 11:21; compare Proverbs 3:13–18). After viewing this, Nephi realizes that (among other things) the tree represents "the love of God" (1 Nephi 11:22) along with the "fountain of living waters, or . . . the tree of life; which waters are a representation of the love of God" (1 Nephi 11:25).

The Veil. The veil setting off the holy of holies was an essential part of the temple; what the veil itself symbolizes is the important thing.

> Inseparable from the veil were the vestments of the high priest, elaborately woven and embroidered in almost the same way as the veil. Veil and vestments were complementary imagery; the veil symbolized all that stood between human perception and the vision of God, and the vestments symbolized the clothing of the divine in that same material world which also concealed it.[77]

While the Book of Mormon never describes the temple veil, two stories use veil imagery to describe the reality that the temple veil symbolizes. These are the stories of Lamoni and the brother of Jared. Lamoni is a Lamanite king whose near-death experience is described this way:

> Now, this was what Ammon desired, for he knew that king Lamoni was under the power of God; he knew that the dark veil of unbelief was being cast away from his mind, and the light which did light up his mind, which was the light of the glory of God, which was a marvelous light of his goodness—yea, this light had infused such joy into his soul, the cloud of darkness having been dispelled, and that the light of everlasting life was lit up in his soul, yea, he knew that this had overcome his natural frame, and he was carried away in God. (Alma 19:6)

It is significant that, in this account, Lamoni's experience[78] beyond the veil points directly to the reality that the high priest's actions behind the temple veil (the atoning Christ) were intended to symbolize.

> And it came to pass that he arose, according to the words of Ammon; and as he arose, he stretched forth his hand unto the woman, and said: Blessed be the name of God, and blessed art thou. For as sure as thou livest, behold, I have seen my Redeemer; and he shall come forth, and be born of a woman, and he shall redeem all mankind who believe on his name. Now, when he had said these words, his heart was swollen within him, and he sunk again with joy; and the queen also sunk down, being overpowered by the Spirit. (Alma 19:12–13)

Redeemer as it is used here points to the atonement. Nephi's earlier vision, which provides the traditional context for this experience, associates the Redeemer, the tree of life, and the woman with both the tree of life and wisdom. These are all temple themes.

M. Catherine Thomas has discussed the experiences of the brother of Jared at the veil, noting the temple implications.[79] While the language of the 3 Nephi account of the risen Lord does not refer to the "veil" directly, it does demonstrate the appropriate reality to which the veil symbolism points. For example, Barker explains:

> The veil was the boundary between earth and heaven. Josephus and Philo agree that the four different colours from which it was woven represented the four elements from which the world was created: earth, air, fire and water. The scarlet thread represented fire, the blue was the air, the purple was the sea, i.e. water, and the white linen represented the earth in which the flax had grown (*War* 5.212–13). In other words, *the veil represented matter*. The high priest wore a vestment woven from the same four colours and this is why the *Book of Wisdom* says that Aaron's robe represented the whole world (*Wisd.* 18.24; also Philo, *Laws* 1.84; *Flight* 110).[80]

Richard Dilworth Rust observes the presence in the 3 Nephi accounts of significant language pointing to the four elements of physical matter and hence, also, pointing to the materials of the veil and of the high priest's robes.

> For example, faith in Jesus Christ the Creator, the Son of God, is shown in the contrast of light and dark and in reference to the four major elements of earth, air, fire, and water. These are brought together in the section of the Book of Mormon that prefigures the Second Coming of Christ. The chaos of things splitting apart and intense darkness— the opposite of creation—is associated with the death of the creator. Cities are sunk in the sea, Zarahemla is burned, and Moronihah is covered with earth. . . .

Those elements that had been destructive before now bring great uplifting and salvation at the coming of "the Son of God, the Father of heaven and of earth, the Creator of all things from the beginning" (Helaman 14:12). Water is represented by baptism by immersion, air and fire by the Holy Ghost, and earth by people being instructed to build on the solidity of Christ's rock.[81]

Many of the simple details in 3 Nephi—such as the man in a white robe, the various titles of Christ (which refer to the anointed high priest), and his being confirmed to be the son of God—though understated and subtle in the text, all resonate vividly in the temple context that Barker describes:

> Thus the veil and the priestly vestments provided the first Christians with ready imagery to convey what they meant by the incarnation. The linen robes worn by the high priest in the sanctuary were also the dress of the angels, those who had left the life of this world and lived in the immediate presence of God. . . .
>
> . . . The veil represented the boundary between the visible world and the invisible, between time and eternity. Actions performed within the veil were not of this world but were part of the heavenly liturgy. Those who passed through the veil were the mediators, divine and human, who functioned in both worlds bringing the prayers and penitence of the people to God and the blessing and presence of God to his people.[82]

During his visit, Jesus is transfigured and angels appear, demonstrating fully that God indeed was present (e.g., 3 Nephi 17:23–4). Barker describes the relevant rituals and symbolic meanings centering on the robes of the high priest:

> He took off this robe when he entered the holy of holies because the robe was the visible form of one who entered the holy of holies. In the Epistle to the Hebrews, which explores

the theme of Jesus as the high priest, there is the otherwise enigmatic line: his flesh was the veil of the temple (Heb. 10.20). In other words, the veil was matter which made visible whatever passed through it from the world beyond the veil. Those who shed the earthly garments, on the other side of the veil, were robed in garments of glory. In other words, they became divine.[83]

One final aspect of the temple veil also deserves mention. Barker explains that the veil was embroidered to depict past, present, and future.[84] During his ministry to the Nephites, Jesus, ultimately the Great High Priest, discourses on the same themes, expounding "all things, even from the beginning until the time that he should come in his glory. . . . And even unto the great and last day" (3 Nephi 26:3–4).

Sacrifice and Atonement

The Book of Mormon prophets keep the law of Moses according to the version they brought with them on the brass plates. "And they also took of the firstlings of their flocks, that they might offer sacrifice and burnt offerings according to the law of Moses" (Mosiah 2:3). A key distinction is that most discussions of the way that the Nephites kept the law emphasize what the law points to, rather than treating it as an end in itself. For example, Lehi explains: "Behold, he offereth himself a sacrifice for sin, to answer the ends of the law, unto all those who have a broken heart and a contrite spirit; and unto none else can the ends of the law be answered" (2 Nephi 2:7).

The constant focus on the atoning sacrifice helps establish the correct context of the Book of Mormon. Hugh Nibley writes:

> The word *atonement* appears only once in the New Testament, but 127 times in the Old Testament. The reason for this is apparent when we note that of the 127 times, all but 5 occur in the books of Exodus, Leviticus, and Numbers, where

they explicitly describe the original rites of the tabernacle or temple on the Day of Atonement; moreover the sole appearance of the word in the New Testament is in the epistle to the Hebrews, explaining how those very rites are to be interpreted since the coming of Christ. . . . [A]tonement (including related terms, atone, atoned, atoneth, atoning) appear[s] . . . 39 times . . . in the Book of Mormon. This puts the Book of Mormon in the milieu of the old Hebrew rites before the destruction of Solomon's Temple.[85]

When the theme of atonement appears in the Book of Mormon, it typically does so in temple contexts.[86] Barker writes: "It is widely agreed that the three autumn festivals of the post-exilic period, (New Year, Day of Atonement and Tabernacles) were derived from an earlier royal festival held every autumn to celebrate the renewal of the year and the enthronement of the king. Nothing can be proved, but Isaiah 40–55 is thought to be based on the liturgies of this festival."[87]

I have already mentioned Szink and Welch's discussion of Benjamin's discourse as pointing to this royal festival. Barker explains how

> Isaiah 53 could have been inspired by the Day of Atonement ritual. A few points must suffice.
>
> 1. "He shall startle many nations" (Isa. 52.15); *yazzeh*, the apparently untranslatable verb, means "sprinkle" in the atonement ritual (Lev. 16.19). The Servant figure does not "startle" many peoples; the original Hebrew says he "sprinkles."
>
> 2. The Servant "carries" the people's sicknesses or weaknesses (Isa. 53.4).
>
> 3. The Servant has been wounded for their transgressions. Wounded, *ḥll*, is a word which carries both the meanings required by Mary Douglas's theory of atonement, viz. to pierce or to defile.
>
> 4. "Upon him was the chastisement that made us

whole" (Isa. 53.5b) can also be translated "The covenant bond of our peace was his responsibility." "With his stripes, *ḥbrt,* we are healed" would then become "By his joining us together we are healed," forming a parallel to *mwsr,* covenant bond. The primary meaning of *ḥbr* is to unite, join together.

5.   The Servant pours out his soul/life as a sin offering, *ʾšm* (Isa. 53.19). The *ʾšm* is, according to Milgrom, the sacrifice which redresses the *mʿl,* which is either sacrilege against holy things or violation of the covenant. The soul/life was in the blood of the sacrifice, hence it was poured out.

All this suggests that the Servant figure was modelled on the one who performed the atonement rites in the first temple.[88]

In light of all the foregoing, it becomes even more significant that Abinadi quotes Isaiah 53 during his Pentecost discourse in the temple city of Nephi near Noah's temple (Mosiah 12–17).[89]

Monarchy

Of the Old World kingship, Barker observes:

> Again, we cannot be certain that the later emphases were direct and legitimate developments of an earlier tradition, but a pattern does emerge from the later contexts of the Enochic material which makes it likely that the tradition originated in the royal cult. The royal cult is something of which the Old Testament tells us very little; we know that there were kings for some four centuries, but the literature which describes that period is curiously silent about several things.[90]

While Nephi showed reluctance to accept formal kingship, his people looked on him as their king and protector, and he formally consecrated his successor as king.[91] Although much of the period of Nephite kings between Nephi and the transition to judges at the end of Mosiah passes in relative silence, we do get fuller accounts of Mosiah, Benjamin, Noah, and Limhi as kings.[92]

Fertility, Prosperity, Justice, and Judgment

Barker explores biblical and Enoch passages that describe the underlying role of the king:

> The creation imagery in Ps. 89 describes the power of the king; the royal mythology set the king figure at the centre of the natural order. Ps. 72 associates justice and fertility with the role of the king; Isa. 11 describes a ruler who brings knowledge and justice, and the harmony of all creation. In Ps. 89 the royal figure has to control the evil forces in the political, the natural and the social order (89.23, 25, 33ff).[93]

All these themes appear conspicuously in Benjamin's discourse in Mosiah. For example, notice that the formula "prosper in the land" in the Book of Mormon encompasses fertility.[94] Benjamin encourages a just and equitable social order and reminds those assembled of their dependence on God for deliverance from their political enemies, to sustain the created order, and for their very lives from moment to moment. In the 3 Nephi accounts of the Lord's ministry, the creation imagery permeates the accounts of the destruction, and the voice of the Lord, identifying himself as the light of the world, begins the new creation for the people (3 Nephi 9:18).

King and Covenant

One of the more interesting aspects of Nephite kingship relates to one of Barker's observations about the Israelite king: "The anointed king was also the bond of the eternal covenant which held all things in their appointed place. I strongly suspect that this eternal covenant was renewed at the great autumn festival for the new year."[95]

Barker explains the significance of the eternal covenant:

In the Hebrew Scriptures there are several covenants: with Noah, with Abraham, with Moses and with David, and Jeremiah looked forward to a new covenant. The Eternal Covenant was the oldest and most fundamental of all and was envisaged as the system of bonds which restrained cosmic forces and maintained an ordered creation where people could live in peace and safety. Nowhere in the Hebrew Scriptures is the establishing of this covenant described, but there are many places where it is assumed.[96]

Given that the covenant is assumed but not described in the Bible, Barker does explain where we should look to find it. "This covenant was part of the judgement-enthronement-renewal cycle associated with the autumn festivals of the Day of Atonement and Tabernacles. . . . Indirect allusions, however, do suggest that the Eternal Covenant was particularly connected with the priests and their role in the temple."[97]

Mosiah's discourse occurred during the autumn festival, and Szink and Welch have illuminated the Day of Atonement aspects of the discourse, just as Tvedtnes has drawn parallels to the Feast of Tabernacles.[98] So in Mosiah, we clearly see the gathering at the temple (Mosiah 2:1) and the creation of the booths for the Feast of Tabernacles:

> And they pitched their tents round about the temple, every man having his tent with the door thereof towards the temple, that thereby they might remain in their tents and hear the words which king Benjamin should speak unto them. (Mosiah 2:6)

Szink and Welch write that

King Benjamin's speech was delivered in the fall, at the time of year when all ancient Israelites, including peoples of the Book of Mormon, would have been celebrating their great autumn festival season, which included many ancient elements that later became enduring parts of the Jewish holidays of Rosh ha-Shanah, Yom Kippur, and Sukkot. Most of the known or surmised ancient elements of these festivals are represented in the text of the Book of Mormon. . . . Benjamin's speech contains numerous elements pertinent to the New Year holy day, the Day of Atonement observances, the Feast of Tabernacles, and the sabbatical or jubilee year.[99]

Barker has explained that while the eternal covenant is never described in the Old Testament, there are several places where it is implied. And in at least two places it seems present in the Book of Mormon. I have previously argued that the overall pattern of 3 Nephi 8–29 suggests the cosmic covenant.[100] More recently, I realized the significance of passages like this in Benjamin's discourse.

> And behold also, if I, whom ye call your king, who has spent his days in your service, and yet has been in the service of God, do merit any thanks from you, O how you ought to thank your heavenly King! I say unto you, my brethren, that if you should render all the thanks and praise which your whole soul has power to possess, to that God who has created you, and has kept and preserved you, and has caused that ye should rejoice, and has granted that ye should live in peace one with another—I say unto you that if ye should serve him who has created you from the beginning, and is preserving you from day to day, by lending you breath, that ye may live and move and do according to your own will, and even supporting you from one moment to another—I say, if ye should serve him with all your whole souls yet ye would be unprofitable servants. (Mosiah 2:19–21)

This image of God as continually sustaining the creation matches the view that Barker develops. And, as we continue to see, the themes appear in the Book of Mormon woven into the same set of associations. One of the places where the concept of the cosmic covenant appears in the Old Testament is in Isaiah 24, in showing the consequences of the violated covenant.

> Behold, the Lord maketh the earth empty, and maketh it waste, and turneth it upside down, and scattereth abroad the inhabitants thereof. . . . The earth also is defiled under the inhabitants thereof; because they have transgressed the laws, changed the ordinance, broken the everlasting covenant. Therefore hath the curse devoured the earth, and they that dwell therein are desolate: therefore the inhabitants of the earth are burned, and few men left. (Isaiah 24:1, 4–5)

These specific images also call to mind the destruction in 3 Nephi 8–10 and the Lord's discussion of the healing covenant that he offers in remedy. Barker explains, "The life of the king, symbolized by the life-blood of the substituted animal, was the sign of the divine presence on earth and this life was used to join together again the spiritual and the material worlds by means of the sprinkling of blood on each side of the temple curtain."[101]

In Benjamin's discourse, the atoning blood serves this function, though the temple curtain is not explicitly described.

> And they had viewed themselves in their own carnal state, even less than the dust of the earth. And they all cried aloud with one voice, saying: O have mercy, and apply the atoning blood of Christ that we may receive forgiveness of our sins, and our hearts may be purified; for we believe in Jesus Christ, the Son of God, who created heaven and earth, and all things; who shall come down among the children of men. (Mosiah 4:2)

In 3 Nephi 11–29, the divine presence on earth becomes literal, and the transfiguration of the resurrected Jesus and the appearance of angels demonstrate the joining of the spiritual and material worlds.

The King and the Name

Szink and Welch note that, with respect to the Name,

> so holy was the Day of Atonement that on this day the ineffable name of God, YHWH, could be pronounced. . . . Later Jewish tradition seems to have the priest utter this name ten times during the Yom Kippur liturgy, and to a similar degree, Benjamin employs the expanded names *Lord God* and *Lord Omnipotent* seven and three times, respectively. Seven of these utterances are in the reported words of the angel to Benjamin. . . . The other three utterances come in the words of Benjamin . . . at important ceremonial breaking points in the speech.[102]

Welch observes that only Benjamin uses the title Lord Omnipotent, and the context suggests in this discourse that these expanded names function as substitutes for the tetragrammaton, or divine name. In calling for his people to assemble, Benjamin offers one of the key reasons for doing so: "And moreover, I shall give this people a name, that thereby they may be distinguished above all the people which the Lord God hath brought out of the land of Jerusalem; and this I do because they have been a diligent people in keeping the commandments of the Lord" (Mosiah 1:11).

Margaret Barker's work again proves to be very useful with respect to the Name:

> Throughout Ps. 118:10–13 Yahweh and the Name of Yahweh seem to be synonymous, and even though other instances are less clear, lines such as these from the psalms still suggest that Name meant something other than what we might mean by it. . . . The Name was the presence and power of Yahweh. *It could be manifested in human form.*[103]

Compare Mosiah 3:5, describing how "the Lord Omnipotent who reigneth, who was, and is from all eternity to all eternity, shall come down from heaven among the children of men, and *shall dwell in a tabernacle of clay.*" Barker explains a "view of the creation where *the Name creates and sustains everything.* The oldest evidence for the Name is exactly this."[104] In Mosiah 2:20, Benjamin explains to those assembled that "God . . . *has created you,* and has kept and preserved you . . . from day to day, by lending you breath, that ye may live and move and do according to your own will, and *even supporting you from one moment to another.*"

On the ritual reaction to hearing the Name, Barker comments:

> According to the Mishnah the Name was only pronounced by the high priest on the Day of Atonement (*Yoma* 3.8): "And when the priests and the people which stood in the Temple Court heard the expressed name, they used to kneel and bow themselves and *fall down on their faces* and say, 'Blessed be the name of the glory of his kingdom forever and ever!'" (*Yoma* 6.2). . . .
>
> . . . The name was Yahweh the creator and renewer made present.[105]

Compare Mosiah 4:1: "And now, it came to pass that when king Benjamin had made an end of speaking the words which had been delivered unto him by the angel of the Lord, that he cast his eyes round about on the multitude, and behold *they had fallen to the earth,* for the fear of the Lord had come upon them."

Again, Barker had explained that the preexilic high priest was called "the anointed," which is what "Christ" and "messiah" both mean. In the discourse, Benjamin describes himself as having been "consecrated" to be king, and during the discourse he acts in the Day of Atonement role as the high priest. And as Szink and Welch note, besides the references to the "name" and the matching seven references to "Christ" (which we ought to read as "anointed high priest who literally wears the Name to show whom he represents—Yahweh") in the words of the angel, "Benjamin uses the root *atone* seven times in this seven-part speech."[106] This all corresponds to Barker's comments on the link between the Name, the creation, the anointed high priest (the Christ), and the actual atonement.

> The name was the nature, the power, the presence of Yahweh. The name was the fundamental bond of creation. . . . But the Name was also present in persons who mediated between the Most High and humankind, and those thus vested had the power of the Name. The high priest's duty of *making atonement and offering life/blood to restore, renew and heal the people and their land* is the clearest expression of the Name at work, *renewing the covenant of peace* which had been entrusted to the high priesthood (Num. 25.12–15). The Epistle to the Hebrews explains how Jesus, as high priest on earth and in heaven, renewed and restored the covenant with his own life/blood (Heb. 9.12).[107]

In Mosiah 4:2, Benjamin's people cry aloud, "saying: O have mercy, and *apply the atoning blood of Christ* that we may receive forgiveness of our sins, and *our hearts may be purified;* for we believe in Jesus Christ, the Son of God, who created heaven and earth, and all things; who shall come down among the children of men."

Begotten Kings/Begotten Israel

Barker observes, "It is significant that the texts which deal with the kingship of Yahweh are also those which deal with the heavenly hosts and the angel mythology."[108] For example, one of the key texts on this topic is Deuteronomy 32:8–9, which has a most significant variation in both the Dead Sea Scrolls and the Septuagint, as compared to the Masoretic Text that underlies the King James Bible. Here is the RSV, which adopts the Dead Scrolls reading: "When the Most High [that is, El Elyon] gave to the nations their inheritance, when he separated the sons of men, he fixed the bounds of the peoples according to the number of the sons of God [the KJV has children of Israel]. For the Lord's portion [that is, Yahweh's portion] is his people, Jacob his allotted heritage."

With this and related passages in mind, Barker looks at Ezekiel:

> If Ezekiel believed that the nations round about Israel had angel princes who walked on the holy mountain, must he not also have believed that Israel had an angel prince?[109] Since Ezekiel was a priest in the temple (Ezek. 1.3), this is an important indication of what the ancient cult believed about the king; he would have been both an earthly king and a heavenly patron, an angelic being. This may be what was meant by the coronation oracle which survives in Ps. 2:
>
> "I have set my king on Zion, my holy hill."
> I will tell you of a decree of the Lord:
> He said to me, "You are my son,
>   Today I have begotten you."[110]

During the monarchy, the most attention was given to the covenant with the king. Barker explores instances where "the king had been the earthly manifestation of the Lord in his temple; he had been addressed as the Lord's son (Pss. 2.7; 72.1) and he had sat upon the Lord's throne as king."[111] While there may be questions about how literally to take this idea, Barker shows that the idealized memory of

> The human figure on the throne is fundamental to our understanding of what was meant by "Messiah." Further, the hostility to this throne tradition explains the hostility between the first Christians and the Judaism from which they eventually separated. From the time of the monarchy when contemporary cultures had described their kings as the image of God, Israel's anointed kings had also sat upon

the divine throne in the temple as the visible manifestation of the Lord, the patron angel of Israel.[112]

Our best understanding of how the Nephites viewed their king is shown during Benjamin's discourse.

> I have not commanded you to come up hither that ye should fear me, or that ye should think that I *of myself* am more than a mortal man. . . . And behold also, if I, whom ye call your king, who has spent his days in your service, and yet has been in the service of God, do merit any thanks from you, O how you ought to thank your heavenly king! (Mosiah 2:10, 19)

Nibley understood these declarations as expressing Benjamin's awareness that "throughout the pagan world the main purpose of the Great Assembly . . . is to hail the king as a god on earth," showing his awareness of "the *conventional* claims of kingship."[113] Were they conventional among the earlier Nephite kings? We can't say for sure. The ambiguity introduced by Benjamin's "of myself" should not mask the fundamental harmony. Barker's examples of the king as divine look back to the early times of the Davidic monarchy. She ties this tradition to his transfiguration during a heavenly ascent, and we should note that Benjamin's report of his encounter with the angel could be understood this way. Lehi leaves Jerusalem during difficult times for the monarchy, and Benjamin's predecessors have a mixed record. The important thing for Barker's reconstruction is that the memory of the divinized king points to the Christian expectation. And her view of Christian secret tradition corresponds well with 3 Nephi when the kingdom of God does indeed appear on earth as it is in heaven.[114]

Later developments in Israel emphasized a democratization of the covenant, in which all Israel makes the covenant. We also see this extension of the covenant to Israel during Benjamin's discourse.[115] "And now, because of the covenant which ye have made ye shall be called the children of Christ, his sons, and his daughters; for behold, this day he hath spiritually begotten you; for ye say that your hearts are changed through faith on his name; therefore, ye are born of him and have become his sons and his daughters" (Mosiah 5:7).

Ricks has observed "a similar idea in the enthronement of Joash. 'And Jehoiada made a covenant between the Lord and the king and the people, that they should be the Lord's people' (2 Kings 11:17). What was once reserved for kings at coronation has now been extended in Nephite culture to the people generally."[116]

Notice that Psalm 82, which is important evidence of the idea of the divine potential of humankind and contains ties to the fallen angel myth,[117] also contains the royal themes that appear in Benjamin's discourse. But in this case, the psalm describes the inverse situation of a broken covenant. Even so, it shows the obligations of the covenant—both social and economic—for individuals and a relationship to cosmic order, as well as the consequences of falling, given the coming judgment:

> God standeth in the congregation of the mighty; he judgeth among the gods [cf. Mosiah 2:28]. How long will ye judge unjustly, and accept the persons of the wicked? Selah. Defend the poor and fatherless: do justice to the afflicted and needy. Deliver the poor and needy: rid them out of the hand of the wicked [cf. Mosiah 4:20–27]. They know not, neither will they understand; they walk on in darkness [cf. Mosiah 2:32–33]: all the foundations of the earth are out of course [cf. Mosiah 2:32–33; 3:21]. I have said, Ye are gods; and all of you are children of the most High [cf. Mosiah 5:7]. But ye shall die like men, and fall like one of the princes [cf. Mosiah 2:36–41]. Arise, O God, judge the earth: for thou shalt inherit all nations [cf. Mosiah 3:10, 13, 20]. (Psalm 82:1–8)

Again, we constantly see that the comparisons we make are not of random parallels, but of interconnected themes, woven together.

Menorah and King

For example, though we have discussed the tree of life in relation to the temple, consider how the tree relates to the king. Barker explains:

> The ancient cult was the original setting of the Menorah. It was a complex symbol of life, light and the presence of God, embodied in the person of the king whom it also represented. There were other agents of God on earth, just as there were other branches of the lamp; each had/was a star, each was a son of God, with access to the divine council and authority to speak in the name of Yahweh. . . . [I]mages of sonship, life, light, kingship, ascent, descent, divine judgement in the presence of Jesus and the prominence of the temple setting can all find a common point of origin in a tradition which remembered the older ways.[118]

These themes appear in Lehi's visions of the divine throne and of the tree of life in 1 Nephi 1 and 8 respectively, showing that Lehi takes us back to the older ways.

Wisdom

The theme of wisdom appears frequently in the Book of Mormon in examples of the distinct genre of wisdom literature, as discussed by Peterson and Nibley,[119] and in direct references to wisdom, as in Benjamin's discourse: "And behold, I tell you these things that ye may learn *wisdom;* that ye may learn that when ye are in the service of your fellow beings ye are only in the service of your God" (Mosiah 2:17). He also la-ments the thought of the Spirit of the Lord having "no place in you to guide you in *wisdom's* paths" (Mosiah 2:36).

Peterson provides a useful description of "wisdom" literature:

> Biblical scholars recognize a genre of writing, found both in the canonical scriptures (e.g., Job, Proverbs, Ecclesiastes, the Song of Solomon) and beyond the canon, that they term "wisdom literature." Among the characteristics of this type of writing, not surprisingly, is the frequent use of the term *wisdom*. But also common to such literature, and very striking in texts from a Hebrew cultural background, is the absence of typically Israelite or Jewish themes, such as the promises to the patriarchs, the story of Moses and the exodus, the covenant at Sinai, and the divine promise to David. There is, however, a strong emphasis on the teaching of parents, and especially on the instruction of the father.[120]

Peterson observes that "careful readers will note that all of these characteristics are present in the accounts of the vision of Lehi and Nephi as they are given in the Book of Mormon."[121] Indeed, Peterson's "Nephi and His Asherah" demonstrates many fascinating connections between the Book of Mormon and Proverbs. For example, he shows the equation of the tree of life and wisdom in Proverbs, the opposition to wisdom by the harlot (a conspicuous theme in 1 Nephi 13–14), and even the name Lemuel, given by Lehi to his second son, which appears in the Bible only in Proverbs.

Barker works to extend the standard definition, building a case that "wisdom was an older form of communication between God and his people. Wisdom was something which the Deuteronomists reformed. This possibility is crucial for my argument."[122] In surveying several other discussions of wisdom, she notes that "all attempts to reconstruct the earlier form of wisdom on the basis of the canonical texts run into great difficulties; massive inconsistencies are all too obvious, and we are obliged to assume that something is seriously amiss in the approach."[123] Further, "Reconstructions of the earliest wisdom use two sources: the basic stratum of Proverbs and the allusions in the prophets. The former has clearly been altered several times."[124] After considering three representative but mutually inconsistent attempts to define wisdom, Barker concludes:

> The weak link in scholarly reconstruction of Israel's ancient wisdom is inconsistency. We find wise men in court or school settings elsewhere in the ancient world, and assume these as the context for Israel's wisdom. But we do not also assume that the manner of operation of the other wise men might have been similar to that of Israel's. Having given the wise men their setting, we then credit them with only the edited texts as evidence for what they were actually about. Thus we fill the courts and schools of Israel with muddled platitudes, which is all that remains of Israel's wisdom, and have then to invent a secular rationalism to explain the prophet's wrath, and an incursion of foreign magicians to explain the rise of apocalyptic.[125]

Considering such unresolved problems in earlier attempts to describe preexilic wisdom, Barker comments: "In studying the pre-Christian Jewish concepts of wisdom, I have never encountered one based upon the evidence of the Enochic literature. This is surprising, since 1 Enoch is quoted in the New Testament, and was used by the Qumran community during the period of Jesus' ministry."[126]

Using Enoch as a key, she argues that "everything points to a development during the exile which radically altered wisdom, but which did not succeed in destroying it. The older tradition reappeared in later works. . . . Wisdom as we know it in the canonical texts was born in the community which Enoch, a later wise man, condemns as impure and apostate."[127] Ultimately she builds the case that "*the simplest, and most likely idea of wisdom to underlie the New Testament is that of the Enoch tradition.*"[128]

How do the reflections of wisdom in the Book of Mormon compare with her definitions and her charge that the Deuteronomists reformed the understanding of wisdom? Although the Book of Mormon shows influence from Josiah's reform, at least with respect to the renewed emphasis on Moses and Deuteronomic law,[129] Barker argues that the key changes to wisdom came in response to the destruction of the monarchy and the exile, after Lehi left. So how was wisdom understood before the exile? "Wisdom was the secrets of creation, learned in heaven and brought to earth, the recurring theme of the apocalypses. There must have been some way in which the king, and the wise men, 'went' to heaven like the prophets in order to learn these secrets by listening in the council of God."[130]

Again, in the Book of Mormon we find that the throne vision given to both Lehi and Nephi demonstrates from the first this same understanding of wisdom. Barker offers a closer look at key passages in Proverbs, the main repository of surviving wisdom in the Bible. Against the context of the later apocalyptic literature, she finds surviving traces of the older scheme and resonance with themes that we have already seen in relation to the temple and the king. For example:

> Proverbs 30 must refer to the world beyond the veil of the temple; it links sonship, ascent to heaven, knowledge of the Holy Ones and the works of Day One:
> Who has ascended to heaven and come down?
> Who has gathered the wind in his fists?
> Who has wrapped up the waters in a garment?
> Who has established all the ends of the earth?
> (Prov. 30.4).
> To which Deuteronomy replies: "(This commandment) is not in heaven, that you should say: Who will go up for

us to heaven, and bring it to us, that we may hear it and do
it?" (Deut. 30.11). Job's arguments were shown to be "words
without knowledge" (Job 38.2) because he had not witnessed the works of Day One.[131]

The account of Jesus in 3 Nephi links these same themes.
He is the "son of God" who has ascended and comes down
(3 Nephi 11:8–10). The descriptions of the destruction explicitly mention his power over the winds and the waters (3 Nephi
8:16 and 9:7). He says "I created the heavens and the earth, and
all things that in them are" (3 Nephi 9:15).

Nephi as an Archetypal Wise Man

The two most conspicuous examples of wise men in the
Bible, Joseph and Daniel, show common traits with Nephi. Referring to the book of Daniel, Barker notes:

> The text itself claims to be about a *wise man* who predicts
> the future, interprets dreams and functions at court. . . .
> Joseph, our only other canonical model [of a wise man], is
> very similar; he functions at court, interprets dreams and
> predicts the future. . . . Daniel is sufficiently Judaized to
> observe the food laws, but how are we to explain his deal-
> ings with heavenly beings, and his use of an inexplicable
> mythology? The elaborate structures of the book suggest
> that it was using a known framework, and not constructing
> imagery as it went along, but there is no hint of such im-
> agery in Proverbs, *except in passages where the text is now
> corrupt.* This suggests that the wisdom elements in the non-
> canonical apocalypses which have no obvious roots in the
> Old Testament may not be foreign accretions, but elements
> of an older wisdom which reformers have purged.[132]

While Nephi does not interact with Zedekiah's court in the
manner of Joseph or Daniel, he does accept kingship, functionally, if not literally, in the New World and anoints a king to suc-

ceed him (2 Nephi 5:18; Jacob 1:9).[133] Nephi also interprets dreams and predicts the future (1 Nephi 10–15). Like Daniel, he shows commitment to the law (1 Nephi 4:14–17; 2 Nephi 5:10), has dealings with angels (1 Nephi 3:29–30; 11:21, 30; 12:1; 2 Nephi 4:24), recognizes the need to seek the interpretation of symbols (1 Nephi 11:11), and speaks of the need to understand the cultural context behind prophetic writing (2 Nephi 25:1–5). Lehi discovers his descent from Joseph in the brass plates (1 Nephi 5:14–16; 2 Nephi 3:4), and the Book of Mormon shows access to Joseph traditions that do not survive in the present Bible (2 Nephi 3 and Alma 46:23–27).[134] Indeed, in Barker's survey the features that early biblical and Enochic writings associated with wisdom correspond neatly to Nephi's own resumé, including his knowledge of writing (1 Nephi 1:2), the wisdom genre in his writing,[135] his mining and metalworking (1 Nephi 17:9–10), his shipbuilding (1 Nephi 17:8–9; 18:1–8), his navigation (1 Nephi 18:12–13, 22–23), and the arts of war (2 Nephi 5:14, 34). He is likely the source of the calendrical calculations his descendants used to determine the holy days and the passage of years related to Lehi's six-hundred-year prophecy of the Messiah (1 Nephi 10:4). Barker further notes, "Wisdom included medicine, taught to Noah (Jub. 10.10) and to Tobit (Tob. 6.6) by angels and brought by the rebels in 1 Enoch 8, where they taught the cutting of roots. In the Old Testament the art of healing belongs to God (Exod. 15.26; Deut. 32.39; Job 5.18) and the gift of healing was given to prophets (1 Kings 17; Isa. 39). We know virtually nothing of the medicines."[136]

The Book of Mormon shows connection to both the spiritual power given to the prophets and the wisdom tradition of medicinal knowledge:

> And it came to pass that they went immediately, obeying the message which he had sent unto them; and they went in

unto the house unto Zeezrom; and they found him upon his bed, sick, being very low with a burning fever; and his mind also was exceedingly sore because of his iniquities; and when he saw them he stretched forth his hand, and besought them that they would heal him. (Alma 15:5)

And there were some who died with fevers, which at some seasons of the year were very frequent in the land—but not so much so with fevers, because of the excellent qualities of the many plants and roots which God had prepared to remove the cause of diseases, to which men were subject by the nature of the climate. (Alma 46:40)

Another aspect of the ancient wisdom tradition involved the arts of divination, of foretelling the future. Barker observes that even though "Deut. 18 prohibits the use of all divination in no uncertain way; . . . such practices are quite consistent with the ways of Daniel and Joseph."[137] For example, she explains: "We have to find a place within Israel's tradition for . . . Urim and Thummim (Num. 27.21; Deut. 33.8) and for the belief that the outcome of any lot was determined by the Lord (Prov. 16.33). Daniel and Joseph both give God the credit for their skills as diviners (Gen. 41.6; Dan. 2.27)."[138]

Looking to the Book of Mormon, we easily find expressions that are at home with these traditions. For instance, Nephi reports how "we cast lots—who of us should go in unto the house of Laban" (1 Nephi 3:11). This story and the description of the function of the Liahona, as strange as it seemed to Joseph Smith's contemporaries, fit nicely into the world of the ancient wise men.

And it came to pass that as my father arose in the morning, and went forth to the tent door, to his great astonishment he beheld upon the ground a round ball of curious workmanship; and it was of fine brass. And within the ball

> were two spindles; and the one pointed the way whither we should go into the wilderness. . . . And it came to pass that I, Nephi, beheld the pointers which were in the ball, that they did work according to the faith and diligence and heed which we did give unto them. And there was also written upon them a new writing, which was plain to be read, which did give us understanding concerning the ways of the Lord; and it was written and changed from time to time, according to the faith and diligence which we gave unto it. And thus we see that by small means the Lord can bring about great things. (1 Nephi 16:10, 28–29)

In *Since Cumorah,* Nibley compared the function of the Liahona to an ancient Semitic practice of divination using arrows.[139] We also have the account of the interpreters in the Book of Mormon, which Joseph Smith later associated with the Urim and Thummim.

> Now Ammon said unto him: I can assuredly tell thee, O king, of a man that can translate the records; for he has wherewith that he can look, and translate all records that are of ancient date; and it is a gift from God. And the things are called interpreters, and no man can look in them except he be commanded, lest he should look for that he ought not and he should perish. And whosoever is commanded to look in them, the same is called seer. . . . But a seer can know of things which are past, and also of things which are to come, and by them shall all things be revealed, or, rather, shall secret things be made manifest, and hidden things shall come to light, and things which are not known shall be made known by them, and also things shall be made known by them which otherwise could not be known. (Mosiah 8:13, 17)

Clearly, the Book of Mormon connects not just to the more traditional understandings of wisdom but also melds with Barker's reconstruction.

Wisdom, the Holy Ones, and Heavenly Ascent

Another significant set of wisdom associations comes with the theme of the Holy Ones in relation to Joseph and Daniel and patterns that appear in comparing them. Barker explains:

> Since the activities of Daniel's Holy Ones are exactly like those found in earlier Old Testament texts, we must not assume that the character they have in Daniel, or their other roles, is late or alien to Israel's traditions. The pattern does not change; they deal with politics, with heavenly decrees from Elyon, they communicate through visions and work through the wise men who advise the king.[140]

The Book of Mormon prophets who use the title Holy One of Israel (or the later shortened Holy One) are Nephi (1 Nephi 19:14–15; 22:5, 18–28, an Isaiah commentary; 2 Nephi 25:29; 27:30, 34; and 28:5, Isaiah paraphrase/commentary; 2 Nephi 30:2; 31:13), Lehi (2 Nephi 1:10; 2:10; 3:2), Jacob (2 Nephi 6:9–10, 15; 9:11–26, 39–41, 51), Amaleki (Omni 1:25–26), Alma$_2$ (Alma 5:52–53), Mormon (Helaman 12:2; Mormon 9:14), and Jesus (3 Nephi 22:5 = Isaiah 54:5). They all show connections to the same patterns from the early tradition. A key aspect of the early tradition is the possibility of seeing God: "The conflict between those who said it was possible to have a vision of God, and those who denied it, was to continue for centuries."[141]

The conflict appears early in the Book of Mormon.

> Now this he spake because of the stiffneckedness of Laman and Lemuel; for behold they did murmur in many things against their father, because he was a visionary man, and had led them out of the land of Jerusalem, to leave the land of their inheritance, and their gold, and their silver, and their precious things, to perish in the wilderness. And this they said he had done because of the foolish imaginations of his heart. . . . And they were like unto the Jews who were at Jerusalem, who sought

to take away the life of my father. (1 Nephi 2:11, 13; cf. Jacob 7:5–7; Alma 30:12–17; Helaman 16:16)

Laman and Lemuel demonstrate sympathy for the Jerusalem party, the same group of people who caused problems for Jeremiah and Ezekiel.[142]

Use and Abuse of Wisdom

While Barker shows a tradition that recognizes the importance of wisdom and vision, she also explains how it fell out of favor during Josiah's reforms. Additionally, some passages in Jeremiah record his conflicts with the wise men who allied themselves to the doomed monarchy:

> How do ye say, We are wise, and the law of the Lord is with us? Lo, certainly in vain made he it; the pen of the scribes is in vain. The wise men are ashamed, they are dismayed and taken: lo, they have rejected the word of the Lord; and what wisdom is in them? (Jeremiah 8:8–9)

> Then said they, Come, and let us devise devices against Jeremiah; for the law shall not perish from the priest, nor counsel from the wise, nor the word from the prophet. Come, and let us smite him with the tongue, and let us not give heed to any of his words. (Jeremiah 18:18)

It is easy to surmise the reaction of those who had taken the advice of the misbehaving wise men in this case and their disillusion while in exile in Babylon. Backlash would be inevitable, particularly by those allied with Josiah's reformers and already hostile to the old wisdom. Barker explains:

> It was what the wise men *did* with their wisdom which caused the conflict with the prophets. Wisdom was not in itself a bad thing, but if misused it was the source of much evil. "The fear of the Lord is the beginning of wisdom" occurs many times, and reminds us that there was some

conflict, now lost to us, which involved wisdom and the attitude to the Lord. One of the strands in the intertestamental literature reflects a similar position; wisdom was not inherently evil, but became so through misuse. The theme of pride and the misuse of wisdom is vitally important to the understanding of Isaiah, and is the basis for Ezek. 28, which describes the fate of the Prince of Tyre when he abused his wisdom.[143]

Jacob shows his awareness of the same potential for mischief:

O that cunning plan of the evil one! O the vainness, and the frailties, and the foolishness of men! When they are learned they think they are wise, and they hearken not unto the counsel of God, for they set it aside, supposing they know of themselves, wherefore, their wisdom is foolishness and it profiteth them not. And they shall perish. But to be learned is good if they hearken unto the counsels of God. But wo unto the rich, who are rich as to the things of the world. For because they are rich they despise the poor, and they persecute the meek, and their hearts are upon their treasures; wherefore, their treasure is their God. And behold, their treasure shall perish with them also. (2 Nephi 9:28–30)

Again, significantly, these Book of Mormon connections to wisdom themes do not occur at random but are all linked. Jacob's "wo unto the rich" passage resonates with conspicuous Enoch themes,[144] and Enoch in turn provides the Ariadne thread that led Barker back to the First Temple.

Temporal and Spiritual: On Earth as It Is in Heaven

Barker discusses the use of parables: "Teaching in parables was a characteristic of wise men, as we have often been told. But the wise men were also visionaries, and this aspect is less emphasized. The Book of Proverbs does not seem to be the work of a visionary, yet the two biblical wise men of whom we know anything, Daniel and Joseph, were both dreamers."[145] Lehi and Nephi fit the same mold, as we have seen.

Another aspect of the wisdom tradition has to do with an approach to teaching and expounding parables.

> Many of the parables, the sayings of the wise men, give the heavenly side of the parallel, in order that the hearer may work out the earthly application. Because of the very nature of the "heavenly" aspect of the parable, it was given in the form of a vision, in Enoch's case called a "vision of wisdom." It was an insight into the secrets of the creation, as that creation was experienced in an earthly, material existence. It was a revelation, an apocalypse. That is what apocalypse means. Often the visions dealt with the great judgement, whether of Israel or of her enemies, but always there was an earthly correspondence.[146]

The prominence of judgment in Nephi's apocalyptic vision (1 Nephi 11:36) needs no comment. But notice how Nephi explains the relationship between the material and the heavenly, or, as he puts it, the temporal and the spiritual:

> And it came to pass that I said unto them that it was a representation of things both temporal and spiritual; for the day should come that they must be judged of their works, yea, even the works which were done by the temporal body in their days of probation. Wherefore, if they should die in their wickedness they must be cast off also, as to the things which are spiritual, which are pertaining to righteousness; wherefore, they must be brought to stand before God, to be judged of their works. (1 Nephi 15:32–33)

Again, we find the same approach to the same themes. Barker explains that the wisdom teachers have a distinctive approach toward identifying the relevance of apocalyptic symbols in the temporal realm. "Nor do we have to think of a parable or vision as having only one specific meaning or application. We tend to think that story parables are relevant again and again, but that visions have a particular message for a particular situation. This is not so."[147]

Nephi shows the appropriate perspective in the way he applies the scriptures: "And I did read many things unto them which were written in the books of Moses; but that I might more fully persuade them to believe in the Lord their Redeemer I did read unto them that which was written by the prophet Isaiah; for I did liken all scriptures unto us, that it might be for our profit and learning" (1 Nephi 19:23).

This "likening" approach can show up in the allusive way that Alan Goff has shown throughout Nephi's account.[148] It also shows in the way that Nephi relates his own vision to that of Lehi. Welch observes: "The two visions are very different in character. Lehi's dream is intimate, symbolic, and salvific; Nephi's vision is collective, historic, and eschatological. Yet both visions embrace the same prophetic elements, only from different angles."[149] Not only the content and genre of their visions but even their modes of teaching demonstrate the influence of the wisdom tradition.

Old World Evidence That Parts of Wisdom Were Lost

Barker clearly indicates the difference between what wisdom became later and what wisdom seemed to be: "The two wise men of whom we know anything in detail, Joseph and Daniel, did have the ability to predict the future. Both interpreted dreams, and Daniel had visions, yet the Book of Proverbs has little to say on the subject of future times. If wisdom was radically modified during the exile, we should have an explanation for this silence."[150]

She acknowledges that one of the difficulties in reconstructing wisdom has been the influence and effectiveness of those making the changes: "The reasons for the changes to wisdom must lie elsewhere, perhaps in those very aspects of wisdom which are no longer extant in the biblical texts as a result of the alterations."[151]

Still, the evidence she surveys demonstrates clearly that wisdom was changed:

> One is also impatient to know what is missing from the text at certain points. Prov. 30.1ff is completely mutilated, and I shall not attempt to translate it, but the LXX of v. 4 reads the plural, *sons*. Given the general theme of the passage, namely ascent to heaven and power over creation, this plural form reminds one immediately of the sons of God in the Enochic mythology. It is these *sons* who have also disappeared from the Hebrew of Deut. 32, suggesting that the opacity of Prov. 30 may not be accidental.[152]

> Texts dealing with Holy Ones and the Holy One have significant elements in common: theophany, judgement, triumph for Yahweh, triumph for his anointed son, ascent to a throne in heaven, conflict with beasts and with angel princes caught up in the destinies of earthly kingdoms. Many of these texts are corrupted; much of their subject matter is that of the "lost" tradition thought to underlie the apocalyptic texts. The textual corruption and the lost tradition are aspects of the same question.[153]

Barker surveys a number of examples and concludes, "The MT has changed 'sons of God' to 'servants,' and removed all explicit references to the heavenly beings who were to be judged. It is important to remember that the changes in the MT always follow the same pattern, and that this pattern distinguishes it from much at Qumran, and also from much in the New Testament."[154] She argues not just from specific examples, but from overall patterns, and from patterns back down to tiny details. Given an awareness of these patterns, a careful reader of Latter-day Saint scriptures may find new insights even with respect to this particular issue.

Jacob and the Deuteronomist Reformers

In "Paradigms Regained," I present arguments that Barker's view fits very nicely with the Book of Mormon in that the very things that Barker says were changed in response to the exile and the monarchy appear intact in the Book of Mormon. However, it had no report of any direct statement in the Book of Mormon referring to the efforts of the Deuteronomist reformers. More recently I realized the significance of Jacob's comments in Jacob 4:4–14. Jacob 4:14 refers to certain Jews at Jerusalem hostile to the prophets[155] who "despised the words of plainness" and "look[ed] beyond the mark." Jacob would have learned from Lehi of the violent rivals that Lehi, Jeremiah, and others faced in Jerusalem. As a consequence of their actions, Jacob reports, "God hath taken away his plainness from them, and delivered unto them many things which they cannot understand, because they desired it." In chapter 4, Jacob reports on the plainness that he emphasizes overall in his ministry, and it is plausible that he would emphasize the very things that he knew had been lost that were all the more precious given his knowledge of that loss. Since Jacob had never been in Jerusalem, he likely obtained from Lehi and Nephi the information about what was lost, or perhaps he drew parallels from Lehi's vision of Jerusalem's destruction (2 Nephi 1:4). It is at least a striking coincidence that Jacob is contemporary with the exile, and his summary of his life teachings in this chapter corresponds point for point to Barker's analysis of what had been lost at that very time and who was responsible.

Remember that Barker writes that "wisdom was an older form of communication between God and his people. Wisdom was something which the Deuteronomists reformed. This possibility is crucial for my argument."[156] Jacob 4:10 emphasizes that the Lord "counseleth in wisdom," and he shows many ties to the lost tradition in his discourses. Barker writes that "the heavenly ascent and the vision of God were abandoned"; Jacob reports that "we have many revelations and the spirit of prophecy" (Jacob 4:6) and urges that his people "despise not the revelations of God" (Jacob 4:8). Barker describes a reaction against "the hosts of heaven and the angels" in favor of a strict monotheism.[157] According to Barker, in the tradition of the First Temple "there was a High God and several Sons of God, one of whom was Yahweh, the Holy One of Israel."[158] Jacob declares that "they believed in Christ and worshiped the Father in his name, and also we worship the Father in his name. And for this intent we keep the law of Moses, it pointing our souls to him; and for this cause it is sanctified unto us for righteousness, even as it was accounted unto Abraham in the wilderness to be obedient unto the commands of God in offering up his son Isaac, which is a similitude of God and his Only Begotten Son" (Jacob 4:5). Barker emphasizes the role of the atoning high priest as a manifestation of Jehovah.[159] Jacob, a temple priest, delivers key discourses on the atonement at the temple that emphasize "the Holy One of Israel" (2 Nephi 9:11) and urges his readers to "be reconciled unto him through the atonement of Christ" (Jacob 4:11).

Other correlations deriving from Jacob's role as a temple priest include some of the specific language he uses. For example, in her essay "Beyond the Veil of the Temple," Barker quotes several writings that emphasize the priestly visionaries' knowledge of the things of the past and future as depicted on the temple veil and as shown to them in their visions.[160] Jacob comments, "For the Spirit speaketh the truth and lieth not. Wherefore, it speaketh of things as they really are, and of things as they really will be; wherefore, these things are manifested unto us plainly, for the salvation of our souls" (Jacob 4:13; cf. D&C 93:24). Barker presents arguments in *The Older Testament* that part of the Deuteronomic reform involved the rejection of a wisdom tradition that predicts the future,[161] and Jacob says, "For, for this intent have we written these things, that they may know that we knew of Christ, and we had a hope of his glory many hundred years before his coming; and not only we ourselves had a hope of his glory, but also all the holy prophets which were before us" (Jacob 4:4). Again, we find not just random parallels, but matching patterns that depend on one specific time and place and one interpretive framework.

Concluding Observations

Barker's own purpose is to illuminate the origins of Christianity. She follows clues from many sources that all lead her back toward the First Temple and the conflicts that arose in ancient Israel in the late seventh and early sixth centuries, right around the time of Lehi. In summary, she explains:

> There appeared very early in Christian writings, references to beliefs that are nowhere recorded in the New Testament and yet clearly originated in the tradition we call apocalyptic. As more is discovered about this tradition, so more and more points of contact can be found between the beliefs of the ancient temple theology and what became Christianity. The secret tradition of the priests probably became the secret tradition of early Christianity; the visions and angel lore suggest this, as does the prohibition in Deuteronomy 29.29. What had the secret things been that were contrasted with the Law? What had been meant by saying that the Law was neither too hard nor too distant? The comparison suggests

that there had been something both hard and distant which had been brought from heaven by one who had ascended (Deut. 30.11–12, cf. John 3.11–12). This suggests that a secret tradition had been banned by the Deuteronomists, who were the temple reformers at the end of the seventh century BCE, and we do not have to look far to discover what this tradition must have been. They offered their Law as a substitute for Wisdom (Deut. 4.6, cf. Gen. 3.5, the Wisdom that made humans like gods). They also said that the Lord was not visible in human form (Deut 4.12), even though a contemporary priest, Ezekiel, had had a vision of a human figure on the throne (Ezek. 1.26–28), and Isaiah had seen the Lord (Isa. 6.5) and someone, of sufficient repute to have his words included in Scripture, had described the vision of God on Sinai (Exod. 24.10).[162]

Putting her efforts in perspective, Barker explains:

What I shall propose . . . is not an impossibility, but only one possibility to set alongside other possibilities, none of which has any claim to being an absolutely accurate account of what happened. Hypotheses do not become fact simply by frequent repetition, or even by detailed elaboration. What I am suggesting does, however, make considerable sense of the evidence from later periods.[163]

Her reconstruction does challenge conventional notions; however, because the texts she uses have now become more available, she has been getting more attention and respect. Her ideas are not completely without precedent or parallel. For example, Nibley writes:

Years ago Hermann Gunkel pointed out that a full-blown gospel of redemption and atonement was in existence among the preexilic Jews, but this claim, so jarring to the prevailing schools of theology, which would only accept an evolutionary pattern of slow and gradual development, was strenuously resisted by the experts. The discovery of the Scrolls has changed all that: "Now that the warning has been given," writes Dupont-Sommer, "many passages of the Old Testament itself must be examined with a fresh eye."[164]

While following along the same kinds of evidence to similar conclusions, Barker brings a fresh eye and offers a substantially new and original viewpoint, particularly with respect to her overarching vision of what happened. Commenting on the distinctiveness and importance of her views, Robert M. Price writes:

> This is what we mean by "paradigm shift." In reading Margaret Barker's wide-ranging investigation one feels the tectonic plates shifting and coming together in a new configuration, or perhaps rather a very old one, as we see the outlines of primal Gondwanaland restored again. Barker strips off the blinders of the canonical redactors of the Old Testament, a job we thought we'd long ago completed.[165]

Thus we see that Barker has raised an important set of questions and has provided a formidable body of scholarship, unsettled though it may be, granted the inevitable controversy that comes when one challenges entrenched positions and vested interests.[166] While comparisons are obviously promising, we also have many questions to explore. Some we cannot yet answer, but we can at least ask. For instance, how did Jeremiah relate to Josiah's reform? Jeremiah received his prophetic call in the thirteenth year of Josiah's reign (Jeremiah 1:2), when Josiah was twenty-one. Jeremiah's father might be the man who reports finding the book of the law, and Jeremiah himself refers to Deuteronomy frequently. But why do even the Jeremiah texts from Josiah's time so rarely refer directly to Josiah after that initial mention?[167] Why does an oracle like the one starting in Jeremiah 3:6, given in the days of Josiah, that is, *during the reform years,* vehemently denounce *both* cultic and moral lapses in Israel?[168] Why the contrast to the rosy picture of the reform

portrayed in 2 Kings and 2 Chronicles? Jeremiah complains bit-
terly: "From the thirteenth year of Josiah the son of Amon king
of Judah, even unto this day, that is the three and twentieth year,
the word of the Lord hath come unto me, and I have spoken
unto you, rising early and speaking; but ye have not hearkened"
(Jeremiah 25:3).

Jeremiah knows the law, yet he complains that those who
"handle the law knew me not" (Jeremiah 2:8), and he even asks,
"How do you say, 'We are wise, and Yahweh's torah is with us'?
In fact, here, it was made for a lie, the lying pen of the scribes"
(Jeremiah 8:8).[169] Some of Jeremiah's ongoing condemnation
of moral and religious corruption seems to fit some goals of
the reformers, especially in renouncing idolatry. Yet we have
no approval, or even acknowledgment, of the reform that fits
with either the Kings or Chronicles account. Many of his comments become more intriguing in light of Barker's thesis:

> Thus saith the Lord, Stand ye in the ways, and see,
> and ask for the old paths, where is the good way, and walk
> therein, and ye shall find rest for your souls. But they said,
> We will not walk therein. (Jeremiah 6:16)

> Because my people hath forgotten me, they have burned
> incense to vanity, and they have caused them to stumble in
> their ways from the ancient paths, to walk in paths, in a way
> not cast up. (Jeremiah 18:15)

Which old paths, which ancient ways, were being abandoned
during Jeremiah's long ministry? The Josianic/Deuteronomic
reform was directed at the high priesthood, the objects in the
holy of holies, and the centralization of worship in Jerusalem.[170]
Yet Jeremiah was from a priestly family and uses language associated with the targets of the reformers. For example, while
he appears to agree with the reform's attack on idolatry in the
high places (Jeremiah 3:6; 2 Kings 23:5), he speaks of personal

revelation (Jeremiah 1:4), the Lord of Hosts (81 times), the tree of life (Jeremiah 1:11; 17:8), the fountain of living waters (Jeremiah 2:13; 17:13), and the glorious high throne of God (Jeremiah 17:12). He also predicts the future. Barker has shown that these were all targeted by the reformers.[171] And clearly, Jeremiah was at odds with most of the religious and political establishment who supported the reforms.

Barker has done most of her work knowing "almost nothing"[172] about Latter-day Saint scripture and scholarship, yet both fields show a striking thematic resemblance to each other, as even a survey of her titles demonstrates.[173] Joseph Smith, of course, dictated the Book of Mormon without the benefit of Barker's language skills and sources (other than the Bible), most of which have been discovered since Joseph Smith died. And we should note that Joseph's critics, from Alexander Campbell on, reserved some of their most withering scorn for Book of Mormon depiction of pre-Christian Jewish temple worship, priesthood, and prophecy. In his 1831 "Delusions," Campbell was quick to claim plagiarism by Joseph Smith from sources like Shakespeare, the Bible, and popular culture.[174] The idea that preexilic Judaism might display differences from later Judaisms never surfaces in Campbell's critique or any other. Only within the past few years has D. Michael Quinn suggested the remote possibility of Joseph Smith gaining access to two relevant texts, the Laurence translations of the *Ascension of Isaiah* and the *Book of Enoch*.[175] All of Joseph's contemporaries had equal physical proximity and better education and financial access, and none of them made a connection to those barely potential (though by themselves inadequate) sources. Remember that the critics made searches and inquiries[176] among Joseph's neighbors sufficient to lead them to the unpublished and ultimately irrelevant Spaulding manuscript. This zeal demonstrates that they would have been alert to any promising rumor and shows that they had the motivation to track down a rare and unpopular text. Yet even the most popular text among current critics, Ethan Smith's *View of the Hebrews,* drew no notice from critics until the turn of the twentieth century.[177]

All the texts contemporary with Joseph Smith ultimately prove inadequate to account for the Book of Mormon, even if he had seen them.[178] Indeed, it is only within the past thirty years, especially in light of recent reevaluations compelled by texts such as the Dead Sea Scrolls and the Pseudepigrapha, that a few Latter-day Saint scholars have begun to seriously explore the implications of the preexilic setting for the first chapters of the Book of Mormon.[179] Despite disclosures in the Book of Mormon that should have set us more directly on this path of research, all have tended to read the Bible and the Book of Mormon in what Barker calls "a deuteronomic manner," assuming an unbroken continuity in the religion of Israel before and after the exile. Barker shows that "The exile in Babylon is a formidable barrier to anyone wanting to reconstruct the religious beliefs and practices of ancient Jerusalem. . . . Enormous developments took place in the wake of enormous destruction."[180]

Barker's work illustrates a complex pattern involving specific historical events, times, places, persons, and teachings. All of this comes in a timely manner and in the appropriate place to be relevant to the Book of Mormon. In my opinion, this correspondence is not accidental but providential (see 1 Nephi 13). "And again, I will give unto you a pattern in all things, that ye may not be deceived" (D&C 52:14). Given that the pattern appears clearly in the Book of Mormon, what should we think?

O then, is not this real?
I say unto you, Yea,
because it is light; and whatsoever is light, is good,
because it is discernible, therefore ye must know that it is
good. (Alma 32:35)

Notes

1. Barker's own emphasis is on understanding the origins of Christianity. Correlation with the Book of Mormon can be seen as either accidental convergence or as inspired confirmation in fulfillment of prophecy in 1 Nephi 13:39–40, depending on your perspective.

2. See Margaret Barker, *The Older Testament: The Survival of Themes from the Ancient Royal Cult in Sectarian Judaism and Early Christianity* (London: SPCK, 1987), 1.

3. William J. Doorly, *Obsession with Justice: The Story of the Deuteronomists* (New York: Paulist, 1994).

4. Barker, *Older Testament*, 7.

5. Ibid., emphasis dropped.

6. See Barker, *Older Testament*.

7. See Ellis T. Rasmussen, "Deuteronomy," in *Encyclopedia of Mormonism,* 1:378–79; and Kevin Christensen, "Paradigms Regained: A Survey of Margaret Barker's Scholarship and Its Significance for Mormon Studies," *FARMS Occasional Papers* 2 (2001): 9–10.

8. Norbert F. Lohfink, "Was There a Deuteronomistic Movement?" in *Those Elusive Deuteronomists: The Phenomenon of Pan-Deuteronomism,* ed. Linda S. Schearing and Steven L. McKenzie (Sheffield: Sheffield Academic, 1999), 60. However, despite the ideals, when one considers the violence during Josiah's reform (2 Kings 23:20) and Barker's references to later memories of Josiah's reform as a time of wrath, "happy" ought not be read here without a sense of irony. Notice that in contrast to the institutional violence that went with the reform, the Nephite tradition says "there was no law against a man's belief" (Alma 30:11).

9. For the Nephite temples, see 2 Nephi 5:15–16. For Nephi's acceptance of kingly roles, see 2 Nephi 5:18. For discussion, see Noel B. Reynolds, "Nephite Kingship Reconsidered," in *Mormons, Scripture, and the Ancient World: Studies in Honor of John L. Sorenson,* ed. Davis Bitton (Provo, Utah: FARMS, 1998), 151–89. For setting up priests, see 2 Nephi 5:26, and for the distinct traditions in which they operate, see Alma 13. For ties to wisdom, see Daniel C. Peter-

son, "Nephi and His Asherah: A Note on 1 Nephi 11:8–23," in *Mormons, Scripture, and the Ancient World,* 191–243, and Christensen, "Paradigms Regained," 54–55.

10. Margaret Barker, *The Great Angel: A Study of Israel's Second God* (London: SPCK, 1992), 12.

11. Barker, *Older Testament,* 7.

12. Barker notes that Isaiah, Ezekiel, and John were all temple priests and knew the ancient tradition. For Isaiah, see Margaret Barker, *The Revelation of Jesus Christ: Which God Gave to Him to Show to His Servants What Must Soon Take Place (Revelation 1.1)* (Edinburgh: Clark, 2000), 124. For Ezekiel, see ibid., 67. For John, see ibid., 10, 79, 124.

13. Margaret Barker, *On Earth as It Is in Heaven: Temple Symbolism in the New Testament* (Edinburgh: Clark, 1995), 4; see also Margaret Barker, *The Lost Prophet: The Book of Enoch and Its Influence on Christianity* (London: SPCK, 1988), 52. Compare Barker's distinction between the law and wisdom with Nibley's discussion of "horizontal and vertical" Judaism and Christianity in Hugh Nibley, *Since Cumorah,* 2nd ed. (Salt Lake City: Deseret Book and FARMS, 1988), 89.

14. Barker, *Older Testament,* 93.

15. Nephi uses the title in 1 Nephi 19 himself and in quotations from Isaiah and from Zenos, a prophet in the northern kingdom.

16. See Peterson, "Nephi and His Asherah," 191–243.

17. See 2 Nephi 25:12–19, in which Nephi discourses on Isaiah, himself a temple priest, on the topic of divine sonship. Later, Benjamin, Abinadi, and the risen Lord discuss other aspects of this theme.

18. Barker, *Older Testament,* 225.

19. Margaret Barker, *The Gate of Heaven: The History and Symbolism of the Temple in Jerusalem* (London: SPCK, 1991), 92.

20. Barker, *Older Testament,* 1.

21. Compare Margaret Barker, *The Great High Priest* (London: Clark, 2003), 294–315.

22. See John W. Welch, "Connections between the Visions of Lehi and Nephi," in *Pressing Forward with the Book of Mormon: The FARMS Updates of the 1990s,* ed. John W. Welch and Melvin J. Thorne (Provo,

Utah: FARMS, 1999), 49–53, showing that Nephi understands Lehi's vision in a historical and apocalyptic sense; Stephen E. Robinson on "Nephi's 'Great and Abominable Church,'" *Journal of Book of Mormon Studies* 7/1 (1998): 32–39; also Mark D. Thomas, *Digging in Cumorah: Reclaiming Book of Mormon Narratives* (Salt Lake City: Signature Books, 2000), 99–104; and Barker, *Great High Priest,* 200–201.

23. Note the temple context and Welch's suggestions regarding the title as the Name. Contrast Alma 34:35.

24. Note that Barker compares the seven-branched candlestick in the temple to the Lord and to the tree of life, in, for example, *Older Testament,* 221–31.

25. Barker, *Revelation of Jesus Christ,* 67.

26. Barker, *Older Testament,* 240.

27. In comparing the Book of Mormon to Barker's account, we must also consider evidence that appears downstream from the preexilic origin but demonstrates thematic connections to the earlier period. For example, Jacob, though never in Jerusalem, was consecrated as a temple priest by Nephi, who had known Jerusalem (2 Nephi 25:5). The most frequently quoted biblical prophet in the Book of Mormon is Isaiah, who was a temple priest in Jerusalem. Therefore, we should expect not only Lehi and Nephi, but also Jacob and subsequent Book of Mormon prophets, to demonstrate influence from the preexilic tradition via Lehi and the brass plates. They should show no influence from the reforms specific to the exile and restoration, while they should and do show influence from the northern kingdom traditions because of Lehi's descent from Joseph. John L. Sorenson, *Nephite Culture and Society* (Salt Lake City: New Sage Books, 1997), 25–39.

28. Barker, *Gate of Heaven,* 7.

29. Barker, *Older Testament,* 6.

30. Barker, *Gate of Heaven,* 13–14.

31. See John W. Welch, "The Temple in the Book of Mormon: The Temples at the Cities of Nephi, Zarahemla, and Bountiful," in *Temples of the Ancient World: Ritual and Symbolism,* ed. Donald W. Parry (Salt Lake City: Deseret Book and FARMS, 1994), 297–387; John W. Welch, "The Melchizedek Material in Alma 13:13–19," in *By*

Study and Also by Faith: Essays in Honor of Hugh W. Nibley, ed. John M. Lundquist and Stephen D. Ricks (Salt Lake City: Deseret Book and FARMS, 1990), 2:238–72; and John W. Welch, *Illuminating the Sermon at the Temple and the Sermon on the Mount* (Provo, Utah: FARMS, 1999).

32. Compare the description of King Noah's temple in Mosiah 11:10.

33. Barker, *Gate of Heaven,* 16.

34. Ibid., 17.

35. See Terrence L. Szink and John W. Welch, "King Benjamin's Speech in the Context of Ancient Israelite Festivals," in *King Benjamin's Speech: "That Ye May Learn Wisdom,"* ed. John W. Welch and Stephen D. Ricks (Provo, Utah: FARMS, 1998), 147–223. See also "Abinadi and Pentecost," in *Reexploring the Book of Mormon,* ed. John W. Welch (Salt Lake City: Deseret Book and FARMS, 1992), 135–38.

36. Mircea Eliade, *Cosmos and History: The Myth of the Eternal Return* (New York: Harper & Brothers, 1959), 77.

37. Barker, *Gate of Heaven,* 63.

38. Stephen D. Ricks "Kingship, Coronation, and Covenant in Mosiah 1–6," in *King Benjamin's Speech,* 261. Ricks cites Walter Brueggemann, "From Dust to Kingship," *Zeitschrift für die alttestamentliche Wissenschaft* 84/1 (1972): 1.

39. See Richard Dilworth Rust, "The Book of Mormon, Designed for Our Day," *Review of Books on the Book of Mormon* 2 (1990): 1–23; Hugh Nibley, *The Prophetic Book of Mormon* (Salt Lake City: Deseret Book and FARMS, 1989), 407–34; Christensen, "Paradigms Regained."

40. See Barker, *Lost Prophet,* 77–78.

41. Compare with Richard E. Friedman, *Who Wrote the Bible?* (New York: Summit Books, 1987), 126.

42. Barker, *Gate of Heaven,* 69.

43. See Friedman, *Who Wrote the Bible?* 126. "Not only is Jeremiah the only prophet to refer to Shiloh and allude to Moses' bronze snake [Jeremiah 8:17–22]; he is the only prophet to refer to Samuel, the priest-prophet-judge who was the greatest figure in Shiloh's history."

44. Ibid., 102; see Donald W. Parry, "Garden of Eden: Prototype

Sanctuary," in *Temples of the Ancient World,* ed. Donald W. Parry (Salt Lake City: Deseret Book and FARMS, 1994), 126–51.

45. See Sorenson, *Nephite Culture and Society,* 25–39. See also Steve St. Clair, "The Stick of Joseph: The Book of Mormon and the Literary Tradition of Northern Israel": "As described in the Bible, the southern kingdom had standard practices in regard to who held the priesthood: it was restricted to members of the tribe of Levi and specifically to descendants of Aaron, the brother of Moses. In the northern kingdom and the peoples descended from it, the picture was much more interesting, and more confusing. They accepted priesthood service by people who did not fit the southern pattern. . . . Priesthood practice among the Rechabites is most instructive as an example of northern Israelite views. When the Prophet Jeremiah, himself perhaps a descendant of northern Israelite priests, praised the covenant-keeping of the Rechabites shortly before the Babylonian captivity, he made them a striking promise in the name of the Lord: 'Jonadab, son of Rechab, shall never lack a man to stand before me.' To 'stand before the Lord' was a technical term with the specific meaning of serving as a priest, because the title 'priest' (Heb. *cohen*) is derived from a word meaning 'to stand upright.' . . . The Rechabites, then, were a group of functioning priests who had no traceable connection with the tribe of Levi or the ancestry of Aaron." Unpublished paper in author's possession. Compare Barker, *Great High Priest,* 122.

46. Barker, *Great Angel,* 15.

47. Barker, *Older Testament,* 257.

48. Compare Noel Reynolds, "The Brass Plates Version of Genesis," in *By Study and Also by Faith,* 2:136–173.

49. See Barker, *Lost Prophet,* 20–24, 36–39.

50. Barker, *Older Testament,* 133.

51. Ibid., 233–34.

52. Ibid., 179.

53. Barker, *Gate of Heaven,* 81. A fourth-century Coptic text (A.D. 380) is also notable when considering the tension between the fallen angel stories and the Genesis Adam story. "Discourse on Abbatôn by

Timothy, Archbishop of Alexandria," in *Coptic Martyrdoms Etc. in the Dialect of Upper Egypt,* ed. E. A. Wallis Budge (London: British Museum, 1914), 474, fuses a postresurrection discourse of Jesus, a ritually elaborate account of Satan's fall, the fallen angel stories, the choice of Jesus as the redeemer from the foundation of the world, and the creation of Adam into a narrative that resonates profoundly with Latter-day Saint Abraham, Moses, and temple accounts.

54. This approach can be concurrent with the insights regarding allusions to the stories in Judges as discussed by Alan Goff in "The Stealing of the Daughters of the Lamanites," in *Rediscovering the Book of Mormon,* ed. John L. Sorenson and Melvin J. Thorne (Salt Lake City: Deseret Book and FARMS, 1991), 67–74, and Brown, *From Jerusalem to Zarahemla,* 99–112.

55. Barker, *Lost Prophet,* 23.

56. Compare Barker, *Older Testament,* 233–45, with Bruce M. Pritchett Jr., "Lehi's Theology of the Fall in Its Preexilic/Exilic Context," *Journal of Book of Mormon Studies* 3/2 (1994): 49–83.

57. Barker, *Older Testament,* 233.

58. Pritchett, "Lehi's Theology of the Fall," 58.

59. Barker, *Older Testament,* 240.

60. Ibid., 238.

61. Pritchett, "Lehi's Theology of the Fall," 61.

62. Margaret Barker, *The Risen Lord: The Jesus of History as the Christ of Faith* (Edinburgh: Clark, 1996), 71.

63. See Christensen, "Paradigms Regained," 71–75.

64. Barker, *Lost Prophet,* 23.

65. Szink and Welch, "King Benjamin's Speech," 178.

66. Barker, *Great High Priest,* 82.

67. Barker, *Gate of Heaven,* 29.

68. Ibid., 29, 92.

69. See Bruce W. Jorgensen, "The Dark Way to the Tree: Typological Unity in the Book of Mormon," in *Literature of Belief: Sacred Scripture and Religious Experience,* ed. Neal E. Lambert (Provo, Utah: BYU Religious Studies Center, 1981), 217–31; Jeanette W.

Miller, "The Tree of Life, a Personification of Christ," *Journal of Book of Mormon Studies* 2/1 (1993): 93–106.

70. See Welch, "Connections between the Visions," 49–53.

71. See C. Wilfred Griggs, "The Book of Mormon as an Ancient Book," in *Book of Mormon Authorship: New Light on Ancient Origins,* ed. Noel B. Reynolds (Provo, Utah: BYU Religious Studies Center, 1982), 77, 81; and Hugh Nibley, *An Approach to the Book of Mormon,* 3rd ed. (Salt Lake City: Deseret Book and FARMS, 1988), 253–64.

72. Barker, *Older Testament,* 224.

73. Barker, *Great High Priest,* 200–201.

74. Barker, *Gate of Heaven,* 95.

75. Peterson, "Nephi and His Asherah," 213.

76. Barker, *Gate of Heaven,* 93.

77. Ibid., 104.

78. This is also true of the experience of the queen and of Abish, although that would lead off on a different tangent. For a suggestion of the mythic/ritual significance of this account, see Kevin and Shauna Christensen, "Nephite Feminism Revisited: Thoughts on Carol Lynn Pearson's View of Women in the Book of Mormon," *FARMS Review of Books* 10/2 (1998): 9–61.

79. M. Catherine Thomas, "The Brother of Jared at the Veil," in *Temples of the Ancient World,* 388–98.

80. Barker, *Great High Priest,* 190.

81. Rust, "The Book of Mormon," 14–15.

82. Barker, *Gate of Heaven,* 104–5.

83. Barker, *Great High Priest,* 190.

84. Ibid., 193.

85. Hugh Nibley, *Approaching Zion* (Salt Lake City: Deseret Book and FARMS, 1989), 566–67.

86. See Welch, "The Temple in the Book of Mormon," 297–387.

87. Barker, *On Earth as It Is in Heaven,* 46. See Christensen, "Paradigms Regained," 77–81, for a discussion of open questions of Isaiah authorship and the Book of Mormon in relation to the Isaiah chapters quoted in the Book of Mormon.

88. Barker, *Great High Priest,* 53–54; also in Margaret Barker,

"Atonement: The Rite of Healing," *Scottish Journal of Theology* 49/1 (1996): 18–19.

89. See "Abinadi and Pentecost," 135–38.

90. Barker, *Older Testament,* 13–14.

91. Reynolds, "Nephite Kingship Reconsidered," 151–89.

92. See, for example, Gordon C. Thomasson, "Mosiah: The Complex Symbolism and Symbolic Complex of Kingship in the Book of Mormon," *Journal of Book of Mormon Studies* 2/1 (1993): 21–38.

93. Barker, *Older Testament,* 113.

94. For example, Benjamin in Mosiah 2:22; the exact phrase occurs twenty-one times in the Book of Mormon, as well as in several other variations.

95. Barker, *Gate of Heaven,* 103.

96. Barker, *Revelation of Jesus Christ,* 41.

97. Barker, *Gate of Heaven,* 80.

98. See Szink and Welch, "King Benjamin's Speech," 147–223; John A. Tvedtnes, "King Benjamin and the Feast of Tabernacles," in *By Study and Also by Faith,* 197–237.

99. Szink and Welch, "King Benjamin's Speech," 199–200.

100. Christensen, "Paradigms Regained," 61–63, also noting comparisons with the Enoch passages in the Pearl of Great Price. Doctrine and Covenants 1:15 also has a strong resonance.

101. Barker, *Gate of Heaven,* 103.

102. Szink and Welch, "King Benjamin's Speech," 179; see Barker, *Great Angel,* 108.

103. Barker, *Great Angel,* 98, emphasis added.

104. Ibid., 104, emphasis added.

105. Ibid., 108, emphasis added.

106. Szink and Welch, "King Benjamin's Speech," 215 n. 111.

107. Barker, *Great Angel,* 111–12, emphasis added.

108. Barker, *Older Testament,* 127.

109. An etymology for Sariah—the name of Lehi's wife, and anciently attested at Elephantine—is "Jehovah is my prince." See Jeffrey R. Chadwick, "Sariah in the Elephantine Papyri," in *Pressing*

Forward, 8; and Paul Y. Hoskisson, "Lehi and Sariah," *Journal of Book of Mormon Studies* 9/1 (2000): 30.

110. Barker, *Gate of Heaven,* 73.

111. Ibid., 134.

112. Ibid., 176.

113. Nibley, *An Approach to the Book of Mormon,* 300, 301.

114. Compare Barker, *Great High Priest,* 1–33, with Nibley, *Prophetic Book of Mormon,* 407–434, and Welch, *Illuminating the Sermon at the Temple,* 32–34.

115. See John W. Welch, "Democratizing Forces in King Benjamin's Speech," in *Pressing Forward,* 110–26.

116. Ricks, "Kingship, Covenant, and Coronation," 254.

117. Daniel C. Peterson, "'Ye Are Gods': Psalm 82 and John 10 as Witnesses to the Divine Nature of Humankind," in *The Disciple as Scholar: Essays on Scripture and the Ancient World in Honor of Richard Lloyd Anderson,* ed. Stephen D. Ricks, Donald W. Parry, and Andrew H. Hedges (Provo, Utah: FARMS, 2000), 471–594.

118. Barker, *Older Testament,* 230.

119. Peterson, "Nephi and His Asherah," 209–18; and Nibley, *Prophetic Book of Mormon,* 551.

120. Peterson, "Nephi and His Asherah," 209.

121. Ibid.

122. Barker, *Older Testament,* 83.

123. Ibid., 82.

124. Ibid., 84.

125. Ibid., 85.

126. Ibid., 81.

127. Ibid., 89.

128. Ibid., 99.

129. See Christensen, "Paradigms Regained," 9–12; Noel Reynolds, "Lehi as Moses," *Journal of Book of Mormon Studies* 9/2 (2000): 26–35.

130. Barker, *Older Testament,* 95. Compare Moses 1 and Abraham 3–4.

131. Barker, *Great High Priest,* 199–200.

132. Barker, *Older Testament,* 91–92.

133. See Reynolds, "Nephite Kingship Reconsidered," 151–89.

134. The material in 2 Nephi 3 has been compared to the Messiah ben Joseph traditions in Joseph F. McConkie, "Joseph Smith as Found in Ancient Manuscripts," in *Isaiah and the Prophets,* ed. Monte S. Nyman (Provo, Utah: BYU Religious Studies Center, 1984), 11–31.

135. See especially Peterson, "Nephi and His Asherah," 209–18.

136. Barker, *Older Testament,* 95.

137. Ibid., 96.

138. Ibid., 97.

139. Nibley, *Since Cumorah,* 251–63.

140. Barker, *Older Testament,* 114.

141. Barker, *Gate of Heaven,* 135.

142. See John A. Tvedtnes, *The Most Correct Book: Insights from a Book of Mormon Scholar* (Salt Lake City: Cornerstone, 1999), 59–75.

143. Barker, *Older Testament,* 90–91.

144. See Nibley, *Approaching Zion,* 325–27.

145. Barker, *Lost Prophet,* 66.

146. Ibid., 67.

147. Ibid.

148. For example, Alan Goff, "Boats, Beginnings, and Repetitions," *Journal of Book of Mormon Studies* 1/1 (1992): 67–84.

149. Welch, "Connections between the Visions," 49.

150. Barker, *Older Testament,* 96.

151. Ibid., 85.

152. Ibid., 84.

153. Ibid., 119.

154. Ibid., 211.

155. See Tvedtnes, *Most Correct Book,* 66–71, on accounts of opposition to Jeremiah and Ezekiel.

156. Barker, *Older Testament,* 83.

157. Barker, *Great Angel,* 46.

158. Ibid., 3.

159. Barker, *Risen Lord,* 57–84.

160. Barker, *Great High Priest,* 188–201.

161. Barker, *Older Testament,* 95–97.

162. Barker, *Great High Priest,* 9, emphasis deleted.

163. Barker, *Great Angel,* 12.

164. Nibley, *Prophetic Book of Mormon,* 77–78.

165. Robert M. Price, review of *The Great Angel: A Study of Israel's Second God,* by Margaret Barker, *Journal of Higher Criticism* 4/1 (1997): 152–55.

166. For instance, on the basis of three or four quotations by three Latter-day Saint authors, Paul Owen felt compelled to devote fully a fifth of his essay on "Monotheism, Mormonism, and the New Testament Witness," in *The New Mormon Challenge: Responding to the Latest Defenses of a Fast-Growing Movement,* ed. Francis J. Beckwith, Carl Mosser, and Paul Owen (Grand Rapids, Mich.: Zondervan, 2002), 271–314, to responding to one of her books (301–8). I counter with an essay, "A Response to Paul Owen's Comments on Margaret Barker," *FARMS Review of Books* 14/1–2 (2002): 193–221, with some excellent help from Margaret Barker herself.

167. Of sixteen verses naming Josiah, most are prefaced by "son of." Three verses mention Josiah in the context of the timing of Jeremiah's prophetic call. Two of these report that Judah had never listened to Jeremiah in all the years since. The only discourse that can be dated with certainty to Josiah's life (Jeremiah 3:6–7) broadly condemns both cultic and moral lapses in Judah and Israel. Only Jeremiah 22:15–16 refers positively to anything about Josiah himself; this passage is a retrospective contrast of Josiah with Jehoiakim, one of his sons, referring to the former judging the cause of the poor and the needy (positive themes of Deuteronomy). Nothing at Josiah's time or later confirms or extends that favorable aside.

168. For example, Jeremiah 3:6–10 denounces idolatry, Jeremiah 5:7 condemns moral lapses, and Jeremiah 5:21 invokes Isaiah's curse in Isaiah 6:8–9 on the refusal of wisdom, pointing to the lack of understanding, seeing, or hearing. Jeremiah 5:27–28 describes economic exploitation and corruption, Jeremiah 5:31 describes false priests and prophets, and Jeremiah 7:4–7 condemns reliance on the temple without moral reformation.

169. Translation in Friedman, *Who Wrote the Bible?* 209. Friedman argues that the passage is criticizing the "P" source.

170. See Margaret Barker, "What Did King Josiah Reform?" in this volume, pages 523–42.

171. See Barker, *Great Angel,* 14–15.

172. Margaret Barker, e-mail to Kevin Christensen, September 2002.

173. See Christensen, "Paradigms Regained," 89.

174. Alexander Campbell, "Delusions," *Millennial Harbinger* 2 (7 February 1831): 85–96.

175. See D. Michael Quinn, *Early Mormonism and the Magic World View,* rev. and enl. ed. (Salt Lake City: Signature Books, 1998), 210–21. Even Quinn does not think Joseph Smith obtained these books. He raises the remote possibility out of professional obligation, rather than plausibility. Compared to Joseph Smith, critics like Abner Cole, the newspaper editor; John Gilbert, the printer; Alexander Campbell, the second-generation religious leader; or Philastus Hurlbut, the disaffected convert, seem to me to be far more likely to have encountered such materials, in terms of both educational background and financial capability. Given how strenuously Campbell objected, for example, it seems reasonable that had he seen the *Ascension of Isaiah,* he would have drawn attention to Joseph's possible use of it in light of pre-Christian knowledge of Christ rather than solely to Joseph's ignorance of the Old Testament. Compare William J. Hamblin on the economics of book buying in "That Old Black Magic," *FARMS Review of Books* 12/2 (2000): esp. 253–76.

176. See Nibley, *Prophetic Book of Mormon,* 170–81.

177. See Andrew H. Hedges, review of *View of the Hebrews,* by Ethan Smith, *FARMS Review of Books* 9/1 (1997): 63–68.

178. See John Gee, "The Wrong Type of Book," in *Echoes and Evidences of the Book of Mormon,* ed. Donald W. Parry, Daniel C. Peterson, and John W. Welch (Provo, Utah: FARMS, 2002), 307–29.

179. See mentions of preexilic issues by Nibley in "New Approaches to Book of Mormon Study," 77–78; Gordon C. Thomasson, "What's in a Name? Book of Mormon Language, Names, and [Metonymic] Naming," *Journal of Book of Mormon Studies* 3/1 (1994): 16; John W.

Welch, "King Benjamin's Discourse in the Context of Ancient Israelite Festivals" (FARMS paper, 1985); Angela Crowell, "Dating the Book of Mormon to Pre-exilic Language Structure" (FARMS reprint, 1996); and Pritchett, "Lehi's Theology of the Fall." Note that Pritchett wrote in response to Blake T. Ostler, "The Book of Mormon as a Modern Expansion of an Ancient Source," *Dialogue* 20/1 (1987): 66–123, which attempted a then state-of-the-art survey that saw extensive conflicts between the Book of Mormon and scholarly views of preexilic Israel. In response to perceived conflicts, Ostler proposed a "prophetic expansion" view of the text. Little noticed by Latter-day Saint scholars, Barker's *Older Testament* was published that same year in England. I find it significant that Ostler, in light of work by Barker and others, has revised his view on the necessity of extensive prophetic expansion, though he still asserts a midrashic view of translation. See also Peterson, "Nephi and His Asherah," 195–204.

180. Barker, *Great Angel,* 12.

Chapter 17

What Did King Josiah Reform?

Margaret Barker

King Josiah changed the religion of Israel in 623 B.C. According to the Old Testament account in 2 Kings 23, he removed all manner of idolatrous items from the temple and purified his kingdom of Canaanite practices. Temple vessels made for Baal, Asherah, and the host of heaven were removed, idolatrous priests were deposed, the Asherah itself was taken from the temple and burned, and much more besides. An old law book had been discovered in the temple, and this had prompted the king to bring the religion of his kingdom into line with the requirements of that book (2 Kings 22:8–13; 2 Chronicles 34:14–20).[1] There could be only one temple, it stated, and so all other places of sacrificial worship had to be destroyed (Deuteronomy 12:1–5). The law book is easily recognizable as Deuteronomy, and so King Josiah's purge is usually known as the Deuteronomic reform of the temple.

In 598 B.C., twenty-five years after the work of Josiah, Jerusalem was attacked by the Babylonians under King Nebuchadnezzar (2 Kings 24:10–16; 25:1–9); eleven years after the first attack, they returned to destroy the city and the temple (586 B.C.). Refugees fled south to Egypt, and we read in the book of Jeremiah how they would not accept the prophet's interpretation of the disaster (Jeremiah 44:16–19). Jeremiah insisted that Jerusalem had fallen because of the sins of her people, but the refugees said it had fallen because of Josiah. The king is not mentioned by name, but there can be no doubt what the refugees had in mind.[2] Until very recently, they said, they and their ancestors in Judah and Jerusalem had worshipped differently and had prospered, but when they changed their manner of worship, disaster had followed.

They had worshipped the Queen of Heaven by offering incense, libations, and special loaves to represent her.[3] Now the Queen of Heaven is not mentioned in the account of Josiah's purge, but the major item removed from the temple was the Asherah, which was dragged out and burned. Later Jewish texts[4] described the Asherah as a stylized tree, and Deuteronomy had forbidden any such tree or any pillar to be placed beside an altar for the Lord (Deuteronomy 16:21). It was these spiritual heirs of Josiah who returned from Babylon to rebuild the temple, and their influence can be found in many of the texts we now read as the Old Testament.[5] These texts do not tell the whole story.

The refugees who fled to Egypt were not the only ones who thought that Josiah's purge had been a disaster. By surveying the extrabiblical texts that still survive, we can begin to piece together what Josiah destroyed. Many of those texts imply that Josiah's purge was a disaster.

In 1897 a text that described a group of covenanters in the land of Damascus was discovered in an old Cairo synagogue. Fragments of the same text were later found among the Dead Sea Scrolls, showing that the text had been known in the time of Jesus. This *Damascus Document*,[6] as it is called, describes the Babylonian destruction of Jerusalem as punishment for the unfaithfulness of the people—Jeremiah would have agreed with that, but it also says that the whole Second Temple era that followed was the age of wrath. Far from restoring the true religion of Jerusalem, the people who returned from Babylon to rebuild the temple were led by false teachers who had not been chosen by God. Israel had gone astray in the hidden things; they had lost the truth. They did not observe the true calendar or the correct forms of worship, and they had corrupt priests. The Damascus Covenant group believed that they were the guardians of the true priestly traditions and that their reward would be to return to the glory of Adam and to be resurrected. They had kept a record of their genealogies and of what they had done.[7]

The book of Enoch known as *1 Enoch*[8] gives a similar account.[9] Preserved within the fifth section of this text is an ancient and cryptic account of the history of Israel. Each period is described as a "week" and so the text is known as the *Apocalypse of Weeks.* In the sixth week, all those who lived in the temple forsook wisdom and lost their vision, and then the temple was burned. Those who returned in the seventh week to rebuild the temple were an apostate generation whose deeds were evil.[10] Elsewhere Enoch records that those who built this second temple made impure and polluted offerings. The people who preserved the Enoch texts looked forward to the Lord destroying that impure temple and building a new and greater temple in its place.[11] They also claimed that the words of scripture had been altered by godless people.[12]

On one of his heavenly journeys, Enoch saw the fragrant tree of life that would one day be planted again in the temple and its fruit given to the righteous. He also saw dismembered branches from the tree, flourishing in a blessed place.[13] In another vision, Enoch saw the fragrant tree as a fiery form, the place where the Lord came when he was in paradise.[14] Yet another text describes the fragrant tree as shining like the sun, and with fruits like clusters of white grapes.[15] Now the book of Proverbs describes wisdom as the tree of life (Proverbs 3:13, 18) and those who are devoted to her as happy, a word play that sounds like the name Asherah.[16] In this way, by piecing together fragments of tradition and folk memory, we can glimpse what Josiah must have removed from the temple. The Asherah must have been the stylized tree of life, the symbol of wisdom.[17] When Moses was told to make the seven-branched lamp for the tabernacle, the menorah, he was told to make it like an almond tree (Exodus 25:31–39), and so it was probably the original menorah that Josiah removed and destroyed.[18]

The work of Josiah was not forgotten. Even mainstream Jewish texts from well into the Christian era record that great changes took place at that time and that the second temple was inferior to the first. The great commentary on the book of Numbers, known as the *Numbers Rabbah*,[19] said that in the time of the Messiah, five things would be restored that had been in the first temple but not in the second: the fire, the ark, the menorah, the spirit, and the cherubim.[20] In other words, the true temple that the Messiah would restore was the first temple, the one Josiah had purged. The mystery here is the menorah: there had been a menorah in the second temple, but it cannot have been the true menorah if this was deemed to be missing from the second temple. The Babylonian Talmud records that Josiah had hidden away the ark, the holy anointing oil, the jar of manna, and Aaron's rod.[21] Most of these items—the ark, the cherubim, the oil, the manna, and Aaron's rod—had been kept in the holy of holies to which only the high priests had access. In other words, Josiah's changes concerned the high priests and were thus changes at the very heart of the temple.

Josiah had not been the first king who attempted to change the religion of Israel and Judah. King Hezekiah, in whose time Isaiah was a prophet in Jerusalem, removed hilltop places of worship, destroyed sacred pillars, and broke down the Asherah (2 Kings 18:4). When the Assyrian envoys came to demoralize the people of Jerusalem, they said that their Lord would no longer protect the city because the king had destroyed his places of worship (Isaiah 36:7). Hezekiah was not seen by his contemporaries as a reformer. Hezekiah's predecessor, King Ahaz, had followed the older religion: he had burned incense at the hilltop shrines and under sacred trees and had even sacrificed his son (2 Chronicles 28:3–4; 2 Kings 16:3). Isaiah had no word of condemnation for Ahaz on these matters; he only rebuked him for his lack of faith in the Lord when Jerusalem was threatened by enemies. Isaiah, it would seem, favored the older ways. He spoke of the great tree that had been felled but preserved the holy seed in its stump (Isaiah 6:13),[22] and he compared the Servant of the Lord to a branch of the menorah, damaged but still able to give light (Isaiah 42:3).[23]

Almost everything that Josiah swept away can be matched in the religion of the patriarchs Abraham, Isaac, and Jacob. They had built shrines all over the land, wherever the Lord had appeared to them, and they had offered sacrifices under great trees (Genesis 12:6–7) and set up pillars to mark holy places (Genesis 28:18). In the Old Testament as we know it, the patriarchs before the time of Moses and the kings after him followed the religion that Deuteronomy condemned and Josiah purged. The custom of child sacrifice, which Josiah abolished, had been required in the oldest of the Hebrew law codes (Exodus 22:29), and only the later modifications permitted a substitute offering of five silver shekels or a Levite for temple service (Exodus 13:15; Numbers 3:40–48).

This change is reflected in the way the story of Abraham and Isaac is told in our Old Testament. Abraham had thought that the sacrifice of his son was necessary, but the Lord told him that a substitute should be offered (Genesis 22:12–13). Another version of this story survived for centuries—namely, that Isaac had actually been sacrificed and then resurrected.[24] Echoes of this version of the story seem to appear in both Jewish and Christian sources—in the *Targum Pseudo-Jonathan* and in the early Christian writings of Barnabas and Clement of Rome[25]—and it is probably implied in the New Testament in the Letter to the Hebrews (Hebrews 11:17–19; also James 2:21). The sacrifice of the Son lies at the heart of Christianity, and the emphasis of the Letter to the Hebrews is that in the case of Jesus, no substitute was offered (Hebrews 9:12). This shows that memories of the older religion and its stories survived for centuries, even though they do not appear in the biblical texts.

Abraham too had paid his tithe to Melchizedek, the priest-king of Jerusalem (Genesis 14:18–20), and so the Melchizedek priesthood must have been part of the older religion.[26] A fragmented text about Melchizedek was found among the Dead Sea Scrolls (11Q13).[27] He was a divine figure, the Messiah, expected to return at just the time when Jesus began his ministry and to make the final great atonement.[28] A damaged portion of the text seems to mention teachers who have been kept hidden and secret.[29] Nothing of the Melchizedek tradition survives in the biblical texts, apart from the Genesis account and one text in Psalm 110, and so we have to ask: Who preserved these Melchizedek traditions?

One way to reconstruct the religion of Jerusalem before Josiah's changes is to note how many of the practices forbidden by Deuteronomy are permitted elsewhere in the Old Testament. Deuteronomy, for example, denies that any vision of

God was seen when the Law was given: "You saw no form; only a voice was heard" (Deuteronomy 4:12), and yet the account in Exodus says that Moses went up the mountain with the leaders and elders of Israel "and they saw the God of Israel" (Exodus 24:10).[30] Isaiah had seen the Lord "high and lifted up and his train filled the temple" (Isaiah 6:1). The vision of God must have been a part of the older faith; there are several accounts of the Lord being in or emerging from his holy place to bring judgment (Deuteronomy 32:43; Habakkuk 2:20; Zephaniah 1:7),[31] and also prayers for the Lord to "shine" upon his people (Numbers 6:25).

Deuteronomy condemns regard for the host of heaven (Deuteronomy 4:19), the angels who were represented by the stars, even though an ancient title for the Lord was the Lord of Hosts. The heavenly host of angels must have been part of the older faith.[32]

Deuteronomy also taught that the Law was to be the wisdom of the chosen people, that the Law would make them wise (Deuteronomy 4:6). The book of Proverbs says that it is Wisdom herself who makes her disciples wise (Proverbs 9:1–6). Wisdom must have been part of the older faith.[33]

All these three—visions of the Lord, the host of heaven, and wisdom—feature in the accounts of Josiah's purge: Enoch says that the priests in the temple lost their vision because they abandoned wisdom, and the account in 2 Kings 23 describes how certain houses in the temple that had belonged to "cult prostitutes" were destroyed. Exactly the same Hebrew letters can be read as "holy ones," angels.[34] What Josiah probably destroyed were the places for the angels, just as he destroyed the Asherah, which was the symbol of Wisdom, the Queen of Heaven. Isaiah saw the Lord among the angels, and he said he had seen the Lord of Hosts in the temple (Isaiah 6:1–5). Except for one mention in the archaic poetry in Deuteronomy 32:8, which scholars do not believe was original to the book, Deuteronomy in the Masoretic tradition does not mention angels.

Another way to reconstruct the older faith is to compare certain Old Testament texts with the parallel accounts elsewhere. To take just one example, let us compare the account of the creation in Genesis 1 with other accounts in ancient texts. According to Genesis 1:3, on day one God said, "Let there be light" and then separated light from darkness. Now in the pattern of temple symbolism, the six days of creation corresponded to the six stages by which Moses erected the tabernacle: thus the first day corresponded to the holy of holies, the second day to the veil of the tabernacle, the third day to the table for the shewbread, and so forth. Whatever we read about day one will have been a secret of the holy of holies, accessible only to the high priests.[35] In Genesis we are told nothing except that God created light and separated it from darkness. However, the book of *Jubilees*[36] (another text found among the Dead Sea Scrolls and preserved by the ancient church in Ethiopia) gives a fuller account of day one, and thus of the holy of holies. On day one the Lord created the angel spirits who serve before him, and the ranks of the angels are listed.[37] A similar list appears in the Song of the Three Young Men in the fiery furnace, which is found in the Greek version of Daniel 3, but not in the Hebrew. The young men call on all creation to praise the Lord, beginning with a detailed account of the angels described in *Jubilees* as the works of day one. It is not until almost halfway through their song that they call on the works of the visible creation to offer praise. The readers of the book of *Jubilees* and the readers of the Greek Daniel knew that the angels had been the work of day one—but we do not learn this from Genesis. It comes as no surprise, though, that the angels were located in the holy of holies, which is where Isaiah saw the heavenly host. Presumably, knowledge of the angels had been a part of what Josiah sought to eliminate. As mentioned earlier, Deuteronomy does not mention angels.

Deuteronomy does, however, warn against the secret things, presumably the knowledge of the holy of holies. "The secret things belong to the Lord our God" (Deuteronomy 29:29). Deuteronomy does not deny that such secret things exist, but all that was necessary was to obey the Law and keep the revealed commandments.[38] The affairs of the holy of holies were the exclusive preserve of the high priests. They alone had charge of the affairs of the altar and the holy of holies (Numbers 18:3), and they alone were permitted to look at the tabernacle furnishings (Numbers 4).[39]

The great angels had been known as the sons of God. It is ironical that, in the first of the two great poems appended to the book of Deuteronomy, we are given the clearest picture of these sons of God. "When the Most High gave to the nations their inheritance, he fixed the bounds of the peoples according to the number of the sons of God" (Deuteronomy 32:8). There was one guardian angel for each nation.[40] The poem goes on to say that Jacob was allotted to the Lord—in other words, that the Lord, the God of Israel, was the Son of God Most High. The older religion had not been monotheism in the way that that word is usually understood today. The Lord, the Son of God, had been the angel of Israel, or, as Isaiah said, the Holy One of Israel, since a holy one is an angel. The Lord as the Son of God Most High became a sensitive matter, and so there were two versions of this text in Hebrew. The Masoretic text on which most English translations are based does not have "sons of God" at this point but "sons of Israel," giving, "He fixed the bounds of the peoples according to the number of the sons of Israel." The Old Greek and the Hebrew texts found among the Dead Sea Scrolls, however, have "sons of God," showing that God Most

High apportioned the nations among his sons and that the Lord, the God of Israel, was the Son of God Most High.[41] The early Christians read the Old Testament in this way; whenever the Lord appeared, for example, to Abraham, they recognized that it was an appearance of the second person of the Trinity, the Messiah, the Son of God.[42]

Once we know that the sons of God were an important part of the first temple religion, other Old Testament texts begin to appear in their original setting. The holy of holies was the place of the angels, and so the rituals of the holy of holies must have been associated with the world of the angels.[43] According to the books of Chronicles, there was in the holy of holies a golden throne in the form of a chariot of cherubim (1 Chronicles 28:18). It was concealed behind the veil of the temple, mentioned in 2 Chronicles 3:14. The account in 1 Kings, influenced by the Deuteronomists, mentions neither the chariot throne nor the veil, so these must have been important items in the older religion. You will recall that the cherubim had been in the first temple but not the second and were to be restored in the time of the Messiah.[44] Chronicles also reveals that when Solomon was made king, he sat on this chariot throne, described as the throne of the Lord, and when he was enthroned, the people worshipped him (1 Chronicles 29:20–23). "The people worshipped the Lord, the king" is the literal translation of 1 Chronicles 29:20. The king "was" the Lord.[45] He was enthroned in the holy of holies, and he was the Lord. One of his titles, according to Isaiah, was Immanuel, "God with us." A human being had entered the holy of holies and become an angel. Isaiah records the song of the angels in the holy of holies as the new angel is born as a son of God: "Unto us a child is born, unto us a son is given, and the government shall be upon his shoulder, and his name shall be called Wonderful Counsellor, Mighty God, Everlasting Father, Prince of Peace" (Isaiah 9:6).[46]

The most complete picture of the first temple religion has been preserved in the Enoch texts.[47] Ancient leaders such as Noah and Moses assumed angelic status while they still lived on earth.[48] Enoch was himself a high priest figure who entered the holy of holies and was transformed into an angel when he stood before the throne and was anointed and clothed by Michael. "He anointed me and he clothed me, and the appearance of that oil is greater than the greatest light, and it is like sweet dew and its fragrance is myrrh, and it is like the rays of the glittering sun. And I looked at myself and I had become like one of the glorious ones."[49] You will recall that the anointing oil had disappeared in the time of Josiah[50] and that there is almost nothing about Enoch in the Hebrew Bible even though he was a major figure among the Dead Sea Scrolls.

All the Enochic visions of the holy of holies must have been memories of the ancient rituals: the high priest taking petitions into the presence of God, the high priest looking out from the holy of holies and seeing all history spread before him so that he knew the future, the blood of the Righteous One being offered before the judgment could begin. This latter must have been a memory of the ancient rite of atonement, when the blood of the royal high priest was offered in the holy of holies, presumably using an animal substitute.[51] Daniel's vision of the Man ascending with clouds to the Ancient of Days says, literally, "He was offered before him," and then he was given dominion (Daniel 7). Atonement is missing from Deuteronomy; the festival calendar in Deuteronomy 16 describes Passover, Pentecost, and Tabernacles—but no Day of Atonement.[52] The final form of the Pentateuch, compiled under the influence of Josiah's party, denies that atonement is even possible. After

Israel had sinned and made the golden calf, Moses went back up the mountain to offer himself as an atonement for their sin. The Lord said to Moses, "Whoever has sinned against me, him will I blot out of my book" (Exodus 32:33). Why had Moses thought that his self-sacrifice could have been an atonement for sin? Presumably there had once been a time when such things were thought possible.

The older faith did not disappear. The people who preserved the Enoch traditions kept the older faith, the community of the Damascus Covenant seems to have kept the older faith, those who wrote the Qumran Melchizedek text knew the date at which the older faith would be restored, and it emerged as the framework of early Christianity.[53] Jesus was proclaimed in the Letter to the Hebrews as Melchizedek (Hebrews 7:14–17, 22),[54] and John, in his vision recorded in the book of Revelation, saw the ark restored to the temple (Revelation 11:19).[55]

Remnants of the older faith survived in many places, preserved by the descendants of those who fled from Josiah's purge. There were the mysterious sons of Rechab whose story was told in the *History of the Rechabites*.[56] Beneath the layers of fantasy and folk tale in this widely known ancient text, we glimpse a group who described themselves as angels and who had fled from Jerusalem after the time of Josiah. Angels had released them from prison, and they had escaped to the desert and crossed the great sea to a paradise land of fruit trees, honey, and abundant water. Angels continued to inform them about events in their former world, and so they knew about the life of Jesus. Zosimus, who visited the Rechabites, brought back stone tablets with an account of them. Now Rechab is an interesting name; it can also mean a chariot, and so the angel sons of Rechab might have been the devotees of the chariot throne in the temple who fled from Jerusalem after Josiah's purge and settled somewhere across a great sea.

Aramaic papyri found at Yeb in the south of Egypt, the Elephantine Papyri,[57] describe a group who worshipped Yahu, another form of the Hebrew name of the Lord, but they also had divine names with feminine forms. None of the names was Egyptian, so they were not the result of local syncretism. They had built themselves a temple and had a priesthood—so they did not accept that there could be only one temple—and they corresponded with the high priest in Jerusalem. Originally they had made no blood sacrifices, just offerings of wine, incense, and cereals, like the refugees who fled to Egypt with Jeremiah. Isaiah had prophesied that there would be an altar for the Lord in the midst of the land of Egypt (Isaiah 19:19) and five cities speaking the language of Canaan and worshipping the Lord of Hosts.

To the south of Yeb (Elephantine) in Ethiopia are the Qemant, another people who have preserved the older faith.[58] They observe the Sabbath and the Old Testament food laws, and they worship one God who can appear in human form, whom they name Adara, not unlike the Hebrew word for "glorious one." They acknowledge seven great angels and expect the day of judgment. They know of Abraham and of Adam. They set up stone pillars and anoint them, and their holy men pray to Adara by sacred trees. Some of them have been taken up to heaven and were never seen again. There is also the tradition that the ark was taken to Ethiopia before the destruction of the first temple.[59] The Christian monks in the Lake Tana monasteries still tell of the time before their people became Christian and how they kept the ark for many centuries until it was taken to Axum.

In western China, bordering Tibet, are the Chiang Min, a people whose way of life was recorded at the beginning of the last century by a Christian missionary. Their religion was identified as that of the Old Testament before Josiah's purge. That missionary's son is Professor Thomas Torrance, the distinguished theologian at the University of Edinburgh, Scotland. He wrote thus: "I myself am convinced of [my father's] main thesis. . . . The religious observances of the Chiang seem to derive from a period in Israel's history . . . before the centralization of the cult in Jerusalem had been carried out, when high place worship was still prevalent."[60] The Chiang Min worship on a high place, with an altar of unhewn stones, a sacred tree behind the altar, and a white stone set between them. God, whom they called Abba Malak, came to his people through the sacred tree. They had remembered that Abba meant father, but had lost the meaning of Malak, which is clearly the Hebrew for angel. They had a sacred rod in the form of a snake twisting round a pole, and they called their faith "the White Religion."[61]

The religion of Abraham was long remembered as distinct from that of the Jews, who also had teachings of Moses. The Qur'an asked: "Do you claim that Abraham, Ishmael, Isaac, Jacob and the tribes were all Jews or Christians?"[62] This "religion of Abraham" must have been the older faith, before Josiah and the Deuteronomists made Moses the more important figure. The earliest account of the life of Muhammad was written by Ibn Ishaq in the middle of the eighth century A.D., and so only about one hundred years after the time of Muhammad. Before the prophet appeared, he wrote, four good men set out to seek the religion of their father Abraham, which they believed their people had corrupted. They accepted neither Judaism nor Christianity but sought the Hanifiya, who had kept the faith of Abraham. One of them went as far as Syria, where a Christian monk told him there was nobody left who kept the faith of Abraham, but that a prophet would soon appear.

On the southwest coast of India are the so-called black Jews, a group that claims to have traveled to India after the destruction of the temple.[63] There seem to have been trading links between Palestine and southern India in the time of the first temple, and early Christian writings say that the apostles Thomas and Bartholomew went to India as missionaries.[64] Pantaenus, who became the head of the Christian academy in Alexandria in the late second century A.D., had in his younger days traveled as a missionary to India. There he found that Bartholomew had left them the Gospel of Matthew in Hebrew, showing that Bartholomew had preached to a Jewish community in India.[65]

Perhaps the most compelling evidence for large numbers of people leaving Jerusalem after Josiah's purge is to be found in the Jerusalem Talmud, which is a compendium of Jewish teaching and traditions compiled around A.D. 400. It describes how a large number of young priests sided with Nebuchadnezzar against Jerusalem and then went to Arabia, where they were denied hospitality by the sons of Ishmael. This is presented in the Talmud[66] as the fulfillment of the prophecy in Isaiah 21:13–15 that those who had been in the forest of Lebanon—that is, the temple complex known as the house of the forest of Lebanon (1 Kings 7:2)—had gone to what Isaiah called "the thickets of Arabia." Jeremiah records that King Zedekiah was more afraid of the people who had deserted to the Babylonians than he was of the Babylonians themselves (Jeremiah 38:19). The priests who supported the Babylonians against Jerusalem must have been those who could not accept what had been done to the temple by Josiah. What they took with them to Arabia must have been the faith of the first temple, the religion Josiah had sought to purge.

We can never know for certain what it was that Josiah purged or why he did it. No original versions of the actual texts or records survive from that period, but even the stories as they have come down to us in various sources show that this was a time of major upheaval that was not forgotten. A thousand years after the events themselves, even mainstream Jewish texts remembered that the temple had been drastically changed, that large numbers of people had left the land, and that the true temple would only be restored in the time of the Messiah.

NOTES

Margaret Barker presented this forum address at Brigham Young University on 6 May 2003. We have added footnotes to some of the sources where Margaret Barker discusses its issues in greater depth. The English translations of the ancient texts in this presentation are by the author.

1. Chronicles reports the timing of the book's discovery differently, six years into the reform. See Margaret Barker, *The Great Angel: A Study of Israel's Second God* (London: SPCK, 1992), 12; also Margaret Barker, *The Older Testament: The Survival of Themes from the Ancient Royal Cult in Sectarian Judaism and Early Christianity* (London: SPCK, 1987), 142–43.

2. See Margaret Barker, *The Great High Priest: The Temple Roots of Christian Liturgy* (London: Clark, 2003), 234–36.

3. Barker, *Great High Priest*, 246–47.

4. Mishnah ʿAbodah Zarah 3.

5. Barker, *Great Angel*, 12–14; Barker, *Older Testament*, 142–48.

6. For the original Cairo Geniza text, see Magen Broshi, ed., *The Damascus Document Reconsidered* (Jerusalem: The Israel Exploration Society and The Shrine of the Book, 1992). For an English translation

of the Cairo and Qumran texts, see Géza Vermès, *The Complete Dead Sea Scrolls in English* (New York: Penguin, 1997), 125–56.

7. Barker, *Great High Priest,* 79, 82.

8. A convenient English translation of the Enoch texts can be found in James Charlesworth, ed., *The Old Testament Pseudepigrapha* (New York: Doubleday, 1983), 1:5–315.

9. See Barker, *Older Testament,* 8–80; and Margaret Barker, *The Lost Prophet: The Book of Enoch and Its Influence on Christianity* (London: SPCK, 1988).

10. *1 Enoch* 93; Barker, *Older Testament,* 59–61.

11. *1 Enoch* 90:29.

12. *1 Enoch* 98, 104.

13. *1 Enoch* 24–26.

14. *2 Enoch* 8.

15. *On the Origin of the World,* Coptic Gnostic Library II,5.110; Barker, *Great High Priest,* 244.

16. Daniel C. Peterson, "Nephi and His Asherah: A Note on 1 Nephi 11:8–23," in *Mormons, Scripture, and the Ancient World: Studies in Honor of John L. Sorenson,* ed. Davis Bitton (Provo, Utah: FARMS, 1998), 212.

17. Barker, *Great High Priest,* 244.

18. Margaret Barker, *Revelation of Jesus Christ: Which God Gave to Him to Show to His Servants What Must Soon Take Place (Revelation 1.1)* (Edinburgh: Clark, 2000), 204–6.

19. An English translation can be found in Judah J. Slotki, *Midrash Rabbah,* ed. H. Freedman and Maurice Simon (London: Soncino, 1939), vols. 5 and 6.

20. *Numbers Rabbah* 15:10.

21. *Horayot* 12a, in Martin S. Jaffee, trans., *The Talmud of Babylonia: An American Translation XXVI. Tractate Horayot* (Atlanta: Scholars Press, 1987), 184–91.

22. Barker, *Great High Priest,* 239–43.

23. Ibid., 244.

24. For further discussion of these accounts, see Hugh Nibley, *Abraham in Egypt,* 2nd ed. (Salt Lake City: Deseret Book and FARMS, 2000), 328–44, 372–75.

25. *Barnabas* 7; *1 Clement* 10 and 31.

26. Barker, *Older Testament,* 257.

27. A translation of 11Q13 can be found in Vermès, *Complete Dead Sea Scrolls,* 500–502.

28. Barker, *Great High Priest,* 37–39. Also, Barker, *Revelation of Jesus Christ,* 4–7.

29. Florentino García Martínez, Eibert J. C. Tigchelaar, and Adam S. Van der Woude, eds., *Qumran Cave 11. II, 11Q2–18, 11Q20–31,* vol. 23, Discoveries in the Judaean Desert (Oxford: Clarendon, 1998).

30. Margaret Barker, *On Earth as It Is in Heaven: Temple Symbolism in the New Testament* (Edinburgh: Clark, 1995), 4–5.

31. *Assumption of Moses* 10.

32. Barker, *Great Angel,* 13–15; Barker, *Older Testament,* 127.

33. Barker, *Great Angel,* 13–15; Barker, *Older Testament,* 81–99, 147; see also Barker, *Great High Priest,* 229–61.

34. Barker, *Great High Priest,* 149.

35. Ibid., 135.

36. A translation of *Jubilees* can be found in Charlesworth, *Old Testament Pseudepigrapha,* 2:35–142.

37. *Jubilees* 2:2.

38. Barker, *Great High Priest,* 224–25.

39. For details of the holy of holies, see Barker, *Great High Priest,* 146–87.

40. Barker, *Great Angel,* 5–6.

41. Ibid.

42. Ibid., 190–95.

43. Barker, *Great High Priest,* 108–9.

44. *Numbers Rabbah* 15:10.

45. Margaret Barker, *Gate of Heaven: The History and Symbolism of the Temple in Jerusalem* (London: SPCK, 1991), 134–35; Barker, *Great Angel,* 8–9; Barker, *Revelation of Jesus Christ,* 36–37.

46. Barker, *Great High Priest,* 242.

47. Barker, *Older Testament,* 12–15, 69; Barker, *Lost Prophet,* 105–6.

48. *1 Enoch* 89:1, 36.

49. *2 Enoch* 22:9–10.

50. Barker, *Great High Priest,* 78.

51. Ibid., 51–55.

52. Ibid., 106.

53. Ibid., 34–41.

54. Margaret Barker, *The Risen Lord: The Jesus of History as the Christ of Faith* (Edinburgh: Clark, 1996), 67.

55. Ibid., 52.

56. A translation of the *History of the Rechabites* can be found in Charlesworth, *Old Testament Pseudepigrapha,* 2:443–61. For further information, see Jeffrey Thompson and John W. Welch, "The Rechabites: A Model Group in Lehi's World," in this volume, pages 611–24.

57. See Bezalel Porten and Ada Yardeni, *Textbook of Aramaic Documents from Ancient Egypt* (Jerusalem: Hebrew University, Department of the History of the Jewish People, 1986).

58. Frederick C. Gamst, *The Qemant: A Pagan-Hebraic Peasantry of Ethiopia* (New York: Holt, Rinehart and Winston, 1969).

59. E. A. Wallis Budge, *The Queen of Sheba and Her Only Son Menyelek: Being the History of the Departure of God and His Ark of the Covenant from Jerusalem to Ethiopia . . . (Kebra Nagast)* (London: Medici Society, 1922), 99–102. Also a full account is found in Graham Hancock, *The Sign and the Seal: The Quest for the Lost Ark of the Covenant* (New York: Crown, 1992).

60. Thomas F. Torrance, *China's First Missionaries: Ancient "Israelites,"* 2nd ed. (Chicago: Shaw, 1988), vii.

61. Ibid., 53, 117, 121.

62. Qurʾan 2:140.

63. Nathan Katz, *Who Are the Jews of India?* (Berkeley: University of California Press, 2000).

64. For example, see "Bartholomew, Saint," and "Thomas, Saint," in *Catholic Encyclopedia,* 2:314 and 14:658.

65. Eusebius, *History of the Church* 5.10.

66. Jerusalem Talmud *Ta'anit* 4.5g.

Chapter 18

A Seething Pot in the North: International Affairs Leading Up to Lehi's Day

John Gee

When Isaiah first became a prophet (ca. 742 B.C.), Egypt was divided in numerous petty states, each led by a different Libyan chieftain.[1] At that time, Judah and Israel were locked in strife with each other and, on occasion, with the Aramaean groups to the north[2] and the Philistine and Phoenician groups to the west. To the east, Mesopotamia was peopled by descendants of the Sumerians, Akkadians, Amorites, and Kassites (who had each ruled Babylon in previous millennia),[3] five Chaldean tribes,[4] and at least forty Aramaean tribes,[5] and the dominant power in the Near East was Assyria. By the time of Jeremiah (626–580 B.C.), just over one hundred years later, the entire political landscape of the Near East had changed. These changes had a significant impact on the political landscape in Lehi's day. The picture that emerges, even the simplified form presented here, is vast in its scope and complex in its details.[6]

Historical Overview

Isaiah maps out the political landscape in his own day (740–701 B.C.) by delineating various international powers and lifting up burdens of doom against them, prophesying that they would be overwhelmed by Assyria.[7] These nations include Babylon, Moab, Damascus, Egypt, the desert of the sea, Dumah, Arabia, the Hizayon valley, Tyre, and Israel.[8] Judah was the exception, as it was to be spared rather than conquered. Isaiah describes the conquests of Assyria (Isaiah 2–12), which was the chosen weapon to conquer all these kingdoms, and conquer it did.

In hindsight, the overall prophetic picture presented by Isaiah seems more logical than remarkable.[9] The king of Israel, Menahem (745–737 B.C.), had paid substantial tribute to Assyria as early as the reign of Tiglath-pileser III (744–727 B.C.; 2 Kings 15:19–20). The significant fragmentation of the various states in the Near East is sufficient to explain why Assyria, driven by ambitious and ruthless rulers, was the dominant empire of Isaiah's day. Furthermore, "the Assyrian military machine was skilled in crushing revolts of cities or of relatively sedentary populations (which could seldom muster sufficient manpower or resources to cope with an Assyrian onslaught)."[10] Yet the ambition and ruthlessness of the rulers and the proficiency of the troops, in and of themselves, do not explain the success of the Assyrian empire. Previous empires had conquered territory only to have the allegiance of the conquered states shift with the slightest change in policy or personal loyalty. The genius of the Assyrian empire was to break the will of the conquered people by uprooting them from their homes and deporting them en masse to other areas of the empire.[11] The result was an eventual allegiance to the empire into which they had been absorbed rather than to the ancestral homeland.[12] The Babylonians learned this lesson from the Assyrians and applied it against Judah and Jerusalem to spectacular effect (the Jews who compiled the Babylonian Talmud around A.D. 700 lived in and remained loyal to Babylon fourteen hundred years later under Muslim rule). Assyria also defeated the coalitions of various states by knocking out members piecemeal when coalition forces were unavailable to assist or were squabbling among themselves.[13]

One might wonder where the Egyptians were when the Assyrians were conquering everything in sight. During Isaiah's day, however, the Egyptians were no longer the united monarchy that they once had been. By 1080 B.C.[14] Egypt was in the hands of invading Libyan tribes. Beginning with the reign of Seti I (1291–1279 B.C.), Libyans began to invade and infiltrate Egypt,[15] principally in the Delta,[16] and "within 250 years of the beginnings of Libyan migration to Egypt, the whole country was ruled by them."[17] During the Twenty-first Dynasty, the Egyptian Delta was divided into a series of principalities ruled by a chief of the Meshwesh/Ma or Libu.[18] Even the noted high priest of Thebes, Herihor (1075 B.C.), had children with Libyan names,[19] showing his ethnic origin. Although the Libyan rulers adopted a veneer of Egyptianization, their essential core remained Libyan,[20] and they still regarded themselves as Libyan over five hundred years later.[21] The chief of the Ma (the highest title of a Libyan ruler) is still attested as late as the middle of the reign of Psammetichus I (664–656 B.C.),[22] four hundred years after the Libyan invasion. The importance of the Libyan invasion for the Old Testament can hardly be overrated: Egypt's Libyan rulers were usually too busy quarrelling among themselves to muster an army to invade anyone else—a common occurrence when Egypt was united both before and after preexilic Israel—and this allowed Israel and later Judah to exist as nations in the first place. Without the invasion of these blond-haired, blue-eyed, North African Libyan tribes, there would have been no kingdom of Israel, no kingdom of Judah, no fulfillment of land covenants to Abraham, Isaac, and Jacob, and consequently no Bible (or Book of Mormon) as we know it.

In 738, in response to the rebellion of Azriyau of Yaudi, the Assyrians under Tiglath-pileser III annexed the Aramaean state of Unqi.[23] Shortly afterwards, during the reign of Pekah in Israel (736–732 B.C.), Tiglath-pileser took a number of cities in northern Israel captive,[24] and Ahaz of Judah (735–715 B.C.) paid tribute to Assyria with many of the treasures from Solomon's temple (2 Kings 16:7–9), refashioning the altar of that temple on Assyrian lines (2 Kings 16:10). In the midst of this Assyrian land grab, the Nubian or Kushite pharaohs of the Twenty-fifth Dynasty conquered Egypt from the south, beginning with the conquest of Piye (sometimes called Pianchi)[25] in 728 B.C., which reunited that country.[26] In about 724, Tiglath-pileser's successor, Shalmaneser V, annexed the Aramaean states of Sam'al and Quwe.[27] In about 721, Shalmaneser took Israel after a three-year siege (2 Kings 17:3–6). Sargon II of Assyria annexed the Aramaean states of Hamath in 720,[28] Carchemish in 717, and Gurgum in about 711. The state Kummukhi, which had already absorbed Milid, was annexed to Assyria in 709 under Sargon II.[29] In 701 Sennacherib struck against Judah, besieging Hezekiah in Jerusalem (2 Kings 18–35; Isaiah 36–37)[30] and finally retreating after feints by the Egyptians under then general, later pharaoh, Taharqa.[31]

Unable to deal with the guerrilla warfare tactics of the Chaldean tribes in southern Mesopotamia,[32] Sennacherib went on the offensive in 694 B.C., building a fleet and sailing to attack the Chaldeans in the swamps north of the Persian Gulf. After five days in a tempest, the fleet reached the Elamite coast and attacked the Elamites and Chaldeans there. Meanwhile, the Elamites attacked Babylon, starting an uprising and capturing Assur-nadin-shumi, Babylon's governor and Assyria's crown prince.[33]

After a five-year siege, Sennacherib conquered Babylon in 689 B.C.[34] Sennacherib—furious over Babylon's betrayal of his son and heir, Assur-nadin-shumi, into the hands of the Elamite king, Hallushu-Inshushinak (694 B.C.), and the city's stubborn rebellion (which had seen two successive kings, Nergal-ushezib and Mushezib-Marduk)—looted the city, smashed or captured its idols, filled its streets with corpses, dispersed its survivors, burned it completely (demolishing its houses, temples, and walls), filled its canals with the debris, and turned it into a swamp "in order that it would not be possible to recognize the site of that city and (its) temples in the future."[35]

In 681 Sennacherib was murdered by his second son, Arda-Mulishshi, who, outmaneuvered by his brother Esarhaddon, failed to gain the throne and fled to Urartu (Ararat),[36] a recalcitrant state on the northeastern border of the Assyrian empire probably led at that time by Rusa II.[37] Urartu controlled major trade networks around Assyria from Elam to the North Syrian Aramaean states, to the Aegean, and to the Black Sea through the Taurus, Zagros, Pontic, and Anti Caucasus Mountains[38] via an elaborate system of mountain routes and fortifications around Lake Van that favored the individual or small group above the army.[39] Esarhaddon continued his conquest down the Levantine littoral, conquering Egypt in 677 and 671 B.C. Esarhaddon also appointed his two sons, Assurbanipal and Shamash-shuma-ukin, to govern Assyria and Babylon respectively, appointments that were to have disastrous consequences for the Assyrian empire. Esarhaddon died in 669 B.C. while campaigning in Egypt.[40] His son Assurbanipal conquered Egypt in 666 and again in 663 B.C.[41]

Ironically, one of the effects of the Assyrian conquest of Egypt was its reunification under Psammetichus I.[42] Psammetichus, who had started as a political vassal of Assyria,[43] once the Assyrian military left, took over the country by 656 B.C.[44] Although of Libyan descent himself,[45] learning from previous experience of the factious nature of the Libyan-style rule of Egypt, Psammetichus emphasized his pharaonic titles, rather than his office as chief of the Ma (a tribal title that previous Libyan rulers had made more important than Pharaoh), and demoted all other chiefs of the Ma to be subordinate to the harbor masters (which had previously been a much lower office).[46] Psammetichus also eliminated regional script variations by making the Demotic script—the standard business script in the Egyptian Delta where he resided—the official script of the realm,[47] as opposed to the Theban cursive hieratic now called "abnormal hieratic."[48] Psammetichus's reformation of Egyptian was to have important consequences ever after.

Psammetichus, however, relied more on Greek mercenaries to unify Egypt[49] and less on the native Egyptians, who had been frozen out of military rank advancement since the Libyan conquest.[50] Because the Egyptian military was a mercenary rather than patriotic force, it was not reliable and its characterization as a "broken reed" is well-merited.[51] Time after time, whenever there was a crucial campaign against a foreign force, the Egyptian forces crumbled.

In 652 B.C., a few years after the successful revolt of Egypt from the Assyrians and after Babylon had mustered sufficient resources, Babylonian ruler Shamash-shuma-ukin broke his oath that he had previously made "not to discuss, propose, or perform any act against [his brother] Ashurbanipal [in Assyria]."[52] It took four years for Assurbanipal to suppress the revolt.[53] The Babylonian revolt inspired other vassals to attempt to throw off the yoke, including the coastal cities of Usu and Acco, which Assurbanipal duly suppressed in 648 B.C. after the Babylonian threat was gone.[54] Assurbanipal appointed Kandalanu to govern

Babylon in Shamash-shuma-ukin's stead, which he did for the next twenty years.[55]

A crucial turning point in the history of the Near East was the fall of Assyria, which shifted the balance of the super powers to Babylon. After the deaths of Assurbanipal and Kandalanu and a year of "insurrections in Assyria and Akkad, [in which] . . . hostilities and warfare continued,"[56] Nabopolassar ascended to the throne of Babylon. He spent the first few years subduing the Assyrians.[57] In 616 B.C., to combat the increasing threat of Babylon, the Egyptians and the Assyrians joined forces but were defeated.[58] In 614 B.C. Cyaxares the Mede took Assur, and two years later (612 B.C.), Nineveh fell to Cyaxares and his Median hosts, accompanied by the Babylonian army and Scythian raiders.[59] Soon afterwards, in 610 B.C., Psammetichus I died and Necho II assumed the Egyptian throne.[60] In 609 Assur-uballit II was struggling to maintain the rule of his country and summoned Necho II for help since it was in Egypt's interest not to have a strong Babylon capable of attempting what the Assyrians had so recently done. In Jerusalem, King Josiah, whether he opposed the alliance of Egypt and Assyria or because he was pro-Babylonian, set out to oppose Necho and was slain at Megiddo (2 Kings 23:29–30). While Necho was away in a vain attempt to help the Assyrians, the kingdom of Judah chose Josiah's son Jehoahaz to rule, but three months later, a returning Necho deposed him in favor of his older brother Eliakim, whom he renamed Jehoiakim (2 Kings 23:31–37). The Scythian horsemen then swept down the Levantine coast; Jeremiah apparently thought that their coming would destroy Jerusalem and fulfill his prophecies, but they only sacked Ashkelon and passed by Jerusalem, giving Jeremiah a temporary crisis of faith.[61] In 606 B.C. the Egyptians again marched against Babylon, crossed the Euphrates at Carchemish, and defeated the Babylonians.[62] This

Reconstruction of the Processional Way leading to the Ishtar Gate at Babylon.

Excavations of ancient Babylon.

action caused Nabopolassar to send his son Nebuchadnezzar against the Egyptians, and he roundly defeated them at Carchemish (605 B.C.).[63] Babylon thus became the master of the Near East and then attacked Egypt's allies, including Judah. The international bully in Isaiah's day had been Assyria, a nation that was still a rising star; but in Lehi's and Jeremiah's day its star set and was completely destroyed. The entire international landscape had changed.

Trade Routes and Foreign Relations

Economic concerns and trade routes had an impact on foreign political policy. To the north, during the time period of the Assyrian empire (745–627 B.C.), Urartu controlled important Anatolian trade routes that effectively circumvented the Assyrian empire.[64] Some of those trade routes went through the Aramaic-speaking Aramaean states of northern Syria.[65] To the west, the seafaring Phoenicians were the dominant trade power on the Mediterranean, based in Sidon and Tyre with trade contacts and colonies as far as the Iberian Peninsula.[66] From the east, Assyria wanted to shut down or take over the Urartian trade routes because they levied taxes on the passage of goods.[67] Thus the Assyrians attacked both Urartu as well as the Aramaean states at the other end of the trade routes. At the same time, they also tried to gain control over the Phoenician cities that controlled so much of the Mediterranean trade.[68] Judah stood at the end of the frankincense trail from Arabia to the south, after which the routes continued north,[69] and the government in Jerusalem gained some income by taxing the caravans.[70] Southwest of Judah, Egypt served as a conduit for goods from locations further south in Africa[71] to the Aegean, Greece, and the Near East (see Isaiah 45:14).[72] As evidence of international connections and contacts during this age, archaeologists have uncovered evidence of Egyptian, Akkadian, and Aramaic scribes who served the Assyrian court at Nimrud.[73]

Israelite and Judean Positions

Curiously, while the Assyrians and Babylonians were the dominant powers in Lehi's century, Judah looked instead to Egypt for cultural influences in artwork, religion, and script.[74] Cylinder seals found in Jerusalem, especially royal cylinder seals, were often decorated with Egyptian and Egyptianizing motifs;[75] only a few cylinder seals from the preexilic period use Babylonian or Assyrian motifs.[76] "An examination of the overall Egyptian(izing) artifact proportions from cultic, mortuary, occupation, and combined contexts at Syro-Palestinian sites yields clear peaks in Egyptian activity during LB 1B (1450–1400 B.C.), LB 2B to Iron 1A (1200–1150 B.C.), early Iron 2B (925–850 B.C.), and late Iron 2B to Iron 2C (750–600 B.C.)."[77] Egyptian amulets proliferated in Judah at this time.[78] Judah also borrowed Egyptian numbers[79]—which are normally called "hieratic" even though the same symbols are also used in Demotic—and Egyptian terms for measurement, such as the *hin* (Egyptian *hnw*) and *ephah* (Egyptian *ip.t*). Judah's prophets continually warned her about relying on Egypt,[80] but the people decided to take the culturally and politically convenient route, which in the long run proved to be anything but convenient.

Out of the Frying Pan

The Near East in the time periods of Lehi and Jeremiah was a complex and complicated place. The sheer variety of political events, posturing, and positions; the number of ethnic and national groups; and the intricacies of feinting and subterfuge politically and militarily all show that Jeremiah's characterization of the area as a "seething pot" (Jeremiah 1:13) was apt. Lehi, because he heeded the warning voice that something wicked this way comes, escaped to a brave new world, while most of the rest of Judah fell into the toil and trouble of that cauldron's bubble.

Notes

1. Piye stele, in N.-C. Grimal, *La stèle triomphale de Pi(ʿankh)y au Musée du Caire JE 48862 et 47086–47089* (Cairo: IFAO, 1981), 2–7, 36–37, 140–41, 142–45, 176–77, pls. I, V; Assurbanipal Rassam cylinder, in Rykle Borger, *Babylonisch-assyrische Lesestücke,* 2nd ed. (Rome: Pontifical Biblical Institute, 1979), 2:336–39; Anthony Leahy, "The Libyan Period in Egypt: An Essay in Interpretation," *Libyan Studies* 16 (1985): 58–59; Robert K. Ritner, "The End of the Libyan Anarchy in Egypt: P. Rylands IX. cols. 11–12," *Enchoria* 17 (1990): 101–2.

2. Such as Unqi, Samʾal, Quwe, Hamath, Carchemish, Gurgum, Kummukhi, and Milid. The Aramaean groups were also called Neo-Hittite; for an overview, see Oliver R. Gurney, *The Hittites* (Harmondsworth: Penguin, 1990), 32–38; Edward Lipiński, *The Aramaeans: Their Ancient History, Culture, Religion* (Louvain: Peeters, 2000), 233–318.

3. Grant Frame, *Babylonia 689–627 B.C.: A Political History* (Leiden: Nederlands Historisch-Archaeologisch Instituut te Istanbul, 1992), 33–36.

4. The Bit-Amukani, Bit-Dakkuri, Bit-Yakin, Bit-Shaʾalli, and Bit Shilani; Frame, *Babylonia 689–627 B.C.,* 36–43.

5. The largest of which were the Gambulu and the Puqudu; Frame, *Babylonia 689–627 B.C.,* 43–48; Lipiński, *Aramaeans,* 409–89.

6. For specific dates, events, and people of this period, see Robert F. Smith, "Book of Mormon Event Structure: The Ancient Near East," *Journal of Book of Mormon Studies* 5/2 (1996): 98–147.

7. The discussion here follows the outline in John Gee, "'Choose the Things That Please Me': On the Selection of the Isaiah Sections in the Book of Mormon," in *Isaiah in the Book of Mormon,* ed. Donald W. Parry and John W. Welch (Provo, Utah: FARMS, 1998), 72.

8. Babylon (Isaiah 13–14), Moab (Isaiah 15–16), Damascus (Isaiah 17–18), Egypt (Isaiah 19–20), the desert of the sea (Isaiah 21:1–10), Dumah (Isaiah 21:11–12), Arabia (Isaiah 21:13–17), Hizayon valley (Isaiah 22), Tyre (Isaiah 23–25), and Israel (Isaiah 28).

9. The reaction of his contemporaries, however, shows that what seems logical in hindsight did not seem logical at the time. Isaiah 7 provides a perfect example as Ahaz's "heart was moved, and the heart of his people, as the trees of the wood are moved with the wind" (Isaiah 7:2) at what turned out to be a phantom menace (the real threat to Judah was not the Syro-Ephraimite confederacy but Assyria and the iniquity and faithlessness of the people of Judah).

10. J. A. Brinkman, "Babylonia under the Assyrian Empire, 745–627 B.C.," in *Power and Propaganda: A Symposium on Ancient Empires,* ed. Mogens T. Larsen (Copenhagen: Akademisk forlag, 1979), 235; cf. Bustenay Oded, *War, Peace and Empire: Justifications for War in Assyrian Royal Inscriptions* (Wiesbaden: Reichert, 1992), 190: "The Assyrian empire came about owing to the formidable military power of Assyria, by taking advantage of discord and internal disorder outside Assyria and by destruction of cities, deportations, pillage and coercion, and a high level of administrative organization and efficiency."

11. Bustenay Oded, *Mass Deportations and Deportees in the Neo-Assyrian Empire* (Wiesbaden: Reichert, 1979), 43–45.

12. Ibid., 46–48.

13. For example, when Kilamuwa of Sam'al hired the king of Assyria, Shalmaneser III, to deal with the king of the Danunians of Quwe; Lipiński, *Aramaeans,* 242.

14. For the date, see Kenneth A. Kitchen, *The Third Intermediate Period in Egypt (1100–650 B.C.),* 2nd ed. (Warminster: Aris & Phillips, 1986), 465.

15. Leahy, "Libyan Period in Egypt," 53.

16. Ibid., 56.

17. Ibid., 54.

18. Ibid., 54; Ritner, "End of the Libyan Anarchy," 101–2; Michel Malinine, Georges Posener, and Jean Vercoutter, *Catalogue des*

stèles du Sérapéum de Memphis (Paris: Imprimerie Nationale, 1968), 1:30–31; 2:pl. X.

19. Kitchen, *Third Intermediate Period,* 253; Leahy, "Libyan Period in Egypt," 55.

20. Leahy, "Libyan Period in Egypt," 51–62; Ritner, "End of the Libyan Anarchy in Egypt," 101.

21. Herodotus, *Histories* 2.18; Leahy, "Libyan Period in Egypt," 55.

22. Ritner, "End of the Libyan Anarchy in Egypt," 104–7.

23. Gurney, *Hittites,* 37.

24. 2 Kings 15:29: "Ijon, and Abel-beth-maachah, and Janoah, and Kedesh, and Hazor, and Gilead, and Galilee, all the land of Naphtali." The number of deportees is given in Assyrian records as 13,200. The captivity is attested archaeologically by destruction levels at "Dan, Hazor, Chinnereth, Bethsaida, Tel Hadar, ʿEn Gev, Beth-Shean, Kedesh, Megiddo, Jokneam, Qiri, Acco, Keisan, Shiqmona, and Dor. Some of these settlements never recovered from this [destruction] and were abandoned for many years (Beth-Shean, Kedesh, ʿEn Gev, Tel Hadar, and Bethsaida)." Ephraim Stern, *Archaeology of the Land of the Bible,* vol. 2, *The Assyrian, Babylonian, and Persian Periods* (New York: Doubleday, 2001), 7, 43.

25. Fundamental to the reading of the name is the discussion in Richard A. Parker, "King *Py,* a Historical Problem," *Zeitschrift für ägyptische Sprache und Altertumskunde* 93 (1966): 111–14. For a gathered list of all the hieroglyphic writings, see Jürgen von Beckerath, *Handbuch der ägyptischen Königsnamen* (Munich: Deutscher Kunstverlag, 1984), 269–70.

26. For details of the campaign, see Grimal, *La stèle triomphale de Pi(ʿankh)y.* For the date, see Kitchen, *Third Intermediate Period in Egypt,* 363–71, 592–91.

27. Gurney, *Hittites,* 37.

28. Ibid. Hamath is mentioned several times in the Bible. A major stop on the trade routes (Numbers 13:21), the border of Hamath marked the northern border of the promised land (Numbers 34:8; Joshua 13:5; Judges 3:3; 1 Kings 8:65; 1 Chronicles 13:5; 2 Chronicles 7:8; Amos 6:14). It had sent embassies to Israel under King David

(2 Samuel 8:9–10; 1 Chronicles 18:9–10) because he vanquished their southern foe Zobah (2 Samuel 8:12; 1 Chronicles 18:3). Hamath became part of Solomon's empire (1 Kings 8:65; 2 Chronicles 8:3–4). Jeroboam reannexed it into the Israelite kingdom (2 Kings 14:25, 28), but afterward it seems to have regained its independence. Inhabitants of Hamath were used to settle Samaria after its conquest by Assyria (2 Kings 17:24–33), and apparently, Assyria settled some of the Israelites in Hamath (Isaiah 11:11). For a more detailed history, see Lipiński, *Aramaeans,* 299–318.

29. Gurney, *Hittites,* 37.

30. Daniel D. Luckenbill, *The Annals of Sennacherib* (Chicago: University of Chicago Press, 1924), 31–34, 69–71, 77, 86.

31. Basic is Kenneth A. Kitchen, "Egypt, the Levant and Assyria in 701 BC," in *Fontes Atque Pontes: Eine Festgabe für Hellmut Brunner,* ed. Manfred Görg (Wiesbaden: Harrassowitz, 1983), 243–53.

32. Brinkman, "Babylonia under the Assyrian Empire," 235–36; J. A. Brinkman, "Merodach-Baladan II," in *Studies Presented to A. Leo Oppenheim* (Chicago: Oriental Institute, 1964), 18–27.

33. Brinkman, "Babylonia under the Assyrian Empire," 236.

34. Frame, *Babylonia 689–627 B.C.,* 52.

35. Ibid., 52–53. The quotation is from Luckenbill, *Annals of Sennacherib,* 83–84, 137–38.

36. Simo Parpola, "The Murderer of Sennacherib," in *Death in Mesopotamia: XXVIᵉ Rencontre assyriologique internationale,* ed. Bendt Alster (Copenhagen: Akademisk forlag, 1980), 171–82; Frame, *Babylonia 689–627 B.C.,* 64.

37. For more on the Urartian state under the reigns of Argishti II (708 B.C.) and Rusa II (673 B.C.), see Friedrich W. König, *Handbuch der chaldischen Inschriften* (Graz: Weidner, 1955–57), 151–61; and Paul E. Zimansky, *Ecology and Empire: The Structure of the Urartian State* (Chicago: Oriental Institute, 1985), 30–31, 54, 60.

38. Susan Frankenstein, "The Phoenicians in the Far West: A Function of Neo-Assyrian Imperialism," in *Power and Propaganda,* 269.

39. Zimansky, *Ecology and Empire,* 28–47.

40. Frame, *Babylonia 689–627 B.C.,* 102.

41. Kitchen, *Third Intermediate Period in Egypt,* 391–95. For Assurbanipal's campaign, see Borger, *Babylonisch-assyrische Lesestücke,* 2:336–39.

42. Nicolas Grimal, *A History of Ancient Egypt,* trans. Ian Shaw (Oxford: Blackwell, 1992), 354–58; Alan B. Lloyd, "The Late Period, 664–323 B.C.," in *Ancient Egypt: A Social History* (Cambridge: Cambridge University Press, 1983), 282–84; Alan B. Lloyd, "The Late Period (664–332 B.C.)," in *The Oxford History of Ancient Egypt,* ed. Ian Shaw (Oxford: Oxford University Press, 2000), 371–72; Erik Hornung, *History of Ancient Egypt,* trans. David Lorton (Ithaca, N.Y.: Cornell University Press, 1999), 137–39. The account in Alan Gardiner, *Egypt of the Pharaohs* (Oxford: Oxford University Press, 1963), 352–57, is now out of date.

43. Borger, *Babylonisch-assyrische Lesestücke,* 2:336–39.

44. Kitchen, *Third Intermediate Period in Egypt,* 400–408.

45. Ritner, "End of the Libyan Anarchy in Egypt," 102.

46. Ibid., 107–8. On Psammetichus I's administrative reforms, see also Hornung, *History of Ancient Egypt,* 139; Grimal, *History of Ancient Egypt,* 357.

47. Mark Depauw, *A Companion to Demotic Studies* (Brussels: Fondation Égyptologique Reine Élisabeth, 1997), 22–23; Ritner, "End of the Libyan Anarchy in Egypt," 102.

48. Michel Malinine, *Choix de textes juridiques en hiératique anormal et en démotique* (Paris: Champion, 1953), 1:iv–xvi; John Gee, "Two Notes on Egyptian Script," *Journal of Book of Mormon Studies* 5/1 (1996): 162–64; Depauw, *Companion to Demotic Studies,* 22.

49. Lloyd, "Late Period (664–332 B.C.)," 372–73; Lloyd, "The Late Period, 664–323 B.C.," 284; Hornung, *History of Ancient Egypt,* 139; Grimal, *History of Ancient Egypt,* 354–55.

50. Lloyd, "The Late Period, 664–323 B.C.," 309, notes that "most, if not all, of the warrior class originated from Libyan mercenaries who had settled in Egypt during the New Kingdom or had subsequently infiltrated the country where they were probably permitted to take up residence on condition that they provided military service to

the Crown when called upon to do so." See also Lloyd, "Late Period (664–332 B.C.)," 372.

51. "Lo, thou trusteth in the staff of this broken reed, on Egypt; whereon if a man lean, it will go into his hand, and pierce it: so is Pharaoh king of Egypt to all that trust in him" (Isaiah 36:6; cf. 2 Kings 18:21).

52. Frame, *Babylonia 689–627 B.C.*, 102, 131–90.

53. Ibid., 188–90.

54. Ibid., 136.

55. Ibid., 191–92.

56. *Akitu Chronicle* 25–26, in Albert K. Grayson, *Assyrian and Babylonian Chronicles* (Locust Valley, N.Y.: Augustin, 1975), 132; Frame, *Babylonia 689–627 B.C.*, 210–13.

57. *Chronicle Concerning the Early Years of Nabopolassar,* in Grayson, *Assyrian and Babylonian Chronicles,* 87–90.

58. *Fall of Nineveh Chronicle,* in Grayson, *Assyrian and Babylonian Chronicles,* 91–92.

59. S. Kent Brown, "History and Jeremiah's Crisis of Faith," in *Isaiah and the Prophets,* ed. Monte S. Nyman (Provo, Utah: BYU Religious Studies Center, 1984), 113.

60. Grimal, *History of Egypt,* 359.

61. Brown, "History and Jeremiah's Crisis of Faith," 105–18.

62. *Chronicle Concerning the Later Years of Nabopolassar* 1–26, in Grayson, *Assyrian and Babylonian Chronicles,* 97–98.

63. *Chronicle Concerning the Later Years of Nabopolassar* 27–28, in Grayson, *Assyrian and Babylonian Chronicles,* 98; *Chronicle Concerning the Early Years of Nebuchadnezzar II* 1–8, in Grayson, *Assyrian and Babylonian Chronicles,* 99.

64. Frankenstein, "Phoenicians in the Far West," 269.

65. Ibid., 271.

66. Ibid., 278–86.

67. J. N. Postgate, "The Economic Structure of the Assyrian Empire," in *Power and Propaganda,* 214.

68. Frankenstein, "Phoenicians in the Far West," 269–73.

69. M. Elat, "The Monarchy and the Development of Trade in

Ancient Israel," in *State and Temple Economy in the Ancient Near East,* ed. Edward Lipiński (Louvain: Departement Oriëntalistiek, 1979), 2:535.

70. Ibid., 2:535–36.

71. Indicative (although it applies to the Ptolemaic period) is François Daumas, "Les textes géographiques du trésor D' du temple de Dendara," in *State and Temple Economy,* 2:689–705.

72. Lloyd, "The Late Period (664–332 B.C.)," 374–76; Grimal, *History of Ancient Egypt,* 355.

73. ND 10048, line 19, in J. V. Kinnier Wilson, *The Nimrud Wine Lists,* Cuneiform Texts from Nimrud 1 (London: British School of Archaeology in Iraq, 1972), pl. 20.

74. Described as "intensive Egyptian activity." Stern, *Archaeology of the Land of the Bible,* 228.

75. Nahman Avigad and Benjamin Sass, *Corpus of West Semitic Stamp Seals* (Jerusalem: Israel Academy of Sciences and Humanities, The Israel Exploration Society, and the Institute of Archaeology, The Hebrew University of Jerusalem, 1997), 50 #3, 51 #4–5, 53 #11, 55 #16, 60 #29, 63 #37, 65 #44, 66 #46, 69 #57, 70 #59, 76–77 #82, 77 #85, 81 #99, 82–83 #103, 83 #104, 84 #108, 85 #112, 86 #116, 89–90 #126–27, 92 #135, 94 #143, 95 #146, 98–99 #159–60, 100 #163, 101 #168, 106 #182, 107 #185, 108 #188, #190, 109 #193–94, 110–11 #198, 112 #203, 113 #206, 118 #226, 122 #243, 128 #267, 133 #284, 137 #298, 142 #316, 143 #320, 144 #325, 145 #328, 149 #343, 150 #345, 157 #369–70, 159 #377, 160 #381, 161–62 #385, 164 #394, 165 #397, 192 #473, 193 #475, 235 #639, 243 #662, 252 #685, 253–54 #689, 263 #711.

76. Examples include Avigad and Sass, *Corpus of West Semitic Stamp Seals,* 49 #2, 62 #34, 81–82 #100, 86 #115, 97 #154, 103 #173, 163 #391, 170–71 #400–402.

77. Gregory D. Mumford, "International Relations between Egypt, Sinai, and Syria-Palestine during the Late Bronze Age to Early Persian Period (Dynasties 18–26: c. 1550–525 B.C.): A Spatial and Temporal Analysis of the Distribution and Proportions of Egyptian(izing) Artifacts and Pottery in Sinai and Selected Sites in Syria-Palestine" (Ph.D. diss., University of Toronto, 1998), 4:3986.

78. See Othmar Keel, *Corpus der Stempelsiegel-Amulette aus Palästina/Israel: Von den Anfängen bis zur Perserzeit* (Freiburg: Vandenhoeck and Ruprecht, 1995), and Claudia Müller-Winkler, *Die ägyptische Objekt-Amulette* (Freiburg: Vandenhoeck and Ruprecht, 1987).

79. Yohanan Aharoni, "The Use of Hieratic Numerals in Hebrew Ostraca and the Shekel Weights," *Bulletin of the American School of Oriental Research* 184 (1966): 13–19; Ivan T. Kaufman, "New Evidence for Hieratic Numerals on Hebrew Weights," *Bulletin of the American School of Oriental Research* 188 (1967): 39–41; Yohanan Aharoni, "A 40-Shekel Weight with a Hieratic Numeral," *Bulletin of the American School of Oriental Research* 201 (1971): 35–36.

80. Isaiah 19–20; 30:2–3; 31:1; 36:6–9; Jeremiah 2:14–19, 31–37; 24:8–10; 25:15–33; 37:6–10; 42:13–22; 43:1–13; 44:1–30; 46:1–28; Ezekiel 17:11–21; 20:5–9; 29:1–21; 30:1–26; 32:1–21; Joel 3:18–21; Nahum 3:1–10.

Chapter 19

The Divine Justification for the Babylonian Destruction of Jerusalem

Bruce Satterfield

In January 588 B.C., Nebuchadnezzar, king of Babylon, laid siege against Jerusalem (see 2 Kings 25; 2 Chronicles 36; Jeremiah 52). For over a year, the Jews suffered the effects of the siege. As famine set in, morale among the Jews sank. Because of their weakened condition, plagues of one kind or another began to afflict the people (Jeremiah 14:12; 27:8, 13). Eventually, the food supply was depleted, and many resorted to cannibalism (Jeremiah 19:9; Lamentations 2:20; 4:10; Ezekiel 5:10). Finally, in July 587 B.C., the Babylonians broke through the walls and began pillaging and looting the city. Many Jews were slaughtered. The city, temple, and walls were razed to the ground. Those not killed were taken captive to Babylon, except for some of the peasantry. All that was left of Jerusalem was ash and rubble. Sadly, the prophet Jeremiah, who had witnessed the destruction, wrote, "How doth the city sit solitary, that was full of people! how is she become as a widow! she that was great among the nations, and princess among the provinces, how is she become tributary!" (Lamentations 1:1).

Why did God allow such horrible misery and destruction to come upon his chosen people? The answer given in the scriptures is because of the wickedness of the people of Jerusalem (e.g., Jeremiah 36:31; Ezekiel 8–9; 22–23; 1 Nephi 1:13; 3:17). But why does the Lord destroy wicked people? At least one reason is offered in the scriptures. Nephi observed: "For the Spirit of the Lord will not always strive with man. And when the Spirit ceaseth to strive with man then cometh speedy destruction, and this grieveth my soul" (2 Nephi 26:11).

This study seeks to identify the spiritual symptoms that accompany the loss of the Spirit of the Lord (or the Light of Christ)[1] and that justify the destruction of a wicked society. After reviewing the teachings of past and present prophets regarding the causes and consequences of losing the Spirit of the Lord, I will show from the writings of Jeremiah and Ezekiel how the people of Jerusalem jeopardized their access to the Light of Christ, thus justifying their destruction.

Accountability and the Loss of the Spirit

Agency of Man

In order to understand why the Lord justifies the destruction of societies who have lost the Light of Christ, one must first understand the relationship between the Light of Christ and agency. The principle of agency is an eternal one essential to all the activities of God regarding his children. In fact, the war in heaven was fought over the issue of agency. The Book of Moses records: "Wherefore, because that Satan rebelled against me, and sought to destroy the agency of man, which I, the Lord God, had given him, . . . I caused that he should be cast down" (Moses 4:3). Elder Bruce R. McConkie explained, "Agency underlies all things—all advancement, all progression, even existence itself."[2] Agency is basic to God's plan of salvation, including the creation of the earth, the fall of Adam, the mortal probation of man, and the atonement of Jesus Christ, all designed to make possible the exaltation of God's children. "Inherent in the whole system of salvation," Elder McConkie taught, "is the eternal law of agency. All of the terms and conditions of the Lord's eternal plan operate because man has his agency, *and none of it would have efficacy, virtue, or force if there were no agency.*"[3]

Lehi set out the conditions that must exist before agency can be exercised. First, there must be opposing choices (2 Nephi 2:15). Second, both choices must be enticing. Said he, "Wherefore, the Lord God gave unto man that he should act for himself. Wherefore, man could not act for himself save it should be that he was enticed by the one or the other" (2 Nephi 2:16). As Elder Harold B. Lee commented, "Father Lehi explained to his son that in order to accomplish that eternal purpose there must be opposition in all things, and that to every individual upon the earth there had to be given the right of free agency and also that *there must be in the world the power to entice to do evil and the power to entice to do good.*"[4]

The Book of Mormon teaches that on the one hand the Spirit of Christ is the agent that entices men and women to do good (Moroni 7:16–17). On the other hand, it is the "the will of the flesh and the evil which is therein, which giveth the spirit of the devil power to captivate" that entices men and women to do evil (2 Nephi 2:29). Without the Spirit of Christ there would be no opposing enticements and, therefore, no agency. With evil as the only enticement, man would forever become evil with no hope of change.

An Immanent Power

What is the Spirit of Christ, the Light of Christ, the Spirit of Truth, or the Spirit of God? President Lee taught that every man born into this world is given "an endowment of that first light which is called the Light of Christ, the Spirit of Truth, or the Spirit of God."[5] What is the nature of this light? This is not easily answered. Elder McConkie wrote:

> There is a spirit—the Spirit of the Lord, the Spirit of Christ, the light of truth, the light of Christ—that defies description and is beyond mortal comprehension. It is in us and in all things; it is around us and around all things; it fills the earth and the heavens and the universe. It is everywhere, in all immensity, without exception; it is an indwelling, immanent, ever-present, never-absent spirit. It has neither shape nor form nor personality. It is not an entity nor a person nor a personage. It has no agency, does not act independently, and exists not to act but to be acted upon.[6]

From the scriptures we learn that this "light proceedeth forth from the presence of God to fill the immensity of space—The light which is in all things, which giveth life to all things, which is the law by which all things are governed, even the power of God who sitteth upon his throne, who is in the bosom of eternity, who is in the midst of all things" (D&C 88:12–13). Thus the Light of Christ is an all-encompassing power that emanates from God. President Joseph F. Smith explained that the Light of Christ "proceeds from the source of intelligence, which permeates all nature, which lighteth every man and fills the immensity of space. You may call it the Spirit of God, you may call it the influence of God's intelligence, you may call it the substance of his power, no matter what it is called, it is the spirit of intelligence that permeates the universe and gives to the spirits of men understanding, just as Job has said. (Job 32:8; Doc. and Cov. 88:3–13.)"[7]

Sometimes the Light of Christ and the Holy Ghost are thought to be the same. This is not so. Elder Joseph Fielding Smith explained:

> The Holy Ghost, as we are taught in our modern revelation, is the third member in the Godhead and a personage of Spirit. These terms are used synonymously: Spirit of God, Spirit of the Lord, Spirit of Truth, Holy Spirit, Comforter; all having reference to the Holy Ghost. The same terms largely are used in relation to the Spirit of Jesus Christ, also called the Light of Truth, Light of Christ, Spirit of God, and Spirit of the Lord; and yet they are separate and distinct things.[8]

Perhaps the reason for the confusion is that the Holy Ghost uses the medium of the Light of Christ to carry out his divine mission. As President Marion G. Romney taught: "There are three phases of the light of Christ that I want to mention. The first one is the light which enlighteneth every man that cometh into the world; The second phase is the gift of the Holy Ghost; And the third is the more sure word of prophecy."[9]

The Light of Christ and Man's Conscience

What must be clear is that any degree of the Light of Christ manifested to man can be nullified through the effects of sin. The difference between losing the influence of the Holy Ghost as opposed to the Light of Christ is this: the Holy Ghost is easily offended whereas the Light of Christ, though sinned against, will continue to strive with man until totally and consistently ignored.

The reason for the persistence of the Light of Christ is that without it there is no agency. In part, the first phase of the Light of Christ manifests itself as man's conscience. According to President Joseph F. Smith, it is by means of this Spirit that "every man is enlightened, the wicked as well as the good, the intelligent and the ignorant, the high and the low, each in accordance with his capacity to receive the light; and this Spirit or influence which emanates from God may be said to constitute man's consciousness."[10] In line with this, Elder McConkie wrote, "By virtue of this endowment all men automatically and intuitively know right from wrong *and are encouraged and enticed to do what is right* (Moro. 7:16.)."[11]

Without the Light of Christ there would be no agency. With no enticement for good, man would naturally give way to the enticement for evil. Therefore, the scriptures teach that the Light of Christ "strives" to be with man (D&C 1:33).

The Loss of the Spirit Brings Destruction

The scriptures teach that it is possible to lose the Light of Christ. The Lord has repeatedly said, "my Spirit shall not always strive with man" (D&C 1:33; cf. Genesis 6:3; 2 Nephi 26:11; Ether 2:15; Moses 8:17). It follows that when the Spirit is lost there is a loss of agency. In such a condition, man is unable to act for himself, a condition that violates the plans of God. When a society as a whole reaches the point that the Light of Christ no longer strives with it, then it is "ripe for destruction." As stated earlier, "For the Spirit of the Lord will not always strive with man. And when the Spirit ceaseth to strive with man *then cometh speedy destruction,* and this grieveth my soul" (2 Nephi 26:11).

Such was the condition of the people in the days of Noah (Moses 8:17–30) and apparently the inhabitants of Sodom and

Gomorrah. Elder Neal A. Maxwell explained: "Being a loving Father, though deeply devoted to our free agency, there are times in human history when He simply could not continue to send spirits to this earth who would have had virtually no chance. This was the case with Sodom and Gomorrah and the cities of the plains."[12] "The children born into these cities had no choice at all left to them. Such was the conformity in wickedness that babes could be born free, but not remain agents unto themselves."[13] Likewise, John Taylor, then an apostle of the church, reasoned:

> Because in forsaking God, they lose sight of their eternal existence, corrupt themselves, and entail misery on their posterity. Hence it was better to destroy a few individuals, than to entail misery on many. And hence the inhabitants of the old world, and of the cities of Sodom and Gomorrah were destroyed, because it was better for them to die, and thus be deprived of their agency, which they abused, than entail so much misery on their posterity, and bring ruin upon millions of unborn persons.[14]

Characteristics of Those Who Have Lost Light

It is pertinent to this study to formalize at least a partial list of features that characterize those who have placed themselves in the position of losing the Light of Christ. In so doing, I am cognizant of the fact that the Lord has not made a full disclosure of this subject. However, the scriptures and the prophets have taught enough to formalize a partial list that can be utilized in examining the writings of Jeremiah and Ezekiel. The following can be deduced:

1. Repetition of sin, making it difficult to repent. As one continues to rationalize sin, it becomes nearly impossible to repent. President Spencer W. Kimball wrote, "A man may rationalize and excuse himself till the groove is so deep he cannot get out without great difficulty. . . . And if the yielding person continues to give way he may finally reach the point of 'no return.' The Spirit will 'not always strive with man.' (D&C 1:33.)"[15] This is the most damnable aspect of continuing in sin. "Free agency," declared President Romney,

> possessed by any one person is increased or diminished by the use to which he puts it. Every wrong decision one makes restricts the area in which he can thereafter exercise his agency. The further one goes in the making of wrong decisions in the exercise of free agency, the more difficult it is for him to recover the lost ground. One can, by persisting long enough, reach the point of no return. He then becomes an abject slave. By the exercise of his free agency, he has decreased the area in which he can act, almost to the vanishing point.[16]

2. Rationalization of sin. The "will" of the sinner is often manifested in rationalizing or excusing sin. President Kimball observed: "When people know right from wrong and find themselves in the broad way to destruction, they have two ways to go. They may repent and cleanse themselves and obtain eventual peace and joy, or they may *rationalize and excuse themselves and try the 'escape' road.* Those who follow the latter road sometimes so completely rationalize that they become calloused and lose the desire to repent, until the Spirit of God ceases to strive with them."[17] Such rationalization is due to an individual's unresponsiveness to the things of God.

3. State of rebellion. Additionally, the attitude of the sinner toward sin plays a major role in the loss of the Spirit. George Albert Smith said: "The spirit of God continues to strive with men everywhere, as long as they make the effort to keep his commandments. *When men abandon the truth, refuse to do the right,* the Lord of necessity withdraws his spirit and men are left to the buffetings of the adversary."[18] Likewise, President Kimball cautioned: "Conscience warns but does not govern. Conscience tells the individual when he is entering forbidden worlds, and it continues to prick until silenced by *the will* or by *sin's repetition*."[19]

4. *Seared conscience.* Those who continually defy the Light of Christ and commit sin sear "their conscience as with a hot iron" (1 Timothy 4:2 JST). Speaking of the Light of Christ, Elder McConkie wrote: "All men receive this Spirit, but not all hearken to its voice. Many choose to walk in carnal paths and go contrary to the enticings of the Spirit. It is possible to sear one's conscience to the point that the Spirit will withdraw its influence and men will no longer know or care about anything that is decent and edifying."[20] The scriptures refer to those who, through seared consciences, have reached this point as "past feeling" (Ephesians 4:19; 1 Nephi 17:45; Moroni 9:20). This is a dangerous position to be in, for the sinner is no longer aware that he is sinning. Elder Maxwell noted, "The more coarse and crude people become, the less they are aware of it. . . . A predator does not know he is a predator, for he is 'past feeling.'"[21]

5. *Rejection of the prophets.* Those who will not heed the warning voice of their own conscience will likewise not listen to the warning voice of God's prophets who are sent to stall their downward fall. Being "past feeling," declared Elder Maxwell, they cannot "'feel' the words of God or his prophets."[22] Indeed, rejecting the Lord's prophets is an indicator that the Light of Christ is nearly gone out or has ceased altogether within a person or society. Nephi observed of the Jews in his day, "For behold, the Spirit of the Lord ceaseth soon to strive with them; for behold, they have rejected the prophets" (1 Nephi 7:14).

6. *Continual sin.* Men lose the Light of Christ when they continually sin against the light. Speaking to the brother of Jared, the Lord said: "Ye shall remember that my Spirit will not always strive with man; wherefore, if ye will sin until ye are fully ripe ye shall be cut off from the presence of the Lord" (Ether 2:15).

Lehi's Jerusalem and the Loss of the Spirit

The writings of Jeremiah and Ezekiel witness that the inhabitants of Jerusalem were "ripe for destruction." They reveal that, generally speaking, the Jews exhibited all the characteristics of those who have jeopardized their access to the Light of Christ. As a consequence, they refused all enticement for good. Therefore, like the Nephites whose "destruction [was] made sure" (Helaman 13:38) because "the Spirit of the Lord hath already ceased to strive with their fathers" (Mormon 5:16), the Lord allowed their destruction.

The century before the prophet Jeremiah began his ministry saw two major religious reforms instituted by the kings of Judah involving the removal of "high places" of worship (whether to Jehovah or pagan deities), the eradication of both foreign and domestic idol worship, a refurbishing of the temple built by Solomon, and a reemphasis of the observance of the Mosaic code. The first was initiated by Hezekiah (ca. 715–687 b.c.) as recorded in 2 Kings 18 and 2 Chronicles 29–31. However, Hezekiah's son, Manasseh (ca. 687–642 b.c.), reversed his father's reform policies (see 2 Kings 21; 2 Chronicles 33). This had the effect of causing "Judah and the inhabitants of Jerusalem to err, *and to do worse than the heathen, whom the Lord had destroyed before the children of Israel*" (2 Chronicles 33:9, emphasis added). Some years after Manasseh's death, his grandson, Josiah (ca. 642–609 B.C.), initiated a second reform (see 2 Kings 22–23; 2 Chronicles 34–35).

Though Josiah's reforms were more aggressive and further reaching than Hezekiah's, their ultimate effects upon the people of Jerusalem were not beneficially lasting. This was so because the reversal of Hezekiah's reforms by Manasseh proved disastrous for Judah. As evidenced by the Lord's intervention against the Assyrians (2 Chronicles 32), Hezekiah's people found themselves in the Lord's good graces after they had eradicated idolatry and refocused their attention toward the law of Moses. But with Manasseh's reversal of his father's religious reforms, Judah's former sins returned. This placed the Jews in a spiritually dangerous position. The Lord has said, "Go your ways and sin no more; but unto that soul who sinneth shall the former sins return" (D&C 82:7). With the return of sins comes a return of punishment. Even worse, a greater darkness envelopes the sinner than experienced before his repentance. Mormon observed, "After a people have been once enlightened by the Spirit of God, and have had great knowledge of things pertaining to righteousness, and then have fallen away into sin and transgression, they become more hardened, and thus their state becomes worse than though they had never known these things" (Alma 24:30). Consequently, Josiah's reforms were not able to dislodge the sinful nature of the people of Judah. The reformation made by Josiah's people was outward only; little inward transformation had taken place (for example, when the prophet Jeremiah taught in the temple that the recently cleansed temple would not preserve them unless they repented of their many sins; Jeremiah 7 and 26). This is why the writer of 2 Kings informs the reader that in spite of Josiah's religious reforms, "The Lord turned not from the fierceness of his great wrath, wherewith his anger was kindled against Judah, because of all the provocations that Manasseh had provoked him withal. And the Lord said, I will remove Judah also out of my sight, as I have removed Israel, and will cast off this city Jerusalem which I have chosen, and the house of which I said, My name shall be there" (2 Kings 23:26–27).

The Witness of Jeremiah

Living in the aftermath of Josiah's reform, Jeremiah witnessed the sinful nature and rebellious heart of Judah. He could see that unless true reform was made, Judah would fall prey to the wrath of Jehovah and would be destroyed. The Lord called Jeremiah to warn the Jews of their eventual destruction if they did not repent. His call came about a year after King Josiah began his reform (compare 2 Chronicles 34:3 and Jeremiah 1:2).[23]

In an early prophecy uttered "in the ears of Jerusalem" (Jeremiah 2:1; cf. 2:1–4:4), Jeremiah levied several charges against the people. This prophecy reveals that the Jews were exhibiting some of the characteristics of those whose actions have minimized the effects of the Light of Christ in their lives. Note the following:

1. Repetition of sin, making it difficult to repent. In Jeremiah 2:20–22, Jeremiah stated that early in Israel's history, all Israel broke the yoke (covenant) they made with Jehovah and said they would not serve God.[24] Israel, including the Jews of Jerusalem, was compared to a harlot "upon every high hill and under every green tree"; a "noble vine . . . turned into the degenerate plant of a strange vine"; and a person who had washed themselves with "much soap" to remove a deep-rooted stain but were unable to do so. William McKane has noted that these verses "agree in their estimate of the deep-seated character of Israel's sinfulness and express a scepticism about the possibility of reformation. . . . Deeply ingrained habits have brought about an inner perversion so fundamental that repentance, a change of heart and new patterns of behaviour, would seem to be ruled out."[25] This seems to be an apt description of perhaps one of the most damnable characteristics of a society losing the Light of Christ. The metaphor of washing with soap but remaining spiritually unclean was an accurate portrayal of the Jew's response to Josiah's reforms. Through Jeremiah, the Lord said, "Judah hath not turned unto me with her whole heart, but feignedly, saith the Lord" (Jeremiah 3:10). Though outward changes had been made, the inner struggle to return to former practices was too great.

2. *Rationalization of sin.* Some justified their actions, feeling it was impossible to get out of the rut they had made, exclaiming, "There is no hope: no; for I have loved strangers [i.e., foreign religious practices], and after them will I go" (Jeremiah 2:25). Others did not believe that what they were doing was wrong: "Because I am innocent, surely his anger shall turn from me" (Jeremiah 2:35). Generally, the Jews had lost their desire to follow God. "We are lords [Heb. *radnu,* 'we wander or roam restlessly'])," they said. "We will come no more unto thee?" (Jeremiah 2:31). These statements of justification reflect a lack of conscience, showing that the Spirit of the Lord was being ignored. Therefore, Jeremiah ended his prophecy with a call for repentance: "Break up your fallow ground, and sow not among thorns. Circumcise yourselves to the Lord, and take away the foreskins of your heart" (Jeremiah 4:3–4). More evidence that the people were losing the Light of Christ is found in another prophecy (Jeremiah 5–6) pronounced proba-bly towards the end of Josiah's reign.

3. *State of rebellion.* Jeremiah berated the wickedness that had saturated Jerusalem, saying, "Run ye to and fro through the streets of Jerusalem, and see now, and know, and seek in the broad places thereof, if ye can find a man, if there be any that

executeth judgment, that seeketh the truth; and I will pardon it [i.e., forgive Jerusalem]" (Jeremiah 5:1). Any real attempt to do this would have been futile for "this people hath a revolting [Heb. *sorer,* 'stubborn'] and a rebellious heart; they are revolted and gone" (Jeremiah 5:23).

4. *Seared conscience.* Neither were they conscience-stricken. "Were they ashamed when they had committed abomination?" the Lord asked. "Nay, they were not at all ashamed, neither could they blush" (Jeremiah 6:15).

5. *Rejection of the prophets.* Since Josiah's religious reforms had little effect on the spiritual nature of his people, Jeremiah warned that the Lord would "bring a nation upon [them] from far" that would "impoverish [their] fenced cities, wherein [they trusted], with the sword" (Jeremiah 5:15, 17). This was a prophecy of the Babylonian siege of 598–597 B.C. (around 600 B.C. in Book of Mormon chronology), the year before Lehi was called to be a prophet. The siege, however, would not render Jerusalem completely destroyed: "Nevertheless in those days, saith the Lord, I will not make a full end with you" (Jeremiah 5:18). This would prove two things. First, Jeremiah's prophecies were true. Second, the Lord still loved his people, for he would allow them one more opportunity to repent. The offer of repentance reveals that though entrenched in sin, there was still hope for the people of Jerusalem. As Josiah's reign came to an end, the Light of Christ was flickering in the winds of sin. Yet the Spirit was still striving with the Jews. But during the reign of Josiah's son, Jehoiakim, who reigned from 609–598 B.C., the light was all but blown out. Under Jehoiakim, Josiah's reform policies came to an end. Immediately, things went from bad to worse.

In the first year of Jehoiakim's reign, Jeremiah stood in the gate of the temple; speaking in the name of the Lord, he delivered a sermon denouncing the wickedness of the Jews and offering them a chance to repent (Jeremiah 7 and 26).[26] The Jews had come to believe that their pretended reforms were enough to turn away Jehovah's wrath. Therefore, they believed they could continue in sin without consequence. Through Jeremiah, the Lord said: "Will ye steal, murder, and commit adultery, and swear falsely, and burn incense unto Baal, and walk after other gods whom ye know not; And come and stand before me in this house, which is called by my name, and say, We are delivered to do all these abominations?" (Jeremiah 7:9–10).

He then reminded them what happened to the tabernacle at Shiloh in the days of Eli, whose sons, as well as all Israel, continually committed sin. Though sinning against Jehovah, they believed that by carrying the ark of the covenant into battle, the Lord would fight in their behalf anyway. Instead, they lost the battle. Additionally, the ark was captured (see 1 Samuel 4) and Shiloh, where the tabernacle was erected, was destroyed. Thus the Lord said, "But go ye now unto my place which was in Shiloh, where I set my name at the first, and see what I did to it for the wickedness of my people Israel" (Jeremiah 7:12; cf. Psalm 78:60–64).

Yet, for all this, the Jews had not passed the point of no return. The Lord offered hope: "Amend your ways and your doings, and I will cause you to dwell in this place" (Jeremiah 7:3).

The initial response of the leaders to Jeremiah's denunciation was to sentence Jeremiah to death, "for he hath prophesied against this city" (Jeremiah 26:11). However, Jeremiah immediately rebuked them, saying, "amend your ways and your doings, and obey the voice of the Lord your God; and repent, and the Lord will turn away the evil that he hath pronounced against you" (Jeremiah 26:13 JST). This unnerved some of the leaders. "This man is not worthy to die," they said, "for he hath spoken to us in the name of the Lord our God" (Jeremiah 26:16). This incident demonstrates that early in the reign of Jehoiakim, there still was some respect for God's prophets among the people. There was still hope.

But hope was diminishing. The Chronicler tells us that Jehoiakim "did that which was evil in the sight of the Lord his God" (2 Chronicles 36:5; also 2 Kings 23:37). The Lord sent prophets, including Jeremiah, warning him to repent. But he refused to hear them. Therefore, Jeremiah said to him: "I have spoken unto you, rising early and speaking; but ye have not hearkened. And the Lord hath sent unto you all his servants the prophets, rising early and sending them; but ye have not hearkened, nor inclined your ear to hear" (Jeremiah 25:3–4). Refusal to heed the Lord's prophets is another sign that the Light of Christ was nearly extinguished in the life of the king.

As the king went, so went the people. They became more stubborn, refusing to follow any of the commands of Jehovah through the prophets. Further, they disregarded the law of Moses, the basis of the covenant made between God and Israel. In response, the Lord told Jeremiah to publicly proclaim to the people: "Hear ye the words of this covenant, and do them" (Jeremiah 11:6). Continuing: "For I earnestly protested unto your fathers in the day that I brought them up out of the land of Egypt, even unto this day, rising early and protesting, saying, Obey my voice. Yet they obeyed not, nor inclined their ear, but walked every one in the imagination of their evil heart" (Jeremiah 11:7–8). Therefore, the Lord said, the curses specified in the covenant (Deuteronomy 28) would be levied against them.

Scriptural history records that these curses often caused Israel to return to the Lord, albeit briefly. In the days of Josiah,

the return to the Lord was emphasized through covenant renewal where the people swore they would obey Jehovah (see
2 Kings 23:3). But in the days of Jehoiakim, the covenant was
purposefully rejected. Therefore, the Lord said: "A conspiracy
is found among the men of Judah, and among the inhabitants
of Jerusalem. They are turned back to the iniquities of their
forefathers, which refused to hear my words; and they went
after other gods to serve them" (Jeremiah 11:9–10). This apostasy was not limited to the rulers, the aristocracy, or the priesthood. Rather, it was widespread among all the people of Judah.
"For according to the number of thy cities were thy gods, O
Judah; and according to the number of the streets of Jerusalem
have ye set up altars to that shameful thing, even altars to burn
incense unto Baal" (Jeremiah 11:13).

6. *Continual sin.* Finally, an incident happened in Jehoiakim's reign that sealed his fate and that of his people.[27] The Lord
had Jeremiah write on a scroll all the prophecies and warnings
that had been given him. He then wanted the scroll read to all
the people. "It may be," the Lord said to Jeremiah, "that the
house of Judah will hear all the evil which I purpose to do unto
them; that they may return every man from his evil way; that I
may forgive their iniquity and their sin" (Jeremiah 36:3).

Jeremiah had his scribe Baruch go to the temple and read
the scroll to the people who had gathered to fast. But there is no
evidence that this had any effect whatsoever. In fact, the Jewish
officials who were present reported the incident to Jehoiakim,
who demanded to hear what was written on the scroll. As the
scroll was being read, Jehoiakim took a small knife and cut each
column that had been read and threw it in the fire. This he did
"until all the roll was consumed in the fire. . . . Yet they were
not afraid, nor rent their garments, neither the king, nor any

of his servants that heard all these words" (Jeremiah 36:23–24). Jehoiakim then sent a guard to arrest Jeremiah and Baruch, "but the Lord hid them" (Jeremiah 36:26).

This was a telling point. Jehoiakim and the other rulers had become past feeling and calloused, paying no head to the Light of Christ. They had no regard for the Lord nor his prophet. Further, there was no evidence that this situation would change. As a consequence, the Lord told Jeremiah to tell the king, "He shall have none to sit upon the throne of David: and his dead body shall be cast out in the day to the heat, and in the night to the frost. And I will punish him and his seed and his servants for their iniquity; and I will bring upon them, and upon the inhabitants of Jerusalem, and upon the men of Judah, all the evil that I have pronounced against them; but they hearkened not" (Jeremiah 36:30–31).

Jerusalem's destruction was now sure. Jehovah's "words of judgments against the people were no longer simply scenarios for warning, but rather plans to be carried out: repentance was no longer to be expected, and the people stood under irrevocable judgment."[28]

Jerusalem being doomed by her wickedness, the Lord commanded Jeremiah,

> Thou shalt not take thee a wife, neither shalt thou have sons or daughters in this place. For thus saith the Lord concerning the sons and concerning the daughters that are born in this place, and concerning their mothers that bare them, and concerning their fathers that begat them in this land; They shall die of grievous deaths; they shall not be lamented; neither shall they be buried; but they shall be as dung upon the face of the earth: and they shall be consumed by the sword, and by famine; and their carcases

shall be meat for the fowls of heaven, and for the beasts of the earth. (Jeremiah 16:2–4)

As prophesied, the Babylonians besieged Jerusalem in December 597 B.C. That same month Jehoiakim died. His son, Jehoiachin, reigned in his place. However, after three months of siege, Jerusalem surrendered. Many Jews, including Jehoiachin, were taken to Babylon. Jehoiachin's brother, Zedekiah, was placed on the throne by Nebuchadnezzar. During the reign of Zedekiah, the Jews were given one more chance for repentance. Like Mormon—who, knowing that "the day of grace was passed" for his people (Mormon 2:15), continued to preach repentance (Mormon 3:2–3)—prophets were sent throughout Jerusalem "prophesying unto the people that they must repent, or the great city Jerusalem must be destroyed" (1 Nephi 1:4).

It may seem strange that the Lord offered the Jews another chance for repentance when their fate was already sealed. However, the fate of the whole is not necessarily the destiny of each individual.[29] Though Jerusalem would be destroyed, repentance by individuals was still possible. This was so because the Light of Christ was not all together extinguished. Evidence of this is found in the Book of Mormon. Many who had survived the Babylonian siege, such as Lehi, had not rebelled against God but had remained faithful. Even after Lehi and his family fled Jerusalem, the Light of Christ was still striving with the people there. Speaking of those living in Jerusalem at this time, Nephi said, "the Spirit of the Lord ceaseth soon to strive with them" (1 Nephi 7:14), suggesting that the Light of Christ was still there to some degree. And where the Light of Christ exists, there is hope.

But the chance for repentance was refused, and hope was vanquished. The people rejected the warnings of the prophets and continued in their wickedness. Therefore, in a letter written during the reign of Zedekiah to the Jews who had been exiled in Babylon after the siege of 597 B.C., Jeremiah wrote the word of the Lord concerning those who remained in Jerusalem:

> Behold, I will send upon them the sword, the famine, and the pestilence, and will make them like vile figs, that cannot be eaten, they are so evil. And I will persecute them with the sword, with the famine, and with the pestilence, and will deliver them to be removed to all the kingdoms of the earth, to be a curse, and an astonishment, and an hissing, and a reproach, among all the nations whither I have driven them: Because they have not hearkened to my words, saith the Lord, which I sent unto them by my servants the prophets. (Jeremiah 29:17–19)

Ezekiel as Another Witness of Jerusalem's Apostasy

About this same time, Jeremiah was shown a vision of two baskets, one full of good figs and the other full of poor figs (Jeremiah 24). He was told that the basket of poor figs represented Zedekiah and all the Jews who remained in Jerusalem. Again, the Lord promised that because they continued in wickedness, "they [would] be consumed from off the land" (Jeremiah 24:10). On the other hand, the basket of good figs represented those who had been exiled to Babylon in 597 B.C. It seems that the Lord allowed these Jews to be exiled to protect them from the further wickedness that would bring about Jerusalem's destruction. This the Lord did in order to prepare a people to return to Jerusalem. He promised that he would give the exiled "an heart to know me, that I am the Lord: and they shall be my people, and I will be their God: for they shall return unto me with their whole heart" (Jeremiah 24:7).

Ezekiel, a priest who had been among those exiled, was called of God to help the Jews undergo the change of heart that would prepare them for their eventual return. He was made "a watchman unto the house of Israel"[30] to warn them of their wicked ways (Ezekiel 3:17). A watchman was a guard or sentry who was to call out the safety of the city from the wall or gate (1 Samuel 14:16; 2 Samuel 18:24; 2 Kings 9:17; Jeremiah 51:12).[31] It was hoped that if Ezekiel warned "the wicked" of the impending consequences of their wickedness, they would "turn from [their] sin, and do that which is lawful and right" (Ezekiel 33:14). Ezekiel's writings add a second witness to Jeremiah's testimony of the wickedness of those living in Jerusalem.

Ezekiel began to receive revelations and visions midway between the 597 B.C. exile (see Ezekiel 1:1–3) and the final siege and destruction of Jerusalem in 588–587 B.C. His first revelations warned of Jerusalem's impending destruction. In 593 B.C., he dramatized the siege and destruction of Jerusalem through a series of symbolic acts (Ezekiel 4–5). Then, in word, he made clear that Jerusalem's destruction was sure: "Thus saith the Lord God . . . Behold, I, even I, will bring a sword upon you, and I will destroy your high places. And your altars shall be desolate, and your images shall be broken: and I will cast down your slain men before your idols" (Ezekiel 6:3–4). The hearts of the people of Jerusalem had turned from serving Jehovah to serving the images of the nations around them. Only through their destruction would they know that Jehovah was their god. In language similar to that used of the people living in the days of Noah before the flood (Genesis 6:13), the Lord said of Judah and Jerusalem: "The end is come upon the four corners of the land [of Judah] . . . for the land is full of bloody crimes, and the city [of Jerusalem] is full of violence" (Ezekiel 7:2, 23). The people of Jerusalem had become like the people in the days of Noah and would therefore experience a similar fate.

In 592 B.C., Ezekiel was taken in vision to Jerusalem, where he witnessed the extent to which wickedness had consumed the hearts of the Jews. He also witnessed that their corruption caused the "glory of the Lord"—certainly an aspect of the Light of Christ—to withdraw from the city (Ezekiel 8–11).[32] The vision was given to Ezekiel in the presence of the elders of Judah, who, after the vision was over, were told all that he, Ezekiel, had seen.

The vision commenced with Ezekiel seeing through successive stages "increasingly greater acts of apostasy."[33] At first he was taken to a gate on the northern wall of the city,[34] where he saw an altar with "the image of jealousy" (Ezekiel 8:3, 5).[35] High places with the images of pagan deities were often placed near the gates of cities (see 2 Kings 23:8), as can be seen, for example, at the Iron Age gates of Tel Dan[36] and at Bethsaida (et-Tel).[37] Just as the northern kingdom saw an increase in the number of altars throughout the land before its destruction (Hosea 8:11; 10:1), Ezekiel witnessed the same proliferation among the Jews in Jerusalem.[38]

Next, Ezekiel was shown a secret chamber in the wall near a gate leading into the inner court directly surrounding the temple.[39] Within the chamber he saw men practicing secret rites associated with images of "every form of creeping things, and abominable beasts, and all the idols of the house of Israel, portrayed upon the wall round about" (Ezekiel 8:10). In an attempt to justify their actions, the men said, "The Lord seeth us not; the Lord hath forsaken the earth" (Ezekiel 8:12). Instead of repenting of their actions and pleading that the Lord would return, the people used Jehovah's absence as a justification for their worship of pagan deities.

From the secret chamber, Ezekiel was brought within the northern gate of the inner court immediately surrounding the temple. The inner court and the temple were designed to be the central place of Jehovah worship. But Ezekiel witnessed that Jehovah was no longer honored or worshipped. Immediately upon his entrance into the inner court, his attention was drawn to the sound of several women sitting near where he stood, who were "weeping for Tammuz" (Ezekiel 8:14), a Mesopotamian fertility deity, whose annual death and resurrection rites were accompanied by weeping mourners.[40]

After gazing on this scene, the Lord told Ezekiel to focus his attention on the area between the altar and the porch of the temple, an area of great sanctity. Only the temple itself was more sacred.[41] In this place of holiness, Ezekiel saw twenty-five men "with their backs toward the temple of the Lord, and their faces toward the east; and they worshipped [Heb. *shahah,* 'to bow down'][42] the sun toward the east" (Ezekiel 8:16). Whether these men were involved in pagan solar worship, such as was found in Egypt or Mesopotamia, or a form of solarized Jehovah worship, as some have suggested,[43] what is clear is that their actions were seen by the Lord as abominable (Ezekiel 8:17). It was a deliberate affront to true Jehovah worship. In the area where priests would pray to Jehovah in behalf of Israel (see Joel 2:17), these men were bowing to the sun rising in the east with their back sides toward the temple of Jehovah.

Ezekiel was told that these contemptible cultic actions were superseded only by the general social corruption of the people. The Lord said: "Is it a light thing to the house of Judah that they commit the abominations which they commit here [in the temple]? for they have filled the land with violence [Heb. *hamas,* 'violence, wrong, injustice'],[44] and have returned to provoke me to anger" (Ezekiel 8:17).

As in Ezekiel 7:23, the language of their social corruptions is reminiscent of the people in the days of Noah. Having turned their backs on the Light of Christ, as represented by the twenty-five men bowing to the rising sun, the people had given themselves over to the "will of the flesh and the evil which is therein" (2 Nephi 2:29). Following the desires of the natural man, like those in the days of Noah, "every imagination of the thoughts of [their] heart[s] was only evil continually" (Genesis 6:5; cf. Moses 8:22). Ignoring the Light of Christ, the Jews gave up their agency. The Lord, therefore, was forced to destroy them for their own good and the good of their children. "Therefore," the Lord told Ezekiel, "will I also deal in fury: mine eye shall not spare, neither will I have pity: and though they cry in mine ears with a loud voice, yet will I not hear them" (Ezekiel 8:18).

As he had seen the wickedness of the Jews in successive degrees, Ezekiel witnessed the withdrawal of the Light of Christ in successive steps. While in the inner court, Ezekiel heard the Lord call for the servants whose assignment was to destroy Jerusalem. Six men came from the north (the direction from which the Babylonian army would come) and stood by the altar, each one holding "a slaughter weapon in his hand" (Ezekiel 9:2). Added to them was a seventh man "clothed with linen, which had the writer's inkhorn by his side" (Ezekiel 9:3).

Then "the glory of the Lord," which had filled the house of the Lord at the time of Solomon's dedication of the temple (1 Kings 8:11) and presumably had remained there, moved from the holy of holies to the threshold of the temple. Remember that those who were worshipping in the hidden chamber justified their actions by claiming that the Lord had abandoned them (see Ezekiel 8:12). But the truth was, the Lord had *not* abandoned them. His glory or light was still there. This is startling in light of the wickedness of the people. But recall what President Kimball taught: "When a person pushes the Spirit away and ignores and puts out the 'unwelcome sign,' eventually the Spirit of the Lord ceases to strive. He does not move away from the individual; it is the person who moves away from the Lord."[45] Ezekiel saw that the spirit of the Lord remained in Jerusalem until *after* it was destroyed.

The moving of the glory of the Lord to the threshold of the temple was the first stage of the Lord's abandonment of his people. But he would not abandon them to their destruction until all the righteous had been removed. He commanded the man with the writer's inkwell attached to his side to go throughout Jerusalem and place a mark (Heb. *taw,* the last letter of the Hebrew alphabet written in the old Hebrew script as an X) on the foreheads of everyone who found the abominations of the people shameful (Ezekiel 9:4). We are not told whether he found any or not. The other six men were told to follow him and destroy all who had no mark. When the man with the inkhorn returned from his assignment, he was told to get coals from between the cherubim, which acted as the throne where the glory of the Lord rested, and "scatter them over the city" (Ezekiel 10:2). The city would now be destroyed by fire.

As the man did so, the glory of the Lord moved from the threshold to the east gate of the temple (Ezekiel 10:18–19). Ezekiel was taken by the Spirit to the same place (Ezekiel 11:1), where he witnessed further apostasy of the people of Jerusalem, further justifying the Lord's destruction of the city. They had come to believe that because they had not been exiled to Babylon in 597 B.C., no further calamities would come upon them (Ezekiel 11:2–3). Their being left behind, however, was not intended to justify their wicked actions, but rather their wickedness would justify their destruction. Ezekiel was commanded to prophesy against them, saying, "And I will bring you out of the midst thereof, and deliver you into the hands of strangers, and will execute judgments among you. Ye shall fall by the sword. . . . And ye shall know that I am the Lord: for ye have not walked in my statutes, neither executed my judgments, but have done after the manners of the heathen that are round about you" (Ezekiel 11:9–10, 12).

Ezekiel asked the Lord, "wilt thou make a full end of the remnant of Israel?" (Ezekiel 11:13). The answer was, No! "Although I have cast them far off among the heathen, and although I have scattered them among the countries, yet will I be to them as a little sanctuary in the countries where they shall come" (Ezekiel 11:16). This is a key verse. Though Jerusalem and the temple would be destroyed, the Lord would still be a little sanctuary or temple to Israel. The temple was a symbol of the fulness of the divine presence of God.[46] But though the fulness of God's presence would be lost for a time, the Lord would still be a small sanctuary to Israel in their scattered condition through the ever-present Light of Christ that fills "the immensity of space—The light which is in all things, which giveth life to all things, which is the law by which all things are governed, even the power of God who sitteth upon his throne" (D&C 88:12–13). If Israel would respond to the Light of Christ and come unto the Lord, the Lord would "give them one heart, and I will put a new spirit within you; and I will take the stony heart out of their flesh, and will give them an heart of flesh: That they may walk in my statutes, and keep mine ordinances, and do them: and they shall be my people, and I will be their God" (Ezekiel 11:19–20).

Ezekiel was later shown that the remnant of Israel who hearken to the Light of Christ would eventually be able to return to Jerusalem with a holy temple wherein the fulness of the glory of the Lord would be found (Ezekiel 40–48). Perhaps to symbolize this, the vision ended with the glory of the Lord making a third movement eastward, to the Mount of Olives (Ezekiel 11:22–23). The Mount of Olives formed Jerusalem's eastern horizon. Babylon, where the exiled Jews were taken, lay to the east of Jerusalem. It may be that the Mount of Olives represented the location of the exiled Jews. There the Lord rested until the return of Israel (see Ezekiel 43).

Conclusion

Sometime between one and two years before Jerusalem was destroyed by the Babylonians, in the land called Bountiful by Lehi and his family, a heated debate took place between Nephi and his rebellious brothers dealing, in part, with the righteousness of the people of Jerusalem whom they had left behind. The brothers claimed: "We know that the people who were in the land of Jerusalem were a righteous people; for they kept the statutes and judgments of the Lord, and all his commandments, according to the law of Moses; wherefore, we know that they are a righteous people" (1 Nephi 17:22). Nephi countered by reviewing Israel's history, showing that "they did harden their hearts from time to time." "And now," he declared, "after all these things, the time has come that they have become wicked, yea, nearly unto ripeness; and I know not but they are at this day about to be destroyed; for I know that the day must surely come that they must be destroyed, save a few only, who shall be led away into captivity" (1 Nephi 17:43).

The writings of Jeremiah and Ezekiel bear out Nephi's assertion. We have seen that the Light of Christ strove with the people of Jerusalem, both enticing and entreating them to repent of their wicked actions and to make reformations in their religious practices in the days of Hezekiah and Josiah. But we also have seen that the changes made by the people were outward only. Inwardly, the draw to sin and idolatry was stronger than their will to follow the Lord. In this condition, the people became rebellious, delighting in that which was evil. Their apostasy included a rejection of the Lord's warnings through his prophets. They justified their sinful actions by claiming that what they were doing was not wrong. Some suggested that Jehovah had abandoned them and therefore did not know what they were doing. In the end, they completely rejected Jehovah and worshipped the pagan deities.

Their utter rejection of Jehovah left them without the influence of the Light of Christ. Though, as Ezekiel saw, the Light of Christ remained until Jerusalem was destroyed, it no longer strove with the people. Their was no enticement for good. Sin prevailed in the hearts of all the people. In this condition, the Jews became ripe for destruction.

Notes

1. The prophets have taught that the Spirit of the Lord has reference to the Light of Christ. For example, see *Doctrines of Salvation: Sermons and Writings of Joseph Fielding Smith,* ed. Bruce R. McConkie (Salt Lake City: Bookcraft, 1999), 1:50–51; Harold B. Lee, *Stand Ye in Holy Places: Selected Sermons and Writings of President Harold B. Lee* (Salt Lake City: Deseret Book, 1974), 117–18; Ezra Taft Benson, *The Teachings of Ezra Taft Benson* (Salt Lake City: Bookcraft, 1988), 343; and Bruce R. McConkie, *Mormon Doctrine,* 2nd ed. rev. (Salt Lake City: Bookcraft, 1966), 446, 752.

2. Bruce R. McConkie, *A New Witness for the Articles of Faith* (Salt Lake City: Deseret Book, 1985), 90.

3. Ibid., 89, emphasis added.

4. Harold B. Lee, in Conference Report, October 1945, 46, emphasis added.

5. Lee, *Stand Ye In Holy Places,* 115.

6. McConkie, *New Witness for the Articles of Faith,* 257.

7. *Gospel Doctrine: Selections from the Sermons and Writings of Joseph F. Smith,* comp. John A. Widtsoe (Salt Lake City: Deseret Book, 1939), 61.

8. Smith, *Doctrines of Salvation,* 50.

9. Marion G. Romney, "The Light of Christ," *Ensign,* May 1977, 43. For other descriptions on the Light of Christ, see C. Kent Dunford, "Light of Christ," in *Encyclopedia of Mormonism,* 2:835; Smith, *Doctrines of Salvation,* 49–54; McConkie, *New Witness for the Articles of Faith,* 257–58; and B. H. Roberts, *The Seventy's Course in Theology,* Fifth Year. Divine Immanence and the Holy Ghost (Salt Lake City: Deseret News, 1912), 1–10.

10. Smith, *Gospel Doctrine,* 61.

11. McConkie, *Mormon Doctrine,* 156, emphasis added.

12. Neal A. Maxwell, *Sermons Not Spoken* (Salt Lake City: Bookcraft, 1985), 91.

13. Neal A. Maxwell, *Look Back at Sodom: A Timely Account from Imaginary Sodom Scrolls* (Salt Lake City: Deseret Book, 1975), 13–14.

14. John Taylor, *The Government of God* (Liverpool: Richards, 1852), 53.

15. Spencer W. Kimball, *The Miracle of Forgiveness* (Salt Lake City: Bookcraft, 1969), 86.

16. Marion G. Romney, "The Perfect Law of Liberty," *Ensign,* November 1981, 45.

17. Ibid., 82, emphasis added. President Kimball often mentioned this point. For example: "The Spirit of God ceases to strive with the man who *excuses himself in wrong-doing*" (ibid., 86, emphasis added). Again, "Self-justification is the enemy of repentance. God's Spirit continues with the honest in heart to strengthen, to help, and to save, but invariably the Spirit of God ceases to strive with the man

who *excuses himself in his wrongdoing.*" Spencer W. Kimball, *Faith Precedes the Miracle* (Salt Lake City: Deseret Book, 1972), 234, emphasis added.

18. George Albert Smith, *Sharing the Gospel with Others,* comp. Preston Nibley (Salt Lake City: Deseret Book, 1948), 29; also in Conference Report, October 1916, 48, emphasis added.

19. Spencer W. Kimball, *The Teachings of Spencer W. Kimball,* ed. Edward L. Kimball (Salt Lake City: Bookcraft, 1982), 162, emphasis deleted and added.

20. McConkie, *New Witness for the Articles of Faith,* 260.

21. Neal A. Maxwell, *Wherefore, Ye Must Press Forward* (Salt Lake City: Deseret Book, 1977), 15.

22. Neal A. Maxwell, *For the Power Is in Them . . . : Mormon Musings* (Salt Lake City: Deseret Book, 1970), 43.

23. I am following the generally accepted chronology of the life of Jeremiah. It should be noted that William Holladay, *Jeremiah 2: A Commentary on the Book of the Prophet Jeremiah* (Minneapolis, Minn.: Fortress, 1989), 24–35, has made a compelling argument for a different chronology.

24. The phrase translated in the KJV, "I will not transgress," should be rendered, "I will not serve." The Hebrew word ʿavad, translated "transgress," means "to work or serve."

25. William McKane, *A Critical and Exegetical Commentary on Jeremiah* (Edinburgh: Clark, 1986), 43.

26. It is assumed by most scholars that Jeremiah chapters 7 and 26 are about the same event.

27. There is some debate as to the exact date of this incident. Jeremiah 36:1 places this in the fourth year of Jehoiakim's reign (604 B.C.). However, the Septuagint (43:9) places it in the eighth year (601 B.C.). William Holladay, *Jeremiah 1: A Commentary on the Book of the Prophet Jeremiah* (Philadelphia: Fortress, 1986), 4–5, argues convincingly for the later date.

28. Holladay, *Jeremiah 1,* 5.

29. The concept that the whole does not necessarily reflect each

individual is seen in the Doctrine and Covenants where the Lord speaks of being pleased with the Church, "speaking unto the church collectively and not individually" (D&C 1:30).

30. Though Ezekiel's message was generally to the house of Israel, his immediate assignment was specifically to warn "them of the captivity, unto the children of thy people, and speak unto them" (Ezekiel 3:11).

31. C. U. Wolf, "Watchman," in *The Interpreter's Dictionary of the Bible,* ed. George A. Buttrick (Nashville: Abingdon, 1962), 4:806.

32. Scholarship is divided as to whether Ezekiel 11 is a continuation of the vision found in Ezekiel 8–10 or a separate vision. For example, Walther Zimmerli, *Ezekiel 1: A Commentary on the Book of the Prophet Ezekiel* (Philadelphia: Fortress, 1979), 257, sees no reason for this being "an originally independent vision," while Keith W. Carley, *The Book of the Prophet Ezekiel* (Cambridge: Cambridge University Press, 1974), 66, views this as a "separate vision." Admittedly, there are problems with the present placement of the scene portrayed in Ezekiel 11 (it would logically fit better before Jerusalem's destruction). However, Daniel I. Block, *The Book of Ezekiel: Chapters 1–24* (Grand Rapids, Mich.: Eerdmans, 1997), 272, has noted: "The editor of Ezekiel's prophecies evidently intended 8:1–11:25 to be treated as a single composition. The boundaries of this literary unit are set by a formal introduction (8:1–4) and a corresponding conclusion (11:22–25)." In this paper, Ezekiel 11 will be considered as a continuation of the vision since the content thematically continues with Ezekiel 8–10.

33. Carley, *Book of the Prophet Ezekiel,* 51.

34. The Hebrew text of Ezekiel 8:3, 5 is difficult, lending itself to various possible translations. The text, however, seems to suggest that the altar and image of jealousy were located next to the northern city gate, which would have been north of the northern gate of the inner court where Ezekiel was first set down. Among those who hold to this view are Solomon Fisch, *Ezekiel* (London: Soncino, 1985), 42; Carley, *Book of the Prophet Ezekiel,* 52; Zimmerli, *Ezekiel 1,* 238. But others,

such as Block, *Book of Ezekiel,* 280, see this gate as the northern gate of the inner court.

35. Many have suggested that the image was the Canaanite fertility goddess, Asherah; see Carley, *Book of the Prophet Ezekiel,* 53; Moshe Greenberg, *Ezekiel 1–20* (Garden City, N.Y.: Doubleday, 1983), 168; Fisch, *Ezekiel,* 42. But Zimmerli, *Ezekiel 1,* 238–39, does not think so.

36. See Avraham Biran, "Dan," in *The New Encyclopedia of Archaeological Excavations in the Holy Land,* ed. Ephraim Stern (New York: Simon & Schuster, 1993), 1:323–32; also Avraham Biran, "Sacred Spaces of Standing Stones, High Places and Cult Objects at Tel Dan," *Biblical Archaeology Review* 24/5 (1998): 38–45, 70.

37. See Rami Arav et al., "Bethsaida Rediscovered," *Biblical Archaeology Review* 26/1 (2000): 45–56.

38. This corroborates Jeremiah's testimony that "according to the number of the streets of Jerusalem have ye set up altars to that shameful thing" (Jeremiah 11:13).

39. For an excellent discussion of the layout of Solomon's temple, including surrounding courts, see Victor V. Hurowitz, "Inside Solomon's Temple," *Bible Review* (April 1994): 24–37, 50. For other discussions, see Roland de Vaux, *Ancient Israel: Its Life and Institutions,* trans. John McHugh (New York: McGraw-Hill, 1961), 2:312–22; Menahem Haran, *Temples and Temple Service in Ancient Israel* (Winona Lake, Ind.: Eisenbrauns, 1985), 189–94. Also helpful is Leslie C. Allen's discussion of Ezekiel's movements within the temple complex, including diagrams, in *Ezekiel 1–19* (Waco, Tex.: Word Books, 1994), 139–41.

40. There is scholarly debate as to the exact nature of Tammuz (Dumuzi) worship. See Oliver R. Gurney, "Tammuz Reconsidered: Some Recent Developments," *Journal of Semitic Studies* 7/2 (1962): 147–60; Thorkild Jacobsen, "Toward the Image of Tammuz," in *Toward the Image of Tammuz and Other Essays on Mesopotamian History and Culture,* ed. William L. Moran (Cambridge: Harvard University Press, 1970), 73–103; Samuel N. Kramer, *The Sacred Marriage Rite* (Bloomington: Indiana University Press, 1969), 107–33; Edwin

M. Yamauchi, "Tammuz and the Bible," *Journal of Biblical Literature* 84 (1965): 283–90.

41. Later rabbis considered the area between the altar and the porch of the temple one of the most sacred areas in the land. The Mishnah describes "ten degrees of holiness" beginning with the land of Israel and ending with the holy of holies, with each degree more holy than the next (see Mishnah *Kelim* 1:6–9). In this list, only the holy place and the holy of holies within the temple itself were more holy than the space between the altar and the temple. According to the Mishnah, it was in this area that the priests blessed the people after performing the daily offering (see Mishnah *Tamid* 7:2). This also was the place where the priests in the days of the Maccabees petitioned the Lord (1 Maccabees 7:36–38).

42. The form of *shahah* found in this verse is *mishtahawithem,* which is unusual. It appears to be a participle with a second masculine singular perfect sufformative. Some scholars, such as Zimmerli, *Ezekiel 1,* 221, and Block, *Book of Ezekiel,* 296 n. 70, assign this to scribal error, feeling the word should be written *mishtahawim,* the normal rendering of worship. However, the rabbis traditionally explained this unusual form as a compound of *mashhithim* (they destroy) and *mishtahawim* (they worship). They see in the word as it is presently rendered the dual nature of the abomination being acted out before the Lord: the worship of the sun god would bring about the destruction of the temple; see Fisch, *Ezekiel,* 45.

43. Zimmerli, *Ezekiel 1,* 243–44.

44. The primary use of *hamas* in the Old Testament is in societal contexts: oppression, injustice, and false accusation based upon greed. But *hamas* can be taken to the point of physical violence and destruction. For a greater understanding of this word, see H. Haag, "Chamas," in *Theological Dictionary of the Old Testament,* ed. G. Johannes Botterweck and Helmer Ringgren (Grand Rapids, Mich.: Eerdmans, 1980), 4:478–87.

45. Kimball, *Teachings of Spencer W. Kimball,* 162.

46. Recall that President Marion G. Romney taught that the Light of Christ may be experienced in three phases: first, the "light which

enlighteneth every man that cometh into the world"; second, the "gift of the Holy Ghost"; and third, the second comforter obtained through the "more sure word of prophecy" when one's calling and election is made sure; see Romney, "Light of Christ," 43–45. In order to obtain the fulness of the Light of Christ one must experience all three phases. These three phases are central to temple worship and are represented in modern temples through various stages of the endowment. These three phases can also be seen in the layout of Solomon's temple. The first phase may be represented by the area outside of the temple including both outer and inner courts. The second phase may be represented by the holy place that housed, among other things, the seven-branched candelabra. The third phase may be represented by the holy of holies with its ark of the covenant.

Chapter 20

How Could Jerusalem, "That Great City," Be Destroyed?

David Rolph Seely and Fred E. Woods

> Neither did they believe that Jerusalem, that great city, could be destroyed according to the words of the prophets. And they were like unto the Jews who were at Jerusalem, who sought to take away the life of my father. (1 Nephi 2:13)

In the opening chapters of the Book of Mormon, Nephi records that his brothers Laman and Lemuel murmured against their father Lehi "because he was a visionary man, and had led them out of the land of Jerusalem, to leave the land of their inheritance, and their gold, and their silver, and their precious things, to perish in the wilderness. And this they said he had done because of the foolish imaginations of his heart" (1 Nephi 2:11). One of the chief complaints the brothers had against their father was that they—like many—did not "believe that Jerusalem, that great city, could be destroyed according to the words of the prophets. And they were like unto the Jews who were at Jerusalem, who sought to take away the life of my father" (1 Nephi 2:13). The biblical record contains much information that helps us to better understand the attitude of

Laman and Lemuel and many of their fellow inhabitants of Jerusalem and to identify the basis for their fervent belief that their city Jerusalem was invincible and impregnable.

At least six interrelated factors, which will be discussed in this article, contributed to the Judahite belief that Jerusalem could not be destroyed: (1) The historical traditions of the spiritual heritage of Jerusalem, "that great city," suggested to many that the Lord would naturally preserve this holy place from destruction and desecration by the enemies of the covenant people. (2) The Jews misunderstood some of the Lord's promises in connection with the covenants that he had made with them. In particular, they misunderstood the promises made to David in the Davidic covenant. (3) The miraculous preservation of Jerusalem and its inhabitants when the Assyrians besieged Jerusalem (2 Kings 18–19) in the days of King Hezekiah (701 B.C.) further reinforced the belief that the Lord would preserve his temple and holy city from the enemy. (4) The city of Jerusalem was fortified and prepared for siege. Hezekiah had heavily fortified the city against the Assyrian siege in 701 B.C. with massive walls and towers (2 Chronicles 32:2–8) and had even prepared a water source inside the city for the inhabitants of the city to endure a long siege (2 Kings 20:20; 2 Chronicles 32:4, 30). Thus the inhabitants of Jerusalem believed they could endure a long siege brought about by their seemingly impregnable walls. (5) The recent reforms of Josiah (640–609 B.C.), who had cleansed the temple and led his people in a ceremony of covenant renewal (2 Kings 22–23), had given certain people of Judah an undue sense of self and community righteousness that they believed would surely preserve them from any threatened destruction. (6) Assurances were given by false prophets, who promised Jerusalem and its inhabitants peace, safety, and preservation from the enemy instead of the destruction and exile prophesied by Jeremiah and Lehi. These false assurances were readily accepted by many since they were the words that they wanted to hear.

1. Historical Tradition

Jerusalem has held a long and exalted place in the biblical tradition. The ancient city Salem was the holy city of the righteous high priest Melchizedek, who blessed Abraham (Genesis 14:18–19; cf. Hebrews 7:2). The Psalmist identified Salem with Jerusalem and with Zion (Psalm 76:2), and in Jewish tradition Jerusalem became known as the "city of peace" (Hebrews 7:2). Jerusalem was also known as Zion—perhaps in remembrance of the city of Enoch, also identified as Zion (Moses 7:19). Under Melchizedek, the "people wrought righteousness, and obtained heaven, and sought for the city of Enoch which God had before taken" (Genesis 14:34 JST). In Genesis 22 the Lord commanded Abraham to sacrifice his son Isaac on one of the mountains in the land of Moriah. The Bible links this sanctified place with the Temple Mount in Jerusalem—called Mount Moriah—"where the Lord appeared unto David" (2 Chronicles 3:1), the same place where David had purchased the threshing floor from Araunah (2 Chronicles 3:1; 2 Samuel 24:18). Thus, according to tradition, the temple was built upon the place where Abraham made his dramatic sacrifice. The city was inhabited by the Jebusites at the time of the conquest and was later conquered by David—who made it the capital of his united kingdom (2 Samuel 5). From that point on it became known as the city of David. David eventually moved the ark of the covenant to Jerusalem (2 Samuel 6) and placed it there inside a tent near his palace, making Jerusalem the political and religious center of Israel. Later, his son Solomon built his splendid temple on the site of Araunah's threshing floor (1 Kings 6–8), which was to stand for over three hundred years as a concrete and permanent symbol of the presence of the Lord in the midst of his people. At the time of Lehi, Jerusalem had been the capital of Judah for over three hundred years and was the political, economic, and spiritual center of the Jews. As the city of David, Jerusalem is portrayed in the scriptures as being part of the marvelous covenants made with the house of David and, indeed, with all of Israel.

2. Misunderstanding the Promises of the Lord

In connection with the covenants of Abraham, Moses, and David, the Lord had made great promises to the covenant people—most of them conditioned on their righteousness. When the children of Israel emerged from their captivity in Egypt, the Jebusites possessed the land and city of Jerusalem (Judges 1:21). Because the Israelites had broken their covenants with the Lord, they were unable to drive out the Jebusites following the death of Joshua (Judges 2:20–21). Israel did not gain possession of the city until King David and his men conquered the Jebusites after selecting Jerusalem as the capital (2 Samuel 5:6–9).

Later, David desired to build a house "unto the name of the Lord," but he was directed not to do so because he had been a man of war (1 Chronicles 22:7–8). Instead, the Lord told David that his son Solomon would build the temple. The Lord made David this promise: "I will appoint a place for my people Israel, and will plant them, that they may dwell in a place of their own, and move no more; neither shall the children of wickedness afflict them anymore, as beforetime" (2 Samuel 7:10).

The Lord promised David: "Thine house and thy kingdom shall be established for ever before thee: thy throne shall be established forever" (2 Samuel 7:16; see Psalm 89:3–4). This promise is called the Davidic covenant and unconditionally promised that kingship would reside in David's seed forever.

As history unfolded, the unconditional part of this covenant turned out to be a prophecy and promise that the Messiah would come through the house of David. This of course was fulfilled by the coming of Jesus Christ—from the lineage of David (Matthew 1:1–17).

The people, however misunderstood this promise. Passages in Psalms connected the Davidic covenant with Jerusalem, the city of David, and identified Jerusalem as the dwelling place of God: "For the Lord hath chosen Zion; he hath desired it for his habitation. This is my rest for ever; here will I dwell; for I have desired it. . . . There will I make the horn of David to bud: I have ordained a lamp for mine anointed. His enemies will I clothe with shame: but upon himself shall his crown flourish" (Psalm 132:13, 17–18). Likewise, Isaiah prophesied that the Lord would fight on behalf of his people and preserve his holy city and the temple: "So shall the Lord of hosts come down to fight for mount Zion, and for the hill thereof. As birds flying, so will the Lord of hosts defend Jerusalem; defending also he will deliver it; and passing over he will preserve it" (Isaiah 31:4–5).[1]

The blessings of protection promised in the covenants of Moses and of David were conditional. In Deuteronomy the Lord warned that disobedience to the covenant would be followed by invasion, siege, destruction, death, and scattering (Deuteronomy 28:45–68). When construction of the temple began, the Lord, speaking to Solomon, further clarified the conditions of the promise made to David: "*If* thou will walk in my statues, and execute my judgments, and keep all my commandments to walk in them; *then* will I perform my word with thee, which I spake unto David thy father: And I will dwell among the children of Israel, and will not forsake my people Israel" (1 Kings 6:12–13, emphasis added). Following Solomon's dedication of the temple, the Lord again emphasized that the blessings were based on obedience and that disobedience would lead to disaster: "But if ye shall at all turn from following me, ye or your children, and will not keep my commandments and my statutes which I have set before you, but go and serve other gods, and worship them: Then will I cut off Israel out of the land which I have given them; and this house, which I have hallowed for my name, will I cast out of my sight" (1 Kings 9:6–7).

Israel, however, constantly broke the covenant through disobedience. The united kingdom was divided into the northern and the southern kingdoms, Israel and Judah, and in 722 B.C. the Assyrians took the Israelites from the northern kingdom into captivity to Assyria from whence they were scattered and lost. Two decades later, the Assyrians, led by King Sennacherib, returned and took possession of much of the southern kingdom of Judah. But many of the people in Judah apparently preferred to put their trust in the temple, both because of the promises of the Davidic covenant and because they perceived that they themselves were righteous. Jeremiah warned these people, "Trust ye not in lying words, saying, The temple of the Lord, The temple of the Lord, The temple of the Lord, are these" (Jeremiah 7:4). They still did not believe Jeremiah, and eventually the temple was destroyed.

3. The Miraculous Preservation of the Jews from the Assyrian Siege in 701 B.C.

Throughout their history, the covenant people Israel had been preserved through many crises, one of which occurred during the reign of King Hezekiah (715–687 B.C.). Hezekiah was a righteous king; upon surveying the idolatry that had grown up in Judah, he set about to remove the high places in Judah and destroy the images of idolatrous worship. In the course of his religious reform, Hezekiah revolted against the

Assyrian masters by refusing to send tribute (2 Kings 18:4–8). In 701 B.C. Sennacherib responded to the revolt of Hezekiah and invaded Judah. "Now in the fourteenth year of king Hezekiah did Sennacherib king of Assyria come up against all the fenced [walled] cities of Judah, and took them" (2 Kings 18:13) and exiled many of them. Indeed, archaeological excavations have documented Sennacherib's capture and destruction of the walled cities in Judah. The savagery of the siege and capture of Lachish and the execution and exile of its inhabitants are dramatically portrayed in Sennacherib's reliefs in his palace in Nineveh, now preserved in the British Museum. But Jerusalem, saved by Sennacherib for last, was miraculously spared from the Assyrian armies. An Assyrian prism inscription of King Sennacherib sheds further light on this biblical account: "As to Hezekiah, the Jew, he did not submit to my yoke, I laid siege to 46 of his strong cities, walled forts and to the countless small villages in their vicinity, and conquered (them) by means of well-stamped (earth-)ramps, and battering rams. . . . Himself I made a prisoner in Jerusalem, his royal residence, like a bird in a cage."[2]

The Bible says King Hezekiah, who had returned righteousness to Judah, consulted with the prophet Isaiah, who in turn promised Hezekiah that the Lord would intervene on behalf of Jerusalem (2 Kings 19:1–13). Hezekiah thus went to the temple to plead with the Lord for protection. In answer to his prayer, the Lord told Hezekiah that his petition would be granted: "For I will defend this city, to save it, for mine own sake, and for my servant David's sake. And it came to pass that night, that the angel of the Lord went out, and smote in the camp of the Assyrians an hundred fourscore and five thousand" (2 Kings 19:34–35). While Judah had been punished for her sins, Jerusalem was preserved—in part because of the righteous reforms of Hezekiah and the mercy of the Lord.

This miraculous display of divine intervention had a tremendous impact on future generations, particularly on those who dwelt securely in Jerusalem, from the time following this deliverance in 701 B.C. until the Babylonian captivity in 586 B.C. Jerusalem's deliverance led to the erroneous belief that the holy city was impregnable. The Jews believed the city enjoyed divine protection, even if they did not abide the law of the covenant. Isaiah observed, "They call themselves of the holy city, and stay themselves upon the God of Israel" (Isaiah 48:2). So while the people counted on divine intervention on their behalf, they failed to realize that the situation presented by the Babylonian invasions in 597 and 586 B.C. had changed from that of 701 B.C. Then King Hezekiah had consulted with the prophet Isaiah and had received divine assurance of the deliverance of Jerusalem. Thus Hezekiah commanded his people to stand fast against the Assyrians. Later, at the time of Lehi, when King Zedekiah consulted with the prophet Jeremiah, the word of the Lord was different—to submit to Babylon in order to preserve Jerusalem (Jeremiah 38:14–28). In addition to the wickedness of the people in Jerusalem, they also failed to heed the word of the Lord delivered through his prophet Jeremiah.

4. Jerusalem's Fortifications and Water Source

After capturing Jerusalem from the Jebusites ca. 1000 B.C., David further fortified the city known as "the strong hold of Zion" (2 Samuel 5:7). The later Judahite kings followed his example and continuously updated the fortifications of the capital city. The Bible notes that Uzziah "built towers" (2 Chronicles 26:9) and that his son Jotham continued the fortifications (2 Chronicles 27:3). In 701 B.C., in the face of the impending

Assyrian invasion and siege, Hezekiah once again heavily fortified Jerusalem against attack and siege: "He . . . built up all the wall that was broken, and raised it up to the towers, and another wall without, and repaired Millo in the city of David, and made darts and shields in abundance" (2 Chronicles 32:5). Remnants of these walls have been found in archaeological excavations in Jerusalem. In ancient warfare, cities' walls were often too strong for an invading army to scale. In many such cases a protracted siege could gain the surrender of a powerful city. In order to avoid this situation, Hezekiah even went so far as to devise a sophisticated tunnel system to make sure his city had an internal supply of water (2 Kings 20:20; 2 Chronicles 32:3–4, 30). This water system was excavated and studied by archaeologists. Later, Hezekiah's son King Manasseh "built a wall without the city of David . . . and raised it up a very great height" (2 Chronicles 33:14).

Thus in the recent memory of the people at the time of Jeremiah and Lehi, the city of Jerusalem had not fallen to the enemy. As they looked around they could see the splendid fortifications: towers, gates, and walls that could protect them from the mighty armies of their enemies. In addition they had the added confidence that they could endure a long siege, if necessary, since they had access to a continuous water source inside their city through Hezekiah's tunnel. This illusion of invincibility was rudely destroyed by the Babylonian siege and capture of Jerusalem in 597 B.C. that resulted in the Babylonians putting Zedekiah on the throne (2 Kings 24:1–18). Laman and Lemuel, as well as many of the other inhabitants of Jerusalem, should have paid attention to this turn of fortunes. Nevertheless, it appears that some still continued to trust in their fortifications instead of in the Lord—for Zedekiah rebelled against Babylon again in 587, resulting in the Babylonian siege and destruction of Jerusalem in 586 B.C. (2 Kings 24:20–25:21).

5. Josiah's Reforms

Two kings in Israel recognized the sins and idolatry of the people and attempted a series of religious reforms. The first was King Hezekiah, who reigned during much of the ministry of Isaiah and threw down the high places and the idolatrous images Israel had set up throughout the temple (2 Kings 18:1–7). Hezekiah's reign was followed by the reign of his son Manasseh, a wicked king who promptly turned Judah back to the worship of idols and all forms of wickedness, including the sacrifice of children (2 Kings 21:1–9).

The second was Josiah, who must have been the king while Lehi's children were growing up in Jerusalem. Josiah came to the throne at the age of eight and early on was influenced by those around him to clean up the religious apostasy left by Manasseh. Like his great-grandfather Hezekiah, Josiah set about to reform the religious practices of Judah. And just like Hezekiah, Josiah's reforms included revolt against the ruling Assyrian empire. Josiah cleansed the temple in Jerusalem, tore down the high places, and began to implement the laws in the newly discovered book of the law, which included the centralization of worship in Jerusalem. From that time forth, according to Josiah's program, all sacrifices, and hence most of the aspects of the religious festivals, were to be offered and observed only at the temple in Jerusalem. This had the dramatic effect of strengthening the power and influence of the temple and its attendant priesthood. In connection with his reforms, Josiah gathered the people together in a ceremony of covenant renewal and pledged to obey the law of Moses as contained in the book of the law, and then he led them in the celebration of a solemn passover (2 Kings 22–23).

The reforms of Josiah—in conjunction with Judah's perception of the invincibility of their city promised in the Davidic covenant and the miraculous deliverance of the city during the reign of Hezekiah—reinforced the people's belief that the great city of Jerusalem could not be destroyed. Their hope of deliverance from the Assyrians was buoyed at this very time by the fact that the Assyrian empire was destroyed by the Babylonians and Medes. In 612 Nineveh fell, and in 605 the final defeat of Assyria occurred at the Battle of Carchemish. In 609 Josiah, attempting to stop the Egyptians from marching to assist the Assyrians against the Babylonians, was killed in battle at Megiddo (2 Kings 23:29–30). What happened to Josiah was a frightening foreshadowing of what would later happen to Judah. In addition, the Babylonians soon conquered the west, and Judah was forced to pay tribute. But King Jehoiakim and later King Zedekiah attempted to follow in the footsteps of Hezekiah and Josiah not in religious reform but in resistance, if not revolt, against the governing empire. Their refusal to pay tribute eventually brought the might of the Babylonian empire to bear on Judah and her capital Jerusalem.

In order to counter the public sentiment of confidence that emerged during the Babylonian threat, the Lord sent prophets to warn the people: "There came many prophets, prophesying unto the people that they must repent, or the great city Jerusalem must be destroyed" (1 Nephi 1:4). Prophets like Lehi and Jeremiah were threatened with death when they spoke what many Jews considered to be blasphemous words against the holy city (1 Nephi 1:20; Jeremiah 26:12–15; 38:4). In fact, the prophet Urijah was put to death by King Jehoiakim for delivering the same message of destruction that Lehi and Jeremiah did (Jeremiah 26:20–23).

Jeremiah delivered a dramatic sermon at the temple that addressed this issue. Isaiah had specifically promised that Jerusalem would be protected from the Assyrians (Isaiah 37:33–35), and apparently the people of Jeremiah's day believed that the Lord would likewise preserve them against the Babylonians. He warned the Jews against believing that the temple was enough to deliver them from destruction: "Trust ye not in lying words, saying The temple of the Lord" (Jeremiah 7:4). Apparently, although Jeremiah observed that the people worshipped the Lord at the temple in the proper fashion, this seemed to be an outward observance since the people still had not repented of their sins. He enumerated their sins, starting with the breaking of the Ten Commandments: murder, adultery, swearing falsely, and walking after other gods (Jeremiah 7:9), as well as not executing justice between themselves and of oppressing the poor (Jeremiah 7:5–6). In short, the Judahites were hypocritically worshipping the Lord outwardly and yet breaking the commandments. Jeremiah repeated the word of the Lord to Judah: "Is this house, which is called by my name, become a den of robbers in your eyes?" (Jeremiah 7:11)—a passage from Jeremiah that Jesus would later quote in Herod's temple in a similar situation in which he prophesied that the hypocrisy of the people would not save that temple from destruction either (Matthew 21:13).

In order to make his point, Jeremiah turned to the sacred history of his people in the past to remind them that a similar situation had been faced at Shiloh: "But go ye now unto my place which was in Shiloh, where I set my name at the first, and see what I did to it for the wickedness of my people Israel" (Jeremiah 7:12). In the days of Samuel, the tabernacle and the ark of the covenant dwelt at Shiloh, and the people faithfully brought their sacrifices there; however, the people had also been disobedient, and the Lord had allowed the Philistines to destroy the holy place and capture the ark of the covenant for a time (1 Samuel 4–7; Psalm 78:56–67).

The public cry was to put Jeremiah to death. Priests and false prophets said of Jeremiah, "This man is worthy to die; for he hath prophesied against this city, as ye have heard with your ears" (Jeremiah 26:11). Jeremiah responded, "The Lord sent me to prophesy against this house and against this city all the words that ye have heard. Therefore now amend your ways and your doings, and obey the voice of the Lord your God, and repent, and the Lord will turn away the evil that he hath pronounced against you" (Jeremiah 26:12–13 JST).

6. False Assurances from False Prophets

At the same time that the Lord sent his prophets to warn the people and call them to repentance, there appeared a host of false prophets prophesying the deliverance of Jerusalem from the Babylonian threat. The Lord told Jeremiah, "The prophets prophesy falsely, and the priests bear rule by their means; and my people love to have it so" (Jeremiah 5:31). In spite of the obvious and visible unrighteousness of the people around them, these prophets came forth and delivered words the people loved to hear. The Lord described this message to Jeremiah: "Then said I, Ah, Lord God! behold, the prophets say unto them, Ye shall not see the sword, neither shall ye have famine; but I will give you assured peace in this place" (Jeremiah 14:13).

The Lord accused these false prophets before Jeremiah of immorality, dishonesty, and supporting the wicked: "I have seen also in the prophets of Jerusalem an horrible thing: they commit adultery, and walk in lies: they strengthen also the hands of the evildoers, that none doth return from his wickedness" (Jeremiah 23:14). The Lord accused these prophets of representing themselves and not the Lord, "I have not sent these prophets, yet they ran: I have not spoken to them, yet they prophesied" (Jeremiah 23:21). And he accused them of delivering words and visions not from the Lord but from themselves, "Hearken not unto the words of the prophets that prophesy unto you: they make you vain: they speak a vision of their own heart, and not out of the mouth of the Lord" (Jeremiah 23:16). Since many of the people believed in these lies and did not repent, many perished in the destruction of the great city of Jerusalem or were taken into exile. At least two of the people who thought the city was invincible—namely Laman and Lemuel—were saved because of their father Lehi.

Summary

Judah did not repent. The books of Kings and Chronicles describe how King Nebuchadnezzar led the Babylonian armies to Jerusalem and besieged and burned the great city and the holy temple and exiled many of its people. In his book, Jeremiah, in lamenting the destruction, describes how the Lord fought with the Babylonians against the people rather than fighting for them (Lamentations 2:3–4; cf. Jeremiah 21:5).

The prophet Ezekiel had a vision in which he learned how in fact the temple at Jerusalem—the house of the Lord—could be destroyed. He records that the presence of the Lord at his temple—which he refers to as "the glory of the God of Israel" (Ezekiel 9:3)—gradually withdrew from the temple, first leaving the cherubim to go to the gate of the temple and then to proceed to the Mount of Olives where the Lord would watch the destruction of his house (Ezekiel 9:3–11:23).

It is not clear if Laman and Lemuel or their descendants were ever convinced that the "great city" of Jerusalem had been destroyed according to Lehi's prophecy. In their murmuring in the wilderness, Laman and Lemuel even expressed that they believed, like the false prophets, that the people in Jerusalem had been righteous: "And we know that the people who were in the land of Jerusalem were a righteous people; for they kept the statutes and judgments of the Lord, and all the commandments, according to the law of Moses" (1 Nephi 17:22). The tradition of the Lamanites that passed from generation to generation was not that their forefathers had been delivered from destruction but rather that Lehi and his followers "were driven out of the land of Jerusalem because of the iniquities of their fathers" (Mosiah 10:12).

Both Lehi and Jacob confirmed that Lehi's prophecy of the destruction of Jerusalem had taken place. After arriving in the promised land, Lehi reported that he had "seen a vision, in which I know that Jerusalem is destroyed" (2 Nephi 1:4). Jacob later added that the Lord showed him that those in Jerusalem were killed and taken captive (2 Nephi 6:8).

Nephi, son of Helaman, later said that the destruction of Jerusalem was common knowledge among the Nephites: "And now we know that Jerusalem was destroyed according to the words of Jeremiah" (Helaman 8:20). He cites as evidence the contact with the people of Mulek, who confirmed the historical reality of the destruction of Jerusalem: "Will ye say that the sons of Zedekiah were not slain, all except it were Mulek? Yea, and do ye not behold that the seed of Zedekiah are with us, and they were driven out of the land of Jerusalem?" (Helaman 8:21; cf. Omni 1:15).

Thus the city of Jerusalem and the splendid temple within were destroyed. The chosen people chose not to repent of their sins and failed to follow the words of the prophet Jeremiah to submit to Babylon. In short, they forgot that the Lord is bound only when they do what he says (see D&C 82:10). In their program to consolidate and regulate the regime of sacrifices at the temple in Jerusalem, they should have remembered the spirit of the Lord and the commandments of righteousness that infused those offerings with meaning, as they should have known from the story of Saul and Agag where the prophet taught that "to obey is better than sacrifice" (1 Samuel 15:22; cf. Jeremiah 7:21–23). The peace that prevailed in Salem during Melchizedek's day and the divine intervention Jerusalem enjoyed during the reign of Hezekiah were conditioned on full obedience to the principles and stipulations of the covenants between God and Israel. And the breaking of those covenants produced the prophesied result of destruction and exile.

NOTES

1. A concise discussion of Israel's reliance on the unconditional covenant given to David in conjunction with Jeremiah's temple sermon in Jeremiah 7 can be found in Jack R. Lundbom, *Jeremiah 1–20* (New York: Doubleday, 1999), 462–63.

2. James B. Pritchard, ed., *Ancient Near Eastern Texts Relating to the Old Testament,* 3rd ed. (Princeton, N.J.: Princeton University Press, 1969), 288.

Chapter 21

THE RECHABITES:
A MODEL GROUP IN LEHI'S WORLD

Jeffrey P. Thompson and John W. Welch

One of the most enigmatic groups briefly mentioned in the Old Testament is the Rechabites. Although (and perhaps precisely because) only a few references to them exist in the entire Old Testament, people throughout the centuries have been fascinated by this extraordinary family group, and scholars have dug for clues in the Bible to explain who they were and where they came from. While many questions remain unanswered about this interesting group, it can be assumed with some confidence that Lehi and Nephi would have been familiar with the Rechabites, if not in person, at least by their general reputation for leading a righteous, covenant-based life in their tents out in the wilderness away from the wickedness in Jerusalem. It is therefore reasonable to surmise that Lehi and his followers may have modeled their behavior in certain respects after this exemplary group of pious but eccentric Israelites.

Several similarities between the Rechabites and the Lehites can be observed. Some are superficial and ordinary; others are interesting and intriguing. Taken together, the few bits and pieces of information that we have about the Rechabites provide evidence that Lehi's group was not completely idiosyncratic or that their behavior would not have been viewed as completely aberrational in the world of Jerusalem in the late seventh century.

In the Wilderness

As early as 1957, Hugh Nibley saw a connection between the Rechabites and the Lehites. In *An Approach to the Book of Mormon,* Nibley characterized the sons of Rechab as "typical of the back-to-the-wilderness movements among the Jews in every age" and suggested that they (and Lehi's group like them) would have been counted "as traitors and outlaws" for having deserted and separated themselves from the holy city of Jerusalem.[1] Nibley argued that Jonadab ben Rekhab and his followers had gone out into the desert "to recapture the spirit of [the ideal Israelite] time,"[2] recalling the years when Israel, having been delivered out of Egypt, was led through the wilderness by God's hovering cloud by day and by his pillar of fire at night. This image invites us to expand on Nibley's suggestion: perhaps, when Lehi saw in vision a "pillar of fire" that came and dwelt on a rock before him (1 Nephi 1:6), his mind was already turning or being directed toward the wilderness, to live like the ancient Israelites in the desert or like the contemporaneous Rechabites in some removed place of refuge away from the wickedness and impending destruction of Jerusalem.

Nibley also linguistically linked Nephite culture to Jonadab the Rechabite on two intriguing but inconclusive grounds: the personal name suffix -*nadab* also appears at the end of the Book of Mormon name of Aminadab, and, in general, "the Rekhabite teachings are strangely like those in the Book of Mormon." From such clues Nibley concluded that "one is forced to admit at very least the possibility that Lehi's exodus *could* have taken place in the manner described, and the certainty that other such migrations actually did take place."[3] Nevertheless, the Rechabites remained for Nibley and for us today a "strange and baffling" group, especially as they come to be represented in later traditions associated with messianic expectations.[4]

A Model of Obedience

How the Rechabite group originated is obscure; some have called it "a mystery."[5] Hints of the origins of the Rechabites are given in 2 Kings and 1 Chronicles, assuming that these texts are speaking of the same group. Back in the ninth century, King Jehu encountered Jehonadab (Jonadab) while traveling toward Mount Carmel and invited him to accompany him and witness his destructive attack on the priests of Baal (2 Kings 10). We can infer from this story, as is also certainly implied in Jeremiah's description of the Rechabites and their reputation for obedience (Jeremiah 35), that these people were known, to a considerable degree, for their pious loyalty to Yahweh.

The only glimpses we have of this obedient group in Lehi's day come from Jeremiah 35. Acting on the Lord's command, "presumably in 599 or 598,"[6] Jeremiah invited the Rechabites to the temple, a place with which they may have been deeply associated,[7] as an example of an obedient people. When Jeremiah offered them wine, they refused declaring, "We will drink no wine: for Jonadab the son of Rechab our father commanded us, saying, Ye shall drink no wine, neither ye, nor your sons for ever" (Jeremiah 35:6). The Rechabites added to this stipulation the command of their father that they were not to be bound to any property, that they were not to "build house, nor sow seed, nor plant vineyard, nor have any: but all your days ye shall dwell in tents; that ye may live many days in the land where ye be strangers" (Jeremiah 35:7). The Lord himself contrasted the obedience of the Rechabites (who obeyed their father) with the disobedience of the men of Judah and the inhabitants of Jerusalem: "Ye have not inclined your ear, nor hearkened unto me.... this people hath not hearkened unto me:... saith the Lord God of hosts" (Jeremiah 35:15–17). For their obedience the Rechabites were blessed: "Because ye have obeyed the commandment of Jonadab your father, and kept all his precepts, and done according unto all that he hath commanded you: therefore thus saith the Lord of hosts, the God of Israel; Jonadab the son of Rechab shall not want a man to stand before me for ever" (Jeremiah 35:18–19).

Saliently, Jeremiah admired the Rechabites for their obedience to the righteous commandments given by Jonadab, their father, and he wished that all of Israel would obey God with the same degree of diligence. No attentive reader of 1 Nephi could miss the similar emphasis placed by Nephi on the principle of obeying the personalized commandments of God issued by a righteous father: Receiving a command of God from his father, Nephi set his face like flint: "I will go and do the things which the Lord hath commanded" (1 Nephi 3:7). Later in the wilderness he again testified "that the commandments of God must be fulfilled" and that if "the children of men keep the commandments of God he doth nourish them, and strengthen them, and provide means whereby they can accomplish the thing which he has commanded them" (1 Nephi 17:3).

Semiurbanized Nomads

Although connected with Jerusalem, both groups seem to have taken up a nomadic or seminomadic lifestyle to distance themselves from the corruptions of city life. We do not know why the Rechabites chose to live away from major towns or cities, but Lehi was instructed by the Lord to take his family and dwell in the wilderness (1 Nephi 2:2) because of the impending destruction of the city (1 Nephi 1:8–13). Nephi made repeated mention of the fact that Lehi dwelt in a tent during this time: "And my father dwelt in a tent" (1 Nephi 2:15; 9:1; 10:16; 16:6; see also 2:6; 3:1; 4:38; 5:7; 7:5, 21, 22; 16:10), which seems to signal something of social significance.[8] His family packed and departed into the desert where they initially set up a camp, like the Rechabites, not in Jerusalem, but close enough so they could return several times to the city to seek records and Ishmael's family (1 Nephi 3–5, 7). This lifestyle allowed them needed mobility and freedom of movement. In this way, Lehi's family spent approximately eight years in the desert (1 Nephi 17:4). Once in the land of promise, Nephi again would "flee into the wilderness" with those who would go with him (2 Nephi 5:5). This pattern of escaping as seminomads into the wilderness, even with flocks, continues well into the Book of Mormon (Mosiah 23:1–3).

Such a temporary lifestyle seems to parallel the regular behavior of the Rechabites, whose code of conduct specifically required that "all your days ye shall dwell in tents" (Jeremiah 35:7). Because of their tent dwelling and their avoidance of agriculture, some scholars have labeled the Rechabites as nomads.[9] Scholars have recognized different kinds of nomadic living in the ancient Near East. The first is the "true nomad or Bedouin" who dwells in the desert and relies solely on the camel. This group has little or no contact with cities. The second breeds sheep and goats and thus is required to move and live where there is rainfall and will usually have some contact with settlements. The third lives a seminomad and semiurban lifestyle. In addition to sheep and goats, this group raises cattle, cultivates a few simple crops, and has some contact with established city centers.[10] Both the Rechabites and the Lehites seem to fit into the second or third group. The Lehites led a more nomadic style of life during their years of trekking through the Arabian Peninsula and later became more settled in the land of Bountiful.

Family Orientation

Both groups made honorific use of the names of their patriarchal founder and also of their guiding teacher. The "house of the Rechabites" had taken their name from an ancestor named Rechab (Jeremiah 35:18). Their way of life, however, seems to have originated with Jehonadab, Rechab's son or descendant, for they had "obeyed the voice of Jonadab the son of Rechab our father in all that he hath charged us" (Jeremiah 35:8).[11] In this group, one ancestor gave the group its name, and another was key in mandating their lifestyle. In the case of the Nephites, something similar occurred, although not until after their settlement in the New World: Lehi was the initial leader of the group and was responsible for their exodus from Jerusalem, while Nephi was the son who shaped their way of life. His followers quickly and easily took their name from his as "the people of Nephi" (2 Nephi 5:9).

Each group was composed of a closely knit full family group. The Rechabites consisted of wives, sons, daughters, and fathers (Jeremiah 35:3, 5, 8). This was a family organization, a type of tribe or clan. Whether there were nonrelatives who joined is not clear; but at least a substantial number, if not all, seem to have been of the same bloodline. Notably, the Rechabites, when they left the wilderness and moved nearer to Jerusalem as Nebuchadnezzar later was invading the land, may have picked up a few outsiders, for the Rechabites appear to have invited others to come up with them at that time (Jeremiah 35:11). Similarly, Lehi's group also consisted initially of a single family. Ishmael's family and Zoram then joined the clan as they fled from danger (1 Nephi 7:2–5; 4:35). It is possible that Ishmael and Lehi were related to each other; soon Ishmael's daughters became the wives of Lehi's sons and of Zoram, and hence they and their children all became part of the family of Lehi (1 Nephi 16:7; 2 Nephi 1–4).

The Rechabites were not gender or age specific; they were not ascetic monks, as they are sometimes cast in light of later Christian narratives.[12] "Wives . . . sons . . . [and] daughters" all lived the Rechabite lifestyle (Jeremiah 35:8), negating the idea that it was a type of monastic life. Lehi's departing group was also organized as a tribe or clan. Following the Lord's command, Lehi took his wife, sons, and daughters with him; the group later included Ishmael's family, whose daughters would become wives for his sons (1 Nephi 2:2–4; 7:1–6; 2 Nephi 5:6).

Sufficient Means

Both the Rechabites and Lehi appear to have been wealthy, having sufficient means. The Rechabites had no fields or vineyards, which meant that they had no means of food production aside from maintaining flocks (something that apparently was not prohibited to them) or some other source of income. Jehonadab's name may even indicate he came originally from the upper class. His name is based on "a variant of the divine name Yahweh" and "the triliteral Hebrew root *n-d-b*."[13] This root has the sense of being "generous" or "noble" and may refer to a member of aristocracy.[14] We know more certainly that Lehi was quite wealthy, for he left "gold and silver, and all manner of riches" behind at his home in Jerusalem (1 Nephi 3:16). The amount of wealth was so "exceedingly great" that when Laban saw it he "did lust" after it (1 Nephi 3:25). Lehi, too, appears to have been a prominent member of Jerusalem society, although it is not clear how he might have been related to the ruling class. The fact that Nephi and his brothers had easy access to Laban, who evidently held a high social position as guardian of the precious brass plates and had command of fifty men (1 Nephi 3:3, 24, 31), further reflects Lehi's adequate economic status.

Metallurgists?

Another possible parallel, also related to economics and commerce, has to do with metallurgy. Clues in the Bible suggest that the Rechabites were familiar with and practiced metalworking.[15] Several historians have assumed that the Rechabites were involved in some kind of metallurgical craft or trade. "The families of the scribes which dwelt at Jabez; the Tirathites, the Shimeathites, and Suchathites. These are the *Kenites* that came of Hemath, the father of the house of Rechab" (1 Chronicles 2:55, emphasis added). The name Kenites is derived from the Semitic root *qyn,* which denotes "fabrication" or "ironworking." In some cases, it is translated as "smiths."[16] In his discussion on the ancient smith, R. J. Forbes draws some parallels with the Rechabites and points out that they may have formed a guild. In preindustrial societies, technical knowledge was carefully protected and handed down from generation to generation. Frick adds that "the smith had to be familiar with many technical procedures, the knowledge of which was handed down and guarded jealously from one generation to the next."[17] Typically, such guilds lasted for many years, even sometimes centuries, in part because guilds often consisted solely of family members.[18] The Rechabites seem to behave in such a familial way. Another marked characteristic of smiths was their itinerant nature.

Egyptian metalsmiths refining copper by pushing the bellows with their feet to provide the draught of air to the furnace. (Wall-painting in the tomb of Rekh-mi-reᶜ, Thebes ca. 1470 B.C.)

They would stay and work in one spot until the ore or fuel was exhausted and then move on. This could also explain why the Rechabites never built homes or planted fields.[19]

Nephi appears to be familiar with metallurgy, as has been suggested, especially by John Tvedtnes.[20] When he is at Irreantum he is commanded by the Lord to "construct a ship, after the manner which I shall show thee" (1 Nephi 17:8). Nephi then proceeds to ask "Lord, whither shall I go that I may find ore to molten, that I may make tools" (1 Nephi 17:9). It has been noted that Nephi did not ask how to make tools, nor did the Lord say he would show Nephi how to make them. Nephi only asked to find the ore so he could make them. This would seem to indicate that Nephi already had the necessary knowledge to make tools. He evidently already knew how to make bellows out of hides without information from the Lord (1 Nephi 17:11). If, as Forbes suggests, metallurgical knowledge was highly guarded, then Nephi must have been taught by a family member or friend—possibly even by someone like a Rechabite, although this cannot be known with any certainty. It is interesting, however, that the Lord did not need to show Nephi how to make the tools just as he showed him how to make the ship. Also noteworthy is the fact that Laman and Lemuel mocked Nephi for trying to build a ship, but nothing was mentioned about his making tools (1 Nephi 17:17–18).

Covenantal Piety

Another similar quality between the two groups is that both appear to have been living a particular law of piety based on a vow or covenant. The Rechabites, we are told, were known for their complete abstinence from wine, for they followed Jehonadab's command that they "drink no wine, neither [they], nor [their] sons for ever" (Jeremiah 35:6, 18).[21] The command was apparently respected by all the Rechabites. Abstinence was not practiced by all the Israelites and was viewed as somewhat peculiar. Only a handful of persons in the Old Testament have been identified as abstaining from wine—most notably the sons of Aaron who held the Levitical priesthood when they were officiating in their duties (Leviticus 10:9) and those who swore the Nazarite vow, such as Samson (Numbers 6:3; Judges 13:4). Both the priests and the Nazarites clearly lived this way in order to maintain a higher level of spirituality and to properly serve God. Lehi and his family were also living a higher law of the gospel. Lehi was the recipient of several magnificent visions, but most importantly, Lehi and his family were deemed righteous enough to be spared the forthcoming destruction of Jerusalem. Whether Lehi's family drank no wine is unclear, but chastity, honesty, and keeping all the Lord's commandments were required and desirable characteristics of Lehi's clan (2 Nephi 9:31–38; Jacob 2:28).

Both groups grounded their religious obligations in a covenant with the Lord. The Rechabites had been promised that if they did not drink wine, build homes, or plant fields, they would "live many days in the land where [they were] strangers" (Jeremiah 35:7). The Lord assured them eternally that, because of their obedience, "Jonadab the son of Rechab shall not want a man to stand before me for ever" (Jeremiah 35:19). Perhaps this promise of the Lord alone motivated their stalwartness in keeping their father's commandments. The Lord's promise to Lehi was similar, namely that "inasmuch as ye shall keep my commandments ye shall be led towards the promised land; and ye shall know that it is by me that ye are led" (1 Nephi 17:13) and that they would "prosper" in the promised land (2 Nephi 1:9). This undoubtedly provided a similar stimulus for the Nephites to be righteous.

Trust in the Lord

In the end, both groups remained calm and confident that the Lord would keep his promises and protect them in the face of serious danger. The Old Testament does not reveal why the Rechabites returned to the vicinity of Jerusalem when they received information about Nebuchadnezzar's plans to invade the land of Judah; but even in the face of impending attack, they maintained their righteousness, came up to the temple, and kept their faith in the Lord.

Lehi and his family, likewise, remained confident and obedient, although in a different way. They knew of the impending destruction of Jerusalem, about which Lehi had read unmistakably in the book shown to him in vision (1 Nephi 1:13). Still, they left their home and went forth, trusting in the Lord, knowing that his "power, and goodness, and mercy are over all the inhabitants of the earth," and that those who will come to God shall not perish (1 Nephi 1:14).

Above all, Lehi knew of the coming of "a Messiah, or, in other words, a Savior of the world" (1 Nephi 10:4). As Nibley notes above, and as has been discussed elsewhere, the Rechabites become the subject of later Jewish and Christian histories and legends that associate them with messianic expectations, looking forward to the time when God will reestablish his righteous covenant with a reunited Israel. Found in several versions, the *History of the Rechabites* is an early Christian text, based on a much earlier Jewish tradition that tells how the Rechabites were led from Jerusalem before the Babylonian captivity to a land across the ocean, having several experiences similar to Lehi's.[22] Whether this religious lore has any historical connection with Lehi and his covenantal group similarly living in a state of messianic expectation and apocalyptic anticipation remains uncertain, but the possibility cannot be completely discounted.

In conclusion, there are many interesting comparisons between the Rechabites and Lehi and his family. Both groups lived more in accord with righteous principles than their fellow Israelites. The two groups certainly could have known each other, since they did live in or around Jerusalem at the same time. Depending on many unknown factors, the Rechabites and Lehites may have had even more in common than these surviving glimpses disclose. Both were, in their own ways, part of the dispersion of Israel in which the Lord leads "away the righteous into precious lands" (1 Nephi 17:38), "scattered upon all the face of the earth" (1 Nephi 10:12).

Notes

The first draft of this chapter was prepared by Jeffrey P. Thompson, a law student assistant working with John W. Welch at the J. Reuben Clark Law School at Brigham Young University. Robert D. Hunt contributed additions.

1. Hugh Nibley, *An Approach to the Book of Mormon*, 3rd ed. (Salt Lake City: Deseret Book and FARMS, 1988), 151.

2. Ibid., 146.

3. Ibid., 69.

4. Ibid., 68.

5. Margaret Barker, *The Great High Priest: The Temple Roots of Christian Liturgy* (London: Clark, 2003), 124.

6. John Bright, *Jeremiah: A New Translation with Introduction and Commentary* (Garden City, N.Y.: Doubleday, 1965), 190.

7. Barker, *Great High Priest,* 29, 124, surmises a connection between the name Rechab and a memory of the *merkavah,* the chariot-throne in the temple.

8. Nibley, *An Approach to the Book of Mormon,* 243.

9. Frank S. Frick, "Rechab," in *Anchor Bible Dictionary,* ed. David Noel Freedman (New York: Doubleday, 1992), 5:631; see also Frank S. Frick, *The City in Ancient Israel* (Missoula, Mont.: Scholars, 1977), 211–17.

10. Frick, *City in Ancient Israel,* 189–90 at 189. See also Roland de Vaux, *Ancient Israel* (New York: McGraw-Hill, 1961), 1:3–4.

11. The term *ben* or *son of* can mean son or descendant; see Francis Brown, S. R. Driver, and Charles A. Briggs, *Hebrew and English Lexicon of the Old Testament* (Peabody, Mass.: Hendrickson, 1999), 120–21.

12. See *Narrative of Zosimus,* concluding sections; Barker, *Great High Priest,* says "ascetics," 28, and "monastic," 124.

13. Frick, "Rechab," 631.

14. Brown, Driver, and Briggs, *Hebrew and English Lexicon,* 621; see also Frick, "Rechab," 631.

15. See R. J. Forbes, *Metallurgy in Antiquity: A Notebook for Archaeologists and Technologists* (Leiden: Brill, 1950), 64–68, 98. See also Frick, "Rechab," 631; John Bright, *A History of Israel,* 3rd ed. (Philadelphia: Westminster, 1981), 125. Frick discusses the Rechabites' association with Ir-nahash in the genealogical lists in 1 Chronicles 4 and with the Kenites in 1 Chronicles 2:55. Both the father Ir-nahash and the Kenite clan were involved in metallurgy.

16. Brown, *Hebrew and English Lexicon,* 883–84. See also Frick, "Rechab," 631.

17. Frick, "Rechab," 631. Frick also discusses this behavior in

relation to their abstinence and nomadism, writing that such "measures . . . were designed to guard the secrets of the trade."

18. Ibid.

19. Forbes, *Metallurgy*, 64–68; see also Frick, "Rechab," 631–32.

20. John A. Tvedtnes, *The Most Correct Book: Insights from a Book of Mormon Scholar* (Salt Lake City: Cornerstone, 1999), 94–97.

21. Although only wine was prohibited, it is assumed that abstinence from all alcohol was practiced since all scriptures in the Old Testament that discuss abstinence preclude both wine and strong drink (see Leviticus 10:9; Numbers 6:3; Judges 13:4, 14).

22. John W. Welch, "The Narrative of Zosimus (History of the Rechabites) and the Book of Mormon," in *Book of Mormon Authorship Revisited: The Evidence for Ancient Origins,* ed. Noel B. Reynolds (Provo, Utah: FARMS, 1997), 323–74, citing several scholarly sources regarding this body of literature; to that material should now be added Chris H. Knights, "A Century of Research into the Story/Apocalypse of Zosimus and/or the History of the Rechabites," *Journal for the Study of the Pseudepigrapha* 15 (1997): 53–66; and "*The History of the Rechabites*—An Initial Commentary," *Journal for the Study of Judaism in the Persian, Hellenistic and Roman Period* 28/4 (1997): 413–36.

Chapter 22

Jerusalem Connections to Arabia in 600 b.c.

S. Kent Brown

At the behest of the Lord, Lehi and Sariah led their family from their home near Jerusalem into the desert of Arabia where they lived for eight long years. Even though for generations their descendants would celebrate their exodus in story and song, the question that invites our attention concerns the connections of the homeland of Lehi and Sariah to Arabia.

The surprise is that Lehi and Sariah fled to Arabia, not to Egypt. As readers of the Old Testament will know, almost all persons known to flee from Jerusalem and its environs went southwest to Egypt, not southeast to Arabia. Given the political climate of 600 b.c., going north or east into Babylonian-controlled areas was not an option because Babylonian authorities would force Lehi back to Jerusalem if Jewish officials requested. In contrast, Egypt was a place of refuge.[1] But Arabia?

As a matter of fact, the Old Testament preserves a number of references to connections between Arabia and ancient Palestine. Other ancient sources do as well, including some recently discovered. Some of these ties were commercial, others were military.

Traditions even claim that Israelites had moved into Arabia long before—and even during—the days of Lehi and Sariah. In this light, should we see Arabia as a known though infrequent destination for travelers from Jerusalem?

Outbound Routes

A reader of the Book of Mormon is left to assume that the Lord had instructed Lehi about where he and his family were to travel from Jerusalem. We do not possess Lehi's report of this experience, and Nephi does not preserve any such instruction in his narrative of the family's move. Evidently knowing the general direction of travel, Lehi led his family "into the wilderness" toward the southeast. How do we know the direction of travel? Because the family's first camping spot lay "in the borders which are nearer the Red Sea" (1 Nephi 2:5).[2]

While Nephi does not indicate the route that he and other family members followed when going south and east toward Arabia, four known roads were open to them, and the likelihood is high that the family followed, or perhaps shadowed, one of these routes that led away from Jerusalem. Two ran south, two ran east. As a point of clarification, one must bear in mind that only one of them ran along the shores of the Dead Sea. On both the east and west sides of the Dead Sea the terrain slopes steeply from cliffs to water's edge and does not allow travelers to pass. The problems would be worse, of course, for pack animals.[3]

South. The only route that skirted any part of the shoreline of the Dead Sea descended the so-called ascent of Ziz (2 Chronicles 20:16 RSV). A major road ran southward from Jerusalem to Hebron through Bethlehem, beginning at the southern gate of Jerusalem, which stood near the Siloam Pool.[4] To reach the ascent of Ziz, a person turned off this main road, bending east near Tekoa, the birthplace of the prophet Amos

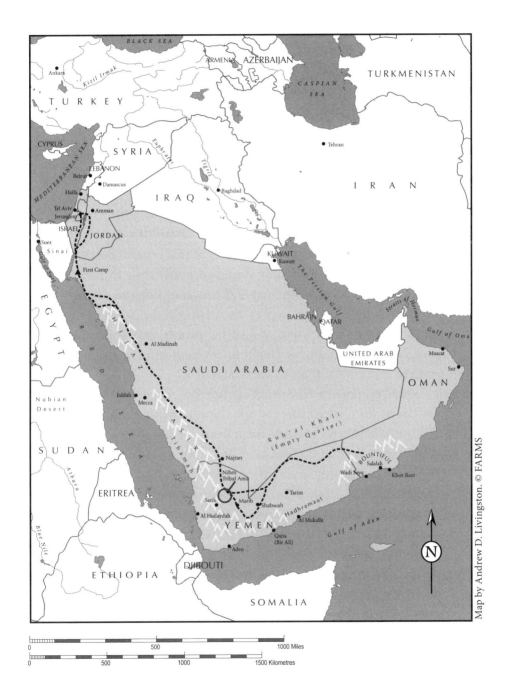

Map by Andrew D. Livingston. © FARMS

(Amos 1:1). From this point the trail descended through the rugged desert hills of Judea to a point near the Ein Gedi oasis next to the Dead Sea. Had the family followed this route, at Ein Gedi they would have turned south toward the northeast arm of the Red Sea where Aqaba and Eilat now sit, keeping the Dead Sea on their left for the next twenty-five miles or so.[5]

A second option consisted in following the same trade route that led south to Hebron. Beyond Hebron, a traveler continued to Arad, then down through the Zohar Valley, and finally into the Arabah Valley. This road would have been more direct and, like the other, would have led the family toward the northeastern tip of the Red Sea. I should emphasize that I do not discount the possibility that the family stayed generally close to a trade route not only for this segment of the journey but for later segments too. Even though Nephi's recounting of the journey does not specifically mention meeting other people, the party surely would have done so. For Nephi offers clear hints that family members ran into others as they traveled.[6]

East, then south. Two other commercial routes led travelers eastward from Jerusalem and then south toward the Red Sea. The more southerly of the two ran from the east side of the city and wound around the southern slope of the Mount of Olives. From that point, it gradually descended eastward through Wadi Mukallik (Nahal Og) and connected with the northeast shore of the Dead Sea. In antiquity this trail was known as the Route of Salt because caravans carried salt, which had been extracted out of the Dead Sea, from its northwest shore up to Jerusalem.[7] If the family had followed this road, they could have broken off at any point after reaching the Jordan Valley and headed eastward to the mountains of Moab where they would have intersected either the King's Highway or another road farther east and turned south.[8]

The other trail ran almost directly eastward from a point north of the temple area. This route climbed the steep western slope of the Mount of Olives, crossing at a point near the modern village of At-Tur, and then plunged downward toward the Wadi Kelt, eventually reaching Jericho. This path, too, carried trade between the Jordan Valley and Jerusalem. One of its spurs on the eastern slope of the Mount of Olives led south to Bethany, a path that Jesus followed when going to raise his friend Lazarus from the tomb (see John 10:40; 11:17–20). For their part, the family of Lehi and Sariah would have exited Wadi Kelt a couple of miles south of Old Testament Jericho. From there, it was an easy trek eastward across the Jordan Valley to the base of the mountains of Moab. The King's Highway or the eastern road would then have led them southward to the tip of the northeastern arm of the Red Sea.

Military Contacts

The nature of military connections between Arabia and ancient Israel is not totally clear. The Old Testament does not treat any such matters directly except for one possible reference in the book of Job, which reads, "The troops of Tema looked, the companies of Sheba waited for them" (Job 6:19), a seeming reference to armies. But the translation is misleading. To be sure, Tema, or Tayma, was an important city in northwestern Arabia and Sheba was the name of an important kingdom in the southwest sector of the peninsula whence the queen of Sheba came to visit Solomon (see 1 Kings 10:1–2). The Revised Standard Version presents a more accurate rendering of Job 6:19: "The caravans of Tema look, the travelers of Sheba hope." Hence, there is nothing of military significance in this passage. Instead, it is the annals of the Assyrian kings that suggest possible military contacts between ancient Israel and Arabia.

The earliest notice of Assyrian military action in the northern kingdom of Israel, which was formed in 922 B.C. after the death of Solomon (see 1 Kings 12:1–20), comes from King Tiglath-pileser III who ruled Assyria from 745 to 727 B.C.[9] Sometime after 736 B.C., the forces of Tiglath-pileser captured Samaria, the capital city of the northern kingdom of Israel. Because Tiglath-pileser's record is incomplete, we do not know the reason for this military action. But we can be reasonably certain that the Assyrian army had come to Samaria because officials there had stopped paying tribute. The Israelite kingdom had already been making such payments during the reign of Menachem (745–737 B.C.), as both the Old Testament and an earlier record from Tiglath-pileser show. By submitting to payment of a heavy tribute, Menahem had effectively surrendered the independence of Israel.[10] The next known military invasion by Assyrians came a decade or so later.

King Shalmaneser V, who ruled Assyria from 726 to 722 B.C., saw a number of small kingdoms attempt to revolt from his control during his first year in office. The kingdom of Israel was one of them. The Israelite king at the time of Shalmaneser was Hoshea, who had come to power by assassinating the prior king (see 2 Kings 15:30). As soon as Hoshea thought he had opportunity to rebel against the Assyrians, he withheld the tribute due to King Shalmaneser and instead tried unsuccessfully to buy military aid from Egypt (see 2 Kings 17:4). It was, however, a fatal mistake. After a siege of more than two years, Israel's capital city, Samaria, fell to the Assyrian army, which promptly marched almost thirty thousand people north and east.[11] These people later became known as the lost ten tribes of Israel.

Shalmaneser's successor, Sargon II (721–705 B.C.), noted in his annals that the Assyrian army faced other forces in the same region, hinting strongly that these clashes occurred during the campaign that destroyed Samaria, or soon thereafter.

They included battles against the rebellious armies of Gaza and Egypt. Then he wrote the following intriguing lines: "I received the tribute . . . from Samsi, queen of Arabia (and) It'amar the Sabaean, gold in dust-form, horses (and) camels."[12] Were these rulers among those who tried to revolt from Sargon's control, effectively collaborating in a general rebellion that the kingdoms of Israel, Gaza, and Egypt initiated? It seems possible. For the Assyrian king forced all the rebel groups and their leaders to pay heavy tributes. And on this occasion the rebels included Queen Samsi of Arabia and It'amar of the Sabaean kingdom, which was likely the same as the biblical Sheba.[13] Hence, it appears that two forces from Arabia had joined the revolts of Israel, Gaza, and Egypt. To be sure, we do not know for certain whether the Arabians had made a formal pact either with King Hoshea of Israel or with the Gazans and Egyptians, or whether they had rebelled on their own. But the observation that Sargon's army apparently met all their armies during the same campaigning season points to a coordinated effort on the part of the rebels.

What must have added insult to injury for both the conquered Israelites and Arabians was the forced migration of nomadic Arab peoples into the former territory of Israel.[14] In the seventh year of his reign, Sargon wrote of "the Arabs who live, far away, in the desert (and) who know neither overseers nor officials." He was evidently referring to Bedouins, who owe no loyalty to rulers unless they are reined in. Next, speaking again of Arab tribesmen, he recorded that "[the Arabs] had not (yet) brought their tribute to any king. I deported their survivors and settled (them) in Samaria." In this context he again mentioned "Samsi, the queen of Arabia, [and] It'amra, the Sabaean."[15] In light of Sargon's assertions that he regularly moved people from one area of his realm to another, as he did with the Israelites and these Arabs, it seems safe to say that on this occasion he forced the Arab "survivors" of war against him to move from their desert homes to the former territory of the Israelites, where he could exercise more control over them and force them to pay tribute.[16]

What does all of this mean for the Book of Mormon story? It is evident that, more than one hundred years before Lehi and Sariah came on the scene, the army of the Assyrian empire had been active in the general region of Jerusalem, both north of the city in the kingdom of Israel and south in Gaza and Egypt. Some of that activity had to do with the intransigence of the Israelites, led by their kings, and some had to do with peoples in Arabia. Two possibilities arise from the military conflicts that occurred in the region over a period of years. First, it is possible—even probable—that Lehi's forebears in the tribe of Manasseh (see Alma 10:3) had moved south to Jerusalem in order to escape the terrors of war with Assyria in the north, eventually establishing an estate that, in time, Lehi came to inherit. Second, it is possible that the Arabs whom Sargon moved into the territory of the former kingdom of Israel became the liaisons for merchants in Arabia who wished to make their exotic goods available to buyers in that general area, including the city of Jerusalem, where Lehi would have had contact with them.

Commercial Ties

According to the Old Testament, by far the largest number of contacts between people in Arabia and those in and around Jerusalem were of a commercial character. Jerusalemites enjoyed prized Arabian imports as diverse as incense, sheep, goats, and gems (see 2 Chronicles 17:11; Isaiah 60:6; Ezekiel 27:21–22). And most of the Old Testament references to this trade date to the era of Lehi and Sariah. But before reviewing these references, we must treat an important person in the book of Job.

Although the date of the composition of the book of Job is a matter of debate, it seems reasonably safe that it was composed before or by the fifth century B.C., not long after the days of Lehi and Sariah.[17] What is significant is that the book features prominently a friend of Job known as Eliphaz the Temanite.[18] Tema, or Tayma, of course, was a crossroads city of northwestern Arabia whose importance blossomed suddenly when Nabonidus, ruler of the ancient Babylonian kingdom, unexpectedly moved his capital there about 550 B.C. For approximately ten years, this desert city was the focus of King Nabonidus's life, even though the city lay many hundreds of miles south of the Mesopotamian valley where his original base of power lay.[19] It was from this city that Eliphaz came to visit the suffering Job. What seems plain in the story of Job is that Eliphaz was a man of means who was able to come to Job in his hour of need. Hence, it seems reasonable to say that Tema was a city of importance that offered opportunity for its citizens to amass a certain amount of wealth. We know, for example, that it was a major center for worship of the moon god in antiquity[20] and sat astride a major junction of trade routes.[21]

In a telling passage written a century before Lehi and Sariah left Jerusalem, the prophet Isaiah wrote of Tema as a place of refuge for those worn weary by war. The passage reads: "In the forest in Arabia shall ye lodge, O ye travelling companies of Dedanim. The inhabitants of the land of Tema brought water to him that was thirsty, they prevented [= met] with their bread him that fled. For they fled from the swords, from the drawn sword, and from the bent bow, and from the grievousness of war" (Isaiah 21:13–15).

Whether this passage alludes to Isaiah's Israelite contemporaries who were fleeing the war waged by the Assyrians against King Hoshea is unknown, although the thought is tempting. For if Isaiah is indeed speaking of Israelites seeking refuge in northwest Arabia, this may constitute the first evidence from an ancient source of such people moving to Arabia. But certainty eludes us. To be sure, later traditions hold that Israelites had begun to live in Arabia as early as the era of Moses and the exodus. But such traditions seem to have no historical basis (more on this subject below).

From the same prophet come words that anticipate events in the latter days when the Lord again gathers his people to his temple for worship. In expressing the varied dimensions of this prophecy, Isaiah appeals to imagery that shows his acquaintance with Arabia. For he writes: "The multitude of camels shall cover thee, the dromedaries of Midian and Ephah; all they from Sheba shall come: they shall bring gold and incense; and they shall shew forth the praises of the Lord. All the flocks of Kedar shall be gathered together unto thee, the rams of Nebaioth shall minister unto thee: they shall come up with acceptance on mine altar, and I will glorify the house of my glory" (Isaiah 60:6–7).

We note that the goods to be offered in the temple will come from Midian, a territory in northwest Arabia; from Sheba, which lies at the edge of the southern desert; and from the people of Kedar and Nebaioth, whose territories lie in north Arabia.[22] The goods are to include "gold and incense" as well as "the flocks" and "the rams" from these areas. From this and other passages we learn that goods from Arabia were prized by Israelites, including those in the era of Lehi and Sariah.[23]

Besides written evidence for extensive ties to Arabia's merchants from Old Testament prophets of the eighth and seventh centuries B.C.—Isaiah, Jeremiah, and Ezekiel—important inscriptions found in Jerusalem date to the same period. According to William Whitt, among the thirty known inscriptions written in the old south Arabian script from this era, some were "found in Jerusalem" on potsherds.[24] Actually, the number of potsherds discovered was three. Archaeologists discovered them in the ancient City of David, the spur of hill that has been inhabited for four thousand years and runs south from the ancient temple area where the Dome of the Rock now sits. Because the potsherds demonstrate the presence of Arabians in Jerusalem, the discoverer, Yigal Shiloh, calls them "extraordinary inscriptions inscribed on sherds from the Iron Age." Maria Höfner of the University of Graz, who is an expert in south Arabian scripts, dates the three inscriptions "to the early stage of the [south Arabian] writing in the eighth–seventh centuries B.C."[25] As is plain, this evidence matches the notices that we have found in the Old Testament about commercial contacts between Arabia and people in and around Jerusalem.

From the above it becomes clear that from a period dating at least one hundred years before Lehi and Sariah, there were extensive commercial contacts between people in Arabia and those in and around Jerusalem. Ancient Israelites sought exotic imported goods as widely diverse as incense and sheep, fabrics and gold, precious gems and spices. If, in fact, Lehi was a trader, as some have suggested,[26] he may have enjoyed commercial relations with counterparts in Arabia. Unfortunately, there is sparse evidence for this observation beyond the fact that with his family he traveled there from Jerusalem.

Traditions

The traditions about Israelites or Jews coming to live in Arabia number essentially three.[27] One holds that some of the Hebrew slaves who came out of Egypt with Moses turned aside from the main migrating group and settled in northern Arabia.[28] There is a certain attraction in this notion because Moses' father-in-law, Jethro, lived in Midian, a region that lay in northwestern Arabia (see Exodus 2:15–16; 3:1). Thus one might suppose that it would be natural for some of Moses' migrants to settle there. But no archaeological or other kind of evidence exists to show that any sizable group of Israelites inhabited Midian in those days.[29] For example, the pottery record for northwest Arabia from the thirteenth to twelfth centuries B.C., about the time of the exodus, consists mostly of remnants of so-called Midianite ware. Researchers have been able to determine that this pottery was manufactured in or around the Arabian town of Qurayyah and spread as far north as Hebron. But no evidence has been uncovered to determine that it was carried farther north, as one might expect if Midianite pottery vessels were being used to carry goods back and forth between Israelites in Midian and Israelites in the land of Canaan.

A second tradition asserts that in the days of Solomon a large group of people migrated from ancient Israel into Arabia. This story attaches itself to the visit of the queen of Sheba (see 1 Kings 10:1–2) and claims that Israelites accompanied her back to her home in south Arabia, eventually settling in the region.[30] While this tale is appealing, chiefly because one can imagine Israelites relocating in order to find commercial opportunities to ship goods to Jerusalem, the evidence falls short of sustaining the story. The biblical record offers no hints about such a migration, and other written and archaeological evidence is lacking.

A third tradition claims that up to seventy-five thousand faithful Jews—a huge number—fled Jerusalem before the Babylonians destroyed the city and the temple in 587 B.C. The same story says specifically that they left forty-two years before the coming of the Babylonians (ca. 629 B.C.). Why did they go? Because these people believed the warning of Jeremiah about the terrible fate of those who remained in Jerusalem (e.g., Jeremiah 38:2).[31] In this case, even allowing for the exaggeration of the number of migrants, they would have departed during the lifetime of Lehi. But as far as we know, no writer took notice of the departure of such a large group. In addition, there is no physical evidence of large numbers of Israelites moving into Arabia in the late seventh century B.C.[32]

Interest in these traditions received a tremendous boost in 1949 when Israelis began to airlift to Israel more than fifty thousand Jews who had been living in Yemen. These Yemenite Jews brought with them fresh versions of these and other traditions, thus fortifying claims that Jews had lived in that region for thousands of years. One of the persons most responsible for recording the stories of Yemenite Jews, even before the airlift, was Shelomo Dov Goitein.[33] While Goitein and his colleagues were thorough in their collecting of stories and their analyses, they turned up no evidence to support these Yemenite Jewish traditions about large numbers of Israelites migrating to Arabia before the fall of the First Temple (587 B.C.), which would roughly coincide with the departure of Lehi and Sariah.[34]

On the other hand, many Jews were living in Arabia by the time of Muhammad, the prophet of Islam, more than a thousand years after Lehi and Sariah. And these people must have come from somewhere. Substantiation for Jews residing in Arabia a few hundred years after the trek of Lehi and Sariah arises in various forms. Four illustrations will suffice, two archaeological and two literary.

The earliest archaeological proof of Jews in Arabia comes from the third century A.D. In 1936, excavations in a cemetery of Bet Shearim in Lower Galilee revealed a series of graves of Jews from Himyar in southern Arabia. Although scholars have challenged the conclusions drawn from this discovery, it seems apparent that prominent Jews living in Himyar were brought to Galilee for burial, much as the remains of Joseph were carried from Egypt to Shechem (see Joshua 24:32).[35] A second witness comes in the form of a Hebrew inscription found in south Arabia and dated to the last quarter of the fourth century A.D. (ca. 380), wherein an Arabian convert to Judaism announces his new house.[36] In light of these remains, it is possible to speak about large numbers of Jews in Arabia, but not until almost a millennium after Lehi and Sariah.

The earliest written account comes from Strabo (ca. 64 B.C.–A.D. 19) who, in referring to the failed Roman military expedition led by Aelius Gallus into Arabia in 25–24 B.C., wrote in his *Geography* that Aelius Gallus "set sail with about ten thousand infantry, consisting of Romans in Egypt, as also of Roman allies, among whom were five hundred Jews." Later, Josephus added a few details about these Jews in his *Antiquities of the Jews:* "at that time [25 B.C.] . . . [King Herod] sent to Caesar five hundred picked men from his bodyguards as an auxiliary force, and these men were very useful to Aelius Gallus, who led them to the Red Sea."[37] Whether these Jewish soldiers accompanied the Roman army in order to contact and seek help from other Jews who were already living in Arabia—an unlikely scenario because the expedition failed—or whether they went because of their skills in desert living and warfare remains an open question. In sum, although the written notices do not demonstrate a significant

Jewish presence in Arabia, the archaeological remains do, but only at a time long after Lehi and Sariah undertook their trek.

The observations of Lehi and Nephi add nothing. They are silent about any contacts with fellow Jews as they moved south. To be sure, Nephi's narrative consistently omits mention of other people whom they surely must have met.[38] But running into fellow Israelites who had moved into Arabia would plausibly have given Nephi reason to note such a meeting. Yet he is silent. In a different vein, the possible reference to Nephi's preaching in Arabia (D&C 33:8) could be construed to mean that he preached to other Israelites. But that need not be so. And even if there were a few Israelites residing in Arabia (and there likely were), it seems reasonable that Lehi and Sariah avoided contact with them so that they would not draw unwanted attention to themselves and their group.

Conclusion

Although at first glance it may seem out of character for refugees from Jerusalem to flee to Arabia rather than to Egypt, a review of ancient sources suggests well-established connections between peoples of Arabia and those who lived in and around the city. At times, the ties evidently linked to military matters; at times, they were of a commercial sort. Whether Lehi himself dealt with Arabian traders or their goods remains unknown. In any event, because of long-standing connections with Arabia, Lehi and Sariah would not have felt completely uncomfortable traveling there. Besides, although Nephi does not mention a commandment of the Lord that the family travel specifically to Arabia (see 1 Nephi 2:1–2), Lehi must have received such a directive, thus pointing him southeast toward Arabia rather than southwest toward Egypt.

We have also learned that there is no evidence to suggest that significant numbers of Israelites were already living in Arabia when Lehi and Sariah began their journey. The first written notation appears in Strabo and the earliest archaeological remains date to the third century A.D., both hundreds of years after Lehi and Sariah. Hence, we should see Lehi and Sariah as pioneers, not relying on others for assistance. Instead, they were to rely on the Lord, who had promised that he would "be [their] light in the wilderness" (1 Nephi 17:13).

NOTES

1. See 1 Kings 11:26–40 (Jeroboam); Jeremiah 43:1–7 (Jeremiah—under protest—and others); compare the journeys of Abraham and Jacob into Egypt (Abraham 2:21; Genesis 12:10; 46:1–7). See also S. Kent Brown, "The Exodus: Seeing It as a Test, a Testimony, and a Type," *Ensign,* February 1990, 54–57. According to the Annals of Sargon II, king of Assyria (721–705 B.C.), rulers of Ashdod twice fled to Upper Egypt to avoid Sargon's army; see James B. Pritchard, ed., *Ancient Near Eastern Texts Relating to the Old Testament,* 3rd ed. with suppl. (Princeton: Princeton University Press, 1969), 285, 286.

2. For estimates of where the family might have camped in northwest Arabia, see Lynn M. Hilton and Hope Hilton, *In Search of Lehi's Trail* (Salt Lake City: Deseret Book, 1976), 63–64 (Al-Badᶜ oasis); and George D. Potter, "A New Candidate in Arabia for the Valley of Lemuel," *Journal of Book of Mormon Studies* 8/1 (1999): 54–63 (Wadi Tayyib al-Ism, the more likely place). On Lehi's record, see S. Kent Brown, *From Jerusalem to Zarahemla: Literary and Historical Studies of the Book of Mormon* (Provo, Utah: BYU Religious Studies Center, 1998), 28–54.

3. The family must have led pack animals—possibly camels—to carry tents and other essentials (1 Nephi 2:4–6). Tent panels can each weigh over a hundred pounds. But camels cannot carry such burdens if they are underfed and tired; see Bertram Thomas, *Arabia*

Felix: Across the "Empty Quarter" of Arabia (New York: Scribner's Sons, 1932), 164–65. That camels were more suited to desert travel than other animals can be seen in the offhanded remark of Ahmed Fakhry, who traveled through southwestern Arabia with camels and mules: "It is impossible for laden mules to walk in that loose sand, and so we had to ride camels." *An Archaeological Journey to Yemen (March–May, 1947)* (Cairo: Government Press, 1952), 1:12. Charles Doughty observes that donkeys "must drink every second day." *Travels in Arabia Deserta,* with an introduction by T. E. Lawrence (New York: Random House, 1936), 1:325.

4. For reconstructions of Jerusalem and its gates at the end of the seventh century B.C., see Dan Bahat, *The Illustrated Atlas of Jerusalem* (New York: Simon and Schuster, 1990), 24–25, 30–31.

5. For the trade routes that brought goods to Jerusalem from the south and the east, see M. Har-El, "The Route of Salt, Sugar and Balsam Caravans in the Judean Desert," *GeoJournal* 2/6 (1978): 549–56. The "ascent of Ziz" route is favored by D. Kelly Ogden in "Answering the Lord's Call (1 Nephi 1–7)," in *1 Nephi to Alma 29,* ed. Kent P. Jackson (Salt Lake City: Deseret Book, 1987), 17–33, especially 23. The first mapping effort was undertaken by Claude R. Conder and Horatio H. Kitchener in *The Survey of Western Palestine: Memoirs of the Topography, Orography, Hydrography, and Archaeology* (London: Palestine Exploration Fund, 1883), 58. For further details on the possible routes from Jerusalem, see S. Kent Brown, "New Light from Arabia on Lehi's Trail," in *Echoes and Evidences of the Book of Mormon,* ed. Donald W. Parry, Daniel C. Peterson, and John W. Welch (Provo, Utah: FARMS, 2002), 56–60.

6. The expression "the place which was called Nahom" indicates that the family learned the name Nahom from others (1 Nephi 16:34). In addition, when family members were some fourteen hundred miles from home at Nahom, some knew that it was possible to return (1 Nephi 16:36), even though they had run out of food twice (16:17–19, 39). Evidently, family members had met people making the journey from south Arabia to the Mediterranean area. Further, the Lord's commandment to Lehi about not taking more than one wife, if Lehi received it

in Arabia, may point to unsavory interaction there (see Jacob 2:23–24). Moreover, Doctrine and Covenants 33:8 hints that Nephi may have preached to people in Arabia, although the reference may be to preaching to members of his own traveling party. See also S. Kent Brown, "A Case for Lehi's Bondage in Arabia," *Journal of Book of Mormon Studies* 6/2 (1997): 205–17.

7. For the routes running east from Jerusalem, see Har-El, "The Route of Salt," 549–56.

8. A series of forts in Edomite territory probably guarded a caravan route that ran to the east of the King's Highway, although they seem not to have been inhabited in 600 B.C. Consult Nelson Glueck, *The Other Side of the Jordan* (New Haven, Conn.: American Schools of Oriental Research, 1940), 128–34. For the route of the King's Highway, see Barry J. Beitzel, "Roads and Highways (Pre-Roman)," in *The Anchor Bible Dictionary,* ed. David Noel Freedman et al. (New York: Doubleday, 1992), 5:779 and the accompanying maps.

9. An army from the northern kingdom of Israel was part of a coalition of forces that opposed the Assyrian king Shalmaneser III at Qarqar in 853 B.C. There is no record that the Assyrians invaded Israel thereafter as punishment. Consult Israel Eph'al, *The Ancient Arabs: Nomads on the Borders of the Fertile Crescent, 9th–5th Centuries B.C.* (Jerusalem: Magnes, 1982), 21.

10. For Tiglath-pileser's records, see Pritchard, *Ancient Near Eastern Texts,* 283; and Eph'al, *Ancient Arabs,* 26–27, 28, 30–33. For Menachem's actions, consult 2 Kings 15:19–20. For an overview of this era, consult John Bright, *A History of Israel,* 3rd ed. (Philadelphia: Westminster, 1981), 269–78.

11. Shalmaneser's successor, Sargon II (721–705 B.C.), records that the number of Israelite exiles was 27,290; see Pritchard, *Ancient Near Eastern Texts,* 285; and Eph'al, *Ancient Arabs,* 38.

12. Pritchard, *Ancient Near Eastern Texts,* 285. Samsi, the Arab queen, is noted by several Assyrian monarchs; consult Eph'al, *Ancient Arabs,* 25–28, 30–32, 36.

13. On the identification of Sheba and Saba or Sabaea, see Gus W.

Van Beek, "Sheba," in *The Oxford Encyclopedia of Archaeology in the Near East,* ed. Eric M. Meyers et al. (New York: Oxford University Press, 1997), 5:18–19.

14. The Old Testament does not specifically mention Arabs among the peoples whom Sargon moved into the former territory of Israel; only Sargon does. Consult 2 Kings 17:24 and Eph‹al, *Ancient Arabs,* 36, 38.

15. Pritchard, *Ancient Near Eastern Texts,* 286. It is not clear whether the difference in spelling between It'amar (Sargon's first Annal) and It'amra (seventh Annal) points to different individuals or not. Also consult Eph‹al, *Ancient Arabs,* 36.

16. In the Annal for his eleventh year, Sargon wrote that "I reorganized (the administration of) these cities (and) settled therein people from the [regions] of the East which I had conquered personally." Compare also his remark that he "led away as prisoners 9,033 inhabitants [of Rapihu, south of Gaza] with their numerous possessions," in Pritchard, *Ancient Near Eastern Texts,* 286, 285.

17. See the review of the evidence for wildly differing estimates of the date of the composition of Job in Roland K. Harrison, *Introduction to the Old Testament* (Grand Rapids, Mich.: Eerdmans, 1969), 1031–42.

18. References to Eliphaz the Temanite occur in Job 2:11; 4:1; 15:1; 22:1; and 42:9.

19. It seems that Nabonidus moved his official residence for religious reasons. See his Chronicle and his so-called Verse Account in Pritchard, *Ancient Near Eastern Texts,* 305–7, 312–15; also consult Bright, *History of Israel,* 352–54, 360.

20. Consult Françoise Briquel-Chatonnet, "Les Arabes en Arabie du nord et au Proche-Orient avant l'Hégire," in Pierre R. Baduel, ed., *L'Arabie antique de Karib'îl à Mahomet: Nouvelles données sur l'histoire des Arabes grâce aux inscriptions.* Revue du Monde Musulman et de la Méditerranée, no. 61 (1991–93): 38.

21. See Ernst A. Knauf, "Tema," in *Anchor Bible Dictionary,* 6:346–47 and accompanying bibliography.

22. See the articles by Ernst A. Knauf, "Kedar" and "Nebaioth," in *Anchor Bible Dictionary,* 4:9–10, 1053.

23. See Jeremiah 6:20; Ezekiel 27:20–24; 38:13; 2 Chronicles 17:11. For other references to Arabia and Arabians, see Joel 3:8, which was composed perhaps between 450 and 400 B.C.; 1 Chronicles 4:39–43; and 2 Chronicles 26:6. On the dating of the book of Joel, consult Harrison, *Introduction to the Old Testament,* 876–79. On the Mehunim or Meunim (Minaeans) of the Chronicler and the likely retrojection of later events into an earlier era, see the summary by Ernst A. Knauf, "Meunim," in *Anchor Bible Dictionary,* 4:801–2. On the importing of luxury goods from Arabia as tribute items, see Ryan Byrne, "Early Assyrian Contacts with Arabs and the Impact on Levantine Vassal Tribute," *Bulletin of the American Schools of Oriental Research* 331 (2003): 11–25.

24. William D. Whitt, "The Story of the Semitic Alphabet," in *Civilizations of the Ancient Near East,* ed. Jack M. Sasson et al. (New York: Scribner's Sons, 1995), 4:2391–92.

25. See Yigal Shiloh, "South Arabian Inscriptions from the City of David, Jerusalem," *Palestine Exploration Quarterly* 119/1 (1987): 9–18 (the quotations, including that from Höfner, come from p. 10); see also the cautionary words of Benjamin Sass, "Arabs and Greeks in Late First Temple Jerusalem," *Palestine Exploration Quarterly* 122/1 (1990): 59–61.

26. Hugh Nibley holds that Lehi knew the desert well and had made his wealth from commerce. See his books *An Approach to the Book of Mormon,* 3rd ed. (Salt Lake City: Deseret Book and FARMS, 1988), 77–80; and *Lehi in the Desert, The World of the Jaredites, There Were Jaredites* (Salt Lake City: Deseret Book and FARMS, 1988), 34–38. The Hiltons, *In Search of Lehi's Trail,* 34–35, suggest that Lehi did business in the desert and thus possessed tents and desert skills. John A. Tvedtnes, "Was Lehi a Caravaneer?" in *The Most Correct Book* (Salt Lake City: Cornerstone, 1999), 76–98, maintains that Lehi did not necessarily go into the desert for commercial purposes.

27. The traditions about Jews in Arabia are summarized in handy

form by Reuben Ahroni in his *Yemenite Jewry: Origins, Culture, and Literature* (Bloomington: Indiana University Press, 1986), 24–37.

28.   See Ahroni, *Yemenite Jewry,* 24–25, where he notes both Arab and Jewish traditions to this effect.

29.   Beno Rothenberg and Jonathan Glass, "The Midianite Pottery," in *Midian, Moab and Edom: The History and Archaeology of Late Bronze and Iron Age Jordan and North-West Arabia,* ed. John F. A. Sawyer and David J. A. Clines (Sheffield: JSOT, 1983), 65–124.

30.   A variant version in Arabic holds that King David himself lived in Arabia for seven years. See Ahroni, *Yemenite Jewry,* 25.

31.   Ahroni, *Yemenite Jewry,* 25–26; consult also Tudor Parfitt, *The Road to Redemption: The Jews of the Yemen 1900–1950* (Leiden: Brill, 1996), 4.

32.   Ahroni, *Yemenite Jewry,* 27, 33–36, makes a special plea—based on no evidence at all except tradition—that "there were Jewish communities in southern Arabia at the very least as far back as the destruction of the First Temple" in 587 B.C. See a similar guess in Bright, *History of Israel,* 353.

33.   For example, consult Shelomo D. Goitein, *Von den Juden Jemens: Eine Anthologie* (Berlin: Schocken, 1937); and *From the Land of Sheba: Tales of the Jews of Yemen* (1947; reprint, New York: Schocken, 1973).

34.   On the approximate date for the departure of Lehi and Sariah from Jerusalem, consult S. Kent Brown and David R. Seely, "Jeremiah's Imprisonment and the Date of Lehi's Departure," *Religious Educator* 2/1 (2001): 15–32.

35.   See Ahroni, *Yemenite Jewry,* 40–42. In this connection, it is worthwhile noting that "nomadic groups . . . carried with them in bags or clay coffins those who died during seasonal migrations, burying them in tombs only when the tribe returned to its traditional burial place. . . . It is also possible that, if the person was killed somewhere far away from his traditional burial place, what was left of him was carried in a container (clay coffin) to the traditional burial place." Khair Yassine, "Social-Religious Distinctions in Iron Age Burial Practice in Jordan," in *Midian, Moab and Edom,* 32.

36. "The first reliable epigraphic testimony to the presence of Jews in Yemen dates to the last two decades of the fourth century [A.D.]." Werner Daum, ed., *Yemen: 3000 Years of Art and Civilisation in Arabia Felix* (Innsbruck: Pinguin-Verlag, 1987), 52. One can consult a photograph of this unusual inscription in Baduel, *L'Arabie antique de Karib'îl à Mahomet*, 30.

37. See Strabo, *Geography* 16.4.23–24; Josephus, *Antiquities of the Jews* 15.9.3 (§317).

38. Consult note 6 above.

Further Reading

Biblical Background

Bible Text and Transmission

Friedman, Richard Elliot. *Who Wrote the Bible?* 2nd ed. San Francisco: HarperCollins, 1997.

Würthwein, Ernst. *The Text of the Old Testament.* 2nd ed. Grand Rapids, Mich.: Eerdmans, 1995.

Ancient Near Eastern Texts

Hallo, William W., ed. *The Context of Scripture.* 3 vols. Leiden: Brill, 1997–2002.

Pritchard, J. B., ed. *Ancient Near Eastern Texts Relating to the Old Testament.* 3rd ed. Princeton: Princeton University Press, 1969.

History and Archaeology

Avigad, Nahman. *Discovering Jerusalem.* Nashville: Nelson, 1980.

Bright, John. *A History of Israel*. 4th ed. Philadelphia: Westminster John Knox, 2000.

Hallo, William W., and William Kelly Simpson. *The Ancient Near East: A History*. 2nd ed. New York: Harcourt Brace, 1998.

Haran, Menahem. *Temples and Temple Service in Ancient Israel: An Inquiry into Biblical Cult Phenomena and the Historical Setting of the Priestly School*. 1978. Reprint, Winona Lake, Ind.: Eisenbrauns, 1985.

King, Philip J. *Jeremiah: An Archaeological Companion*. Louisville: Westminster John Knox, 1993.

Lipschits, Oded, and Joseph Blenkinsopp, eds. *Judah and the Judeans in the Neo-Babylonian Period*. Winona Lake, Ind.: Eisenbrauns, 2003.

Mazar, Amihai. *Archaeology of the Land of the Bible*. Vol. 1, *10,000–586 B.C.E.* Anchor Bible Reference Library. New York: Doubleday, 1990.

Shanks, Hershel, ed. *Ancient Israel: From Abraham to the Roman Destruction of the Temple*. Rev. ed. Washington, D.C.: Biblical Archaeology Society, 1999.

Smelik, Klaas A. D. *Writings from Ancient Israel: A Handbook of Historical and Religious Documents*. Louisville: Westminster John Knox, 1991.

Stern, Ephraim. *Archaeology of the Land of the Bible*. Vol. 2, *The Assyrian, Babylonian, and Persian Periods (732–332)*. Anchor Bible Reference Library. New York: Doubleday, 2001.

Stern, Ephraim, ed. *The New Encyclopedia of Archaeological Excavations in the Holy Land*. 4 vols. New York: Simon & Schuster, 1993.

Sweeney, Marvin A. *King Josiah of Judah: The Lost Messiah of Israel*. Oxford: Oxford University Press, 2001.

Vaughan, Andrew G., and Ann E. Killebrew, eds. *Jerusalem in Bible and Archaeology: The First Temple Period*. Atlanta: Society of Biblical Literature, 2003.

Atlases

Aharoni, Yohanan, Michael Avi-Yonah, Anson R. Rainey, and Ze'ev Safrai. *The Carta Bible Atlas*. 4th ed. Jerusalem: Carta, 2002. Formerly *The Macmillan Bible Atlas*.

Bahat, Daniel. *The Illustrated Atlas of Jerusalem*. New York: Simon & Schuster, 1990.

Beitzel, Barry J. *The Moody Atlas of Bible Lands*. Chicago: Moody, 1985.

Ben-Dov, Meir. *Historical Atlas of Jerusalem*. New York: Continuum, 2002.

Life in Biblical Times

Borowski, Oded. *Daily Life in Biblical Times*. Atlanta: Society of Biblical Literature, 2003.

de Vaux, Roland. *Ancient Israel: Its Life and Institutions*. 1961. Reprint, Grand Rapids, Mich.: Eerdmans, 1997.

Falk, Ze'ev W. *Hebrew Law in Biblical Times: An Introduction*. 2nd ed. Provo, Utah: Brigham Young University Press, 2001.

Haran, Menachem. *Temples and Temple Service in Ancient Israel: An Inquiry into Biblical Cult Phenomena and the Historical Setting of the Priestly School*. 1978. Reprint, Winona Lake, Ind.: Eisenbrauns, 1985.

King, Philip J., and Lawrence E. Stager. *Life in Biblical Israel*. Louisville: Westminster John Knox, 2001.

Levy, Thomas E., ed. *The Archaeology of Society in the Holy Land*. London: Leicester University Press, 1995.

Matthews, Victor H. *Manners and Customs in the Bible: An Illustrated Guide to Daily Life in Bible Times*. Rev. ed. Peabody, Mass.: Hendrickson, 1991.

Matthews, Victor H. *Social World of the Hebrew Prophets*. Peabody, Mass.: Hendrickson, 2001.

Matthews, Victor H., and Don C. Benjamin. *Social World of Ancient Israel: 1250–587 BCE*. Peabody, Mass.: Hendrickson, 1993.

Perdue, Leo G., Joseph Blenkinsopp, John J. Collins, and Carol Meyers, eds. *Families in Ancient Israel*. Louisville: Westminster John Knox, 1997.

Thompson, J. A. *Handbook of Life in Bible Times*. Downers Grove, Ill.: InterVarsity, 1986.

Commentaries on Biblical Books

Cogan, Mordechai, and Hayim Tadmor. *II Kings: A New Translation*. Anchor Bible 11. Garden City, N.Y.: Doubleday, 1988.

Hobbs, T. R. *2 Kings*. Word Bible Commentary. Nashville: Nelson, 1985.

Holladay, William L. *Jeremiah: A Commentary on the Book of the Prophet Jeremiah*. 2 vols. Hermeneia. Philadelphia: Fortress, 1986, 1989.

Japhet, Sara. *I and II Chronicles: A Commentary*. Old Testament Library. Louisville: Westminster John Knox, 1993.

Jones, Douglas Rawlinson. *Jeremiah*. New Century Bible Commentary. Grand Rapids, Mich.: Eerdmans, 1992.

Lundbom, Jack R. *Jeremiah 1–20: A New Translation with Introduction and Commentary.* Anchor Bible 21A. New York: Doubleday, 1999.

Thompson, J. A. *The Book of Jeremiah.* New International Commentary on the Old Testament. Grand Rapids, Mich.: Eerdmans, 1979.

Williamson, H. G. M. *1 and 2 Chronicles.* New Century Bible Commentary. Grand Rapids, Mich.: Eerdmans, 1982.

Book of Mormon Studies

Abunuwara, Ehab. "Into the Desert: An Arab View of the Book of Mormon." *Journal of Book of Mormon Studies* 11 (2002): 60–65, 111.

Adams, William J., Jr. "Lehi's Jerusalem and the Writings on Metal Plates." *Journal of Book of Mormon Studies* 3/1 (1994): 204–6.

Adams, William J., Jr. "More on the Silver Plates from Lehi's Jerusalem." *Journal of Book of Mormon Studies* 4/2 (1995): 136–37.

Adams, Williams J., Jr. "Synagogues in the Book of Mormon." *Journal of Book of Mormon Studies* 9/1 (2000): 4–13, 76.

Bokovoy, David. "From Distance to Proximity: A Poetic Function of Enallage in the Hebrew Bible and the Book of Mormon." *Journal of Book of Mormon Studies* 9/1 (2000): 60–63.

Brown, S. Kent. *From Jerusalem to Zarahemla: Literary and Historical Studies of the Book of Mormon.* Provo, Utah: BYU Religious Studies Center, 1998.

Brown, S. Kent, and David Rolph Seely. "Jeremiah's Imprisonment and the Date of Lehi's Departure." *Religious Educator* 2/1 (2001): 15–31.

Gee, John. "A Note on the Name 'Nephi.'" *Journal of Book of Mormon Studies* 1 (1992): 189–91.

Hoskisson, Paul Y. "By What Authority Did Lehi, a Non-Levite Priest, Offer Sacrifices?" *Ensign*, March 1994, 54.

Jackson, Kent P., ed. *1 Nephi to Alma 29*. Studies in Scripture 7. Salt Lake City: Deseret Book, 1987. The relationship of the Book of Mormon to its biblical background is explored in chapters 3, 6, 11.

Johnson, Mark J. "The Exodus of Lehi Revisited." *Journal of Book of Mormon Studies* 3/2 (1994): 123–26.

Largey, Dennis L., ed. *Book of Mormon Reference Companion*. Salt Lake City: Deseret Book, 2003.

Meservy, Keith H. "Jerusalem at the Time of Lehi and Jeremiah." *Ensign*, January 1988, 22–25.

Nibley, Hugh W. *An Approach to the Book of Mormon*. Salt Lake City: Deseret Book and FARMS, 1988.

Nibley, Hugh W. *Lehi in the Desert, The World of the Jaredites, There Were Jaredites*. Salt Lake City: Deseret Book and FARMS, 1988.

Nibley, Hugh W. *The Prophetic Book of Mormon*. Salt Lake City: Deseret Book and FARMS, 1989.

Nibley, Hugh W. *Since Cumorah*. Salt Lake City: Deseret Book and FARMS, 1988.

Nyman, Monte S., and Charles D. Tate Jr., eds. *The Book of Mormon: First Nephi, The Doctrinal Foundation*. Provo, Utah: BYU Religious Studies Center, 1988. Articles dealing with the biblical background of the Book of Mormon are found in chapters 3, 4, 6, 13, 18, 19.

Nyman, Monte S., and Charles D. Tate Jr., eds. *The Book of Mormon: Second Nephi, The Doctrinal Structure.* Salt Lake City: Bookcraft, 1989. Insights into the biblical background of the Book of Mormon are found in chapters 4, 8, 11, 12, 13.

Ostler, Blake T. "The Throne-Theophany and Prophetic Commission in 1 Nephi: A Form-Critical Analysis." *BYU Studies* 26/4 (1986): 67–95.

Parry, Donald W., Daniel C. Peterson, and John W. Welch, eds. *Echoes and Evidences of the Book of Mormon.* Provo, Utah: FARMS, 2002. Numerous points surrounding the world around 600 B.C. are discussed on pp. 56–69, 130, 142, 155–89, 198, 214, 311, 338–72, 374, 389–407, 422, 425, 456–62, 466–72, 474–78, 480–83.

Parry, Donald W., and John W. Welch, eds. *Isaiah in the Book of Mormon.* Provo, Utah: FARMS, 1998.

Peterson, Daniel C. "Nephi and His Asherah." *Journal of Book of Mormon Studies* 9/2 (2000): 16–25, 80–81.

Potter, George D. "A New Candidate in Arabia for the 'Valley of Lemuel.'" *Journal of Book of Mormon Studies* 8/1 (1999): 54–63, 79.

Pritchett, Bruce M., Jr. "Lehi's Theology of the Fall in Its Preexilic/Exilic Context." *Journal of Book of Mormon Studies* 3/2 (1994): 49–83.

Reynolds, Noel B. "The Brass Plates Version of Genesis." In *By Study and Also by Faith: Essays in Honor of Hugh W. Nibley*, edited by John M. Lundquist and Stephen D. Ricks, 2:136–73. Salt Lake City: Deseret Book and FARMS, 1990.

Reynolds, Noel B. "Lehi as Moses." *Journal of Book of Mormon Studies* 9/2 (2000): 26–35, 81–82.

Reynolds, Noel B., ed. *Book of Mormon Authorship: New Light on Ancient Origins.* 1982. Reprint, Provo, Utah: FARMS, 1996. Articles relating to the biblical background of the Book of Mormon are found in chapters 2, 3, 4, 5, 6.

Reynolds, Noel B., ed. *Book of Mormon Authorship Revisited: The Evidence for Ancient Origins.* Provo, Utah: FARMS, 1997. Factors that point to ancient Israelite origins are found in chapters 8, 11, 13, 14, 16.

Ricks, Stephen D., and John A. Tvedtnes. "The Hebrew Origin of Some Book of Mormon Place Names." *Journal of Book of Mormon Studies* 6/2 (1997): 255–59.

Rolph, Daniel N. "Prophets, Kings, and Swords: The Sword of Laban and Its Possible Pre-Laban Origin." *Journal of Book of Mormon Studies* 2/1 (1993): 73–79.

Seely, David Rolph. "Abinadi, Moses, Isaiah, and Christ: O How Beautiful upon the Mountains Are Their Feet." In *The Book of Mormon: The Foundation of Our Faith: The 28th Annual Sidney B. Sperry Symposium,* 201–16. Salt Lake City: Deseret Book, 1999.

Seely, David Rolph. "Lehi's Altar and Sacrifice in the Wilderness." *Journal of Book of Mormon Studies* 10/1 (2001): 62–69, 80.

Smith, Robert F. "Book of Mormon Event Structure: The Ancient Near East." *Journal of Book of Mormon Studies* 5/2 (1996): 98–147.

Sorenson, John L. "The Brass Plates and Biblical Scholarship." *Dialogue* 10/4 (1977): 31–39.

Sorenson, John L. "The Composition of Lehi's Family." In *By Study and Also by Faith: Essays in Honor of Hugh W. Nibley*, edited by John M. Lundquist and Stephen D. Ricks, 2:174–96. Salt Lake City: Deseret Book and FARMS, 1990.

Sorenson, John L. *Metals and Metallurgy Relating to the Book of Mormon Text*. Provo, Utah: FARMS, 1992.

Sorenson, John L. "The Significance of an Apparent Relationship between the Ancient Near East and Mesoamerica." In *Man across the Sea: Problems of Pre-Columbian Contact,* edited by Carroll L. Riley, 219–41. 1971. Reprint, Provo, Utah: FARMS, 1981.

Sorenson, John L., and Melvin J. Thorne, eds. *Rediscovering the Book of Mormon: Insights You May Have Missed*. Salt Lake City: Deseret Book and FARMS, 1991. Meaningful topics pertinent to Lehi's Jerusalem are discussed in chapters 5, 8, 10, 13, 15, 19, 21.

Spackman, Randall P. "The Jewish/Nephite Lunar Calendar." *Journal of Book of Mormon Studies* 7 (1998): 48–59, 71.

Sperry, Sidney B. "The Book of Mormon and the Problem of the Pentateuch." *Journal of Book of Mormon Studies* 4/1 (1995): 119–28.

Sperry, Sidney B. "Hebrew Idioms in the Book of Mormon." *Journal of Book of Mormon Studies* 4/1 (1995): 218–25.

Sperry, Sidney B. "The 'Isaiah Problem' in the Book of Mormon." *Journal of Book of Mormon Studies* 4/1 (1995): 129–52.

Sperry, Sidney B. "The Isaiah Quotation: 2 Nephi 12–24." *Journal of Book of Mormon Studies* 4/1 (1995): 192–208.

Studia Antiqua: The Journal of the Student Society for Ancient Studies (Summer 2003), special issue on Hebrew law in the Book of Mormon, copublished with FARMS.

Szink, Terrence L. "Further Evidence of a Semitic Alma." *Journal of Book of Mormon Studies* 8/1 (1999): 70.

Tate, George S. "The Typology of the Exodus Pattern in the Book of Mormon." In *Literature of Belief: Sacred Scripture and Religious Experience,* edited by Neal E. Lambert, 245–62. Provo, Utah: BYU Religious Studies Center, 1981.

Tvedtnes, John A. *The Book of Mormon and Other Hidden Books: "Out of Darkness unto Light."* Provo, Utah: FARMS, 2000.

Tvedtnes, John A. *The Most Correct Book: Insights from a Book of Mormon Scholar.* Salt Lake City: Cornerstone, 1999.

Tvedtnes, John A. "'A Visionary Man.'" *Journal of Book of Mormon Studies* 6/2 (1997): 260–61.

Tvedtnes, John A. "'The Workmanship Thereof Was Exceedingly Fine.'" *Journal of Book of Mormon Studies* 6/1 (1997): 73–75.

Tvedtnes, John A., John Gee, and Matthew Roper. "Book of Mormon Names Attested in Ancient Hebrew Inscriptions." *Journal of Book of Mormon Studies* 9/1 (2000): 40–51, 77.

Welch, John W. "Legal Perspectives on the Slaying of Laban." *Journal of Book of Mormon Studies* 1/1 (1992): 119–41.

Welch, John W. "Lehi's Last Will and Testament." In *The Book of Mormon: Second Nephi, The Doctrinal Structure,* edited by Monte S. Nyman and Charles D. Tate Jr., 61–82. Provo, Utah: BYU Religious Studies Center, 1989.

Welch, John W. "The Temple in the Book of Mormon: The Temples at the Cities of Nephi, Zarahemla, and Bountiful." In *Temples of the Ancient World: Ritual and Symbolism,* edited by Donald W. Parry, 297–387. Salt Lake City: Deseret Book and FARMS, 1994.

	CLASSICAL WORLD			ISRAEL	
	ROME	GREECE/ ASIA MINOR	EGYPT	JUDAH	ISRAEL
750	Traditional founding of Rome by Romulus (753)	P=Poet Ph=Philosopher L=Lawgiver		Ahaz (735–715)	Pekah (735–732) Hoshea (732–724) ← INVASIO 732 B.C
725			DYNASTY 25 Shabaka (716–701)	*Isaiah* Hezekiah (715–687)	**Fall of Samaria** 722 B.C. ←
700			Shabataka (701–689) Taharqa (689–664)	Manasseh (687–642)	← INVASION (Jerusalem Preserv 701 B.C.
675			Tanutamani (664–656) DYNASTY 26 Saite Renaissance (716–701) Psammetichus I (664–609)	← SACK OF MEMPHIS 671 B.C. ← SACK OF THEBES 663 B.C.	
650		Archilochus of Paros (P, 650) Solon of Athens (L, 630–560) Thales of Miletus (Ph, 624–545)		Amon (642–640) Josiah (640–609) *Zephaniah Jeremiah Nahum*	
625		Draco of Athens (L, 621) Alcaeus of Mytilene (P, 620–580) Sappho of Lesbos (P, 610–550)	Necho II (609–594)	*Habakkuk Huldah* Jehoahaz (609) Jehoiakim (609–598) *Lehi, Urijah Daniel*	
600		Anaximander of Miletus (Ph, 610–546) Peisistratus of Athens (L, 600–527) Pythagoras of Samos (Ph, 582–500)	Psammetichus II (594–588) Apries (588–568)	Jehoiachin (598) Zedekiah (597–586) Lehi leaves *Ezekiel* **Jerusalem Destroyed** 586 B.C.	← JERUSALEM CAPTURED 597 B.C.
575		Cleisthenes of Athens (L, 570–508)			
550					
525	Prepared by David Rolph Seely			← EGYPT CONQUERED 525 B.C.	